Study Guide
for
The Economy Today

Fourth Edition

Bradley R. Schiller

Prepared by

Michael M. Tansey
Rockhurst College

and

Lawrence F. Ziegler
University of Texas at Arlington

RANDOM HOUSE
BUSINESS DIVISION
NEW YORK

To the Instructor

This *Study Guide* is an important part of the complete and fully integrated textbook package called *The Economy Today*. Students who use this *Study Guide* on a continuous basis should be able to remember what they have read in their textbook and heard in your lecture. It should enable them to apply to examinations the principles they learn and, more important, should help them recognize the same principles at work in their daily experiences. Each section of each chapter has a particular objective, which is described in the following paragraphs.

The *Quick Review* and *Learning Objectives* sections provide brief summaries of the basic contents of the corresponding text chapters and outline the important areas of the *Study Guide*. Each learning objective is keyed to specific pages in the text and to specific questions and problems that follow. Look at page 2 for examples.

Economic terminology is often an obstacle to new students in economics. Thus the *Key-Term Review* and *Crossword Puzzle* sections of the *Study Guide* provide practice in the use of terminology. Both sections help the students to link economic terms to the appropriate economic concepts. The *Study Guide* reinforces the terminology by repetition. However, we have taken pains not to make the repetition burdensome. The crossword puzzles we have introduced in some of the chapters, for example, help to make the repetition fun.

The *True or False* and *Multiple Choice* sections help the student advance from memorizing terminology to applying economic principles in a familiar problem-solving setting. This will help greatly in their preparation for exams.

The *Problems and Applications* sections let the students discover economic principles for themselves. Students not only learn the techniques that economists use, but they also discover the basis for the economic principles they have learned.

The section called *Common Errors* was introduced in the first edition of this book in 1980, and at that time it was unique to this *Study Guide*. Since then a number of competing books have begun including similar sections, a strong indicator of its usefulness to students and its popularity with instructors. It is our feeling that, semester after semester, students have difficulty with the same concepts and make the same mistakes; hence, the name *Common Error*. We've tried to draw attention to some of these problem areas and provide explanations using the appropriate economic principles. You may wish to add to those we have provided.

Another unique feature of this *Study Guide* is what we call the "media exercise." The media exercises are contained in the *Problems and Applications* section of each chapter. Each one directs the students to reread a certain newspaper, magazine, or other media article from among those interspersed throughout the text. The students then answer a series of questions based on the article, using the economic principles they have learned in the chapter. The media exercises should help the students see economic principles at work in the world around them, and make them aware of how to get the "economics" out of a critical reading of the "news" long after they leave the economics classroom.

The *Study Guide* provides an alternative to the memorization: it directs the student in applying economic principles. The exercises and crossword puzzles should actually stimulate interest in economics. We have found that our students showed great satisfaction from the discovery of the ideas embedded in the exercises as well as the neatness of completed problems and mathematical calculations. The exercises focusing on current or historic events also generated interest among the students. We also found that our students enjoyed making up their own crossword puzzles.

To the Student

This *Study Guide* is designed to be used with *The Economy Today*, Fourth Edition, by Bradley R. Schiller. Working through the *Study Guide* should reinforce what you have learned in the textbook and help you to recognize economic principles in your daily experiences.

Note the following points in the various sections of each of the chapters:

- The *Quick Review* provides a brief summary of the concepts in the corresponding text chapter. If you are not comfortable with the terminology and concepts in this review, you should reread the appropriate sections of the text chapter.
- The *Learning Objectives* focus on the basic information in each text chapter and provide outlines for material to be covered in the *Study Guide*. The learning objectives are keyed to questions and problems that follow and to pages in the text. If you have difficulty with a particular idea, you can quickly find the text material and review it.
- The *Key-Term Review* and *Crossword Puzzles* give you practice in the use of terminology in the specific chapters. As a learning aid, you are encouraged to write out the definitions of the key economic terms.
- The *True or False* and *Multiple Choice* questions test your understanding of the basic economic principles discussed in the text chapter.
- The *Problems and Applications* section contains one or more real-world problems, which allow you to work out in a practical way the economic principles that you have been studying.
- Nearly all chapters contain a "media exercise" that refers you to specific newspaper, magazine, or other articles reprinted in the text. These exercises will assist you in developing your critical thinking skills.
- The *Common Errors* section identifies some of the errors that students often make and explains the correct principles. This is a very effective way to help you discover and correct your mistakes.
- *Answers* to *all* problems, exercises, and questions are provided at the end of each chapter of the *Study Guide*, so you can quickly check your answers and go back and review where necessary.

Acknowledgments

This *Study Guide* is now in its fourth edition, and we have many people to thank for their contributions. Our greatest thanks must go to our students, upon whom the exercises in the first edition of the *Study Guide* were tested. Their patience, creativity, and astuteness provided a much better *Study Guide*, one from which other students will benefit. Contributors of the crossword puzzles include Sidi Habi, Patricia Eason, Margaret Gatchell, Louise Oller, and Robin Burdette. Richard Bayer originated two excellent exercises in the macroeconomics section. All these contributions have been retained in this edition.

The teachers enrolled in the 1982 University of Texas at Arlington Summer Institute in Economics worked through the first fifteen chapters of an early draft of the second edition manuscript. The participants are too numerous to cite individually, but their thoroughness is certainly appreciated. Any errors that remain are, of course, our responsibility. Bryce Jones, Sheldon Stahl, and Gerald Miller, all of Rockhurst College, provided comments and support that helped make the project possible.

We happily acknowledge the help and support of the Random House staff. We know of no other publisher that has made a greater commitment to a book of this type. Special thanks on this edition are extended to June Smith, Bonnie Binkert, and Catherine Woods. We appreciate their gracious attitude, calm demeanor, and competence displayed throughout the entire process. Project editor Barbara Gerr was delightful to work with, and copy editor Elaine Romano was outstanding as well.

We remember with special fondness the late Mary Griffin, who was the project editor for the first edition. The success of the *Study Guide* is due to her role as a relentless taskmaster who set high standards for two rookie authors. The typists for each of the four editions—Nancy Bloodgood Sproba, Mildred Simms, Cyndy Carver, and Eileen Garland—were superb. Finally we continue to value the friendship of Paul Shensa, who got us started with Random House over ten years ago.

Michael M. Tansey
Rockhurst College
Lawrence F. Ziegler
*University of Texas
at Arlington*

Contents

Chapter 1
An Overview

Quick Review

The output of the U.S. economy is well over $4 trillion per year. This is simply the economist's way of summarizing the total volume of goods and services produced in the economy by market participants like you and me. In other words, "The economy is us."

Although our annual production of goods and services is impressive, our resources are not sufficient to satisfy all of our wants. Society's wants are infinite and insatiable while our available resources are relatively fixed. As a result, we (like all societies) are forced to choose which goods and services will be produced and which will not. Economists illustrate these choices by drawing a production-possibilities curve. This curve shows the combinations of goods and services a society could produce if it were operating efficiently and all of its resources were fully employed. The production-possibilities curve appears bowed out from the origin because of the law of increasing opportunity costs.

Every society has to decide what goods and services it wants to produce. In the United States our choices are determined by the market mechanism. Through the market mechanism the production and consumption decisions of individuals directly affect the allocation of resources. These individual decisions are supplemented with generous doses of public-sector activity. When the market mechanism leaves some of our needs unmet—our desire for clean air and water, for example—the public sector must do the job. Market systems do not automatically generate pollution-control mechanisms. Such market imperfections must be overcome by government activity. In some economies the market mechanism is not allowed to work efficiently. Planned economies, like that of the Soviet Union, are good examples of this.

In studying the economy, it is useful to break economics into two categories: microeconomics and macroeconomics. Microeconomics focuses on a specific individual, firm, industry, or government agency; macroeconomics focuses on the entire economy.

Learning Objectives

After reading Chapter 1 and doing the following exercises, you should:	True or false	Multiple choice	Problems and applications	Common errors	Pages in the text
1. Know what the science of economics is concerned with.	10	1–3,5		2,3	19–23
2. Know the factors of production.	2	9		1	
3. Understand opportunity costs and how to represent them.	1,3,12	6–8	2,3		6–8
4. Be able to draw and interpret a production-possibilities curve.	4,16	12,13	1,3		8–10
5. Be able to explain the law of increasing opportunity costs.	11	14	2,3		11–13
6. Know how to represent growth and technological change in terms of shifts of the production-possibilities curve.	13,14	9,10	1		14–15
7. Be able to describe different mechanisms for allocating resources.	6,8	4			16–19
8. Know how the market mechanism allocates resources.	9				16–18
9. Know several different types of market imperfections.	5,7	11			17–18
10. Be able to differentiate between microeconomics and macroeconomics.	15,17	15,16			19–20

Key-Term Review

Review the following terms; if you are not sure of the meaning of any term, write out the definition and check it against the Glossary in the text.

ceteris paribus
economic growth
economics
externalities
factors of production
law of increasing opportunity costs

macroeconomics
market mechanism
microeconomics
mixed economy
opportunity cost
production possibilities

Fill in the blank following each of the statements below with the appropriate term from the list above.

1. A Latin phrase meaning "all other things being equal" is _____.

   1. _CETERIS PARIBUS_

2. The branch of economics that focuses on the activities of individual decision-making units is _____.

   2. _MICRO ECONOMICS_

3. When economists say that to have more schools we must give up houses, they are illustrating the principle of _____.

   3. _OPPORTUNITY COSTS_

4. When market prices signal what goods and services should be produced, the allocation of resources is being accomplished by the _____.

4. _MARKET mechanism_

5. Those things that are transformed into final goods and services desired by society are _____.

5. _factors of Production_

6. The branch of economics that focuses on the behavior of the entire economy is _____.

6. _MACro economics_

7. A curve showing the various combinations of goods and services that a society can produce with its scarce resources is a _____ curve.

7. _Production Possibilities_

8. The production-possibilities curve is bowed out because of the _____.

8. _LAW OF increasing_ _opportunity_ _costs_

9. When the activity of a producer or consumer imposes costs or benefits on someone else, these costs or benefits are called _____.

9. _Externalities_

10. The science that studies how societies allocate scarce resources is _____.

10. _Economics_

11. Much of the resource allocation in the United States is done through the public sector, indicating that we have a _____.

11. _Mixed economy_

12. Where there is an increase in real output there is _____.

12. _economic Growth_

True or False: *Circle your choice.*

T (F) 1. Students do not pay tuition in elementary school, so in this case education is a free good.

(T) F 2. Goods are scarce because society's desire for them exceeds society's ability to produce them.

(T) (F) 3. If a commodity has a market price that is greater than zero, it must be scarce.

(T) (F) 4. A production-possibilities curve can only be drawn if a scarce resource prevents production of as much as we want of a commodity.

(T) (F) 5. The market-directed or price-directed economy is capable of solving the problems created by externalities without intervention by government.

(T) F 6. The U.S. economy is referred to as a mixed economy because some of our resources are allocated by the public sector (government).

(T) F 7. When a factory pollutes the air we breathe, this situation is known in economics as an externality.

T (F) 8. In the U.S. market system, the signals for deciding how to use resources are given by the Council of Economic Advisers.

(T) F 9. The distribution of income largely determines the kinds of goods and services the economy will produce.

(T) F 10. The task of economic theory is to explain and predict the economic behavior of market participants.

(T) F 11. One reason that the production-possibilities curve is bowed out is that the efficiency with which resources are used in production varies.

(T) F 12. If the economy is fully and efficiently employing its resources, then the only way to acquire more of one good is to accept less of something else.

T (F) 13. Technological advance shifts the production-possibilities curve inward.

T F 14. When the economy experiences declining productivity, then the production-possibility curve is likely to be shifting inward.

T F 15. Microeconomics focuses on the economy as a whole.

T F 16. The slope of the production-possibilities curve is related to the idea of opportunity cost.

T F 17. Economic growth is a major economic goal in macroeconomics.

Multiple Choice: *Select the correct answer.*

____ 1. Which of the following *best* describes the subject matter covered by principles of economics?
   (a) How the stock market works.
   (b) How to go into business for yourself.
   (c) How the economy allocates its scarce resources.
   (d) Why the U.S. economy outperforms the Soviet economy.

____ 2. Which of the following *best* describes the term "resource allocation"?
   (a) How one spends one's income.
   (b) How one decides which bank to patronize.
   (c) How one decides which stocks and bonds to buy.
   (d) Which goods and services society will produce with the land, labor, and capital available.

____ 3. In economics, what does scarcity mean?
   (a) That when there is a shortage of a particular good, the price will rise.
   (b) That very few buggy whips are being manufactured nowadays.
   (c) That society's desires exceed the want-satisfying capability of the resources available to satisfy those desires.
   (d) None of the above.

____ 4. Which of the following *best* describes the way resources are allocated in the U.S. economy?
   (a) By tradition.
   (b) By command.
   (c) By markets.
   (d) By government.

____ 5. Which of the following are considered scarce in the U.S. economy?
   (a) Hamburgers.
   (b) Automobiles.
   (c) Petroleum products.
   (d) All of the above.

____ 6. I plan on going to a $5 movie this evening instead of studying for an exam. The total opportunity cost of the movie:
   (a) Depends on how I score on the exam.
   (b) Is $5.
   (c) Is what I could have purchased with the $5 plus the study time I forgo.
   (d) Is the forgone studying I could have done in the same time.

____ 7. The opportunity cost of installing a traffic light at a dangerous intersection is:
   (a) Negative, since it will reduce accidents.
   (b) The cost of the stoplight plus the cost savings from a reduction in the number of accidents.
   (c) The time lost by drivers who approach the intersection when the light is red.
   (d) The best possible alternative bundle of other goods or services that must be forgone in order to build and install the traffic light.

_D_ 8. The often-used phrase "time is money" is a way of stating:
(a) "The economy is us."
(b) The fee for a visit to the doctor's office has increased.
(c) Parking meters have been installed.
(d) The idea of opportunity cost.

_D_ 9. Which of the following events would cause the production-possibilities curve to shift *inward*?
(a) The labor supply grows.
(b) New factories are built.
(c) A technological breakthrough occurs.
(d) None of the above.

_D_ 10. Which of the following events would cause the production-possibilities curve to shift *outward*?
(a) The economy grows.
(b) A new, strong plastic is developed for use in building houses.
(c) More women enter the labor force.
(d) All of the above would cause such a shift.

_D_ 11. The market mechanism in the United States generates a distribution of income that is viewed as:
(a) Equal, since everyone gets the same income.
(b) Equitable, since public policy does not tamper with it.
(c) Both equal and equitable, since they mean the same thing.
(d) Inequitable, apparently, since we change it through the activities of the public sector.

_C_ 12. The *slope* of the production-possibilities curve provides information about:
(a) The growth of the economy.
(b) Technological change in the economy.
(c) Opportunity costs in the economy.
(d) All of the above.

_A_ 13. The bowed-out shape of the production-possibilities curve indicates:
(a) Increasing opportunity costs.
(b) Externalities.
(c) Market imperfections.
(d) A mixed economy.

_B_ 14. The law of increasing opportunity costs explains:
(a) How everything becomes more expensive as the economy grows.
(b) The shape of the production-possibilities curve.
(c) Inflation.
(d) All of the above.

_D_ 15. Which of the following are major economic goals?
(a) Full employment.
(b) Price stability.
(c) An equitable distribution of income.
(d) All of the above.

_D_ 16. Macroeconomics focuses on the performance of:
(a) Individual consumers.
(b) Firms.
(c) Government agencies.
(d) None of the above.

Problems and Applications

Exercise 1

This exercise is similar to the problem at the end of Chapter 1 in the text. It provides practice in drawing and interpreting a production-possibilities curve and demonstrating shifts of such a curve.

1. A production-possibilities schedule showing the production alternatives between corn and lumber is presented in Table 1.1. Graph combination A in Figure 1.1 and label it. Do the same for combination B. In going from combination A to combination B, the economy has sacrificed ___2___ billion board feet of lumber production per year and has transferred the land resources to production of ___1___ billion bushels of corn per year. The opportunity cost of corn in terms of lumber is ___2___ board feet per bushel.

Table 1.1

Combination	Quantity of corn (billions of bushels per year)	Quantity of lumber (billions of board feet per year)
A	0	50
B	1	48
C	2	44
D	3	38
E	4	30
F	5	20
G	6	0

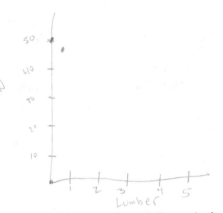

2. You have determined the opportunity cost of corn when the economy is initially producing no corn (combination A). Using the information in Table 1.1, graph the rest of the production-possibility combinations in Figure 1.1 and label each of the points with the appropriate letter.

Figure 1.1

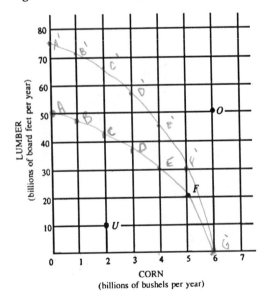

LUMBER (billions of board feet per year)

CORN (billions of bushels per year)

3. When Table 1.2 is completed, it should show the opportunity cost of corn at each possible combination of lumber and corn production in the economy. Opposite "1st billion bushels" insert the number of board feet per year of lumber that is sacrificed when the economy shifts from combination A to combination B. Complete the table for each of the remaining combinations.

Table 1.2

Corn production (billions of bushels per year)	Opportunity cost of corn in terms of lumber (billions of board feet per year)
1st billion bushels	2
2nd billion bushels	4
3rd billion bushels	6
4th billion bushels	8
5th billion bushels	10
6th billion bushels	20

4. From Table 1.2 it is apparent that as more corn is produced (as the economy moves from combination A toward combination G), the opportunity cost of corn __RISES__ (falls, rises, remains the same), which illustrates the law of _INC OPP COST_.

5. Suppose that lumber companies begin to clear-cut forest areas instead of cutting them selectively. Clear-cutting improves the economy's ability to produce lumber but not corn. Table 1.3 describes such a situation. Using the information in Table 1.3, sketch the new production-possibilities curve in Figure 1.1 as you did the initial production-possibilities curve based on Table 1.2. In the adoption of which combination does the use of clear-cutting fail to change the amount of corn and lumber? __G-G'__

Table 1.3

Combination	Corn (billions of bushels per year)	Lumber (billions of board feet per year)
A'	0	75
B'	1	72
C'	2	66
D'	3	57
E'	4	45
F'	5	30
G'	6	0

6. The production-possibilities curve after the introduction of clear-cutting is __OUTSIDE__ (outside, inside, the same as) the earlier curve. As a result of clear-cutting, the opportunity cost of corn has __Increased__ (increased, decreased).

7

7. Study Figure 1.1 and decide which of the combinations shown (*U, F, O*) demonstrates each of the following. (*Hint:* Check the answers at the end of the chapter to make sure you have diagrammed the production-possibility curve in Figure 1.1 correctly.)
   (a) Society is producing at its maximum potential. Combination _F 20, 5_ .
   (b) Society may have some unemployed or underemployed resources. Combination ___U___ .
   (c) Society cannot produce this combination. Combination ___O___ .
   (d) Society might be able to produce this combination if technology improved but cannot produce it with current technology. Combination ___O___ .
   (e) If society produces this combination, some of society's wants will go unsatisfied unnecessarily. Combination ___U___ .

Exercise 2

The following exercise shows how to recognize and infer the concept of production possibilities from statements of public officials.

In a speech before the American Society of Newspaper Editors on April 16, 1953, President Eisenhower stated:

> Every gun that is made, every warship launched, every rocket fired signifies, in the final sense, a theft from those who hunger and are not fed, those who are cold and are not clothed. This world in arms is not spending money alone. It is spending the sweat of its laborers, the genius of its scientists, the hopes of its children. . . . This is not a way of life at all in any true sense. Under the cloud of threatening war, it is humanity hanging from a cross of iron.

Answer the following questions on the basis of the preceding quotation:

1. What factors of production did Eisenhower point to as the resources that limit our production possibilities?
   (a) Guns, warships, rockets.
   (b) Food, clothes.
   (c) Money.
   (d) Laborers, scientists, and the hopes of our children.

2. What are the final goods and services that society desires?
   (a) Guns.
   (b) Warships.
   (c) Clothes.
   (d) All of the above.

3. What would be placed on one of the axes of the production-possibilities curve that Eisenhower has implicitly described?
   (a) Guns, warships, rockets, and other armaments.
   (b) Laborers, scientists, and other labor.
   (c) Money.
   (d) None of the above.

4. Which of the following is the opportunity cost of armaments (guns, warships, and rockets)?
   (a) The amount of clothing or food given up to produce a given quantity of armaments.
   (b) The dollar value of armaments to the national defense.
   (c) The amount of money that Congress appropriates for purchasing armaments.
   (d) None of the above.

5. Implicitly, President Eisenhower recommended that there be greater:
   (a) Expenditure on armaments relative to clothing.
   (b) Expenditure on clothing and on food relative to armaments.
   (c) Development of labor, genius, and hopes to make more armaments, food, and clothing possible.
   (d) Expenditure of money for all of society's needs.

6. If Eisenhower's speech achieved a cutback in production of armaments and greater production of food and clothing, then, assuming the law of increasing opportunity costs applies, the opportunity cost of:
   (a) Both armaments and clothing–food should rise.
   (b) Both armaments and clothing–food should fall.
   (c) Armaments should fall while the opportunity cost of food–clothing should rise.
   (d) Armaments should rise while the opportunity cost of food–clothing should fall.

Exercise 3

Newspaper articles contain a great deal of information about the trade-offs necessary in producing different goods and services. To describe the trade-off, the articles should provide certain information. By using one of the articles in the text, this exercise will show the kind of information to look for. If your professor makes a newspaper assignment for this chapter, this exercise will provide an example of how to do it.

Reread the article in Chapter 1 entitled "Looting the Means of Production" from the *New York Times*. Then answer the following questions:

1. Find the two goods or services (or two groups of goods or services) mentioned in the article between which a trade-off must be made in their production.

2. What passage indicates that a trade-off exists between the two goods or services? For example, does the article indicate some resources that are in limited supply?

3. What evidence is there in the article about the applicability or inapplicability of the law of increasing opportunity cost?

4. What passage in the article indicates a possible shift of the production-possibilities curve or a movement along it? (The shift or movement may have occurred already, may be occurring now, or may occur in the future. Or, the author of the article may be implicitly advocating a shift or a movement.)

5. What would the production-possibilities curve between the two goods in Question 1 look like? Carefully and neatly draw a production-possibilities curve for the two goods using Figure 1.2. Don't use any numbers. However, be very careful to label both of your axes properly and to draw a production-possibilities curve with the correct shape, showing evidence of the applicability or inapplicability of the law of increasing opportunity costs.

Figure 1.2

6. In your diagram of a production-possibilities curve, in what direction would there be a movement along the curve or in what direction would the curve shift based on the passage in Question 4 above? Draw an arrow to indicate the movement or shift.

Common Errors

The first statement in each "common error" below is incorrect. Each incorrect statement is followed by a corrected version and an explanation.

1. Words mean the same thing in economics that they do in our everyday conversation. WRONG!

   Words used in everyday conversation *very often* have different meanings when they are used in economics. RIGHT!

   You'll have to be very careful here. Words are used with precision in economics. You'll have difficulty if you confuse their everyday meanings with their economic meanings. For example, the term "capital" in economics means simply "man-made instruments of production." In everyday usage it may mean money, machines, a loan, or even the British response to the question "How are you feeling?"

2. Economic models are abstractions from the real world and are therefore useless in predicting and explaining economic behavior. WRONG!

   Economic models are abstractions from the real world and *as a result* are useful in predicting and explaining economic behavior. RIGHT!

   You have to be willing to deal with abstractions if you want to get anything accomplished in economics. By using economic models based on specific assumptions, we can make reasonable judgments about what's going on around us. We try not to disregard any useful information. However, to try to include everything (such as what we ate for breakfast) would be fruitless. For example, the production-possibilities frontier is an abstraction. No economist would argue that it is an economy! But it certainly is useful in focusing on public-policy choices, such as whether to produce guns or butter.

3. Because economics is a "science," all economists should come up with the same answer to any given question. WRONG!

   Economics is a science, but there is often room for disagreement in trying to answer a given question. RIGHT!

   Economics is a social science, and the entire society and economy represent our laboratory. Economists cannot run the kind of experiments that are done by physical scientists. As a result, two economists may attack a given problem or question in different ways using different models. They may come up with different answers, but since there is no answer book, you cannot say which is right. The solution is, then, to do more testing, refine more models, compare results, and so on. By the way, the recent space probes have given physicists cause to reevaluate much of their theory concerning the solar system, and there is much controversy concerning what the new evidence means. But physics is still a science!

■ ANSWERS ■

Key-Term Review

1. *ceteris paribus*
2. microeconomics
3. opportunity cost
4. market mechanism
5. factors of production
6. macroeconomics
7. production-possibilities
8. law of increasing opportunity cost
9. externalities
10. economics
11. mixed economy
12. economic growth

True or False

1. F	4. T	7. T	10. T	13. F	16. T
2. T	5. F	8. F	11. T	14. T	17. T
3. T	6. T	9. T	12. T	15. F	

Multiple Choice

1. c	4. c	7. d	10. d	13. a	16. d
2. d	5. d	8. d	11. d	14. b	
3. c	6. c	9. d	12. c	15. d	

Problems and Applications

Exercise 1

1. 2, 1, 2

2. **Figure 1.1 answer**

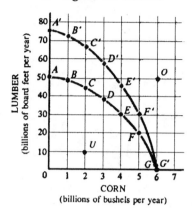

3. **Table 1.2 answer**

Corn production (billions of bushels per year)	Opportunity cost of corn in terms of lumber (billions of board feet per year)
1st billion bushels	2
2nd billion bushels	4
3rd billion bushels	6
4th billion bushels	8
5th billion bushels	10
6th billion bushels	20

4. rises, increasing opportunity costs
5. See Figure 1.1 answer; combination G.
6. outside, increased
7. a, *F;* b, *U;* c, *O;* d, *O;* e, *U*

Exercise 2

1. d
2. d
3. a
4. a
5. b
6. c

Exercise 3

1. "The concentration of capital on the military portends sharply diminished opportunity for a productive livelihood for most Americans." This sentence indicates two general groups of goods: (a) "military" goods, and (b) those goods which provide for the "productive livelihood" of Americans.
2. The resources that constrain production of both types of goods are "machinery, tools, engineers, energy, raw materials, skilled labor, and managers." The "finite" amount of these resources is the cause of the trade-off between military and other goods. The last paragraph of the article explicitly refers to the "trade-offs."
3. "This looting of the means of production on behalf of the military economy can only be accelerated as a consequence of the unprecedented size of the war budgets advocated by the Reagan Administration." The

article suggests that a "deterioration" has already occurred because of big expenditures on defense; but additional military expenditure would cause this deterioration to "accelerate," which suggests the deterioration would occur at a quickening rate, not just a proportionately higher rate.

4. Melman explicitly recognizes the impossibility of shifting the production-possibilities curve outward and is implicitly recommending a move along a production-possibilities curve toward fewer military goods.

5. **Figure 1.2 answer**

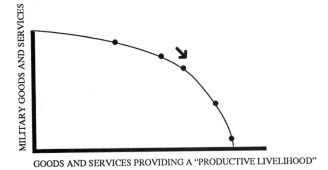

6. See arrow in Figure 1.2 answer.

Chapter 2
Supply and Demand

Quick Review

Every economy must answer the same basic questions:

- WHAT goods and services should the economy produce?
- HOW should they be produced?
- FOR WHOM should they be produced?

In the U.S. economy we rely heavily on markets to answer these questions. In this chapter we focus on markets and market participants and seek answers to three subsidiary questions:

- What determines the price of a good or service?
- How much of a specific product will be produced?
- Why do prices and production levels often change?

Let's look at some market participants and see how they interact. Households and firms exchange factors of production in factor markets and goods and services in product markets. The quantity supplied of factors or products in a market is the quantity that sellers are willing and able to sell at a particular price. Market prices are likely to affect the quantity supplied. Economists represent the relationship between price and the quantity supplied in a supply schedule or supply curve. Supply represents the ability and willingness to sell specific quantities of a good at alternative prices in a given time period, *ceteris paribus.*

The quantity demanded of factors or products in a market is the quantity that buyers are willing and able to buy at a particular price. When prices fall, people tend to buy more. Economists represent the relationship between price and the quantity purchased in the form of a demand schedule or demand curve. Demand is the ability and willingness to buy specific quantities of a good at alternative prices in a given time period, *ceteris paribus.* Demand and supply do not determine what is actually exchanged, nor do they tell why an exchange occurs.

Market-supply and market-demand curves can be used to find the equilibrium price and rate of production in a market. A market-supply curve is the sum of the supply curves of the sellers in the market. Similarly, a market-demand curve is the sum of the individual demand curves of buyers in the market. When the market-demand curve intersects the market-supply curve, the market is in equilibrium. The market mechanism moves price toward the equilibrium price level:

1. If the market price is above the equilibrium price, surpluses appear. To get rid of the surplus, sellers lower prices and production rates. Buyers buy more at lower prices.
2. If the market price is below equilibrium price, shortages occur. Buyers bid up the price of the commodity and sellers raise production rates in response to the increased price.

In both cases price and production rates change until the market reaches the equilibrium price and equilibrium production rate. This is the price and production rate that clears the market efficiently. The market mechanism may fail if there are externalities, and it may not allocate income in a desirable way, but it does tell us WHAT to produce, HOW to produce, and FOR WHOM to produce.

13

Market-demand and market-supply curves shift for a variety of reasons. Changes in the price or availability of other goods, tastes, income, expectations, and the price of a given good can alter market demands. Changes in resource prices, in technology, in expectations, in taxes, and in the number of sellers can alter market supply. With each shift the market finds its way through trial and error back to equilibrium.

Learning Objectives

After reading Chapter 2 and doing the following exercises, you should:	True or false	Multiple choice	Problems and applications	Common errors	Pages in the text
1. Know the basic questions in economics and how the U.S. economy answers the questions.	1,2	2–4,8,9			30–31
2. Be able to describe the different types of markets and the participants in those markets.	3,4	5,6,11			31–34
3. Understand how a demand schedule represents demand and how a supply schedule represents supply.	7,8	24,28	1,3,4		34–38
4. Be able to define and graph supply and demand curves.	5,6,9,10	7,32	1,4	1	34–44
5. Know why supply and demand curves shift.	18–20	10,16,21, 22,26,29–31	2–5	7	38–39,44
6. Know the difference between individual demand and market demand and between individual supply and market supply.	10	23,25	1,3		34–44
7. Be able to describe how and why markets move toward equilibrium.	11,13, 15–17	12–14,27	4,5	2–4	44–46
8. Be able to explain shortages and surpluses.	12,14	15,20	3,4,5		46–49
9. Know what causes movement along supply and demand curves.		17–19	4,5	5,6	38–39,44
10. Understand the concept of laissez faire.		1			50–53

Key-Term Review

Review the following terms; if you are not sure of the meaning of any term, write out the definition and check it against the Glossary in the text.

ceteris paribus
demand
demand curve
demand schedule
equilibrium price
factor market
factors of production
laissez faire
law of demand
law of supply
market

market demand
market economy
market mechanism
market shortage
market supply
market surplus
opportunity cost
product market
shift in demand
supply

Fill in the blank following each of the statements below with the appropriate term from the list above.

1. The sum of the quantities demanded by all of the individual buyers in a market at every price is called _____.

   1. _MARKET DEMAND_

2. The relationship between prices and the quantity a buyer is willing and able to purchase at those prices is shown in tabular form as a _____.

   2. _DEMAND Schedule_

3. The value of the next most desirable use of resources is called the _____.

   3. _OPPORTUNITY COSTS_

4. Any place where individuals get together to buy or sell is referred to as a _____.

   4. _MARKET_

5. By adding together all the quantities that individual suppliers are willing and able to sell at different prices, you can find _____.

   5. _MARKET SUPPLY_

6. A French term meaning "let alone" is _____.

   6. _LAISSEZ FAIRE_

7. What a buyer is willing and able to buy at various prices is called _____.

   7. _DEMAND_

8. What a seller is willing and able to sell at various prices is called _____.

   8. _SUPPLY_

9. When quantity demanded equals quantity supplied, this correspondence establishes the _____.

   9. _Equilibrium PricE_

10. Changes in tastes, income, or prices of other goods may cause a _____.

    10. _Shift IN DEmand_

11. The quantities that buyers are willing and able to buy at various prices are shown graphically in a _____.

    11. _DEMAND CURVE_

12. When prices are determined by buyers and sellers in a market, the economy is using the _____.

    12. _market mechanism_

13. A decline in market prices below the market equilibrium level causes a _____.

    13. _MARKET Shortage_

14. Finished goods are exchanged in a _____.

    14. _Product market_

15. A rise in market price above the market-equilibrium price level causes a _____.

    15. _MARKET surplus_

16. Resources are exchanged for money in a _____.

    16. _factor market_

17. A Latin phrase meaning "all other things remaining equal" is _____.

    17. _ceteris Paribus_

18. The idea that quantity demanded increases as price falls, *ceteris paribus*, is known as the _____.

    18. _LAW OF Demand_

19. The idea that quantity supplied increases when price increases, *ceteris paribus*, is known as the _____.

    19. _LAW OF Supply_

20. Households are suppliers of _____ in the factor market.

    20. _factors OF production_

21. Supply and demand are the driving forces in a _____.

    21. _MARKET economy_

True or False: *Circle your choice.*

T (F) 1. In a market economy, prices are determined by the consumer; in a planned or command economy, prices are determined by the seller.

(T) F 2. Firms, consumers, and government all have goals, and they also have constraints that prevent them from realizing these goals.

(T) F 3. People who are producers at work may be consumers when they go to the store to buy groceries.

T (F) 4. Exchange of goods and services occurs only when money is available to bring about the exchange.

(T) F 5. Supply curves reflect the potential behavior only of the sellers or producers of a good or service, not of buyers.

(T) F 6. Demand curves reflect the potential behavior only of the buyers of a good or service, not of sellers.

T (F) 7. Transactions in a command economy reflect the willingness and ability of sellers to supply a product.

T (F) 8. Transactions in a command economy reflect the willingness and ability of buyers to demand a product.

T (F) 9. The demand curve shows how much of a good a buyer will actually buy at a given price.

(T) F 10. A market-demand curve can always be found by adding, horizontally, the demand curves of all of the buyers in a given market.

(T) F 11. The equilibrium price occurs at the price where the supply and demand curves intersect.

T (F) 12. In a planned economy the market moves the price toward the equilibrium price.

(T) F 13. The equilibrium price is determined through the process of trial and error by both the buyers and the sellers in a market.

(T) F 14. There are never shortages or surpluses when the price in a market is equal to the equilibrium price for the market.

T (F) 15. At the equilibrium price, sellers receive signals to increase production rates while buyers receive signals to increase purchases in a given time period.

T (F) 16. The people who demand goods and services are constrained by their incomes from achieving the goal of satisfying their desires for goods and services.

(T) F 17. An economy run with a laissez-faire policy permits the invisible hand to direct prices for all goods and services toward their equilibrium levels.

(T) F 18. When the number of suppliers in a market changes, the market-supply curve for goods and services also changes, even if the individual supply curves of original suppliers do not shift.

(T) F 19. Changes in technology, prices of resources, taxes, and expectations cause market-supply curves to shift.

(T) F 20. Changes in variables that shift individual demand curves (such as tastes and income) also shift market-demand curves.

Multiple Choice: *Select the correct answer.*

___A___ 1. A laissez-faire policy may not create as much satisfaction as might otherwise be obtainable because of the existence of:
   (a) Public goods, inequitable distributions of income, and market power of businesses.
   (b) Public goods, government intervention, and competitiveness of businesses.
   (c) Government intervention, welfare for the poor, and lobbying by unions and businesses.
   (d) Government taxation, government regulation, and government enterprise.

_____ B 2. The principal actors in an economy are all constrained from achieving their goals:
   (a) Consumers by income, businesses by profits, and government by taxes.
   (b) Consumers by available goods and services, businesses by scarce resources, government by resources not used by businesses.
   (c) Consumers by the satisfaction derived from purchasing goods and services, businesses by profits, and government by the general welfare.
   (d) Consumers by available goods and services, businesses by scarce resources, and government by the general welfare.

_____ 3. The goals of the principal actors in the economy are:
   (a) Income for consumers, profits for businesses, and taxes for government.
   (b) Goods and services for consumers, scarce resources for businesses, and resources not used by businesses for government.
   (c) Satisfaction from the purchase of goods and services for consumers, profits for businesses, and general welfare for government.
   (d) Available goods and services for consumers, scarce resources for businesses, and general welfare for government.

_____ 4. Since not all goals can be achieved because of our limited resources, economists find the significant questions to be answered are:
   (a) When something should be produced, how long it should be produced, and who should produce it.
   (b) Why something should be produced, who should receive the production or services, and how they should receive them.
   (c) What can be produced, how often it should be produced, and who should produce it.
   (d) What should be produced, how it should be produced, and who should receive it.

_____ 5. The three factors of production are:
   (a) Labor, natural resources, and equipment.
   (b) Rent, wages, and profit.
   (c) Land, labor, and capital.
   (d) None of the above.

_____ 6. Product markets differ from factor markets in that:
   (a) Product markets involve finished goods and services.
   (b) Supply and demand curves can be applied only to product markets.
   (c) Products can be used to produce factors of production.
   (d) None of the above is the case.

_____ 7. The emphasis on "willingness and ability" in the definitions of supply and demand warns us that supply and demand do not necessarily tell us:
   (a) The actual quantities produced and bought in a market.
   (b) The reasons that a particular quantity is demanded or supplied.
   (c) Who actually produces or receives the quantity demanded or supplied.
   (d) All of the above.

_____ C 8. Market-supply and market-demand curves are similar in that both:
   (a) Involve the willingness and ability of a supplier to sell a product or service.
   (b) Involve the willingness and ability of a buyer to buy a product or service.
   (c) Have price on the y-axis and production rate (quantity) on the x-axis.
   (d) Can be derived by adding vertically all of the curves of the individuals in the market.

_____ 9. Equilibrium prices include:
   (a) List prices that firms post on their products or in catalogs to inform the buyer of the price that is being offered.
   (b) Bid prices by buyers to inform the seller of the highest price that a buyer is willing and able to pay for a product.
   (c) Transaction prices that leave no shortages or surpluses at the end of the transaction period.
   (d) Prices at which there is excess supply.

10. A downward shift in demand and a leftward shift in demand are both characterized by (two answers):
    (a) A smaller quantity demanded at every price.
    (b) A greater quantity demanded at every price.
    (c) A higher price at each quantity demanded.
    (d) A lower price at each quantity demanded.

11. The goal of the supplier of a product or service in a market economy is:
    (a) The use of scarce resources subject to the constraint of taxes.
    (b) The use of scarce resources subject to the constraint of available profit.
    (c) Profits subject to the constraint of scarce resources.
    (d) Profits subject to the constraint of income.

12. The equilibrium price in a market is found where:
    (a) The supply curve intersects the demand curve.
    (b) The supply curve intersects the y-axis.
    (c) The demand curve intersects the y-axis.
    (d) The supply curve intersects the x-axis.

13. In a market not at equilibrium:
    (a) Excess supply corresponds to surpluses, and excess demand to shortages.
    (b) Excess supply corresponds to shortages, and excess demand to surpluses.
    (c) Excess demand corresponds to an excessive price.
    (d) None of the above.

14. In a market economy, when there is a surplus in a market a firm has an incentive to:
    (a) Raise prices.
    (b) Lower prices.
    (c) Raise production.
    (d) None of the above.

15. What may happen when a competitive market is in equilibrium?
    (a) There may be shortages.
    (b) There may be surpluses.
    (c) Firms will have an incentive to raise prices.
    (d) None of the above.

16. A movement along the supply curve is the same as:
    (a) A shift in the supply curve.
    (b) A change in the quantity supplied.
    (c) A change in the quantity demanded.
    (d) All of the above.

17. A change in the price of a good corresponds to a:
    (a) Change in the quantity demanded of the good.
    (b) Shift in the supply curve for the good.
    (c) Shift in the demand curve of the good.
    (d) None of the above.

18. The determinant of demand that does not shift a demand curve is:
    (a) Income.
    (b) Taste.
    (c) The price of the good itself.
    (d) The prices of other goods.

19. According to the law of demand, the quantity of a good demanded in a given time period:
    (a) Increases as its price rises, ceteris paribus.
    (b) Decreases as its price falls, ceteris paribus.
    (c) Increases as its price falls, ceteris paribus.
    (d) Does none of the above.

____ 20. A market shortage is:
   (a) The amount by which the quantity demanded exceeds the quantity supplied at a given price.
   (b) Excess demand.
   (c) A situation in which market price does not equal equilibrium price, so that people cannot buy all of the goods that they are willing and otherwise able to buy.
   (d) All of the above.

____ 21. A shift in demand is defined as a change in the:
   (a) Quantity demanded.
   (b) Quantity demanded due to a change in price.
   (c) Quantities demanded at alternative prices.
   (d) Equilibrium quantity.

____ 22. A shift of supply is defined as a change in the:
   (a) Quantity supplied.
   (b) Quantity supplied due to a change in price.
   (c) Quantities supplied at alternative prices.
   (d) Equilibrium quantity.

____ 23. By definition, market demand is:
   (a) The sum of individual demands.
   (b) The total quantity of a good or service people are willing and able to buy at alternative prices over a given period of time, *ceteris paribus.*
   (c) The total quantity of a good or service people are willing and able to buy at a given price over a given period of time.
   (d) a and b.

____ 24. By definition, supply reflects:
   (a) The ability and willingness to sell a specific quantity of a good at a given price over a given time period, *ceteris paribus.*
   (b) The ability and willingness to sell specific quantities of a good at alternative prices over a given time period, *ceteris paribus.*
   (c) The ability and willingness to produce a specific quantity of a good at a given price in a given time period, *ceteris paribus.*
   (d) All of the above.

____ 25. Market supply represents:
   (a) The total quantity of a good that sellers are willing and able to sell at alternative prices in a given time period, *ceteris paribus.*
   (b) The horizontal sum of individual supply curves.
   (c) The combined willingness and ability of market suppliers to sell goods and services at various prices, in a given time period, *ceteris paribus.*
   (d) All of the above.

____ 26. A downward shift in the supply curve and a rightward shift in the supply curve are both characterized by:
   (a) A smaller quantity supplied and a greater price.
   (b) A greater quantity supplied and a greater price.
   (c) A smaller quantity supplied and a lower price.
   (d) A greater quantity supplied and a lower price.

____ 27. By definition, the equilibrium price in a market:
   (a) Occurs when the supply and demand curves are the same, *ceteris paribus.*
   (b) Is the price at which the quantity of a good or service demanded in a given time period equals the quantity supplied.
   (c) Is the market price.
   (d) All of the above.

_B_ 28. *Ceteris paribus* means:
    (a) Everything being equal.
    (b) Everything else being equal.
    (c) Only one thing changes.
    (d) Only one thing remains the same.

_B_ 29. Which of the following would generally cause an increase in the demand for automobiles?
    (a) A decrease in the price of automobiles.
    (b) An increase in consumers' income.
    (c) The new models are perceived as ugly compared to old models.
    (d) Consumer expectation that the price of automobiles will be lower next year.

_D_ 30. Which of the following would you expect to cause a decrease in the demand for automobiles?
    (a) A rise in the price of gasoline.
    (b) Consumer expectation that the price of automobiles will be lower next year.
    (c) Consumer expectation that a significant recession will develop that could last for a year.
    (d) All of the above.

_U_ 31. Which of the following would *not* cause the market supply of telephones to increase?
    (a) Telecommunications are deregulated, and anyone who wants to can produce and sell telephones.
    (b) A new and cheaper technology for producing plastics is developed.
    (c) A reduction in the demand for telephones causes their prices to fall.
    (d) Taxes levied on telephone production are reduced.

_D_ 32. Which of the following *best* provides an example of the law of supply?
    (a) Falling labor costs cause an increase in supply.
    (b) An improved technology shifts the supply curve to the right.
    (c) Some producers leave the industry, and the supply curve shifts upward.
    (d) Demand falls and the quantity supplied decreases.

Problems and Applications

Exercise 1

This exercise provides practice in graphing demand and supply curves for individual buyers and sellers as well as graphing market-demand and market-supply curves.

1.   Suppose you were willing and able to buy 20 gallons of gasoline per week if the price were $1, but if the price were $3 you would be willing and able to buy only the bare minimum of 10 gallons. Complete the demand schedule in Table 2.1.

Table 2.1
Your demand schedule for gasoline

Price (dollars per gallon)	Quantity (gallons per week)
$1	20
3	10

2.   Use your demand schedule for gasoline in Table 2.1 to diagram the demand curve in Figure 2.1. Assume your demand curve is a straight line.

Figure 2.1
Your demand curve for gasoline

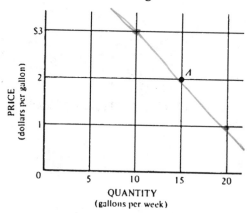

If you have drawn your demand curve correctly, it should go through point A.

3. Suppose that 999 other people in your town have demand curves for gasoline that are just like yours in Figure 2.1. Fill out the town's market-demand schedule in Table 2.2 at each price. (Remember to include your own quantity demanded along with everyone else's at each price.)

Table 2.2
Market demand schedule for gasoline in your town

Price (dollars per gallon)	Quantity (gallons per week)
$1	20,000
3	10,000

4. Using the market-demand schedule in Table 2.2, draw the market-demand curve for gasoline for your town in Figure 2.2. Assume that the curve is a straight line, and label it D.

Figure 2.2
Market supply and demand curves for gasoline in your town

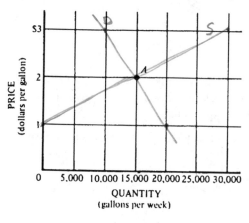

If you have drawn the demand curve correctly, it should pass through point A.

5. Suppose the friendly neighborhood gas station will not sell anything at $1 per gallon, but at $3 it would be willing to sell 1,500 gallons per week. Fill in the supply schedule for this gas station in Table 2.3.

21

Table 2.3
Supply schedule for neighborhood gas station

Price (dollars per gallon)	Quantity (gallons per week)
$1	0
3	1,500

6. Graph the supply curve in Figure 2.3 based on the information in Table 2.3 and label it S. Assume that the supply curve is a straight line through both points.

Figure 2.3
Supply curve for neighborhood gas station

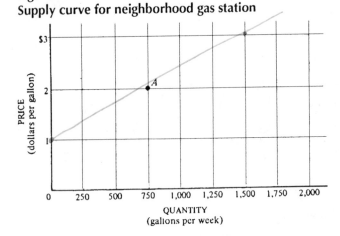

7. Suppose that nineteen other gas stations in your town have the same supply schedule as your neighborhood gas station (Table 2.3). Fill out the market-supply schedule for gasoline of the twenty gas stations in your town in Table 2.4.

Table 2.4
Market supply schedule for gasoline in your town

Price (dollars per gallon)	Quantity (gallons per week)
$1	0
3	30,000

8. Using the market supply schedule in Table 2.4, draw the market-supply curve for gasoline for your town on Figure 2.2. Assume that the market-supply curve is a straight line. If you have drawn the curve correctly, it should pass through point A. Label the supply curve S.

9. The equilibrium price for gasoline for your town's twenty gas stations and 1,000 buyers of gasoline (see Figure 2.2) is:
   (a) Above $2.
   (b) Exactly $2.
   (c) Below $2.

10. At the equilibrium price there are:
    (a) Shortages.
    (b) Surpluses.
    (c) Excess inventories.
    (d) None of the above.

Exercise 2

This exercise shows the market mechanics at work in shifting market-demand curves.

1. In Figure 2.4, the supply (S_1) and demand (D_1) curves for gasoline as they might appear in your town are presented. The equilibrium price is:
   (a) $3 per gallon.
   (b) $2 per gallon.
   (c) $1 per gallon.
   (d) $0 per gallon.

Figure 2.4
Market demand and supply curves for gasoline in your town

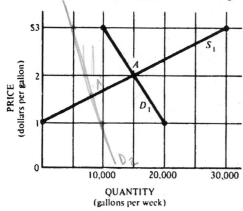

2. Assume that one-half of the people in your town move away. Because of this suppose that buyers are willing and able to buy only half as much gasoline at each price as was bought before. Draw the new demand curve in Figure 2.4 and label it D_2.

3. T   F   When the number of buyers in a market changes, the market-demand curve for goods and services shifts.

4. When half of the buyers move from your town, the equilibrium price:
   (a) Rises above the old equilibrium price.
   (b) Equals the old equilibrium price.
   (c) Falls below the old equilibrium price.
   (*Hint:* See the second demand curve, D_2, in Figure 2.4.)

5. If the old market price ($2) does not change to the new equilibrium price, there will be:
   (a) A larger quantity demanded than is supplied at the old equilibrium price.
   (b) A smaller quantity demanded than is supplied at the old equilibrium price.

6. If the market price does not adjust to the new equilibrium price after the potential buyers leave, there will be:
   (a) A market shortage.
   (b) A market surplus.
   (c) Neither shortage nor surplus.

7. When there is a surplus in a market, prices are likely to fall:
   (a) Because buyers do not wish to buy as much as sellers want to sell.
   (b) Because sellers are likely to offer discounts to eliminate expensive excess inventories.
   (c) Because buyers who cannot buy commodities at the current market price are likely to make offers to buy at lower prices that sellers will accept.
   (d) For all of the above reasons.

8. Whenever there is a leftward shift of the market-demand curve, market forces should push:
   (a) Market prices upward and market quantity downward.
   (b) Market prices upward and market quantity upward.
   (c) Market prices downward and market quantity upward.
   (d) Market prices downward and market quantity downward.

9. Whenever there is a rightward shift of the market-demand curve, market forces should push:
   (a) Market prices upward and market quantity downward.
   (b) Market prices upward and market quantity upward.
   (c) Market prices downward and market quantity upward.
   (d) Market prices downward and market quantity downward.

Exercise 3

This exercise gives practice in computing market-demand and market-supply curves using the demand and supply curves of individuals in a market. It is similar to the problem at the end of Chapter 2 in the textbook.

1. Table 2.5 shows the weekly demand and supply schedules for various individuals. Fill in the total market quantity that these individuals demand and supply.

Table 2.5
Individual demand and supply schedules

	Price			
	$4	$3	$2	$1
Buyers				
Al's quantity demanded	2	3	5	6
Betsy's quantity demanded	2	2	2	3
Casey's quantity demanded	1	2.5	3	3.5
Total market quantity demanded	5	7.5	10	12.5
Sellers				
Alice's quantity supplied	8	3	2	0
Butch's quantity supplied	7	5	4	0
Connie's quantity supplied	9	7	3	0
Ellen's quantity supplied	6	5	1	0
Total market quantity supplied	30	20	10	0

Use the data in Table 2.5 to answer Questions 2–4.

2. Construct and label market-supply and market-demand curves in Figure 2.5.

3. Identify the equilibrium price and label it *EQ* in Figure 2.5.

4. What is the amount of shortage or surplus that would exist at a price of $1? _____

Figure 2.5
Market-supply and market-demand curves for buyers and sellers

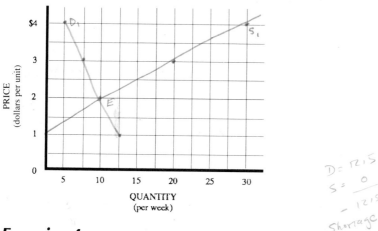

Exercise 4

This exercise provides examples of events that would shift demand or supply curves. It is similar to the exercise at the end of Chapter 2 in the text.

Choose the letter of the appropriate diagram in Figure 2.6 that best describes the type of shift that would occur in each of the following situations. The shifts are viewed as occurring in the market for U.S. defense goods. (*Hint:* Ask yourself if the change occurs initially through the buyers or the sellers. Then look for the determinant that is changing. Finally, ask yourself how the quantity or price should change due to the hypothesized event. Use common sense. With these three pieces of information it should be possible to determine the shift that occurs. The nonprice determinants of demand are tastes and preferences, incomes, buyer expectations, prices and availability of other goods, and number of buyers. The nonprice determinants of supply are technology, price and availability of resources, expectations, taxes, and number of suppliers.)

Figure 2.6
Shifts of curves

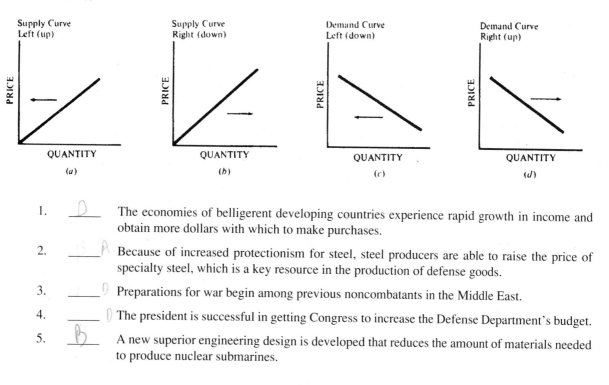

1. ___D___ The economies of belligerent developing countries experience rapid growth in income and obtain more dollars with which to make purchases.

2. ___A___ Because of increased protectionism for steel, steel producers are able to raise the price of specialty steel, which is a key resource in the production of defense goods.

3. ___D___ Preparations for war begin among previous noncombatants in the Middle East.

4. ___D___ The president is successful in getting Congress to increase the Defense Department's budget.

5. ___B___ A new superior engineering design is developed that reduces the amount of materials needed to produce nuclear submarines.

25

6. __B__ New firms enter the market to produce defense goods.

7. __A__ A large firm in the defense industry goes into liquidation when it loses a defense contract and becomes bankrupt.

8. __D__ Consumers expect gun-control legislation to be enacted that will make it more difficult to purchase handguns in the future.

9. When you know what is shifting, you should be able to tell how equilibrium price and quantity will change. Fill in the blanks in Table 2.6 with "Rises" or "Falls."

Table 2.6
Response of equilibrium price and quantity to shifts in market supply and demand

Type of shift (ceteris paribus)	Equilibrium price	Equilibrium quantity
Market supply shifts leftward	Rises	Falls
Market supply shifts rightward	Falls	Rises
Market demand shifts leftward	Falls	Falls
Market demand shifts rightward	Rises	Rises

Exercise 5

The media often provide information about supply and demand shifts. Using one of the articles in the text, this exercise will show the kind of information to look for. If your professor makes a newspaper assignment for this chapter, this exercise will provide an example of how to do it.

Reread the article in Chapter 2 entitled "Surplus Punches Hole in Oil Price" from *USA Today*. Then answer the following questions:

1. Which of the four diagrams in Figure 2.6 (p. 25) best represents the shift caused by the Norwegian oil strike?
   a   b   c   d   (circle one)

2. Find the sentence that indicates the market is an international, national, regional, or local market.

3. What single word describes the change in the determinant of demand or supply that has caused the shift you chose in Figure 2.6?

4. Is it the buyer or the seller of crude oil who is initially affected by the change? How do you know?

5. What phrase (no more than a sentence) indicates the change in price or quantity that results from the Norwegian oil strike?

6. Although the article indicates prices were headed down because of the "world surplus," does it provide any indication about which determinants of demand and supply caused the world surplus?

Crossword Puzzle

Select the economic term in the following list that corresponds with each of the definitions and descriptions below. Then fit the term or one of the words within it into the crossword puzzle at the numbers indicated.

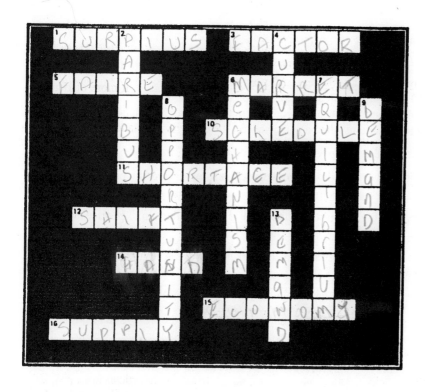

ceteris paribus
command
  economy
demand
demand curve
demand
  schedule
equilibrium
  price
factor market
invisible hand
laissez faire
market
market demand

market economy
market
  mechanism
market shortage
market supply
market surplus
opportunity cost
product market
shift in demand
shift in supply
supply
supply curve
supply schedule

Across

1. What occurs when market price is above the market-equilibrium price level.
3. Where resources are exchanged for money.
5. A non-English way of saying "let alone."
6. The total quantity that all sellers in a market are willing and able to make available at various prices.
10. A table that shows the relationship between prices and the quantities a buyer is willing and able to buy at various prices.
11. What occurs when market price is below the market-equilibrium price level.
12. Changes in tastes, incomes, or opportunity costs cause this to happen.
14. What guides market prices if the government does not interfere.
15. The type of system in which the invisible hand determines prices.
16. The quantities a seller is willing and able to sell at various prices.

Down

2. A non-English term meaning "all other things being equal."
4. A graph representing the quantities that buyers are willing to buy at various prices, *ceteris paribus*.
6. When prices are determined by buyers and sellers in a market, the economy is using the _____ market mechanism
7. When quantity demanded equals quantity supplied, the _____ is established.
8. The value of the next best alternative that must be forgone as a result of the decision to use resources in a particular way.
9. What a buyer is willing and able to buy at various prices.
13. The total quantity demanded by all of the individual buyers in a market at every price.

Common Errors

The first statement in each "common error" below is incorrect. Each incorrect statement is followed by a corrected version and an explanation.

1. If a large number of people petition the government in order to get something, then there is a large demand for that item. WRONG!

27

If a large number of people desire a commodity *and have the ability to pay for it,* then there is a large demand for that commodity in a particular time period. RIGHT!

People may want something, but there is no "demand" for it unless they are able to pay for it. Economists use the word "demand" in a way that is quite different from normal usage. People who want (desire, have preferences, a taste or liking for) a commodity are seen as going to a market to purchase the commodity with money or through bargaining. As economists use the word, "demand" has no connotation of stridency or imperiously claiming the right to something when a person hasn't the ability to buy it.

2. Market price is the same thing as equilibrium price. WRONG!

The market price moves by trial and error (via the market mechanism) toward the equilibrium price. RIGHT!

When demand and supply curves shift, the market is temporarily out of equilibrium. The price may move along a demand or supply curve toward the new equilibrium.

3. Since the quantity bought must equal the quantity sold, every market is always in equilibrium by definition. WRONG!

Although quantity bought equals quantity sold, there may be shortages or surpluses. RIGHT!

Although the quantity *actually* bought does equal the quantity *actually* sold, there may still be buyers who *are willing and able* to buy more of the good at the market price (shortages exist) or sellers who are willing and able to sell more of the good at the market price (surpluses exist). If the market price is above the equilibrium price, there will be queues of goods (inventories). Prices will be lowered by sellers toward the equilibrium price. If the market price is below the equilibrium price, there will be queues of buyers (shortages). Prices will be bid up by buyers toward the equilibrium price.

4. The intersection of the supply and demand curves determines how much of a good or service will actually be exchanged and the actual price of the exchange. WRONG!

The intersection of supply and demand curves only shows where buyers and sellers *intend* and have the *ability* to exchange the same amount of a commodity. RIGHT!

Many institutional interferences may prevent the market from ever reaching the equilibrium point, where supply and demand curves intersect. All that can be said is that, given a free market and no other changes, prices and production will tend to move toward equilibrium levels.

5. A change in price changes the demand for goods by consumers. WRONG!

A change in price changes the quantity demanded by consumers in a given time period. RIGHT!

Economists differentiate between the terms "quantity demanded" and "demand." A change in the quantity demanded usually refers to a movement along the demand curve due to a change in price or production rate. A change in demand refers to a shift of the demand curve due to a change in incomes, tastes, prices of other goods, or expectations.

6. A change in price changes the supply of goods produced by a firm. WRONG!

A change in price changes the quantity of a good supplied by a firm in a given time period. RIGHT!

Economists differentiate between the terms "quantity supplied" and "supply." A change in the quantity supplied usually refers to a movement along a supply curve due to a change in price or production rate. A change in supply refers to a shift of the supply curve due to a change in technology, prices of resources, number of sellers, expectations, or taxes.

7. A rise in the supply curve is the same as an increase in supply. WRONG!

An upward shift in the supply curve implies a decrease in supply. RIGHT!

In Figure 2.7 the *rise* of the supply curve from S_1 to S_2 will result in a fall in quantity from Q_1 to Q_2 at any price, P^*. Supply is *lower*. A fall in the supply curve means an increase in supply.

Figure 2.7

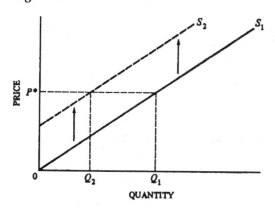

Be careful: When a shift in the supply curve is mentioned, it may help to think of the shift as a movement to the left or right, not up or down.

■ ANSWERS ■

Key-Term Review

1. market demand
2. demand schedule
3. opportunity cost
4. market
5. market supply
6. laissez faire
7. demand
8. supply
9. equilibrium price
10. shift in demand
11. demand curve
12. market mechanism
13. market shortage
14. product market
15. market surplus
16. factor market
17. *ceteris paribus*
18. law of demand
19. law of supply
20. factors of production
21. market economy

True or False

1. F	5. T	9. F	12. F	15. F	18. T
2. T	6. T	10. T	13. T	16. T	19. T
3. T	7. F	11. T	14. T	17. T	20. T
4. F	8. F				

Multiple Choice

1. a	7. d	13. a	18. c	23. d	28. b
2. b	8. c	14. b	19. c	24. b	29. b
3. c	9. c	15. d	20. d	25. d	30. d
4. d	10. a, d	16. b	21. c	26. d	31. c
5. c	11. c	17. a	22. c	27. b	32. d
6. a	12. a				

Problems and Applications

Exercise 1

1. Table 2.1 answer

p	q
$1	20
$3	10

2. **Figure 2.1 answer**

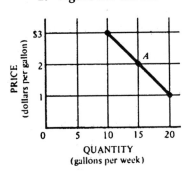

QUANTITY
(gallons per week)

3. **Table 2.2 answer**

p	q
$1	20,000
$3	10,000

4. **Figure 2.2 answer**

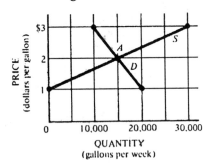

QUANTITY
(gallons per week)

5. **Table 2.3 answer**

p	q
$1	0
3	1,500

6. **Figure 2.3 answer**

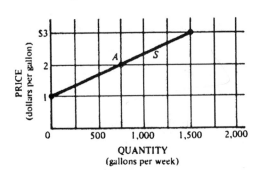

QUANTITY
(gallons per week)

7. **Table 2.4 answer**

p	q
$1	0
3	30,000

8. See Figure 2.2 answer.
9. b
10. d

Exercise 2

1. b
2. **Figure 2.4 answer**

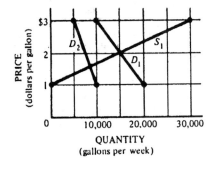

QUANTITY
(gallons per week)

3. T
4. c
5. b
6. b
7. d
8. d
9. b

Exercise 3

1. **Table 2.5 answer**

	Price			
	$4	*$3*	*$2*	*$1*
Buyers				
Total market quantity demanded	5	7.5	10	12.5
Sellers				
Total market quantity supplied	30	20	10	0

2. **Figure 2.5 answer**

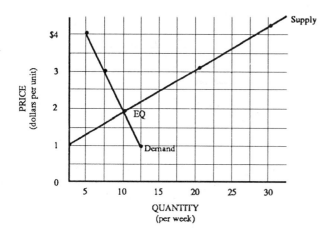

3. See point *EQ* in Figure 2.5.
4. Since the quantity supplied is zero at a price of $1, the shortage is the same as the quantity demanded (12.5 units).

Exercise 4

1. d   A rise in income shifts the demand curve upward (to the right).
2. a   An increase in the price of a resource shifts the supply curve upward (to the left).
3. d   An increase in the number of buyers shifts the demand curve upward (to the right).
4. d   A larger budget (income) for defense shifts the demand curve upward (to the right).
5. b   An improvement in technology shifts the supply curve downward (to the right).
6. b   An increase in the number of suppliers shifts the supply curve downward (to the right).
7. a   A decrease in the number of suppliers shifts the supply curve to the left.
8. d   Buyers' expectations that guns will be more difficult to obtain in the future shift the demand curve to the right today.

9. **Table 2.6 answer**

Type of shift (ceteris paribus)	Equilibrium price	Equilibrium quantity
Market supply shifts leftward	Rises	Falls
Market supply shifts rightward	Falls	Rises
Market demand shifts leftward	Falls	Falls
Market demand shifts rightward	Rises	Rises

Exercise 5

1. a   Supply shifts to the left because there will be less oil available at every price.
2. The fact that the Norwegian oil strike can affect West Texas crude oil suggests an international market.
3. The word "strike" indicates the resources used to produce crude oil are no longer available, which means a reduced supply of crude oil.
4. The sellers of crude oil will experience the effects of the strike first because they cannot get the crude oil to bring to the market.
5. "Fueling the earlier price rally" indicates that prices were rising in response to the strike.
6. No, the article provides information telling why prices went up, but it gives no information on the major theme of the article, "surplus punches hole in oil price." Such incomplete information is likely when the media deliberately keep news short. Incompleteness is an important reason for using the *Wall Street Journal, New York Times, Business Week,* and other news sources that provide more background information.

Crossword Puzzle Answer

Across

1. market *surplus*
3. *factor* market
5. laissez *faire*
6. *market*
10. demand *schedule*
11. market *shortage*
12. *shift* in demand
14. invisible *hand*
15. market *economy*
16. *supply*

Down

2. ceteris *paribus*
4. demand *curve*
6. market *mechanism*
7. *equilibrium* price
8. *opportunity* cost
9. *demand*
13. market *demand*

Chapter 3
The Public Sector

Quick Review

The combined levels of government—federal, state and local—have a tremendous impact on the answers to the questions WHAT, HOW, and FOR WHOM IN the U.S. economy. In this chapter we focus initially on the following questions:

- Do we need a public sector?
- What goods and services are best produced by government?
- How large a public sector is desirable?

There are several ways to justify the existence of the public sector. One justification is market failure, the failure of the market mechanism when left on its own to produce an "optimal mix" of output. This first justification for government intervention resides in the concept of "public goods." These goods and services are consumed jointly, both by those who pay and by those who don't. Those who don't pay are termed "free riders." National defense is a good example, because the consumption of national defense is communal. Consumption by one person does not preclude consumption by another. Public goods are different from private goods, for consumption of a private good by one person generally does preclude consumption by another.

The existence of externalities—costs or benefits of a market activity that are borne by a third party—is often cited in justifying public-sector activity, too. Externalities can be negative (such as the pollution from a steel mill) or positive (such as the enrichment of the surrounding community when education is produced and consumed). Because the market has no way of accounting for all costs and all benefits of some forms of economic activity, it tends to underproduce those that generate external benefits and overproduce those that generate external costs.

The existence of market power—the ability of a single firm to alter the market price of a specific product—also justifies public-sector intervention. Market power—whether bestowed by a legal sanction (copyrights, patents, etc.), efficiencies of large-scale production, or some other factor—can be used to restrict output and raise prices. The public sector counters market power by antitrust activity and/or regulation.

Finally, equity in the answer to the FOR WHOM question is the basis for a large measure of public-sector activity. The market mechanism, left on its own, would provide too little for some (the aged, the infirm, some of the very young) than is thought fair. Since the public at large is thought to benefit from expenditures made to address this problem, income redistribution—for example, through transfer payments—is considered a public good.

Although the examples above focus on micro failures (i.e., where we are on the production-possibilities curve), macro failure can occur too, as when we fail to reach our production-possibilities curve or suffer from inflation. Thus, government is expected to intervene at the macro level to alleviate the problem of unemployment and monitor the price level.

The role of government has grown dramatically in recent decades. The budget of the federal government is over $1 trillion, but it still takes only about the same share (of the now much larger economy) as it did in 1950. State and local government activity exceeds that of the federal government and has grown much more rapidly in recent decades. Transfer payments have increased much faster than purchases of goods and services, and they account for the largest part of the observed increase in the size of the entire public sector.

Federal expenditures on goods and services, transfer payments, interest on the public debt, and general aid to state and local governments in fiscal year 1989 exceeded $1 trillion. These expenditures are supported by the federal personal income tax, social security taxes, corporate income taxes, excise taxes, and other taxes.

State and local governments rely most heavily on sales and on property taxes, respectively. Their expenditures go primarily to education, streets and highways, and other services we find close to home.

Whether government is "too big" depends on one's perception of the private-sector activity forgone when government absorbs resources and changes the mix of the economy's output. Cost–benefit analysis and mechanisms that allow taxpayers to vote on projects are ways of trying to ensure that we get the amount and kind of government we want.

Critics of public-sector activity emphasize the role of public officials' self-interest in the decision-making process. In fact, public-choice theory essentially extends the analysis of market behavior to political behavior. Public officials are viewed as utility maximizers pursuing their own individual goals rather than public goals.

Learning Objectives

After reading Chapter 3 and doing the following exercises, you should:	True or false	Multiple choice	Problems and applications	Common errors	Pages in the text
1. Be able to explain the several kinds of micro failure that justify the public sector.	1,13–15,22	4,6,17, 20,22	2	1	57–63
2. Understand how macro failure justifies public-sector activity.	15	5,7,18			63–64
3. Recognize the opportunity costs of public-sector activity.	1,2,20	10	2,4,5	1	75–77
4. Know several different kinds of taxation and the level of government for which they are particularly important.		16	4		67–73
5. Be able to determine whether a type of tax is progressive or regressive.	7,8,11,23	11–15	3		70–72
6. Know how the mechanism of public decision making differs from the market mechanism.	21,22	22	4		78–79
7. Be able to compute and use cost–benefit ratios.	16		2		77–78
8. Know the effects of externalities and how they should be handled in the economy.	17,18,21,22	21		2	60
9. Know some of the important policy issues connected with taxation, expenditure, and borrowing.	3,6,10	7–9	4	1,2	74–77
10. Understand the outlines of the new theory of public choice.	24	19			77–80
11. Know the relative sizes of government budgets, sources of revenue, and expenditure categories.	4,5,9, 12,19	1–3,6	1	2	67,69,70,72

Key-Term Review

Review the following terms; if you are not sure of the meaning of any term, write out the definition and check it against the Glossary in the text.

antitrust
categorical grants
externalities
factors of production
fiscal year (FY)
free rider
government failure
inflation
interest
market failure
market mechanism
market power
monopoly

opportunity cost
optimal mix of output
private good
production possibilities
progressive tax
public choice
public goods
regressive tax
regulation
transfer payment
unemployment
user charge

Fill in the blank following each of the statements below with the appropriate term from the list above.

1. The existence of public goods represents, in a way, our inability to produce the best mix of outputs entirely through the _____.

1. _____

2. When a retired person receives a social security check; a veteran, a benefit check; and a poor person, a welfare payment, each is receiving a _____.

2. _____

3. The budget submitted by the president in January 1988 was really for the period from October 1, 1988, to September 30, 1989, a period called the government's _____.

3. _____

4. The dollar value of the private goods forgone in order to produce public goods is a measure of their _____.

4. _____

5. When you borrow money, the lender expects to get back the amount lent plus _____.

5. _____

6. When one person cannot be prevented from receiving benefits from another person's purchase, the first person is said to be a _____.

6. _____

7. Tuition payments made by college students are an example of a _____.

7. _____

8. Those goods that cannot be provided efficiently or in the right amount by the private sector are called _____.

8. _____

9. Because the fraction of income paid in taxes rises with income, the personal income tax is a _____.

9. _____

10. When consumption of a good by one person precludes consumption by someone else, such a good is called a _____.

10. _____

11. The theory of _____ emphasizes the self-interest of government decision makers.

11. _____

12. When revenue sharing is limited to specific purposes, the funds are called _____.

12. _____

13. Those outputs of goods and services that the economy can produce are referred to as its _____.

13. _____

14. A sales tax takes a higher fraction of a poor person's income than a rich person's income; thus it is a _____.

14. _____

15. Immunization clinics not only prevent a person from getting a disease but reduce the incidence of the disease generally; that is, they have effects on third parties. Such effects are called _____.

15. _____

16. The existence of a patent or copyright may give the holder a _____.

16. _____

17. _____ enforcement or _____ is used to counter the problem of monopoly power.

17. _____

_____

18. _____ and _____ are examples of macro failure.

18. _____

_____

19. _____ occurs when public-sector intervention fails to move the economy closer to its goals.

19. _____

20. _____ means that the market mechanism has not led to production of the _____.

20. _____

_____

21. _____ is the ability to alter market outcomes.

21. _____

22. When government absorbs _____, they are denied to the private sector.

22. _____

True or False: *Circle your choice.*

T F 1. The term "public sector" refers only to federal government purchases of goods and services.

T F 2. Income transfers are payments to individuals for which nothing is currently rendered in return.

T F 3. When federal government expenditures exceed federal tax revenues, the federal debt grows.

T F 4. State and local government employment exceeds federal government employment.

T F 5. Grants by the federal government to state and local governments for specific purposes are called "block grants."

T F 6. The larger the federal debt, the greater will be the interest expense on it, *ceteris paribus.*

T F 7. The federal income tax is progressive because the tax rates increase at higher income levels.

T F 8. Progressive tax rates mean a larger fraction of income is taken in the form of taxes as income increases.

T F 9. The federal government's share of the U.S. economy has grown in both relative and absolute terms since the 1950s.

T F 10. Increased government borrowing means increased government debt, *ceteris paribus.*

T F 11. State and local property taxes tend to be regressive.

T F 12. State and local government spending is less than federal government spending in the U.S. economy.

T F 13. A public good is a good or service for which consumption by one person excludes consumption by others.

T F 14. Police protection is an example of a service that involves the free-rider problem.

T F 15. If public goods were produced and marketed like private goods, the market would very likely fail to provide them in the quantity society is willing and able to pay for.

T F 16. If the cost–benefit ratio for a given project is greater than 1, that indicates that for each dollar of expenditure on the project, society gets benefits worth less than $1 from the project.

T F 17. If you burn garbage in your backyard and the smoke damages a neighbor's house, the damage is considered an externality.

T F 18. If your neighbors spray the weeds in their yard and this activity prevents weed seeds from blowing into your yard, the benefit you receive is an externality.

T F 19. The public sector in the United States is greater in absolute size than is the public sector of any European country.

T F 20. The production-possibilities curve sets a limit on the amount of public services we should produce, not what we can produce.

T F 21. Externalities come into existence only when the social costs of a market activity exceed the social benefits of a market activity.

T F 22. For any given market activity, if the social cost exceeds the private cost, that activity should be curtailed.

T F 23. The tax that is implicit in the transfer of state lottery proceeds to state treasuries appears quite regressive.

T F 24. The theory of public choice relies on the rational self-interest of both voters and government decision makers.

Multiple Choice: *Select the correct answer.*

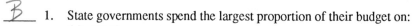

B 1. State governments spend the largest proportion of their budget on:
   (a) Welfare programs.
   (b) Education.
   (c) Highways.
   (d) Environmental protection.

A 2. Local governments spend the largest proportion of their budgets on:
   (a) Education.
   (b) Welfare.
   (c) Highways.
   (d) Environmental protection.

D 3. The federal government spends the largest proportion of its budget for goods and services on:
   (a) Education.
   (b) Welfare.
   (c) Agriculture.
   (d) National defense.

A 4. Which of the following public-sector services is *best* justified by the existence of the free-rider problem?
   (a) Expenditures for national defense.
   (b) Expenditures for veterans' benefits.
   (c) Expenditures on the agricultural sector.
   (d) Expenditures on regulation of public utilities.

_____ 5. Which of the following federal government expenditures can be justified on the basis of the free-rider problem?
(a) Welfare payments.
(b) Social security payments.
(c) Veterans' benefits.
(d) None of the above.

_____ 6. Which of the following is the form of grant made by the federal government to a state or local government which is limited to a specific purpose?
(a) A block grant.
(b) A general-purpose grant.
(c) A categorical grant.
(d) None of the above.

_____ 7. Which of the following have been tried in attempting to reduce the size of the federal government's role in the economy?
(a) Transferring federal government functions back to state and local governments.
(b) Cutting federal government expenditures.
(c) Cutting federal taxes.
(d) All of the above.

_____ 8. When federal government expenditures exceed federal government revenues, the effect is:
(a) To increase federal government borrowing.
(b) To increase federal government debt.
(c) To increase the interest expense on the federal government's debt, _ceteris paribus._
(d) All of the above.

_____ 9. The increased interest expense on the federal debt may reflect higher interest rates and:
(a) A reduction in federal borrowing.
(b) Government expenditures in excess of government revenues.
(c) A balanced budget.
(d) A decline in the federal debt.

_____ 10. Which of the following statements concerning the opportunity costs of public-sector activity is true?
(a) They can be measured in terms of the private-market activity forgone.
(b) They are represented as the slope of a production-possibilities curve showing public versus private goods.
(c) They reflect the limited resources available for public and private activity.
(d) All of the above statements are true.

_____ 11. Which of the following can be classified as a regressive tax?
(a) The federal corporate income tax.
(b) The federal personal income tax.
(c) The federal gasoline tax.
(d) All of the above.

_____ 12. Which of the following is an example of a progressive tax?
(a) The excise tax on distilled spirits.
(b) The federal tax on gasoline.
(c) The federal personal income tax.
(d) All of the above.

_____ 13. A tax is regressive if it takes a:
(a) Larger number of dollars as income rises.
(b) Larger number of dollars as income falls.
(c) Smaller fraction of income as income falls.
(d) Smaller fraction of income as income rises.

_____14. The social security tax is:
   (a) A progressive tax at all income levels.
   (b) A regressive tax above a certain income level.
   (c) A proportional tax at all income levels.
   (d) None of the above.

_____15. Suppose that if your income is $10,000, your tax is $1,000, but if your income is $50,000, your tax is $4,000. Such a tax is:
   (a) Regressive.
   (b) Progressive.
   (c) Proportional.
   (d) None of the above.

_____16. The tuition paid by college students is a:
   (a) Progressive tax.
   (b) Regressive tax.
   (c) User charge.
   (d) Categorical grant.

_____17. The free-rider dilemma is:
   (a) Exemplified by thrill seekers who follow fire trucks.
   (b) A distinguishing characteristic of public goods.
   (c) An issue with every good produced in the public sector.
   (d) An argument for a laissez-faire policy.

_____18. Inflation and unemployment are indicators of:
   (a) Micro failure.
   (b) Macro failure.
   (c) Antitrust activity.
   (d) Regulation.

_____19. Which of the following would *not* support the theory of public choice?
   (a) The governor of the state vetoes a highway bill even though the highway would enhance the value of property he owns.
   (b) The local mayor campaigns in favor of a bond issue for the construction of sewer lines that will raise the value of his property.
   (c) The local police chief fails to give the mayor a speeding ticket because the mayor might fire him.
   (d) A college president asks the board of regents to allow her to remain in office so she can bolster her retirement income, even though she has reached the mandatory retirement age.

_____20. Market failure means that the market mechanism, left alone, will:
   (a) Produce too many public goods and too few private goods.
   (b) Produce too many private goods and too few public goods.
   (c) Produce the optimal mix of output.
   (d) Result in too few resources being allocated to private goods.

_____21. Which of the following demonstrates the concept of externalities? While dining in a restaurant, the person at the next table lights up a cigar and:
   (a) You don't like the smell of the cigar smoke.
   (b) You enjoy the smell of the cigar smoke.
   (c) The cigar smoke doesn't bother you.
   (d) a and b.

_____22. Which of the following is *not* an example of economic regulation of monopoly power?
   (a) You write a hit song and obtain a copyright for the words and music.
   (b) You invent a telephone with digital readout of long-distance charges and obtain a patent for it.
   (c) Texaco is ordered by the court to pay Pennzoil several billion dollars for interfering with Pennzoil's purchase of Getty Oil.
   (d) All of the above are examples of economic regulation.

Problems and Applications

Exercise 1

This exercise gives you an opportunity to observe the growth in federal government expenditures from 1980 through 1989. Only a few of the categories (representing over 50 percent of the budget) have been selected from the budget. Most are those that come up frequently in political discussions. The entire budget expanded by over 80 percent during this period. See Table B.77 in the 1988 *Economic Report of the President* for the complete budget. (FY 1989 figures are estimates.)

1. Calculate the percentage increases in Table 3.1 and answer the following questions.

[*Hint:* Column 3 = ((column 2/column 1) – 1) x 100.]

Table 3.1
Projected federal budget outlays for selected categories of expenditure, FY 1980–89

	(1) 1980 (billions of dollars per year)	(2) 1989 (billions of dollars per year)	(3) Percent increase, 1980–89
National defense	$133.9	294.0	_____
Agriculture	8.8	21.7	_____
Social security	118.5	233.4	_____
Medicare	32.1	84.0	_____
Income security	86.5	135.6	_____
Education, training, employment, and social services	31.8	37.4	_____
Net interest	52.5	151.8	_____

2. Which of the categories grew most rapidly? _____

3. Which grew faster, Medicare or social security? _____

4. Which category is largest in absolute dollars? _____

5. Did any category *decline* from FY 1980 to FY 1989? _____

Exercise 2

This exercise examines a form of public good and provides practice in the kind of cost–benefit analysis that government analysts use when evaluating projects.

The Army Corps of Engineers lists the benefits and costs of a water project as shown in Table 3.2. The project is a dam in Brown's Valley.

Table 3.2
Benefits and costs of a dam in Brown's Valley

Cost items	Cost (millions of dollars)	Benefit items	Benefits (millions of dollars)
Purchase of land	$2.0	Irrigation	$4.0
Land preparation	4.0	City water supply	4.0
Fill material	2.0	Flood control	1.0
Construction company services	1.0	Future recreation	5.0
Future maintenance cost	1.0		
Total	$____	Total	$ ____

1. Fill in Table 3.2. What is the benefit–cost ratio for the Brown's Valley dam? _____

2. If the resources were available would the project be worth doing? _____

3. Suppose the people in Brown's Valley object to the new dam. They commission their own study, which shows that the value of future recreation will be only $3 million rather than $5 million. They also find that putting in recreation facilities will cost an additional $4 million. Compute the new benefit–cost ratio. _____

4. Is the project worth doing if these new estimates are correct? _____

5. Because there is such a controversy over the figures, one of the civic leaders, Mr. Collins, initiates a study to examine a new Brown's Valley Project and alternative sites for a dam that would be more acceptable to the majority of people. The engineers return with the three recommended project sites shown in Table 3.3. Compute the benefit–cost ratios of each project and fill in Table 3.3.

Table 3.3
Benefit–cost ratios (millions of dollars)

	Virginia Ranch	Yuba	New Brown's Valley
Benefits	$15.0	$18.0	$10.0
Costs	7.5	10.0	6.0
Benefit–cost ratio	_____	_____	_____

6. Which site would be chosen for construction?
   (a) Virginia Ranch.
   (b) Yuba.
   (c) New Brown's Valley.

7. Which of the following reasons *best* explains why the other projects might not be undertaken?
   (a) Their benefit–cost ratios are less than 1.
   (b) Brown's County cannot afford more than one project and must select the one with the highest benefit–cost ratio.
   (c) Brown's County can earn a 10 percent return for investing in the stock or money markets.

8. The county decides to raise the money for the new dam by instituting a sales tax. Such a tax would most likely be:
   (a) Progressive.
   (b) Regressive.

9. The reason that people in Brown's Valley would not be able to raise the money privately and would have to do it through taxes is:
   (a) The free-rider problem.
   (b) The dam is a public good.
   (c) User charges cannot be levied on a project that does not yet exist.
   (d) All of the above.

10. Communities downriver from the dam want to bid for the water. However, because these new demands would raise the price of water, the farmers prevent sale of the water to those communities. This suggests that the dam:
   (a) Should have been provided by private enterprise through the market mechanism instead of big government.
   (b) Has externalities that have not been included in the cost part of the benefit–cost ratio.
   (c) Has externalities that have not been included in the benefit part of the benefit–cost ratio.

11. What type of government is *best* suited to manage water projects, considering the existence of significant externalities that affect residents in multiple government jurisdictions?
   (a) City government.
   (b) County government.
   (c) State government.
   (d) Federal government.

Exercise 3

The following problem shows how to determine whether a tax is progressive or regressive. The problem is similar to the one at the end of Chapter 3 in the text.

Suppose that Table 3.4 describes the spending and saving behavior of individuals at various income levels.

1. Assuming that a tax of 40 percent is levied on savings, calculate the following:
   a. The amount of taxes paid at each income level (column 3 of Table 3.4).
   b. The fraction of income paid in taxes at each income level (column 4 of Table 3.4).

Table 3.4
Taxes on income and savings

(1) Income	(2) Total savings	(3) Savings tax (at 40 percent)	(4) Savings tax as percent of income	(5) Income tax (at 10 percent)
$ 1,000	$ −50	$ _____	% _____	$ _____
2,000	0	_____	_____	_____
3,000	50	_____	_____	_____
5,000	100	_____	_____	_____
10,000	1,000	_____	_____	_____
100,000	20,000	_____	_____	_____

2. Is the tax on savings progressive or regressive in relation to income? _____

3. Alternatively, assume that a flat-rate income tax of 10 percent is levied. Compute the amount of taxes paid at each income level (column 5 of Table 3.4).

4. Work the problem at the end of Chapter 3 in the text and then consider these questions: Which of the following—a flat-rate income tax, a tax on savings, or a tax on spending—would provide:
   a. The greatest incentive for taxpayers to earn higher incomes? _____
   b. The most equitable outcome if society wishes to redistribute income to the poor? _____
   c. The most equitable outcome if society assumes that everyone should make the same percentage contribution to the maintenance of our government? _____

Exercise 4

Waste and inefficiency frequently provide good stories for the media. Using one of the articles in the text, this exercise will show the kind of information to look for. If your professor makes a newspaper assignment for this chapter, this exercise will provide an example of how to do it.

Reread the article in Chapter 2 entitled "Fed Up with the Food Fight: Forced to Queue Endlessly for Supplies, the Poles Are Boiling" from *Time* magazine. Then answer the following questions:

1. What passage in the article indicates a good or service that is being wasted?

2. Assume that the production-possibilities curve pictured in Figure 3.1 represents the production-possibilities curve for all goods in the Polish economy. The y-axis indicates the good or service that is being wasted. Label the y-axis with this good or service.

Figure 3.1
Production-possibilities curve

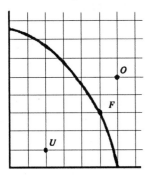

ALL OTHER GOODS
AND SERVICES

3. What single word, phrase, or sentence (no more than a sentence) in the article indicates the efficiency or inefficiency of resource use?

4. Which of the points in Figure 3.1 would best characterize where the economy is given the inefficiency described in the article?   U   F   O   (circle one)

5. Indicate a point that would show where the economy would be with the elimination of the inefficiency described in the article, and label it A. Assume other goods and services are used efficiently.

Common Errors

The first statement in each "common error" below is incorrect. Each incorrect statement is followed by a corrected version and an explanation.

1. Fire protection, police protection, and other services can be produced more efficiently by the private sector than by the public sector. WRONG!

   The public sector can produce many services more efficiently than the private sector. RIGHT!

   You should recognize now that the existence of externalities and the free-rider problem force society to produce some goods and services through public-sector expenditures. Many of the goods and services we take for granted (such as education) would not be produced in sufficient quantities if left to the private sector. And can you imagine trying to provide for your own defense against foreign countries?

2. The national debt only grows when expenditures on goods and services exceed revenues. WRONG!

   The national debt can grow simply because interest rates rise. RIGHT!

   The interest on the outstanding debt was projected at over $148 billion for FY 1988. Since the government is constantly borrowing to refund its debt, when interest rates rise, the cost of servicing the debt goes up too. This has to be paid for by either tax revenues or (you guessed it) additional borrowing.

43

■ ANSWERS ■

Key-Term Review

1. market mechanism
2. transfer payment
3. fiscal year
4. opportunity cost
5. interest
6. free rider
7. user charge
8. public goods
9. progressive tax
10. private good
11. public choice
12. categorical grants
13. production possibilities
14. regressive tax
15. externalities
16. monopoly
17. antitrust, regulation
18. unemployment, inflation
19. government failure
20. market failure, optimal mix of output
21. market power
22. factors of production

True or False

1. F	5. F	9. F	13. F	17. T	21. F
2. T	6. T	10. T	14. T	18. T	22. T
3. T	7. T	11. T	15. T	19. T	23. T
4. T	8. T	12. F	16. T	20. F	24. T

Multiple Choice

1. b	5. d	9. b	13. d	17. b	20. b
2. a	6. c	10. d	14. b	18. b	21. d
3. d	7. d	11. c	15. a	19. a	22. c
4. a	8. d	12. c	16. c		

Problems and Applications

Exercise 1

1. Table 3.1 answer

	(3) Percent increase, 1988–89
National defense	119.6
Agriculture	146.6
Social security	97.0
Medicare	162.7
Income security	56.8
Education, training, employment, and social services	17.6
Net interest	189.1

2. Net interest.
3. Medicare.
4. National defense.
5. No.

Exercise 2

1. See Table 3.2 answer.
2. yes
3. $\dfrac{\$12,000,000}{\$14,000,000} = .86$
4. no
5. See Table 3.3 answer.

6. a
7. b
8. b
9. d
10. c
11. d

Table 3.2 answer

Cost	Benefit	Benefit–cost ratio
$10,000,000	$14,000,000	1.4 = ($14,000,000/$10,000,000)

Table 3.3 answer

	Virginia Ranch	Yuba	New Brown's Valley
Benefit–cost ratio	2.0	1.8	1.67

Exercise 3

1a and b. See columns 3 and 4.

Table 3.4 answer

(3) Savings tax	(4) Savings tax as percentage of income	(5) Income tax
$ −20	−0.2%	$ 100
0	0.0	200
20	0.67	300
40	0.8	500
400	4.0	1,000
8,000	8.0	10,000

2. Progressive. With greater income a higher percentage of income goes to taxes (from 0 to 8 percent in column 4).
3. See Table 3.4 answer, column 5.
4. a. A regressive tax such as the tax on spending would provide an incentive for people to earn higher incomes because a smaller percentage of their income will be taxed at higher income levels.
    b. A progressive tax such as the tax on saving would provide the most equitable outcome if society wishes to redistribute income to the poor.
    c. If equity is defined in terms of equal contribution in terms of percentage of income to the maintenance of government, then the flat-rate income tax would be most equitable.

Exercise 4

1. "The government officially maintains that the average Pole spends four hours queueing up each day." This suggests labor services are being wasted.

2. **Figure 3.1 answer**

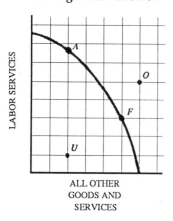

3. "The state-run supply system on the verge of collapse" is one of the many phrases in the article that indicate the inefficiency of resource use.
4. U
5. See Figure 3.1 answer. The Poles could move to any point on the production possibilities curve.

Chapter 4
National-Income Accounting

Quick Review

In this chapter, we begin the task of measurement in the economy. We need to have some basic information to know where the economy is relative to society's goals, that is, where we want the economy to be. We want to know some basic information about the economy, including:

- How much output do we produce in a year?
- How much income is generated from production of these goods and services?
- Where does all of the output and income go?

We begin by discussing national-income accounting, which is concerned with the measurement of the nation's economic activity. Several national-income aggregates allow the national-income accountant to add together the production of literally millions of goods and services using a single common denominator, dollar value.

The most often used economic aggregate is gross national product (GNP), which is the total market value of all final goods and services produced by the economy over a certain period, such as a year. When our total output is calculated in dollar terms and compared with *what could have been* produced by the economy over the same period, appropriate economic policies can be developed. Those policies should be aimed at getting the economy to operate as close to its potential as possible.

The GNP does not include all types of transactions. It includes only transactions of new products and services; for example, sales of new cars are included, but not sales of used cars. The transactions must be arm's length; for example, paying an allowance to Junior for mowing the lawn is not included in the GNP. Illegal transactions, which are not recorded, or transactions for which no exchange of money for services occurs are also likely to be missing from the GNP. For example, the transactions in illegal drugs, the services of homemakers, and bartering for many services and products are not included in the GNP. There is a large underground economy that the GNP never captures. The underground economy could be as large as 20 percent of the nation's GNP. Finally, only transactions of goods and services that are sold for final consumption are included—whether it is personal consumption, business consumption (investment), government consumption (government expenditures), or foreign consumption (exports). Intermediate goods are not included in the GNP in order to avoid distortions due to double counting.

There are several alternative measures of output, each with a different purpose. The GNP shows how much output is produced during a given year, which serves as an excellent basis for comparing different economies and the changes in the welfare of a single economy over time. However, the net national product (NNP) corrects for the disappearance—or depreciation—of capital; therefore, it serves as a better measure of the actual production possibilities of the economy. The GNP includes gross investment; the NNP includes only the net investment in capital goods for the economy. When indirect business taxes are subtracted from net national product, it is possible to find a measure of income, the national income, which shows what different factors of production earn for generating the nation's income. Finally, we might not be interested so much in which factors earn income as in which households receive it. For this purpose there are two measures of income—one before taxes are paid (personal income) and one after taxes are paid (disposable income).

GNP is a price-times-quantity measurement. Therefore, it can go up because prices go up, because quantities produced go up, or both. Because our standard of living is based on real goods and services, we have to distinguish between real GNP and nominal GNP. In periods when prices are rising, we deflate the GNP by dividing by an appropriate index. When prices fall, we inflate it in the same fashion. Also, when comparisons are made of different economies, the GNP is divided by the population to show how much per capita income there is.

To summarize, national-income accounting allows the economist to see how the economy is doing in relation to how we would like it to perform.

Learning Objectives

After reading Chapter 4 and doing the following exercises, you should:	True or false	Multiple choice	Problems and applications	Common errors	Pages in the text
1. Know the purposes of national-income accounting.	1,2	20		3	83–85
2. Be able to describe the different measures of output and income.	10,11,17–20, 22–24,27	1,2,4, 16,17		1,3	83–92
3. Know why the GNP per capita is computed.	1,2			2	85
4. Be able to explain the conceptual problems encountered in estimating GNP.	4–6,12,25	10–12,18		3	86–88
5. Be familiar with the underground economy.	26,28	10			87
6. Know the difference between real GNP and nominal GNP and be able to convert the latter to the former.	7–9	9,13,14	1		88–89
7. Know the definitions and uses of the important national-income aggregates.	3,11,13	3,15			88–97
8. Be able to calculate GNP and other aggregates from a given set of data.	14–16, 18–21	5–8,19	2		94–97

Key-Term Review

Review the following terms; if you are not sure of the meaning of any term, write out the definition and check it against the Glossary in the text.

depreciation
disposable income (*DI*)
exports
GNP per capita
gross investment
gross national product (GNP)
imports
inflation
intermediate goods
investment

national income (*NI*)
national-income accounting
net investment
net national product (NNP)
nominal GNP
personal income (*PI*)
production possibilities
real GNP
saving
value added

Fill in the blank following each of the statements below with the appropriate term from the list above.

1. Those goods that are to be processed further before final sale are _____.

1. _Intermediate Goods_

2. Final purchases of goods and services by the business sector are referred to as _____.

2. _____investment_____

3. The major national-income aggregate used to measure an economy's total economic activity is _____.

3. _____GNP_____

4. The major aggregate used to compare economic well-being across international boundaries is _____.

4. _____GNP per capita_____

5. Gross national product unadjusted for changes in the price level is called _____.

5. _____nominal GNP_____

6. At each stage of production there is an increase in _____.

6. _____Value added_____

7. An increase in the general level of prices is referred to as _____.

7. _____Inflation_____

8. The value of the capital stock used up in producing this year's GNP, measured in dollars, is _____.

8. _____depreciation_____

9. Gross national product adjusted for changes in the general level of prices is referred to as _____.

9. _____Real GNP_____

10. That part of GNP that is "earned" by factors of production is called _____.

10. _____National income NI_____

11. That national-income aggregate that measures what the household sector has left to spend or save after taxes is _____.

11. _____Disposable income DI_____

12. If you add net investment to depreciation, you get _____.

12. _____gross investment_____

13. That aggregate that measures the addition to the nation's capital stock is called _____.

13. _____net investment_____

14. Disposable income plus personal taxes is called _____.

14. _____personal income_____

15. Technology and resources are the most important constraints on the economy's _____.

15. _____production possibilities_____

16. U.S. goods and services purchased by foreigners are _____.

16. _____exports_____

17. Foreign goods and services purchased by people in the United States are _____.

17. _____imports_____

18. _____ is the process of measuring aggregate economic activity.

18. _____national income accounting_____

19. The amount of current output that society can consume without reducing next year's production possibilities is best measured by _____.

19. _____net national product_____

20. Whatever households do not spend out of their disposable income is referred to as _____.

20. _____savings_____

True or False: *Circle your choice.*

T F 1. Per capita GNP is commonly used to compare economic welfare across international boundaries.

T F 2. Comparisons of per capita GNP across international boundaries provide no information on the distribution of GNP within each country. T

T F 3. GNP is the total market value of all goods produced in the economy. F

T F 4. Nonmarket activities, such as the work of a homemaker, are excluded in the calculation of the nation's GNP. T

T F 5. GNP can be calculated by summing up the "value added" at every stage of production. T

T F 6. Eliminating intermediate goods from the calculation of GNP results in double-counting. F

T F 7. In periods of rising prices, real GNP will rise more slowly than nominal GNP. T

T F 8. In periods of falling prices, nominal GNP must be inflated to obtain real GNP. F

T F 9. Real GNP and nominal GNP are equal during the base year for which an index is constructed. T

T F 10. The difference between GNP and national income is measured by depreciation. F

T F 11. Depreciation figures used in the calculation of GNP are based on actual measures of the deterioration of equipment, plant, capital, and the like. F

T F 12. For the nation's capital stock to grow, net investment must be positive. T

T F 13. Net investment cannot be negative. F

T F 14. Government spending in the national-income accounts refers only to expenditures at the federal level. F

T F 15. The reason state and local government expenditures are left out of GNP calculations is that they are expenditures for intermediate goods and services. F

T F 16. When exports exceed imports, net exports are negative. F

T F 17. Total output and total income differ by the amount of depreciation. F

T F 18. GNP minus indirect business taxes equals net national product. F

T F 19. National income is a measure of the incomes "earned" by the factors of production in the process of producing the GNP. T

T F 20. Net national product (NNP) minus indirect business taxes equals national income (NI). T

T F 21. Social security taxes are an example of an indirect business tax because they are taken out of the employee's paycheck. F

T F 22. Personal income is what households have to spend or to save. F

T F 23. If you add consumption expenditures to personal savings, you get disposable income.

T F 24. Undistributed corporate profits are an example of income that is earned but not received by the owners of the factors of production. T

T F 25. Many things that add to the quality of life are not included in the calculation of GNP. T

T F 26. Economic activity in the underground economy can be estimated from reported income. F

T F 27. Gross domestic product for the United States exceeds gross national product. F

T F 28. Most of the income earned in the underground economy results from illegal activities. F

49

Multiple Choice: *Select the correct answer.*

A 1. Those who are interested in assessing the overall performance of the economy over time are most likely to look at:
  (a) GNP.
  (b) NNP.
  (c) *NI.*
  (d) *DI.*

B 2. Those who are interested in observing how the economy is doing on a sustainable basis are most likely to look at:
  (a) GNP.
  (b) NNP.
  (c) *NI.*
  (d) *DI.*

C 3. The addition to the economy's capital stock can be found by:
  (a) Subtracting NNP from GNP.
  (b) Subtracting depreciation from GNP.
  (c) Subtracting depreciation from gross investment.
  (d) None of the above.

B 4. National income is a measure of:
  (a) How well the economy is doing on a gross basis.
  (b) The incomes earned by the factors of production in producing GNP.
  (c) The incomes received by the factors of production in producing GNP.
  (d) None of the above.

D 5. Which of the following must be subtracted from national income to obtain personal income?
  (a) Undistributed corporate profits. ✓
  (b) Social security taxes. ✓
  (c) Corporate profit taxes. ✓
  (d) All of the above. ✓

D 6. Personal income differs from national income by an amount equal to:
  (a) Social security taxes. ✓
  (b) Transfer payments.
  (c) Personal taxes.
  (d) None of the above.

A 7. Disposable income is:
  (a) The amount households have to spend or to save.
  (b) The amount the household sector earns in producing the GNP.
  (c) The amount households have left to spend after savings are subtracted.
  (d) None of the above.

D 8. GNP can be found by:
  (a) Adding up the spending by business, government, households, and foreigners, and subtracting imports.
  (b) Adding up the "value added" at every stage of production in the economy.
  (c) Adding up all of the receipts of households, government, and business.
  (d) All of the above.

C 9. Which of the following describes how to calculate real GNP?
  (a) Divide nominal GNP by the current price level.
  (b) Divide an index of price changes by nominal GNP.
  (c) Divide current GNP by the GNP deflator.
  (d) Divide the current price level by nominal GNP.

C 10. Which of the following items is *always* part of the underground economy?
(a) Payments to family members for performing household tasks.
(b) Income from legal pursuits.
(c) Unreported income.
(d) None of the above.

C 11. Which of the following nonmarket values is *excluded* from calculations of GNP?
(a) Food grown by farmers for their own consumption.
(b) The rental value of owner-occupied homes.
(c) The value of services performed by housewives.
(d) All of the above.

D 12. Steel sold by U.S. Steel to General Motors is excluded from the calculation of GNP:
(a) Because it is an intermediate good.
(b) Because it is an input into the final product, automobiles.
(c) Because its value will be included in the price of the final good, automobiles.
(d) For all of the above reasons.

D 13. If both the prices and the quantities of all final goods and services produced doubled from one year to the next and population remained constant, then:
(a) Nominal GNP would be four times as large in the second year as in the first.
(b) Real GNP would be twice as large in the second year as in the first.
(c) On the average, the population could be twice as well off in the second year as in the first.
(d) All of the above would be the case.

A 14. In periods of rising prices, percentage increases in nominal GNP will:
(a) Exeed percentage increases in real GNP.
(b) Equal percentage increases in real GNP.
(c) Be less than percentage increases in real GNP.
(d) It's difficult to generalize about the relationship between nominal and real GNP.

B 15. Which of the following statements about net investment is true?
(a) It is always positive in the U.S. economy.
(b) It can be negative if the economy wears out capital faster than it replaces it.
(c) It is often negative in the U.S. economy.
(d) None of the above statements is true.

D 16. The total value of output produced by the economy and the total value of incomes generated by the economy:
(a) Differ by the amount of profits earned by corporations.
(b) Differ by the amount of taxes collected by all levels of government.
(c) Differ by the amount of depreciation that occurs in the economy.
(d) Are equal.

C 17. Someone who is interested in the fraction of total output purchased by the private sector would be interested in which of the following ratios?
(a) C/GNP
(b) I/GNP
(c) $(C + I)$/GNP
(d) $(I + G)$/GNP

A 18. Transfer payments are part of personal income but not of national income because:
(a) Personal income is a "receipts concept."
(b) Personal income is an "earnings concept."
(c) National income is a "receipts concept."
(d) None of the above is an adequate explanation.

19. Social security payments are:
    (a) Transfer payments.
    (b) Added, along with other things, to national income to get personal income.
    (c) Payments received for which no current good or service is rendered.
    (d) All of the above.

20. GNP most closely measures:
    (a) The quality of life in the United States.
    (b) Social welfare.
    (c) The economic value of the resources used in the production of all final goods and services.
    (d) Consumption expenditures plus saving.

Problems and Applications

Exercise 1

This exercise shows the relationship between nominal GNP and real GNP, and it provides practice in computing percentage changes over time. This will help you with the problems at the end of Chapter 4 in the text.

Each January the president has the Council of Economic Advisers prepare an economic report on the state of the U.S. economy called *The Economic Report of the President*. National-income accounts* form the basis of much of the analysis that goes into this report. It summarizes the essential features of the economy's performance and the policy initiatives that are likely to be undertaken. This exercise shows the kind of information that is developed for this publication.

Table 4.1 presents the Commerce Department estimates of GNP.

1. Table 4.1 shows the real GNP and the GNP deflator for each of the years indicated. Calculate nominal GNP (GNP unadjusted for price changes for each year), and write it in the appropriate column.

Table 4.1
Real GNP, GNP deflator, and per capita GNP, 1978–87

(1) Year	(2) GNP deflator	(3) Real GNP (in billions of dollars per year)	(4) Nominal GNP (in billions of dollars per year)	(5) Percentage growth in nominal GNP	(6) Percentage growth in real GNP	(7) U.S. population (in millions)	(8) Real GNP per capita
1978	72.2	3,115.2	$ 2249.2	— %	— %	222.6	$ 13,994
1979	78.6	3,192.4	2509.2	11.5	2.50%	225.1	14,82
1980	85.7	3,187.1	2731.3	8.8%	~.2	227.1	
1981	94.0	3,248.8	3053.8	11.8	1.9	229.1	
1982	100.0	3,166.0	3166.0	3.7	-2.6	232.1	
1983	103.9	3,279.1	3407.0	7.6	3.6	234.2	
1984	107.7	3,501.4	3771.0	10.7	6.8	237.0	
1985	111.2	3,607.5	4007.9	6.6%	3%	239.3	
1986	114.1	3,713.3	4236.9	5.7	2.9	241.6	
1987	117.5	3,819.6	4488.0	5.9	2.9	243.8	

Source: *The Economic Report of the President*, 1988.

*The Commerce Department provides information on the national accounts in the *Survey of Current Business*, the *U.S. Statistical Abstract*, and other readily available publications.

2. From the information in Table 4.1, calculate the percentage growth in nominal and real GNP for each of the years 1978–87 and insert your answers in the appropriate columns. Use the following formula:

$$\text{Percentage growth in real GNP} = \frac{GNP_{n+1} - GNP_n}{GNP_n} \times 100\%$$

where n = beginning year
   $n + 1$ = next year.

[handwritten: $\frac{3192.4 - 3115.2}{3115.2} \times 100\%$]

For example, from 1978 to 1979 the real GNP increased by the following percentage:

$$\frac{GNP_{n+1} - GNP_n}{GNP_n} \times 100\% = \frac{3,192.4 - 3,115.2}{3,115.2} \times 100\% = 2.5\%$$

[handwritten: $\frac{c - p}{p} \times 100$]

3. T (F) When nominal GNP grows, real GNP grows.

4. By what nominal dollar amount did nominal GNP grow from 1978 to 1987? $ _2338_

5. By what constant dollar amount did real GNP grow from 1978 to 1987? $ _204_ billion

6. The U.S. population for various years is presented in column 7 of Table 4.1. Calculate the real GNP per capita in column 8.

7. T (F) When real GNP rises, real GNP per capita must also rise.

Exercise 2

This problem is designed to help you learn the way the national-income aggregates are determined and to reinforce your understanding of their relationship to one another. It will also help you with the problem at the end of Chapter 4 in the text.

Table 4.2
U.S. national-income aggregates, 1984
(billions of dollars per year)

1. Personal consumption expenditures	$2,342
2. Gross private domestic investment	637
3. Exports	364
4. Imports	430
5. Federal government purchases	296
6. State and local government purchases	452
7. Depreciation	403
8. Indirect business taxes	304
9. Social security taxes	306
10. Retained earnings	118
11. Corporate profits tax liability	88
12. Net interest	150
13. Transfer payments	418
14. Personal taxes	435

Source: *The Economic Report of the President,* 1985.

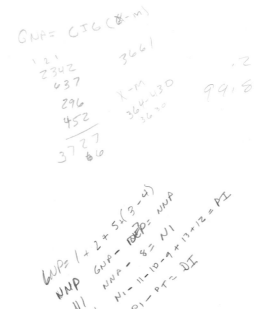

1. On the basis of the information provided in Table 4.2, calculate the national-income aggregates required to complete the column headed 1984 in Table 4.3, and calculate the percentage growth in each aggregate from 1984 to 1987. (See page 96 of the text for an example.)

Table 4.3
U.S. national-income aggregates, 1984 and 1987
(billions of dollars per year)

Economic aggregate	1984	1987	Percent increase in nominal value
GNP	$ 3661	$4,486	19.4 %
NNP	3258	4,007	
NI	2954	3,636	
PI	3010	3,746	
DI	2675	3,181	

2. Which national-income aggregate increased by the greatest percentage? _____

3. What was the ratio of federal government purchases to GNP in 1984? __8.1%__ In 1987? __8.5%__
(*Note:* Federal government purchases were $381 billion in FY 1987.)

Common Errors

The first statement in each "common error" below is incorrect. Each incorrect statement is followed by a corrected version and an explanation.

1. Income and output are two entirely different things. WRONG!

   Income and output are two sides of the same coin. RIGHT!

   This is fundamental. Every time a dollar's worth of final spending takes place, the seller must receive a dollar's worth of income. It could not be otherwise. Remember, profits are used as a balancing item. Don't confuse the term "income" with the term "profit." Profits can be negative, whereas output for the economy cannot.

2. Comparisons of per capita GNP between countries tell you which population is better off. WRONG!

   Comparisons of per capita GNP between countries are only indicators of which population is better off. RIGHT!

   Simple comparisons of per capita GNP ignore how the GNP is distributed. A country with a very high per capita GNP that is unequally distributed may well provide a standard of living that is much below that of another country with a lower per capita GNP that is more equally distributed. There are other problems with comparisons of per capita GNP as a result of exchange-rate distortions, differences in mix of output in two countries, and organization of the economy. GNP per capita is only an indicator of how much goods and services each person could have, not what they do have.

3. Value added is a measure of a firm's profit. WRONG!

   Value added includes all factor payments to land, labor, and capital in addition to the residual (profit) that goes to the entrepreneur for taking risks. RIGHT!

   In computing value added, a firm subtracts *from* total revenue the cost of items sold to the firm in "arm's-length" transactions. There are additional cost items that normally would be subtracted to calculate "profit" but are not subtracted in the computation of value added. Those items include the cost of capital, land, and labor. When value added for all economic units is combined, the total of payments to capital (interest), land (rent), labor (wages), and risk taking (profits) will equal the total gross national product.

■ ANSWERS ■

Key-Term Review

1. intermediate goods
2. investment
3. gross national product (GNP)
4. GNP per capita
5. nominal GNP
6. value added
7. inflation
8. depreciation
9. real GNP
10. national income (*NI*)
11. disposable income (*DI*)
12. gross investment
13. net investment
14. personal income (*PI*)
15. production possibilities
16. exports
17. imports
18. national-income accounting
19. net national product (NNP)
20. saving

True or False

1. T	6. F	11. F	16. F	21. F	25. T
2. T	7. T	12. T	17. F	22. F	26. F
3. F	8. F	13. F	18. F	23. T	27. F
4. T	9. T	14. F	19. T	24. T	28. F
5. T	10. F	15. F	20. T		

Multiple Choice

1. a	5. d	9. c	12. d	15. b	18. a
2. b	6. d	10. c	13. d	16. d	19. d
3. c	7. a	11. c	14. a	17. c	20. c
4. b	8. d				

Problems and Applications

Exercise 1

1. **Table 4.1 answer**

Year	Nominal GNP (in billions of dollars per year)	Percentage growth in nominal GNP	Percentage growth in real GNP	Real GNP per capita per year
1978	$2,249.2	— %	— %	$13,995
1979	2,509.2	11.6	2.5	14,182
1980	2,731.3	8.9	−0.2	14,034
1981	3,053.9	11.8	1.9	14,181
1982	3,166.0	3.7	−2.6	13,641
1983	3,407.0	7.6	3.6	14,001
1984	3,771.0	10.7	6.8	14,774
1985	4,011.5	6.4	3.0	15,075
1986	4,236.9	5.6	2.9	15,370
1987	4,488.0	5.9	2.9	15,667

2. See Table 4.1 answer, columns 5 and 6.
3. F
4. $2,238.8 billion
5. $704.4 billion
6. See Table 4.1 answer, column 8.
7. F

Exercise 2

1. GNP = $C + I + G + (X - M)$
   GNP = $2{,}342 + 637 + (296 + 452) + (364 - 430)$
   GNP = $3{,}661$

Gross national product (GNP)	3,661
Less depreciation	(403)
Net national product	3,258
Less indirect business taxes	(304)
National income (*NI*)	2,954
Less corporate taxes	(88)
Less retained earnings	(118)
Less social security taxes	(306)
Plus transfer payments	(418)
Plus net interest	(150)
Personal income (*PI*)	3,010
Less personal taxes	(435)
Disposable incomes (*DI*)	2,575

Table 4.3 answer

Economic aggregate	1984 (billions of dollars per year)	1987 (billions of dollars per year)	Percent increase in nominal value
GNP	$3,661	$4,486	22.5%
NNP	3,258	4,007	23.0
NI	2,954	3,636	23.1
PI	3,010	3,746	24.4
DI	2,575	3,181	23.5

2. *PI*

3. $1984 = \dfrac{296}{3{,}661} = 8.1\%$

   $1987 = \dfrac{381}{4{,}486} = 8.5\%$

SECTION II MACROECONOMICS
PART A MAJOR PROBLEMS

Chapter 5
The Business Cycle

Quick Review

The Great Depression of the 1930s was a world-wide phenomenon. No market economy seemed to avoid it. High unemployment and low production for a decade led to despair nearly everywhere. They also caused a major rethinking of our views on the U.S. economy. Serious questions were raised, including:

- How stable is the U.S. economy?
- What forces cause instability?
- What, if anything, can the government do to promote steady economic growth?

The basic purpose of macroeconomics is to answer these questions—that is, explain the alternating periods of expansion and contraction known as the business cycle. If we can develop a macro theory to explain such changes, perhaps we can develop macro policies to control them.

The Classical school of thought, which was largely in vogue prior to the 1930s, stressed the self-adjusting nature of the economy. Automatic adjustment mechanisms—such as flexible wages and prices, falling interest rates, and the like—were thought to ensure that any downswing would be short if the economy was left alone.

The Great Depression lasted a long time, and economists and politicians everywhere began to question Classical theory. The great British economist John Maynard Keynes developed an alternative theory that took issue with the self-adjusting view of Classical economics. Keynes asserted that the economy was, in fact, inherently *unstable*. To leave the economy alone was poor policy. Instead, he prescribed increased government spending, income transfers, and lower interest rates to get the economy moving again. The arguments about business cycles are still not settled, but we have learned a great deal and agree to measure the cycle from peak to trough by watching the fluctuation in real GNP. Two consecutive quarters of decline in real GNP is a recession. Growth for a period below the 3 percent long-run trend of the economy is called a "growth recession." The statistics presented in this chapter make clear that business cycles vary greatly in length, frequency, and intensity.

Today economists focus on aggregate demand and aggregate supply to explain how the economy works. These concepts are the macroeconomic counterparts to demand and supply in individual markets. The aggregate demand curve slopes downward and to the right when plotted against the price level. The aggregate supply curve slopes upward to the right. The macro equilibrium that is defined by their intersection may or may not be the employment level we desire. Even if the macro equilibrium is at the output, employment, and price levels we desire, it may not last for long. The forces lying behind the equilibrium can change. Shifts in aggregate demand and/or aggregate supply can lead to unemployment, inflation, or worse yet, stagflation—a combination of the two.

The aggregate demand–supply framework provides a convenient way to compare various theories about how the economy works. The theories can be classified as demand side, supply side, or "eclectic," which draws on both. The three policy levers used to discuss and demonstrate the several theories are:

1. Fiscal policy—changes in taxes and government spending to alter economic outcomes
2. Monetary policy—the use of money and credit to control economic outcomes
3. Supply-side policies—those that favor tax cuts to increase incentives for producers

Much of what follows in the next several chapters is devoted to explaining the theory of macroeconomic behavior introduced in this chapter.

Learning Objectives

After reading Chapter 5 and doing the following exercises, you should:	True or false	Multiple choice	Problems and applications	Common errors	Pages in the text
1. Understand the dimensions of the business cycle.	3,4,13,18, 19,24,25	2–4, 17–21			106–114
2. Have in mind a historical perspective on the business cycle from the Great Depression to the present.	1				110–114
3. Be able to distinguish the Keynesian and Classical positions on how the macro economy works.	2,14	5,9,13,16, 22,23			108–109
4. Understand the definitions of aggregate demand and aggregate supply and the implications of macroeconomic equilibrium.	5–11,15	1,6–8,10,14, 15, 24,25	1,2	1,2	114–121
5. Be aware that there are several explanations of the business cycle —demand side, supply side, and eclectic.	12,13,16, 17,21,22	3,9,11,12	2		121–123
6. Be able to differentiate the policy levers advocated in the various business cycle theories.	20,23,26	16	1,2		123–125

Key-Term Review

Review the following terms; if you are not sure of the meaning of any term, write out the definition and check it against the Glossary in the text.

aggregate demand
aggregate supply
business cycle
equilibrium (macro)
fiscal policy
growth recession
inflation
law of demand

macroeconomics
monetary policy
real GNP
recession
Say's Law
supply-side policy
stagflation

Fill in the blank following each of the statements below with the appropriate term from the list above.

1. The idea that "supply creates its own demand" is known as _____.

    1. _____Says Law_____

2. When substantial inflation and unemployment occur at the same time, this is called _____.

    2. _____Stagflation_____

3. The idea that greater quantities will be demanded at lower prices, *ceteris paribus,* is the _____.

    3. _____law of Demand_____

4. When GNP grows, but at a rate less than the long-term trend, this is called a _____.

    4. _____growth recession_____

5. A _____ is said to occur when real GNP declines for two consecutive quarters.

5. _Recession_

6. The price at which _____ and _____ are equal determines macroeconomic equilibrium.

6. _aggregate supply + demand_

7. _____ is the use of money and credit controls to influence macroeconomic activity.

7. _monetary policy_

8. _____ is the use of government taxes and spending to influence macroeconomic activity.

8. _fiscal policy_

9. The first Reagan administration emphasized tax cuts as a _____.

9. _supply side policy_

10. The observed period of alternative economic growth and contraction is known as the _____.

10. _Business cycle_

11. The branch of economics that focuses on the behavior of the entire economy is _____.

11. _macroeconomics_

12. Nominal GNP adjusted for inflation is called the _____.

12. _real GNP_

13. _____ is the combination of price level and real output where aggregate demand and aggregate supply are equal.

13. _equilibrium_

14. When the average level of prices increases continuously, the process is known as _____.

14. _inflation_

True or False: *Circle your choice.*

T F 1. During World War II, real GNP expanded rapidly.

T **F** 2. In the Classical view of the economy, the product market is brought into equilibrium by flexible wages, the factor market by flexible prices.

T F 3. During a growth recession, real output actually increases.

T **F** 4. Unlike a growth recession, a recession is defined as occurring when the unemployment rate increases for two consecutive quarters.

T **F** 5. Aggregate demand refers to the quantities of all goods and services that an individual is willing and able to purchase.

T **F** 6. The quantity of real output demanded rises with price, *ceteris paribus.*

T F 7. The quantity of real output supplied rises with price, *ceteris paribus.*

T F 8. For macroeconomic equilibrium to occur, aggregate demand must equal aggregate supply.

T F 9. A stable equilibrium means that there is no tendency for price or output to change.

T F 10. If, at the prevailing price level, aggregate supply exceeds aggregate demand, the price level will tend to fall.

T **F** 11. A stable equilibrium means that the economy is at full employment.

T F 12. Those theories emphasizing the role of spending in the economy are called demand-side theories.

T **F** 13. During the business cycle, unemployment and production typically move in the same direction.

T **F** 14. John Maynard Keynes is known best for his work on the supply-side theory of the business cycle.

T **F** 15. A stable macro equilibrium is the same as a desirable macro equilibrium for the economy.

59

T F 16. Both Keynesian and monetarist theories of the business cycle are demand-side theories.

T F 17. Supply-side theories of the business cycle focus on the unwillingness of producers to supply more goods and services at existing prices.

T F 18. Business cycles are measured using the real GNP.

T F 19. Unemployment and inflation tend to rise and fall together.

T F 20. Price instability and unemployment are reasons that government may try to change a macro equilibrium.

T F 21. A disequilibrium occurs at prices where aggregate demand equals aggregate supply.

T F 22. The Classical approach to the business cycle was for government to do nothing.

T F 23. Fiscal policy is the use of tax and spending powers to alter economic outcomes.

T F 24. To have a recession, real output must actually fall.

T F 25. The "Crash of '87" occurred in many industrial countries, including the United States.

T F 26. The "crowding out" phenomenon is associated with the monetarist theory of business cycle control.

Multiple Choice: *Select the correct answer.*

___ 1. Macroeconomics tries to explain:
  (a) Unemployment rates.
  (b) Inflation rates.
  (c) Interest rates.
  (d) All of the above.

___ 2. The Great Depression:
  (a) Followed a period of apparent prosperity.
  (b) Led to an unemployment rate that reached 25 percent.
  (c) Caused President Roosevelt to declare a "bank holiday" in 1933.
  (d) Did all of the above.

___ 3. When real GNP declines for two consecutive quarters, this is known as:
  (a) Stagflation.
  (b) A recession.
  (c) A growth recession.
  (d) All of the above.

___ 4. A growth recession is said to occur when the economy grows at:
  (a) A rate less than that of population.
  (b) A rate less than the long-term average.
  (c) A slower rate in the current year than the preceding year.
  (d) None of the above.

___ 5. Which of the following characterizes the Classical view of the economy?
  (a) Wages are flexible and prices are not.
  (b) The economy is inherently unstable.
  (c) The economy will "self-adjust" if we let it alone.
  (d) None of the above is characteristic.

___ 6. In the aggregate demand–aggregate supply diagram:
  (a) The vertical axis measures the average price level.
  (b) The horizontal axis measures real output.
  (c) The horizontal axis measures real income.
  (d) All of the above are true.

C 7. *Both* the aggregate supply and aggregate demand curves are drawn on the assumption that:
   (a) People will buy more at lower prices than at higher prices.
   (b) Firms will supply more at higher prices than at lower prices.
   (c) All other things are held constant except prices.
   (d) None of the above is the case.

C 8. Macro equilibrium always occurs:
   (a) When aggregate supply is greater than aggregate demand.
   (b) When the labor force is fully employed.
   (c) When aggregate demand equals aggregate supply at the average price level of the economy.
   (d) Under none of the above conditions.

D 9. Keynes argued that deficient aggregate demand might originate with:
   (a) Increased consumer savings.
   (b) Inadequate business investment.
   (c) Insufficient government spending.
   (d) All of the above.

D 10. Starting from an equilibrium at less than full employment:
   (a) If aggregate demand increases, *ceteris paribus*, the economy will experience inflation.
   (b) If aggregate supply increases, *ceteris paribus*, the economy is unlikely to experience inflation.
   (c) If both aggregate demand and aggregate supply increased, output and employment should increase, but the price level movement would be uncertain.
   (d) All of the above are the case.

D 11. Which of the following is emphasized in the eclectic approach to solving the business cycle?
   (a) The money supply.
   (b) Taxes and government spending.
   (c) Incentives for producers.
   (d) All of the above.

C 12. An aggregate demand curve most likely shifts to the left when:
   (a) Taxes fall.
   (b) Savings fall.
   (c) Government spending falls.
   (d) All of the above occur.

D 13. Which of the following are inherent in the Classical view of a self-adjusting economy?
   (a) Flexible wages.
   (b) Flexible prices.
   (c) Say's Law.
   (d) All of the above.

C 14. Which of the following causes the aggregate supply curve to shift?
   (a) Changes in consumer income.
   (b) Changes in consumer savings.
   (c) Changes in costs experienced by American businesses.
   (d) None of the above.

C 15. When aggregate supply exceeds aggregate demand, what will happen to the price level?
   (a) Prices will rise to a new equilibrium.
   (b) Prices will remain the same at equilibrium
   (c) Prices will drop to a new equilibrium.
   (d) Interest rates will adjust but not prices.

_____ 16. Keynes viewed the economy as inherently unstable and suggested that during a downturn policy makers should:
(a) Cut taxes, increase government spending, and reduce transfers.
(b) Cut taxes, reduce government spending, and increase transfers.
(c) Raise taxes, increase government spending, and increase transfers.
(d) Cut taxes, increase government spending, and increase transfers.

_____ 17. Which of the following countries experienced the greatest reduction in industrial production during the Great Depression?
(a) The United States.
(b) England.
(c) The Soviet Union.
(d) Japan.

_____ 18. Business cycles in the United States:
(a) Are remarkably similar in length but vary greatly in intensity.
(b) Vary greatly in length, frequency, and intensity.
(c) Are similar in frequency and intensity.
(d) Are similar in length, frequency, and intensity.

_____ 19. The average annual upward trend in real GNP is approximately:
(a) 10 percent.
(b) 3 percent.
(c) 5 percent.
(d) 2 percent.

_____ 20. The peak of a business cycle should be accompanied by:
(a) The lowest unemployment rate over the cycle.
(b) The highest rate of increase in the price level over the cycle.
(c) The greatest rate of growth in output of goods and services over the cycle.
(d) All of the above.

_____ 21. Which of the following would be a "growth recession"?
(a) Real GNP contracts for two consecutive quarters.
(b) Real GNP grows for a period at a rate less than 3 percent.
(c) The unemployment rate stays constant at the long-run rate of 6 percent.
(d) Prices rise steadily but at a rate less than the long-run trend of 4 percent.

_____ 22. The "real balance" effect relies on the idea that as the price level falls:
(a) Each dollar you own will purchase more goods and services.
(b) Each bond you own will increase in value, thus increasing your wealth.
(c) You will begin to save less because your wealth has increased.
(d) All of the above are the case.

_____ 23. When the price level falls in our economy, consumers tend to:
(a) Buy more imported goods and fewer domestically produced goods, *ceteris paribus*.
(b) Buy more imported goods and more domestic goods, *ceteris paribus*.
(c) Buy fewer imported goods and more domestic goods, *ceteris paribus*.
(d) Buy fewer imported goods and fewer domestic goods, *ceteris paribus*.

_____ 24. The upward slope of the aggregate supply curve can best be explained by:
(a) The "real balance" effect.
(b) The interest-rate effect.
(c) Higher costs associated with higher-capacity utilization rates.
(d) None of the above.

___ 25. Starting from macro equilibrium at full employment, which of the following would cause stagflation to develop?
(a) Aggregate demand shifts right; aggregate supply does not shift.
(b) Aggregate supply shifts to the right, aggregate demand does not shift.
(c) Aggregate supply and aggregate demand both shift to the right.
(d) Aggregate supply shifts to the left; aggregate demand does not shift. ✓

Problems and Applications

Exercise 1

This exercise examines the effects of tax policy using aggregate supply and demand curves.

Assume the aggregate demand and supply curves are those shown in Figure 5.1. Then suppose the government reduces taxes, which causes the quantity of output demanded in the economy to rise by $1 trillion per year at every price level. Decide whether the tax change shifts aggregate demand or aggregate supply from its initial position.

Figure 5.1

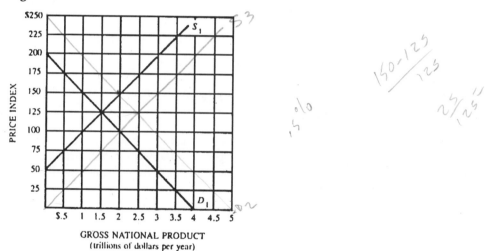

GROSS NATIONAL PRODUCT
(trillions of dollars per year)

1. Draw the new aggregate demand curve (label it D_2) or aggregate supply curve (label it S_2) in Figure 5.1 that results from the tax change.

2. Compute the percentage change in equilibrium GNP caused by the shift. _____ %

3. Suppose that the unemployment rate drops by one percentage point for every 5 percent increase in GNP. If the unemployment rate was 15 percent before the shift occurred, what would it be after the shift? _____ %

4. What is the percentage change in the equilibrium price level as a result of the tax change? _____ %

5. The shift that occurred in Question 1 (above) is consistent with:
(a) Stagflation.
(b) Inflation and a lower unemployment rate.
(c) Deflation and a higher unemployment rate.
(d) Lower inflation and a lower unemployment rate.

Now suppose the lower taxes also induce productivity changes and generate incentives that cause firms (sellers) to lower prices by $50 per unit of output per year after the tax change. (In Questions 6–11, compare the new equilibrium to that in Questions 1–5.)

63

6. Draw the new aggregate demand curve (label it D_3) or aggregate supply curve (label it S_3) in Figure 5.1. Compare the new equilibrium to that used in Problems 1–5.

7. Compute the percentage change (on curve S_2 or D_2) in equilibrium GNP caused by the shift. _____ %

8. Suppose that the unemployment rate drops by one percentage point for every 5 percent increase in GNP. If the unemployment rate was 8.4 percent before the shift occurred, what would it be after the shift? _____ %

9. What would be the percentage change in the equilibrium price level associated with the new level of output? _____ %

10. This shift is consistent with:
    (a) Stagflation.
    (b) Inflation and a lower unemployment rate.
    (c) Deflation and a higher unemployment rate.
    (d) A lower price level and lower unemployment rate.

11. The tax cut can best be characterized as:
    (a) Monetary policy only.
    (b) Fiscal policy only.
    (c) Supply-side policy only.
    (d) Both fiscal and supply-side policy.
    (e) None of the above.

Exercise 2

This exercise shows how government policy can be used to alleviate problems brought on by natural disasters. Aggregate supply and demand curves are used.

Assume the aggregate demand and supply curves are those shown in Figure 5.2. Suppose drought causes massive destruction of crops, which results in a decrease of $1 trillion of goods and services (GNP) that sellers are willing and able to provide. Decide whether the change shifts aggregate demand or supply from the initial equilibrium.

Figure 5.2

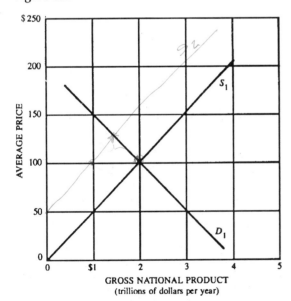

1. Draw the new aggregate demand (label it D_2) or aggregate supply curve (label it S_2) in Figure 5.2 that results from the drought.

2. With which of the following is the move to the new equilibrium in Question 1 consistent?
   (a) Stagflation.
   (b) Inflation and a lower unemployment rate.
   (c) Deflation and a higher unemployment rate.
   (d) Deflation and a lower unemployment rate.

3. If the average price was held down to 100 by government price controls, would there be a shortage or a surplus after the drought? _Shortage_

4. Which curve would shift if the government released some of its inventories to push the equilibrium to a GNP of $2 trillion at an average price of 100? _$S_2 - S_1$_

5. Draw the new aggregate demand (label it D_3) or supply curve (label it S_3) in Figure 5.2 that would result from the government's inventory release program.

Exercise 3

The media frequently provide information on macroeconomic events that affect aggregate demand and supply. To describe such shifts the media should provide certain kinds of information. Because it uses one of the articles in the textbook, this exercise will show the kind of information to look for. If your professor makes a newspaper assignment for this chapter, this exercise will provide an example of how to do it.

Reread the article in Chapter 3 entitled "Some Taxing Facts about Lotteries." Then answer the following questions:

1. What statement (no more than a sentence) indicates the cause of a shift in aggregate demand or supply?

2. What statement (no more than a sentence) indicates the recipients of the initial impact of the change in aggregate demand or supply?

3. What phrase indicates an actual change in quantity or price that results from the shift?

4. Which of the diagrams in Figure 5.3 best represents the shift in aggregate demand or supply?

   a   b   c   d   (circle one)

Figure 5.3

Shifts of aggregate demand and supply

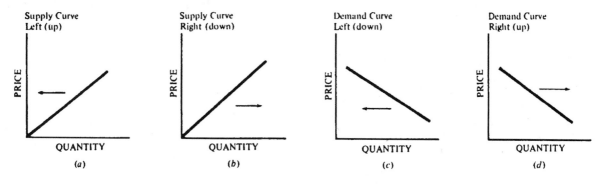

65

Common Errors

The first statement in each "common error" below is incorrect. Each incorrect statement is followed by a corrected version and an explanation.

1. The full-employment GNP is the same as the equilibrium GNP. WRONG!

    The full-employment GNP is not necessarily the same as the equilibrium GNP. RIGHT!

    The full-employment GNP refers to the capacity of the economy to produce goods and services. When resources are fully employed, no additional goods and services can be produced. However, the equilibrium GNP refers to the equality between the aggregate demand for goods and services and the aggregate supply of those goods and services, not to any particular level of resource employment.

2. Aggregate demand (supply) and market demand (supply) are the same. WRONG!

    Aggregate demand (supply) and market demand (supply) involve very different levels of aggregation. RIGHT!

    Market demand can be found for specific markets only. Products in that market must be homogeneous. The firms in that market are competitors. The market demand is used for microeconomic applications. Aggregate demand applies to all products within the economy and involves their average prices. It is not even possible to sum the market demand curves to find the aggregate demand curve because the prices of different commodities cannot be measured in the same units; an average price must be computed. Aggregate demand is used for macroeconomic applications, not microeconomic ones. The distinction between aggregate supply and market supply is similar to that between aggregate demand and market demand.

■ANSWERS■

Key-Term Review

1. Say's Law
2. stagflation
3. law of demand
4. growth recession
5. recession
6. aggregate demand, aggregate supply
7. monetary policy
8. fiscal policy
9. supply-side policy
10. business cycle
11. macroeconomics
12. real GNP
13. equilibrium (macro)
14. inflation

True or False

1. T	6. F	11. F	15. F	19. F	23. T
2. F	7. T	12. T	16. T	20. T	24. T
3. T	8. T	13. F	17. T	21. F	25. T
4. F	9. T	14. F	18. T	22. T	26. T
5. F	10. T				

Multiple Choice

1. d	6. d	10. d	14. c	18. b	22. d
2. d	7. c	11. d	15. c	19. b	23. c
3. b	8. c	12. c	16. d	20. d	24. c
4. b	9. d	13. d	17. a	21. b	25. d
5. c					

Problems and Applications

Exercise 1

1. See Figure 5.1 answer, D_2.

Figure 5.1 answer

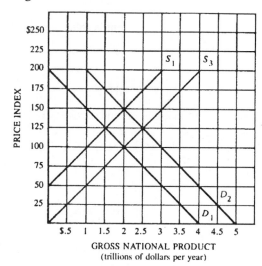

GROSS NATIONAL PRODUCT
(trillions of dollars per year)

2. Equilibrium GNP before the shift is $1.5 trillion each year.
   Equilibrium GNP after the shift is $2.00 trillion each year.
   Percentage change = (2.0 – 1.5)/1.5 = 33%

3. $\dfrac{33\% \text{ change in output}}{5\%}$ = 6.6% drop in the unemployment rate.

   The new unemployment rate is 8.4% (= 15% – 6.6%).
4. Equilibrium price before the shift is 125.
   Equilibrium price after the shift is 150.
   Percentage change = (150 – 125)/125 = 20%.
5. b
6. See Figure 5.1 answer, S_3.
7. Equilibrium GNP before the shift is $2.0 trillion.
   Equilibrium GNP after the shift is $2.5 trillion.
   Percentage change = (2.5 – 2.0)/2.0 = 25%.

8. $\dfrac{25\% \text{ change in output}}{5\%}$ = 5% drop in the unemployment rate.

   The new unemployment rate is 3.4% (= 8.4% – 5%).
9. Equilibrium price before the shift is 150.
   Equilibrium price after the shift is 125.
   Percentage change = (125 – 150)/150 = –17%.
10. d
11. d

Exercise 2

1. See Figure 5.2 answer, S_2.

Figure 5.2 answer

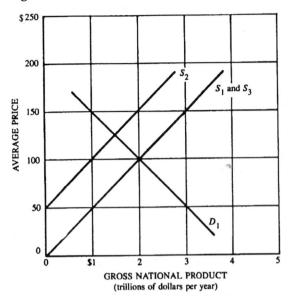

GROSS NATIONAL PRODUCT
(trillions of dollars per year)

2. Since the drought causes prices to rise and the GNP to fall, its effects on the economy are consistent with stagflation.
3. Shortage. The price is below the new equilibrium price of 125.
4. The supply curve would have been shifted back to its original position.
5. See Figure 5.2 answer, S_3.

Exercise 3

1. "Per capita lottery ticket sales average $88 in 1985, up from $23 in 1975. . . . " This statement indicates an increase in taxes.
2. "The transfer of these revenues to state treasuries is an implicit tax on lottery bettors, and that tax is decidedly regressive." Consumers—the buyers of goods—are experiencing the impact of the new tax.
3. ". . . Net revenues from lotteries were $30 per capita." This statement is the closest that the article comes to an indication of the magnitude of the change in aggregate demand that results from the tax on lotteries.
4. d Aggregate demand shifts to the left because of the lower after-tax incomes resulting from the tax.

Chapter 6
Unemployment

Quick Review

Unemployment concerns policy makers because it can cause people to lose their income and create social unrest. Society also loses its potential output. In the Employment Act of 1946 a low unemployment rate became one of the important national goals. But unemployment is difficult to measure, its causes are numerous, and its impact is hard to gauge. Thus, we need to answer several questions:

- When are resources "unemployed"?
- What are the consequences of unemployment for individuals and for the larger economy?
- What causes unemployment?
- What is "full employment"?

Unemployment is measured only in terms of those people in the labor force who have no job but are actively seeking employment. If you're a civilian under 16 or you're not looking for work, then you're not in the labor force and you are not considered unemployed. This criterion eliminates children, mothers at home, and people in the armed forces. The number of unemployed is determined through surveys of households across the country. To find the unemployment rate, the number of unemployed is divided by the number in the labor force.

Economists typically distinguish four kinds of unemployment: frictional (short-term unemployment between jobs), seasonal (unemployment that varies with the seasons), structural (caused by a mismatch of available labor with skill requirements or job locations), and cyclical (caused by deficient aggregate demand). For these reasons, several million people are unemployed in the United States during any period of time.

During the 1960s the Council of Economic Advisers thought that an unemployment rate of 4 percent provided the optimal balance between employment and price-level goals. In the 1970s and 1980s this figure was revised upward to 6 percent to reflect the increased importance of structural unemployment. Changes in the age–sex composition of the labor force, more liberal transfer payments, and so on necessitated this revision.

The unemployment rate does not provide a complete view of the problem of joblessness. Some of the costs of unemployment are psychological and show up in ways other than low or zero income—alcoholism, hypertension, suicide, divorce. Unemployment also strikes some groups—teenagers, minorities, the uneducated—harder than others. Finally, those who get discouraged and quit looking for work are not counted as unemployed.

Making the distinction between the labor force and the total population allows us to distinguish also between physical production possibilities, the maximum amount that could be produced if we put the entire population to work, and institutional production possibilities, which defines the annual output we could produce if we efficiently employed our entire labor force. The labor force is smaller than the entire population because of institutional constraints such as compulsory education or child labor laws. The institutional production-possibilities curve lies inside the physical production-possibilities curve.

Learning Objectives

After reading Chapter 6 and doing the following exercises, you should:	True or false	Multiple choice	Problems and applications	Common errors	Pages in the text
1. Know who is included in the labor force.	1–3, 5, 7,10,12	2,3, 11,12			129–130
2. Know the reasons why physical production possibilities and institutional production possibilities differ.	6–8	4,5	3		130–132
3. Know why unemployment is a major social concern.	20		2,3	1	132–136
4. Know how the unemployment rate is calculated.	9	1	1,4	1	136–138
5. Know how the unemployment rate varies with age, sex, education, and race.	4,11,19	8,9			136–137
6. Be able to distinguish between unemployment and underemployment.		10,12,21	3		136–137
7. Be aware of programs designed to alleviate unemployment.		6,7			134
8. Be aware of the ways in which the unemployment rate may understate the true dimensions of the unemployment problem.		11,21	3	2	136–137
9. Know the meaning of "full" employment.	21,23	19,21			139–142
10. Be able to distinguish the causes of cyclical, frictional, structural, and seasonal unemployment.	13–18	13–18	1,3	2	139–142
11. Know how to calculate the GNP gap.		20	2		145–146
12. Understand why the number of young workers is declining.	22				144

Key-Term Review

Review the following terms; if you are not sure of the meaning of any term, write out the definition and check it against the Glossary in the text.

cyclical unemployment
discouraged worker
frictional unemployment
full employment
full-employment GNP
GNP gap
institutional production possibilities

labor force
physical production possibilities
seasonal unemployment
structural unemployment
underemployment
unemployment
unemployment rate

Fill in the blank following each of the statements below with the appropriate term from the list above.

1. When people are employed below their capabilities, they are said to be victims of _____.

1. _Underemployment_

2. The loss of jobs when the economy fails to reach its potential is called _____.

2. _cyclical unemployment_

3. Unemployment statistics sometimes understate the magnitude of the problem because they do not take into account the _____.

3. _discouraged worker_

4. Dividing the number of unemployed people by the entire labor force yields the _____.

4. _unemployment Rate_

5. When the economy is operating below its potential, there is said to be a _____.

5. _GNP Gap_

6. The Council of Economic Advisers has revised upward its estimate of what constitutes _____, variously estimated to be between 6 and 7 percent unemployment.

6. _full Employment_

7. The economy's physical production possibilities exceed its _____.

7. _Institutional Production Possibilities_

8. When society imposes limitations on the efficient use of workers, the result is that it cannot produce at the limit of its _____.

8. _Physical Production Possibilities_

9. Every person 16 years of age or older who is either employed for pay or actively seeking employment is considered a part of the _____.

9. _Labor force_

10. When the unemployment rate increases after schools close for the summer, the increase is referred to as _____.

10. _Seasonal unemployment_

11. Those who cannot find jobs because they do not possess the skills that jobs currently require suffer from _____.

11. _Structural unemployment_

12. Adding together structural, frictional, seasonal, and cyclical unemployment gives a gross estimate of the amount of total _____.

12. _Unemployment_

13. Joblessness that occurs as people move from one job to another is _____.

13. _Frictional unemployment_

14. One of the goals of economic policy is to see that the economy produces a _____.

14. _full employment GNP_

True or False: *Circle your choice.*

T **(F)** 1. Full employment means everyone in the labor force has a job.

(T) F 2. To be counted as part of the labor force, one must be at least 16 years old.

(T) F 3. A homemaker with part-time paid employment is part of the labor force; one without paid employment (and who is not looking for employment) is not part of the labor force.

(T) F 4. In recent years the rapid increase in the number of teenagers and women in the labor force has led to increased structural and frictional unemployment.

T **(F)** 5. Those who get discouraged and no longer seek work are counted as unemployed.

(T) F 6. The institutional production-possibilities curve lies inside the physical production-possibilities curve.

(T) F 7. Child labor laws restrict the economy's production to less than what is physically possible.

(T) F 8. The institutional production-possibilities curve reflects the restrictions society has placed on the use of resources and technology.

71

T F 9. To obtain the unemployment rate, divide the number counted as unemployed by the population.

T F 10. Everyone who is willing to work and seeking work but cannot find a job is considered unemployed.

T F 11. There is a direct relationship between educational level attained and the unemployment rate.

T F 12. A person who is employed part-time but seeks a full-time job is underemployed.

T F 13. The unemployment rate was as high as 25 percent during the depression of the 1930s.

T F 14. Those who make their livings by driving snowplows are likely to suffer from seasonal unemployment.

T F 15. Someone who quits one job to take another after a short vacation is among those who are classified as "frictionally unemployed."

T F 16. When telephone operators were replaced by direct dialing, one could predict the development of structural unemployment.

T F 17. The development of the disco, with its recorded music, could be expected to result in the structural unemployment of musicians.

T F 18. Cyclical unemployment stems from insufficient aggregate demand.

T F 19. One of the main reasons for revising the full-employment rate was a change in the age and sex structure of the labor force.

T F 20. Discouraged workers are counted as part of the labor force.

T F 21. In 1987 the unemployment rate dipped below 6 percent for the first time in a decade.

T F 22. The number of young people in our economy has been declining and will continue to do so into the 1990s.

T F 23. When the unemployment rate reaches 6 percent, the labor force is said to have reached full employment.

Multiple Choice: *Select the correct answer.*

___ 1. Who among the following would be counted among the unemployed?
(a) Someone who is on vacation but will return to a job.
(b) Someone who is on strike.
(c) An unpaid employee of a family enterprise such as a farm.
(d) None of the above.

___ 2. Which of the following would be counted as a member of the labor force?
(a) A hard-working homemaker who is not employed outside the home.
(b) A man doing ten years for armed robbery.
(c) A retired commander of a U.S. Navy nuclear submarine.
(d) The president of General Motors.

___ 3. The number of persons in the labor force is:
(a) About half of the total population.
(b) Equal to the number in the population.
(c) Less than half of the population.
(d) None of the above.

___ 4. Which of the following would cause the institutional production-possibilities curve to shift *inward*?
(a) The FDA approves a chemical that is efficient in fighting forest fires.
(b) The FDA bans a chemical useful in producing potatoes.
(c) Child labor laws are abolished.
(d) None of the above would cause such a shift.

_D_ 5. The existence of unemployment means that the economy is:
  (a) Producing beyond the physical production-possibilities curve.
  (b) Producing beyond the institutional production-possibilities curve.
  (c) Producing beyond both the physical and institutional production-possibilities curves.
  (d) Doing none of the above.

_B_ 6. The maximum amount of unemployment benefits one may receive is determined by:
  (a) The federal government.
  (b) The state government.
  (c) The local government.
  (d) None of the above.

_C_ 7. The amount of weekly unemployment benefits you receive depends largely on:
  (a) The amount you've been able to build up in your savings account.
  (b) The number of consecutive years you've held your job.
  (c) Your previous weekly wage.
  (d) How long you've been unemployed.

_C_ 8. Which of the following groups typically has the highest unemployment rate?
  (a) White teenagers.
  (b) Black adults.
  (c) Black teenagers.
  (d) White adult females.

_D_ 9. Which of the following typically have unemployment rates above the national average?
  (a) Black teenagers.
  (b) White teenagers.
  (c) Black adult males.
  (d) All of the above.

_A_ 10. Which of the following statements *best* describes the relationship between educational level and the unemployment rate?
  (a) An inverse relationship.
  (b) A positive relationship.
  (c) No relationship.
  (d) The relationship cannot be determined.

_D_ 11. Which of the following would typically be classified as a discouraged worker?
  (a) Someone who has recently been disciplined by his or her employer.
  (b) Someone who does not like his or her job.
  (c) Someone who is employed part-time.
  (d) Someone who is not actively seeking employment but who would do so if it seemed possible to find a job.

_C_ 12. Underemployment means:
  (a) The same thing as unemployment.
  (b) A person is lazy and not working hard at his or her job.
  (c) The job a person has does not require that person to work to his or her full capabilities.
  (d) None of the above.

_D_ 13. Which of the following contributed to an increase in the perceived level of structural unemployment?
  (a) More youth and women in the labor force.
  (b) Increased transfer payments.
  (c) Structural changes in demand.
  (d) All of the above.

_B_ 14. When migrant workers seek employment after the crops have been picked, the unemployment rate goes up. This situation is an example of:
    (a) Frictional unemployment.
    (b) Seasonal unemployment.
    (c) Structural unemployment.
    (d) Cyclical unemployment.

_C_ 15. Which of the following situations is characteristic of frictional unemployment when other forms of unemployment are low?
    (a) There are not enough jobs for those frictionally unemployed.
    (b) Those who are frictionally unemployed cannot perform the jobs available.
    (c) The period of job search will be relatively short.
    (d) All of the above are characteristic.

_D_ 16. Frictional unemployment is thought to be typically in the neighborhood of:
    (a) 0 to 1 percent.
    (b) 3 to 4 percent.
    (c) 1 to 2 percent.
    (d) 2 to 3 percent.

_A_ 17. Automobile workers in Detroit who are unemployed because of foreign imports at the same time that job vacancies exist for coal miners in West Virginia would most likely be classified as:
    (a) Structurally unemployed.
    (b) Cyclically unemployed.
    (c) Frictionally unemployed.
    (d) Seasonally unemployed.

_D_ 18. Which of the following is a cause of cyclical unemployment?
    (a) Bicycle manufacturers' inventories are too large.
    (b) Workers do not possess the appropriate skills for the vacancies that exist.
    (c) Unemployment benefits are too high and given for too long a period.
    (d) There is simply not enough demand for workers at the present wage rate.

_D_ 19. Which of the following statements provides a rationale for treating a 6 percent unemployment rate rather than a 4 percent unemployment rate as the "full-employment target"?
    (a) The number of teenagers seeking jobs has increased.
    (b) The proportion of women in the labor force is higher than it used to be.
    (c) The number of persons reentering the labor force has increased dramatically.
    (d) All of the above provide such a rationale.

_D_ 20. The amount by which full-employment GNP exceeds actual GNP is called:
    (a) The high-employment budget.
    (b) The potential GNP.
    (c) The institutional GNP.
    (d) The GNP gap.

_C_ 21. Which of the following is considered by the Reagan administration to be the inflation threshold unemployment rate?
    (a) 2–3 percent.
    (b) 4–5 percent.
    (c) 6–7 percent.
    (d) 9–10 percent.

Problems and Applications

Exercise 1

This exercise shows how to calculate the unemployment rate and indicates the relationship between the unemployment rate and GNP.

1. Compute the unemployment rate based on the information in Table 6.1, and insert it in column 4.

Table 6.1
Unemployment and real GNP, 1970–1987

Year	(1) Noninstitutional population	(2) Civilian labor force	(3) Unemployment	(4) Unemployment rate (percent)	(5) Percent change in real GNP (percent)
	(Thousands of persons 16 and over)				
1970	140,273	82,771	4,093	4.9 %	−0.2%
1971	143,032	84,382	5,016	5.9	3.4
1972	146,575	87,034	4,882	5.6	5.7
1973	149,422	89,429	4,365	4.9	5.8
1974	152,349	91,949	5,156	5.6	−0.6
1975	153,333	93,775	7,929	8.5	−1.2
1976	158,294	96,158	7,406	7.7	5.4
1977	161,166	99,009	6,991	7.1	5.5
1978	164,027	102,251	6,202	6.1	5.0
1979	166,951	104,962	6,137	5.8	2.8
1980	167,745	106,940	7,637	7.1	−0.3
1981	170,130	108,670	8,273	7.6	2.5
1982	172,271	110,204	10,678	9.7	−2.1
1983	174,215	111,550	10,717	9.6	3.7
1984	176,383	113,544	8,539	7.5	6.8
1985	178,206	115,461	8,312	7.2	3.0
1986	180,587	117,834	8,237	7.0	2.9
1987	182,753	119,865	7,425	10.62% 6.2%	2.9

2. In Figure 6.1 graph both the unemployment rate (column 4 of Table 6.1) and the percentage change in the real GNP (column 5).

Figure 6.1

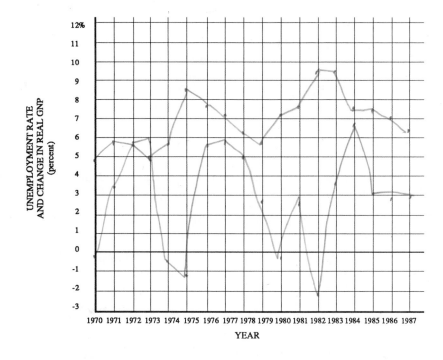

UNEMPLOYMENT RATE AND CHANGE IN REAL GNP (percent)

YEAR

75

3. The relationship between the unemployment rate and the percentage change in the real GNP is best characterized as:
   (a) A direct relationship (the two indicators go up and down together).
   (b) An inverse relationship (the two indicators move in opposite directions).

4. Which indicator seems to change direction first through time?
   (a) Real GNP.
   (b) The unemployment rate.

5. Which of the following kinds of unemployment is suggested in Figure 6.1?
   (a) Structural unemployment.
   (b) Seasonal unemployment.
   (c) Cyclical unemployment.
   (d) Frictional unemployment.

6. Which of the following government programs would be *most* appropriate to counteract this kind of unemployment?
   (a) Increase job-placement services.
   (b) Stimulate economic growth.
   (c) Make school last all year long.
   (d) Provide more job training.

7. In what years was full employment, as defined by the Reagan administration, achieved between 1970 and 1987? _____

Exercise 2

This exercise shows the relationship between unemployment and the level of GNP. It is similar to the problem at the end of Chapter 6 in the text.

Suppose the labor force of a country consists of 1 million people, of whom 900,000 are employed. Assume that each employed worker contributes an annual average of $50,000 worth of goods and services and that the full-employment level occurs at a 3 percent unemployment rate.

1. What is the unemployment rate? ____10____ %

2. How far is the economy from full employment? ____7____ %

3. What is the GNP gap? $_____

Exercise 3

The following exercise provides practice in categorizing the various kinds of unemployment.

Identify each of the following cases as an example of seasonal unemployment, frictional unemployment, structural unemployment, cyclical unemployment, or underemployment.

1. The immigration service faces its greatest problem during the summer when illegal immigrants cross the border to pick crops. _Seasonal_

2. While the Soviet Union boasts of no unemployment and a high education level for its population, the productivity of the population and the quality of their production are extremely low. _underemployment_

3. People who are fired from jobs with high salaries take longer to find new jobs than those with low salaries. _frictional_

4. In the depression unemployment affected one-fourth of the labor force. _cyclical_

5. In some cities there are extreme shortages of labor at the same time that there is substantial unemployment. The problem is that the shortages occur in high-tech industries while the unemployment occurs for unskilled laborers. _structural_

Exercise 4

Articles on unemployment provide information that is often politically sensitive. Using one of the articles in the text, this exercise will show the kind of information to look for. If your professor makes a newspaper assignment for this chapter, this exercise will provide an example of how to do it.

Reread the article in Chapter 6 entitled "Taiwanese Jobless Rate Falls to a Five-Year Low" from the *Wall Street Journal*. Then answer the following questions:

1. What sentence provides the latest unemployment data? To what group or community does the data apply? _____

2. What sentence indicates the trend in the unemployment rate prior to the most recent data?
   _____

3. What statement indicates the government's interpretation of the numbers? _____

Common Errors

The first statement in each "common error" below is incorrect. Each incorrect statement is followed by a corrected version and an explanation.

1. The government should eliminate unemployment. WRONG!
   The government must lower unemployment at the same time that it accomplishes other goals. RIGHT!
   Under the Full Employment and Balanced Growth Act of 1978, the government sets an unemployment goal for itself, but this goal is well short of a zero unemployment rate. As we shall see in subsequent chapters, the government may have to sacrifice such goals as price stability if it lowers unemployment too much. In this chapter we have seen that it would be very difficult and even undesirable to eliminate frictional or seasonal unemployment.

2. A rise in the unemployment rate of 0.1 or 0.2 percent for a month is bad. WRONG!
   Monthly changes in the unemployment rate may not have any significant economic implications. RIGHT!
   The weaknesses of the unemployment rate as an economic measure should be clear by this time. Small changes in the unemployment rate tell us nothing about what is happening to disguised unemployment, discouraged workers, or changes in the labor force; and large changes in seasonal or frictional unemployment are not necessarily bad and could not be easily remedied even if they were. Be careful in interpreting changes in the unemployment rate.

■ ANSWERS ■

Key-Term Review

1. underemployment
2. cyclical unemployment
3. discouraged worker
4. unemployment rate
5. GNP gap
6. full employment
7. institutional production possibilities
8. physical production possibilities
9. labor force
10. seasonal unemployment
11. structural unemployment
12. unemployment
13. frictional unemployment
14. full-employment GNP

True or False

1. F	5. F	9. F	13. T	17. T	21. F
2. T	6. T	10. F	14. T	18. T	22. T
3. T	7. T	11. F	15. T	19. T	23. T
4. T	8. T	12. T	16. T	20. F	

Multiple Choice

1. d	5. d	9. d	13. d	16. d	19. d
2. d	6. b	10. a	14. b	17. a	20. d
3. c	7. c	11. d	15. c	18. d	21. c
4. b	8. c	12. c			

Problems and Applications

Exercise 1

1. Table 6.1 answer

Year	(4) Unemployment Rate (percent)
1970	4.9%
1971	5.9
1972	5.6
1973	4.9
1974	5.6
1975	8.5
1976	7.7
1977	7.1
1978	6.1
1979	5.8
1980	7.1
1981	7.6
1982	9.7
1983	9.6
1984	7.5
1985	7.2
1986	7.0
1987	6.2

2. Figure 6.1 answer

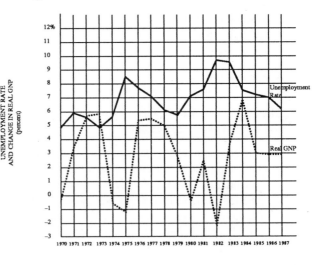

3. b
4. a
5. c
6. b
7. 1970–74, 1978, 1979, and 1987

Exercise 2

1. The unemployment rate is found as follows:

$$\text{Unemployment rate} = \frac{\text{Unemployed}}{\text{Labor force}} = \frac{\text{Labor force} - \text{Employed}}{\text{Labor force}}$$

$$= \frac{(1,000,000 - 900,000)}{1,000,000} = 10\%$$

78

2. Since the full employment rate occurs at 3 percent, 7 percent more of the labor force (10% – 3%) must be employed before full employment is reached.
3. Since 7 percent of the labor force is not employed and the unemployed could produce an average of $50,000 a year, the unemployed could add $3.5 billion (7% x 1,000,000 x $50,000) to the GNP. In other words, there is a $3.5 billion GNP gap.

Exercise 3

1. seasonal
2. underemployment
3. frictional
4. cyclical
5. structural

Exercise 4

1. The statement "Taiwanese unemployment fell to 1.7% of the labor force in April" indicates the unemployment rate for Taiwan.
2. In that same sentence, unemployment in April is said to be "the lowest rate in five years, down from 2.3% a year earlier."
3. The statement "Officials of the Council of Economic Planning and Development attributed the low rate to Taiwan's booming exports" gives the government's interpretation of the numbers as well as the probable cause for the low unemployment rate.

Chapter 7
Inflation

Quick Review

Inflation is viewed as a serious problem by presidents, politicians, and citizens in general. In this chapter we focus on the following topics:

- What kind of price increases are referred to as "inflation"?
- How does inflation affect individual households and the larger economy?
- How is inflation measured?
- What are the major causes of inflation?

Inflation is an increase in the average price level of goods and services. Some prices rise faster than the inflation rate; others rise more slowly. At the microeconomic level, inflation causes redistribution of real income among individuals and businesses; it is not an equal-opportunity phenomenon. At the macroeconomic level, inflation inhibits some production and consumption decisions, often promotes wasteful buying, and encourages unproductive speculation.

There are several types of inflation and three types of measures of it. The types of inflation are named for the disturbances that bring about inflation:

1. Cost-push inflation results when increases in costs initiate increases in inflation.
2. Demand-pull inflation occurs when excess aggregate demand leads to bidding up of prices by buyers.

The three measures of inflation are:

1. The Consumer Price Index, which reflects cost increases experienced by the consumer
2. The Producer Price Index, which reflects prices received by producers of goods and services
3. The GNP deflator, which shows the percentage of nominal GNP growth that is attributable to price increases

A zero inflation rate would inflict heavy costs on the economy in the form of unemployment. In 1978 the goal of price stability was defined by the U.S. government as a 3 percent inflation rate.

Learning Objectives

After reading Chapter 7 and doing the following exercises, you should:	True or false	Multiple choice	Problems and applications	Common errors	Pages in the text
1. Be able to describe differences in inflation rates among different countries and give examples of hyperinflations.		1	3		148–149
2. Know the meaning of, and how to to measure, inflation.	2,8,12, 14,15	3,4,11,12, 14,15,19,20		1,2	149–150, 162–166
3. Be able to list the micro consequences of inflation.	4,5,9–11, 16,18	2,16			150–158
4. Be able to distinguish and compute nominal and real income, and know how they are related to money illusion.	17	7,8	2		151–154, 158
5. Be able to list the macro consequences of inflation.	6,7	5,6,9,10	1		158–162
6. Know how COLA clauses protect real income.	13	13,21		3	165
7. Know the history of inflation and deflation in the United States.	1,3				166–168
8. Know how the goal of price stability is related to the inflation rate, product quality changes, and full employment.	19,21	17			168–170
9. Know the different types and causes of inflation.	20	18			169–170

Key-Term Review

Review the following terms; if you are not sure of the meaning of any term, write out the definition and check it against the Glossary in the text.

bracket creep
Consumer Price Index (CPI)
cost-of-living adjustment (COLA)
cost-push inflation
deflation
demand-pull inflation
inflation

inflation rate
money illusion
nominal income
price stability
real income
relative price

Fill in the blank following each of the statements below with the appropriate term from the list above.

1. One measure of the _____ is the _____, which measures the average price increases that consumers face.

2. When the inflation rate is negative, there is _____.

3. When the inflation rate is low and does not vary much, we say there is _____.

1. _____Inflation Rate_____

2. _____Deflation_____

3. _____Price Stability_____

4. A positive rate of increase in the average price level is called _____.

4. _inflation_

5. This may occur because of excessive demand for final goods and services, which results in _____.

5. _demand pull inflation_

6. When organized labor obtains large wage increases, the type of inflation that may result is referred to as _____.

6. _Cost push inflation_

7. Unions may try to protect members' incomes from inflation by having a _____ clause in their contracts.

7. _COLA_

8. When inflation occurs, _____ grows at a greater rate than _____.

8. _Nominal income_
Real income

9. The measures of inflation do not provide information on how the _____ of a good changes with respect to other prices.

9. _relative price_

10. When people fail to recognize changes in their real income because they look only at their nominal income, they are victims of _____.

10. _money illusion_

11. When inflation pushes nominal income of taxpayers into higher marginal tax brackets, the process is called _____.

11. _Bracket creep_

True or False: *Circle your choice.*

T **F** 1. Inflation above 10 percent per year has occurred frequently in the United States.

T **F** 2. Inflation always occurs when a weighted average of prices of manufacturing industries rises.

T **F** 3. Since 1940 the purchasing power of the U.S. dollar has increased.

T F 4. Relative price changes are essential in order for the market mechanism to function efficiently.

T **F** 5. Buyers usually respond to inflation by cutting back on purchases of goods and services.

T F 6. Inflation may cause society to produce inside the production-possibilities curve.

T F 7. Sudden speculative withholding of commodities due to inflation ties up resources, causing real income to fall.

T **F** 8. Some price increases do not contribute to inflation because they are below the inflation rate.

T F 9. If all individuals were able to anticipate inflation correctly and make appropriate adjustments in their market behavior, there would be no redistribution of real income or real wealth due to inflation.

T F 10. The microeconomic effect of inflation is the redistribution of income.

T **F** 11. Fortunately for college students, increases in tuition cost have lagged behind the average rate of inflation in recent years.

T F 12. The Consumer Price Index usually increases before the Producer Price Index (formerly the Wholesale Price Index).

T F **13.** A COLA counteracts the effects of inflation on the economy by lowering the inflation rate.

T F 14. The base year for a price index is the year against which other years are compared.

82

T F 15. An index of 1.05 for a particular year means that prices are 5 percent higher than in the base year.

T F 16. When doctors' prices rise faster than aspirin prices, real income falls for people who visit a doctor relative to those who prescribe aspirin for themselves.

T F 17. If the prices of things you buy do not increase, but the inflation rate is 10 percent, then your real income falls.

T F 18. If all prices and wages in the economy rose by the same percentage at the same time, there would be no redistribution of income.

T F 19. The Full-Employment and Balanced Growth Act of 1978 suggests a target rate of inflation of about 3 percent.

T F 20. Demand-pull inflation occurs when business and labor raise wages and prices above their equilibrium levels.

T F 21. The undesirable effects of bracket creep can be eliminated by indexing tax rates.

Multiple Choice: *Select the correct answer.*

____ 1. Inflation rates above 10 percent have rarely occurred:
   (a) In the world today.
   (b) In the United States.
   (c) During wartime periods.
   (d) In or during all of the above.

____ 2. Relative prices are more useful than absolute prices in:
   (a) Determining the redistribution of income due to inflation.
   (b) Determining the inflation rate.
   (c) Deflating nominal income.
   (d) All of the above.

____ 3. When the inflation rate is zero, a decrease in the absolute price of a specific product is similar to:
   (a) No increase in the price of the product when there is deflation.
   (b) The price of the product increasing faster than the inflation rate.
   (c) The price of the product rising at the same rate as the inflation rate.
   (d) The price of the product remaining unchanged during inflation.

____ 4. When the price of a good is decreasing more slowly than an index of average prices generally, then:
   (a) The good's relative price has risen while its absolute price has fallen.
   (b) The good's relative price and absolute price have risen.
   (c) The good's relative price and absolute price have fallen.
   (d) The good's relative price has fallen while its absolute price has risen.

____ 5. Which of the following happenings can characterize the reactions of consumers or businesses to the uncertainties caused by inflation?
   (a) Consumers cut back on consumption because they fear that future cost increases will make it difficult to make payments on what they consume.
   (b) Consumption increases as consumers try to buy products before their prices rise.
   (c) Businesses decrease investment spending in an attempt to avoid being caught with unprofitable plant and equipment.
   (d) All of the above characterize their reactions.

_____ 6. Inflation may cause the economy to operate inside the production-possibilities curve because:
   (a) People waste resources when they hoard in anticipation of inflation.
   (b) Firms withhold resources in anticipation that the relative price of resources will be higher than the inflation rate.
   (c) The government takes strong inflationary countermeasures that result in less than full-employment real income.
   (d) All of the above are the case.

_____ 7. Nominal income always falls when real income:
   (a) Falls and there is inflation.
   (b) Falls and there is deflation.
   (c) Rises and there is inflation.
   (d) Rises and there is deflation.

_____ 8. We can always compute real income if we know:
   (a) The inflation rate and growth rate of nominal income.
   (b) The inflation rate and nominal income.
   (c) The price index and nominal income.
   (d) The price index and the growth rate of nominal income.

_____ 9. When the price of a product rises faster than the inflation rate, what must always be true?
   (a) The nominal incomes of the users of that product fall.
   (b) The users of that product have higher real incomes than people who do not use the product.
   (c) The nominal incomes of the users of that product rise.
   (d) None of the above is true.

_____ 10. Which of the following occurrences is *not* an effect of a sudden burst of inflation?
   (a) The economy is pushed inside the production-possibilities curve.
   (b) Morale in the economy is lowered.
   (c) Government receives lower taxes because of lower real incomes.
   (d) Production and consumption incentives are distorted.

_____ 11. To construct the Consumer Price Index, the Bureau of Labor Statistics must:
   (a) Find out what people buy with their incomes and how the prices of what they buy change.
   (b) Find out why people buy what they do and how the prices of what they buy change.
   (c) Find out what is in the typical consumer market basket on the basis of what producers produce.
   (d) Conduct consumer expenditure surveys to determine how much prices rise.

_____ 12. The CPI (Consumer Price Index) and PPI (Producer Price Index) do not rise simultaneously because:
   (a) They are based on prices at different stages of the *production* process.
   (b) One index represents prices immediately after production while the other represents the prices seen by the final consumer.
   (c) They do not measure prices of the same physical goods.
   (d) All of the above are the case.

_____ 13. COLAs are desired because:
   (a) The real value of wages can be maintained, since a COLA corrects for the effects of inflation.
   (b) COLA helps to dampen inflation.
   (c) COLA helps to stimulate employment.
   (d) All of the above are true.

_____ 14. The base year used in computing a price index is:
   (a) The year in which prices were at their lowest level.
   (b) The year in which prices were at their average level.
   (c) A recent year from which meaningful comparisons can be made.
   (d) The earliest year for which data are available.

_____15. A Consumer Price Index that has the value 105 means that:
  (a) Average prices that the typical consumer pays have risen 105 percent over base-year average prices.
  (b) Average prices at which producers sell goods have risen 105 percent over base-year average prices.
  (c) Average prices that the typical consumer pays have risen 5 percent over base-year average prices.
  (d) Average prices at which producers sell goods have risen 105 percent over the average prices of the previous year.

_____16. Income redistribution occurs during inflation because:
  (a) Not all prices rise by the same amount as average prices.
  (b) Taxes cause inflation to hit certain income groups harder than others.
  (c) Not all groups can protect their incomes against inflation.
  (d) All of the above are the case.

_____17. The reason that policy makers are reluctant to force the economy to a zero percent inflation rate is that:
  (a) There would be unacceptable levels of unemployment if the economy were controlled by fiscal policy.
  (b) Wasteful quality changes and new products would be designed to escape price controls if controls were used.
  (c) Shortages of some products would be likely if there were wage–price controls.
  (d) All of the above are true.

_____18. Which of the following terms gives no indication of the source of the type of average price change it describes?
  (a) Inflation.
  (b) Demand-pull inflation.
  (c) Deflation.
  (d) Stagflation.

_____19. Which of the following indexes gives the *best* indication of the inflation rate faced by consumers?
  (a) The GNP deflator.
  (b) The industrial production index.
  (c) The PPI (formerly the Wholesale Price Index).
  (d) The CPI.

_____20. How is the impact of a given price change on the Consumer Price Index computed?
  (a) Multiply the base year times the weight assigned to the item.
  (b) Divide the weight assigned to the item by the change in the price of the item.
  (c) Multiply the weight assigned to the item by the percentage change in the price of the item.
  (d) None of the above is correct.

_____21. Bracket creep occurs when marginal tax rates are based on:
  (a) Nominal income.
  (b) Real income.
  (c) Per capita income.
  (d) Real disposable income.

Exercise 1

The following exercise shows the relationship between inflation and interest rates.

1. On the back inside cover of the text you will find data on the prime interest rate and percentage changes in both the Consumer Price Index and the price deflator for the gross national product. On Figure 7.1, graph these indices, showing time on the horizontal axis (*x*-axis) from 1970 to the present and percentage changes on the vertical axis (*y*-axis).

Figure 7.1
Inflation and interest rates, 1970–1987

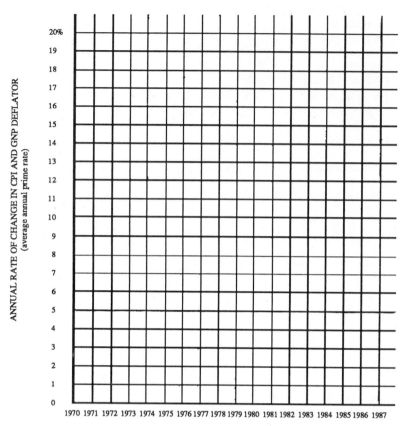

ANNUAL RATE OF CHANGE IN CPI AND GNP DEFLATOR
(average annual prime rate)

1970 1971 1972 1973 1974 1975 1976 1977 1978 1979 1980 1981 1982 1983 1984 1985 1986 1987

YEAR

2. Indicate whether each of the following indices moves directly (in the same direction) with the others or inversely (in opposite directions):

   a. The Consumer Price Index   D   I
   b. The price deflator for the GNP   D   I
   c. The prime interest rate   D   I

3. Which index tends to have the widest swings?
   (a) The Consumer Price Index.
   (b) The price deflator for the GNP.
   (c) The prime interest rate.

4. Which index usually is highest?
   (a) The Consumer Price Index.
   (b) The price deflator for the GNP.
   (c) The interest rate.

5. When the inflation rate is above the prime interest rate:
   (a) Borrowers gain purchasing power by borrowing.
   (b) Lenders lose purchasing power by lending.
   (c) The economy experiences price, wealth, and income effects.
   (d) All of the above are the case.

86

6. Assume that real income for the entire economy is going to be computed using the following formula:

$$\text{Real income} = \frac{\text{Nominal income}}{\text{Index}}$$

Which of the three indices in Figure 7.1 would you use in the formula?
(a) The Consumer Price Index.
(b) The price deflator for the GNP.
(c) The prime interest rate.

7. If you were computing the real income of a household, which index would you use?
(a) The Consumer Price Index.
(b) The price deflator for the GNP.
(c) The prime interest rate.

Exercise 2

This exercise shows how to compute changes in real income. It is similar to the problem at the end of Chapter 7 in the text.

Suppose that between 1980 and 2000, the average consumer's nominal income increases from $18,000 to $36,000. Table 7.1 lists the prices of a small market basket purchased in both of those years. Assuming that this basket of goods is representative of all goods and services purchased, compute the percentage change in real income between 1980 and 2000. _____ %

Table 7.1
Price of a small market basket in 1980 and 2000

Item	Quantity (units per year)	Price in 1980 (dollars per unit)	Price in 2000 (dollars per unit)
Coffee	20 pounds	$ 3	$ 8
Tuition	1 year	4,000	20,000
Pizza	100 pizzas	8	6
VCR rental	75 days	15	4
Vacation	2 weeks	300	1,000

Exercise 3

Articles on inflation are as politically sensitive as those reporting unemployment numbers. The former often provide selected information on average price increases throughout the economy. By using one of the articles in the text, this exercise will show the kind of information to look for. If your professor makes a newspaper assignment for this chapter, this exercise will provide an example of how to do it.

Reread the article in Chapter 7 entitled "Inflation and the Weimar Republic" from the *Wall Street Journal*. Then answer the following questions:

1. What sentence provides the inflation data for the worst period of inflation? To what group or community do these data apply?

2. What sentences indicate the trend in the inflation rate prior to the hyperinflation?

3. What statement indicates the government's interpretation of the numbers?

Crossword Puzzle

Select the economic term in the following list that corresponds to each of the definitions and descriptions below the crossword puzzle. Then fit the term or one of the words within it into the puzzle at the number indicated.

absolute price level
base-year price
bracket creep
Consumer Price Index
cost-of-living adjustment
cost-push inflation
deflation
demand-pull inflation
GNP deflator

GNP gap
inflation rate
money illusion
nominal income
price stability
Producer Price Index
profit margin
real income
relative price
speculation

Across

5. The measure you would use if you wanted to find the average price increases charged directly by businesses for commodities.
6. The average price increases of goods and services.
7. If you wanted a measure of GNP that was not distorted by inflation, you would compute this.
11. A clause you might want in a contract to protect you from the effects of inflation.
13. Producers contribute to supply-side inflation when they attempt to raise prices faster than costs to raise this.
15. If you want to find how much your household costs are rising, this measure of price movements will be just what you're looking for.
16. Movements in average prices induced by increases in the prices of resources, particularly those of labor.
17. Movements in average prices that occur when goods and services become scarce as a consequence of people's increased willingness and ability to pay for goods and services.

Down

1. What you might engage in if you expected prices of certain commodities to increase greatly in the future—enough to make it worthwhile to hold the commodities off the market.
2. Even when all prices are going down, this price may go up.
3. The price index used to calculate real income from nominal income.
4. The difference between what the economy could produce and what it actually produces.
8. One of three goals established in the Employment Act of 1946 and the Full-Employment and Balanced Growth Act of 1978.
9. What you look at when you want to know how much money to shell out to buy a product.
10. The measure of national welfare that many people look at and are impressed by without realizing that it grows because of inflation, not just because of increased production.
12. A decrease in average prices.
14. The use of nominal income, not real income, as a basis for market choice.

Common Errors

The first statement in each "common error" below is incorrect. Each incorrect statement is followed by a corrected version and an explanation.

1. When the price of a product rises, there is inflation. WRONG!

    When an average of prices rises, there is inflation. RIGHT!

    The price of a single product may rise while an average of prices of all products falls. Such adjustment in relative prices is essential to the most *efficient* distribution of goods and services through the market. When an average of all prices is rising, however, distribution may not be efficient and capricious redistributions of income may occur.

2. As long as price increases do not exceed the inflation rate, they do not contribute to inflation. WRONG!

    Every price increase contributes to a rise in the inflation rate. RIGHT!

    Since the inflation rate is an average of all price increases, the increase in any price by any amount raises the average. Firms that buy commodities from another firm that raises prices will in turn pass the increase on to their own customers; an increased price may have indirect effects in raising the inflation rate.

3. Indexation such as a COLA clause in a contract protects the economy against the effects of inflation. WRONG!

    Indexation institutionalizes inflation. RIGHT!

    Indexation can protect the real incomes of specific groups for which indexation is applied. In other words, it can address some of the micro consequences of inflation. However, if everyone's income is not indexed, then even the micro consequences may not be adequately addressed. In fact, indexation can lead under such circumstances to dramatic changes in relative prices. Furthermore, indexation may lead to anticipation of higher rates of inflation; high current inflation rates may guarantee higher future rates due to indexation.

■ ANSWERS ■

Key-Term Review

1. inflation rate
2. deflation
3. price stability
4. inflation
5. demand-pull inflation

6. cost-push inflation
7. cost-of-living adjustment(COLA)
8. nominal income
   real income

9. relative price
10. money illusion
11. bracket creep

True or False

1. F	5. F	9. T	13. F	16. T	19. T
2. F	6. T	10. T	14. T	17. F	20. F
3. F	7. T	11. F	15. T	18. T	21. T
4. T	8. F	12. F			

Multiple Choice

1. b	5. d	9. d	13. a	16. d	19. d
2. a	6. d	10. c	14. c	17. d	20. d
3. d	7. b	11. a	15. c	18. d	21. a
4. a	8. c	12. b			

Problems and Applications

Exercise 1

1. **Figure 7.1 answer**

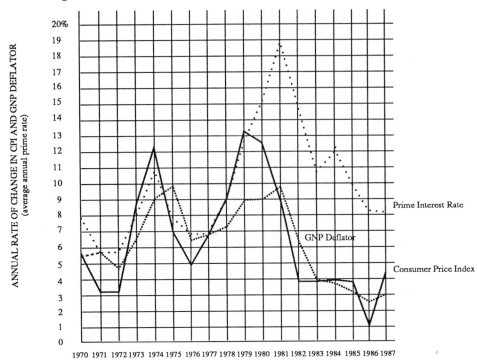

ANNUAL RATE OF CHANGE IN CPI AND GNP DEFLATOR (average annual prime rate)

Prime Interest Rate

GNP Deflator

Consumer Price Index

1970 1971 1972 1973 1974 1975 1976 1977 1978 1979 1980 1981 1982 1983 1984 1985 1986 1987

2. D is the correct answer for all three indices.
3. a, although c is also technically correct. 1980 was an exceptional case.
4. c
5. d
6. b
7. a

Exercise 2

The first step is to find the total expenditure on the items for each year.

In 1980 it is:

20 pounds	x	$3 per pound	=	$	60
1 year	x	$4,000 per year	=		4,000
100 pizzas	x	$8 per pizza	=		800
75 days	x	$15 per day	=		1,125
2 weeks	x	$300 per week	=		600
					$6,585

In 2000 it is:

20 pounds	x	$8 per pound	=	$	160
1 year	x	$20,000 per year	=		20,000
100 pizzas	x	$6 per pizza	=		600
75 days	x	$4 per day	=		300
2 weeks	x	$1000 per week	=		2,000
					$23,060

The percentage change in real income is:

$$\frac{36,000/18,000}{23,060/6,585} - 1 = -42.9\%$$

Exercise 3

1. The last sentence of the second paragraph describes the worst period of the hyperinflation. The data apply to Germany.
2. The first two paragraphs describe the trend of inflation before and after World War I.
3. The government is only mentioned at the end of the article in an understatement; "57 years later government policy is still colored by this experience with hyperinflation."

Crossword Puzzle Answer

Across

5. *Producer* Price Index
6. inflation *rate*
7. real *income*
11. cost-of-living *adjustment*
13. *profit* margin
15. Consumer Price *Index*
16. cost-push *inflation*
17. *demand*-pull inflation

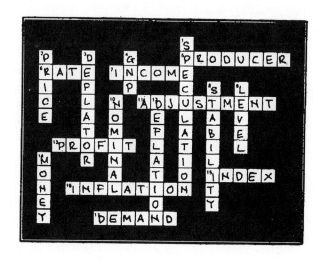

Down

1. *speculation*
2. relative *price*
3. GNP *deflator*
4. *GNP* gap
8. price *stability*
9. absolute price *level*
10. *nominal* income
12. *deflation*
14. *money* illusion

Chapter 8
Aggregate Spending

Quick Review

The Employment Act of 1946, as currently amended, has made full employment, price stability, and continued economic growth the basic goals of macroeconomic policy. According to the Keynesian explanation, our success in achieving these goals depends in part on our ability to maintain a balance between the rate of desired expenditure and the rate of full-employment production (full-employment GNP). The keys to an intelligent discussion concerning the achievement of these goals reside in the answers to the following questions:

- What are the components of aggregate demand?
- What determines the level of spending for each component?
- Will there be enough demand to maintain full employment?

Aggregate spending includes consumption expenditures by households (C), investment expenditures by businesses (I), government expenditures (G), and net foreign expenditures (X–M). Consumption expenditure levels are affected by disposable income. This relationship is summarized in the consumption function, $C = a + bY_D$, where a and b refer to important characteristics of consumer behavior. Investment, however, is affected more by interest rates, expectations of future income levels, and technology than by current income levels. It is difficult to tell what government expenditures depend on. Net foreign spending, discussed in a later chapter, depends on the level of income, exchange rates, and the like.

One thing is certain: the components of aggregate spending $[C + I + G + (X - M)]$ behave in very different ways. Aggregate spending can hardly be expected always to match the full-employment production rates. Sometimes aggregate spending at full employment is below full-employment GNP; the difference between the two is then called the "recessionary gap." People want to save and do not buy as much as firms expect them to buy. Businesses are then stuck with undesired inventories (undesired investment). Production must then be cut back, and people are laid off their jobs.

The inflationary gap is hardly an improvement. If aggregate spending at full employment exceeds full-employment GNP, the difference between the two is the inflationary gap. Now people want to consume more than businesses are willing and able to produce at full employment; businesses are caught short of inventories. As inventories are depleted, consumers frantically bid prices upward. If businesses increase investment expenditures to raise inventories, however, they only add fuel to the demand-pull inflation.

The economy must balance the leakages from income (savings, taxes, and imports) with the injections into income (investment, government expenditures, and exports). If the government does not take an active role in balancing aggregate demand with full-employment GNP, then the economy may fall short of full-employment GNP and may experience unintended investment in inventories. However, government may increase aggregate demand too much, which then leads to inflation and depleted inventories.

Learning Objectives

After reading Chapter 8 and doing the following exercises, you should:	True or false	Multiple choice	Problems and applications	Common errors	Pages in the text
1. Know the Keynesian theory and history of aggregate spending.	19,20				174
2. Understand the difference between aggregate demand (a spending–price level relationship) and aggregate spending (a spending–income relationship).			1–4	3–6	175–176
3. Know how the concept of derived demand relates incomes in product markets to employment in factor markets.			1–5		178–179
4. Know how to find the average and marginal propensity to consume.	7–9,21	8,9,12,15	1	4	179–182
5. Be able to interpret the consumption function.	5,6	11,19–26	1,3		182–187
6. Know how to use the aggregate spending function and the 45-degree line to calculate saving or dissaving at a given income.	10,15,16		2–4	5	182–185
7. Be able to describe how the components of aggregate spending are affected by income, interest rates, expectations, and technology.	5,12,13,22	10,14	4,5	2	185–187
8. Be able to explain the concept of leakages.	11	6	3–4		173–174
9. Be able to explain the concept of full-employment GNP.	1–3,16	1,2			188
10. Know and be able to graph the components of aggregate spending and full-employment income.	4,14,23	5,7, 19–26	2,3	3,6	188–191
11. Be able to portray, diagrammatically, a recessionary and an inflationary gap, explain what occurs in both situations, and describe how the government can influence either type of gap.		3,4,16–18	2,5		196–198
12. Explain the role of savings (a leakage), its relationship to investment (an injection), the effect it has on equilibrium income, and its relationship to consumption.	17,18	13	2,4,5	1	197–198

Key-Term Review

Review the following terms; if you are not sure of the meaning of any term, write out the definition and check it against the Glossary in the text.

aggregate demand ✓
aggregate supply ✓
aggregate spending ✓
average propensity to consume (APC) ✓
consumption ─
consumption function ✓
cyclical unemployment ✓
demand-pull inflation ✓
derived demand ✓
disposable income (DI)
dissaving ✓

equilibrium (macro) ✓
full employment
full-employment GNP ─
imports
inflationary gap ✓
investment ─
leakage ─
marginal propensity to consume (MPC) ─
marginal propensity to save (MPS)
recessionary gap ✓
saving

Fill in the blank following each of the statements below with the appropriate term from the list above.

1. The formula $C = a + bY_D$ is referred to as the _____.

1. __Consumption function__

2. In this formula, b is the same thing as the _____.

2. __MPC__

3. The formula $C + I + G + (X - M)$ represents _____.

3. __Aggregate Spending__

4. I in this formula represents _____.

4. __Investment__

5. C in the formula represents _____.

5. __Consumption__

6. Dividing C by _____ gives the _____, which shows what percentage of the consumer's income is spent on consumption.

6. __Disposable incom | APC__

7. The excess of disposable income over consumption is _____.

7. __Savings__

8. Saving is considered a _____ because it is income not spent directly on domestic output.

8. __leakage__

9. When consumption exceeds disposable income, there is _____.

9. __Dissavings__

10. When desired aggregate spending is less than _____, then there is a _____, which means that inventories will accumulate and there will be fewer jobs. This type of unemployment is often referred to as _____.

10. __full employment GNP__
__Recessionary Gap__
__Cyclical__

11. _____ is established at the price–output combination at which _____ equals _____.

11. __Equilibrium__
__Aggregate Supply__
__aggregate Demand__

12. If the economy is at full employment and aggregate demand rises above full-employment GNP, then there is an _____.

12. __inflationary Gap__

94

13. Average prices will rise due to excessive demand for goods and services, which is called _____.

13. demand pull inflation

14. As the demand for goods and services rises, the _____ for labor will also rise.

14. derived demand

15. The ratio of the change in saving to any change in disposable income is known as the _____.

15. MPS

16. The Classical economists believed the economy would automatically seek an equilibrium at _____.

16. full employment

17. _____, goods and services purchased from foreigners, are a leakage from the circular flow of income.

17. Imports

True or False: *Circle your choice.*

T F 1. If the economy is on the institutional production-possibilities curve, then it is producing at the full-employment rate.

T F 2. Full-employment GNP is any rate of production that allows prices to remain stable.

T F 3. Full employment with price stability always occurs when production is at the full-employment GNP.

T F 4. The largest component of aggregate spending is government spending.

F T F 5. Consumption is completely determined by current income. $C =$

T F 6. An individual, like an economy, cannot spend more than current income.

T F 7. If consumers are optimistic, the marginal propensity to save rises.

T F 8. The marginal propensity to consume (*MPC*) is related to the marginal propensity to save (*MPS*) by the formula $MPC = 1 - MPS$.   MPC + MPS = 1

T F 9. The average propensity to consume (*APC*) is related to the average propensity to save (*APS*) by the formula $APC = 1 - APS$.

T F 10. All market supply curves are 45-degree lines.

T F 11. Because saving is a leakage, additional saving necessarily results in lower equilibrium income for for society, *ceteris paribus*.

T F 12. Favorable expectations about future sales may cause higher investment, *ceteris paribus*.

T F 13. Current income is the major determinant of investment.

T F 14. Government spending is larger than investment spending.

T F 15. If there is an inflationary gap, then the 45-degree line exceeds aggregate spending at the full-employment level of imcome.

T F 16. Full employment always occurs whenever aggregate spending and the 45-degree line are equal.

T F 17. Undesired investment occurs in the form of excess inventories.

T F 18. Cyclical unemployment is caused by saving that exceeds desired investment at full-employment income.

T F 19. Unlike the Classical economists, Keynes felt that if the economy was at less than full employment, it would automatically adjust to full employment.

T F 20. Keynes, like the Classical economists, viewed the aggregate supply curve as being horizontal in a recession.

95

T (F) 21. When all disposable income is spent on consumption, the marginal propensity to consume is zero.

(T) F 22. The stock market crash of 1987 caused a great reduction in household wealth, and, as a result, many households indicated they would cut back on consumption expenditures.

(T) F 23. Exports, like investment, are an injection into the income stream.

Multiple Choice: *Select the correct answer.*

____C____ 1. The full-employment GNP is the GNP level at which:
(a) The lowest possible rate of unemployment is obtained.
(b) The lowest rate of unemployment possible occurs with stable economic growth.
(c) The lowest rate of unemployment possible occurs with price stability.
(d) None of the above is the case.

____A____ 2. Which of the following is eliminated when production rates are equal to full-employment GNP?
(a) Cyclical unemployment.
(b) Demand-pull inflation.
(c) Cost-push inflation.
(d) All of the above.

____C____ 3. What results when the spending on final goods and services exceeds full-employment GNP?
(a) Inventory accumulation.
(b) Unemployment.
(c) Inflation.
(d) All of the above.

____A____ 4. What results when the aggregate spending for final goods and services at full employment is below full-employment GNP?
(a) Undesired investment.
(b) An excess of desired investment over desired saving.
(c) Dissaving.
(d) Entry of new firms as a result of increased profits.

____D____ 5. Consumer spending depends mostly on:
(a) Investment.
(b) Government expenditure.
(c) Imports.
(d) Disposable income.

____D____ 6. Which of the following are leakages?
(a) Savings.
(b) Imports.
(c) Taxes.
(d) All of the above.

____A____ 7. Disposable income can be computed most easily using:
(a) Consumption and saving.
(b) Consumption, saving, imports, and exports.
(c) Consumption, saving, imports, exports, and taxes.
(d) Consumption, government expenditures, investment, and saving.

____C____ 8. The average propensity to consume can be found by dividing:
(a) Total consumption by total saving.
(b) Total consumption by the number of people consuming.
(c) Total consumption by disposable income.
(d) Disposable income by total consumption.

_D_ 9. The amount of additional consumption that will occur in the economy when disposable income increases by a certain amount in a given time period is the:
 (a) Total consumption in the economy.
 (b) Disposable income in the economy.
 (c) Average propensity to consume.
 (d) Marginal propensity to consume.

_D_ 10. The reason that consumption is not entirely determined by current income is:
 (a) That people do not cut consumption in proportion to a cut in income.
 (b) That people may spend today in anticipation of earning more income in the future.
 (c) That people may spend earlier savings in addition to their current incomes.
 (d) All of the above.

_B_ 11. The part of consumption that is independent of disposable income is found where the consumption function intersects the:
 (a) Horizontal axis.
 (b) Vertical axis.
 (c) 45-degree line.
 (d) Aggregate spending curve.

_B_ 12. The marginal propensity to consume always corresponds to the slope of:
 (a) The 45-degree line.
 (b) The consumption function curve.
 (c) The aggregate demand curve.
 (d) None of the above.

_D_ 13. Which of the following counteracts the effect of circular-flow leakage?
 (a) Fixed investment.
 (b) Inventory investment.
 (c) Exports.
 (d) All of the above.

_A_ 14. Which of the following is *not* thought to be an important determinant of investment?
 (a) Current disposable income.
 (b) Expectations.
 (c) Interest rates.
 (d) Technological change.

In Questions 15–18 choose the appropriate diagram in Figure 8.1, where Y_f = full-employment disposable income. Assume that aggregate spending consists solely of consumption expenditures and that the economy is at full employment.

Figure 8.1

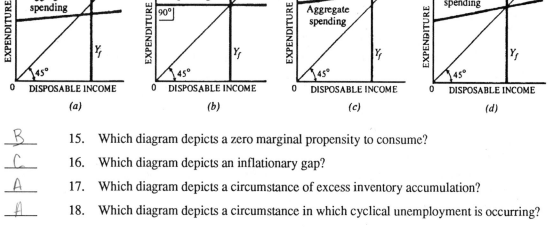

_B_ 15. Which diagram depicts a zero marginal propensity to consume?

_C_ 16. Which diagram depicts an inflationary gap?

_A_ 17. Which diagram depicts a circumstance of excess inventory accumulation?

_A_ 18. Which diagram depicts a circumstance in which cyclical unemployment is occurring?

97

Use Figure 8.2 to answer Questions 19–26.

Figure 8.2

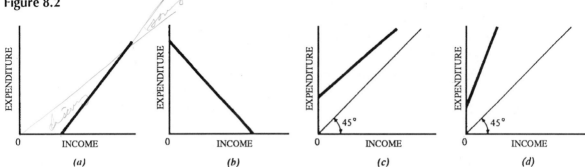

| | (a) | (b) | (c) | (d) |

_C_ 19. Which of the diagrams in Figure 8.2 best represents a plausible graph of the consumption function?

_a_ 20. Which diagram suggests that there is no consumption expenditure at an income level of zero?

_B_ 21. Which diagram shows that consumption does not rise with income?

_D_ 22. Which diagram shows that the economy always consumes more than its income?

_B_ 23. In which diagram is the marginal propensity to consume negative?

q _B_ 24. For which diagram would a in the consumption function be negative?

_b_ 25. For which diagram would b in the consumption function be negative?

_b_ 26. For which diagram is there an inverse relationship between consumption and income?

$C = a + by$

Problems and Applications

Exercise 1

The following exercise emphasizes the use of definitions in computing marginal propensity to consume, average propensity to consume, and saving.

1. The consumption function is:
   (a) $C = a + bY_D$.
   (b) A mathematical relationship indicating the rate of consumer spending that will take place at various income levels.
   (c) An algebraic relationship that shows consumption is influenced by disposable income.
   (d) All of the above.

2. Personal saving is:
   (a) That part of disposable income not spent on goods and services in a given time period.
   (b) Disposable income less consumption.
   (c) Positive above the break-even level of income.
   (d) All of the above.

3. Net investment:
   (a) Occurs when money is used to purchase stocks.
   (b) Includes expenditure only on new plant and equipment (capital) and changes in inventories in a given time period.
   (c) Includes expenditure on all plant and equipment (capital) and changes in inventories in a given time period.
   (d) Is saving minus depreciation and equipment expenditure.

4. Personal consumption expenditure is:
   (a) All purchases of goods and services by consumers.
   (b) Purchases of newly produced final goods and services by consumers.
   (c) Nontaxed income of consumers.
   (d) All of the above.

5. The average propensity to consume is:
   (a) Total consumption in a given period divided by total disposable income.
   (b) The percentage of total disposable income spent on consumption.
   (c) That part of the average consumer dollar that goes to the purchase of final goods.
   (d) All of the above. *(circled)*

6. The marginal propensity to consume is:
   (a) That part of the average consumer dollar that goes to the purchase of final goods.
   (b) The change in consumption divided by the change in disposable income. *(circled)*
   (c) The fraction of each additional (marginal) dollar of consumption spent on disposable income.
   (d) All of the above.

7. Using the consumption schedule in Table 8.1, compute the average propensity to consume and then the marginal propensity to consume.

Table 8.1
Marginal and average propensity to consume
(billions of dollars per year)

(1) Disposable income	(2) Total consumption	(3) Average propensity to consume (2) ÷ (1)	(4) Change in consumption	(5) Change in income	(6) Marginal propensity to consume (4) ÷ (5)	(7) Saving
$ 0	$ 200	—	$300	$400	.75	$ (200)
400	500	1.25	600	800	.75	(100)
1,200	1,100	.91	2100	1925	.75	100

8. What is the equilibrium level of disposable income if investment is $100 billion and government spending and net exports are zero? $ ~~$650~~ 1200

(handwritten: $C + I + G + (X-M)$ *, $100 B$, MPC, $1100 + 100 = 1200$)*

Exercise 2

This exercise shows how market forces lead the economy to equilibrium income. It is similar to an exercise at the end of Chapter 8 in the text.

Use Figure 8.3 in the following problems.

Figure 8.3
Full employment and equilibrium

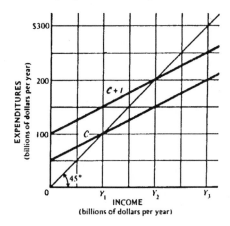

99

Problems 1–8 concern an economy starting at an annual income level of Y_3 in Figure 8.3.

1. People save $_____100_____ billion worth of income.

2. Businesses desire to invest $_____50_____ billion worth of income.

3. There is $_____50_____ billion of undesired investment.

4. Because of undesired investment, inventories will (accumulate, fall).

5. Firms will (raise, lower) production to eliminate inventories.

6. Employment will (rise, fall) as inventories are eliminated.

7. Income (GNP) will tend to (rise, fall) as inventories are eliminated.

8. If full-employment income were at Y_3, there would be:
   (a) A recessionary gap of $50 billion.
   (b) An inflationary gap of $50 billion.

Problems 9–16 concern an economy at income level Y_1 over a single year.

9. People save $_____0_____ billion of income.

10. Firms desire to invest $_____50_____ billion of income.

11. There is:
    (a) $50 billion of unused output (undesired investment).
    (b) $50 billion shortage of output to meet investment desires.

12. Inventories will (accumulate, fall).

13. Firms will (raise, lower) production as they replenish inventories.

14. Employment will (rise, fall) as firms raise inventories.

15. GNP will (rise, fall) as firms raise inventories.

16. If full-employment income were at Y_1, there would be:
    (a) A recessionary gap of $50 billion.
    (b) An inflationary gap of $50 billion.

Exercise 3

This exercise provides practice in using the consumption function and in identifying shifts and movements along the consumption expenditure curve.

1. Assume the following consumption function:

   $C = \$200$ billion $+ 0.75\, Y_D$

Table 8.2 should help you to compute a consumption schedule from the formula.

Table 8.2
Computation of a consumption schedule
(billions of dollars per year)

Disposable income (Y_D)	Consumption not changing with income (a)	+	Additional spending at higher income (bY_D) (0.75 x col. 1) =	Total consumption (C)
$ 0	200		0.75 x 0 = 0	$ 200
400	200		0.75 x 400 = 300	500
1,200	200		0.75 x 1,200	1,100

$\Delta C / \Delta Y_D = MPC$

$200 / 400$

100

2. From the consumption schedule in Table 8.2, draw the consumption function in Figure 8.4 and label it 1. The curve should pass through point *B* if it is correctly drawn.

3. Fill in the schedule (Table 8.3) for the consumption function, $C = \$300$ billion $+ 0.75\ Y_D$.

4. What is the marginal propensity to consume in Table 8.3?

Table 8.3
Consumption function shift
(billions of dollars per year)

Disposable income (Y_D)	changing with income (a)		Additional Consumption not higher income (bY_D) $(0.75 \times col.\ 1)$	=	Total spending at consumption (C)
$\$\ \ \ 0$	$\$300$	+	$.75 \times 0 = 0$		$\$\ \ \ 300$
400	300		$.75 \times 400 = 300$		600
800	300		$.75 \times 800 = 600$		900
1,200	300		$.75 \times 1200 = 900$		1200

5. Graph the consumption function in Figure 8.4 (label it 2) and draw a 45-degree line from the origin.

6. (T) F   In Figure 8.4 the shift in the consumption function shows that at any given level of disposable income, consumption will be greater and savings will be less.

Figure 8.4

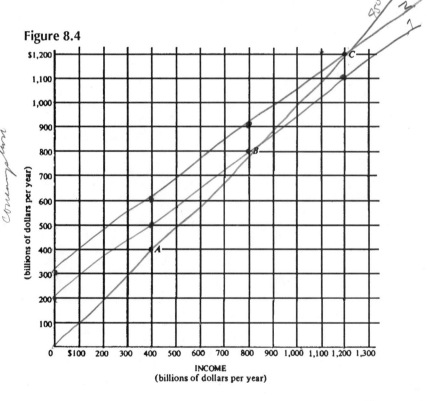

Choose the appropriate diagram in Figure 8.5 to represent the shift of or movement along a consumption curve that accompanies each of the events described in Problems 7–10. (*Hint:* Try to figure out how each event affects the quantity of consumption goods demanded. Remember, if only income is changing, there is a movement along the function.)

101

7. Income falls. ___D___

8. Imports into the United States increase (so that there is less consumption of U.S. goods at every level of income). ___A___

9. People expect that inflation will get out of hand, so they decide to buy more goods today, before prices rise, even if they do not need them now. ___B___

10. People have more disposable income and so they consume more. ___C___

Figure 8.5

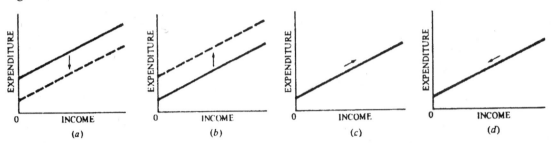

(a)   (b)   (c)   (d)

Exercise 4

This exercise offers practice in graphing aggregate spending curves from information about consumption and investment. It also relates the level of aggregate spending to interest rates.

1. Table 8.4 is a demand schedule for investment goods. In Figure 8.6 graph the demand curve for investment goods.

Table 8.4
Demand schedule for investment goods

Interest rate (percent)	Investment goods (billions of dollars per year)
20%	$ 0
15	50
10	100
5	200
0	300

Figure 8.6

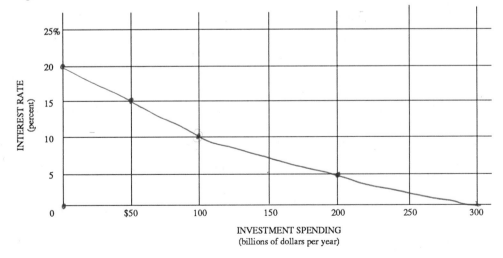

INVESTMENT SPENDING
(billions of dollars per year)

2. As interest rates climb, the investment-demand curve shows, *ceteris paribus:*
   (a) That people find it worthwhile to invest in capital goods that will appreciate in value.
   (b) That since capital goods must have a higher rate of return to be worth investing in, fewer new capital goods and inventories are bought.
   (c) That as it becomes more expensive to borrow, savings are put into investment goods and the total amount of investment therefore increases.
   (d) All of the above.

3. Use Figure 8.6 to determine investment at each of the income levels in Table 8.5 when the interest rate is 10 percent. (*Hint:* Remember that investment is insensitive to current income.)

$$C = I + G + (x - m)$$

Table 8.5
Investment schedule
(billions of dollars per year)

Disposable income	Investment goods
$ 0	$ 100
400	11
800	11
1,200	11

4. Assume that the consumption function is $C = \$200$ billion $+ 0.75\, Y_D$ and that the interest rate is 20 percent. Fill in Table 8.6 to find the aggregate spending schedule. (Assume that government expenditures and net exports are zero.)

Table 8.6
Aggregate spending schedule
(billions of dollars per year)

(1) Disposable income	(2) Consumption	(3) Investment	(4) Aggregate spending (2) + (3) = (4)
$ 0	$ 200	$ 0	$ 200
400	50,0	0	500
800	800	0	800
1,200	1100	0	1200

5. In Figure 8.7, diagram the aggregate spending curve from the schedule in Table 8.6 and label it 1; then draw a 45-degree line through the origin.

6. What is the equilibrium income? __800__

Figure 8.7

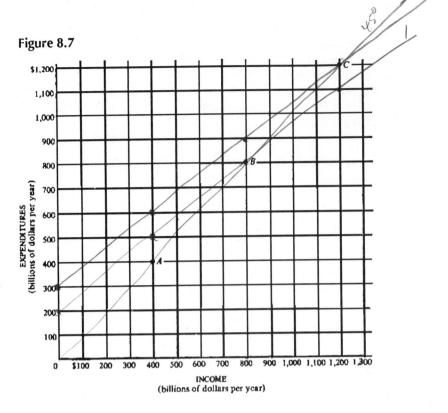

7. Suppose that in Table 8.4 the interest rate fell to 10 percent and the consumption function remained $C = \$200$ billion $+ 0.75\ Y_D$. Fill in Table 8.7 to find the new aggregate spending curve.

Table 8.7
Aggregate spending schedule
(billions of dollars per year)

| *(1)* | *(2)* | *(3)* | *(4)* |
Disposable income	Consumption	Investment	Aggregate spending (2) + (3) = (4)
$ 0	$ 200	$ 100	$ 300
400	500	100	600
800	800	100	900
1,200	1100	100	1200

8. Draw the aggregate spending curve based on Table 8.7 in Figure 8.7 and label it 2.

9. What is the new equilibrium income? $ 1200

10. When the interest rate fell by 10 percentage points, then:
   (a) Investment rose by $100 billion and equilibrium income rose by $100 billion per year.
   (b) Investment rose by $100 billion and equilibrium income rose by $400 billion per year.
   (c) Investment fell by $100 billion and equilibrium income fell by $100 billion per year.
   (d) Investment fell by $100 billion and equilibrium income fell by $400 billion per year.

104

Exercise 5

The media continually provide information that can help us determine if the economy is experiencing an inflationary or recessionary gap. By using one of the articles in the text, this exercise will show the kind of information to look for. If your professor makes a newspaper assignment for this chapter, this exercise will provide an example of how to do it.

Figure 8.8
Inflationary and recessionary gaps

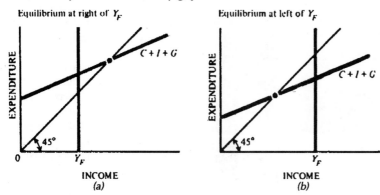

Reread the article in Chapter 8 entitled "Exports Boost U.S. Industrial Capacity Usage" from the *Washington Post*. Then answer the following questions, using Figure 8.8 for Question 1:

1. Which of the two diagrams in the figure best represents the condition of the economy based on the information in the article?   a   b   (circle one)

2. What is the word, phrase, or sentence (no more than a sentence) in the article that provides evidence for your choice?

3. What sentence in the article describes governmental or professional interpretation of the information in the article?

Crossword Puzzle

Select the economic term in the following list that corresponds with each of the definitions and descriptions below the crossword puzzle. Then fit the term or one of the words within it into the puzzle at the numbers indicated.

aggregate spending
average propensity to consume
average propensity to save
consumption
consumption function
cyclical unemployment
demand-pull inflation
derived demand
disposable income
dissaving

45-degree line
full-employment GNP
inflationary gap
investment
leakage
marginal propensity to consume
marginal propensity to save
market demand
nominal income
potential GNP
recessionary gap
saving
stabilization problem

Across

1. The value of goods and services that people can buy after their taxes have been deducted.
6. The proportion of the next extra dollar of income that people tend to put aside so that they can consume in the future.
7. The excess of aggregate spending over a 45-degree line at full-employment income.
10. Consumption + government + investment + net exports.
11. An algebraic representation that shows what people consume depends on their disposable-income level.
13. Diversion of income from the circular flow.
14. The percentage of the next extra dollar of income that is spent for final goods and services by households.
17. The one type of inflation for which excessive buying is responsible.
20. Expenditures for capital (including inventories).
22. The percentage of total income spent on final goods and services by households.
23. What people are willing and able to buy of a particular commodity.

Down

2. The part of disposable income that is not consumed.
3. The percentage of total income devoted to purposes other than consumption (assuming there are no taxes).
4. The shortfall of aggregate spending from a 45-degree line at full-employment income.
5. When aggregate demand fails to reach full-employment levels, the labor force suffers from _____.
8. A synonym for full-employment GNP.
9. The trade-off between growth and price stability.
12. The extinction of final goods and services.
15. Demand for factors reflects demand for products and is therefore called _____.
16. When income is low, people have to engage in _____ (live off what has already been produced in the society); consumption is higher than income.
18. A measure of income that can be distorted by sudden changes in inflation.
19. The curve that shows that income equals expenditures.
21. The total market value of goods and services at maximum employment with stable prices.

Common Errors

The first statement in each "common error" below is incorrect. Each incorrect statement is followed by a corrected version and an explanation.

1. The economy can spend no more than its income. WRONG!

   The economy can spend more than its income. RIGHT!

   The economy can spend more than its income by drawing down inventories of both public and private goods or by consuming capital (allowing it to depreciate) without replacing it. If the economy consumes more than income, it will actually dissave and experience negative investment.

2. When a person invests in stocks, investment expenditure is increased. WRONG!

   Personal investing in stocks has only an indirect relationship to investment expenditure in the economy. RIGHT!

   Investment expenditure refers to purchases of new capital goods (plant, machinery) or inventories. A purchase of stock represents a transfer of ownership from one person to another. Sometimes such purchases are called "financial investments," but they do not represent economic investment.

3. The aggregate spending curve is the sum of the aggregate demand concepts. WRONG!

   The aggregate spending curve and aggregate demand curve are only indirectly related to each other. RIGHT!

   Aggregate spending and aggregate demand are two quite different curves. They should not be confused with each other. They have different units on the axes: aggregate spending represents the intended expenditures at each *income* level; aggregate demand represents what buyers are willing and able to buy at average prices for all goods and services.

4. The marginal propensity to consume is consumption divided by income. WRONG!

   The average propensity to consume is consumption divided by income. RIGHT!

   There is a big difference between total consumption and a change in consumption. While the average propensity to consume involves totals of consumption and income, the marginal propensity to consume involves changes in consumption and income.

5. Dissaving is the difference between the 45-degree line and aggregate spending curves. WRONG!

   Dissaving is the difference between the consumption curve and the 45-degree line and occurs only when the consumption curve is above the 45-degree line. RIGHT!

6. Aggregate spending rises when people buy more imports. WRONG!

Aggregate spending falls when people buy more imports. RIGHT!

Students often think of imports as expenditures and therefore believe that imports will have the same effect on the economy as an increase in consumption. Expenditures on imports, however, do not generate domestic income. If imports increase, they do so at the expense of U.S. goods, meaning fewer jobs in the United States. Because employment declines, there is less income with which to consume goods; consumption falls and so does aggregate spending.

■ ANSWERS ■

Key-Term Review

1. consumption function
2. marginal propensity to consume (*MPC*)
3. aggregate spending
4. investment
5. consumption
6. disposable income average propensity to consume (*APC*)
7. saving
8. leakage
9. dissaving
10. full-employment GNP recessionary gap cyclical unemployment
11. equilibrium (macro) aggregate demand aggregate supply
12. inflationary gap
13. demand-pull inflation
14. derived demand
15. marginal propensity to save (*MPS*)
16. full employment
17. imports

True or False

1. T	5. F	9. T	13. F	17. T	21. F
2. F	6. F	10. F	14. T	18. T	22. T
3. F	7. F	11. T	15. F	19. F	23. T
4. F	8. T	12. T	16. F	20. F	

Multiple Choice

1. c	6. d	11. b	15. b	19. c	23. b
2. a	7. a	12. b	16. c	20. a	24. a
3. c	8. c	13. d	17. a	21. b	25. b
4. a	9. d	14. a	18. a	22. d	26. b
5. d	10. d				

Problems and Applications

Exercise 1

1. d	3. b	5. d
2. d	4. b	6. b

7. **Table 8.1 answer**
   (billions of dollars per year)

Average propensity to consume	Change in consumption	Change in income	Marginal propensity to consume	Saving
undefined	$300	$400	0.75	–$200
1.25	600	800	0.75	– 100
0.92				100

8. $1,200 billion. Aggregate spending is the sum of C, I, G, and $(X - M)$. By adding $100 billion to column 2 (total consumption), we can compute aggregate spending for the year. It equals disposable income at $1,200 billion for the year.

$C + I + G$

Exercise 2

1. $100 (= $300 [45-degree line] – $200 [$C$ line]) billion per year
2. $50 (= $250 [$C + I$ line] – $200 [$C$ line]) billion per year
3. $50 (= $100 [Problem 1] – $50 [Problem 2]) billion per year
4. accumulate
5. lower
6. fall
7. fall
8. a
9. $0 (= $100 [45-degree line] – $100 [$C$ line]) billion per year
10. $50 (= $150 [$C + I$ line] – $100 [$C$ line]) billion per year
11. b
12. fall
13. raise
14. rise
15. rise
16. b

Exercise 3

1. Table 8.2 answer
   (billions of dollars per year)

(Y_D)	(a)	+ (bY_D) =	(C)
$ 0	$200	0.00	$ 200
400	200	0.75 x 400	500
1,200	200	0.75 x 1,200	1,100

2. Figure 8.4 answer

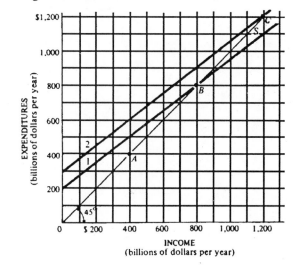

109

3. **Table 8.3 answer**
   (billions of dollars per year)

(Y_D)	(a)	+ (bY_D) =	(C)
$ 0	$300	0.75 x 0	$ 300
400	300	0.75 x 400	600
800	300	0.75 x 800	900
1,200	300	0.75 x 1,200	1,200

4. 0.75. The marginal propensity to consume is the change in consumption (for example, $600 – $300 billion per year) divided by the corresponding change in income ($400 – 0 billion per year).
5. See Figure 8.4 answer, line 2.
6. T
7. d
8. a
9. b
10. c

Exercise 4

1. **Figure 8.6 answer**

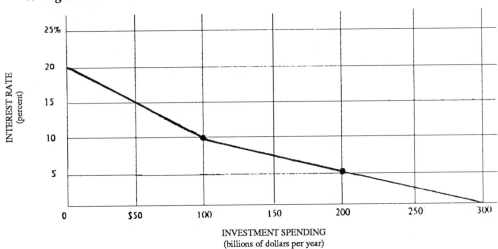

2. b
3. **Table 8.5 answer**
   (billions of dollars per year)

Disposable income	Investment goods
$ 0	$100
400	100
800	100
1,200	100

4. **Table 8.6 answer**
(billions of dollars per year)

Disposable income	Consumption	Investment	Aggregate spending
$ 0	$ 200	$0	$ 200
400	500	0	500
800	800	0	800
1,200	1,100	0	1,100

5. **Figure 8.7 answer**

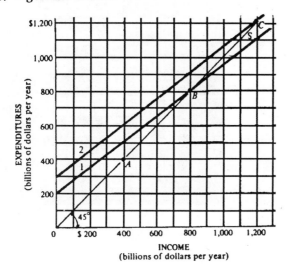

6. $800 (where the 45-degree line and the aggregate spending curve cross) billion per year

7. **Table 8.7 answer**
(billions of dollars per year)

Disposable income	Consumption	Investment	Aggregate spending
$ 0	$ 200	$100	$ 300
400	500	100	600
800	800	100	900
1,200	1,100	100	1,200

8. See Figure 8.7 answer, line 2.
9. $1,200 (where the 45-degree line and the aggregate spending curve cross) billion per year
10. b

Exercise 5

1. Diagram *a*. The article indicates a probable inflationary gap.
2. "The Federal Reserve said . . . that steel and other primary metal manufacturers . . . were operating at the highest rate in almost six years."
3. "Analysts credited the rebound to the 40 percent decrease in the value of the dollar over the past two years."

Crossword Puzzle Answer

Across

1. *disposable* income
6. marginal propensity to *save*
7. inflationary *gap*
10. *aggregate* spending
11. consumption *function*
13. *leakage*
14. *marginal* propensity to consume
17. demand-*pull* inflation
20. *investment*
22. average propensity to *consume*
23. market *demand*

Down

2. *saving*
3. *average* propensity to save
4. *recessionary* gap
5. *cyclical* problem
8. *potential* GNP
9. stabilization *problem*
12. *consumption*
15. *derived* demand
16. *dissaving*
18. nominal *income*
19. 45-degree *line*
21. *full*-employment GNP

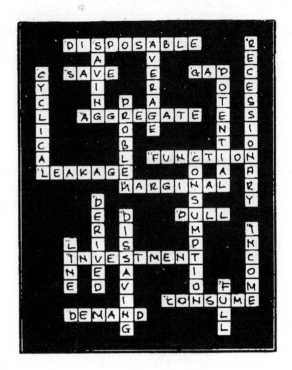

Chapter 9
Potential Instability

Quick Review

This chapter deals with how the economy responds to imbalances between desired spending and output. Specifically, we seek answers to the following questions:

- How do producers respond to an imbalance between output and sales?
- How do consumers respond to changes in output and income?
- What macro outcomes will these responses create?

Let's consider the last question first. This is the question over which Classical and Keynesian economists went to battle. The Classical economists believed that two mechanisms naturally adjusted aggregate spending to the full-employment level:

1. Flexible interest rates, which balanced desired saving with desired investment
2. Flexible prices and wages, which would adjust to changes in demand and supply

The Keynesian economists believed that the two mechanisms did not ensure self-adjustment of the economy because:

1. Expectations of declining income would result in lower investment by businesses, which would offset the effects of interest rates.
2. Declining wages and prices would mean a decline in aggregate spending, which would move the economy away from full employment, not toward it, as Classical economists had predicted. Furthermore, wages and prices are not flexible; they rarely decline.

The economy is potentially unstable because small changes in aggregate spending are multiplied into large changes in income. The multiplier depends on the marginal propensity to consume (*MPC*). The key formula for computing the multiplier is

$$\text{Multiplier} = \frac{1}{1 - MPC}$$

The multiplier occurs in the economy because of successive rounds of spending. When there is a sudden $100 billion drop in aggregate spending, there is suddenly $100 billion less in income received by those who would normally purchase the goods and services that make up aggregate output.

With $100 billion less in income, these people must reach into their savings or consume less. If the marginal propensity to consume is 0.80, then people will consume $80 billion less and will save $20 billion less. However, the multiplier begins to work again. With $80 billion less in consumption, there is now $80 billion less in income received by those who normally generate the consumption. These people in turn cut back consumption. How much do they now cut back? Multiply the marginal propensity to consume (0.80) by the change in income ($80 billion) to find the loss in consumption ($64 billion). When the losses of income in these rounds and more are added together, they total $500 billion. The initial $100 billion loss of aggregate spending has been translated into a total loss of $500 billion in income. Therefore, small changes in the economy are potentially destabilizing.

Learning Objectives

Key-Term Review

Review the following terms; if you are not sure of the meaning of any term, write out the definition and check it against the Glossary in the text.

consumption function

cyclical unemployment

demand-pull inflation

derived demand

equilibrium GNP

inflationary gap

marginal propensity to consume (*MPC*)

marginal propensity to save (*MPS*)

multiplier

recessionary gap

Fill in the blank following each of the statements below with the appropriate term from the list above.

1. When the economy is experiencing cyclical unemployment, the difference between aggregate spending and income at full employment is equal to the _____.

   1. _RECESSIONARY GAP_

2. $C = a + bY_D$ is the formula for the _____.

   2. _CONSUMPTION FUNCTION_

3. The marginal propensity to consume and the _MPS_ must add up to one.

   3. _MPS_

4. The income level at which aggregate spending equals income is known as _E_ _____.

   4. _EQUILIBRIUM GNP_

5. $1 - MPS$ indicates the _____.

   5. _MPS_

6. The type of inflation that can be caused by too much government spending is known as _____.

   6. _Demand Pull_

7. The resources that firms are willing and able to buy as a result of the demand for products that consumers are willing and able to buy is known as _____.

7. _Derived demand_

8. $\dfrac{1}{1-MPC}$ is the _____.

8. _multiplier_

9. When total desired spending at full employment exceeds full-employment output, there is an _____.

9. _Inflationary gap_

10. The type of unemployment that is reduced by expanding aggregate spending is _____.

10. _Cyclical_

True or False: *Circle your choice.*

T F 1. The Classical economists believed that aggregate spending adjusted quickly to equal full-employment output.

T **F** 2. Say's Law says that demand creates its own supply.

T F 3. The Great Depression destroyed the credibility of Classical theory on the speed of the self-adjustment of aggregate spending to full-employment income.

T F 4. Keynes believed that investment may be influenced more by expectations than by interest rates.

T **F** 5. A change in expectations is represented by a movement along the aggregate spending curve.

T F 6. Equilibrium occurs when the aggregate spending curve intersects the 45-degree line.

T **F** 7. Equilibrium GNP occurs only when there is full employment in an economy.

T **F** 8. Equilibrium GNP is the most desired level of GNP for an economy.

T **F** 9. The "paradox of thrift" shows that saving is undesirable for an economy.

T **F** 10. The multiplier is applicable only to a recessionary gap, because nominal income cannot increase beyond the full-employment level when there is an inflationary gap.

$\dfrac{1}{1-mpc}$

T F 11. In the short run it is not possible to close an inflationary gap by increasing real output.

T F 12. When there is an inflationary gap, there is excess investment, and investors bid up the interest rate by competing for savings.

T F 13. When there is an inflationary gap, there are excess purchases of goods and services, and consumers bid up prices by competing for those goods and services.

T F 14. When there is an inflationary gap, there are not enough resources available, and so wages are bid up by employers to keep available employees.

T **F** 15. According to Keynes, an inflationary gap can be eliminated only if prices, wages, and interest rates are downwardly flexible.

T F 16. Keynes recommended increased government expenditure to get the country out of its stagnation.

T **F** 17. Government can curb inflation by increasing government expenditures, according to Keynes.

T F 18. A Classical economist would say that the Great Depression would have to come to an end without government interference if the free market had simply been allowed a chance to adjust.

T **F** 19. A recessionary gap is the same as a GNP gap.

T F 20. Total spending, aggregate spending, and total expenditure mean the same thing.

T **F** 21. Aggregate spending and aggregate demand mean the same thing.

T F 22. Aggregate demand is related to the price level, and aggregate spending is related to the level of income.

115

Multiple Choice: *Select the correct answer.*

D 1. Classical economists believed that there would be a quick adjustment of aggregate spending and full-employment output as a result of changes in:
    (a) Interest rates.
    (b) Prices.
    (c) Wages.
    (d) All of the above.

A 2. According to Classical economists, the reason that interest rates helped to close a recessionary GNP gap is:
    (a) That borrowers lower the interest rate paid to savers, causing investment to rise and some savers to switch from saving to consumption, thus raising aggregate spending.
    (b) That borrowers raise the interest rate paid to savers, thus stimulating investment, which raises aggregate spending.
    (c) That borrowers raise the interest rate paid to savers, so that investments decline and aggregate spending in turn is lowered.
    (d) None of the above.

C 3. Producers respond to excess inventories by:
    (a) Increasing production.
    (b) Increasing prices.
    (c) Investing less.
    (d) Increasing employment.

a 4. Say's Law is:
    (a) A tenet of the Classical position.
    (b) A tenet of the Keynesian position.
    (c) A statement about the French economy only.
    (d) None of the above.

B **D** 5. The Classical economists differed from Keynes in believing that wages, prices, and interest rates would:
    (a) Cause cyclical unemployment if they were determined through the market mechanism.
    (b) Adjust so that unemployment would be eliminated through the market mechanism.
    (c) Lower aggregate spending instead of raising it when there is a recessionary gap.
    (d) Do both b and c.

B 6. Keynes believed that:
    (a) Investment is unresponsive to changes in interest rates.
    (b) The response of investment to falling interest rates may be overwhelmed by expectations about changes in income.
    (c) Investment decreases when there is a recessionary gap because interest rates fall.
    (d) Investment increases when there is a recessionary gap because interest rates fall.

Figure 9.1 shows four demand curves for investment goods. Choose the diagram that best answers each of the questions in Questions 7–10.

Figure 9.1

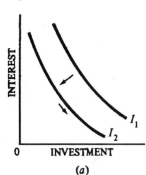 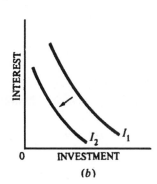  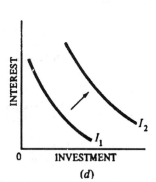

_B_ 7. Which diagram shows how investment responds to the expectation that the economy is about to enter a recession, causing firms to expect a decline in sales?

_C_ 8. Which diagram shows what happens to investment as interest rates fall?

_a_ 9. Which diagram illustrates the Keynesian view about the way investment responds to a recessionary gap?

_b_ 10. Which diagram illustrates the Classical view about the way investment responds to a recessionary gap?

_A_ 11. According to Keynes, the market mechanism may not lead to full employment because of:
    (a) Lower disposable incomes when wages fall.
    (b) Downward flexibility of wages and prices.
    (c) Higher prices as full employment is reached.
    (d) The insensitivity of investment to prices and wages.

_C_ 12. The multiplier is:
    (a) *MPC*.
    (b) *MPS*.

    (c) $\dfrac{1}{1 - MPC}$

    (d) $\dfrac{1}{1 - MPS}$

_C_ 13. Which of the following occurrences is an example of the multiplier at work as a result of an increase in government expenditures?
    (a) Consumers compete with the government by increasing their expenditures, thus causing businesses to increase their investments in order to satisfy the increased demand.
    (b) Government expenditures increase inflation, thus lowering real incomes, so that consumer expenditures and investment decline, thus lowering aggregate spending.
    (c) Households and businesses receive income from government expenditures; they spend a portion of this new income; these expenditures in turn generate income for other businesses and households, which in turn spend a portion of the new income, and so on.
    (d) Government expenditures stimulate investment in new plant and equipment in order to produce goods and services for the government, which provides jobs and increases incomes.

_D_ 14. The impact of the multiplier depends on:
    (a) The time period over which the multiplier works.
    (b) The size of the marginal propensity to consume.
    (c) The size of the initial change in expenditure.
    (d) All of the above.

<u>C</u> 15. The equilibrium GNP occurs at the point where the total (aggregate) spending curve intersects:
  (a) The horizontal axis.
  (b) The vertical axis.
  (c) A 45-degree line.
  (d) None of the above.

A <u>B</u> 16. The economy tends to move toward equilibrium GNP because:
  (a) Above equilibrium GNP inventories are too large, and below equilibrium GNP desired investment exceeds desired saving.
  (b) Above equilibrium GNP inventories are too large, and below equilibrium GNP desired saving exceeds desired investment.
  (c) Above equilibrium GNP inventories are declining, and below equilibrium GNP desired investment exceeds desired saving.
  (d) Above equilibrium GNP inventories are declining, and below equilibrium GNP desired saving exceeds desired investment.

D <u>A</u> 17. If the economy is below full-employment income:
  (a) The economy is inside its institutional production-possibilities curve.
  (b) Unemployment is unnecessarily high.
  (c) Prices tend to be dampened.
  (d) All of the above are the case.

D <u>A</u> 18. When the economy is not at the equilibrium GNP level:
  (a) Desired investment does not equal desired saving.
  (b) Inventories are not at their desired levels.
  (c) The economy is not at a GNP level where the aggregate spending curve intersects the 45-degree line.
  (d) All of the above are the case.

<u>A</u> 19. The paradox of thrift occurs chiefly because:
  (a) Saving is a leakage.
  (b) Investment does not equal saving.
  (c) The multiplier effect counteracts increased consumption and saving.
  (d) Consumption rises with saving.

In answering questions 20–25 refer to the diagrams in Figure 9.2. Assume the consumption function has the same slope as the aggregate spending curve. (Some questions have more than one correct answer.)

Figure 9.2

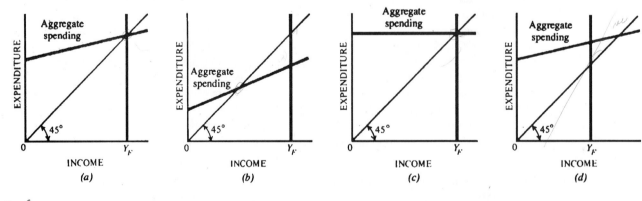

(a) (b) (c) (d)

<u>A, C</u> 20. In which diagrams is full-employment income equal to the equilibrium income?

<u>B</u> 21. In which diagram is a recessionary gap in evidence?

<u>D</u> 22. In which diagram is an inflationary gap in evidence?

<u>C</u> 23. In which diagram is marginal propensity to consume the lowest?

118

_B_ 24. In which diagram would aggregate spending be lowest if there were no income?

_C_ 25. In which diagram would the multiplier be lowest?

_D_ 26. In the Keynesian view of the adjustment process, which of the following is true?
   (a) When output is greater than desired spending, producers reduce output and employment.
   (b) Declining income causes consumers to spend less.
   (c) Reductions in consumer spending cause further reductions in output and employment.
   (d) All of the above are true.

_B_ 27. Which of the following statements is true?
   (a) Investment, saving, and imports are leakages from the income stream.
   (b) Saving, imports, and taxes are leakages from the income stream.
   (c) Investment, spending, government spending, and exports are leakages from the income stream.
   (d) Investment, government spending, and imports are leakages from the income stream.

Problems and Applications

$$\frac{1}{1-mpc}$$

Exercise 1

You will know the difference between Keynesian and Classical economics after doing this exercise.

Fill in the spaces in Table 9.1 with the appropriate choices from the pairs in parentheses after each item, contrasting the Classical and Keynesian views on the effect of a recessionary gap.

Table 9.1
Classical and Keynesian views of a recessionary gap

		Classical view	Keynesian view
1.	Expected duration of recessionary gap without government interference (long, short)	Short	LONG
2.	Does the economy self-adjust? (yes, no)	YES	NO
3.	Reaction of interest rates to a recessionary gap (rise, fall).	FALL	FALL
4.	What happens to investment in a recessionary gap? (rises, falls)	RISES	FALLS
5.	. . . because of changes in (expectations, interest rates)	INTEREST RATES	expectations
6.	This causes a _____ investment demand (movement along, shift of)	movement along	shift of
7.	The reaction of prices and wages to a recessionary gap (lower, inadequate change)	lower	inadequate change
8.	. . . because of (rigid prices, unemployment)	unemployment	Rigid prices
9.	After prices adjust in a recessionary gap, what happens to consumption? (rises, falls)	Rises	falls
10.	This causes a _____ the consumption-demand curve (movement along, shift of)	Movement along	Shift off

Exercise 2

This exercise shows both the graphic and algebraic ways to compute the influence of aggregate spending on aggregate income. It shows how to use and compute the multiplier. It also provides practice in the skills needed to solve one of the exercises at the end of Chapter 9 in the text.

1. Assume that an economy is characterized by the following consumption function:

Consumption = $30 billion + 0.75 Y_D

While investment equals $30 billion, government expenditures and net exports are assumed to be zero. Finish Table 9.2 and then draw the aggregate spending curve and 45-degree line in Figure 9.3. Both curves should pass through point *A*. Label aggregate spending TE_1.

Table 9.2
Aggregate spending schedule
(billions of dollars per year)

Disposable income (Y_D)	Consumption (C)	Investment (I)	Aggregate spending (C+I)	MPC
$ 0	30	30	60	—
120	120	30	150	.75
240	210	30	240	.75

$C = 30 + 0.75Y$

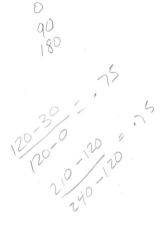

Figure 9.3

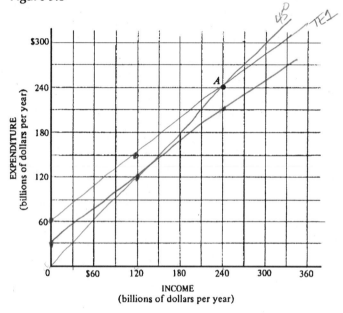

2. Fill in the marginal propensity to consume for each shift of income level in Table 9.2. For example, using the *MPC* formula between $0 and $120 billion of income, we find the change in income is $120 billion while the change in consumption is only $90 billion ($120 – $30).

   Therefore $MPC = \dfrac{\$90}{\$120} = 0.75$.

3. T **F** The marginal propensity to consume changes with income in this example.

4. Businesses abruptly invest $30 billion less in capital formation. Complete Table 9.3, which shows this change. Graph the new aggregate spending curve in Figure 9.3 and label it TE_2.

Table 9.3
Aggregate-spending schedule with a fall of $30 billion in investment (billions of dollars per year)

(1) Disposable income	(2) Consumption	(3) Investment	(4) Aggregate spending (2) + (3) = (4)
$ 0	$ 30	$ 0	$ 3̶6̶
120	120	0	120
240	210	0	210

5. Fill in Table 9.4, which shows the changes in equilibrium income when the businesses suddenly fail to invest.

Table 9.4
Changes in equilibrium income due to the change in business expenditure (billions of dollars per year)

(1) (see TE₁ in Figure 9.3) Equilibrium income before decreased business expenditure	(2) (see TE₂ in Figure 9.3) Equilibrium income after decreased business expenditure	(3) Change in income due to decreased business expenditure (2) – (1) = (3)
$ 240	$ 120	$ –120

6. Which of the following formulas best represents the multiplier?

(a) $\dfrac{1}{MPC}$

(b) $\dfrac{MPS}{MPC}$

(c) $1 - MPC$

(d) $\dfrac{1}{1 - MPC}$

7. If the $MPC = 0.75$ and investment expenditures fall by $30 billion, then when we use the multiplier, we find that equilibrium income will change annually by:
   (a) $40 billion.
   (b) $22.5 billion.
   (c) $120 billion.
   (d) $30 billion.

8. Does your answer correspond to the third column in Table 9.4? ___yes___

9. (T) F   The diagram of a shift in aggregate spending predicts the same change in income as would be predicted using the multiplier.

10. (T) F   As long as full employment is not reached, the multiplier magnifies abrupt changes in aggregate spending into much larger changes in real income.

Exercise 3

The following exercise shows how the multiplier works and two ways of calculating it—an easy way and a hard way.

1. Suppose the economy were at full employment but suddenly experienced a $216 billion recessionary gap due to abrupt cancellation of investment plans. Follow the impact of this sudden change through the economy in Table 9.5, as in Table 9.2 in your text (p. 208). Assume the marginal propensity to consume is 5/6.

Table 9.5

Spending cycles		Amount (billions of dollars per year)	Cumulative decrease in aggregate spending (billions of dollars per year)
First cycle:	recessionary gap emerges	$216	$216
Second cycle:	consumption drops by MPC x gap	180	396
Third cycle:	consumption drops by MPC^2 x gap	150	546
Fourth cycle:	consumption drops by MPC^3 x gap	125	671
Fifth cycle:	consumption drops by MPC^4 x gap	105	775
Sixth cycle:	consumption drops by MPC^5 x gap	87.50	862.5
Seventh cycle:	consumption drops by MPC^6 x gap	73	935.4
		60	995

2. What will be the final cumulative impact on aggregate spending? (*Hint:* The eighth cycle is $[5/6]^7$ x $216 billion = $60 billion, which brings the cumulative change in aggregate spending to $994. Continue the cycles.) 1294   1296

3. Compute the multiplier. 6

4. Multiply the $216 billion by the multiplier. 1296

Note: The multiplier provides an easy way of finding out how the economy will be affected by a sudden change in aggregate spending. It saves calculations such as those in Problem 1 of this exercise and allows simple calculation of the cumulative effect on aggregate spending.

Exercise 4

The media often provide information on multiplier effects in the economy. By using one of the articles in the text, this exercise will show the kind of information to look for. If your professor makes a newspaper assignment for this chapter, this exercise will provide an example of how to do it.

Reread the article in Chapter 9 entitled "Plants Plan December Shutdowns as the Recession Spreads Rapidly" from the *Wall Street Journal*. Then answer the following questions:

1. What phrase or sentence indicates the cause of the change in income in the economy? In other words, where does the article indicate a change in a leakage or injection?

2. What passage (no more than a sentence) indicates who initially experiences the change in income?

3. What sentence illustrates the change in spending habits resulting from the change in income?

4. What passage mentions the people whose incomes are secondarily affected because of the changes in spending?

Common Errors

The first statement in each "common error" below is incorrect. Each incorrect statement is followed by a corrected version and an explanation.

1. Since saving and investment must be the same by definition, the economy must be at equilibrium because investment equals saving. WRONG!

   Intended investment equals intended saving at equilibrium. RIGHT!

   If there are excess inventories or if people are forced to save because they cannot spend on desired goods and services, then income may be different from equilibrium income. Do not confuse actual investment and actual saving with intended investment and intended saving.

2. If consumers save more, interest rates will fall and investment will rise. WRONG!

   When consumption falls due to increased saving, investment may be discouraged. RIGHT!

   Interest rates *may* fall because of increased saving. However, Keynes showed that businesses may invest less when they expect to sell less. The lower consumption may actually cause them to lower investment.

3. Equilibrium GNP and full-employment GNP are always the same. WRONG!

   Equilibrium GNP and full-employment GNP are determined in different ways. RIGHT!

   Equilibrium GNP occurs where the aggregate spending curve and the 45-degree line intersect. The full-employment GNP occurs at the GNP level where the market-supply and market-demand curves for labor are in equilibrium. For most purposes, we can consider the two levels to be independent of each other.

   Be careful! While it is possible to determine the equilibrium GNP or income level by glancing at the aggregate spending curve and the 45-degree line, it is not possible to determine full-employment GNP this way. Full-employment GNP is shown simply as a vertical line.

■ ANSWERS ■

Key-Term Review

1. recessionary gap
2. consumption function
3. marginal propensity to save (*MPS*)
4. equilibrium GNP
5. marginal propensity to consume (*MPC*)
6. demand-pull inflation
7. derived demand
8. multiplier
9. inflationary gap
10. cyclical unemployment

True or False

1. T	5. F	9. F	13. T	17. F	20. T
2. F	6. T	10. F	14. T	18. T	21. F
3. T	7. F	11. T	15. F	19. F	22. T
4. T	8. F	12. T	16. T		

Multiple Choice

1. d	6. b	11. a	16. a	20. a, c	24. b
2. a	7. b	12. c	17. d	21. b	25. c
3. c	8. c	13. c	18. d	22. d	26. d
4. a	9. a	14. d	19. a	23. c	27. b
5. b	10. c	15. c			

Problems and Applications

Exercise 1

Table 9.1 answer

	Classical view	Keynesian view
1. Expected duration of recessionary gap	short	long
2. Does the economy self-adjust?	yes	no
3. Reaction of interest rates to a recessionary gap	fall	fall
4. What happens to investment?	rises	falls
5. ... because of changes in	interest rates	expectations
6. This causes a _____ investment demand	movement along	shift of
7. Reaction of prices and wages to recessionary gap	lower	inadequate change
8. ... because of	unemployment	rigid prices
9. What happens to consumption?	rises	falls
10. This causes a _____ the consumption-demand curve	movement along	shift of

Exercise 2

1. **Table 9.2 answer**
   (billions of dollars per year)

Disposable income (Y_D)	Consumption (C)	Investment (I)	Aggregate spending (C+I)	MPC
$ 0	$30 + 0.75 \times 0 = 30$	$30	$ 60	—
120	$30 + 0.75 \times 120 = 120$	30	120	$\frac{120 - 30}{120 - 0} = 0.75$
240	$30 + 0.75 \times 240 = 210$	30	240	$\frac{210 - 120}{240 - 120} = 0.75$

Figure 9.3 answer

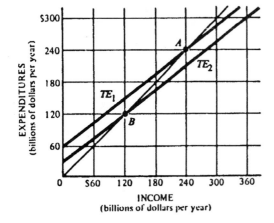

2. See Table 9.2 answer, last column.
3. F
4. See Figure 9.3 answer, TE_2.

Table 9.3 answer
(billions of dollars per year)

Disposable income	Aggregate spending
$ 0	$ 30
120	120
240	210

5. **Table 9.4 answer**
   (billions of dollars per year)

(1)	(2)	(3)
$240	$120	−$120

6. d   7. c   8. yes   9. T   10. T

Exercise 3

1. **Table 9.5 answer**
   (billions of dollars per year)

Spending cycles	Amount	Cumulative decrease in aggregate spending
First cycle	$216	$216
Second cycle	180	396
Third cycle	150	546
Fourth cycle	125	671
Fifth cycle	104	775
Sixth cycle	87	862
Seventh cycle	72	934

2. $1,296 billion per year.

3. $\text{Multiplier} = \dfrac{1}{1 - MPC} = \dfrac{1}{1 - (5/6)} = 6$

4. 6 x $216 billion per year = $1,296 billion per year

Exercise 4

1. "All over the United States, manufacturers are waiting for interest rates to come down some more and for consumer confidence to return." This quotation indicates that two injections, investment and consumption, are low.
2. The passage "The hard-hit auto, truck, farm equipment and construction machinery industries..." identifies whose income is being hurt by the low levels of consumption and investment.
3. "There will be a lot of shutdowns and short workweeks this month as companies adjust to the rapidly spreading recession." This sentence indicates loss of income of both firms and their employees who depend on consumption and investment.
4. "The hard-hit auto, truck, farm equipment and construction machinery industries...will take a lot of extra time off this year, as will a number of their suppliers." The last phrase indicates the multiplier effect, as firms feeling the initial impact of the recession reduce orders from their suppliers.

Chapter 10
Fiscal Policy

Quick Review

The basic questions confronted in this chapter are:

- Can government spending and tax policies help stabilize the economy?
- What kinds of policy changes will produce desired macro outcomes?
- How do those policies affect the government's budget balance?

The questions above relate to the stabilization function of fiscal policy. The stabilization function attempts to achieve and sustain full employment and stable prices. Government changes fiscal policy by changing its spending or tax rates. Government can move aggregate spending toward full-employment GNP and price stability if it cuts taxes or raises expenditures (expansionary fiscal policy) when there is a recessionary gap, or if it raises taxes or cuts spending (contractionary fiscal policy) when there is an inflationary gap. The multiplier assures that even modest changes in government spending or taxes will have a significant impact on total spending.

Certain "uncontrollable" parts of the budget automatically adjust aggregate spending toward full-employment GNP. These are the built-in stabilizers, such as unemployment compensation and welfare. Because of the multiplier effect, any change in government spending creates a much larger change in GNP. Any change in government expenditures also alters the type of goods and services produced and the distribution of income to individuals.

The government frequently pursues its stabilization function through deficit spending. The stabilization function of government therefore often makes it difficult to balance the budget. Even when the government attempts to balance the budget by cutting discretionary fiscal spending, "uncontrollable" items of the budget may offset the cutbacks. If the government succeeds in cutting back expenditures, the multiplier will lower income by even more than the cutbacks. While the government may offset this multiplying effect by cutting taxes an equal amount, people do not raise consumption by the amount of the returned taxes; they save some of the returned income. This balanced-budget multiplier guarantees that a government spending cutback lowers income even when taxes fall by the same amount as the government expenditure cutback. Historically, the stabilization function of fiscal policy has outweighed the importance of a balanced budget.

The government finds the full-employment-budget concept more useful than the balanced-budget concept in pursuing its stabilization function. The full-employment budget is the budget that would exist at full employment based on current fiscal policy.

Both the president and Congress work together to determine the budget. The Office of Management and Budget sends forward the administration's proposed budget. Congressional committees investigate and hold hearings on the budget. Congress authorizes the expenditures to be made and appropriates the money for them. The president may accept the resulting budget or veto it and return it to the Congress to be reworked.

Learning Objectives

After reading Chapter 10 and doing the following exercises, you should:	True or false	Multiple choice	Problems and applications	Common errors	Pages in the text
1. Know what fiscal policy is and who makes it.	4,5	10,16,18, 21,24	3		221–222
2. Know what fiscal policy should be in different economic circumstances.		3,6–8, 11,15,19	3		222–242
3. Know how the government pays for its expenditures.	13,19	9,17			223
4. Be able to use the multiplier, full-employment, and the aggregate spending curve in explaining how the government can stabilize the economy.	3,7,9–11, 15–18	2,3,12,14, 19,24,29	1,2		222–228
5. Be able to illustrate how leakages such as taxes affect aggregate spending.		25	1,2		222–224
6. Know the arguments for increasing public or private spending with fiscal policy.		7,9	3		236–238
7. Understand how the government determines a budget.		21–23			238–239
8. Know the difference between discretionary fiscal spending and uncontrollable items in the government's budget.		6,22	3		238–239
9. Be able to explain how built-in stabilizers counteract the effects of cyclical unemployment.	8	1,5			238
10. Be able to explain why the stabilization function may conflict with the goal of balancing the budget.	19	17,19, 26,27		1	239–241, 244–246
11. Know what is meant by the balanced-budget multiplier.	1,2,6, 12,20	13,20,28	2	2	232
12. Understand what is meant by the full-employment budget.		17			239–242
13. Understand how a change in income affects the budget balance.	14	1,7	2,3		239–242, 244–246
14. Understand how transfer payments affect the economy.	21–24				229,244

Key-Term Review

Review the following terms; if you are not sure of the meaning of any term, write out the definition and check it against the Glossary in the text.

aggregate spending	fiscal year (*FY*)
automatic stabilizer	income transfers
budget surplus	inflationary gap
deficit spending	marginal propensity to consume (*MPC*)
discretionary fiscal spending	marginal propensity to save (*MPS*)
disposable income	multiplier
equilibrium GNP	recessionary gap
fiscal policy	

Fill in the blank following each of the statements below with the appropriate term from the list above.

1. The production rate at which planned aggregate spending equals the production rate is called _____.

1. _____

2. When the equilibrium GNP occurs at an income level below full-employment GNP, there is likely to be a _____.

2. _____

3. Many programs of the government will immediately counteract the resulting effects of recession without requiring Congress or the president to act. Any such program is called an _____.

3. _____

4. Congress may initiate new spending programs to counteract the effects of recession; this is referred to as the use of _____.

4. _____

5. However, such programs are likely to increase government debt, which means the government is engaging in _____.

5. _____

6. Many people disapprove of such spending and urge the government to bring expenditures below government revenues for a _____.

6. _____

7. The government, however, has only limited authority to cut back spending. Its _____ is only a small part of its total budget.

7. _____

8. When the government cuts back its spending, the _____ causes household after-tax _____ to fall by more than the cutback in government expenditures.

8. _____

_____

9. If you know the _____, you can always calculate the multiplier.

9. _____

10. The government _____ begins in October.

10. _____

11. When the equilibrium GNP occurs at an income level above the full-employment level of output, there will be an _____.

11. _____

12. A downward shift in the _____ curve lowers the equilibrium level of income.

12. _____

13. As a fiscal policy measure, _____ of a given size will have a smaller impact on GNP than an equal change in government spending.

13. _____

14. _____ is equivalent to one minus the MPC.

14. _____

True or False: *Circle your choice.*

T F 1. When increases in government spending are offset by equal increases in taxes, the level of income remains constant.

T F 2. The balanced-budget multiplier has a numeric value of one.

T F 3. Private expenditures include C, I, G, and imports.

T F 4. Fiscal policy involves changes in government spending and taxes but not regulation of prices or production.

T F 5. By not changing spending, the government can avoid redistributing income, changing growth rates, and changing price levels.

T F 6. By attempting to balance the budget during a recession, the government is likely to worsen the recession.

T F 7. If equilibrium income is $400 million below full-employment income, then the government can increase expenditures by $400 million to make equilibrium income equal full-employment income.

T F 8. Because of automatic stabilizers, the federal budget automatically adjusts so that equilibrium GNP equals full-employment GNP.

T F 9. When government spending increases, consumption also increases via the multiplier process.

T F 10. When government spending increases, saving also increases through the multiplier process.

T F 11. The multiplier ensures that equilibrium GNP equals full-employment GNP.

T F 12. The budget must be balanced for the balanced-budget multiplier to equal one.

T F 13. By running a deficit, the government is necessarily increasing the federal debt.

T F 14. When income falls, the budget deficit rises because of automatic increases in government spending and because tax revenues decline with unemployment.

T F 15. An increase in investment has the same multiplier effect as an increase in government spending.

T F 16. Increases in government spending intended to close a recessionary gap should equal the size of the gap.

T F 17. If the economy is at full employment and there is a recessionary gap, undesired inventories accumulate.

T F 18. The consumption function is the same as the aggregate spending curve.

T F 19. The government deficit is simply the difference between government expenditures and tax revenues.

T F 20. The balanced-budget multiplier refers to the impact of equal *increases* or *decreases* in taxing and spending by the federal government.

T F 21. An increase in transfer payments of $10 million would have the same impact as a $10 million increase in government spending.

T F 22. Income transfers are payments to individuals for which no current goods or services are exchanged.

T F 23. To raise income by a given amount, an increase in transfer payments would have to be larger than an increase in government spending to achieve the same result.

T F 24. An increase in transfer payments by a given amount would have the same impact on the level of income as a reduction in taxes of the same amount.

Multiple Choice: *Select the correct answer.*

_____ 1. Automatic stabilizers tend to stabilize the level of economic activity because:
(a) They are changed quickly by Congress.
(b) They increase the size of the multiplier.
(c) When the level of GNP rises, stabilizing expenditures fall.
(d) They control the rate of change in prices.

_____ 2. If the marginal propensity to consume out of disposable income were 0.66, a $1 billion decrease in taxes would raise national income by an amount:
(a) Equal to $1 billion.
(b) Less than $1 billion.
(c) Greater than $2 billion.
(d) Equal to $2 billion.

_____ 3. Suppose the economy is at full employment and prices are reasonably stable. If the government wants to increase spending for public transportation systems, which of the following actions will have the *least* inflationary impact?
(a) Taxes are increased by an amount greater than the increase in spending.
(b) Taxes are increased by an amount smaller than the increase in spending.
(c) Taxes are increased by an amount equal to the increase in spending.
(d) Tax rates are not changed at all when expenditures increase.

_____ 4. Suppose the economy is operating at a point below full employment. If the government wishes to expand aggregate spending but does not wish to increase the size of the government in the process, which of the following policy actions should it undertake?
(a) Increase government spending and leave tax rates unchanged.
(b) Decrease tax rates and leave government spending unchanged.
(c) Increase government spending and taxes by the same amount.
(d) Increase government spending by more than the increase in taxes.

_____ 5. Which of the following is *not* an automatic stabilizer?
(a) Income taxes.
(b) Unemployment benefits.
(c) Welfare payments.
(d) Defense spending.

_____ 6. Examples of discretionary fiscal spending include:
(a) Income taxes.
(b) Unemployment benefits.
(c) Social security payments.
(d) Expenditures for highways.

_____ 7. When the government changes its spending only, which of the following is likely to change?
(a) The mix and rate of production in the economy.
(b) The distribution of income.
(c) Growth of the economy.
(d) All of the above.

_____ 8. The government can best eliminate a recessionary gap by:
(a) Increasing government spending and raising taxes.
(b) Increasing government spending and lowering taxes.
(c) Decreasing government spending and raising taxes.
(d) Decreasing government spending and lowering taxes.

_____ 9. Crowding out occurs when the government:
(a) Increases taxes, thus causing a decrease in consumption.
(b) Issues debt, thus making it more difficult for the private sector to issue debt.
(c) Prints money, which displaces currency.
(d) Does all of the above.

_____ 10. Fiscal policy may not work because:
(a) The effect of the policy may not be felt until some time after it is needed.
(b) The federal budget must be balanced.
(c) It changes the money supply in unpredictable ways.
(d) Government regulations are counterproductive.

_____ 11. The amount of government spending needed to make equilibrium income rise to full-employment income equals:
(a) The difference between full-employment income and equilibrium income.
(b) The inflationary gap.
(c) The recessionary gap.
(d) The amount of saving at full-employment income levels.

_____ 12. The amount of additional income caused by increased government spending depends on:
   (a) The marginal propensity to consume.
   (b) The number of spending cycles that occur in a given period of time.
   (c) The size of the multiplier.
   (d) All of the above.

_____ 13. The reason a tax cut of $100 has a different impact on income than an increase in government spending of $100 is that:
   (a) People spend only a part of the $100 tax cut on consumption.
   (b) Government spending is less productive than consumption spending.
   (c) Government bureaucracy is expanded by the increase in government spending but wouldn't be if taxes were lowered.
   (d) All of the above are the case.

_____ 14. It is inflationary for government to increase spending if:
   (a) It will have to increase taxes to pay for the increased spending.
   (b) Increased government spending will result in deficits.
   (c) The economy is at full employment.
   (d) Equilibrium income is thereby lowered.

_____ 15. When there is an inflationary gap:
   (a) Inventories accumulate.
   (b) There is excess saving.
   (c) Unemployment is likely to be high.
   (d) None of the above is the case.

_____ 16. Fiscal policy may consist of:
   (a) Raising and lowering taxes.
   (b) Raising government spending.
   (c) Lowering government spending.
   (d) All of the above.

_____ 17. Deficit spending is financed by:
   (a) Increased taxes.
   (b) Government bonds.
   (c) Decreased government spending.
   (d) None of the above.

_____ 18. When government increases spending to eliminate a recessionary gap:
   (a) The government is performing its stabilization function.
   (b) The national debt is reduced.
   (c) Government spending must exceed taxes.
   (d) All of the above are the case.

_____ 19. When there is an inflationary gap, it is appropriate for the government to:
   (a) Make budget surpluses smaller.
   (b) Make budget deficits smaller.
   (c) Make budget deficits larger.
   (d) Do none of the above.

_____ 20. If the government increases spending and maintains a balanced budget at the same time:
   (a) There will be no effect on the economy, since taxes balance government spending.
   (b) Income will increase by the amount of the increase in government spending.
   (c) Income will increase through the multiplier effect by more than the increase in government spending.
   (d) Income will actually decrease by the amount that taxes have to be increased to offset the effects of the government spending.

_____21. Which of the following presided over the largest tax cuts in U.S. history?
  (a) President Kennedy.
  (b) President Nixon.
  (c) President Johnson.
  (d) President Reagan.

_____22. Observers of the federal budget suggest that about:
  (a) One-fourth of the expenditures are discretionary.
  (b) One-half of the expenditures are discretionary.
  (c) One-third of the expenditures are discretionary.
  (d) Three-fourths of the expenditures are discretionary.

_____23. The government's fiscal year begins:
  (a) September 30.
  (b) October 1.
  (c) June 1.
  (d) January 1.

_____24. The government is pursuing an expansionary policy if, whatever the value of the budget:
  (a) It increases its spending and/or reduces its tax rates.
  (b) It increases its spending or increases its tax rates.
  (c) It decreases its spending or reduces its tax rates.
  (d) It decreases its spending and increases its tax rates.

_____25. A change in tax laws will initially:
  (a) Cause a movement along the aggregate spending curve.
  (b) Shift the aggregate spending curve.
  (c) Shift the government spending curve.
  (d) Do none of the above.

_____26. Which of the following is an argument for balancing the federal budget by cutting expenditures?
  (a) Fiscal policy can be used to stabilize the economy during recessions.
  (b) Federal spending causes inflation.
  (c) The government can safely issue more money and issue more debt when the budget is balanced.
  (d) An equivalent increase in government spending and taxes has no effect on income.

_____27. Which of the following is an argument against balancing the federal budget?
  (a) The federal government spends and interferes with the economy too much.
  (b) The government may not be able to pay off its debts.
  (c) The government may be unable to pull the economy out of recession.
  (d) An equivalent increase in government spending and taxes has no effect on income.

_____28. For the balanced budget multiplier to equal one:
  (a) The budget must be balanced before the change in taxes and spending takes place.
  (b) The budget need not be balanced, but the changes in taxes and spending must be equal.
  (c) The budget must be balanced and the change in spending must equal the change in taxes.
  (d) The budget must be balanced but the change in taxes and spending may be unequal amounts.

_____29. Which of the following would cause the level of income to *change* by the greatest amount, *ceteris paribus*?
  (a) An increase in social security payments of $10 billion.
  (b) A reduction in personal income taxes of $10 billion.
  (c) An increase in defense spending of $10 billion.
  (d) The changes suggested in a, b, and c have equal impacts on the level of income.

Problems and Applications

Exercise 1

This exercise shows how government spending affects aggregate income and gives practice in shifting the aggregate spending curve. It is similar to exercises at the end of Chapter 10 in the text.

1. T   F   The recessionary gap is the amount by which desired spending falls short of full-employment GNP.

2. Assume the consumption function for the economy is:

   Consumption = $50 billion + 0.5 Y_D

   Further assume that investment is $50 billion per year and government expenditures are $100 billion per year. Complete Table 10.1.

Table 10.1
Relationship of income and expenditure
(billions of dollars per year)

Income (Y_D)	Consumption	Investment	Government spending	Aggregate spending
$ 0	_____	_____	_____	_____
200	_____	_____	_____	_____
400	_____	_____	_____	_____
600	_____	_____	_____	_____

3. Graph the aggregate spending curve in Figure 10.1, using the data in Table 10.1. Label the aggregate spending curve TE_1. The curve should go through point A. Refer to Figure 10.1 to answer Problems 4–6.

Figure 10.1

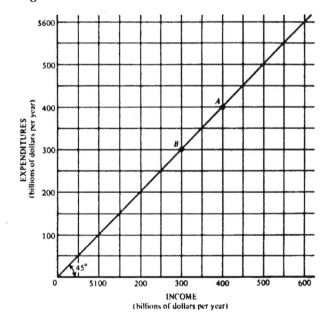

4. Equilibrium income equals $_____ billion per year.

5. Compute the recessionary gap when full-employment income is $500 billion per year. $_____ .

6. Suppose a new president persuades Congress to cut government spending to $50 billion per year in order to balance the budget. The resulting income expenditures table is shown in Table 10.2. Compute aggregate spending in Table 10.2.

Table 10.2
Relationship of income and spending after reduction in government expenditures of $50 billion (billions of dollars per year)

Income	Consumption	Investment	Government spending	Aggregate spending
$ 0	$ 50	$50	$50	$_____
200	150	50	50	_____
400	250	50	50	_____
600	350	50	50	_____

7. Graph the new aggregate spending curve in Figure 10.1 and label it TE_2. The new curve should pass through point B.

8. Complete Table 10.3, which shows the changes due to the cut in government spending.

Table 10.3
Effects of a cut in government spending (billions of dollars per year)

	(1) Before cut	(2) After cut	(3) Change (1) – (2)
Equilibrium income	$_____ (see Problem 4)	$_____ (see TE_2 in Figure 10.1)	$_____
Recessionary gap (full employment = $500 billion)	_____ (see Problem 5)	_____	_____

9. On the basis of Table 10.3, and assuming full employment occurs at $500 billion, we may conclude that cuts in government spending to balance the budget cause (an increase, a decrease) in income, which causes a (rise, decline) in the unemployment rate, (excess, inadequate) inventories, and a tendency toward (inflation, deflation).

10. T F The policy trade-off for elimination of the deficit is a worsening of the recession.

Exercise 2

This exercise shows how the balanced-budget multiplier works. It also shows the relationship between a balanced budget and income. It will help you with the second exercise at the end of Chapter 10 in the text.

1. Figure 10.2 shows the aggregate spending curve, TE_1, facing an economy in the first year of a new administration. Government expenditures are $100 billion while taxes are only $50 billion. In order to balance the budget, Congress decides to cut government spending from $100 to $50 billion. Draw the new aggregate spending curve and label it TE_2. (*Hint:* It should pass through one of the three points in Figure 10.2.)

Figure 10.2

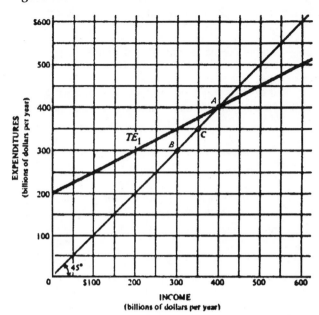

INCOME
(billions of dollars per year)

2. Suppose the new president discovers Congress has acted too severely and decides to stimulate the economy by proposing tax rebates. Since government expenditures were cut $50 billion, the president proposes to give $50 billion back to consumers in tax rebates during the next year. What is the marginal propensity to consume on the basis of Figure 10.2? (*Hint:* Look at the slope of the aggregate spending curve.) _____

3. How much of the rebate will be spent on consumption? $_____ billion per year. (*Hint:* The *MPC* tells how much consumption changes for an extra dollar of disposable income.)

4. Assume that only $25 billion out of the $50 billion rebate appears as increased consumption; draw the new aggregate spending curve in Figure 10.2 and label it TE_3. (*Hint:* It should pass through one of the three points in Figure 10.2.)

5. T   F   When cuts in government expenditures are balanced by tax rebates of an equal amount, equilibrium income remains unchanged. (*Hint:* Compare TE_1 and TE_3 in Figure 10.2.)

6. Let's see if these fiscal policy actions (the cut in government expenditures and taxes) are an improvement over doing nothing. Complete Table 10.4. Assume full-employment income is $500 billion per year.

Table 10.4
Effects of cutback and rebate on the economy
(billions of dollars per year)

	(1) Before cutback and rebate	(2) After cutback and rebate	(3) Change (2) – (1)
Equilibrium income (Figure 10.2)	$400	$_____	$_____
Recessionary gap (Figure 10.2)	50	_____	_____
Government spending	100	50	50
Taxes	50	$50 – $50 rebate = $0	_____
Deficit	50	_____	_____

135

7. T F In this example, by taking actions that would seem to move toward a balanced budget, the government does not change the deficit at all, lowers income, and increases unemployment.

8. T F In this example, taxes are lowered, but more people are out of work or are receiving lower incomes.

9. T F If there were automatic stabilizers such as unemployment insurance and welfare, the government deficit would be smaller than it was before the cut in government expenditures and the tax rebate.

Exercise 3

The media continually present information about events that shift aggregate expenditures for our economy. By using one of the articles in the text, this exercise will show the kind of information to look for. If your professor makes a newspaper assignment for this chapter, this exercise will provide an example of how to do it.

Reread the article in Chapter 10 entitled "Japan Adopts Package to Prime Economy" from the *Washington Post*. Then answer the following questions using Figure 10.3 for question 1:

Figure 10.3

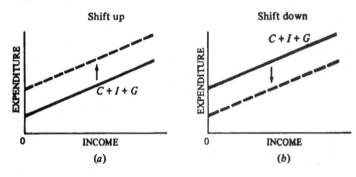

1. Which of the two diagrams in Figure 10.3 best represents the shift in aggregate expenditure that the article is describing?   a   b   (circle one)

2. What phrase or sentence in the article indicates the change in a leakage (savings, taxes, or imports), an injection (investment, government expenditure, or exports), or consumption that provides evidence of the shift?

3. What passage (no more than a sentence) indicates the change in income that results from the shift?

4. Assume that Japan's marginal propensity to consume is 85 percent. Compute the cumulative aggregate spending effects of the government's pump priming.

Crossword Puzzle

Select the economic term in the following list that corresponds with each of the definitions and descriptions below. Then fit the term or one of the words within it into the crossword puzzle at the numbers indicated.

aggregate spending
built-in stabilizer
budget surplus
crowding out
cyclical unemployment
demand-pull inflation
discretionary fiscal spending
disposable income
equilibrium GNP
fiscal policy
fiscal year
full-employment budget
full-employment GNP
inflationary gap
injections
leakage
marginal propensity to consume
multiplier
recessionary gap
uncontrollable expenditure

Across

1. The factor that is used to find the total impact on income of an increase in government expenditures.
6. The state of government finances if the economy is producing at the potential GNP level under prevailing fiscal policy.
7. The state of government finances if actual expenditures are less than actual taxes.
10. The change in consumption divided by the change in income.
12. The government's use of taxes and expenditures to stabilize the economy.
15. What you have left to spend after taxes.
18. If the government decides to increase expenditures when aggregate demand equals income at full employment, the increased expenditures will produce an _____.
19. Uncontrollable expenditures or automatic taxes that push the economy toward full-employment income.

Down

2. Flows of income that are not included in expenditures for goods and services that are currently produced.
3. Increases in aggregate expenditures at each level of income.
4. Expenditures that the president and Congress can increase or cut back relatively easily.
5. The government's _____ begins on October 1.
8. While the president may be blamed for not balancing the budget, there is actually little he can do about this aspect of the budget.
9. Increases in average prices due to excessive expenditures.
11. The income level at which aggregate demand equals the 45-degree line.
13. What occurs in private bond markets when government has to finance a large debt.
14. Loss of jobs due to inadequate aggregate demand.
16. The excess of income over aggregate demand at full-employment income.
17. Potential GNP.

Common Errors

The first statement in each "common error" below is incorrect. Each incorrect statement is followed by a corrected version and an explanation.

1. Government deficits always lead to inflation. WRONG!

   Government deficits may result from government spending to reach full employment with price stability. RIGHT!

   You should focus on what is happening to aggregate spending, not just deficits, when looking for the sources of inflation. By looking at the deficit, you cannot tell if there is an inflationary or recessionary gap in the economy. If there is a recessionary gap, government spending and resulting deficits may restore full employment with price stability! If there is an inflationary gap, demand-pull inflation can result from increased consumption, investment, or export expenditures, just as much as from increased government spending. It is possible that a government deficit will increase due to increased government expenditure while other expenditures fall and inflation will not occur. It is all too easy to point the finger at the government and forget the contribution to inflation of all of the sectors of the economy.

2. If the government increases spending and taxes by the same amount, there will be no effect on income. WRONG!

   Income increases by the amount of government spending, even if taxes are increased by the same amount. RIGHT!

   The full impact of the increased government spending turns into income for the people who provide goods and services to the government. Part of the increased taxes, however, comes from people's savings, which had been leakages from the economy. So consumption decreases by less than the loss of taxes. This in turn means that income generated by consumption spending is not cut back by the amount of taxes. Therefore, the economy experiences a smaller cutback in incomes as a result of increased taxes than from stimulus from increased government spending.

■ ANSWERS ■

Key-Term Review

1. equilibrium GNP	7. discretionary fiscal spending	11. inflationary gap
2. recessionary gap	8. multiplier	12. aggregate spending
3. automatic stabilizer	disposable income	13. income transfers
4. fiscal policy	9. marginal propensity to	14. marginal propensity to
5. deficit spending	consume (*MPC*)	save (MPS)
6. budget surplus	10. fiscal year (*FY*)	

True or False

1. F	5. F	9. T	13. T	17. T	21. F
2. T	6. T	10. T	14. T	18. F	22. T
3. F	7. F	11. F	15. T	19. T	23. T
4. T	8. F	12. F	16. T	20. T	24. T

Multiple Choice

1. c	6. d	11. c	16. d	21. d	26. b
2. d	7. d	12. d	17. b	22. a	27. c
3. a	8. b	13. a	18. a	23. b	28. b
4. b	9. b	14. c	19. b	24. a	29. c
5. d	10. a	15. d	20. b	25. b	

Problems and Applications

Exercise 1

1. T

2. **Table 10.1 answer**
   (billions of dollars per year)

Income (Y_D)	Consumption	Investment	Government spending	Aggregate spending
$ 0	$ 50	$50	$ 100	$ 200
200	150	50	100	300
400	250	50	100	400
600	350	50	100	500

3. **Figure 10.1 answer**

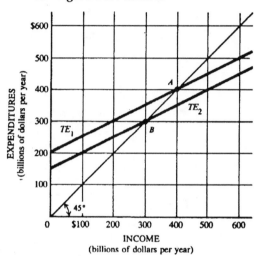

4. $400, at point A, where the aggregate spending curve intersects the 45-degree line
5. $50 (= $500 [45-degree line at $500] – $450 [aggregate spending at $500]) billion per year

6. **Table 10.2 answer**
   (billions of dollars per year)

Income	Aggregate spending
$ 0	$150
200	250
400	350
600	450

7. See Figure 10.1 answer, line TE_2.

8. **Table 10.3 answer**
   (billions of dollars per year)

	Before cut	After cut	Change
Equilibrium income	$400	$300	$100
Recessionary gap	50	100	–50

9. a decrease; rise; excess; deflation
10. T

Exercise 2

1. **Figure 10.2 answer**

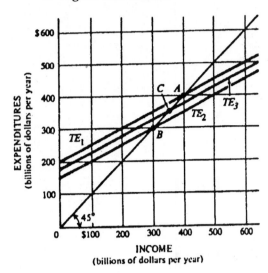

2. $$0.5 = \frac{150 - 50}{200 - 0} = \frac{\text{Change in consumption}}{\text{Change in income}}$$

3. \$25 billion per year = MPC x \$50 billion per year
4. See Figure 10.2 answer, TE_3.
5. F

6. **Table 10.4 answer**
   (billions of dollars per year)

	Before cutback and rebate	After cutback and rebate	Change
Equilibrium income	\$400	\$350	−\$50
Recessionary gap	50	75	25
Government expenditures	100	50	50
Taxes	50	0	− 50
Deficit	50	50	0

7. T
8. T
9. F

Exercise 3

1. a
2. "The Japanese Cabinet . . . today adopted a nearly \$24 billion package of pump-priming measures." Government expenditure is the injection that is being increased.
3. The previous quotation continues: "to prop up its sagging economy." Income is a typical measure of the health of the economy and is likely to increase if the Japanese pump priming succeeds.
4. \$24 billion x 1/(1 − .85) = \$160 billion.

Crossword Puzzle Answer

Across

1. m*ultiplier*
6. full-*employment* budget
7. *budget* surplus
10. marginal propensity to *consume*
12. *fiscal* policy
15. *disposable* income
18. *inflationary* gap
19. *built*-in stabilizer

Down

2. *leakage*
3. *injections*
4. aggregate *spending*
5. fiscal *year*
8. uncontrollable *expenditure*
9. demand-*pull* inflation
11. *equilibrium* GNP
13. *crowding* out
14. *cyclical* unemployment
16. recessionary *gap*
17. full-employment *GNP*

Chapter 11

Money and Banks

Quick Review

Money is clearly very important to the operation of the U.S. economy. The study of money begins with some very basic questions:

- What is money?
- How is money created?
- What role do banks play in the circular flow of income and spending?

Let's begin by examining what money does for us. Money has three functions; it serves as a

1. Medium of exchange, permitting goods and services to be exchanged without the complications of barter

2. Standard of value, permitting the prices of disparate goods and services to be compared

3. Store of value, permitting people to hold it in order to buy goods and services in the future

Money consists of all of those things that are generally acceptable as a medium of exchange. The most often used definition of "money supply" is $M1$, the sum of currency held by the public and balances held in transactions accounts. Other money-supply concepts include "near money," such as savings deposits.

Most of the basic money supply, $M1$, is in the form of transactions deposits, commonly referred to as checking accounts or demand deposits. Most of the checking accounts come into existence when banks perform their lending function. When you borrow from a bank, you receive an increase in your checking account. You have more money, and no other member of the public has less. Thus the money supply expands.

Our banking system is based on the fractional-reserve principle. The Federal Reserve System (the "Fed") requires banks to maintain reserves equal to some fraction of their transactions-deposit liabilities. As a result of this reserve requirement and the fact that banks may lose reserves to other banks via the check-clearing process, a single bank can safely make loans only to the extent of its excess reserves. The banking system, however, can make loans equal to a multiple (1/reserve requirement) of any existing reserves.

Banks and other depository institutions control the money supply by making loans and creating deposits. Banks also hold savings accounts and thus assist in the transfer of purchasing power from savers (those who choose not to spend all of their incomes) to borrowers (those who wish to spend more than their disposable incomes).

The Monetary Control Act of 1980 ended a set of regulations that, one way or the other, discriminated among financial institutions. The changes set in motion by the act (which continue today) have blurred the distinction between commercial banks and other depository institutions.

Learning Objectives

After reading Chapter 11 and doing the following exercises, you should:	True or false	Multiple choice	Problems and applications	Common errors	Pages in the text
1. Know the basic characteristics and functions of money.	1–3	22,23			248–249
2. Know some of the differences between various accounts permitting transfer by check.	5				251–252
3. Know the difference between a transactions account and other accounts.					251
4. Understand that the Monetary Control Act of 1980 caused changes in the way financial institutions conduct their business.		6,20			251
5. Be familiar with the composition and various definitions of the money supply.	4,6,7,9, 11,13,14	4,7, 21	3		251–254
6. Be able to summarize the important differences between banks and other financial institutions.	12	9,19			255
7. Know how banks create money with new loans.	8,10, 24,26	3,10, 11,17	1,2,4	1,2	254–256
8. Know the reason for the reserve requirement.	15,16	1,5,16,17			256–259
9. Know the difference between required and excess reserves.	20,21	3,11–15	1,2		259
10. Be able to work through the steps of deposit creation using balance sheets (T-accounts).	17–19, 21	8,17,18	3	1	260–262
11. Be able to calculate the money multiplier.	22–25	2,8	1,2		262–265

Key-Term Review

Review the following terms; if you are not sure of the meaning of any term, write out the definition and check it against the Glossary in the text.

aggregate spending
bank reserves
barter
demand deposit
deposit creation
excess reserves

money
money multiplier
money supply (M1)
required reserves
reserve ratio
transactions account

Fill in the blank following each of the statements below with the appropriate term from the list above.

1. To exchange goods and services, an economy without a monetary system must use _____.

1. _____

2. When banks make loans, they expand the money supply by balancing loan creation with _____.

2. _____

3. A bank account that permits direct payment to a third party is called a _____.

3. _____

4. The reserves that a bank must have on its books are its _____.

4. _____

5. Something that is generally accepted in exchange for goods and services and that can be used as a standard and store of value is _____.

5. _____

6. The ratio of reserves to deposits is the _____.

6. _____

7. Bank reserves beyond those required by government regulation are known as _____.

7. _____

8. Currency held by the public plus balances in transactions accounts define the _____.

8. _____

9. The inverse of the reserve ratio is sometimes called the _____.

9. _____

10. A checking-account balance is known as a _____.

10. _____

11. _____ are assets held by a bank to fulfill its deposit obligations.

11. _____

12. Changes in the supply of money can be used to influence _____.

12. _____

True or False: *Circle your choice.*

T F 1. Money eliminates the need to exchange goods directly through barter.

T F 2. When you purchase $5 worth of gasoline, money is serving as a medium of exchange.

T F 3. In times of rising prices, money serves well the function of a store of value.

T F 4. Coins and cash are clearly money, but checking accounts are not.

T F 5. The terms "demand deposit" and "checking account" mean the same thing.

T F 6. To determine $M1$ you add up the dollar value of all the coin, currency, and demand deposits in existence.

T F 7. Transactions accounts permit direct payment to third parties.

T F 8. When you get a loan at a bank, the bank creates money.

T F 9. Currency and coin are the largest components of $M1$.

T F 10. Banks transfer money from savers to spenders by lending funds held on deposit.

T F 11. Time deposits at commercial banks are part of $M1$.

T F 12. A commercial bank is one that accepts deposits only from commercial establishments.

T F 13. When you withdraw money from your checking account, the money supply gets smaller.

T F 14. When you deposit $100 worth of coins in your checking account, $M1$ gets larger.

T F 15. A bank's reserve ratio is the value of its required reserves divided by its transactions deposits.

T F 16. The minimum-reserve ratio is established by the Federal Reserve System.

T F 17. The higher the legal minimum-reserve ratio, the greater the lending power of the banks.

T F 18. To calculate required reserves, multiply the minimum-reserve ratio by the amount of transactions deposits on the bank's balance sheet.

T F 19. If the minimum-reserve ratio is 20 percent, then $1 of reserves can support $5 in transactions deposits.

T F 20. Excess reserves are reserves over and above those that are legally required.

T F 21. Total reserves minus required reserves equal excess reserves.

T F 22. If the required-reserve ratio is 20 percent, the money multiplier is 20.

T F 23. If the required-reserve ratio is 25 percent, the money multiplier is 4.

T F 24. Each bank in a multibank system is free to expand its loans by an amount equal to the money multiplier times its excess reserves.

T F 25. The amount any bank in a multibank system can lend is equal to its excess reserves.

T F 26. Increases in the money supply occur with net borrowing.

Multiple Choice: *Select the correct answer.*

_____ 1. Which of the following sets the legal minimum-reserve ratio?
   (a) The commercial banks.
   (b) The U.S. Treasury.
   (c) The Federal Reserve System.
   (d) None of the above.

_____ 2. If the minimum-reserve ratio is 25 percent, the money multiplier is:
   (a) 25.
   (b) 5.
   (c) 4.
   (c) None of the above.

_____ 3. Which of the following is the correct way to calculate excess reserves?
   (a) Total reserves minus required reserves.
   (b) The minimum-reserve requirement times transactions deposits.
   (c) Both a and b.
   (d) None of the above.

_____ 4. *M*1 refers to:
   (a) The money-supply concept.
   (b) Currency held by the public plus transactions accounts balances.
   (c) The smallest of the money-supply aggregates watched by the Fed.
   (d) All of the above.

_____ 5. The purpose of the legal minimum-reserve requirement is:
   (a) To provide safety to depositors.
   (b) To provide control of the money supply by the Fed.
   (c) To prevent bankers from calling in loans.
   (d) None of the above.

_____ 6. The Monetary Control Act of 1980:
   (a) Created greater competition among various financial institutions.
   (b) Allowed more institutions to offer "checking account" services.
   (c) Allowed thrift institutions (e.g., savings and loan associations) and banks to pay interest on checking accounts.
   (d) Did all of the above.

_____ 7. Which of the following is the *largest* monetary aggregate?
   (a) Coin.
   (b) Currency.
   (c) Checking accounts.
   (d) NOW accounts.

_____ 8. When you pay off a loan at the bank:
   (a) The money supply becomes smaller.
   (b) The money supply becomes larger.
   (c) There is no change in the money supply.
   (d) The amount of transactions deposits gets larger.

_____ 9. Which of the following is *not* an essential function of a "bank"?
   (a) It must accept deposits.
   (b) It must offer certificates of deposit to be included in $M2$.
   (c) It must offer check-writing privileges.
   (d) It must make loans.

_____ 10. Which of the following categories of financial institutions "creates" the most money?
   (a) Commercial banks.
   (b) Savings and loan associations.
   (c) Mutual savings banks.
   (d) Credit unions.

_____ 11. Suppose a bank has no excess reserves when someone deposits $100. The bank will then:
   (a) Be able to lend $100.
   (b) Be able to lend $80.
   (c) Not be able to lend anything.
   (d) Be able to lend an amount equal to $100 minus required reserves.

_____ 12. If none of the banks in the banking system have any excess reserves before the Fed lowers the minimum legal reserve ratio from 16 percent to 12 percent:
   (a) The banks will then be able to make loans.
   (b) Excess reserves will then exist.
   (c) The Fed is engaging in an expansionary policy.
   (d) All of the above are the case.

_____ 13. Suppose the total amount of transactions deposits on the books of all of the banks in the system is $1 million and that the minimum-reserve ratio is 0.10. The amount of required reserves is then:
   (a) $100,000.
   (b) $10,000.
   (c) $1,000,000.
   (d) None of the above.

_____ 14. Suppose that conditions remain as in Question 13 and the minimum-reserve requirement is raised to 20 percent. In order to meet the new requirement the banks in the system will need an *additional:*
   (a) $100,000 of reserves.
   (b) $10,000 of reserves.
   (c) $200,000 of reserves.
   (d) $15,000 of reserves.

_____ 15. If the banking system described in Question 13 (the reserve requirement is 0.10) has no excess reserves and you deposit $100 in cash:
   (a) Your bank can lend $90.
   (b) Your bank can lend $10.
   (c) Your bank can lend $900.
   (d) Your bank can lend none of the above.

_____ 16. Given the situation in Question 15, all of the banks in the banking system could expand loans by:
   (a) $1,000.
   (b) $900.
   (c) $100.
   (d) $10.

_____17. If the banks lend the maximum legal amount in Questions 15 and 16, the total maximum expansion in the money supply is:
(a) $1,000.
(b) $100.
(c) $900.
(d) None of the above.

_____18. When the minimum-reserve ratio is 10 percent, the money multiplier is:
(a) 10.
(b) 1.
(c) 0.01.
(d) None of the above.

_____19. Which of the following is a source of profits for banks?
(a) Securities.
(b) Reserves.
(c) Cash in the vault.
(d) All of the above.

_____20. The Monetary Control Act of 1980:
(a) Created sharper distinctions among various financial institutions.
(b) Eliminated many forms of competition among financial institutions.
(c) Required banks to pay interest on checking accounts.
(d) Did none of the above.

_____21. The alternative measures of the money supply are all intended to reflect:
(a) Variations in liquidity and accessibility of assets.
(b) Whether deposits are domestic or international.
(c) How often depositors use their accounts.
(d) All of the above.

_____22. In Poland many consumers prefer to use cigarettes rather than money as:
(a) A medium of exchange.
(b) A standard of value.
(c) A store of value.
(d) All of the above.

_____23. For the Polish people, using cigarettes rather than zlotys allows them to:
(a) Avoid long lines in stores.
(b) Buy the items they wish from others who prefer to have cigarettes rather than goods.
(c) Maintain wealth in a form not subject to change by the government.
(d) All of the above.

Problems and Applications

Exercise 1

Use the information from the T-account in Table 11.1 to answer Problems 1–10.

Table 11.1
Bank of Arlington

Assets		Liabilities	
Loans	$1,000,000	Transaction deposits	$1,000,000
Securities	200,000		
Member bank reserves	200,000		
Other assets	100,000		
		Ownership claims	500,000
Total	$1,500,000	Total	$1,500,000

1. Suppose that the Bank of Arlington is just meeting its reserve requirement. The reserve requirement must be _____.

2. To be in a position to make loans, the Bank of Arlington must acquire some (required reserves/excess reserves).

3. If we assume that the reserve ratio is changed to 10 percent, the Bank of Arlington would have required reserves of _____ and excess reserves of _____.

4. With a 10 percent reserve ratio the Bank of Arlington is in a position to make new loans totaling _____.

5. Suppose the Bank of Arlington makes a loan of $100,000. The $100,000 is then spent so that it does not return to the Bank of Arlington but goes instead to the Bank of Cambridge. After this transaction, transactions deposits of the Bank of Arlington will be _____; its total reserves will be _____; its excess reserves will be _____; its required reserves will be _____.

6. The Bank of Cambridge had zero excess reserves before receiving the $100,000 deposits. Because of the 10 percent reserve requirement, the required reserves for the bank rise by _____.

7. Excess reserves for the Bank of Cambridge after the $100,000 deposit are _____.

8. If it makes the full amount of loans possible under the reserve requirement, the Bank of Cambridge will cause $M1$ to increase by _____.

9. Altogether the Bank of Arlington and the Bank of Cambridge made loans and created deposits of _____.

10. If this process were to continue to the maximum, the amount of loans made on the basis of the $100,000 initial excess reserves of the Bank of Arlington would be _____, and the amount of deposits created would be _____.

Exercise 2

This exercise is very much like Table 11.4 in the text (p. 264), but the reserve requirement has been changed. Assume Bank A, below, is a monopoly bank.

1. Complete Table 11.2 on the basis of the following:
   - $100 in cash is deposited in Bank A. (Assume cash is counted as reserves.)
   - The reserve requirement is 0.10.
   - The bank begins with zero excess reserves.

Table 11.2
Transactions-deposit creation

	Change in transactions deposits	Change in total reserves	Change in required reserves	Change in excess reserves	Change in lending capacity
...ish is deposited in ...ien Bank A acquires	$_____	$_____	$_____	$_____	$_____
...e and deposited in ...nen Bank B acquires	_____	_____	_____	_____	_____
...e and deposited in ...hen Bank C acquires	_____	_____	_____	_____	_____
...le and deposited else- ...nen Bank D acquires	_____	_____	_____	_____	_____
...de and deposited else- ...hen Bank E acquires	_____	_____	_____	_____	_____
...ide and deposited else- ...then Bank F acquires	_____	_____	_____	_____	_____
...ade and deposited else- ...then Bank G acquires	_____	_____	_____	_____	_____
...ocess continues indefi- ...changes will total	_____	_____	_____	_____	_____

2. The money multiplier in Table 11.3 in the text was 5 and the money multiplier in this exercise is _____.

3. Suppose that the initial transaction had been a withdrawal of $100 in cash (reserves) and the banking system had been all loaned up (had no excess reserves). As a result of the initial withdrawal, _____ of reserves would have been lost. Required reserves would have been reduced by _____ and the banking system would be deficient by _____. Assuming no other way to get reserves, the banking system would have to call in loans of _____.

Exercise 3

The following exercise shows how to use supply and demand curves to analyze money-market outcomes. You will observe the connection between the supply of money, the demand for money, and interest rates. You may postpone this exercise until you have read Chapter 13.

For each of the following eight statements decide what shift would occur in the money market. Choose the letter of the diagram in Figure 11.1 that matches the shift. Then indicate with an arrow whether the equilibrium interest rate and equilibrium quantity of money should rise (↑) or fall (↓) as a result of the shift you identified.

Figure 11.1   Money market

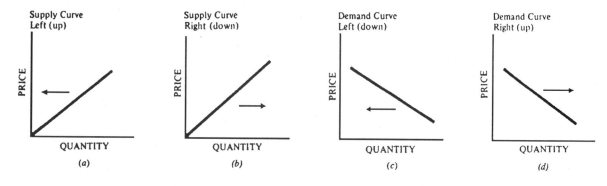

(a) Supply Curve Left (up)   (b) Supply Curve Right (down)   (c) Demand Curve Left (down)   (d) Demand Curve Right (up)

149

Keep in mind that the demand for money changes as people receive larger incomes, as the velocity of money changes, and as the inflation rate changes. The supply of money is determined by the actions of the Federal Reserve System, the willingness of the financial system to make loans, and individual perceptions of the future course of the economy. Also, the interest rate can be considered the price of money. It shows the additional payment required in the future when one borrows in the present.

	SHIFT	EQUILIBRIUM INTEREST RATE	EQUILIBRIUM QUANTITY OF MONEY

1. Economists have discussed and have tried to verify the existence of a "political business cycle" in which the Federal Reserve tries to prevent excessive unemployment in an election year. What is the effect of such actions by the Fed?

2. In the 1972 election year such an expansion of the money supply did occur, and it contributed to a very high rate of inflation. What should the Fed chairman have done to curb the inflation rate?

3. In 1974, OPEC raised the price of oil precipitously. A recession occurred in the United States.

4. The dollar declined in value relative to other currencies. Foreigners were worried about holding dollars because of the high U.S. inflation rate and tried to obtain West German marks, gold, and so on, to hold as substitutes for the dollar.

5. During the 1974–75 recession, the U.S. banking system was shocked as foreign debts became difficult to collect, real estate investments went bad, and the oil market collapsed. Fear of further collapses made bankers less willing to lend.

6. The new chairman of the Federal Reserve Board of Governors applied a "credit crunch" to the economy to prevent unnecessary borrowing and to slow down the double-digit rate of inflation.

7. The economy entered a recession in 1980.

8. The Reagan administration found itself running huge deficits that had to be financed with additional money.

Exercise 4

The media often feature articles about changes in government policies that affect the money supply or about events that change the demand for money. By using one of the articles in the text, this exercise will show the kind of information to look for. If your professor makes a newspaper assignment for this chapter, this exercise will provide an example of how to do it.

Read the article in Chapter 13 entitled "Money Is Free" from the *Wall Street Journal*. Then answer the following questions:

1. Which of the four diagrams in Figure 11.1 (p. 149) best represents what the author wants the Fed to do?
   a   b   c   d   (circle one)

2. What passage (no more than a sentence) specifically indicates what the author suggests should be done to the money supply?

3. What passage indicates the determinant of the recommended change in money supply or demand?

4. What single sentence indicates the change in interest rates or quantity of money that results from the shift of supply or demand?

Common Errors

The first statement in each "common error" below is incorrect. Each incorrect statement is followed by a corrected version and an explanation.

1. Banks can't create money. WRONG!

   Banks can and do create money. RIGHT!

   It should be obvious by now that banks and other depository institutions are very important participants in the money-supply process. They create money by granting loans to borrowers and accomplish their role by adding to their customers' transactions accounts. The accounts are money just as much as the printed money in your wallet is money. The banks create (supply) money, but only in response to borrowers' demands for it. Without customers "demanding" loans, banks wouldn't be able to create money at all.

2. Banks hold your deposits in their vaults. WRONG!

   Banks don't hold your deposits in their vaults. (And neither do other depository institutions.) RIGHT!

   You can look at this two ways. First, when you deposit your paycheck there's nothing for the bank to "hold" in its vault, except the check, and that is returned to the person who wrote it. Second, if you deposited coin or cash, it's all put together and you can't distinguish any one person's deposit from any other person's deposit. Even then, when "cash in vault" becomes too large, much of it is shipped away by armored truck to the Federal Reserve Bank. (This is described in Chapter 12.) Thus, banks don't hold your deposits in their vaults.

■ ANSWERS ■

Key-Term Review

1. barter
2. deposit creation
3. transactions account
4. required reserves
5. money
6. reserve ratio
7. excess reserves
8. money supply (*M*1)
9. money multiplier
10. demand deposit
11. bank reserves
12. aggregate spending

True or False

1. T	6. F	11. F	15. F	19. T	23. T
2. T	7. T	12. F	16. T	20. T	24. F
3. F	8. T	13. F	17. F	21. T	25. T
4. F	9. F	14. F	18. T	22. F	26. T
5. T	10. T				

Multiple Choice

1. c	5. b	9. b	13. a	17. c	21. a
2. c	6. d	10. a	14. a	18. a	22. d
3. a	7. c	11. d	15. a	19. a	23. d
4. d	8. a	12. d	16. b	20. d	

Problems and Applications

Exercise 1

1. 0.20
2. excess reserves
3. $100,000; $100,000
4. $100,000
5. $1,000,000; $100,000; 0; $100,000
6. $10,000
7. $90,000
8. $90,000
9. $190,000
10. $1,000,000; $1,000,000

Exercise 2

1.

Table 11.2 answer

	Change in transactions deposits	Change in total reserves	Change in required reserves	Change in excess reserves	Change in lending capacity
If $100 in cash is deposited in Bank A, then Bank A acquires	$ 100.00	$100.00	$ 10.00	$ 90.00	$ 90.00
If loan made and deposited in Bank B, then Bank B acquires	90.00	90.00	9.00	81.00	81.00
If loan made and deposited in Bank C, then Bank C acquires	81.00	81.00	8.10	72.90	72.90
If loan made and deposited elsewhere, then Bank D acquires	72.90	72.90	7.29	65.61	65.61
If loan made and deposited elsewhere, then Bank E acquires	65.61	65.61	6.56	59.05	59.05
If loan made and deposited elsewhere, then Bank F acquires	59.05	59.05	5.91	53.15	53.15
If loan made and deposited elsewhere, then Bank G acquires	53.15	53.15	5.32	47.84	47.84
And if process continues indefinitely, changes will total	1,000.00		100.00		900.00

2. 10
3. $100; $10; $90; $900

Exercise 3

	TYPE OF SHIFT (by Figure 11.1 diagram letter)	INTEREST RATE	MONEY
1.	b	↓	↑
2.	a	↑	↓
3.	c	↓	↓
4.	c	↓	↓
5.	a	↑	↓
6.	a	↑	↓
7.	c	↓	↓
8.	b	↓	↑

Exercise 4

1. a Tighten the money supply.
2. The last sentence beginning "The longer the Fed delays in starting to curb money growth . . . ." suggests the author's opinion of what should be done.
3. This passage is indicative: "In particular, the observation ought to be of interest to the Federal Reserve's Open Market Committee, which meets today to set money growth targets . . . ." The *determinant* is the Federal Reserve System in its role of specifying the supply of money targets and therefore its purchases or sales of bonds.
4. "That is why interest rates will not go down, nor the dollar recover meaningfully, until inflation is reduced." By tightening the money supply, the Fed should reduce inflation, which would eventually allow the interest rate to fall. The author implicitly assumes the reader understands these relationships.

Chapter 12
The Federal Reserve System

Quick Review

In the preceding chapter we saw how money was created, and we got some hints that money must be controlled. In this chapter we examine these questions:

- How does government control the amount of money in the economy?
- Which government agency is responsible for exercising this control?
- How are banks and bond markets affected by the government's policies?

The answer to all of these questions begins with the Federal Reserve System. The Federal Reserve System is the central bank of the United States. All banks are subject to the reserve requirements imposed by it.

The Federal Reserve System has three basic tools with which to control the money supply: open-market operations, changes in the reserve requirement, and changes in the discount rate. Open-market operations, implemented by the Open Market Committee, are the most important. To increase the size of the money supply, the Open Market Committee orders the purchase of government securities (bonds) in the open market. These purchases increase bank reserves and lending potential and may have the additional effect of raising bond prices (lowering yields).

The Fed could accomplish the same objective, although with less certainty, by lowering the discount rate. A lower discount rate encourages member banks to borrow reserves and acquire lending potential. The Fed could also modify reserve requirements. Reserve requirements, however, are not changed often or by large amounts. When the reserve requirement is raised, excess reserves are transformed into required reserves; when the reserve requirement is lowered, required reserves are transformed into excess reserves. In addition, there is an inverse relationship between the size of the reserve requirement and the size of the money multiplier.

The Fed effectively controls the money supply. Its policy actions can have a significant impact on the level of economic activity.

The Monetary Control Act of 1980 had two objectives:

1. To foster competition among financial institutions.

2. To provide the Fed with tighter controls on the nation's money supply.

Among other things, the act provides for a phase-out of interest-rate ceilings, allows many depository institutions to offer accounts that are transferable by check, and allows the payment of interest on checking accounts.

Learning Objectives

After reading Chapter 12 and doing the following exercises, you should:	True or false	Multiple choice	Problems and applications	Common errors	Pages in the text
1. Be familiar with the organization, structure, and purpose of the Federal Reserve System.	1,3,4, 17,19,21	2,9, 10,24		1	269–272
2. Know how the reserve requirement can be changed to achieve a money-supply objective.	6,7,8,11, 16–18	3–7, 11,13	1	1	272, 283–284
3. Know several deposit insurance funds.		25			274
4. Know how the discount rate can be changed to achieve a given policy objective.	2,5,6, 8,9	15	3		275–277
5. Know the meaning of "federal funds" and the "federal funds rate."	10	8,14, 19,20			276
6. Know how the Open Market Committee can achieve a given policy objective by buying or selling securities.	12–14	20	2	2	278–283
7. Understand how the Fed's activities in the bond market alter portfolio decisions of bond sellers and buyers.	15	12	6		279–282
8. Understand the distinction between the interest rate on a bond and the yield from a bond.	15	1,16,18			280–281
9. Be able to demonstrate the inverse relationship between interest rates and bond prices.			4–6	3	280–281
10. Know several "interest rates."		17,19			278
11. Know what the money multiplier is and how it is used.			1	2	273
12. Know the major provisions of the Monetary Control Act of 1980.	4,16, 18,20	21–23			285–288

Key-Term Review

Review the following terms; if you are not sure of the meaning of any term, write out the definition and check it against the Glossary in the text.

bond
discount rate
discounting
excess reserves
monetary policy
money multiplier

money supply ($M1$)
open-market operations
portfolio decision
required reserves
yield

Fill in the blank following each of the statements below with the appropriate term from the list above.

1. When a member bank borrows from the Federal Reserve bank in its district, it is engaged in _____.

1. _____

2. When the Federal Reserve System engages in open-market operations, it must do so by inducing banks and individuals to make the appropriate _____.

2. _____

3. Those reserves a bank holds over and above what are required are called _____.

3. _____

4. The rate of interest that the Fed charges on loans to member banks is called the _____.

4. _____

5. When the Fed buys or sells government securities, the policy tool it uses is called _____.

5. _____

6. A certificate acknowledging the existence of a debt and the amount of interest to be paid each year until the agreed date of repayment is called a _____.

6. _____

7. The Open Market Committee attempts to elicit the appropriate portfolio responses from banks and members of the public by altering the bond _____.

7. _____

8. Those reserves that a bank must hold against its demand liabilities are referred to as _____.

8. _____

9. The inverse of the required-reserve ratio is the _____.

9. _____

10. The discount rate, reserve requirements, and open-market operations are all instruments of _____.

10. _____

11. The main function of the Federal Reserve System is to control the _____.

11. _____

True or False: *Circle your choice.*

T F 1. The Federal Reserve System consists of one central bank and eleven branches.

T F 2. When commercial banks borrow from a Federal Reserve bank, the process is called "discounting."

T F 3. The Federal Reserve banks hold deposits of banks and other business firms.

T F 4. All depository institutions are required to be members of the Federal Reserve System.

T F 5. The most powerful monetary policy tool available to the Fed is the power to change the discount rate.

T F 6. If the Fed wishes to create the conditions under which the money supply can be increased, it can reduce the reserve requirement.

T F 7. When the reserve requirement is increased, excess reserves are reduced.

T F 8. The Fed changes the reserve requirement very frequently.

T F 9. The discount rate is the rate of interest charged by banks that lend in the federal funds market.

T F 10. The federal funds rate is announced by the Federal Reserve Board just like the discount rate.

T F 11. Banks that are short of reserves can acquire reserves by selling securities.

T F 12. The buying and selling of federal government securities by the Fed is known as "open-market operations."

T F 13. To increase the lending capacity of banks, the Fed buys securities.

T F 14. The Fed's activities in the bond market influence bankers' portfolio decisions.

T F 15. The value of a bond is found by dividing the face amount of the bond by the current market rate of interest.

T F 16. All U.S. banks are subject to reserve requirements established by the Fed.

T F 17. The size of the reserve requirement is positively related to the dollar volume of the transactions accounts on a bank's balance sheet.

T F 18. Federal Reserve System requirements are structured so as to give a competitive advantage to smaller banks.

T F 19. The phrase "the interest rate" refers to an average of several interest rates.

T F 20. The United States returned to the gold standard with the passage of the Monetary Control Act of 1980.

T F 21. Paul Volcker is the chairman of the Federal Reserve Board of Governors.

Multiple Choice: *Select the correct answer.*

_____ 1. Suppose a one-year bond has a face value of $1,000 and the current market rate of interest is 5 percent. The price of that bond is:
   (a) ($1,000) (0.05).
   (b) ($1,000) (1.05).
   (c) $1,000/0.05.
   (d) None of the above.

_____ 2. Which of the following is *not* one of the tools of monetary policy used by the Fed?
   (a) Expulsion from Fed membership.
   (b) Changing the reserve requirement.
   (c) Changing the discount rate.
   (d) Performing open-market operations.

_____ 3. Suppose the banking system has $1 million of reserves when the reserve requirement is 0.20. What is the volume of demand deposits in the system if there are no excess reserves to begin with?
   (a) $200,000.
   (b) $500,000.
   (c) $5,000,000.
   (d) $2,000,000.

_____ 4. Suppose the Fed raised the reserve requirement to 0.25 in Question 3. Then the banks in the system would be deficient in reserves by:
   (a) $2,500,000.
   (b) $1,250,000.
   (c) $250,000.
   (d) $1,000,000.

_____ 5. Suppose the banking system is in the condition described in Question 3, and the Fed lowers the reserve requirement to 0.15. Then the banking system has:
   (a) Excess reserves of $250,000.
   (b) Required reserves of $750,000.
   (c) The potential to create $250,000 x $\frac{1}{0.15}$ dollars of loans.
   (d) All of the above.

_____ 6. In Question 5, the money multiplier is:
   (a) 1 ÷ 0.15.
   (b) 0.15 ÷ 1.
   (c) (1) (0.15)
   (d) None of the above.

_____ 7. When the Fed wishes to increase the excess reserves of the member banks, it:
  (a) Sells securities.
  (b) Buys securities.
  (c) Raises the discount rate.
  (d) Raises the reserve requirement.

_____ 8. Federal funds are:
  (a) Tax revenues collected by the Fed.
  (b) Bank deposits held in Federal Reserve banks.
  (c) The source of funds for revenue sharing.
  (d) Reserves loaned by one bank to another.

_____ 9. Which of the following are services performed by the Federal Reserve banks?
  (a) Clearing checks between commercial banks.
  (b) Holding reserves of commercial banks.
  (c) Providing currency to commercial banks.
  (d) All of the above.

_____ 10. Bank reserves can take the form of which of the following?
  (a) Deposits at the district Federal Reserve bank.
  (b) Cash in the bank's own vault.
  (c) Deposits held at other commercial banks.
  (d) a and b.

_____ 11. The Federal Reserve System can provide reserves to the banking system by all of the following except:
  (a) Buying securities in the open market.
  (b) Lending to member banks.
  (c) Lending federal funds to member banks.
  (d) Reducing the reserve requirements.

_____ 12. Which of the following is included in the M1 definition of the money supply?
  (a) Coins owned by the public.
  (b) Currency owned by the public.
  (c) Demand-deposit balances owned by the public.
  (d) All of the above.

_____ 13. The reserve requirements imposed by the Fed:
  (a) Are the same for all member banks.
  (b) Vary with the size of the bank's capital account.
  (c) Vary with the value of the bank's transactions-account liabilities.
  (d) Vary from as low as 2 percent to as high as 25 percent.

_____ 14. If a bank in New York borrows federal funds from a bank in San Francisco:
  (a) Lending potential goes up in New York.
  (b) Lending potential goes down in San Francisco.
  (c) Lending potential for the banking system does not change.
  (d) All of the above.

_____ 15. When the Fed raises the discount rate, this action:
  (a) Raises the cost of borrowing reserves to member banks.
  (b) Is a signal that the Fed is moving toward a slower growth rate for the money supply.
  (c) Is a signal that interest rates may rise generally.
  (d) Does all of the above.

_____ 16. Suppose you buy a bond issued by General Motors. Which of the following best describes your financial situation?
  (a) General Motors will have to redeem the bond at maturity for an amount stated on the face of the bond.
  (b) General Motors owes you an amount equal to the market value of the bond.
  (c) General Motors owes you an amount equal to the interest on the bond.
  (d) You own part of General Motors.

_____17. Which of the following would you expect to be able to borrow at the prime rate?
    (a) A textile company on the verge of bankruptcy.
    (b) IBM.
    (c) The typical college professor.
    (d) The City of New York.

_____18. Eurodollars are:
    (a) Typically dollars spent by U.S. residents traveling in Europe.
    (b) Dollar deposits on the books of European financial institutions.
    (c) Dollars owed by European borrowers to U.S. lending institutions.
    (d) Dollars borrowed by U.S. firms to make investments in European financial institutions.

_____19. The federal funds market is a market in which:
    (a) Overnight loans are popular.
    (b) Government securities are bought and sold.
    (c) Loans tend to be for $1 million or less.
    (d) There are no transactions costs.

_____20. When the Fed wishes to slow the rate of consumer and investor spending, it will most likely:
    (a) Reduce the absolute supply of money.
    (b) Reduce the "rate of growth" in the money supply.
    (c) Increase the reserve requirement.
    (d) Do none of the above.

_____21. The basic reason Congress passed the Monetary Control Act of 1980 was that:
    (a) Banks demanded authority to pay interest on checking accounts.
    (b) Credit unions demanded to be subject to Federal Reserve regulation.
    (c) Savings and loan associations paid rates of interest that gave them a competitive advantage over mutual funds.
    (d) The Fed's ability to control the money supply had diminished.

_____22. Which of the following are subject to regulation by the Fed?
    (a) All commercial banks.
    (b) Savings and loan associations.
    (c) Savings banks.
    (d) All of the above.

_____23. As a result of loopholes in the Monetary Control Act of 1980:
    (a) "Nonbanks" developed that accept deposits and make only commercial loans.
    (b) "Nonbanks" developed that make both consumer loans and commercial loans but do not accept deposits.
    (c) "Nonbanks" developed that behave like other depository institutions but offer a much wider variety of services.
    (d) None of the above developed.

_____24. Alan Greenspan was appointed by President Reagan to serve:
    (a) A fourteen-year term on the Federal Reserve Board of Governors.
    (b) A fourteen-year term as chairman of the Federal Reserve Board of Governors.
    (c) A fourteen-year term as a member, and a four-year term as chairman, of the Federal Reserve Board of Governors.
    (d) As the Comptroller of the Currency to supervise federally chartered banks.

Problems and Applications

The first three exercises demonstrate how monetary policy might work in a hypothetical situation.

Exercise 1

This exercise is similar to the problem at the end of Chapter 12 in the text, which shows how to understand the accounts for the entire banking system. The focus of this exercise is the reserve requirement.

Suppose the Fed wishes to expand M1. Carefully read the assumptions below and then work through the exercise step by step to achieve the policy objective. Assume:

- The banks in the system have initially $240 million of transactions-deposit liabilities.
- The banking system has initially no excess reserves.
- The initial reserve requirement is 0.25.
- The banks make loans in the full amount of any excess reserves that they acquire.
- No cash is drained out of the system.

The combined balance sheet of the banks in the system is as shown in Table 12.1.

Table 12.1
Balance sheet of banking system
when reserve requirement is 0.25
(millions of dollars)

Total reserves	$ 60	Transactions accounts	$240
Required, $60			
Excess, $0			
Securities	80		
Loans	100		
Total	$240	Total	$240

1. Suppose the Fed lowers the reserve requirement to 0.20. How much excess reserves does this create? $_____.

2. How large are required reserves now? $_____.

3. How large are total reserves? $_____.

4. What is the additional lending capacity of the banking system due to the change in the reserve requirement from 0.25 to 0.20? $_____.

5. If the banks fully utilize their new lending capacity, reconstruct the balance sheet in Table 12.2 to show the new totals for the accounts affected in the total banking system.

Table 12.2
Balance sheet of banking system
when reserve requirement is 0.20
(millions of dollars)

Total reserves	$_____	Transactions accounts $_____	
Required, _____			
Excess, _____			
Securities	_____		
Loans	_____		
Total	$_____	Total	$_____

6. So far the money supply (M1) has expanded by $_____.

7. Total reserves have gone up by $_____.

8. Loans have gone up by $_____.

Exercise 2

Like the problem at the end of Chapter 12 in the text, this exercise shows how the money supply can be changed. The focus of this exercise is open-market policy.

Suppose the Fed wants to expand the money supply using open-market operations and it is faced with the balance sheet of the banking system as shown in Table 12.3. Suppose further that:

- The banking system initially has no excess reserves.
- The reserve requirement is 0.20.
- The banks make loans in the full amount of any excess reserves that they acquire.
- No cash is drained out of the system.

Table 12.3
Balance sheet of banking system
(millions of dollars)

Total reserves	$ 60	Transactions accounts	$300
Required, $60			
Excess, $0			
Securities	80		
Loans	160		
Total	$300	Total	$300

1. Suppose the Open Market Committee buys $10 million of securities from the commercial banking system. In Table 12.4 show the changes and new totals for the various accounts on the balance sheet of the commercial banks after this transaction but before any new loans are made or called in.

Table 12.4
Balance sheet of commercial banking system
after OMC buys $10 million of securities
(millions of dollars)

Total reserves	$_____	Transactions accounts $_____	
Required, _____			
Excess, _____			
Securities	_____		
Loans	_____		
Total	$_____	Total	$_____

2. Suppose the banking system now expands its loans and transactions accounts by the maximum amount it can on the basis of its $_____ in excess reserves.

3. In Table 12.5 complete the balance sheet for the banking system showing the new totals for all of the accounts after loans have been made. (*Remember:* The reserve ratio is 0.20.)

Table 12.5
Balance sheet of banking system
after expansion of loans and deposits
(millions of dollars)

Total reserves	$_____	Transactions accounts	$_____
Required, _____			
Excess, _____			
Securities	_____		
Loans	_____		
Total	$_____	Total	$_____

4. As a result of the open-market operations, the money supply has expanded by a total of $_____.

5. Total reserves have gone up by $_____.

6. Loans have increased by $_____.

Exercise 3

This exercise demonstrates what might happen when the Fed lowers the discount rate.

Suppose the Fed wants to expand the money supply by changing the discount rate. It is faced with the balance sheet of the banking system as shown in Table 12.6. Carefully read the assumptions below and then work through the exercise step by step to achieve the policy objective. Assume that:

- The banking system initially has no excess reserves.
- The initial reserve requirement is 0.20.
- The banks in the system respond to each percentage point drop in the discount rate by borrowing $2 million from the Fed.
- The banks make loans in the full amount of any excess reserves that they acquire.
- No cash is drained out of the system.

Table 12.6
Balance sheet of banking system
(millions of dollars)

Total reserves	$ 70	Transactions accounts	$350
Required, $70			
Excess, $0			
Securities	70		
Loans	210		
Total	$350	Total	$350

1. Suppose that the Fed now lowers the discount rate by one percentage point and that the banking system responds as indicated in the third assumption above. As a result of this policy initiative, the banks in the system will now borrow $_____ from the Fed, all of which is (excess/required) reserves. On the basis of this lending potential, the banks together can expand their loans by $_____.

2. In Table 12.7 assume the banks have made the additional loans. Complete the balance sheet to show the final effect of the change in the discount rate.

Table 12.7
Final balance sheet of banking system
(millions of dollars)

Total reserves	$_____	Transactions accounts $_____	
Required, _____			
Excess, _____			
Securities	_____	Discounts payable	
Loans	_____	to Fed	_____
Total	$_____	Total	$_____

3. The effect of lowering the discount rate is an increase in the money supply of $_____.

Exercise 4

It is very important that the inverse relationship between bond prices and bond yields be understood. The following problems will help you to nail down this important concept.

1. Suppose that today you purchased from AT&T a $1,000 bond that would mature in one year bearing interest at 8 percent. In one year AT&T would pay you $_____ for return of principal and $_____ of interest for letting them use your purchasing power. The yield on the bond is _____ percent.

2. Suppose that a company called Similar Firm was offering $1,000 bonds paying 10 percent interest. If you bought a bond from Similar Firm, at the end of one year you would receive $_____ for return of principal and $_____ in interest, and the yield would be _____ percent.

3. All other things being equal, which bond would be the best buy? _____

4. In order to earn a yield of 10 percent, how much would the price of the AT&T bond have to fall? (*Hint:* The formula for finding the new bond price is:

$$\frac{(principal + interest)}{new\ price\ of\ bond} = (1 + bond\ yield)$$

When the bond was first issued, we know, the principal was $1,000 and interest was $80. To be competitive with Similar Firm, the price must fall enough to give a yield of 10 percent. It remains only to find the new price of the bond.) Answer: _____

5. T F Although the interest rate on the AT&T bond is 8 percent, its price will fall enough to raise the yield to 10 percent.

6. As the price of the AT&T bond goes down, the yield goes (down/up), even though the face value and interest rate do not change.

(The message here is clear. Bond prices and bond yields move in opposite directions. When interest rates on new bonds have risen, you won't be able to sell old bonds for what you paid for them. But there is a lower price that will make them just as good a buy as the new bonds.)

Exercise 5

The following exercise shows how to use supply and demand curves to analyze what happens in the bond market. It also demonstrates how the bond market is related to deficits, debt, and the interest rate.

In each of the circumstances discussed below, analyze the impact and decide what would happen in the market for bonds. Match the letter of the appropriate diagram in Figure 12.1 with each of the shifts in the supply and demand for bonds listed below.

Remember that the demand for bonds will increase as people receive larger incomes, desire greater wealth, or try to increase their savings. The supply of bonds is determined by government or private firms as they attempt to increase or decrease their debts.

Figure 12.1   Shifts of curves

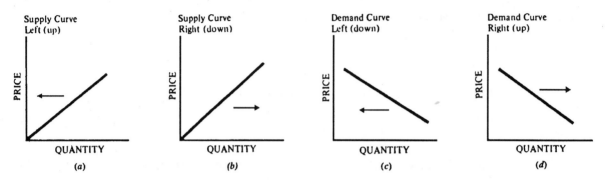

Supply Curve Left (up)	Supply Curve Right (down)	Demand Curve Left (down)	Demand Curve Right (up)
(a)	*(b)*	*(c)*	*(d)*

In each circumstance described below, indicate with an arrow whether the equilibrium price of bonds in the United States will rise (↑) or fall (↓). Do the same for interest rates and the equilibrium quantity of bonds. Interest rates move in the opposite direction to bond prices. To learn why, see Exercise 4 of this chapter.

	SHIFT	BOND PRICES	INTEREST RATES	NO. OF BONDS
1. The Reagan administration is running large federal deficits that must be financed with new debt.				
2. Foreigners view the United States as a safe haven to park their unused cash. There is a sudden shift in preferences toward holding debt of the U.S. government and U.S. corporations.				
3. The auto industry must make massive purchases of new technology to compete with the Japanese. They enter the capital markets to "float" their new debt.				
4. A major nuclear facility fails to be built and a municipality defaults on the debt used to finance this nuclear project. Bondholders suddenly flee from the bond market.				

	SHIFT	BOND PRICES	INTEREST RATES	NO. OF BONDS
5. Foreign interest rates fall, but American rates remain the same. Foreign investors switch their preferences from foreign debt to American debt to earn a higher return.				
6. A predicted recession scares firms away from financing and installing new capital equipment.				
7. The stock market takes a sudden plunge. Anticipating a further plunge, investors sell stock and buy bonds.				
8. There is a sudden surge in the inflation rate. Anticipating higher interest rates investors steer clear of the bond market.				
9. The United States issues bonds with smaller denominations, which makes it possible for a larger number of buyers to hold U.S. securities.				

Exercise 6

The media often provide information on changes in the demand and supply of bonds. By using one of the articles in the text, this exercise will show the kind of information to look for. If your professor makes a newspaper assignment for this chapter, this exercise will provide an example of how to do it.

Reread the article in Chapter 13 entitled "Money Is Free" from the *Wall Street Journal*. Then answer the following questions:

1. Which of the four diagrams in Figure 12.1 best represents what the author wants the Fed to do?
   a   b   c   d   (circle one)

2. What phrase or sentence specifically indicates what the author suggests the Fed should do in the government bond market?

3. What passage indicates the determinant of the change in the supply or demand of bonds?

4. What single sentence indicates a change in interest rates or in the quantity of bonds that results from the shift in demand or supply?

Common Errors

The first statement in each "common error" below is incorrect. Each incorrect statement is followed by a corrected version and an explanation.

1. Bank reserves are required for the safety of depositors' money. WRONG!

   Bank reserves are for control of the money supply. RIGHT!

   Many people have the idea that bank reserves provide for the safety of depositors' money. They don't. The statistics in Chapter 11 indicate that the amount of demand deposits is several times larger than that of reserves. Reserves are for control of the money supply. The FDIC provides for safety of deposits by insuring them. Reserves are not principally for depositors' safety.

2. Deposits of cash are necessary to start the process of lending and deposit creation. WRONG!

   To start the lending process, the banks must acquire reserves from outside of the banking system. RIGHT!

   Many find it difficult to understand that for deposit creation to occur, the banking system needs only to acquire reserves from outside of the system. It may acquire reserves by selling off a security to the Fed or by borrowing from the Fed. An individual bank, however, may acquire reserves from another bank. So to the extent that it has increased its reserves, another bank's reserves have shrunk. Thus, the system has no more reserves after the transaction than it had before, and so the system's lending capacity is unchanged.

3. Interest rates are the same thing as the price of bonds. WRONG!

   Interest rates are inversely related to the price of bonds. RIGHT!

   The relationship between the price of a bond maturing in one year and the "yield" (which is usually close to current market interest rates) is given by:

$$\text{Current bond market price} = \frac{\text{face value of the bond} \times (1 + \text{bond interest rate})}{(1 + \text{current interest rate})}$$

   There are two interest rates involved here: the interest rate stated on the bond when it is first issued and the current market interest rate that occurs at any time before the bond matures. It is the current market interest rate that is inversely related to the value of the bond (i.e., to the bond's current market price).

■ ANSWERS ■

Key-Term Review

1. discounting
2. portfolio decision
3. excess reserves
4. discount rate

5. open-market operations
6. bond
7. yield
8. required reserves

9. money multiplier
10. monetary policy
11. money supply ($M1$)

True or False

1. F	5. F	9. F	13. T	16. T	19. T
2. T	6. T	10. F	14. T	17. T	20. F
3. F	7. T	11. T	15. F	18. T	21. F
4. F	8. F	12. T			

Multiple Choice

1. d	5. d	9. d	13. c	17. b	21. d
2. a	6. a	10. d	14. d	18. b	22. d
3. c	7. b	11. c	15. d	19. a	23. d
4. c	8. d	12. d	16. a	20. b	24. b

Problems and Applications

Exercise 1

1. $12 million
2. $48 million
3. $60 million
4. $60 million
5. See Table 12.2 answer
6. $60 million
7. Zero
8. $60 million

Table 12.2 answer
(millions of dollars)

Total reserves	$ 60	Transactions accounts	$300
Required, $60			
Excess, $0			
Securities	80		
Loans	160		
Total	$300	Total	$300

Exercise 2

1. **Table 12.4 answer**
   (millions of dollars)

Total reserves	$ 70	Transactions accounts	$300
Required, $60			
Excess, $10			
Securities	70		
Loans	160		
Total	$300	Total	$300

2. $10 million

3. **Table 12.5 answer**
   (millions of dollars)

Total reserves	$ 70	Transactions accounts	$350
Required, $70			
Excess, $0			
Securities	70		
Loans	210		
Total	$350	Total	$350

4. $50 million
5. $10 million
6. $50 million

Exercise 3

1. $2 million; excess; $10 million

2. **Table 12.7 answer**
   (millions of dollars)

Total reserves	$ 72	Transactions accounts	$360
Required, $72			
Excess, $0			
Securities	70		
Loans	220	Discounts payable to Fed	2
Total	$362	Total	$362

3. $10 million

Exercise 4

1. $1,000; $80; 8
2. $1,000; $100; 10
3. Similar Firm
4. $982 [= ($1,000 + $80)/1.10]
5. T
6. up

Exercise 5

	TYPE OF SHIFT (by Figure 12.1 diagram letter)	BOND PRICES	INTEREST RATES	NO. OF BONDS
1.	b	↓	↑	↑
2.	d	↑	↓	↑
3.	b	↓	↑	↑
4.	c	↓	↑	↓
5.	d	↑	↓	↑
6.	a	↑	↓	↓
7.	d	↑	↓	↑
8.	c	↓	↑	↓
9.	d	↑	↓	↑

Exercise 6

1. b By selling bonds, the Fed withdraws reserves from the banking system which reduces the money supply.
2. The reference to the "Federal Reserve's Open Market Committee" suggests that the purchase or sale of bonds should be used to alter the money supply.
3. "In particular, the observation ought to be of interest to the Federal Reserve's Open Market Committee, which meets today to set money growth targets." The determinant is the Federal Reserve in its role of specifying monetary targets and therefore its purchases of bonds.
4. "That is why interest rates will not go down, nor the dollar recover meaningfully, until inflation is reduced." By tightening the money supply, the Fed should reduce inflation, which would eventually allow the interest rates to fall.

Chapter 13
Monetary Policy

Quick Review

In this chapter, we focus on monetary policy and the Fed's role in attempting to move the economy toward its macroeconomic goals. Specifically, we look for answers to the following questions:

- What is the relationship between the amount of money and aggregate expenditure?
- How can the Fed use its control of the money supply to alter macro outcomes?
- How effective is monetary policy, compared to fiscal policy?

The Federal Reserve System controls the lending capacity of the banking system. By controlling the banks' ability to make loans ("create money"), the Federal Reserve System controls the money supply. The amount of money in the economy, however, reflects money demand as well as money supply.

In the Keynesian view, the demand for money has three components:

1. The transactions demand, which reflects people's normal needs for coin and currency in order to buy and sell goods and services

2. The precautionary demand, which is what people feel they need for emergencies and other needs that may arise

3. The speculative demand, in which money is held temporarily as a secure liquid asset in anticipation of changes in interest rates

The level of GNP and interest rates influence transactions and precautionary demand. Speculative demand, however, is most influenced by interest rates. It is the interest rate (price of money) that connects the demand for money with the supply of money. The equilibrium rate of interest is the rate that equates the quantity of money demanded with the quantity of money supplied.

If the Fed wishes to stimulate aggregate spending, it will drive down interest rates by expanding the money supply. This lower interest rate stimulates components of aggregate spending (e.g., investment), which are influenced by interest rates. The success of monetary policy depends on the elasticity of the demand for money and the sensitivity of the expenditure decisions to changes in interest rates.

There is substantial controversy over the transmission mechanism in monetary policy. Monetarists, viewing the velocity component in the equation of exchange ($MV = PQ$) as a constant, assert that "only money matters"; extreme Keynesians argue that V can change so that monetary policy is completely stymied. As a result "money doesn't matter" in determining total employment and income. In reality, V does fluctuate and both monetary and fiscal policy are important.

Learning Objectives

After reading Chapter 13 and doing the following exercises, you should:	True or false	Multiple choice	Problems and applications	Common errors	Pages in the text
1. Understand the opportunity cost of holding idle funds.	1	3,7,9			293
2. Understand the concept of portfolio decisions.	2	3	1		297–300
3. Know the determinants of the transactions, precautionary, and speculative demand for money.	3–11	4,5,7,8			292–293
4. Be able to graph money-market equilibrium.	12,13	11–15	1		294
5. Know and understand the three distinct steps in the Keynesian theory of monetary policy.	13,14, 17,18	1,10,16	1,3,4		295–297
6. Be aware of the limitations of Keynesian monetary policy in closing an inflationary and a recessionary gap.	15,19–21, 23,31–33	17–21	1,3,4		297–298
7. Understand the equation of exchange and the assumptions on which it is based.	29,30	24,25	3,5		301–303
8. Know the mechanism by which changes in M affect GNP in the monetarist model.	27	2,6,16,24, 26,28	5		301–302
9. Be able to calculate the nominal and real rates of interest.	22,24,35		2	2	305
10. Be able to prescribe monetarist policy to close both an inflationary gap and a recessionary gap.	28	29–32	3	3	304–307
11. Be aware of the uneven impact that changes in interest rates have on the economy.	25,26	22,23	5	1	291,307
12. Know the implications for monetary and fiscal policy of the Keynesian–monetarist debate.	32	2,26,27, 30,32,33		3	307–311
13. Understand the controversy over the stability of velocity in the short run and the long run.	27,29	27,28,31, 32,33	3	3	311–313
14. Understand the inverse relationship between interest rates and bond prices.	14,16				299–300
15. Understand the meaning of the phrase "natural rate of unemployment."	34				303

Key-Term Review

Review the following terms; if you are not sure of the meaning of any term, write out the definition and check it against the Glossary in the text.

aggregate spending
crowding out
demand for money
equation of exchange
equilibrium rate of interest
income velocity of money (V)
interest rate
liquidity trap

monetary policy
natural rate of unemployment
portfolio decision
precautionary demand for money
real rate of interest
speculative demand for money
transactions demand for money

Fill in the blank following each of the statements below with the appropriate term from the list above.

1. The implicit cost of holding money in idle balances is measured by the _____.

1. _____

2. The total quantity of money the public is willing and able to hold at various rates of interest, *ceteris paribus*, is called the _____.

2. _____

3. When the average level of prices is rising, the nominal rate of interest exceeds the _____.

3. _____

4. Dividing GNP by the number of dollars in circulation yields the _____.

4. _____

5. The belief that when government expands the size of its budget it merely replaces private spending that would otherwise have taken place is embodied in the concept of _____.

5. _____

6. Choosing among alternative ways of holding assets is essentially a _____.

6. _____

7. That part of the money balances that the public holds in anticipation of making normal market purchases is referred to as the _____.

7. _____

8. That part of one's money balances held in case an emergency should arise is called the _____.

8. _____

9. That part of the money supply held with the idea of capitalizing on interest rate (bond-price) movements is called the _____.

9. _____

10. When the Fed wishes to close a recessionary gap by purchasing securities in the open market, it is engaging in an "easy" _____.

10. _____

11. One reason that monetary policy may be unable to lower interest rates is the possible existence of a _____.

11. _____

12. That rate of interest that equates the demand for money with the supply of money is called the _____.

12. _____

13. The mathematical statement that $MV = PQ$ is called the _____.

13. _____

14. Structural forces in the economy establish the _____.

14. _____

15. To be effective in achieving price and employment goals monetary policy must influence the level of _____.

15. _____

True or False: *Circle your choice.*

T F   1. People who hold idle money balances incur no costs.

T F   2. The term "portfolio decision" refers to the way one chooses to allocate one's assets between various earning and nonearning assets.

T F   3. Money held for the purpose of making normal expenditures is called the transactions demand.

T F   4. The transactions demand for money depends primarily on the level of GNP.

T F   5. The precautionary demand for money depends partly on the expected future level of GNP.

T F   6. Precautionary balances are held to make anticipated expenditures.

T F   7. The speculative demand for money depends on the rate of interest.

T F   8. The speculative demand for money depends on anticipated changes in bond prices.

T F   9. The speculative demand curve for money flattens out when the interest rate is very low.

T F 10. The speculative demand curve for money flattens out when bond prices are very high.

T F 11. The liquidity trap occurs when bond prices are very low.

T F 12. If the interest rate in the money market is above equilibrium, the quantity of money supplied exceeds the quantity of money demanded.

T F 13. If the interest rate in the money market is below equilibrium, bond prices will fall when the market moves toward equilibrium.

T F 14. When interest rates fall, bond prices rise.

T F 15. If the Fed wishes to pursue an expansionary monetary policy, it can sell securities in the open market.

T F 16. When the Fed increases the supply of securities (by selling in the open market), interest rates rise.

T F 17. When the Fed buys securities, causing interest rates to fall, investment spending increases, thus expanding GNP.

T F 18. Both consumer spending and local government spending are insensitive to changes in the interest rate.

T F 19. If the interest rate is in the liquidity-trap range, monetary policy is likely to be ineffective.

T F 20. To close an inflationary gap, the Fed can sell securities and raise the discount rate.

T F 21. Whether restrictive monetary policy is effective or not depends on its ability to reduce aggregate spending.

T F 22. If you lend $100 at the beginning of the year at 8 percent and prices are constant, at the end of the year you'll have $108 of real purchasing power.

T F 23. The Fed has missed monetary targets for the money supply by wide margins.

T F 24. To find the real rate of return on an investment, subtract the nominal interest rate from the rate of inflation.

T F 25. One of the advantages of monetary policy is that it affects all components of aggregate demand equally.

T F 26. An advantage of monetary policy is that, since it operates by changing market rates of interest, it leaves the competitive structure of other markets unchanged.

T F 27. If velocity grows at 3 percent per year, inflation is 3 percent per year, and the money supply grows at 3 percent per year, real GNP cannot grow at all.

172

T F 28. Monetarists argue that fiscal policy is ineffective in changing the level of aggregate spending.

T F 29. The monetarist proposition that "only money matters" rests on the assumption that velocity (V) is constant.

T F 30. From the monetarist point of view, increased government spending merely "crowds out" an equivalent amount of private spending.

T F 31. Monetarists feel the Fed should control interest rates; the Keynesians feel the Fed should control the money supply.

T F 32. Under Alan Greenspan, the Fed has adopted the monetarist philosophy—that is, steady growth rates for $M1$.

T F 33. Consumer expectations regarding future price levels are important in determining the effectiveness of monetary policy.

T F 34. The natural rate of unemployment is the rate of unemployment that occurs if monetary and fiscal policies are optimally applied.

T F 35. Keynesians view high interest rates as a symptom of inflation, not a cure.

Multiple Choice: *Select the correct answer.*

_____ 1. In the Keynesian model, the effectiveness of monetary policy depends on which of the following?
    (a) The Fed's ability to influence bond prices.
    (b) The sensitivity of interest rates to changes in the money supply.
    (c) The sensitivity of investment spending to changes in interest rates.
    (d) All of the above.

_____ 2. The Shadow Open Market Committee:
    (a) Takes an eclectic point of view.
    (b) Takes a Keynesian point of view.
    (c) Takes a monetarist point of view.
    (d) Takes a supply-side point of view.

_____ 3. Which of the following statements is correct?
    (a) When bond prices fall, the opportunity cost of holding idle balances increases.
    (b) When bond prices rise, the opportunity cost of holding idle balances increases.
    (c) When interest rates fall, the opportunity cost of holding idle balances increases.
    (d) None of the above is correct.

_____ 4. Which of the following is thought to be *most* sensitive to changes in the rate of interest?
    (a) The transactions demand for money.
    (b) The speculative demand for money.
    (c) The precautionary demand for money.
    (d) None of the above.

_____ 5. Which of the following is thought to be *least* sensitive to changes in bond prices?
    (a) The precautionary demand for money.
    (b) The transactions demand for money.
    (c) The speculative demand for money.
    (d) All of the above are equally sensitive to changes in bond prices.

_____ 6. Which of the following positions can be attributed to the Monetarists?
    (a) "Only money matters."
    (b) "Velocity is constant."
    (c) "Government expenditures crowd out private expenditures."
    (d) All of the above are monetarist positions.

_____ 7. Those who hold idle balances for speculative purposes incur no cost because:
   (a) They expect interest rates are going to rise.
   (b) They expect interest rates are going to fall.
   (c) They expect bond prices are going to fall.
   (d) They expect none of the above.

_____ 8. Precautionary balances are held:
   (a) To take advantage of future changes in bond prices.
   (b) To make anticipated expenditures.
   (c) To handle emergencies.
   (d) To do none of the above.

_____ 9. The cost of holding idle balances is:
   (a) Nothing if you hold it in the form of cash.
   (b) Equal to the service charge collected by the bank.
   (c) The return that could have been earned had the funds been lent out at interest.
   (d) None of the above.

_____ 10. Which of the following is a series of events that accurately describes the steps by which expansionary monetary policy is alleged to work in the short run?
   (a) Increase in M, decrease in interest rate, increase in I.
   (b) Decrease in interest rate, increase in M, increase in I.
   (c) Increase in M, decrease in I, decrease in interest rate.
   (d) Increase in M, increase in interest rate, increase in I.

_____ 11. By adding together the speculative, transactions, and precautionary demands for money, one can obtain:
   (a) The market demand curve for money.
   (b) The Keynesian liquidity trap.
   (c) The monetarist demand-for-money curve.
   (d) None of the above.

_____ 12. The market demand-for-money curve:
   (a) Is perfectly flat.
   (b) Is perfectly vertical.
   (c) Slopes downward and to the right.
   (d) Slopes upward and to the right.

_____ 13. There is an inverse relationship between the quantity of money demanded and:
   (a) The price of money.
   (b) The interest rate.
   (c) The opportunity cost of owning money.
   (d) All of the above.

_____ 14. Equilibrium in the market for money is found where:
   (a) Planned saving equals planned investment.
   (b) Aggregate spending equals full-employment output.
   (c) Leakages equal injections.
   (d) The quantity of money demanded equals the quantity of money supplied.

_____ 15. Starting from a position of equilibrium, if the Fed reduces the reserve requirement, we may infer that:
   (a) The demand for money will increase.
   (b) The demand for money will decrease.
   (c) the interest rate will rise.
   (d) The interest rate will fall.

_____16. When the Fed increases the money supply and causes interest rates to fall:
 (a) The rate of investment spending may increase.
 (b) Some consumer spending may increase.
 (c) Some spending by state and local governments may increase.
 (d) All of the above may occur.

_____17. Monetary policy will be effective if:
 (a) The demand for money is sensitive to changes in the interest rate, and the investment demand is not.
 (b) The demand for money is very sensitive to changes in the interest rate, but investment demand is sensitive to changes in the interest rate.
 (c) Interest rates are sensitive to the quantity of money supplied, and investment spending is sensitive to changes in the interest rate.
 (d) None of the above is the case.

_____18. To close an inflationary gap, the Fed can:
 (a) Raise the reserve requirement.
 (b) Raise the discount rate.
 (c) Sell bonds in the open market.
 (d) Do all of the above.

_____19. To be effective, monetary policy must:
 (a) Cause the interest rate to change.
 (b) Cause a shift in the aggregate spending curve.
 (c) Cause the money supply to change.
 (d) Do all of the above.

_____20. The effectiveness of restrictive monetary policy will be lessened by the existence of:
 (a) High real rates of interest.
 (b) High nominal rates of interest.
 (c) Low real rates of interest.
 (d) Low nominal rates of interest.

_____21. Which of the following is thought to be *most* sensitive to changes in the interest rate?
 (a) Federal spending for national defense.
 (b) Spending for residential construction.
 (c) Spending by local governments.
 (d) Spending by households.

_____22. Which of the following impacts characterize monetary policy?
 (a) Uneven effects across various industries and governments.
 (b) No effect on government spending, but across-the-board effects on industries and households.
 (c) No effect on consumption.
 (d) No generalizations can be made about the influence of monetary policy.

_____23. During periods of "tight money":
 (a) Credit dries up for all firms.
 (b) Banks must find ways to allocate credit among potential creditworthy borrowers.
 (c) Large and small firms have equal access to credit.
 (d) Small firms have an advantage in getting credit, since their demands are small relative to the total market.

_____24. The equation of exchange can be stated in which of the following ways?
 (a) $MV = PQ$.
 (b) $P = \dfrac{MV}{Q}$.
 (c) $V = \dfrac{PQ}{M}$.
 (d) All of the above.

_____ 25. Monetarists argue that:
  (a) *M* is constant.
  (b) *V* is constant.
  (c) *P* is constant.
  (d) *Q* is constant.

_____ 26. Which of the following *most* accurately describes the monetarist view on the effectiveness of economic policy tools?
  (a) Fiscal policy is very powerful.
  (b) Fiscal policy and monetary policy are very effective.
  (c) Monetary policy is very powerful.
  (d) Wage and price controls are more effective than monetary policy.

_____ 27. The Keynesian counterargument to monetarism is based largely on which of the following ideas?
  (a) The Fed can alter interest rates and therefore economic activity.
  (b) "Crowding out," even if it did occur, would not be important because people would be working.
  (c) Velocity is certainly not constant and may even by quite volatile.
  (d) All of the above are Keynesian arguments.

_____ 28. Which of the following seems borne out by monetary statistics?
  (a) Over short periods velocity seems constant, but over long periods it is volatile.
  (b) Over long and short periods velocity seems volatile.
  (c) Velocity seems unstable over short periods but fairly stable over long periods.
  (d) Over both long and short periods, velocity is stable.

_____ 29. The Fed adopted fixed money-supply targets as a policy goal from 1979 to 1982. The Fed abandoned the money-supply targets:
  (a) Because interest rates rose to undesired levels.
  (b) Because the economy went into a deep recession.
  (c) Because it wanted greater flexibility in policy making.
  (d) For all of the above reasons.

_____ 30. Which of the following is correct?
  (a) Monetarists favor growth in the money supply at a steady rate.
  (b) Keynesians favor monetary targets, which take on a range of values (e.g., 3–8 percent).
  (c) The Fed has recently been using the monetarist approach.
  (d) The eclectic approach favors a steady rate of growth in the money supply.

Problems and Applications

Exercise 1

1. Suppose conditions in the money market are as indicated in Table 13.1. Plot the demand and supply of money in Figure 13.1. The demand curve should pass through point *A*. Label the curves *D* and S_1.

Table 13.1

Interest rate (percent)	Total demand for money (billions of dollars)	Supply of money (billions of dollars)
0	$160	$110
1	150	110
2	140	110
3	130	110
4	120	110
5	110	110
6	100	110

Figure 13.1

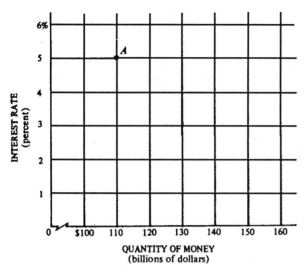

QUANTITY OF MONEY
(billions of dollars)

2. What is the equilibrium rate of interest in Problem 1? _____ percent

3. What is the equilibrium quantity of money in Problem 1? $_____ billion

Now suppose that:

- For every one percentage point decline in the interest rate, the aggregate spending schedule shifts upward by $20 billion.
- The spending multiplier has a value of 2.
- There is a recessionary gap of $40 billion.

Use these assumptions to answer the following questions.

4. If the Fed wishes to close the recessionary gap, it should (increase/decrease) the money supply.

5. Suppose the Fed increases the money supply by $10 billion. The interest rate will fall to _____. (Illustrate this in Figure 13.1 by drawing a second money-supply curve; label it S_2.)

6. This decline would cause the aggregate spending curve to shift by $_____ billion and raise the level of income by $_____ billion.

7. This would still leave a recessionary gap of $_____ billion.

8. To close the recessionary gap completely, the Fed should increase the money supply by another $_____ billion. This action would cause an upward shift in the aggregate spending curve of $_____ billion and raise income by $_____ billion more.

Exercise 2

This exercise will help you understand the difference between real and nominal rates of interest.

Table 13.2 lists the annual rate of interest charged to prime bank borrowers and the Federal Housing and Loan Board (FHLB) rate charged by mortgage lenders for selected years from 1960 to 1984. Column 4 also gives the annual average rate of increase in the CPI for the same years.

1. Calculate the real rate of return to banks and to mortgage lenders by subtracting the inflation rate from the appropriate interest rate. Place the answers in columns 5 and 6 in Table 13.2.

Table 13.2

(1) Year	(2) Bank prime rate (percent per annum)	(3) New home (FHLB) mortgage yield (percent per annum)	(4) Rate of inflation in CPI (percent per annum)	(5) Real rate of return to banks (percent per annum)	(6) Real rate of return to mortgage lenders (percent per annum)
1960	4.8%	NA	1.5%	_____ %	_____ %
1965	4.5	5.8%	1.9	_____	_____
1970	7.9	8.5	5.5	_____	_____
1975	7.9	9.0	7.0	_____	_____
1977	6.8	9.0	6.8	_____	_____
1979	12.7	10.8	13.3	_____	_____
1981	18.9	14.7	8.9	_____	_____
1982	14.9	15.1	3.9	_____	_____
1983	10.8	12.6	3.8	_____	_____
1984	12.0	12.4	4.0	_____	_____

2. In Figure 13.2, plot the real rate of return to the lenders indicated.

Figure 13.2

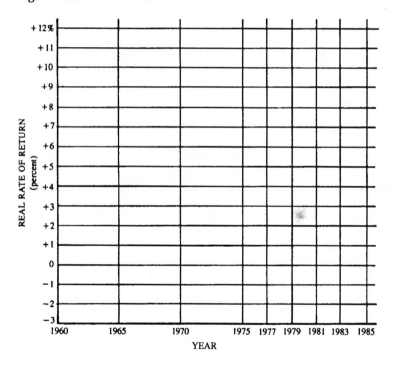

3. The nominal interest rate was exactly equal to the real rate of return for bank lenders in _____.

4. Bank lenders experienced a negative real rate of return in _____.

5. The real rate of return to mortgage lenders was negative in _____.

6. In which year was the inflation rate the highest? _____.

7. When was the real rate of return to banks and mortgage lenders lowest? _____.

8. T   F   High nominal rates of interest may be accompanied by negative real rates of return.

9. T   F   High rates of inflation seem to be accompanied by high nominal interest rates.

10. T   F   The bank prime rate and the mortgage lending rate seem to have an inverse relationship.

178

Exercise 3

This exercise will help you check your understanding of how monetary and fiscal policy affect the economy.

Consider the following statements. Decide whether you think they were made by a Monetarist or a Keynesian and place a check in the appropriate column in Table 13.3. If you have difficulty, reread Table 13.1 and 13.2 in the text (pp. 310–311).

Table 13.3
Comparing Keynesian and monetarist views on monetary policy

	MONETARIST	KEYNESIAN
1. An increase in government spending will raise total spending.		
2. A reduction in taxes will leave real output unaffected.		
3. Real interest rates are determined by real growth.		
4. Prices may be affected by increases in G or reductions in T.		
5. Changes in the money supply definitely affect both the price level and aggregate spending.		
6. Changes in M definitely affect changes in the nominal interest rate.		
7. Changes in M may cause changes in V and Q.		
8. Changes in M definitely cannot lower the unemployment rate.		
9. The liquidity trap may prevent the nominal interest rate from falling.		
10. Monetary and fiscal policy must be used together to stabilize aggregate demand.		

Exercise 4

The following exercise should provide practice in understanding how monetary policy affects the banking system and the economy. The exercise is similar to the one in the text at the end of Chapter 13.

Suppose the Federal Reserve decides to sell $20 billion worth of government securities in the open market and the bonds are purchased by an insurance company.

1. $M1$ will initially _____ (increase, decrease) by $_____ billion.

2. If the reserve requirement is 5 percent the lending capacity of the banking system will _____ (increase, decrease) by $_____ billion.

3. Banks will induce investors to adjust to this changed lending capacity by (two answers):
   (a) Paying higher interest rates for investors' funds.
   (b) Paying lower interest rates for investors' funds.
   (c) Lending at higher interest rates.
   (d) Lending at lower interest rates.

4. If the economy is at full employment, then the above change in the money supply will cause:
   (a) Either aggregate spending or prices to fall.
   (b) Either aggregate spending to fall or prices to rise.
   (c) Either aggregate spending or prices to rise.
   (d) Either aggregate spending to rise or prices to fall.

5. The reserve requirement would have to be _____ (raised, lowered) to achieve the same total effect on the money supply as a $20 billion purchase of government securities.

6. The discount rate would have to be _____ (raised, lowered) to achieve the same total effect on the money supply as a $20 billion purchase of government securities.

Exercise 5

The media often provide information about changes in policy by the Federal Reserve System. By using one of the articles in the text, this exercise will show the kind of information to look for. If your professor makes a newspaper assignment for this chapter, this exercise will provide an example of how to do it.

Reread the article in Chapter 12 entitled "Fed, Banks Increase Key Interest Rates" from the *Washington Post*. Then answer the following questions:

1. What central monetary authority is mentioned in the article?

2. What phrase in the article indicates the monetary instrument that is being used by the central monetary authority?

3. Which instrument is being used?
    (a) Reserve requirement.
    (b) Open-market operations.
    (c) Discount rate.
    (d) Other (Specify: _____)

4. Which of the following *best* summarizes the effect of this monetary policy on the quantity of money?
    (a) It speeds an increase.
    (b) It slows an increase.
    (c) It speeds a decrease.
    (d) It slows a decrease.

5. Which of the following *best* describes the effect of the change in monetary policy on inflation according to the equation of exchange?
    (a) It speeds up inflation.
    (b) It slows inflation.
    (c) It speeds deflation.
    (d) It slows deflation.

Common Errors

The first statement in each "common error" below is incorrect. Each incorrect statement is followed by a corrected version and an explanation.

1. When the interest rate goes down, the demand for money increases. WRONG!

    When the interest rate goes down, the quantity of money demanded increases. RIGHT!

    Don't fail to recognize the difference between a change in demand and a change in quantity demanded. Remember that each demand schedule (speculative, transactions, precautionary) is drawn on the assumption of *ceteris paribus*. Unless there is a change in one of the things held constant (e.g., expectations), there will be no change in demand when the interest rate falls, only a change in quantity demanded.

2. High nominal rates of interest mean high real rates of interest. WRONG!

    High nominal interest rates and high real interest rates do not necessarily coincide. RIGHT!

    High nominal interest rates and high real interest rates will coincide only if the average level of prices is not changing rapidly enough to offset the differential. For example, if the nominal rate is 10 percent and prices are rising at 10 percent, the real rate of interest is zero.

3. Monetary policy is easy to determine and to administer. WRONG!

Monetary policy is difficult to determine and to administer. RIGHT!

One could easily get the idea that monetary policy is easy to administer and that the Fed always knows the rate at which the money supply should grow. This is not so. Many variables intervene to make monetary policy difficult to prescribe and implement. Such variables include timing and the duration of a given policy, unanticipated events on the fiscal side, and problems abroad. The Fed's policy makers analyze the data available and do the best they can to achieve a given objective, which often involves compromises. The process is much more difficult than turning a printing press on and off.

■ ANSWERS ■

Key-Term Review

1. interest rate	6. portfolio decision	11. liquidity trap
2. demand for money	7. transactions demand for money	12. equilibrium rate of interest
3. real rate of interest	8. precautionary demand for money	13. equation of exchange
4. income velocity of money (V)	9. speculative demand for money	14. natural rate of unemployment
5. crowding out	10. monetary policy	15. aggregate spending

True or False

1. F	7. T	13. T	19. T	25. F	31. F
2. T	8. T	14. T	20. T	26. F	32. F
3. T	9. T	15. F	21. T	27. F	33. T
4. T	10. T	16. T	22. T	28. T	34. F
5. T	11. F	17. T	23. T	29. T	35. F
6. F	12. T	18. F	24. F	30. T	

Multiple Choice

1. d	6. d	11. a	16. d	21. b	26. c
2. c	7. d	12. c	17. c	22. a	27. c
3. a	8. c	13. d	18. d	23. b	28. c
4. b	9. c	14. d	19. d	24. d	29. d
5. a	10. a	15. d	20. c	25. b	30. a

Problems and Applications

Exercise 1

1. **Figure 13.1 answer**

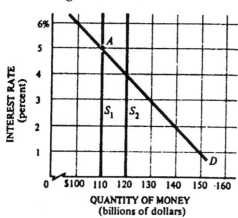

INTEREST RATE (percent)

QUANTITY OF MONEY
(billions of dollars)

2. 5 percent
3. $110 billion
4. increase
5. 4 percent; see Figure 13.1 answer, line S_2.
6. $20 billion; $40 billion (= $20 billion x multiplier = $20 billion x 2)
7. $20 billion [$40 billion (recessionary gap) – $20 billion (new aggregate spending)]
8. $10 billion; $20 billion; $40 billion.

Exercise 2

1. Table 13.2 answer

Year	Real rate of return to banks (percent)	Real rate of return to mortgage lenders (percent)
1960	3.3%	—%
1965	2.6	3.9
1970	2.4	3.0
1975	0.9	2.0
1977	0.0	2.2
1979	– 0.6	– 2.5
1981	10.0	5.8
1982	11.0	11.2
1983	7.0	8.8
1984	8.0	8.4

3. No year
4. 1979
5. 1979
6. 1979
7. 1979
8. T
9. T
10. F

2. Figure 13.2 answer

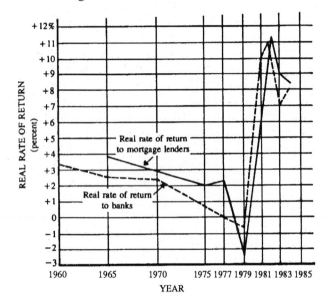

Exercise 3

Table 13.3 answer

	MONETARIST	KEYNESIAN
1.		✓
2.	✓	
3.	✓	
4.		✓
5.	✓	
6.	✓	
7.		✓
8.	✓	
9.		✓
10.		✓

Exercise 4

1. Decrease; $20 billion. This action also withdraws reserves from the banking system.
2. Decrease; $400 billion. The product of the money multiplier (20) and the decrease in reserves ($20 billion) is therefore $400 billion.
3. a and c   The banks must charge a higher interest rate to ration the remaining credit to borrowers who take out loans. They will also acquire more deposits with higher interest rates.
4. a   Full employment is irrelevant in this case because the money supply is going down. The quantity equation suggests that either aggregate spending or prices or both will fall.
5. raised
6. raised

Exercise 5

1. The Federal Reserve System of the United States is the central bank featured in the article.
2. The phrase "... raised the discount rate from 5 1/2 percent to 6 percent" indicates the Fed is using the discount rate.
3. c
4. b
5. b

Chapter 14

Supply-Side Policies

Quick Review

Supply-side economics and supply-side policies played a very important role during the first Reagan presidential campaign and the two Reagan administrations that followed. In this chapter we focus on the rationale and form of supply-side initiatives. We first take up the questions:

- How can the aggregate supply curve be shifted?
- How do shifts of the aggregate supply curve affect macroeconomic outcomes?

A trade-off between unemployment and inflation makes stabilization goals difficult to attain. This trade-off is represented by the Phillips curve. When the trade-off worsens with significant degrees of both inflation and unemployment, we have stagflation.

The four major sources of stagflation are:

1. Profit-push pricing behavior on the part of powerful producers
2. Inflationary wage demands by labor unions (cost-push inflation)
3. Structural unemployment
4. Government regulation

Each of these sources contributes to stagflation by causing price increases before full employment is reached. As a consequence, increases in aggregate demand (MV) often lead to increases in prices (P) rather than in output (Q).

There are three major policy approaches for attacking stagflation—Keynesian, monetarist, and supply-side. Each approach views the aggregate supply curve in a different way. The supply-side policies directly attempt to shift the aggregate supply curve for all goods and services outward so that greater production can be obtained. This is accomplished through four types of supply-side policies:

1. Supply-side tax cuts
2. Deregulation
3. Elimination of structural bottlenecks
4. Wage–price controls

Each type of policy change has been used at one time or another to combat stagflation.

Supply-side tax cuts are incentive based—that is, they work on the assumption that people and firms will produce more if they get to keep a larger fraction of what they earn. Keynesian demand-side tax cuts emphasize the spending that takes place when more of every dollar earned becomes disposable income. In both cases the marginal tax rate plays a pivotal role. Some have even gone so far as to suggest that tax cuts will cause such an increase in productivity that tax revenue (generated by increased output) might actually increase. This is the idea behind the Laffer curve.

The supply-side policies help to shift the Phillips curve down and to the left—in other words, toward lower inflation and lower unemployment. However, wage–price controls may also lead to market distortions and reduce efficiency. Government human-resource programs are expensive. Nevertheless, there have been frequent experiments with both types of programs.

Learning Objectives

After reading Chapter 14 and doing the following exercises, you should:	True or false	Multiple choice	Problems and applications	Common errors	Pages in the text
1. Know what is meant by supply-side policies and how to combat stagflation.		5,12			327–341
2. Be able to contrast supply-side policies with demand-side monetary policies.	3	6,8	2		321–328
3. Know the meaning and measure of stagflation.	17	10	3	5	325
4. Describe the Phillips curve and explain what makes it shift.	4,7	9	1–3	4	323–326
5. Be able to contrast the Keynesian, monetarist, and supply-side views on the nature of the aggregate supply curve.		11, 23–26			322
6. Be able to list the different supply-side policies and show how they affect aggregate supply.	20	12		3	327–341
7. Know why marginal tax rates affect work incentives, investment, and saving.	13,19	13			329–335
8. Be able to show why deregulation can increase aggregate supply.	1				335–338
9. Know the source of major bottlenecks to the smooth functioning of the economy and how supply-side economics would eliminate the bottlenecks.	6,8–12, 14,18	1,14, 16–19,22			338–341
10. Describe when wage–price controls may appropriately be used and how they may have been used in the past.	2,5, 15,16	2–4,7,15, 20,21	4	1,2	341–346

Key-Term Review

Review the following terms; if you are not sure of the meaning of any term, write out the definition and check it against the Glossary in the text.

aggregate supply
cost-push inflation
derived demand
equation of exchange
investment
labor force
labor productivity
Laffer curve
marginal tax rate
market power

Phillips curve
profit-push inflation
saving
stagflation
structural unemployment
tax elasticity of supply
tax rebate
transfer payment
unit labor cost
wage–price controls

Fill in the blank following each of the statements below with the appropriate term from the list above.

1. The cornerstone of an incomes policy often consists of _____.

    1. _____

2. The relationship between the rate of inflation and the unemployment rate is shown in graphic form by a _____.

    2. _____

3. People above the age of 16 who are working or are seeking work make up the _____.

    3. _____

4. Output per unit of labor time is known as _____.

    4. _____

5. A worsening of both inflation and unemployment is called _____.

    5. _____

6. The total quantity of final goods sellers are willing and able to sell at alternative price levels is _____.

    6. _____

7. A rise in the average price level, often resulting from union wage demands, is known as _____.

    7. _____

8. Joblessness caused by lack of skills or a mismatch between skills and job locations is known as _____.

    8. _____

9. An increase in the average level of prices caused by businesses' attempts to increase the percentage of the revenues that they receive above costs is called _____.

    9. _____

10. When the demand for a particular good reflects the demand for another good, then the demand is _____.

    10. _____

11. Although often mistaken as being identical to wages, _____ may be quite different, depending on productivity.

    11. _____

12. The ability to alter prices or wages in a market is called _____.

    12. _____

13. Disposable income minus consumption is _____.

    13. _____

14. A lump-sum refund of taxes from the government is a _____.

    14. _____

15. The tax rate imposed on the last dollar of income is the _____.

    15. _____

16. Expenditures on new plant and equipment constitute _____.

    16. _____

17. The relationship $MV = PQ$ is called the _____.

    17. _____

18. The ratio of the percentage change in quantity supplied to the percentage change in tax rates is called the _____.

    18. _____

19. The _____ shows the relationship between tax revenues and tax rates.

    19. _____

20. Unemployment compensation is a good example
of a _____.   20. _____

True or False: *Circle your choice.*

T F 1. Deregulation shifts the aggregate supply curve by lowering costs and releasing supplies of goods.

T F 2. Price controls may dampen consumers' expectations of inflation.

T F 3. Monetary policy focuses on the quantity of money; fiscal policy focuses on the velocity of money.

T F 4. The Phillips curve shows an inverse relationship between unemployment and the rate of inflation.

T F 5. Major corporations with market power are principally responsible for profit-push inflation.

T F 6. Labor productivity is measured by the wage earned per hour of labor worked.

T F 7. In the 1970s the Phillips curve shifted upward and to the right.

T F 8. If wages keep pace with productivity, unit labor costs remain unchanged.

T F 9. Cost-push inflation occurs when labor raises wages by the amount of productivity increases in the economy.

T F 10. Income is redistributed from business to labor when labor raises wages to reflect increases in productivity.

T F 11. Education increases the productivity of the labor force.

T F 12. Young workers are usually more productive than older workers.

T F 13. By lowering marginal tax rates, governments can make taxes more progressive and therefore stimulate spending.

T F 14. Women and blacks contribute to structural unemployment to the extent that they are less experienced than their male and white counterparts.

T F 15. John F. Kennedy's wage standard of 3.2 percent in the early 1960s guaranteed that inflation would be at least 3.2 percent.

T F 16. The cost of price controls is the inefficiency that results.

T F 17. The "discomfort index" is a measure of stagflation.

T F 18. Equal opportunity programs increase efficiency by eliminating discriminatory barriers that might otherwise prevent the most qualified people from getting particular jobs.

T F 19. The marginal tax rate can be found by dividing taxes by income.

T F 20. Supply-siders feel that current unemployment compensation and welfare benefits inhibit labor supply.

Multiple Choice: *Select the correct answer.*

_____ 1. Which of the following is the policy used to combat structural unemployment?
   (a) A decrease in tax rates for the purpose of increasing aggregate demand.
   (b) An increase in the discount rate.
   (c) Government intervention in labor markets for the purpose of holding wage increases down to 5.5 percent annually.
   (d) Job training programs.

187

_____ 2. The "guideposts" that were in effect during the Kennedy and Johnson administrations were designed for the purpose of achieving stability in the level of prices. The government reasoned that this goal could be attained if:
(a) No wage increases were granted to labor.
(b) No profit increases were allowed among businesses.
(c) Average wage increases were no greater than average productivity increases.
(d) Average wage increases were no greater than the average increase in producer prices.

_____ 3. If productivity (output per worker-hour) rises at the annual rate of 3.5 percent, average wage increases of 6.0 percent will imply annual price increases of about:
(a) 9.5 percent.
(b) 6.0 percent.
(c) 2.5 percent.
(d) 3.5 percent.

_____ 4. During 1972, when President Nixon announced that wage increases would be held down to a rate of 5.5 percent in order to achieve a target rate of inflation of 2.5 percent:
(a) He miscalculated; if wages rise by 5.5 percent, inflation will also rise by 5.5 percent.
(b) An increase in productivity equal to 5.5 percent was required if the target rate of inflation was to be achieved.
(c) He could reasonably expect to achieve the target rate of inflation if productivity were to increase by 3.0 percent.
(d) He could reasonably hope to achieve the target rate of inflation if productivity were to increase by 2.5 percent.

_____ 5. Supply-side policies are designed to cause which of the following shifts?
(a) A shift of the Phillips curve to the left.
(b) A shift of the Phillips curve to the right.
(c) A movement along the Phillips curve.
(d) No changes in inflation.

_____ 6. Demand-side policies alone result in which of the following?
(a) A shift of the Phillips curve to the left.
(b) A shift of the Phillips curve to the right.
(c) A movement along the Phillips curve.
(d) No changes in inflation.

_____ 7. If labor receives wage increases in the amount of productivity increases:
(a) The business share of income will fall, but the wage increases will not be inflationary.
(b) The business share of income will be the same, and the wage increases will not be inflationary.
(c) The business share of income will be the same, and the wage increases will be inflationary.
(d) None of the above is the case.

_____ 8. When the money supply grows and fiscal policy is expansionary, it can definitely be said that:
(a) P rises.
(b) Q rises.
(c) PQ rises.
(d) Q remains the same.

_____ 9. The labels for axes found on the graph of the Phillips curve are:
(a) Y-axis with inflation rate and x-axis with unemployment rate.
(b) Y-axis with prices and x-axis with employment.
(c) X-axis with prices and y-axis with unemployment rate.
(d) X-axis with inflation rate and y-axis with employment.

_____ 10. Which of the following causes stagflation?
   (a) Workers push costs upward and thereby initiate profit-push inflation.
   (b) Labor unions negotiate wage increases equal to productivity increases, thereby setting off cost-push inflation.
   (c) Structural unemployment or other bottlenecks limit the expansion of output.
   (d) Government deregulation raises costs and limits production.

_____ 11. What type of inflation occurs when the economy is at full employment and the government suddenly initiates massive new expenditures?
   (a) Profit-push inflation.
   (b) Demand-pull inflation.
   (c) Cost-push inflation.
   (d) None of the above.

_____ 12. Which of the following policies is a supply-side policy?
   (a) Tax cuts.
   (b) Deregulation.
   (c) Elimination of structural unemployment by job programs.
   (d) All of the above.

_____ 13. What type of inflation occurs if oil companies apply an increased markup over the cost of the imported oil?
   (a) Profit-push inflation.
   (b) Demand-pull inflation.
   (c) Cost-push inflation.
   (d) None of the above.

_____ 14. What type of inflation occurs when labor unions get wage increases in excess of productivity increases?
   (a) Profit-push inflation.
   (b) Demand-pull inflation.
   (c) Cost-push inflation.
   (d) None of the above.

_____ 15. Unit labor costs depend on:
   (a) The wage rate.
   (b) The productivity of a worker.
   (c) Technological change.
   (d) All of the above.

_____ 16. Cost-push inflation definitely occurs:
   (a) When productivity rises more quickly than wages.
   (b) When productivity rises slowly and wages rise more slowly.
   (c) When productivity rises quickly and wages rise more quickly.
   (d) Under none of the above conditions.

_____ 17. Structural unemployment is likely when:
   (a) The labor force is highly educated.
   (b) The labor force is very experienced.
   (c) Many young people enter the labor force for the first time.
   (d) All of the above occur.

_____ 18. The decrease in the proportion of adult males in the labor force is due mainly to:
   (a) World War II.
   (b) The entrance of women and minorities into the labor force.
   (c) Increased immigration.
   (d) All of the above.

_____19. Which of the following programs cause(s) unemployment?
  (a) Agricultural acreage restrictions by the government.
  (b) The minimum wage.
  (c) Price controls.
  (d) All of the above.

_____20. The reason we do not know if price controls work is that:
  (a) They have never been given a fair trial in this country.
  (b) It is difficult to compare controlled prices with the prices that would have been charged if there had been no price controls.
  (c) They have never been used except in wartime, and at those times there are too many distortions in the economy.
  (d) All of the above are true.

_____21. When price controls are lifted, prices shoot upward very quickly:
  (a) Because aggregate demand shifts upward as people seek to buy needed goods.
  (b) Because prices are adjusting to market equilibrium levels, which are above price-control levels.
  (c) Because businesses wish to gouge the public and make up for losses under the price-control program.
  (d) For all of the above reasons.

_____22. The method for eliminating structural unemployment when the economy is at full employment is through:
  (a) Fiscal policy.
  (b) Monetary policy.
  (c) Wage and price controls.
  (d) Human-resource programs.

Using the diagram in Figure 14.1, answer Questions 23–26.

Figure 14.1

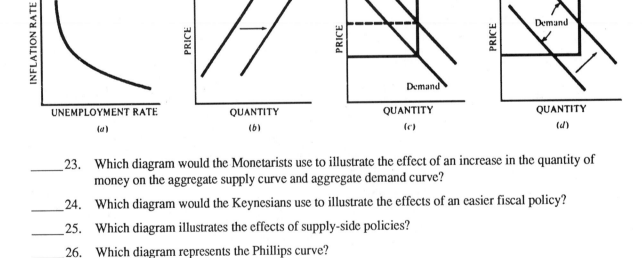

_____23. Which diagram would the Monetarists use to illustrate the effect of an increase in the quantity of money on the aggregate supply curve and aggregate demand curve?

_____24. Which diagram would the Keynesians use to illustrate the effects of an easier fiscal policy?

_____25. Which diagram illustrates the effects of supply-side policies?

_____26. Which diagram represents the Phillips curve?

Problems and Applications

Exercise 1

This exercise will help to show the relationship of the Phillips curve to the tools you already know. The aggregate demand curve and aggregate supply curve for all of the goods in an economy are presented in Figure 14.2. The economy is assumed to be on aggregate demand curve B in the current fiscal year.

Figure 14.2

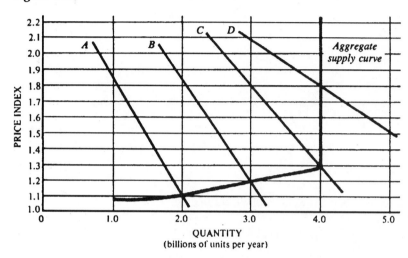

1. Four aggregate demand curves are shown in Figure 14.2, corresponding to four alternative government policies for the coming fiscal year.

   For the following four government policies, choose the aggregate demand curve in Figure 14.2 that best portrays the expected impact of each policy. Place the letter of your choice in each blank provided.

   _____ Money supply is expanded, taxes are cut, government increases its expenditures.

   _____ Government does nothing.

   _____ Government decides to balance the budget by eliminating its deficit by reducing government spending and raising taxes.

   _____ Government increases expenditures and cuts taxes.

2. Indicate the equilibrium price index for each policy in Table 14.1.

Table 14.1
Equilibrium prices for four government policies

Aggregate demand curve	A	B	C	D
Equilibrium price index	___	___	___	___

3. Suppose the price index is currently 1.2 as shown by demand curve B in Figure 14.2. Compute the inflation rate under each of the four policies assuming the supply curve remains the same. The formula is:

$$100 \times \left(\frac{\text{equilibrium price index} - 1.2}{1.2} \right)$$

191

Enter your answers for each policy in the appropriate blank of column 1 in Table 14.2.

Table 14.2
Inflation rates, equilibrium output, and unemployment rates under four government policies

Aggregate demand curve	(1) Equilibrium price change	(2) Equilibrium output (billions of units per year)	(3) Unemployment rate
A	_____%	_____	_____%
B	_____	_____	_____
C	_____	_____	_____
D	_____	_____	_____

4. In Table 14.2 (column 2) indicate the equilibrium output associated with each of the policies. Use Figure 14.2 to find this information.

Unemployment Rate

5. Which of the following *best* represents the U.S. unemployment rate?
   (a) The number of people divided by the U.S. labor force.
   (b) The number of people employed divided by the U.S. population.
   (c) The number of people counted as unemployed divided by the U.S. labor force.
   (d) The number of people unemployed divided by the U.S. population.

6. Table 14.3 shows a *hypothetical* U.S. population, the labor force, the number of people who are employed, and the number of people who are unemployed at each production rate for the economy. Compute the unemployment rate at each production rate in the table.

Table 14.3
Computation of the unemployment rate

Production rate (billions of units per year)	2	3	4
U.S. population (millions)	200	200	200
Labor force (millions)	100	100	100
Number of people unemployed (millions)	15	8	5
Number of people employed (millions)	85	92	95
Unemployment rate (percent)	_____	_____	_____

7. Using the information in Table 14.3, complete column 3 in Table 14.2, which shows the unemployment rate corresponding to each government policy.

8. The government's dilemma is:
   (a) That it cannot reach an unemployment level of 5 percent without experiencing inflation of at least 8 percent.
   (b) That it cannot reach stable prices (0 percent increase) without experiencing an unemployment rate of 8 percent or more.
   (c) That when it makes gains in holding inflation below 8 percent, unemployment increases.
   (d) Expressed by all of the above statements.

9. Which of the four aggregate demand curves places the economy closest to full-employment output and moderate inflation?
    (a) Aggregate demand curve A.
    (b) Aggregate demand curve B.
    (c) Aggregate demand curve C.
    (d) Aggregate demand curve D.

10. In Figure 14.3 graph the points that represent the data in columns 1 and 3 of Table 14.2 and then connect them with a curved line. What is this curve called? _____

Figure 14.3

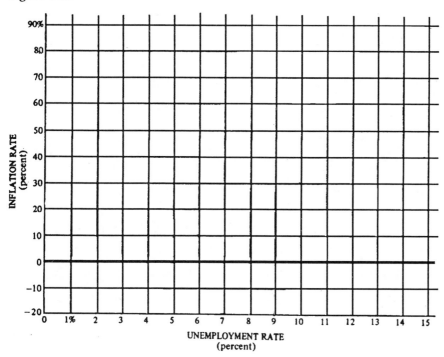

Exercise 2

The following exercise provides practice on shifts of the Phillips curve and the effects of monetary, fiscal, and the supply-side policies.

1. Which of the following is the *best* indication that stagflation is occurring?
    (a) Rising unemployment rate, falling inflation rate.
    (b) Rising unemployment rate, rising inflation rate.
    (c) Falling unemployment rate, falling inflation rate.
    (d) Falling unemployment rate, rising inflation rate.

2. Stagflation is most likely occurring when there is:
    (a) A movement up along the Phillips curve.
    (b) A movement down along the Phillips curve.
    (c) A shift outward of the Phillips curve to a new position.
    (d) A shift of the Phillips curve to a new position closer to the origin.

Each of the events described in Problems 3–9 results in a change involving the Phillips curve. Choose the diagram in Figure 14.4 that most likely represents the change that should occur.

_____ 3. Labor unions make wage demands in excess of productivity, forcing businesses to raise prices and even forcing some businesses into bankruptcy.

_____ 4. Government safety restrictions cause cost increases to manufacturers, forcing some of them out of business and consequently causing prices to rise.

_____ 5. The economy is below full employment and prices are stable. The government begins to subsidize businesses that employ and train people who are otherwise hard to employ, *ceteris paribus*.

Figure 14.4

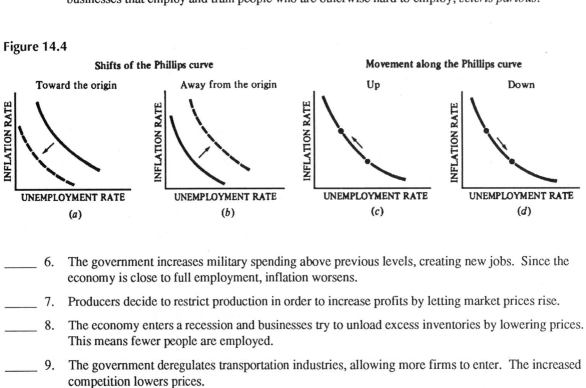

_____ 6. The government increases military spending above previous levels, creating new jobs. Since the economy is close to full employment, inflation worsens.

_____ 7. Producers decide to restrict production in order to increase profits by letting market prices rise.

_____ 8. The economy enters a recession and businesses try to unload excess inventories by lowering prices. This means fewer people are employed.

_____ 9. The government deregulates transportation industries, allowing more firms to enter. The increased competition lowers prices.

Exercise 3

On the inside back covers of the text you will find data on the unemployment rate and the percentage change in the Consumer Price Index. Using Figure 14.5, graph both series. Label one curve *U* (for unemployment) and the other *I* (for inflation).

Figure 14.5

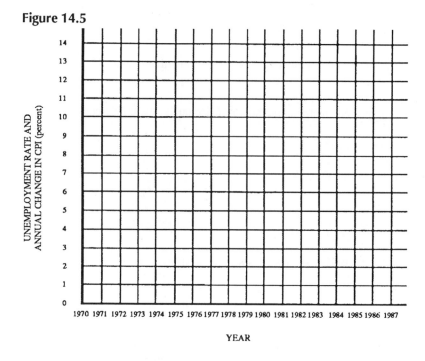

UNEMPLOYMENT RATE AND ANNUAL CHANGE IN CPI (percent)

YEAR

1. The unemployment rate and inflation rate appear to be:
    (a) Inversely related.
    (b) Directly related.

2. Compare your graph to the Phillips curve in Figure 14.3 in the text. Does one graph provide information different from that of the other graph?   yes   no   (circle one)

3. Why might the Phillips curve be a better way to provide information than the graph that you have drawn? For example, is it easier to see a change in one type of graph rather than the other?

Exercise 4

The media often provide information about changes in supply-side policies and the effects of such changes. By using one of the articles in the text, this exercise will show the kind of information to look for. If your professor makes a newspaper assignment for this chapter, this exercise will provide an example of how to do it.

Reread the article in Chapter 14 entitled "Mexico Freezes Peso, Prices to Slow Rampant Inflation" from the *Washington Post*. Then answer the following questions:

Figure 14.6 Possible shifts of aggregate demand or supply

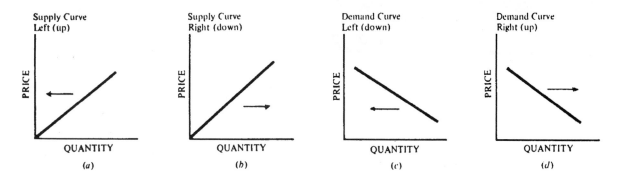

1. What part of the article indicates a supply-side policy change?

2. In what way does the article indicate the government agency or representative responsible for making or enforcing the policy?

3. Is there evidence of an actual or expected change in quantity or price due to the policy change?

4. What prices will be affected by the change?

5. Who is first affected by the change in the market?
   (a) The buyer.
   (b) The seller.

6. What determinants of demand and supply are changing?

7. Examine the diagrams in Figure 14.6. Which one best represents the shift?   a   b   c   d   (circle one)

Crossword Puzzle

Select the economic term in the following list that corresponds with each of the definitions and descriptions below. Then fit the term or one of the words within it into the crossword puzzle at the numbers indicated.

aggregate
  demand
cost-push
  inflation
cyclical
  unemployment
demand-pull
  inflation
inflation rate
investment
labor
labor force
marginal tax
  rates
market power
market shortage
natural rate of
  unemployment

nominal income
opportunity cost
Phillips curve
productivity
profit-push
  inflation
real income
relative
  price
saving
stagflation
structural
  unemployment
tax rebate
unit labor cost
wage–price
  control

196

Across

1. The quantity of the next most desirable commodity or service that must be forgone in order to produce a particular good.
4. Often the cornerstone of an incomes policy.
7. Taxes returned by the government.
11. A graph of the relationship between inflation and unemployment.
13. The change in taxes for a change in income.
16. A measure of the rise in average prices.
17. The dollar value of the goods and services that can be bought in a particular year.
18. A rise in average prices often resulting from union wage demands.
21. People above the age of 16 who are working or are seeking work.
24. The gap between demand and supply of a product, often induced by price controls.
25. Output per unit of labor time.

Down

2. A worsening of both inflation and unemployment.
3. Nominal GNP corrected for inflation.
5. Long-term rate of unemployment determined by structural features of labor and product markets, if government does not interfere.
6. One of the three factors of production; often the source of cost-push inflation.
8. Expenditures on capital.
9. Lack of work because people's skills or locations do not mesh with the needs of the job market.
10. An average increase in prices caused by businesses' attempts to increase the percentage of the revenues that they make above costs.
12. An average increase in prices caused by excess of expenditures above income when the economy is fully employed.
14. Lack of jobs because of inadequate aggregate demand.
15. The unit value of one good in comparison with the unit value of other goods.
19. Often mistaken as being identical to wages, but may be quite different, depending on productivity.
20. $C + I + G +$ net exports.
22. Disposable income that is not consumed.
23. The ability to alter prices or wages in a market.

Common Errors

The first statement in each "common error" below is incorrect. Each incorrect statement is followed by a corrected version and an explanation.

1. Labor productivity increases when more is produced per dollar of wages. WRONG!

   Labor productivity increases when more units of product are produced per unit of labor. RIGHT!

   Productivity changes are not directly related to wage levels. Wage levels reflect a large number of influences embodied in the demand and supply curves for labor. Productivity, however, is a physical measure of the relation between units of product and the amount of labor needed to produce them.

2. Price controls are ineffective and cause distortions. WRONG!

   Price controls may be effective, but when they are, they cause distortions. RIGHT!

   If price controls do not have an effect, it is hard to argue that they can cause distortions. Price controls cause distortions in production, profits, and other measures of performance through their effect on prices. If price controls are ineffective in altering prices, the economy continues to function through the market mechanism. If controls are effective, relative prices will be distorted.

3. Higher wages cause inflation. WRONG!

   Any wage settlement that increases wages less than productivity increases is not necessarily inflationary. RIGHT!

   Remember that a firm does not lose profits if it can offset wage increases with productivity increases. By the same logic, wages in the amount of productivity increases do not force prices to increase.

197

4. The Phillips curve is simply a demand curve. WRONG!

    Although the Phillips curve is related to supply and demand curves, it is not the same as either a demand or a supply curve. RIGHT!

    Table 14.4 shows some of the major differences separating Phillips curves, market demand curves, and aggregate demand curves. The axes of the three curves are very different.

Table 14.4
Characteristics of three types of demand curve

Source of differences			
Type of curve	X-axis	Y-axis	Market
Phillips curve	Unemployment	Inflation	Aggregate labor market
Market demand curve	Quantity per time period	Price	Single market
Aggregate demand curve	Output per time period	Price index	Aggregate product market

5. We can't have full employment with price stability. WRONG!

    Full employment with price stability is possible, although it may be difficult to achieve. RIGHT!

    Look at the definition of full employment again. It is the lowest rate of unemployment with price stability. Although we may be able to increase production above full employment, it will cause inflation.

■ ANSWERS ■

Key-Term Review

1. wage–price controls
2. Phillips curve
3. labor force
4. labor productivity
5. stagflation
6. aggregate supply
7. cost-push inflation
8. structural unemployment
9. profit-push inflation
10. derived demand
11. unit labor cost
12. market power
13. saving
14. tax rebate
15. marginal tax rate
16. investment
17. equation of exchange
18. tax elasticity of supply
19. Laffer curve
20. transfer payment

True or False

1. T	5. T	9. F	12. F	15. F	18. T
2. T	6. F	10. F	13. F	16. T	19. F
3. T	7. T	11. T	14. T	17. T	20. T
4. T	8. T				

Multiple Choice

1. d	6. c	11. b	15. d	19. d	23. c
2. c	7. b	12. d	16. c	20. b	24. d
3. c	8. c	13. a	17. c	21. b	25. b
4. c	9. a	14. c	18. b	22. d	26. a
5. a	10. c				

Problems and Applications

Exercise 1

1. D, B, A, C

2. **Table 14.1 answer**

Aggregate demand curve	A	B	C	D
Equilibrium price index	1.1	1.2	1.3	1.8

3. See Table 14.2 answer, column 1.

Table 14.2 answer

Aggregate demand curve	(1) Equilibrium price change	(2) Equilibrium output (billions of units per year)	(3) Unemployment rate
A	− 8.3%	2.0	15%
B	0.0	3.0	8
C	8.3	4.0	5
D	50.0	4.0	5

4. See Table 14.2 answer, column 2.
5. c

6. **Table 14.3 answer**

Production rate (billions of units per year)	2	3	4
Unemployment rate (percent)	15	8	5

7. See Table 14.2 answer, column 3.
8. d
9. c
10. Phillips curve

Figure 14.3 answer

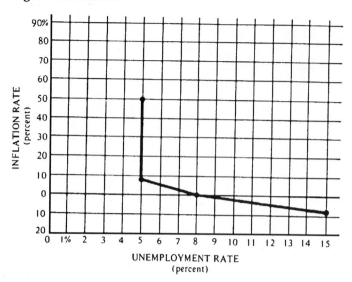

Exercise 2

1. b
2. c
3. b
4. b
5. a
6. c
7. b
8. d
9. a

Exercise 3

Figure 14.5 answer

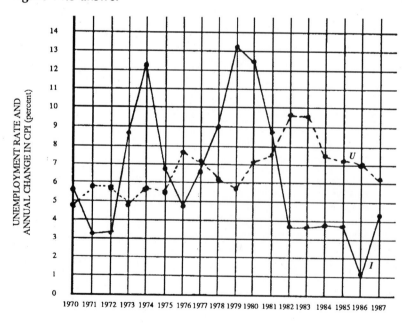

1. a
2. No
3. The Phillips curve presents all of the information in one curve, not two separate curves. The negative slope or positive slope of this curve indicates whether the variables are directly or inversely related to each other. If the unemployment rate and inflation rate are drawn over time, it is more difficult to see the inverse or direct relationship.

Exercise 4

1. The title "Mexico Freezes Peso, Prices" indicates the supply-side policy change.
2. The article only states that the "Mexican Government" or "the administration of President Miguel de la Madrid" is taking the action.
3. Again words in the title "to slow rampant inflation" indicate the anticipated effect.
4. The changes will include "the peso's exchange rate and the prices of all state-controlled goods and services" as well as moderation of "wage increases."
5. a
6. Costs of resources and the prices of goods and services are changing.
7. b To the extent that resource costs change, the shifts involve supply.

Crossword Puzzle Answer

Across

1. opportunity *cost*
4. wage-price *control*
7. tax *rebate*
11. *Phillips* curve
13. marginal tax *rates*
16. *inflation* rate
17. nominal *income*
18. cost-*push* inflation
21. labor *force*
24. *market* shortage
25. *productivity*

Down

2. *stagflation*
3. *real* income
5. *natural* rate of unemployment
6. *labor*
8. *investment*
9. *structural* unemployment
10. *profit*-push inflation
12. demand-*pull* inflation
14. cyclical *unemployment*
15. relative *price*
19. *unit* labor cost
20. aggregate *demand*
22. *saving*
23. market *power*

Chapter 15
Theory and Reality

Quick Review

Designing economic policy for an economy as large and diverse as that of the United States is a very difficult job, and using the available tools in a complementary fashion to implement the policy adds to the complexity. It is thus appropriate that we consider the following questions:

- What is the ideal "package" of macro policies?
- How well does our macro performance live up to the promises of that package?
- What kinds of obstacles prevent us from achieving all of our economic goals?

We begin by noting that the president and Congress are responsible for making economic policy and achieving economic goals. One goal that is unanimously supported is that of eliminating the business cycle because achieving that goal alone would solve many problems all at once.

There are a number of policy tools in the arsenal that can be used to fight upswings and downswings in the economy. Monetary policy tools (open-market operations, changing reserve requirements, etc.) and fiscal policy tools (changing taxes and spending) are the most powerful ones. Economic forecasters, who advise policy makers, follow a variety of indicators and use econometric models to predict problems. Many, many economic resources are devoted to the study and development of economic policy. Yet our policies seem to fail. Why? There are many reasons. One is the lack of unanimity within the economics profession about how the economy works. There are several "groups" of economists that have been identified—Keynesians, Monetarists, Supply-siders, Rational Expectationists, and so on—who have somewhat different views about how to achieve economic stability.

Other serious problems plague us, too:

1. *Measurement problems.* It's difficult to measure what we want to know, to find current measurements when measurement is possible, or to make accurate forecasts even with current information.
2. *Design problems.* We don't know *exactly* how the economy responds to specific policies. Perverse reaction to government policies may actually worsen the problem the policy was intended to solve.
3. *Implementation problems.* It takes time for Congress and the president to agree on an appropriate plan of action. Four types of lag seem to prevent policies from being implemented quickly: recognition lag, lag in formulation of a response, lag in the response itself, and lag in the impact of the policy.

For all of these reasons the fine-tuning of economic performance rarely lives up to its theoretical potential. In addition, the continual changes of policy lead to a lack of credibility on the part of policy makers. Because of their rational expectations about the continually changing policies, people are likely to act in ways that defeat policy initiatives of the government.

Learning Objectives

After reading Chapter 15 and doing the following exercises, you should:	True or false	Multiple choice	Problems and applications	Common errors	Pages in the text
1. Know the three basic types of policies and each of the policy instruments.		12,22	3		352–357
2. Know how the concept of opportunity cost defines the basic policy trade-offs facing the economy.		13	1,2		353–357
3. Be able to prescribe policies to eliminate a recessionary gap.	1,6,11	2	3	1	357–358
4. Be able to design policies to deal with an inflationary gap.		3,11	3		358–359
5. Be able to suggest policies to control stagflation.	2	4	3	2	360–361
6. Know the general beliefs of several groups of economists.	15	16–19			359
7. Evaluate how effective policy makers have been in battling inflation and unemployment.	3–5	1,15		3	361–363
8. Be able to explain how measurement problems impede policy.	7–10,17	5,23			364–369
9. Understand the concept of a leading indicator.		5,20,21			367
10. Understand the design problems encountered in administering policy and the problems of forecasting.	13,14	6,7,15, 23,24	1,2,4		368–369
11. Know the "rational expectations" argument about the effectiveness of policy.	12,15	8			376–377
12. Recognize the lags involved in policy implementation.		9,10,23	4		370–374
13. Know the advantages and problems of rules and discretion in policy.	16	14			375–377
14. Review Chapters 4–14.			1		

Key-Term Review

Review the following terms; if you are not sure of the meaning of any term, write out the definition and check it against the Glossary in the text.

automatic stabilizer	natural rate of unemployment
business cycle	opportunity costs
fine-tuning	rational expectations
fiscal policy	recessionary gap
inflationary gap	structural deficit
monetary policy	supply-side policy
multiplier	velocity of money (V)

Fill in the blank following each of the statements below with the appropriate term from the list above.

1. During a downswing in economic activity, unemployment compensation supports disposable income and is an _____.

1. _____

2. When the government has to sacrifice production of consumer goods in order to produce weapons, then the weapons have _____ which can be measured in terms of consumer goods forgone.

2. _____

3. When the government adjusts policies to maintain full employment, it is engaging in _____.

3. _____

4. Because of the inability of policy makers to eliminate the _____ completely and because of the resulting changes in unemployment, many feel that economic theory is in error.

4. _____

5. Changes in taxes and expenditures are changes in _____.

5. _____

6. Only if the economy is at full employment will the _____ and the actual deficit be equal.

6. _____

7. The chairman of the Federal Reserve Board of Governors is the most powerful figure in making _____.

7. _____

8. Monetarists argue that the unemployment rate can go below the _____ in the short run only.

8. _____

9. _____ rests on the assumption that individuals and firms will respond to changes in incentives.

9. _____

10. To close a _____, a Keynesian would likely suggest cutting taxes and increasing spending.

10. _____

11. The greater the *MPC* is, the greater will be the _____.

11. _____

12. Monetarists argue that fiscal policy doesn't matter as long as the _____ is constant.

12. _____

13. It can be argued that when government policy loses credibility, people act according to their _____, which counteracts any policy initiatives.

13. _____

14. The _____ is the amount by which desired spending exceeds output at full employment.

14. _____

True or False: *Circle your choice.*

T F 1. To attain the economy's goals, fiscal and monetary policy should be consistent. For example, when the money supply is increased, fiscal policy should be expansionary.

T F 2. When the economy is experiencing stagflation, it is appropriate to ease monetary policy and cut taxes.

T F 3. "Fine-tuning" refers to the ability of policy makers to make slight adjustments to the economy in order to attain economic goals.

T F 4. Since the Employment Act of 1946, the government has kept unemployment below 5 percent for all but three years.

T F 5. In defending monetary policy for 1986, during which the money supply grew by 15 percent, the Fed cited an increase in velocity as a justification.

T F 6. A major change in the personal income tax during the 1980s was the reduction in marginal tax rates.

T F 7. The CBO and OMB tend to underestimate budget deficits and economic growth rates.

T F 8. The reason it is said that the government tends to solve only those problems it can measure is that policy makers need information to show that something is wrong before they can act.

T F 9. The reason the policy makers wanted to compile statistics after the Great Depression was that they hoped that if another depression came, they would be able to identify it soon enough to do something about it.

T F 10. Appropriations bills set forth amounts and purposes for which revenues can be spent.

T F 11. Either fiscal policy or monetary policy can be used in attempts to maintain levels of aggregate demand.

T F 12. Rational expectations about the effect of a government policy may lead to private-sector actions that defeat the policy.

T F 13. Because President Reagan reappointed Paul Volcker, we may infer that the Fed consistently supports the administration's economic policy initiatives.

T F 14. One of the constraints on policy makers is that the economy is characterized by groups that have the same goals.

T F 15. The New Classical economists developed a synthesis of conflicting views and feel that they have rescued discretionary economic policy.

T F 16. The structural deficit declines as the economy moves toward full employment.

T F 17. Democratic administrations appear to have achieved higher real economic growth rates than their Republican counterparts when measured over four-year terms.

Multiple Choice: *Select the correct answer.*

_____ 1. Which of the following statements is an accurate description of our success in attaining the nation's stated goals?
   (a) Since the passage of the Employment Act of 1946, we have fallen short of our full-employment target—a 4 percent rate of unemployment—only twice; until 1968 the price level was completely stable.
   (b) The price level has risen continuously since World War II at an annual rate in excess of 5 percent; the full-employment target has almost never been attained.
   (c) During the 1960s and early 1970s, the economy moved progressively toward its full-employment target, with a very tolerable 1.5 percent annual increase in the level of prices.
   (d) None of the statements above is an accurate description.

_____ 2. The government's best policy during a recession is to:
   (a) Expand the money supply and increase federal spending.
   (b) Expand the money supply and lower federal spending.
   (c) Contract the money supply and increase federal spending.
   (d) Contract the money supply and lower federal spending.

_____ 3. The government's best policy during an inflationary period is to:
   (a) Expand the money supply and increase federal spending.
   (b) Expand the money supply and lower federal spending.
   (c) Contract the money supply and increase federal spending.
   (d) Contract the money supply and lower federal spending.

_____ 4. Wage and price controls are most appropriately used during periods of:
   (a) Stagflation.
   (b) Inflation and low unemployment.
   (c) Recession and deflation.
   (d) Rising prices for imports.

_____ 5. Many economists argue that the CPI overstates inflation by 2 to 3 percent. From the point of view of those designing economic policy, this is an example of:
   (a) A goal conflict.
   (b) A measurement problem.
   (c) A design problem.
   (d) An implementation problem.

_____ 6. Which of the following is a reason that many economic policies fail, even if they are properly designed to achieve economic goals?
   (a) Measurement difficulties prevent policy makers from correctly identifying what is happening in the economy.
   (b) People often react in perverse ways that may undercut new government policies.
   (c) There are important lags in response to policy.
   (d) All of the above are reasons for economic policy failure.

_____ 7. The reason that economic forecasting of the economy is most important and useful is that:
   (a) Economists need employment.
   (b) Business managers need to be able to anticipate government actions that will affect their firms and industries.
   (c) Policy makers need to be able to anticipate what needs to be done and take action in time to be effective in achieving the desired result.
   (d) Consumers can find out when they are going to lose their jobs and income.

_____ 8. The economic reason that the government must purposely surprise the economy with a new policy is:
   (a) To avoid perverse behavior that worsens the economic problem that the policy is designed to solve.
   (b) To overcome the resistance of malicious bureaucrats.
   (c) To attract people's attention so they will know there is a new policy.
   (d) To allow everyone to get the information.

_____ 9. Which of the following is the *appropriate order* in which lags cause policy actions to be tardy in their effects?
   (a) Response design, recognition, impact, and implementation.
   (b) Recognition, response design, implementation, and impact.
   (c) Impact, implementation, recognition, and response design.
   (d) Impact, recognition, response design, and implementation.

_____ 10. Which of the following actions would cause the longest lag between recognition of a problem and appropriate stabilization responses to it?
   (a) Congress takes the authority over stabilization so that it does not need to wait for the executive branch to respond.
   (b) The appropriation and authorization responsibilities of Congress are transferred to the executive branch in order to eliminate congressional lags.
   (c) Congress writes legislation providing more built-in stabilizers in the economy.
   (d) Congress provides limited authority to the president to alter fiscal or monetary policy for the purpose of stabilization.

_____ 11. Why might Congress or the president hesitate to apply restrictive fiscal policies?
   (a) Monetary policy is always more effective.
   (b) Voters might lose jobs and income.
   (c) Fiscal policy is too complex.
   (d) Fiscal-year appropriations are not under the authority of Congress.

_____12. Which of the following is *not* one of the three basic types of policies mentioned in the textbook?
   (a) Monetary policy.
   (b) Rational expectations policy.
   (c) Fiscal policy.
   (d) Supply-side policy.

_____13. Which of the following concepts does *not* represent basic trade-offs faced by a government?
   (a) Production-possibilities curve.
   (b) Phillips curve.
   (c) Opportunity costs.
   (d) Fine-tuning.

_____14. Because of rational expectations about government policy changes, it has been recommended that government policy consist of:
   (a) Unalterable rules.
   (b) Discretion.
   (c) Faster measurement.
   (d) Shorter lags in policy.

_____15. At one time, the Carter administration proposed a $50 tax rebate and then withdrew it when conditions changed. Which of the following were most likely involved in making that decision?
   (a) Measurement problems.
   (b) Design problems.
   (c) Implementation problems.
   (d) All of the above.

_____16. Which of the following groups of economists would argue that the American economy is inherently unstable because of its capitalist structure?
   (a) Neo-Keynesians.
   (b) Supply-siders.
   (c) Marxists.
   (d) Monetarists.

_____17. Which of the following feels that once the private sector figures out what the government is doing, it takes actions based on rational expectations to offset it?
   (a) Keynesians.
   (b) New Classicists.
   (c) Supply-siders.
   (d) Marxists.

_____18. Which of the following groups feels that output and employment gravitate to their "natural levels"?
   (a) Keynesians.
   (b) Monetarists.
   (c) New Classical economists.
   (d) Marxists.

_____19. Which groups agree on the way a tax cut can cure a recessionary gap?
   (a) Monetarists and Keynesians.
   (b) Monetarists and Supply-siders.
   (c) Supply-siders and New Classicists.
   (d) None of the above.

_____20. Which of the following is *not* a leading indicator for economic activity?
   (a) Average workweek.
   (b) Delivery times.
   (c) Natural rate of unemployment.
   (d) Money supply.

_____21. The index of leading indicators is an index of twelve indicators that:
- (a) Move in the same direction at the same time.
- (b) Frequently move in different directions at the same time.
- (c) Are given equal weights in the index.
- (d) Generally lead the economy with a lag of about twelve months.

_____22. Congress is responsible for:
- (a) Monetary policy.
- (b) Fiscal policy.
- (c) Monetary and fiscal policy.
- (d) Monetary, fiscal, and supply-side policy.

_____23. The Fed allowed the money supply to grow at a well-above-target rate of 15 percent in 1986. Which of the following could *not* be used to justify this policy?
- (a) Deregulation of the banking system.
- (b) The availability of interest-bearing checking accounts, which reduced the opportunity cost of holding transactions deposits.
- (c) The low inflation rate, which improved money's performance as a store of value.
- (d) None of the above.

_____24. Which act established the following goals for the economy: 4 percent unemployment; 4 percent economic growth; 3 percent inflation?
- (a) The Gramm-Rudman Act of 1985.
- (b) The Employment Act of 1946.
- (c) The Employment and Balanced-Growth Act of 1978.
- (d) The Omnibus Reconciliation Act of 1988.

Problems and Applications

Exercise 1

This exercise shows the relationship between income and various economic aggregates that have been studied in Chapters 4–14.

Table 15.1 presents data on interest rates, government expenditures, taxes, exports, imports, investment, consumption, the GNP deflator, unemployment, and pollution for four levels of equilibrium income (GNP). These items appear frequently in newspaper articles about the economy. In the following questions you should be able to explain some of the relationships apparent in Table 15.1.

Table 15.1
Level of key economic indicators, by GNP level
(billions of dollars per year)

	30%	20%	10%	0%
Interest rate	30%	20%	10%	0%
Government expenditures	$ 100	$ 100	$ 100	$ 100
Taxes	$ 25	$ 75	$ 125	$ 175
Budget balance	$____	$____	$____	$____
Exports	$ 300	$ 300	$ 300	$ 300
Imports	$ 260	$ 280	$ 300	$ 320
Balance of trade	$____	$____	$____	$____
Investment	$ 10	$ 90	$ 170	$ 250
Consumption	$ 750	$ 790	$ 830	$ 870
Nominal GNP	$____	$____	$____	$____
Saving	$____	$____	$____	$____
GNP deflator (index)	1.00	1.00	1.02	1.10
Real GNP (constant dollars)	$____	$____	$____	$____
Unemployment rate	15%	7%	4%	3.5%
Pollution index	1.00	1.80	1.80	1.80

1. Compute the federal budget balance, balance of trade, nominal GNP, saving, and real GNP in Table 15.1, for each level of nominal GNP. (*Hint:* Remember the formula $C + I + G + [X - M] =$ GNP; see Chapter 4.)

2. Which of the following policies is the government most likely changing to reach each of the income levels in Table 15.1?
   (a) Fiscal policy.
   (b) Monetary policy.
   (c) Wage and price controls.
   (d) Labor policy.

3. Which of the following statements is *not* likely to explain why pollution changes with income, as indicated in Table 15.1?
   (a) Normal waste facilities are unable to handle the extra waste when the economy approaches capacity production.
   (b) When income rises, people have the money to dispose of waste more efficiently.
   (c) As income rises, people buy more houses; thus more land is cleared and streams are polluted.
   (d) Increased economic activity (higher GNP) naturally generates more waste.

4. Which of the following statements best explains why taxes might change with income, as shown in Table 15.1?
   (a) Taxpayers experience bracket creep.
   (b) As taxpayers' incomes rise, their taxes rise.
   (c) The income tax is regressive.
   (d) Automatic stabilizers link taxes with income.

5. Which of the following statements best explains why imports change with income, as shown in Table 15.1?
   (a) People consume more foreign goods as their incomes rise.
   (b) People consume more domestic goods as their incomes rise.
   (c) Government buys fewer domestic goods as incomes rise.
   (d) People consume fewer domestic goods as their incomes rise.

6. Which of the following statements best explains why exports *do not* change with GNP?
   (a) Exports are determined by the incomes (GNP) of people in other countries.
   (b) Exports increase with GNP because firms can afford to produce more.
   (c) Exports decrease with GNP because people at home need goods and can pay for them.
   (d) Exports equal imports at all levels of income as the dollar adjusts to bring them into equilibrium.

7. The reason that the price index changes with income, as shown in Table 15.1, is most likely that:
   (a) As people receive greater income, they can be more discriminating buyers and find the lowest prices.
   (b) As businesses receive more orders, they make greater profits, which show up in the form of higher prices.
   (c) As people receive greater income, they spend it even with the economy is at full capacity, thus bidding up prices.
   (d) As businesses receive greater income, they are stimulated to expand capacity and must pass the cost of the increased capacity to consumers through higher prices.

8. The reason that unemployment changes with income, as shown in Table 15.1, is most likely that:
   (a) As incomes rise, people do not need jobs and therefore leave the labor force.
   (b) As incomes rise, automatic stabilizers provide increased benefits to the unemployed, keeping them out of the labor force.
   (c) As incomes rise, inflation causes real income and employment to fall.
   (d) As incomes rise, aggregate demand rises, stimulating the derived demand for labor.

9. As income increases, the balance of trade worsens, which lowers the value of the dollar, because with higher income:
   (a) People buy more imports.
   (b) Businesses produce more goods for U.S. exports.
   (c) Businesses take goods out of export in order to sell them domestically.
   (d) None of the above is the case.

10. Referring to Table 15.1, draw the Phillips curve in Figure 15.1. Compute the inflation rate from the base year price index (remember the index in the base year is 1.0) for each level of income.

Figure 15.1

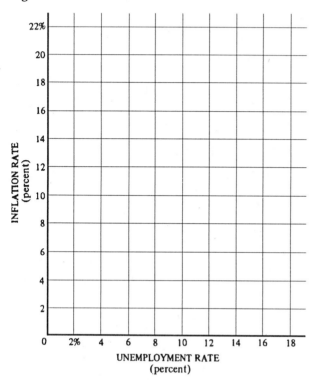

Exercise 2

This exercise shows the difficulties facing policy makers because of trade-offs in the economy.

Table 15.2 presents data on government expenditure, taxes, exports, imports, GNP deflator, unemployment, and pollution for four levels of equilibrium income (GNP). These items appear frequently in newspaper articles about the economy.

Table 15.2
Level of key economic indicators, by GNP level
(billions of dollars per year)

Indicator	Nominal GNP			
	$120	$160	$200	$240
Government expenditure	$ 0	$ 20	$ 35	$ 50
Taxes	$ 18	$ 24	$ 30	$ 36
Budget balance	$___	$___	$___	$___
Exports	$ 10	$ 10	$ 10	$ 10
Imports	$ 0	$ 10	$ 15	$ 20
Balance of trade	$___	$___	$___	$___
GNP deflator (index)	1.00	1.00	1.02	1.20
Real GNP (constant dollars)	$___	$___	$___	$___
Unemployment rate	15%	7%	4%	3.5%
Pollution index	1.00	1.10	1.80	1.90

1. Compute the federal budget balance, balance of trade, and real GNP in Table 15.2 for each level of nominal GNP.

2. What government expenditure level would best accomplish all of the following goals according to Table 15.2? $_____

   - Lowest taxes.
   - Largest trade surplus.
   - Lowest pollution.
   - Lowest inflation rate.

3. Which of the following reasons might induce a policy maker to choose a higher government expenditure level than the one that answers Problem 2?
   (a) High unemployment.
   (b) Government inability to provide public goods and services.
   (c) Low real income.
   (d) All of the above.

4. What government expenditure level would best accomplish all of the following goals? $_____

   - Lowest unemployment rate.
   - Highest amount of public goods and services.
   - Highest real income.

5. For the policy that best satisfies the goals in Problem 4, there would most likely be:
   (a) A recessionary gap.
   (b) An inflationary gap.
   (c) A GNP gap.
   (d) None of the above.

6. At what level of government expenditure is the value of the dollar in greatest danger? (*Note:* If there is a large trade deficit, the value of the dollar would fall.) $_____

7. Which government expenditure level would best accomplish all of the following goals? $_____

   - Balancing the federal budget.
   - Balancing the balance of trade.
   - Maintaining pollution at reasonably low levels.
   - Maintaining price stability.

8. At which government expenditure level does full employment occur? (*Hint:* Look at the definition of full employment. Use 4 percent unemployment as full employment.) $_____.

9. If you were a policy maker faced with the alternatives in Table 15.2, would you be able to say that one of the alternative government expenditure levels was clearly best? _____

Exercise 3

This exercise checks to see if you can find the appropriate policy action for various undesirable economic conditions.

Choose the policy actions from the list below that would be appropriate to correct the economic conditions at the top of Table 15.3. Mark the letter of each item only once in Table 15.3.

a. Deregulation.
b. Discount rate lowered.
c. Discount rate raised.
d. Government spending decreases.
e. Government spending increases.
f. Open-market operations (Fed buys government securities).
g. Open-market operations (Fed sells government securities).

h. Reserve requirement higher.
i. Reserve requirement lower.
j. Skill training and other labor market aids.
k. Tax cuts.
l. Tax incentives to alter the structure of supply and demand
m Tax incentives to encourage saving.
n. Tax increases.
o. Wage–price controls.

Table 15.3
Economic policies

	Recessionary gap	Inflationary gap	Stagflation
Fiscal policy	1. _____	6. _____	
	2. _____	7. _____	
Monetary policy	3. _____	8. _____	
	4. _____	9. _____	
	5. _____	10. _____	
Supply-side policy		11. _____	12. _____
			13. _____
			14. _____
			15. _____

Exercise 4

The media often provide information about the government's slowness in responding to the economy's needs. By using one of the articles in the text, this exercise will show the kind of information to look for. If your professor makes a newspaper assignment for this chapter, this exercise will provide an example of how to do it.

Reread the article in Chapter 7 entitled "Yugoslavs Jam Food Stores to Beat Steep Price Boosts" from the *Wall Street Journal*. Then answer the following questions:

1. What passage in the article provides evidence of an implementation lag?

2. What sentence indicates who is responsible for the policy?

3. What phrase indicates the reason or event that requires a policy response?

4. What sentence shows the undesirable effect of the lag?

Common Errors

The first statement in each "common error" below is incorrect. Each incorrect statement is followed by a corrected version and an explanation.

1. Fiscal and monetary policy should be consistently applied to stimulate the economy. WRONG!

   Fiscal and monetary policies must be tailored to the specific economic problems faced by the government. RIGHT!

   The government sometimes needs to apply apparently contradictory monetary and fiscal policies in order to attain quite different goals. For example, an expansionary fiscal policy may be needed to stimulate the economy, but a contractionary monetary policy may be needed to raise interest rates so that foreign capital will be enticed into the United States. A policy maker must weigh the various goals and decide on the appropriate mix of tools to achieve them.

2. Fiscal, monetary, and stagflation policies are effective regardless of the income level of the economy. WRONG!

   The state of the economy in relation to full employment is important in determining the effectiveness of the various policies. RIGHT!

   If the economy is experiencing an inflationary gap, wage–price controls will prove ineffective in curbing demand-pull inflation. At relatively low levels of GNP, however, wage–price controls can be effective in holding down cost-push and profit-push inflation. Work force policies are often more effective in matching people with jobs when many people are looking for work than when unemployment is low. It is easier for the government to increase expenditures to stimulate the economy when there is a recession than to cut them back when there is an inflationary gap.

3. The government has the power to prevent unemployment and inflation, but it just doesn't want to use it. WRONG!

   While the government has the power to move the economy closer to any one goal, it faces a trade-off between different goals that prevents it from achieving all of them. RIGHT!

   Remember that the Phillips curve shows that a trade-off exists between unemployment and inflation. Government policies to lower unemployment may lead to a worsening of inflation. The government must choose between the different goals.

■ ANSWERS ■

Key-Term Review

1. automatic stabilizer
2. opportunity costs
3. fine-tuning
4. business cycle
5. fiscal policy
6. structural deficit
7. monetary policy
8. natural rate of unemployment
9. supply-side policy
10. recessionary gap
11. multiplier
12. velocity of money (V)
13. rational expectations
14. inflationary gap

True or False

1. F	4. F	7. F	10. T	13. F	16. F
2. F	5. F	8. T	11. T	14. F	17. F
3. T	6. T	9. T	12. T	15. F	

Multiple Choice

1. d	5. b	9. b	13. d	17. b	21. b
2. a	6. d	10. a	14. a	18. b	22. b
3. d	7. c	11. b	15. d	19. d	23. d
4. a	8. a	12. b	16. c	20. c	24. c

Problems and Applications

Exercise 1

1. **Table 15.1 answer**
   (billions of dollars per year)

Interest rate	30%	20%	10%	0%
Budget balance	– $ 75	– $ 25	$ 25	$ 75
Balance of trade	40	20	0	– 20
Nominal GNP	900	1,000	1,100	1,200
Saving	125	135	145	155
Real GNP (constant dollars)	900	1,000	1,078	1,091

At the 30 percent interest rate, the following calculations should have been made, in billions of dollars per year:

budget balance = $25 – $100 = –$75
balance of trade = $300 – $260 = $40
nominal GNP = $750 + $10 + $100 + $40 = $900
saving   = disposable income – consumption
   = (GNP – taxes) – consumption = $900 – $25 – $750 = $125

2. b
3. b
4. b
5. a
6. a
7. c
8. d
9. a
10. For example, when income is $1,200 the price index is 1.10. The inflation rate is

$$\left(\frac{1.10}{1.00} - 1.00\right) \times 100\% = 10\%.$$

Figure 15.1 answer

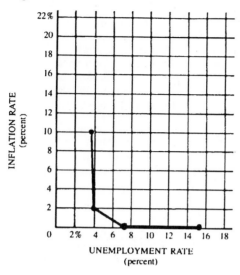

Exercise 2

1. **Table 15.2 answer**
   (billions of dollars per year)

| | Nominal GNP | | | |
Indicator	$120	$160	$200	$240
Budget balance	$ 18	$ 4	$ –5	$ –14
Balance of trade	10	0	–5	–10
Real GNP (constant dollars)	120	160	196	200

2. $0
3. d
4. $50 billion
5. b

6. $50 billion
7. $20 billion
8. $35 billion
9. No

Exercise 3

1. **Table 15.3 answer**

	Recessionary gap	Inflationary gap	Stagflation
Fiscal policy	1. k Tax cuts	6. n Tax increases	
	2. e Government spending increases	7. d Government spending decreases	
Monetary policy	3. b Discount rate lowered	8. c Discount rate raised	
	4. f Open-market operations (Fed buys government securities)	9. g Open-market operations (Fed sells government securities)	
	5. i Reserve requirement lower	10. h Reserve requirement higher	

(continued)

Table 15.3 answer (continued)

	Recessionary gap	Inflationary gap	Stagflation
Supply-side policy		11. m Tax incentives to encourage saving	12. a Deregulation 13. l Tax incentives to alter the structure of supply and demand 14. o Wage–price controls 15. j Skill training and other labor market aids

Exercise 4

1. "Yugoslavs jammed Belgrade food stores yesterday to buy food before it could be marked up." Because the price increases could not be implemented quickly enough, people were lining up.
2. "The government . . . announced an anti-inflation package that will initially push up prices of essential goods."
3. "fighting inflation of 135%"
4. "Yugoslavs poured into shops yesterday and began hoarding food supplies."

Chapter 16
The National Debt

Quick Review

The U.S. government has been in debt on a virtually continuous basis ever since the Continental Congress borrowed money to fight the Revolutionary War, and the debt grows every year. This chapter focuses on the relationship between annual deficits that created the national debt and such questions as:

- How did we get so far in debt?
- Who bears the burden of our national debt?
- Should we require balanced budgets and gradual elimination of the debt?

When the federal government's revenues fall short of its expenditures in any fiscal year, the U.S. Treasury issues some IOUs (e.g., Treasury bonds) and sells them to cover the difference. The difference between receipts and expenditures is called a "deficit." It is a "flow" concept because it has a time dimension. If you add up all of the Treasury's IOUs that are outstanding at any point in time, the sum is the national debt—currently in the neighborhood of $3 trillion. While the deficit is a flow measured over a period of time, the national debt is a stock concept, which means it can be measured or viewed at a single instant in time, like a photograph.

Most of the debt that accrued in the first 200 years of our history was incurred to fight wars or fight recessions. In the 1980s, however, the explosive growth of the debt largely resulted from the recessions in 1981 and 1984 and also the massive tax cuts from 1981–84. In spite of the unprecedented growth in the debt, the ratio of the national debt to the GNP, which is a measure of our ability to pay the interest on that debt, has been falling recently because the GNP has grown rapidly in nominal terms; it doubled between 1978 and 1987.

Most citizens are overwhelmed by the size of the debt and concerned about its effects both in the present and in the future. Some of the apprehension concerning the burden of the debt is unfounded. After all, while the national debt is a liability of the government (and its citizen-taxpayers), it is just as much of an asset to those who hold the debt. Nearly 90 percent of the federal government's debt is owned "internally" by banks and other financial institutions, the Federal Reserve, the social security trust fund, private individuals, and the like. The interest earned from holding government debt becomes an important source of income and security for many private individuals.

Only about 10 percent of the debt is owned externally, by foreigners. However, this foreign ownership is an important concern. Payments on their holdings of our debt mean that dollars must flow out of the country, which in turn has an impact on exchange rates. Debt that is purchased and held by foreigners allows us to avoid opportunity costs in the present, by providing us the wherewithal to import goods and services (and use foreign-owned resources). If foreigners in the future, however, turn in their bonds for dollars and use them to increase their imports from us, then future generations will have less output to consume. This would be a real burden. We are consuming today and paying tomorrow.

The national debt will never be paid off: when some of it comes due, the Treasury just issues more to obtain funds to pay it off. This "refinancing" is done routinely. Of course, the debt also has to be "serviced"—interest must be paid to those who own the debt. The required interest payments restrict the U.S. government's ability to spend and redistribute income from taxpayers to bondholders (many of whom are the same people) without imposing opportunity costs on society.

Only when the debt uses resources that would be employed other places *or* causes resources to be misallocated does society incur an opportunity cost. When government purchases goods and services, the resources used are denied to the rest of society. But society owns what the government buys, so the cost is borne in the present, and future generations will reap some of the benefits from the sacrifice today (e.g., they can use the bridge that was built today). Even when transfer payments are financed by selling bonds, few resources are used and the real cost borne today is very small.

The debt, however, raises questions. When government uses resources that would otherwise be used by the private sector, the mix of output is definitely changed. This is referred to as "crowding out" private output. If the rates of investment and economic growth are both slowed when government borrowing pushes interest rates up, this crowding out has a serious impact on the economy. Because of crowding out, future generations will have less capital to work with and thus less productive capacity. Of course, some of the things that government purchases—highways, schools, defense systems—benefit future generations too. The debate, then, is less about passing a burden on to future generations than about the relative role of public versus private spending.

Most discussions of the debt gloss over these reflections and focus only on the aggregate size of the debt. Some believe that "deficit ceilings" are a way to slow down or eliminate growth in the debt. The Gramm-Rudman-Hollings Act of 1985, for example, called for lower deficits each year until a balanced budget is achieved, and for automatic spending cutbacks if Congress fails to keep the deficit below the ceiling.

Learning Objectives

After reading Chapter 16 and doing the following exercises, you should:	True or false	Multiple choice	Problems and applications	Common errors	Pages in the text
1. Understand the history of the national debt and how it reached its present size.	1	1,6,12, 13,15	2	1,2	381–383
2. Know the relationship between annual deficits and the national debt.	2,16,20	5,10,13	1,2,3	1,2	385–389
3. Know the principal owners of the debt, and understand the implications of internal and external debt ownership.	5–12,20	1,2,3, 17,21			383–385, 390–392
4. Understand why the debt will be continually refinanced and thus *never* paid off.	13–15	5–8,16	1,2	1,2,3	385–390
5. Be able to articulate the opportunity-cost argument concerning the burden of the debt.	17–19,21	9,11,14, 15,17–20	2	1	385–390
6. Know the difference between deficit ceilings and debt ceilings.	1,3,4,6, 13,14,18,20	4,6–8,10, 13,15,18	1,2	1	392–394

Key-Term Review

Review the following terms; if you are not sure of the meaning of any term, write out the definition and check it against the Glossary in the text.

asset
budget deficit
budget surplus
crowding out
debt ceiling
debt servicing
deficit ceiling
external debt
internal debt

liability
national debt
open-market operations
opportunity cost
optimal mix of output
production possibilities
refinancing
Treasury bonds
transfer payments

Fill in the blank following each of the statements below with the appropriate term from the list above.

1. When the federal government spends more than it receives in tax revenue, the difference is called a _____.

    1. _____

2. The sum total of all the deficits accumulated by the federal government is referred to as the _____.

    2. _____

3. The bonds that are owned by foreign households and institutions are known as _____.

    3. _____

4. The bonds that are owned by U.S. households and institutions are known as _____.

    4. _____

5. Most discussions concerning the national debt focus on the debt as a _____.

    5. _____

6. People often neglect the fact that the debt is an _____ to those who own it.

    6. _____

7. If the federal government were to run a _____, then the debt could be reduced.

    7. _____

8. To provide funds for _____ and to retire bonds that may mature, the Treasury engages in _____, that is, selling new bonds to retire old bonds.

    8. _____

    _____

9. _____ on the balance sheet of the Federal Reserve System are used to conduct _____.

    9. _____

    _____

10. Any real burden of the debt must result in an _____ for society.

    10. _____

11. Many people feel that budget deficits result in a less than _____.

    11. _____

12. The Gramm-Rudman-Hollings Act sought to address this problem by imposing a _____ on Congress.

    12. _____

13. The imposition of a _____ has been unsuccessful in halting growth in the national debt.

    13. _____

14. The _____ hypothesis suggests that the debt influences where the economy is on the _____ curve.

    14. _____

    _____

15. _____ are payments to individuals for which no currently produced goods or services are exchanged.

    15. _____

True or False: *Circle your choice.*

T F 1. The national debt is a stock concept, as opposed to annual deficits, which are a flow concept.

T F 2. When the GNP grows faster than the debt, the debt's relative size increases.

T F   3. The only way to prevent the national debt from growing is to balance the federal budget annually.

T F   4. The national debt grows when state and local governments spend in excess of their tax revenues.

T F   5. When we speak of the national debt, we refer to the debt of the federal government only.

T F   6. The national debt is an asset to those who own it and a liability of the federal government.

T F   7. Less of the federal debt is owned by state and local governments than is owned by foreigners.

T F   8. Nearly one-half of the national debt is owned by the private sector.

T F   9. When foreigners add to their debt holdings U.S. residents can consume more than they produce.

T F 10. Bonds owned by financial institutions represent indirect ownership of the national debt by the private sector.

T F 11. Internal ownership of the debt refers to that part of the national debt owned by government agencies.

T F 12. Externally held debt refers to that part of the national debt owned by private individuals, and internally held debt refers to that part owned by the public sector.

T F 13. The last time the national debt actually decreased in size was over thirty years ago.

T F 14. When the government refinances a portion of the debt, the debt must grow larger, *ceteris paribus*.

T F 15. Each part of the national debt is paid off when it comes due.

T F 16. Debt servicing refers to the payment of interest and repayment of principal on the debt.

T F 17. National wealth is reduced when the federal government borrows money by selling bonds.

T F 18. Because the government must pay interest on the public debt, its ability to balance the budget or fund public-sector activities is reduced.

T F 19. If those receiving interest payments on the debt have a higher marginal propensity to consume than those paying the taxes for debt servicing, aggregate demand should increase.

T F 20. When the Fed sells bonds in the open market, the national debt goes up.

T F 21. The opportunity cost of government purchases is greater when financed by borrowing than when financed by taxes.

Multiple Choice: *Select the correct answer.*

_____ 1. Which of the following owns the largest amount of the federal debt?
   (a) Foreigners.
   (b) Federal agencies in the executive branch of government.
   (c) State and local governments.
   (d) The Federal Reserve System.

_____ 2. What proportion of the national debt is owned by the private sector?
   (a) Nearly half.
   (b) About ninety percent.
   (c) About ten percent.
   (d) About twenty-five percent.

_____ 3. Which of the following would represent internal ownership of the national debt?
   (a) Bonds owned by the Federal Reserve System.
   (b) Bonds owned by the Social Security Administration.
   (c) Bonds owned by private individuals.
   (d) All of the above.

_____ 4. There has been an absolute increase but not a relative increase (relative to the GNP) in the size of:
 (a) The deficit but not the debt.
 (b) The debt but not the deficit.
 (c) The deficit and the debt.
 (d) Neither the deficit nor the debt.

_____ 5. Treasury bonds are:
 (a) An asset on the balance sheet of the Federal Reserve System.
 (b) A liability on the balance sheet of the U.S. Treasury.
 (c) An asset on the balance sheet of a commercial bank.
 (d) All of the above.

_____ 6. _Ceteris paribus_, when the Treasury refinances the debt:
 (a) The debt gets larger.
 (b) The debt gets smaller.
 (c) The size of the debt does not change.
 (d) It is not possible to determine what happens to the debt.

_____ 7. An increase in the value of bonds owned by U.S. households could indicate that, _ceteris paribus:_
 (a) They have added to their wealth by purchasing newly issued bonds.
 (b) The have added to their wealth by purchasing previously issued bonds.
 (c) Interest rates have fallen generally.
 (d) All of the above are the case.

_____ 8. When the U.S. Treasury issues new bonds to replace bonds that have matured, it is engaging in:
 (a) Debt refinancing.
 (b) Debt servicing.
 (c) Income transfers.
 (d) None of the above.

_____ 9. The cost of servicing the debt has risen sharply in recent years:
 (a) Because the debt has grown rapidly.
 (b) Because the deficits have been very large.
 (c) Because interest rates were at historical highs.
 (d) For all of the above reasons.

_____ 10. The debt would cease to grow if:
 (a) The federal government balanced its budget.
 (b) Federal expenditures equaled federal receipts.
 (c) Debt refinancing was unnecessary.
 (d) All of the above were the case.

_____ 11. Which of the following statements concerning the opportunity cost of financing a government project with the proceeds of a bond sale is true?
 (a) It will be greater the lower the amount of unemployed resources available.
 (b) It will be smaller the lower the amount of unemployed resources available.
 (c) It is unaffected by the amount of resources that are unemployed.
 (d) None of the above statements is true.

_____ 12. The existence of the national debt is largely a product of:
 (a) War.
 (b) Recession.
 (c) Tax cuts.
 (d) All of the above.

_____ 13. When the Federal Reserve System buys bonds in the open market:
 (a) The national debt must increase.
 (b) The national debt must increase as long as it buys only newly issued bonds.
 (c) The national debt will decrease because the Fed is a government agency.
 (d) None of the above is the case.

_____ 14. Selling bonds to finance government leads to an opportunity cost that:
   (a) Is less than when government is financed with taxes.
   (b) Is greater than when government is financed with taxes.
   (c) Is the same as financing government with taxes.
   (d) Depends on who buys the bonds.

_____ 15. If the federal government balanced its budget every year, it would have to:
   (a) Raise taxes and spending in a recession.
   (b) Lower taxes and spending in a recession.
   (c) Lower spending and raise taxes in a recession.
   (d) Do none of the above.

_____ 16. Which of the following statements concerning the national debt is true?
   (a) It is paid off each fiscal year when the debt is refinanced.
   (b) It is never going to be paid off in any given year, but it will be entirely paid off when it is refinanced over a number of years.
   (c) It will be paid off when the budget is balanced for a sufficient number of years.
   (d) None of the above statements is true.

_____ 17. The real burden of externally held debt is:
   (a) Incurred when the newly issued bonds are sold to foreigners.
   (b) Incurred in the future when foreigners sell the bonds and use the proceeds to buy goods and services from the United States.
   (c) Incurred by third countries if those who own the bonds sell them and use the proceeds to purchase goods and services from third countries.
   (d) None of the above.

_____ 18. The key to understanding the "real burden" of the debt is understanding:
   (a) The idea of opportunity cost.
   (b) The difference between internally held debt and externally held debt.
   (c) The relationship between the Treasury and the Federal Reserve System.
   (d) How transfers redistribute income.

_____ 19. When is "crowding out" most likely to occur?
   (a) When the federal government runs a surplus and pays off part of the debt.
   (b) When the federal government has a balanced budget but refinances a portion of the debt that matures.
   (c) When the federal government runs a deficit and raises taxes to generate more revenue.
   (d) When the federal government has run a deficit, and sells bonds to make up the difference.

_____ 20. The "crowding out" hypothesis refers to the possibility that:
   (a) Foreigners will turn in the bonds they own and use the proceeds to purchase goods and services desired by U.S. residents.
   (b) State and local governments will sell the bonds they own and lower their taxes as a result.
   (c) The sale of bonds by the federal government will raise interest rates and cause firms to invest less.
   (d) The Federal Reserve System will be unwilling to lend to member banks because they own so many Treasury bonds.

_____ 21. If all of the national debt was owned internally, then:
   (a) We would not have to worry about raising taxes to pay the interest on the debt.
   (b) We would still have to worry about the effect of interest payments on the distribution of income.
   (c) The federal government would have to stop refinancing the debt.
   (d) The Federal Reserve System would have to use some other asset to conduct open-market operations.

Problems and Applications

Exercise 1

After doing this exercise you should understand the relationships among deficits, bonds, debt, and interest payments. You should see how continual deficits lead to larger and larger interest payments and larger and larger debt. Keep in mind that it is difficult to eliminate deficits when interest payments are an important factor contributing to the deficit. This problem is similar to the problem at the end of Chapter 16 in the text.

1. Suppose the federal government expenditures in the year 2000 are $1 trillion and taxes are $800 billion. Compute the deficit and place the answer in column 1 of Table 16.1 for the year 2000.

Table 16.1
Deficits, bonds, debts, and interest payments
(billions of dollars per year)

Year	(1) Deficit	(2) Newly issued bonds	(3) Total debt	(4) Interest payment
1999	$0	$0	$0	$0
2000	_____	_____	_____	_____
2001	_____	_____	_____	_____
2002	_____	_____	_____	_____
2003	_____	_____	_____	_____
2004	_____	_____	_____	_____
2005	_____	_____	_____	_____
2006	_____	_____	_____	_____
2007	_____	_____	_____	_____

2. To finance the deficit the government must sell bonds of an equivalent amount to cover the revenue shortfall. What is the dollar amount necessary to finance the debt? Place the answer in column 2 of Table 16.1 for the year 2000.

3. Assume that up to 1999 the government had zero debt (as shown in the 1999 row of Table 16.1). What is the total debt after the government has borrowed to cover the deficit in the year 2000? Place the answer in column 3 of Table 16.1 for the year 2000.

4. What will be the interest payment on the total debt in the year 2000 if the interest rate is 10 percent per year? Place the answer in column 4 of Table 16.1 for the year 2000.

5. For the years 2001 through 2007, the government spends $1 trillion each year plus any interest payment on the previous years' debt and receives tax revenues of only $800 billion each year. The interest rate is still 10 percent per year. Fill in the rest of Table 16.1.

6. Graph the deficit (column 1 of Table 16.1) and interest payment (column 4) in Figure 16.1.

Figure 16.1

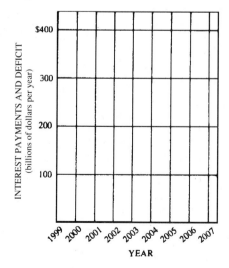

7. T F With continual deficits, interest payments on past deficits will become a bigger part of current deficits, *ceteris paribus.*

8. T F In this example, if both taxes and government expenditures increased at 5 percent per year due to bigger government, both the deficit and the debt would become smaller.

9. T F If taxes and government expenditures increased at 5 percent per year and the inflation rate was 5 percent per year, the nominal debt would become larger.

Exercise 2

This exercise focuses on the ratio of the debt to GNP, which is an important measure of the burden of the public debt. It shows, too, how important inflation rates are to this burden. Finally, it demonstrates how inflation is an alternative to taxation as a mechanism to finance government deficits. This exercise builds on the data from the previous exercise.

1. Column 1 of Table 16.2 shows the growth of the nominal debt resulting from continual deficits (numbers are from the previous exercise). Graph the nominal debt in Figure 16.2. Assume that the government is disciplining itself to a deficit ceiling of $200 billion per year on noninterest payments each year (see previous exercise).

Table 16.2
Debt, income, and inflation
(billions of dollars per year)

Year	(1) Nominal debt	(2) Real debt	(3) Nominal GNP	(4) Real GNP	(5) Debt/ GNP
1999	$ 0	$0	$ 800	$960	s _____
2000	200	_____	1,000	_____	_____
2001	420	_____	1,250	_____	_____
2002	662	_____	1,563	_____	_____
2003	928	_____	1,953	_____	_____
2004	1,221	_____	2,441	_____	_____
2005	1,543	_____	3,052	_____	_____
2006	1,897	_____	3,815	_____	_____
2007	2,287	_____	4,768	_____	_____

Figure 16.2

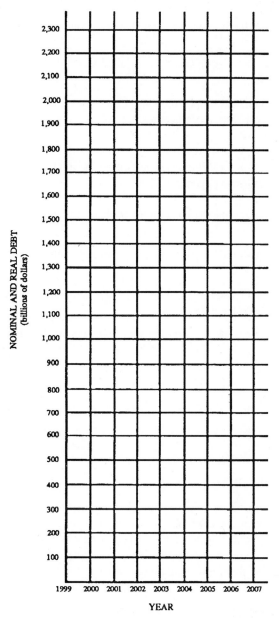

NOMINAL AND REAL DEBT
(billions of dollars)

YEAR

2. Suppose the inflation rate is 20 percent per year. Assuming that the base year for computing inflation rates is the year 2000, compute the real value of the debt in constant dollars (for the year 2000) for each year in column 2 of Table 16.2. This is done by dividing the debt figure by the price index, which rises from 1.2 in 2001 to 1.2^2 in 2002, and so on.

3. Graph the real value of the debt in Figure 16.2.

4. T F As the price level rises in this example, the real value of the debt also rises.

5. T F Inflation and holding down the size of the deficit both lower the real value of the debt immediately.

6. In column 3 of Table 16.2 the nominal GNP for each year is presented. It grows at the rate of 25 percent per year. Compute the real GNP in column 4 the same way you computed the real value of the debt in column 2.

7. T F The economy is in a recession over the period of 2000 to 2007.

8. The ratio of the nominal debt (column 1) to the nominal GNP (column 3) is a measure of the burden that the debt places on the economy. Compute this ratio in column 5 of Table 16.2.

9. T F While the real value of the debt continues to rise, the burden of the debt on the economy eventually begins to fall.

Exercise 3

The media often provide information on changes in the demand and supply of bonds. Using one of the articles in the text, this exercise will show the kind of information to look for. If your professor makes a newspaper assignment for this chapter, this exercise will provide an example of how to do it.

Reread the article in Chapter 16 entitled "Reagan Decision to Sign Deficit Measure Portends Budget Battles with Congress" from the *Wall Street Journal*. Then answer the following questions:

1. Which phrase mentions the authority responsible for making the decision on the trade-offs involved in balancing the budget?

2. Which sentence indicates the expenditure (or taxes) that would be given up to help bring the budget into balance?

3. Which sentence describes who is fighting to make the increased expenditure or who is demanding to lower the taxes? In other words, who is willing to increase the deficit?

4. By contrast, which sentence describes who is fighting to cut the expenditure or raise the taxes? In other words, who is trying to balance the budget?

Common Errors

The first statement in each "common error" below is incorrect. Each incorrect statement is followed by a corrected version and an explanation.

1. Our grandchildren will feel the burden of the deficit. WRONG!

   Our grandchildren may feel the burden of the debt. RIGHT!

   Deficit and debt are concepts that are often confused. While deficits occur due to the excess of expenditures over taxes during a given year, the debt can be calculated at any given point in time and represents the cumulative effect of running deficits over our entire history. It is the debt on which transfers such as interest payments are made, not the deficit. Such transfers may result in opportunity costs. However, a deficit may reflect expenditures on capital that future generations will need and thus may not be the source of the burden.

2. The national debt must be paid off eventually. WRONG!

   The national debt is paid off continually through refinancing. RIGHT!

   No Treasury bond has a maturity date more than thirty years in the future. Some bonds have maturity dates that come much sooner—in ten or twenty years. Treasury bills are sold at auction and have maturity dates of thirty, sixty, or ninety days. Suppose the federal government had balanced budgets for the next thirty years. The entire debt would have come due at some point. What would happen? It would be refinanced as it came due and replaced with new debt with other maturities.

3. There is nothing "behind" the national debt. WRONG!

   The federal government owns many physical assets and has the ability to tax. RIGHT!

   The proceeds of bond sales by the federal government are used to do many things, including the purchase of many assets. Every item owned by the federal government—from the White House to Old Faithful—is an asset that could be sold to help pay off the national debt. Stealth bombers, office buildings, computers, and the like are all assets that were needed over the years and are as much an asset as the debt is a liability. By raising taxes the government can at least theoretically run a surplus and pay off the debt.

■ ANSWERS ■

Key-Term Review

1. budget deficit	7. budget surplus	11. optimal mix of output
2. national debt	8. debt servicing	12. deficit ceiling
3. external debt	refinancing	13. debt ceiling
4. internal debt	9. Treasury bonds	14. crowding out
5. liability	open market operations	production possibilities
6. asset	10. opportunity cost	15. transfer payments

True or False

1. T	5. T	9. T	13. T	16. F	19. T
2. F	6. T	10. T	14. F	17. F	20. F
3. T	7. F	11. F	15. T	18. T	21. F
4. F	8. T	12. F			

Multiple Choice

1. b	5. d	9. d	13. d	16. d	19. d
2. a	6. c	10. d	14. c	17. b	20. c
3. d	7. d	11. b	15. c	18. a	21. b
4. c	8. a	12. d			

Problems and Applications

Exercise 1

1–5.

Table 16.1 answer
(billions of dollars per year)

Year	(1) Deficit	(2) Newly issued bonds	(3) Total debt	(4) Interest payment
2000	$200	$200	$ 200	$ 20 = (.10 x 200)
2001	220	220	420 = (200 + 220)	42 = (.10 x 420)
2002	242	242	662 = (420 + 242)	66 = (.10 x 662)
2003	266	266	928 = (662 + 266)	93 = (.10 x 928)
2004	293	293	1,221 = (928 + 293)	122 = (.10 x 1,221)
2005	322	322	1,543 = (1,221 + 322)	154 = (.10 x 1,543)
2006	354	354	1,897 = (1,543 + 354)	190 = (.10 x 1,897)
2007	390	390	2,287 = (1,897 + 390)	229 = (.10 x 2,287)

Figure 16.1 answer

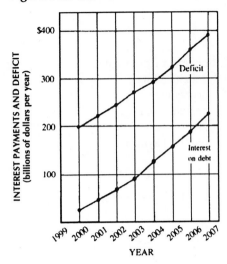

7. T Compare relative sizes of columns 1 and 4 in Table 16.1 answer.
8. F
9. T

Exercise 2

1. **Figure 16.2 answer**

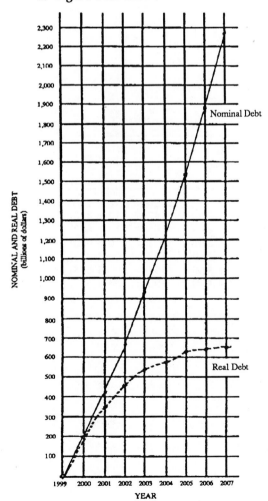

2. See Table 16.2 answer, column 2.

Table 16.2 answer
(billions of dollars per year)

Year	(1) Nominal debt	(2) Real debt		(3) Nominal GNP	(4) Real GNP	(5) Debt/ GNP
1999	$ 0	$ 0		$ 800	$ 960	
2000	200	200 =	$200/(1.2)^0$	1,000	1,000 = 1,000/1.0	.20
2001	420	350 =	$420/(1.2)^1$	1,250	1,042 = 1,250/1.2	.34
2002	662	460 =	$662/(1.2)^2$	1,563	1,085 = 1,563/1.44	.42
2003	928	537 =	$928/(1.2)^3$	1,953	1,130 = 1,953/1.73	.48
2004	1,221	589 =	$1,221/(1.2)^4$	2,441	1,177 = 2,441/2.07	.50
2005	1,543	620 =	$1,543/(1.2)^5$	3,052	1,227 = 3,052/2.49	.51
2006	1,897	635 =	$1,897/(1.2)^6$	3,815	1,278 = 3,815/2.99	.50
2007	2,287	638 =	$2,287/(1.2)^7$	4,768	1,331 = 4,768/3.58	.48

(*Hint:* To calculate the real value of the debt, divide the nominal debt for each year by the appropriate price index, which grows as follows: $1 \times 1.2 = 1.2$; $1.2 \times 1.2 = 1.44$; $1.2 \times 1.44 = 1.7$, etc. For the year 2000, the real value of the debt is 200 divided by 1.2^0; 2001, 420 divided by 1.2^1; 2002, 662 divided by $1.2^2 = 1.44$, etc.)

3. See Figure 16.2 answer.
4. T   Notice that a positive inflation rate dampens the increase in the real value of the debt in Figure 16.2 answer.
5. F   While the real debt grows at a lower rate due to both instruments, the change is very gradual.
6. See Table 16.2 answer, column 4.
7. F   Notice that column 4 is rising at about 5 percent per year, which is relatively fast growth for the United States.
8. See Table 16.2 answer, column 5.
9. T   Notice how column 5 starts to fall in the year 2006, while the real debt is still rising by 2007.

Exercise 3

1. The first sentence refers to "funding battles with Congress." The ultimate authority over the budget is the Congress.
2. The main expenditure category cut back by Gramm-Rudman mentioned in the article is defense: "Congressional Democrats have predicted that in order for Mr. Reagan to maintain the defense spending he wants, he will have to accept a $10 billion to $12 billion revenue increase."
3. See the quotation in Question 2 above: Reagan wanted the increased expenditure.
4. The same sentence in Question 2 indicates the Democrats want to raise revenue or cut defense.

Chapter 17

Global Views

Quick Review

Up to this point, we have not paid much attention to economic events in the rest of the world. However, the economies of all nations are increasingly interdependent. We need to know:

- How does the U.S. economy interact with the rest of the world's economies?
- How does the rest of the world affect U.S. macro outcomes?
- How does our global interdependence limit or change our macro policy options?

One facet of our interaction with other countries is the export and import of goods and services. Exports (X) are an injection (like investment or government expenditures) and imports (M) are a leakage (like saving or taxes).

The additional leakage from imports reduces the size of the income multiplier by lowering the amount of *additional* spending on domestic output that results from any increase in our income. In a model of the closed economy, the multiplier can be calculated using the marginal propensity to save (MPS); the multiplier is $1/MPS$. However, the multiplier in a model of an open economy must reflect people's desire to spend a little out of every extra dollar for imports, which is called their marginal propensity to import (MPM). The multiplier for the open economy becomes $1/(MPS + MPM)$. The graphic equivalent of this is a reduced slope of the aggregate spending curve in an open economy as compared to a closed economy.

The marginal propensity to import may hinder our application of fiscal policy to achieve domestic goals. Because the multiplier is smaller in an open economy than in a closed economy, any tax or spending change will have to be larger to achieve a given income or employment goal.

In an open economy we must also consider exports of our goods. When we import goods, foreigners receive dollars, which they turn around and spend on goods that we produce. When they decide to buy more goods from us, the aggregate spending curve will shift upward, with a resulting multiplier effect on income.

Naturally, our exports (determined abroad) are not always equal to our imports (determined at home). We expect either a trade surplus $(X - M) > 0$ or trade deficit $(X - M) < 0$. While the trade deficit permits us to consume goods valued at more than the goods we produce, it may complicate fiscal policy. A fiscal expansion will increase any trade deficit, *ceteris paribus*.

While we're worrying about our domestic goals and the impact foreign trade has on our potential to achieve them, foreigners are doing the same thing. Our exports are their imports; our imports their exports. If we have a trade deficit $(X - M) < 0$ and consume more than we produce, our trading partners must have an overall trade surplus $(X - M) > 0$ and consume less than they produce. Our domestic goals may be incompatible with theirs or theirs with ours. This may mean that our economy competes with their economies with respect to employment and inflation goals.

While trade flows involve the movement of new goods across international boundaries, capital flows involve the purchase of various forms of wealth or of titles to capital across international boundaries. Individuals and corporations purchase securities, bonds, and property in foreign countries or repatriate earnings from abroad. Their actions result in massive dollar flows—capital inflows when foreigners lend to us (e.g., by purchasing a Treasury bond) and outflows when we purchase securities from them (e.g., building up a bank account abroad).

Like trade flows, capital flows are seldom in balance. When the outflow of dollars exceeds the inflow of dollars,

Capital imbalances can alter macro outcomes too. Inflationary pressures can be fought, *ceteris paribus*, by slowing the growth of the money supply, which in turn pushes up domestic interest rates. But this action would make our bonds attractive to foreigners, which they would purchase with accumulated dollars. Their purchase would frustrate the Fed's attempt to reduce the money supply.

The critical link between economies in both trade and finance is the exchange rate, the price of one country's currency in terms of another's. The expected imbalance between trade and capital flows implies that the exchange rates fluctuate like other prices determined by supply and demand. For example, if the United States runs persistent trade deficits and foreigners suddenly begin to withdraw their investments from the United States, the value of the dollar in terms of other currencies will drop.

The exchange rate also responds to changes in the specialization and productivity of firms world-wide. Specialization and trade increase world efficiency and output. Trade also stimulates improvements in productivity as producers anywhere must compete with producers everywhere. However, if one country makes dramatically greater improvements in productivity than other countries, then it is likely to run persistent trade surpluses, which in turn will cause its currency to become more valuable. Significant "swings" in exchange rates can sometimes overwhelm productivity changes and decrease the competitiveness of many firms within a country.

Thus, three kinds of rates must be watched very carefully in an open economy: inflation rates, interest rates, and exchange rates. Changes in these rates reflect changes in trade and capital flows, and they also play a role in triggering changes in trade and capital flows. The effectiveness of both fiscal and monetary policy is powerfully affected by changes in these rates.

Learning Objectives

After reading Chapter 17 and doing the following exercises, you should:	True or false	Multiple choice	Problems and applications	Common errors	Pages in the text
1. Understand how international transactions affect U.S. economic performance and the ability to use macroeconomic policy.	1,6, 12,20	3,18	1–3	3	411–412
2. Be able to explain why the open-economy multiplier is smaller than the closed-economy multiplier.	1,2,4, 10,13	1–3, 5,6	1–3		397–399
3. Understand why the marginal propensity to import *changes the slope* of the aggregate spending curve.	2,3, 5,6	2,4–6	1–3		397–399
4. Be able to demonstrate how a change in exports *shifts* the aggregate spending curve.	4,5,8, 19,20	3,6	1–3		399–401
5. Be able to show how trade and capital flows counteract normal macro policy tools.	1,7,9, 11,12, 15,18	7–9, 14–16	4	4	401–402
6. Be aware of the foreign repercussions of U.S. policy initiatives.	12,14, 19	11		3	402–404
7. Know the principal vocabulary of the trade and capital accounts.	15–19	7,10, 14–16			404–409
8. Be able to relate exchange rate changes to the question of competitiveness in international trade.	21–24	17,19,20		1,2	409–410
9. Understand how OPEC activities in the 1970s upset the macro equilibrium of the U.S. economy.	14	12,13			404–405

Key-Term Review

Review the following terms; if you are not sure of the meaning of any term, write out the definition and check it against the Glossary in the text.

capital deficit
capital surplus
equilibrium GNP
exchange rate
exports
growth recession
imports
leakage
marginal propensity to import (*MPM*)

marginal propensity to save (*MPS*)
money supply (*M1*)
multiplier
net exports
open-market operations
production possibilities curve
productivity
trade deficit
trade surplus

Fill in the blank following each of the statements below with the appropriate term from the list above.

1. Through trade, an open economy allows consumption to exceed the _____ of a closed economy.

    1. _____

2. An open economy includes flows of goods and services across borders of different countries. Inflows are called _____.

    2. _____

3. Outflows of goods and services are called _____.

    3. _____

4. When _____ are positive, there is a _____, which means that the value of a country's exports exceeds the value of what it imports.

    4. _____
    _____

5. When there is a _____, the value of a country's imports exceeds the value of its exports.

    5. _____

6. A trade deficit can be financed by a _____, which means that more money for investments and other nontrade purposes is flowing into the country than is being withdrawn.

    6. _____

7. A _____ can result when citizens of a country wish to invest more abroad or when foreigners withdraw funds from the country.

    7. _____

8. When the Fed uses _____ to increase the _____, which in turn lowers the interest rate, investors may want to obtain higher returns by buying securities of other countries where interest rates are higher.

    8. _____

9. Trade deficits and capital deficits both tend to lower the _____ for a country's currency.

    9. _____

10. The exchange rate may also fall if a country's _____ in producing goods efficiently deteriorates.

    10. _____

11. With a lower-valued currency a country's goods become cheaper and thus more competitive abroad, which leads to increased exports and, through the _____, increases its income.

    11. _____

12. The open economy multiplier will be smaller, the larger is the _____, *ceteris paribus*.   12. _____

13. The open economy multiplier will be smaller, the larger is the _____, *ceteris paribus*.   13. _____

14. A _____ in the United States economy would reduce the level of _____ in many of our trading-partner countries, because United States imports, a _____, would be reduced causing their exports, an injection, to fall.   14. _____

_____

_____

True or False: *Circle your choice.*

T F 1. Imports are an injection into the circular flow of economic activity.

T F 2. The existence of imports changes the slope of the domestic consumption expenditure curve.

T F 3. A larger marginal propensity to import (*MPM*) means a larger multiplier, *ceteris paribus*.

T F 4. Increases in exports increase the size of the multiplier; decreases reduce it, *ceteris paribus*.

T F 5. Changes in exports shift the aggregate spending curve but do not change its slope.

T F 6. The marginal propensity to import is the ratio of the change in imports to a given change in income.

T F 7. If the *MPM* is 0.1 and the *MPS* is 0.1, the multiplier is 0.2.

T F 8. A reduction in net exports will lower the equilibrium level of income.

T F 9. When the United States has a trade deficit, the value of what the United States produces is more than the value of what it consumes.

T F 10. Import leakages help reduce inflationary pressures, *ceteris paribus*.

T F 11. Fiscal policy to cure unemployment will worsen a trade surplus, *ceteris paribus*.

T F 12. Restrictive fiscal policy will simultaneously reduce an inflationary gap and a trade deficit, *ceteris paribus*.

T F 13. OPEC activities in the 1970s caused both the U.S. aggregate demand curve and the U.S. aggregate supply curve to shift downward.

T F 14. The aggregate supply curve shifted upward when OPEC raised the price of crude oil, because crude oil is a major input into the U.S. economy.

T F 15. If the United States runs a trade deficit, the rest of the world must have a trade surplus.

T F 16. The purchase of Treasury bonds by foreigners results in a capital outflow.

T F 17. The repatriation of profits on U.S. investments abroad causes a capital inflow.

T F 18. Capital inflows to the U.S. economy can be used to finance a U.S. trade deficit.

T F 19. A trade deficit should be accompanied by a capital inflow; a trade surplus, by a capital outflow.

T F 20. When U.S. interest rates rise relative to foreign interest rates, capital flows out of the United States.

T F 21. An exchange rate is the price of a country's currency in terms of another country's currency.

T F 22. A strong dollar makes our exports attractive to foreign buyers.

T F 23. When the dollar gets weaker, the United States becomes less competitive in the world markets.

T F 24. The persistent trade deficits of the U.S. economy are evidence that our producers are less efficient than foreign producers.

Multiple Choice: *Select the correct answer.*

_____ 1. The open-economy multiplier is smaller than the closed-economy multiplier:
(a) Because imports are a leakage from the circular flow.
(b) Because the marginal propensity to import is greater than zero.
(c) Because the denominator is greater for the open-economy multiplier than for the closed-economy multiplier.
(d) For all of the above reasons.

_____ 2. The marginal propensity to import relates:
(a) Domestic consumption to the foreign level of income.
(b) Changes in the domestic level of income to changes in the foreign level of income.
(c) Changes in the domestic level of income with changes in domestic imports.
(d) Changes in domestic consumption with changes in imports.

_____ 3. An increase in U.S. exports:
(a) Must increase unemployment in the rest of the world.
(b) Means the rest of the world must be importing more.
(c) Means the rest of the world must have a trade deficit.
(d) Means the rest of the world must have a trade surplus.

_____ 4. If the marginal propensity to import is 0.2 and the marginal propensity to save is 0.2, the multiplier is:
(a) 0.4.
(b) 2.5.
(c) 4.0.
(d) 2.0.

_____ 5. An increase in the marginal propensity to import will:
(a) Reduce the size of the open-economy multiplier.
(b) Increase the size of the closed-economy multiplier.
(c) Shift the domestic consumption expenditure curve upward.
(d) Change the slope of the domestic consumption expenditure curve.

_____ 6. The equilibrium condition in an open economy is (all in desired terms):
(a) $I = S$
(b) $I + G = S + T$
(c) $I + G + X = S + T + M$
(d) $I + G + M = S + T + X$

_____ 7. A trade surplus implies that the United States is:
(a) Consuming more than it produces, and its net exports are positive.
(b) Consuming more than it produces, and net exports are negative.
(c) Consuming less than it produces, and net exports are positive.
(d) Consuming less than it produces, and net exports are negative.

_____ 8. If the economy has a recessionary gap and a trade surplus, which of the following would be an appropriate policy to follow?
(a) A tax cut, with government spending cut by the same amount.
(b) A tax cut, accompanied by an increase in government spending.
(c) A tax increase, accompanied by a cut in government spending.
(d) A tax increase, with no change in government spending.

_____9. With an open economy, rather than a closed economy:
   (a) Smaller tax or spending changes will be required to achieve the same employment goals.
   (b) Monetary policy will more easily control inflation.
   (c) The multiplier will be smaller.
   (d) All of the above are the case.

_____10. All nations can run trade surpluses simultaneously when all of their economies are:
   (a) Below full employment.
   (b) At full employment.
   (c) Above full employment.
   (d) None of the above.

_____11. If the U.S. economy has an inflationary gap and a zero trade balance:
   (a) A tax increase would reduce the inflationary gap and push the trade account into surplus, *ceteris paribus.*
   (b) A tax increase would reduce the inflationary gap and push the trade account into deficit, *ceteris paribus.*
   (c) An open-market purchase of bonds would worsen the inflationary gap and would push the trade account into surplus, *ceteris paribus.*
   (d) An open-market sale of bonds would improve the inflationary gap and push the trade account into deficit, *ceteris paribus.*

_____12. The oil shocks of the 1970s:
   (a) Caused the U.S. aggregate demand curve to shift to the left.
   (b) Caused the aggregate supply curve to shift to the right.
   (c) Lowered cost-push inflationary pressures.
   (d) Did all of the above.

_____13. The Nixon administration clearly focused on the inflationary problem caused by OPEC because:
   (a) It followed fiscal and monetary policies aimed at shifting the aggregate supply curve to the right.
   (b) It followed fiscal and monetary policies designed to shift the aggregate demand and supply curves to the left.
   (c) It followed fiscal and monetary policies that shifted the aggregate demand curve to the left.
   (d) It encouraged the Fed to increase the money supply to offset contractionary fiscal policy.

_____14. A capital inflow occurs when:
   (a) Foreign investors purchase Treasury bonds.
   (b) The Fed increases bank reserves.
   (c) Taxes are increased and our imports fall.
   (d) All of the above occur.

_____15. A capital outflow occurs when, *ceteris paribus:*
   (a) Citizens of the United States buy foreign stock.
   (b) U.S. corporations abroad repatriate their profits.
   (c) Foreigners purchase real estate in the United States.
   (d) All of the above occur.

_____16. The existence of a trade deficit can be financed by:
   (a) A capital surplus.
   (b) A strengthening of the exchange rate for the currency.
   (c) Stimulation of the economy to full employment.
   (d) None of the above.

_____17. When exchange rates are free to fluctuate, a stronger dollar means:
   (a) Imports become more expensive.
   (b) U.S. producers become more competitive in foreign markets.
   (c) U.S. exports should increase.
   (d) None of the above.

18. The basic argument for trading with other countries is that trade:
    (a) Increases our production possibilities above consumption possibilities.
    (b) Decreases our production possibilities below consumption possibilities.
    (c) Increases our consumption possibilities above production possibilities.
    (d) Decreases our consumption possibilities below production possibilities.

19. Between 1981 and 1985 the value of the U.S. dollar in international trade:
    (a) Rose by about 50 percent.
    (b) Rose by about 25 percent.
    (c) Did not change.
    (d) Fell by about 50 percent.

20. The U.S. trade gap in the 1980s was the result of:
    (a) The strong dollar.
    (b) The weakness of foreign currencies.
    (c) Lagging productivity in some of our export industries.
    (d) All of the above.

Problems and Applications

Exercise 1

This exercise uses aggregate spending curves to examine the effect of adding the export sector to a closed economy.

Suppose that an economy is characterized by a consumption function (C) in terms of disposable income (Y_D) such that

$$C = 100 + 0.8\, Y_D$$

where all figures are in billions of dollars. Furthermore, government expenditures (G) amount to $200 billion, and investment (I) is $40 billion.

1. Fill in Table 17.1 for each of the macroeconomic variables at the disposable income levels shown in column 1, assuming that this is a closed economy.

Table 17.1
Aggregate spending schedule for a closed economy
(billions of dollars per year)

(1) Disposable income (Y_D)	(2) Consumption (C)	(3) Investment (I)	(4) Government expenditures (G)	(5) Aggregate spending (2) + (3) + (4)	(6) Saving (1) − (2)
$ 0	$_____	$_____	$_____	$_____	$_____
2,000	_____	_____	_____	_____	_____
4,000	_____	_____	_____	_____	_____

2. Calculate the marginal propensity to save. _____

3. Using the data from Table 17.1, graph the aggregate spending curve in Figure 17.1 and label it AD_1.

236

Figure 17.1

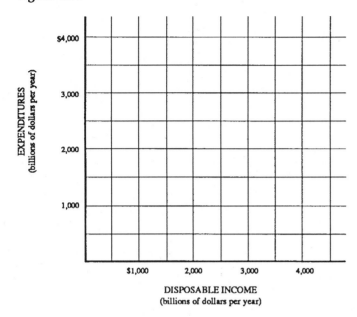

DISPOSABLE INCOME
(billions of dollars per year)

4. Fill in Table 17.2 for each of the variables at the different disposable income levels shown in column 1. Assume this economy has exports of $210 billion and other injections as shown in Table 17.1. Imports equal zero.

Table 17.2
Aggregate spending schedule for an economy with exports
(billions of dollars per year)

(1) Disposable income (Y_D)	(2) Consumption (C)	(3) Investment (I)	(4) Government expenditures (G)	(5) Exports (X)	(6) Aggregate spending (2) + (3) + (4) + (5)
$ 0	$_____	$_____	$_____	$_____	$_____
2,000	_____	_____	_____	_____	_____
4,000	_____	_____	_____	_____	_____

5. In Figure 17.1 graph the aggregate spending curve for the open economy represented by Table 17.2 and label it AD_2.

T F 6. When exports increase, aggregate spending falls because consumers are able to buy less of domestic production.

T F 7. When exports increase, the aggregate spending curve shifts up in a parallel fashion because exports vary with foreign income.

8. Compute the multiplier for the closed economy. _____

T F 9. When exports are added to the closed economy, the multiplier changes.

Exercise 2

In this exercise the effect of imports on aggregate expenditure is examined in a Keynesian model of the economy. The open economy in this exercise has the same injections as the closed economy in the previous exercise.

Suppose again the consumption function is

$$C = 100 + 0.8\ Y_D$$

where all figures are in billions of dollars. Furthermore, government expenditures (G) are $200 billion, investment (I) is $40 billion, and exports (X) are $210 billion.

1. Find the equilibrium for the economy by doing the following:
   a. Determine aggregate spending in Table 17.3.

Table 17.3
Aggregate spending schedule without imports, G=$200
(billions of dollars per year)

(1) Disposable income (Y_D)	(2) Consumption (C)	(3) Investment (I)	(4) Government expenditures (G)	(5) Exports (X)	(6) Aggregate spending (2) + (3) + (4) + (5)
$ 0	$_____	$_____	$_____	$_____	$_____
2,000	_____	_____	_____	_____	_____
4,000	_____	_____	_____	_____	_____

   b. In Figure 17.2 graph the aggregate spending curve from Table 17.3, and label it AD_1.

Figure 17.2

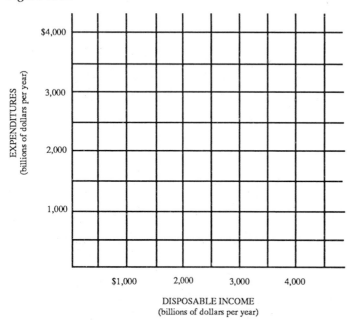

   c. Draw a 45-degree line in Figure 17.2.
   d. Find the intersection of the 45-degree line with AD_1, and label this equilibrium income, EQ_1.

2. Suppose government expenditures were to *increase* by $250 billion to a total of $450 billion, *ceteris paribus*. Find the new equilibrium for the economy by doing the following:
   a. Determine aggregate spending in Table 17.4.

238

Table 17.4
New aggregate spending schedule without imports, G=$450
(billions of dollars per year)

(1) Disposable income (Y_D)	(2) Consumption (C)	(3) Investment (I)	(4) Government expenditures (G)	(5) Exports (X)	(6) Aggregate spending (2) + (3) + (4) + (5)
$ 0	$_____	$_____	$_____	$_____	$_____
2,000	_____	_____	_____	_____	_____
4,000	_____	_____	_____	_____	_____

   b.   In Figure 17.2 graph the aggregate spending curve based on Table 17.4 and label it AD_2.

   c.   Find the intersection of the 45-degree line with AD_2 and label this equilibrium income level EQ_2.

3.   In response to the $250 billion increase in government expenditures, the equilibrium income rose from EQ_1 of $_____ billion to EQ_2 of $_____ billion, which is _____ (a decrease, an increase) of $_____ billion of income for the economy.

4.   Suppose the economy has been opened up to imports and has the import function

$$M = 50 + 0.3\,Y_D$$

where all figures are in billions of dollars. Find the equilibrium level of income by doing the following:

   a.   Determine aggregate spending in Table 17.5 assuming the same injections shown in Table 17.3.

Table 17.5
Aggregate spending schedule for an open economy: G=$200
(billions of dollars per year)

(1) Disposable income (Y_D)	(2) Consumption (C)	(3) Investment (I)	(4) Government expenditures (G)	(5) Exports (X)	(6) Imports (M)	(7) Aggregate spending*
$ 0	$_____	$_____	$_____	$_____	$_____	$_____
2,000	_____	_____	_____	_____	_____	_____
4,000	_____	_____	_____	_____	_____	_____

*Remember: Aggregate spending = C + I + G + X − M.

   b.   In Figure 17.2 graph the aggregate spending curve from Table 17.5 and label it AD_3.

   c.   Find the intersection of the 45-degree line with AD_3 and label this equilibrium income level EQ_3.

5.   Because imports have been added, what has happened to the model? (*Hint:* Compare curves AD_1 and AD_3.)

   (a) There has been a parallel upward shift in the aggregate spending curve.

   (b) There has been a parallel downward shift in the aggregate spending curve.

   (c) There has been a movement of the aggregate spending curve upward and to a flatter position.

   (d) There has been a movement of the aggregate spending curve downward and to a flatter position.

6.   Suppose government expenditures were to increase by $250 billion to a total of $450 billion, *ceteris paribus*. Find the new equilibrium for the economy by doing the following:

   a.   Determine aggregate spending in Table 17.6.

Table 17.6
Aggregate spending schedule for an open economy: G=$450
(billions of dollars per year)

(1) Disposable income (Y_D)	(2) Consumption (C)	(3) Investment (I)	(4) Government expenditures (G)	(5) Exports (X)	(6) Imports (M)	(7) Aggregate spending*
$ 0	$_____	$_____	$_____	$_____	$_____	$_____
2,000	_____	_____	_____	_____	_____	_____
4,000	_____	_____	_____	_____	_____	_____

*Remember: Aggregate spending = $C + I + G + X - M$.

    b.   In Figure 17.2 graph the aggregate spending curve from Table 17.6, and label it AD_4.
    c.   Find the intersection of the 45-degree line with your AD_4 and label this equilibrium income level EQ_4.

  7. In response to the $250 billion increase in government expenditure, the equilibrium level of income has risen from $_____ billion at EQ_3 in Figure 17.2 to $_____ billion at EQ_4 which is _____ (a decrease, an increase) of $_____ billion for the economy.

  8. For a given $250 billion dollar increase in government expenditure, the existence of imports causes _____ (an increase, a decrease, the same amount) of stimulus to the economy. (*Hint:* Compare your answers in Question 3 with those in Question 7.)

Exercise 3

All of the work you did in Exercises 1 and 2 can be done much more easily with the use of multipliers.

Again assume that an economy is characterized by the consumption function

$$C = 100 + 0.8\,Y_D$$

where all figures are in billions of dollars.

  1. Compute the marginal propensity to consume for this closed economy. _____

  2. Compute the marginal propensity to save for the closed economy. _____

  3. Compute the multiplier for this closed economy. _____

  4. If government expenditures were to increase by $250 billion, by how much would income increase in this closed economy? _____

  5. Again suppose the economy has been opened up to imports and has the import function

$$M = 50 + 0.3\,Y_D$$

where all figures are in billions of dollars. The import function is very much like a consumption function except that it shows how much foreign production is consumed rather than how much domestic output is consumed at any level of income. What is the marginal propensity to import? _____

  6. Assuming that the consumption function is the same as in Problem 1, compute the multiplier for this open economy. _____

7. If government expenditures increase by $250 billion, how much does income increase in this open economy? _____

8. T   F   The import sector dampens the effectiveness of fiscal policy. (Compare your answers in Problems 4 and 7.)

Using multipliers you have made the same calculations as in Exercise 2, but you have done so much more quickly. (Compare your answers to Problems 3 and 7 of Exercise 2 with your answers to Problems 4 and 7 of this exercise.)

Exercise 4

This exercise shows why trade deficits get worse as income increases. It uses the import equation and export values from Exercises 1–3 to illustrate the idea.

Again suppose an economy has imports (M) that can be described by the import function

$$M = 50 + 0.3\, Y_D$$

where all figures are in billions of dollars. Exports are assumed to be $210 billion per year.

1. In Table 17.7 compute imports, exports, and the balance of trade at the various levels of disposable income in column 1.

Table 17.7
Trade for an open economy
(billions of dollars per year)

(1) Disposable income (Y_D)	(2) Exports (X)	(3) Imports (M)	(4) Balance of trade (4) = (2) – (3)
$ 0	$_____	$_____	$_____
500	_____	_____	_____
1,000	_____	_____	_____

2. Graph imports against income in Figure 17.3 and label this line M.

Figure 17.3

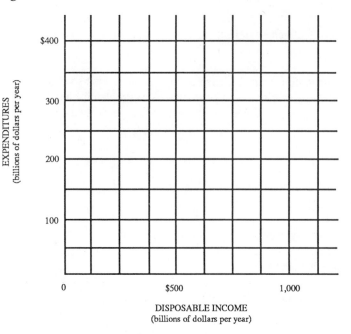

EXPENDITURES (billions of dollars per year) — vertical axis, marked $400, 300, 200, 100

DISPOSABLE INCOME
(billions of dollars per year) — horizontal axis, marked 0, $500, 1,000

3. In previous exercises we assumed that exports were constant at $210 billion. Draw a line in Figure 17.3 that shows exports at each income level and label it *X*. (*Hint:* The line should be flat.)

4. Show the balance of trade at disposable income levels of $0, $500, and $1,000. Use a bracket to indicate the trade deficit or trade surplus at each income level.

5. Indicate with an arrow where exports equal imports in Figure 17.3.

6. At what disposable income level does the trade balance equal zero? _____

7. T F At disposable income levels below the level at which trade is balanced, there are trade deficits.

8. T F As the government stimulates the economy to higher income levels, the trade deficit will become worse, *ceteris paribus*, because consumer spending on imports increases.

Common Errors

The first statement in each "common error" below is incorrect. Each incorrect statement is followed by a corrected version and an explanation.

1. A stronger dollar means American firms are stronger and more competitive. WRONG!

   A stronger dollar puts U.S. firms at a competitive disadvantage, *ceteris paribus*. RIGHT!

   The problem is how the word "competitive" is used. It is quite possible that because American firms were strong, productive, and competitive *in the past,* many countries bought U.S. goods and the dollar was strengthened. However, when the dollar strengthens *in the present* and nothing else changes (*ceteris paribus*), American firms are placed at a competitive disadvantage. It may be true that the strengthening dollar will force them to be more competitive *in the future,* but they may also simply go out of business. Generally, a strengthened dollar today means American firms are less able to compete with foreign companies today, because their output becomes more expensive relative to foreign goods.

2. The reason American firms can't compete is that foreign wages are so low. WRONG!

American firms compete with other American firms for American dollars abroad, not just with foreign firms. RIGHT!

In a **given** market, an American firm competes with other American firms as well as with foreign firms. However, the firm is also competing indirectly with *all* American firms.

When Americans buy foreign goods and send American dollars abroad, they provide the money with which foreigners can buy American goods. If American goods are being bought in large quantities by foreigners and Americans are buying few foreign goods, a trade imbalance will develop. The value of the dollar will rise as foreign exchange markets move to eliminate such an imbalance. This rise in the value of the dollar makes all American goods less competitive internationally—*even if productivity has risen for companies producing those goods.*

It is not surprising that a manager who makes a firm more productive will become angry when foreign costs seem to be dropping faster than foreign productivity changes. However, the firm may really be experiencing the effects of a strengthening currency. The strengthened currency reflects the productivity gains of *all* American firms. The manager's firm is effectively racing with other American firms in all other markets for the dollars held by foreigners.

3. Trade surpluses are good for the economy, and trade deficits are bad for the economy. WRONG!

Trade surpluses and deficits are neither *inherently* bad nor *inherently* good. RIGHT!

When we run a trade deficit, we get the benefits of foreign resources **net**. That's good. But, persistent deficits can be bad for the economy if they lead to restrictive policies designed to cut down on imports and to a continual depreciation of the exchange rate. Our persistent trade deficits (foreigners' trade surpluses) mean foreigners will eventually accumulate too much of our currency. Capital inflows will not be able to stem the glut of the currency. As a result our currency will depreciate and foreign goods will become more expensive.

4. The U.S. trade deficit means U.S. producers are inefficient. WRONG!

The U.S. trade deficit means U.S. producers are having difficulty competing. RIGHT!

The trade deficit reflects more than our (in)efficiency. As an example, U.S. agricultural producers are extremely efficient, but they have had difficulty exporting because the dollar was so strong for so long. A weaker dollar helps our producers compete. Before we believe the rhetoric concerning competitiveness, we need to know what is happening to exchange rates.

■ ANSWERS ■

Key-Term Review

1. production possibilities
2. imports
3. exports
4. net exports
   trade surplus
5. trade deficit
6. capital surplus
7. capital deficit
8. open-market operations
   money supply (*M*1)
9. exchange rate
10. productivity
11. multiplier
12. marginal propensity to save (*MPS*)
13. marginal propensity to import (*MPM*)
14. growth recession
    equilibrium GNP
    leakage

True or False

1. F	5. T	9. F	13. F	17. T	21. T
2. F	6. T	10. T	14. T	18. T	22. F
3. F	7. F	11. F	15. T	19. T	23. F
4. F	8. T	12. T	16. F	20. F	24. F

Multiple Choice

1. d	5. a	9. c	12. a	15. a	18. c
2. c	6. c	10. d	13. c	16. a	19. a
3. b	7. c	11. a	14. a	17. d	20. d
4. b	8. b				

Problems and Applications

Exercise 1

1. **Table 17.1 answer**
   (billions of dollars per year)

(1) Disposable income (Y_D)	(2) Consumption (C)	(3) Investment (I)	(4) Government expenditures (G)	(5) Aggregate spending (2) + (3) + (4)	(6) Saving (1) – (2)
$ 0	$ 100	$40	$200	$ 340	–100
2,000	1,700	40	200	1,940	300
4,000	3,300	40	200	3,540	700

2. The marginal propensity to consume (*MPC*) is 0.8 based on the consumption function. The marginal propensity to save is equal to $1 - MPC$, which is 0.2.

3. **Figure 17.1 answer**

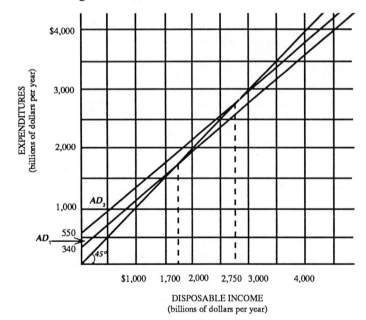

4. **Table 17.2 answer**
(billions of dollars per year)

(1) Disposable income (Y_D)	(2) Consumption (C)	(3) Investment (I)	(4) Government expenditures (G)	(5) Exports (X)	(6) Aggregate spending (2) + (3) + (4)
$ 0	$ 100	$40	$200	$210	$ 550
2,000	1,700	40	200	210	2,150
4,000	3,300	40	200	210	3,750

5. See AD_2 in Figure 17.1 answer.
6. F   Table 17.2 shows higher aggregate spending, not less.
7. T   Exports do not change in column 5 of Table 17.2, which means that aggregate spending rises by the same amount at each level of disposable income. A parallel shift is indicated.
8. $1/MPS = 1/0.2 = 5$
9. F   The foreign marginal propensity to import determines our exports, and it does not change the American marginal propensity to consume. The multiplier does not change when exports increase, *ceteris paribus*.

Exercise 2

1. a.

Table 17.3 answer
(billions of dollars per year)

(1) Disposable income (Y_D)	(2) Consumption (C)	(3) Investment (I)	(4) Government expenditures (G)	(5) Exports (X)	(6) Aggregate spending (2) + (3) + (4) + (5)
$ 0	$ 100	$40	$200	$210	$ 550
2,000	1,700	40	200	210	2,150
4,000	3,300	40	200	210	3,750

b–d.   See AD_1, the 45-degree line, and EQ_1 in Figure 17.2 answer.

Figure 17.2 answer

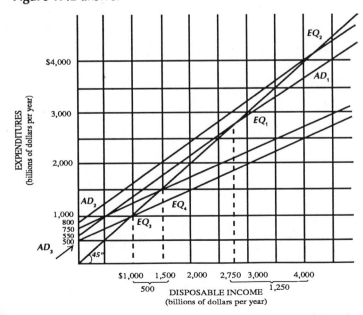

2. a

Table 17.4 answer
(billions of dollars per year)

(1) Disposable income (Y_D)	(2) Consumption (C)	(3) Investment (I)	(4) Government expenditures (G)	(5) Exports (X)	(6) Aggregate spending (2) + (3) + (4) + (5)
$ 0	$ 100	$40	$450	$210	$ 800
2,000	1,700	40	450	210	2,400
4,000	3,300	40	450	210	4,000

b and c. See AD_2 and EQ_2 in Figure 17.2 answer.
3. $2,750 billion; $4,000 billion; an increase; $1,250 billion.
4. a.

Table 17.5 answer
(billions of dollars per year)

(1) Disposable income (Y_D)	(2) Consumption (C)	(3) Investment (I)	(4) Government expenditures (G)	(5) Exports (X)	(6) Imports (M)	(7) Aggregate spending
$ 0	$ 100	$40	$200	$210	$ 50	$ 500
2,000	1,700	40	200	210	650	1,500
4,000	3,300	40	200	210	1,250	2,500

b and c. See AD_3 and EQ_3 in Figure 17.2 answer.
5. d
6. a.

Table 17.6 answer
(billions of dollars per year)

(1) Disposable income (Y_D)	(2) Consumption (C)	(3) Investment (I)	(4) Government expenditures (G)	(5) Exports (X)	(6) Imports (M)	(7) Aggregate spending
$ 0	$ 100	$40	$450	$210	$ 50	$ 750
2,000	1,700	40	450	210	650	1,750
4,000	3,300	40	450	210	1,250	·2,750

b and c. See AD_4 and EQ_4 in Figure 17.2 answer.
7. $1,000 billion; $1,500 billion; an increase; $500 billion
8. a decrease

Exercise 3

1. 0.8. See the consumption function.
2. $1 - .08 = 0.2$
3. $1/MPS = 5$
4. $1,250 billion ($250 billion x 5)

5. 0.3
6. $1/(MPS + MPM) = 1 (0.2 + 0.3) = 2$
7. $250 billion x 2 = $500 billion
8. T

Exercise 4

1. **Table 17.7 answer**
   (billions of dollars per year)

(1) Disposable income (Y_D)	(2) Exports (X)	(3) Imports (M)	(4) Balance of trade (2) – (3)
$ 0	$210	$ 50	$ 160
500	210	200	10
1,000	210	350	– 140

2–5.   See Figure 17.3 answer.

Figure 17.3 answer

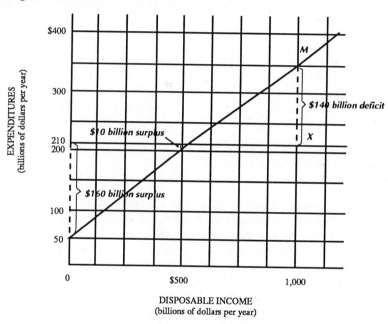

6. $533 billion. In Figure 17.3 the two lines cross at this disposable income level.
7.   F   For example, at an income level of $500 billion there is a surplus of 10 billion.
8.   T   For example, above $533 billion in Figure 17.3 there are only trade deficits.

Chapter 18

Long-Term Growth: Sources and Limits

Quick Review

Economic growth has been the major source of the ever-rising standard of living of the human race. However, the nature of growth and possible limits to it have long been debated. In this chapter we focus on the following concerns:

- Can the U.S. and world economies continue to grow?
- What are the sources of past and future economic growth?
- Will future growth destroy the environment?

Although short-term growth may be accomplished by moving to the production-possibilities frontier, long-term growth requires an expansion of an economy's productive capacity. For a nation's people to become better off, real GNP must increase at a rate that exceeds the rate of population growth. Growth is a complex process and is not completely understood, but the best sources of increased productivity appear to be in the saving–investment process: improved quality of labor, new management techniques, research and development expenditures, and the like. Government can do much to influence all of these.

Not everyone feels growth is necessarily good or sustainable. This feeling is best exemplified by the writing of the "doomsday prophets." In this regard, every generation of students rediscovers the work of the eighteenth-century clergyman Thomas R. Malthus. His message was unmistakable: the means of subsistence could not keep ahead of population growth. Hence, the human race was doomed to starvation unless steps were taken to stave off disaster. Doomsday prophets captured large audiences again in the 1970s. The widespread popularity of *The Limits to Growth,* a study by a group of M.I.T. scientists, and the works of Barry Commoner, Paul Ehrlich, and others again raised the question, "Is the human race doomed?"

The argument that growth has identifiable limits is founded on two concerns: (1) We are depleting the resources necessary for survival, and (2) we are polluting our environment so badly that further growth may make life increasingly unpleasant, or worse, biologically impossible.

The general weakness of these arguments is that they incorporate good arithmetic with a faulty sense of economics and history and a lack of appreciation for the adaptive capacity of our institutions.

Technological advance and adaptive capacity are automatically encouraged by economic forces. As resources become relatively scarce, their prices rise. These higher prices discourage resource use and provide incentives for exploration of new sources of supply and the substitution of alternative resources. From the perspective of resource requirements, growth may be limitless.

The pollution problem is perhaps more serious because the market mechanism does not adequately allocate the costs of pollution and thus does not provide the incentives necessary for its correction. Public policy to allocate costs or to set standards is needed to correct for this weakness.

Growth is possible for the foreseeable future. But is it desirable? Most seem to think it is, as long as it means a higher standard of living. On the other hand, an argument can be made that rather than continued growth, we simply need to change the mix of outputs we are producing to bring about an increase in economic well-being.

Many of the problems alluded to in this chapter caused many to advocate what has been called "industrial policy." Industrial policy envisions direct government intervention in investment, consumption, and resource use decisions by planning groups. Advocates say it would help eliminate short-run problems. Opponents view the suggestions as unwarranted intrusions into private matters by bureaucrats who would bring no additional expertise and slow down the decision making. The debate continues.

Learning Objectives

After reading Chapter 18 and doing the following exercises, you should:	True or false	Multiple choice	Problems and applications	Common errors	Pages in the text
1. Know the difference between the way output changes in the short run and the long run.	3–5, 23		1		416–417, 436–437
2. Know and be able to calculate some indices of growth.	1,2,5,6, 7,12,23	3	2	1,3	417–420
3. Understand some of the sources of productivity growth.	1,8,9,21	1,2,4,19	3		420–428
4. Be familiar with the history of the doomsday prophets.	10,11,14–16	5,10,12			428–431
5. Be aware of the shortcomings of the analyses of the doomsday prophets.	10,11, 13–16	6,8,12, 14,15	2	2,4	431–433
6. Understand the nature of environmental constraints that can limit growth.		7,13,16		3	434–435
7. Recognize what society can do to mitigate the external costs imposed by economic growth.	20,21	9,11,17		4	434–436
8. Know the basic arguments for and against an "industrial policy."	17–19,22	18			437

Key-Term Review

Review the following terms; if you are not sure of the meaning of any term, write out the definition and check it against the Glossary in the text.

arithmetic growth
economic growth
geometric growth
GNP per capita
growth rate
labor force

net investment
nominal GNP
production possibilities
productivity
real GNP
substitution effect

Fill in the blank following each of the statements below with the appropriate term from the list above.

1. The dollar value of an economy's final output divided by total population may be defined as _____.

1. _____

2. A series such as 2, 4, 6, 8 represents _____.

2. _____

3. A series such as 3, 9, 27, 81 represents _____.

3. _____

4. Total output divided by the number of units of input is a measure of that input's _____.

4. _____

5. A change in a purchasing pattern due to changes in relative prices is called a _____.

5. _____

6. The money value of GNP unadjusted for price changes is called _____.

6. _____

7. An increase in real GNP is referred to as _____.

7. _____

8. When nominal GNP is adjusted for price changes, the resulting aggregate is called _____.

8. _____

9. In the 1970s the population grew much more slowly than the working-age population, which makes up the _____.

9. _____

10. Percentage change in real GNP from one period to another is the _____.

10. _____

11. When an economy's productivity increases, there is an increase in its _____.

11. _____

12. To increase an economy's capital stock requires _____.

12. _____

True or False: *Circle your choice.*

T F 1. The United States is among the leading Western countries in improving average yearly productivity.

T F 2. When an economy moves from a point within its production-possibilities curve to a point on its production-possibilities curve, no economic growth takes place.

T F 3. Once an economy is on its production-possibilities curve, further increases in output require an expansion of productive capacity.

T F 4. An increase in nominal GNP is always accompanied by an outward shift in the production-possibilities curve.

T F 5. To achieve long-term economic growth requires an increase in potential GNP.

T F 6. Growth in GNP per capita is achieved only when population grows more rapidly than GNP.

T F 7. One result of the post–World War II baby boom was that in the 1970s the population grew more rapidly than the labor force.

T F 8. One of the results of the influx of teenagers and women into the U.S. labor force was a decline in the average productivity of the work force.

T F 9. While the average absolute price of a man's suit has risen over the past thirty years, its cost in terms of "work effort" has fallen.

T F 10. Scarcity of food was viewed by Malthus as a "natural check" on population growth.

T F 11. Malthus believed that the means of subsistence could not be expanded to accommodate continuous population growth.

T F 12. Malthus believed that population grew arithmetically and that the means of subsistence grew geometrically.

T F 13. Modern doomsday prophets emphasize that the productivity increases that have staved off starvation are not guaranteed to continue.

T F 14. The M.I.T. scientists who produced *The Limits to Growth* compared only known reserves and expected use to determine when we would run out of certain resources.

T F 15. Higher food prices will have the beneficial effect of stimulating research on ways to improve agricultural productivity.

T F 16. As some food prices rise, substitution effects in diets can be expected.

T F 17. Industrial policy is a program designed to save U.S. smokestack industries.

T F 18. Industrial policy advocates cooperative planning by business, government, and labor to rationalize the process of resource allocation.

T F 19. Opponents of industrial policy would rather risk small mistakes without government intervention than the larger risks they see as inherent in bureaucratic planning.

T F 20. Increases in the rate at which we utilize our productive capacity move the economy toward our production-possibilities curve.

T F 21. Sustained increases in GNP per capita are more likely to come from increases in productivity than from increases in the labor force.

T F 22. Since saving is a leakage from the income stream, it tends to inhibit improvements in productivity.

T F 23. Increases in the size of the labor force and capital stock have been less important than productivity advances in causing U.S. GNP to grow.

Multiple Choice: *Select the correct answer.*

_____ 1. Which of the following would likely contribute to an improvement in the productivity of labor?
(a) Greater expenditures on training and education.
(b) Policies to stimulate the saving and investment process.
(c) Greater expenditures on research and development.
(d) All of the above.

_____ 2. Which of the following is thought to have been the *greatest* source of advances in productivity?
(a) Improvement in management.
(b) Increases in capital per worker.
(c) Spending on research and development.
(d) Improvements in the quality of labor.

_____ 3. A sustained net growth in real output of 3.5 percent per year will cause real output to double in about:
(a) 10 years.
(b) 20 years.
(c) 30 years.
(c) 35 years.

_____ 4. Which of the following may be cited as a cause of the U.S. economy's poor performance in advancing labor productivity?
(a) A relatively low saving rate.
(b) Changes in the age–sex composition of the labor force.
(c) The trend away from manufacturing and toward services in our industrial structure.
(d) All of the above.

_____ 5. Which of the following statements can be attributed to Malthus?
   (a) Population grows geometrically and the means of subsistence arithmetically.
   (b) Starvation serves as a natural check to population growth.
   (c) Moral restraint, in the form of delayed marriage and childbearing, is necessary if humankind is to avoid misery.
   (d) All of the above are Malthusian statements.

_____ 6. Which of the following would be brought about automatically by changes in relative prices?
   (a) Substitution of polluting goods for nonpolluting goods.
   (b) Substitution of high-priced resources for low-priced resources in the production process.
   (c) Substitution of low-priced foods for high-priced foods.
   (d) None of the above.

_____ 7. In the pollution doomsday model, the variable that reaches its peak first is:
   (a) Population.
   (b) Pollution.
   (c) Industrial output per capita.
   (d) Food production per capita.

_____ 8. Which of the following results automatically from the working of the market system?
   (a) People do not pollute because all costs of consumption are borne directly by the consumer.
   (b) Producers are precluded from polluting because all costs of production are borne directly by the producer.
   (c) Neither producers nor consumers are forced to incur all of the costs of their activities.
   (d) None of the above results automatically.

_____ 9. Which of the following can help to stave off ecological disaster?
   (a) Changes in the output mix of GNP.
   (b) Government policy to control pollution.
   (c) Economic forces that lead to a reduction in population growth.
   (d) All of the above.

_____ 10. The description of economics as the "dismal science" refers to the:
   (a) Uninteresting subjects of the discipline.
   (b) Early predictions of world overpopulation and starvation.
   (c) Dull way the subject material is presented.
   (d) Absence of humor in the textbooks.

_____ 11. One reason that we can be somewhat more optimistic than the doomsday economists is that:
   (a) Land is not in finite supply.
   (b) Population is actually decreasing.
   (c) Technology continues to advance.
   (d) We have less demand for food now than we had years ago.

_____ 12. The M.I.T. scientists included in their computer calculations of the growth of food production:
   (a) Optimistic estimations of potential productivity improvements.
   (b) The production incentive of high profits.
   (c) Substitution effects in food consumption.
   (d) None of the above.

_____ 13. The doomsday theorists regard technological change as:
   (a) A diversion from the fundamental problem of growth in a finite system.
   (b) The only salvation from the dire consequences of their calculations.
   (c) A cure for the fundamental problem of growth in a finite system.
   (d) Unlikely.

14. An answer to the doomsday theorists is that:
    (a) Past experience and present knowledge support their thesis about productivity and technology.
    (b) We know exactly the limits to technological advancement.
    (c) Past experience and present knowledge suggest that there is hope for increased productivity and substitution.
    (d) We know when and where the technological limits will recur.

15. The profit incentive tends to:
    (a) Encourage productivity research and pollution abatement.
    (b) Discourage pollution abatement.
    (c) Discourage productivity research and pollution abatement.
    (d) Reduce the need for laws or fines to reduce pollution.

16. The benefits of pollution abatement:
    (a) Are external to the consumer or firm incurring the abatement costs.
    (b) Are directly experienced by the firm incurring the abatement costs.
    (c) Create the incentive for firms to take action on their own to stop pollution.
    (d) Are minimal and not worth economic consideration.

17. One probable short-run result of the cost of pollution being reflected in the cost of production is:
    (a) Increased pollution.
    (b) Higher prices for many consumer goods and services.
    (c) More goods produced at lower costs.
    (d) None of the above.

18. Industrial policy advocates envision:
    (a) Cooperation by business, labor, and government in the planning process.
    (b) A master plan to rationalize trade regulation, tax laws, and so on.
    (c) Direct government intervention in consumption, investment, and resource use decisions.
    (d) All of the above.

19. Which of the following are sources of productivity increase?
    (a) Research and development.
    (b) Improvements in labor quality.
    (c) Capital investment.
    (d) All of the above.

Problems and Applications

Exercise 1

This exercise focuses on the supply-and-demand effects of the energy crisis that occurred in the early 1970s.

The energy crisis should have an impact on the various markets listed below. Match the letter of the appropriate diagram in Figure 18.1 with each of the markets and events listed below and place it in the box marked "Shift." Then indicate with an arrow in the boxes "Price" and "Quantity" whether the equilibrium price and equilibrium quantity in each market should rise (↑) or fall (↓) because of the shift in demand or supply. Finally list the determinant of demand or supply that changed. (*Hint:* The nonprice determinants of demand are income, buyer expectations, the prices of related goods and availability of other goods, and the number of buyers. The nonprice determinants of supply are technology, the price and availability of resources, expectations, taxes and subsidies, and the number of suppliers.) *Make sure you decide which market is affected before deciding which shift occurs.*

Figure 18.1

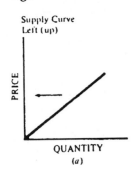

Supply Curve
Left (up)

PRICE

QUANTITY

(a)

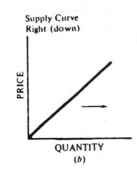

Supply Curve
Right (down)

PRICE

QUANTITY

(b)

Demand Curve
Left (down)

PRICE

QUANTITY

(c)

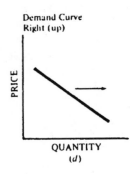

Demand Curve
Right (up)

PRICE

QUANTITY

(d)

---

1. **Market**

   Shingles

   Change

   OPEC announces it will increase the price of crude oil by 25 percent over the next six months. Crude oil is an input in the production of shingles.

   Figure 18.2

   QUANTITY PER UNIT OF TIME

SHIFT	PRICE	QUANTITY
DETERMINANT:		

---

2. **Market**

   Drilling rigs

   Change

   Government removes price controls on crude oil and the price of crude oil rises.

   Figure 18.3

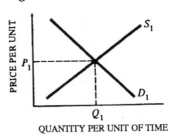

   QUANTITY PER UNIT OF TIME

SHIFT	PRICE	QUANTITY
DETERMINANT:		

---

3. **Market**

   Apartments in the suburbs

   Change

   Higher commuting costs convince the public it's better to live downtown.

   Figure 18.4

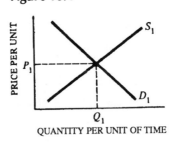

   QUANTITY PER UNIT OF TIME

SHIFT	PRICE	QUANTITY
DETERMINANT:		

---

4. **Market**

   Gas-run clothes dryers

   Change

   Canada and Mexico announce they will no longer sell the United States any natural gas.

   Figure 18.5

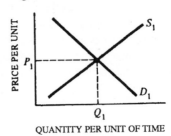

   QUANTITY PER UNIT OF TIME

SHIFT	PRICE	QUANTITY
DETERMINANT:		

254

5. **Market**
Coal miners

Change
Government bans the use of crude oil in new electrical generating plants. New plants use coal.

Figure 18.6

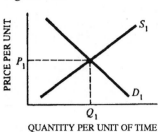

QUANTITY PER UNIT OF TIME

SHIFT	PRICE	QUANTITY
DETERMINANT:		

6. **Market**
Home insulation

Change
The *Farmer's Almanac* forecasts an unusually warm winter and the price of natural gas falls.

Figure 18.7

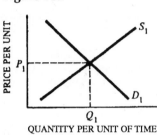

QUANTITY PER UNIT OF TIME

SHIFT	PRICE	QUANTITY
DETERMINANT:		

7. **Market**
Crude oil

Change
A huge oil deposit is discovered off the Atlantic coast.

Figure 18.8

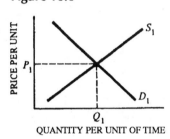

QUANTITY PER UNIT OF TIME

SHIFT	PRICE	QUANTITY
DETERMINANT:		

8. **Market**
Natural gas

Change
New technology improves the probability of hitting natural-gas wells.

Figure 18.9

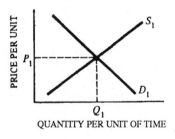

QUANTITY PER UNIT OF TIME

SHIFT	PRICE	QUANTITY
DETERMINANT:		

9. **Market**
Shrimp

Change
A Mexican oil well blows out in the Gulf of Mexico and the resulting oil slick damages commercial shrimp beds along the Texas coast.

Figure 18.10

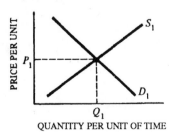

QUANTITY PER UNIT OF TIME

SHIFT	PRICE	QUANTITY
DETERMINANT:		

10.   **Market**   **Change**   **Figure 18.11**

Marine insurance   The world fleet of super-
tankers expands, increas-
ing the probability of
collisions.

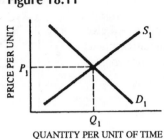

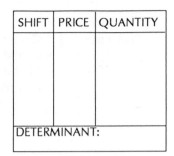

SHIFT	PRICE	QUANTITY
DETERMINANT:		

Exercise 2

The following exercise gives practice in recognizing the difference between arithmetic and geometric growth rates.

Assume that the population of a country is 1 million people in the year 2000 and that it is increasing at the rate of 10 percent per decade. Assume that food production is 1 million tons per year and grows by 100,000 tons every decade.

1.   In Figure 18.12 graph the tons of food per capita over a century.

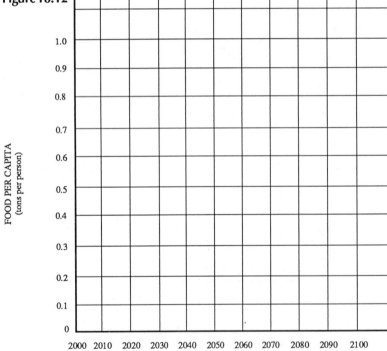

2.   The population growth is:
      (a) Geometric.
      (b) Arithmetic.

3.   The increase in food is:
      (a) Geometric.
      (b) Arithmetic.

256

4. After one century by what percentage has food consumption *per capita* declined as a result of the population increase? _____%

Exercise 3

The media often provide information about events that affect productivity. By using one of the articles in the text, this exercise will show the kind of information to look for. If your professor makes a newspaper assignment for this chapter, this exercise will provide an example of how to do it.

Reread the article in Chapter 18 entitled "R & D Spending Seen Growing at Slower Rate" from the *Washington Post*. Then answer the following questions:

1. What phrase indicates the event that would alter productivity?

2. Which of the following statements *best* indicates the effect the event has on productivity?
   (a) The productivity growth rate is reduced compared to what it would have been if R & D had not been cut.
   (b) The productivity growth rate rises compared to what it would have been if R & D had not been cut.

3. Which of the four diagrams in Figure 18.1 (p. 254 in the text) *best* represents the effect of the event on aggregate supply or demand?   a   b   c   d   (circle one)

4. What statement indicates the effect of the event on production rates, prices, unit costs, or productivity?

Common Errors

The first statement in each "common error" below is incorrect. Each incorrect statement is followed by a corrected version and an explanation.

1. Zero economic growth treats everyone equally. WRONG!

   Zero economic growth treats groups unequally. RIGHT!

   Zero economic growth in its simplest dimensions means that GNP would not grow from year to year. Income per capita could therefore not grow unless population declined. Yet we know that U.S. population is growing, although slowly, as a result of new births and increased longevity, and more recently as a result of immigration. If GNP were not to grow, the only way for those at the bottom of the income distribution to have more would be for someone at the top to take less.

2. There is no way to hold off the doomsday prophecy. WRONG!

   Much has been done in the last decade to avoid the cataclysmic predictions of the doomsday prophets. RIGHT!

   It's about two decades since the deluge of new doomsday literature hit the newsstands. Before that, pollution, the environment, and ecology were issues popularized in the turbulent 1960s. Since then much has been done by federal, state, and local governments to overcome some of the problems that seemed most acute. The air is cleaner in many areas. So is water. Even the OPEC actions of the 1970s and early 1980s were of help in this regard. Higher oil prices spurred research into new sources of power and new ways to conserve energy. All of this activity helped us to meet the doomsday challenge once again.

3. Zero economic growth will alleviate the pollution problem. WRONG!

   Zero economic growth will maintain the rate of pollution. RIGHT!

   Some people mistakenly think that stifling economic growth is a way to cut down on pollution. It isn't. The best that a ZEG policy could do is cut down on the *growth* in pollution. With the same output level and output mix, the rate of pollution would be the same from year to year. To cut pollution would require cutting GNP—that is, a *negative* economic growth policy! The economy has the capability of cleaning up pollution as well as generating pollution as it grows.

257

4. The world must run out of resources sooner or later. WRONG!

So long as recycling occurs, substitutions are made, and advances in technology take place, we won't run out of resources. RIGHT!

We'll stop relying on most presently used, theoretically exhaustible resources long before they are completely gone. The costs of obtaining them would be too great. At some point it will be cheaper to recycle, substitute new resources, and devise new technologies than to rely on hard-to-get-at supplies of resources. We won't run out of everything!

■ ANSWERS ■

Key-Term Review

1. GNP per capita	5. substitution effect	9. labor force
2. arithmetic growth	6. nominal GNP	10. growth rate
3. geometric growth	7. economic growth	11. production possibilities
4. productivity	8. real GNP	12. net investment

True or False

1. F	5. T	9. T	13. T	17. F	21. T
2. F	6. F	10. T	14. T	18. T	22. F
3. T	7. F	11. T	15. T	19. T	23. T
4. F	8. T	12. F	16. T	20. T	

Multiple Choice

1. d	5. d	8. c	11. c	14. c	17. b
2. c	6. c	9. d	12. d	15. b	18. d
3. b	7. d	10. b	13. a	16. a	19. d
4. d					

Problems and Applications

Exercise 1

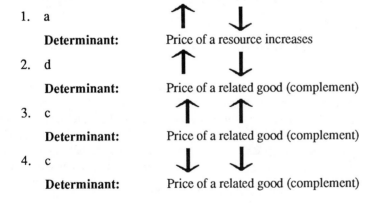

	Shift	Price	Quantity
1.	a	↑	↓
	Determinant:	Price of a resource increases	
2.	d	↑	↓
	Determinant:	Price of a related good (complement)	
3.	c	↑	↑
	Determinant:	Price of a related good (complement)	
4.	c	↓	↓
	Determinant:	Price of a related good (complement)	

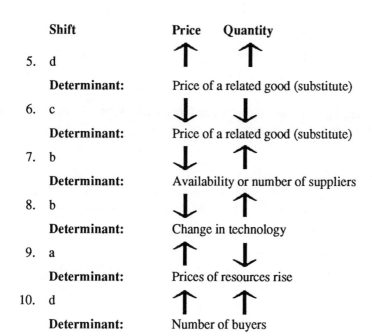

	Shift	**Price**	**Quantity**
5.	d	↑	↑
	Determinant:	Price of a related good (substitute)	
6.	c	↓	↓
	Determinant:	Price of a related good (substitute)	
7.	b	↓	↑
	Determinant:	Availability or number of suppliers	
8.	b	↓	↑
	Determinant:	Change in technology	
9.	a	↑	↓
	Determinant:	Prices of resources rise	
10.	d	↑	↑
	Determinant:	Number of buyers	

Exercise 2

Figure 18.12 answer

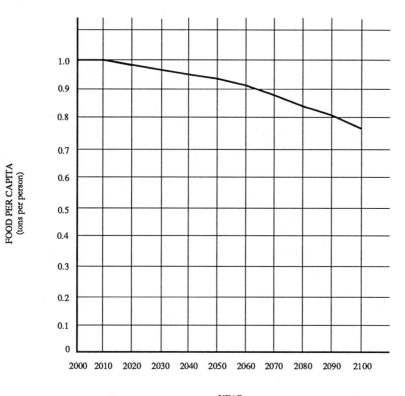

FOOD PER CAPITA (tons per person) vs YEAR

2. a
3. b
4. nearly 25% [(1 – 0.7711) x 100%]

Exercise 3

1. The phrase "federal budget constraints, economic uncertainty and short term corporate outlooks" indicates the original problems that will curb R & D and thereby curb productivity.
2. a
3. a
4. "Growth of research and development spending in the United States is likely to slip" indicates a slowing in research and development, which in turn should lower productivity rates. Notice that the term "productivity" is never even mentioned in the article. It has to be discovered by reading between the lines.

SECTION III MICROECONOMICS
PART A PRODUCT MARKETS: BASIC THEORY

Chapter 19
The Demand for Goods

Quick Review

Demand and supply were introduced in Chapter 2 to demonstrate how markets operate. In this chapter we look at demand in greater depth. (Supply is considered in Chapter 21.) Specifically, the chapter looks at the following questions:

- Why do we buy certain goods and not others?
- How do we decide how much of any good to buy?
- What factors change our consumption patterns?

Other concepts are developed too, but these three questions organize our early discussion.

Demand refers to the willingness and ability of buyers to buy goods and services. It has nothing to do with the sellers of those goods or services or even with the availability of the goods or services. It refers only to buyers. In fact, demand can exist even if there are no purchases by buyers at all.

Demand for goods and services is more than just the desire for goods and services. When people starve as a result of a drought, they have the desire for food but not the ability to pay for it. Demand reflects both the willingness and the ability to buy goods and services. Consumers' tastes, their incomes, the price of the product, the prices (and availability) of other goods, and people's expectations (about tastes, incomes, and prices) determine what individuals are willing and able to buy. If any of these determinants of demand change, then the demand curve shifts. Shifts in the demand curve are likely to cause changes in price and purchases in the marketplace. To understand the market, we must look carefully at tastes, incomes, prices, and expectations.

Utility theory helps to clarify much of what we know about consumer tastes and preferences. Consumers buy only those things that give them satisfaction or utility. Since consumers have a limited income, they must ask what gives them maximum satisfaction for that income. Usually a variety of goods and services is available. Consumers compare the available goods and services—and their relative prices—then choose the amounts that will give them the greatest satisfaction, or utility, for the income available. As a consumer consumes more and more of any one product, other goods and services begin to look relatively more desirable. Here we see the law of diminishing marginal utility at work: as we consume more of a product, we receive smaller and smaller increments of pleasure from it.

The law of diminishing marginal utility translates readily into the law of demand. The law of demand asserts that we will be willing to buy increasing quantities of a product as its price falls; that is, an inverse relationship exists between quantity demanded and price. This law is graphically illustrated by a downward-sloping demand curve. The demand curve itself relates the quantity of a good demanded to its price, under the assumption that all other things are held constant (*ceteris paribus*). The downward slope of the demand curve indicates that larger quantities of a good will be purchased at lower prices.

The demand curve gives information about the total revenue that a firm could receive. By computing the price elasticity of demand, the firm can even determine how its total revenue changes for a given change in price. Elasticities are also useful in describing how sensitive the quantity demanded of a good is to changes in its own price.

Learning Objectives

After reading Chapter 19 and doing the following exercises, you should:	True or false	Multiple choice	Problems and applications	Common errors	Pages in the text
1. Be able to distinguish the demand for a good from the desire for it.	1,2,20	4–6,16		7	445–447
2. Know how the law of diminishing marginal utility and the law of demand relate to each other.	3,7–9,16, 18,19,21	1–3,13	3,4	1,5,7	447–450
3. Be able to draw a demand curve from a demand schedule and create a demand schedule by looking at a demand curve.	1		1,2	2	450–452
4. Be able to distinguish between a change in demand (a shift of the curve) and a change in quantity demanded (a movement along the demand curve).	2,5, 6,11	5,6	5	6	452–457
5. Be able to show how any change in the price of a good, in the price of a substitute, in the price of a complement, in incomes, in tastes, or in expectations will affect the demand curve.	4	4,9,15, 16,20			454–457
6. Be able to compute the price elasticity of demand between two points on the demand curve.	10	7	2	3,4	457–461
7. Be able to determine on the basis of the the elasticity of demand what will happen to total revenue when prices change.	12–15	8,11,12, 14, 17–19			461–465
8. Know how a consumer makes the optimal consumption decision.	17,20	10	3,4		465–469

Key-Term Review

Review the following terms; if you are not sure of the meaning of any term, write out the definition and check it against the Glossary in the text.

ceteris paribus	optimal consumption
complementary goods	price elasticity of demand
demand	quantity demanded
demand curve	shift in demand
demand schedule	substitute goods
law of demand	total revenue
law of diminishing marginal utility	total utility
marginal utility	utility
opportunity cost	

Fill in the blank following each of the statements below with the appropriate term from the list above.

1. When the price of one type of good is raised, consumers buy more of _____.   1. _____

2. "All other determinants of demand are held constant except for the price of the good itself" is expressed by the phrase _____.

    2. _____

3. If a firm raises the price of a good and finds that fewer units of the good are purchased, there has been a change in _____.

    3. _____

4. This change in quantity demanded in response to a change in price illustrates the _____.

    4. _____

5. If a firm raises prices 10 percent but people buy 20 percent less of its product, the firm experiences a decline in _____.

    5. _____

6. The decline in revenue because of the price increase could have been anticipated if the firm had known its _____.

    6. _____

7. As you drink more and more soda, you begin to feel less comfortable, in accordance with the _____.

    7. _____

8. The relationship between price and quantity is summarized in a table called the _____.

    8. _____

9. When a person increases the quantities of goods and services purchased according to his or her marginal utility until the budget constraint is reached, that person is attaining _____.

    9. _____

10. The various quantities that people are willing and able to purchase at various prices in a given time period, *ceteris paribus*, is known as _____.

    10. _____

11. The inverse relationship of quantity and price is expressed graphically in a _____.

    11. _____

12. The satisfaction a person gains from consuming an extra unit of a product is _____.

    12. _____

13. Satisfaction is also known as _____.

    13. _____

14. Goods that are used or consumed together, such as cream with coffee, are _____.

    14. _____

15. A change in the price of a substitute good is followed by a _____.

    15. _____

16. The next best use of resources that must be forgone in order to produce a good is called the good's _____.

    16. _____

17. The amount of satisfaction obtained from your entire consumption of a product is known as _____.

    17. _____

True or False: *Circle your choice.*

T F 1. It is not possible to draw a demand curve for a good or service if the good or service is not available at any price.

T F 2. Sellers use advertising to change the consumer's tastes, thus causing a shift in the consumer's demand curve.

T F 3. The law of demand differs from the law of diminishing marginal utility in that it considers what a person is able to pay for a good or service, not just the person's desire for a good or service.

T F 4. A rise in the price of a good causes the demand curve for substitute goods to shift in a direction opposite to that of a shift for complementary goods, *ceteris paribus.*

T F 5. In order to find the demand curve for a consumer, we can design an experiment in which all determinants of demand are held constant except for price. We locate the demand curve by observing the quantity of a good or service that the consumer buys at each price.

T F 6. A change in the quantity demanded occurs only when the demand curve shifts.

T F 7. According to the law of diminishing marginal utility, the total utility we obtain from a product decreases as we consume more of it.

T F 8. In general, the total utility we derive from consuming all products increases with the number of products we obtain.

T F 9. If the law of demand holds, the demand curve of a consumer must slope downward to the right.

T F 10. An increase in price does not necessarily increase total revenue.

T F 11. Advertising causes a company to move along its demand curve.

T F 12. If demand is elastic, a rise in price raises total revenue.

T F 13. If the elasticity of demand is equal to 1, then a 1 percent increase in price will shift the demand curve 1 percent to the left.

T F 14. Elasticity of demand is constant along straight-line demand curves.

T F 15. Since a flat (horizontal) demand curve is inelastic, consumers are unlikely to change their purchasing habits when the price changes.

T F 16. According to the law of demand, quantity demanded rises as price rises.

T F 17. Optimal consumption implies that consumers are all satisfied.

T F 18. When there are food riots because people are starving, the demand for food is increasing.

T F 19. By the law of demand, when people expect the price of a commodity to rise in the future, they buy less of the commodity in the present.

T F 20. Optimal consumption implies that a consumer has achieved as much satisfaction as possible with his or her available income.

T F 21. When a buyer purchases a good, the demand for the good falls at the same time.

Multiple Choice: *Select the correct answer.*

_____ 1. The law of demand says that, *ceteris paribus:*
  (a) The lower the price, the less buyers will purchase.
  (b) The lower the price, the more buyers will purchase.
  (c) The lower the income of a buyer, the more the buyer will purchase.
  (d) The lower the income of a buyer, the less the buyer will purchase.

_____ 2. Which of the following statements exemplifies the law of diminishing marginal utility?
  (a) Garbage gives me no satisfaction, so I won't spend my income for any of it.
  (b) The more soda I drink, the more I want to drink.
  (c) The more I go to school, the more I want to do something else.
  (d) Since we need water more than we need diamonds, water is more valuable.

_____ 3. *Ceteris paribus* means (in demand theory):
    (a) Nothing is allowed to change.
    (b) The determinants of demand may change, but all else must be held constant.
    (c) Only one determinant (for example, price) is being changed while all other determinants remain unchanged.
    (d) Consumers try to keep all things constant so that prices will be lower.

_____ 4. Which of the following is *not* a determinant of the demand for Frisbees?
    (a) Income.
    (b) Prices of goods related to Frisbees.
    (c) Tastes and preferences for Frisbees.
    (d) A change in the technology of producing Frisbees.

_____ 5. Which of the following would *not* cause a change in the demand for soda?
    (a) A change in your salary.
    (b) A change in the price of a substitute, such as mineral water.
    (c) A change in the price of soda itself.
    (d) All of the above.

_____ 6. A decline in the price of a good, *ceteris paribus,* causes:
    (a) A change in the demand for the good.
    (b) A change in quantity demanded of the good.
    (c) Both a and b.
    (d) None of the above.

_____ 7. The midpoint formula for price elasticity is:
    (a) $\dfrac{(q_1 - q_2)/q_1}{(p_1 - p_2)/p_1}$

    (b) $\dfrac{(q_1 - q_2)/q_2}{(p_1 - p_2)/p_2}$

    (c) $\dfrac{(q_1 - q_2)/[1/2\,(q_1 + q_2)]}{(p_1 - p_2)/[1/2\,(p_1 + p_2)]}$

    (d) None of the above.

_____ 8. Total revenue declines:
    (a) When price rises and supply is elastic, *ceteris paribus.*
    (b) When price rises and demand is inelastic, *ceteris paribus.*
    (c) When price falls and demand is elastic, *ceteris paribus.*
    (d) Under none of the above conditions.

_____ 9. When the price of a substitute for commodity X rises, *ceteris paribus*:
    (a) The demand curve for commodity X shifts to the right.
    (b) The demand curve for commodity X shifts to the left.
    (c) The consumer increases the quantity demanded of good X (in other words, the consumer moves down along the demand curve for good X).
    (d) The consumer decreases the quantity demanded of good X (in other words, the consumer moves up along the demand curve for good X).

_____ 10. Which of the following statements does *not* exemplify the opportunity cost of buying popcorn at a movie theater?
    (a) We won't be able to play pinball because the popcorn took all the money we had left.
    (b) We won't be able to ride the bus home after the movie because the popcorn took our bus money.
    (c) We will be able to see the movie, eat popcorn, and ride the bus home after the movie, but we won't be able to spend all day sitting at the drugstore with friends, spending money on magazines and milk shakes.
    (d) We like to eat popcorn only when we go to the movies.

_____ 11. One of the airline industry's arguments against deregulation of air fares was that the resulting fall in prices would lower airline total revenue. Instead, total revenue rose. It can be concluded that:
(a) Airline representatives thought demand for plane trips was elastic.
(b) Quantity demanded of airline service increased by a greater percentage than the percentage fall in price.
(c) Demand for airline service increased with the fall in prices.
(d) Airlines were more profitable after deregulation.

_____ 12. Each member of a union pays dues of 5 percent of his or her wage. In a contract negotiation the union succeeds in raising wages. But it finds that total union dues have actually decreased after the increased wage settlement. This is consistent with which of the following statements?
(a) The demand for the labor services of union members is elastic.
(b) Because of automation, more workers are hired.
(c) Because of a recession, more workers are hired elsewhere.
(d) It is consistent with all of the above statements.

_____ 13. Both the law of demand and the law of diminishing marginal utility:
(a) State that quantity and price are inversely related.
(b) Reflect declining satisfaction from consuming additional units of product.
(c) Reflect both the willingness and the ability of buyers to buy goods and services.
(d) Can be illustrated by means of demand curves.

_____ 14. The concept of elasticity:
(a) Compares the change in quantity with the change in price.
(b) Provides evidence on the way total revenue changes when price changes.
(c) Shows what the slope of the demand curve is.
(d) Does both a and b.

_____ 15. When a man is fired from his job and is unable to find another job:
(a) His demand curve for goods should shift to the left.
(b) His demand curve for goods should shift to the right.
(c) He will move up along his demand curve.
(d) He will move down along his demand curve.

_____ 16. When an employee is fired and cannot find work, the determinant of his or her demand for goods that has changed is:
(a) Income.
(b) Prices of related goods.
(c) Tastes and preferences.
(d) Technology.

_____ 17. A university's football games usually bring larger crowds than its stadium can seat. By which of the following means can the university reduce the size of the crowd and simultaneously earn more revenue to finance a new stadium?
(a) By raising ticket prices when demand for tickets is inelastic.
(b) By raising ticket prices when demand for tickets is elastic.
(c) By lowering ticket prices when demand for tickets is inelastic.
(d) By lowering ticket prices when demand for tickets is elastic.

_____ 18. If a state legislature wishes to raise revenue by increasing certain excise taxes, it would increase excise taxes on goods that:
(a) Are illegal.
(b) Are bought by rich people.
(c) Have inelastic demand.
(d) Have elastic demand.

_____19. A politician states that price controls would induce people to increase their demand, with resultant benefits to both firms and consumers. Which of the following criticisms of this claim is valid?
   (a) If demand for goods is inelastic, firms may receive lower total revenues.
   (b) The quantity demanded of goods will change, but not demand.
   (c) Businesses need to know how costs will change before they increase production.
   (d) All of the above criticisms are valid.

_____20. If consumers expect automakers to offer rebates next month, they will:
   (a) Increase their demand for cars today.
   (b) Decrease their demand for cars today.
   (c) Keep demand the same but increase the quantity demanded of cars.
   (d) Keep demand the same but decrease the quantity demanded of cars.

Problems and Applications

Exercise 1

This exercise will help you to draw demand curves from demand schedules. It should also give you practice in constructing market demand curves.

   1. Market demand is:
      (a) The total quantity of a good or service that people are willing and able to buy at alternative prices in a given period of time, *ceteris paribus.*
      (b) The sum of individual demands.
      (c) Represented as the horizontal sum of individual demand curves.
      (d) All of the above.

   2. Table 19.1 presents a *hypothetical* demand schedule for cars manufactured in the United States in 1989.

Table 19.1
Demand for U.S. cars, 1989

Price	Number of new U.S. cars (millions per year)
$ 8,600	9.7
10,000	9.0

Graph this demand curve in Figure 19.1.

Figure 19.1

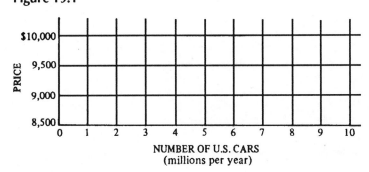

NUMBER OF U.S. CARS
(millions per year)

3. Table 19.2 presents a similar demand schedule for imported cars.

Table 19.2
Demand for foreign cars, 1989

Price	Number of new foreign cars (millions per year)
$ 8,600	2.4
10,000	1.5

Graph this demand curve in Figure 19.2.

Figure 19.2

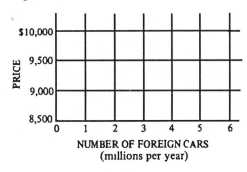

NUMBER OF FOREIGN CARS
(millions per year)

4. Suppose that foreign-car prices are always kept competitive with domestic-car prices, so that they are the same. In Table 19.3 indicate the number of cars (both foreign and domestically produced) at the two prices shown.

Table 19.3
Market demand for new cars, 1989

Price	Number of new cars (millions per year)
$ 8,600	_____
10,000	_____

5. In Figure 19.3 draw the domestic market demand curve for both foreign and domestic cars. (The curve should pass through point A.)

Figure 19.3

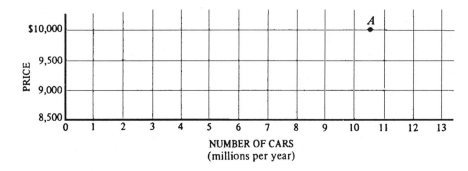

NUMBER OF CARS
(millions per year)

Exercise 2

This exercise should give you practice in computing and interpreting the elasticity of demand. This exercise is similar to the first exercise at the end of Chapter 19 in the text.

1. T   F   The midpoint formula for the price elasticity of demand is:

$$\frac{(p_1 - p_2) / [1/2 \, (p_1 + p_2)]}{(q_1 - q_2) / [1/2 \, (q_1 + q_2)]}$$

2. If you answered "True" to Problem 1, you goofed. The percentage change in quantity, $(q_1 - q_2) / [1/2 \, (q_1 + q_2)]$, should be on the top, not the bottom. The correct formula is:

$$\frac{(q_1 - q_2) / [1/2 \, (q_1 + q_2)]}{(p_1 - p_2) / [1/2 \, (p_1 + p_2)]}$$

Apply this formula to the information in Table 19.4, which represents a hypothetical demand schedule for cars.

Table 19.4
Hypothetical demand schedule for cars

Price	Number of new cars (millions per year)	Elasticity of demand
$ 10,000	10.5	_____
8,600	12.1	_____
7,000	14	_____
5,500	15.6	_____
4,000	17.4	_____

3. Graph the first two columns in Table 19.4 in Figure 19.4.

Figure 19.4

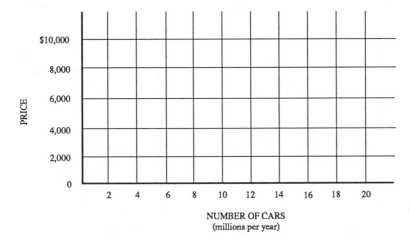

4. T   F   The curve is a linear demand curve.

5. What is the slope of the demand curve? _____

6. Moving down a linear demand curve results in:
   (a) More inelastic demand and a changing slope.
   (b) More inelastic demand but a constant slope.
   (c) More elastic demand and a changing slope.
   (d) More elastic demand and a constant slope.

7. T   F   While the concept of elasticity reflects a ratio of percentage changes in two variables, the slope reflects only changes in the variables, not percentage changes.

Exercise 3

This exercise shows the relationship between total and marginal utility. It also gives practice in identifying the law of diminishing marginal utility.

Suppose there are two types of entertainment that you enjoy—an evening at home with friends and an "event" entertainment, such as a sports event or a rock concert. The number of times that you experience each type of entertainment during a month determines the total utility of each type of entertainment for that month. Suppose Table 19.5 represents the total utility you achieve from consuming various quantities of the two types of entertainment.

Table 19.5
Total and marginal utility of two types of entertainment per month

Days of entertainment per month	Evening at home		Event	
	Total utility	Marginal utility	Total utility	Marginal utility
0	0	_____	0	_____
1	180	_____	600	_____
2	360	_____	1,200	_____
3	530	_____	1,680	_____
4	670	_____	2,040	_____
5	810	_____	2,400	_____
6	950	_____	2,760	_____
7	1,050	_____	3,120	_____
8	1,150	_____	3,120	_____
9	1,250	_____	3,120	_____
10	1,250	_____	3,120	_____
11	1,150	_____	2,920	_____
12	1,030	_____	2,700	_____

1. Compute the marginal utility of each type of entertainment and complete Table 19.5.

Law of diminishing marginal utility

2. The law of diminishing marginal utility means:
   (a) The total utility of a good declines as more of it is consumed in a given time period.
   (b) The marginal utility of a good declines as more of it is consumed in a given time period.
   (c) The price of a good declines as more of it is consumed in a given period of time.
   (d) All of the above.

3. The law of diminishing marginal utility is in evidence in Table 19.5:
   (a) For both types of entertainment.
   (b) For home entertainment only.
   (c) For event entertainment only.
   (d) For neither type of entertainment.

   (*Hint:* You should be able to tell by looking at the marginal utility columns in Table 19.5. Does the marginal utility become smaller as you go down the column?)

4. In Figure 19.5 graph the *total* utility curve for evenings at home.

Figure 19.5

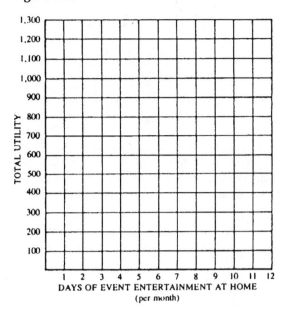

5. In Figure 19.6 graph the *marginal* utility curve for evenings at home.

Figure 19.6

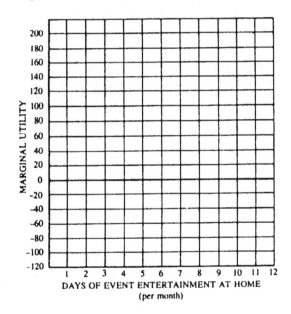

6. On the basis of the two graphs, marginal utility becomes zero only when:
    (a) Total utility is zero.
    (b) Total utility reaches a maximum.
    (c) Total utility is positive.
    (d) Total utility is negative.

7. When total utility is rising, then:
   (a) Marginal utility is rising.
   (b) Marginal utility is negative.
   (c) Marginal utility is positive.
   (d) Marginal utility is zero.

Exercise 4

The principle of utility maximization is applied to find optimal consumption. This exercise builds on the previous exercise.

Suppose you hold a part-time job that gives you $120 a month extra spending money. On any day of the month you can spend that money on either of two types of entertainment—an evening at home with friends, for which you usually spend $10 for snacks and drinks, or an "event" entertainment, which can cost $20 and up to $10 more for gas to get to and from the event. Table 19.6 shows the hypothetical marginal utility that each type of entertainment provides for you during the month.

Table 19.6
Total and marginal utility of two types of entertainment per month

Days of entertainment per month	Evening at home (price = $10)		Event entertainment (price = $30)	
	Marginal utility	MU / price	Marginal utility	MU / price
0	0	0	0	—
1	180	18	600	_____
2	180	18	600	_____
3	170	17	480	_____
4	140	14	360	_____
5	140	14	360	_____
6	140	14	360	_____
7	100	10	360	_____
8	100	10	0	_____
9	100	10	0	_____
10	0	0	0	_____

Maximization of utility and optimal consumption

1. Finding the optimal level of consumption with a given income involves choosing successive *increments* of a good (service), *each of which* yields:

   (a) The largest total utility.
   (b) The largest marginal utility per unit of product or activity purchased.
   (c) The largest marginal utility for each dollar spent.
   (d) All of the above.

2. Divide marginal utility by the price of the "event" entertainment to complete Table 19.6.

   Before you spend any money on any activity:

3. Which activity has the highest MU/p ratio? _____

4. Judging by the MU/p ratio, how many days of event entertainment should you buy before spending anything on "at-home" entertainment? _____

5. If you had $120, how much money would you have left after buying two days of "event" entertainment? $ _____

6. Should you spend the rest on "at-home" entertainment? _____

7. After you have bought three "at-home" nights and two "events," how much income is left from the original $120? $_____

8. Which activity offers a higher MU/*p* ratio for this remaining income? _____

9. T   F   When your income is $120, optimal consumption occurs with three evenings of each type of entertainment.

Exercise 5

The media often provide information that suggests shifts in a market demand curve or a movement along such a curve. By using one of the articles in the text, this exercise will show the kind of information to look for. If your professor makes a newspaper assignment for this chapter, this exercise will provide an example of how to do it.

Reread the article in Chapter 2 entitled "Surplus Punches Hole in Oil Price" from *USA Today*. Then answer the following questions:

1. Which of the four diagrams in Figure 19.7 best represents the movement or shift that the article describes?   a   b   c   d   (circle one)

Figure 19.7

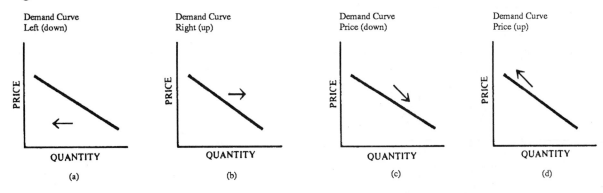

2. What phrase indicates the *market* in which the demand shift occurs?

3. What passage describes the change in the determinant of demand or price that caused the shift you chose in Figure 19.7?

4. What passage indicates who the buyer is?

5. Where does the article mention a change in price or quantity that resulted from the shift in demand or that caused the movement along the demand curve?

Common Errors

The first statement in each "common error" below is incorrect. Each incorrect statement is followed by a corrected version and an explanation.

1. The law of demand and the law of diminishing marginal utility are the same. WRONG!

   The law of demand and the law of diminishing marginal utility are not the same. RIGHT!

   Do not confuse utility and demand. Utility refers only to expected satisfaction. Demand refers to both preferences and ability to pay. This distinction should help you to keep the law of diminishing marginal utility separate from the law of demand.

2. Figures 19.8*a* and 19.8*b* represent simple graphs drawn from a demand schedule.

Figure 19.8*a*

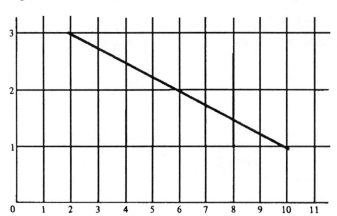

WRONG!

Figure 19.8*b*

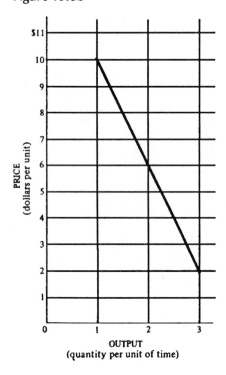

OUTPUT
(quantity per unit of time)

The first graph has been drawn without any units indicated. It is something of an accidental tradition in economics to show price on the *y*-axis and quantity on the *x*-axis. This convention is sometimes confusing to mathematicians, who want to treat quantity as a function of price, according to the definition in the text. In Figure 19.8*a* the axes have been reversed and incorrect points have been chosen.

Be careful! When you are learning a new graph, make a special effort to understand the units that are placed on the axes. Also make sure you know the kinds of units in which each quantity is measured. If you are drawing a graph from a table (or schedule), you can usually find what should be on the axes by looking at the heading above the column from which you are reading the numbers.

Make sure price is shown on the *y*-axis (vertical) and quantity on the *x*-axis (horizontal). If you mix up the two, you may confuse a graph showing perfectly elastic demand with one showing perfectly inelastic demand.

3. The formula for the price elasticity of demand is:

$$\frac{\text{Change in price}}{\text{Change in quantity}}$$

The formula for the price elasticity of demand is:

$$\frac{\text{Percentage change in quantity}}{\text{Percentage change in price}}$$

The concept of elasticity allows us to compare relative changes in quantity and price without having to worry about the units in which they are measured. In order to do this, we compute percentage changes of both price and quantity. A change in price *causes* people to change the quantity they demand in a given time period. By putting the quantity changes in the numerator, we can see that if quantity response is very large in relation to a price change, the elasticity will also be very large. If the quantity response is small in relation to a price change, then demand is inelastic (elasticity is small).

Be careful! Do not confuse slope and elasticity. The formula for the slope of the demand curve is the *wrong* formula shown above. The formula for the price elasticity of demand is the *right* formula.

4. A flat demand curve has an elasticity of zero. WRONG!

A flat demand curve has an infinite elasticity. RIGHT!

When price remains constant even when quantity changes, the elasticity formula requires us to divide by a zero price change. In fact, as demand curves approach flatness, the elasticity becomes larger and larger. By agreement we say it is infinite.

5. The person for whom a good or service has the greatest utility has the greatest desire for more of it. WRONG!

The good that has the greatest *marginal* utility for a person, with respect to price, is the good of which he or she desires more. RIGHT!

Utilities of one good for many people cannot be compared. Utilities of various goods for one person can be compared. Marginal utility with respect to price, however, is the basis on which a choice will be made, not total utility.

6. An expected price change has the same effect as a change in the current price. WRONG!

An unexpected price change shifts the demand curve, whereas a current price change is a movement along the demand curve. RIGHT!

If prices are expected to rise in the near future, people will demand more of the commodity today in order to beat the rise in price. Demand increases and the quantity demanded will rise. However, if the price rises today, by the law of demand people reduce the quantity demanded! Furthermore, demand itself does not change. A current price change and an expected price change have very different effects.

7. When a buyer buys a good, the demand for the good decreases. WRONG!

When a buyer buys a good, demand is not affected. RIGHT!

Demand refers only to the *willingness* and *ability* of a buyer to buy. The potential for purchase is the focus of demand, not the actual purchase. Demand is defined over a given period of time. If a buyer buys a good during that period of time, he or she is still counted as demanding the good—even after it is purchased.

■ ANSWERS ■

Key-Term Review

1. substitute goods
2. *ceteris paribus*
3. quantity demanded
4. law of demand
5. total revenue
6. price elasticity of demand
7. law of diminishing marginal utility
8. demand schedule
9. optimal consumption
10. demand
11. demand curve
12. marginal utility
13. utility
14. complementary goods
15. shift in demand
16. opportunity cost
17. total utility

True or False

1. F	5. T	9. T	13. F	16. F	19. F
2. T	6. F	10. T	14. F	17. F	20. T
3. T	7. F	11. F	15. F	18. F	21. F
4. T	8. T	12. F			

Multiple Choice

1. b	5. c	9. a	12. a	15. a	18. c
2. c	6. b	10. d	13. b	16. a	19. d
3. c	7. c	11. b	14. b	17. a	20. b
4. d	8. d				

Problems and Applications

Exercise 1

1. d
2. **Figure 19.1 answer**

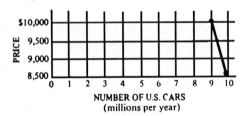

NUMBER OF U.S. CARS
(millions per year)

3. **Figure 19.2 answer**

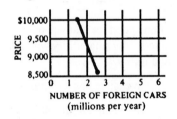

NUMBER OF FOREIGN CARS
(millions per year)

4. **Table 19.3 answer**

Price	Number of new cars (millions per year)
$ 8,600	12.1
10,000	10.5

5. **Figure 19.3 answer**

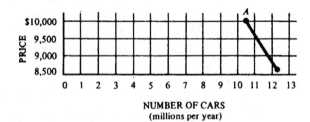

NUMBER OF CARS
(millions per year)

276

Exercise 2

1. F

2. **Table 19.4 answer**

Price	Number of new cars (millions per year)	Elasticity of demand
$ 10,000	10.5	—
8,600	12.1	0.94
7,000	14	0.71
5,500	15.6	0.45
4,000	17.4	0.35

3. **Figure 19.4 answer**

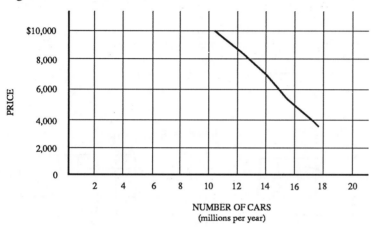

4. T
5. The slope can be estimated by using the coordinates of any two points on the demand curve. The slope is computed by dividing the change on the variable on the y-axis by the change in the variable on the x-axis. For example, using the first two points in Table 19.4, we would have:

$$\frac{\text{Change in y-axis}}{\text{Change in x-axis}} = \frac{p_1 - p_2}{q_1 - q_2} = \frac{10,000 - 8,600}{10.5 - 12.1} = \frac{1,400}{1.6} = -875$$

Regardless of what pair of points is chosen the slope should be the same except for rounding error.

6. b   As noted in the previous problem, the slope is the same regardless of which pair of points is tried.
7. T

Exercise 3

3. Table 19.5 answer

Days of entertainment per month	Evening at home Marginal utility	Event Marginal utility
0	—	—
1	180	600
2	180	600
3	170	480
4	140	360
5	140	360
6	140	360
7	100	360
8	100	0
9	100	0
10	0	0
11	−100	−200
12	−120	−220

2. b
3. a

4. Figure 19.5 answer

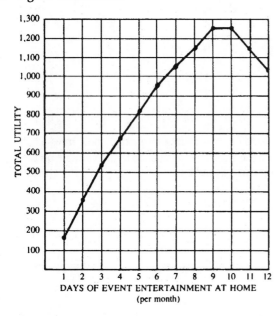

DAYS OF EVENT ENTERTAINMENT AT HOME
(per month)

5. Figure 19.6 answer

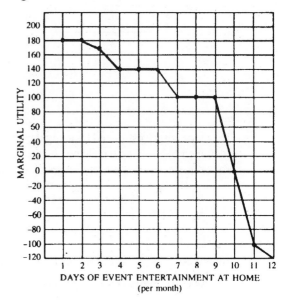

DAYS OF EVENT ENTERTAINMENT AT HOME
(per month)

6. b
7. c

Exercise 4

1. c
2. **Table 19.6 answer**

Days of entertainment per month	Event entertainment (price = $30)	
	Marginal utility	$\dfrac{MU}{price}$
0	0	0
1	600	20
2	600	20
3	480	16
4	360	12
5	360	12
6	360	12
7	360	12
8	0	0
9	0	0
10	0	0

3. "event"
4. 2
5. $60 = $120 – ($30 x 2)
6. no
7. $30 = $120 – $60 – (3 x $10)
8. "event"
9. T

Exercise 5

1. a (shift of demand to the left) or c (movement down along the demand curve) or d (movement up along the demand curve), depending on which piece of information is examined. Most of the information in the article is about supply shifts. The only information about a demand shift is the description of the reasons for the earlier price rise—the summer driving season (b) and the strike, which changed supply and caused (d). However, the drop in oil prices could also cause a movement down along the demand curve (c). It is necessary to separate the various shifts that are mentioned and focus on just one shift at a time. For this exercise we will choose the demand shift caused by the summer driving season.
2. The article refers to "West Texas intermediate, the USA's highest quality grade of crude."
3. For b, the appropriate passage would be "Fueling the earlier price rally expected strong demand for gasoline for this summer's driving season..." For the movement down the demand curve, c, we can look at the headline, "Surplus Punches Hole in Oil Price."
4. The previous quotation indicates one of the markets for oil is for private transportation.
5. See the quotation in Question 3 for the information on price changes. The quantity changes are implied by the fact that the summer driving season means a greater quantity of fuel will be demanded at every price, as in shift (b).

Chapter 20

The Costs of Production

Quick Review

In this chapter we attempt to identify the costs of producing goods and services. We begin by looking at some basic questions:

- What are the costs of producing a good or a service?
- How do costs change as the rate of output varies?
- How does company size and productivity affect production costs?

Business managers must know how costs change when output is changed. Without such knowledge they cannot know what they would be willing and able to supply in the marketplace. Costs can be computed at different levels of production if management keeps track of all factors that are used in producing output. The production function establishes the quantity that can be produced from a given amount of factors. The production function is therefore the cornerstone to the computation of a firm's costs at different output levels.

If we know the production function, it is possible to determine factor productivity, efficiency, and various categories of costs. Productivity is simply the amount of output per unit of input that can be produced by a firm. Efficiency is attained if the firm is able to achieve the maximum output from its given resources. The law of diminishing returns says that the marginal output of any factor decreases as more of it is used to produce output when other factors are held constant. These concepts have important implications for the behavior of cost.

In the short run (when firms are unable to vary some factors of production), the law of diminishing returns causes the marginal costs and average variable costs of production to rise with increased output. In effect, the variable factors of production are limited by the fixed factors, which cannot be expanded. Even though average fixed costs fall with increased output, the limitation eventually causes average total costs to rise.

In the long run (when there are no fixed factors), changes in average total cost may occur when the rate of output is increased. If an increase in plant size (scale) causes average total cost to rise, there are diseconomies of scale. If average total cost falls with increased plant size, there are economies of scale. However, it is quite possible that average costs will not change over a wide range of output, in which case there are constant returns to scale.

The short-run cost curves are related to the long-run cost curves. The long-run average total cost curve runs along the bottom of the lowest of all possible short-run average total cost curves at each level of output.

Certain rules relate the different cost curves, whether they are long run or short run. Whenever the marginal curve is below the average curve, then the average curve will be falling as output increases. However, if the marginal curve is above the average curve, the average curve will be rising. The marginal cost curve always intersects the average cost curve at its lowest point.

Learning Objectives

After reading Chapter 20 and doing the following exercises, you should:	True or false	Multiple choice	Problems and applications	Common errors	Pages in the text
1. Know the relationship between the production function and the firm's ability to produce goods and services.	3–5,7	2,4	1,6		484–487
2. Understand the relationship between the production function and the short-run cost curves.	1,2	1			490–497
3. Understand the nature and determinants of marginal productivity.	9	3		2	488–490
4. Be able to draw a graph relating the marginal physical product and total product curves.	10	5	1		488
5. Be able to define and explain the law of diminishing returns.	1,2,16	6–8,10	1	1	490
6. Understand the difference between variable costs and fixed costs.	1,2	14,16,20	3		493
7. Know how to define and calculate the total, average, and marginal costs of production and be able to show their relationship to marginal productivity.	1,2,11,12, 16,17	13,15,17	2,3	4,5	494–499
8. Understand the relationship between average and marginal cost curves.	18,19,22	9,18,19	2,3		494–500
9. Understand the distinction between economic costs and accounting costs.	14,20		5		501–502
10. Know the distinction between long-run costs and short-run costs.	1,2,6,8, 13,15,21	1,11,12			503–504
11. Be able to explain economies of scale, diseconomies of scale, and constant returns to scale.	23,24			3	504–506
12. Understand the impact of technological improvements on the production function.	25		4,6		506–508

Key-Term Review

Review the following terms; if you are not sure of the meaning of any term, write out the definition and check it against the Glossary in the text.

average fixed cost (AFC)
average total cost (ATC)
average variable cost (AVC)
constant returns to scale
economic cost
economies of scale
efficiency (technical)
factors of production
fixed costs
law of diminishing returns

long run
marginal cost (MC)
marginal physical product (MPP)
opportunity cost
production function
productivity
short run
total cost
variable costs

Fill in the blank following each of the statements below with the appropriate term from the list above.

1. The addition to total cost incurred if the firm produces an additional unit of output is called _____.

1. _____

2. When you divide total variable cost by the quantity produced, you get _____.

2. _____

3. By adding _____, which do not change with the rate of output, to _____, which do change with the rate of output, one can calculate the _____ of producing at any level of output.

3. _____

_____

_____

4. When long-run average costs do not change, the firm is achieving _____.

4. _____

5. When the long-run average costs of production are decreasing as output increases, there are _____.

5. _____

6. The *additional* total output attributable to one more unit of a variable input is known as _____.

6. _____

7. When the marginal physical product of a variable input begins to decline, it is the result of the _____.

7. _____

8. If you divide total output by the amount of labor used to produce it, you measure labor's _____.

8. _____

9. The relationship showing the maximum outputs attainable from given input combinations is called the _____.

9. _____

10. In the _____ there are both fixed costs and variable costs.

10. _____

11. The _____ is the market value of inputs used to produce any output, whether the costs are explicitly paid by the producer or not. It may be quite different from a similarly named concept used by accountants.

11. _____

12. _____ is attained when the maximum output is obtained from the resources used in production.

12. _____

13. The best alternative use of resources forgone is a measure of _____.

13. _____

14. In order to supply goods and services, a firm must employ _____.

14. _____

15. By dividing fixed costs by the quantity of output, one can find the _____.

15. _____

16. By dividing total costs by the quantity of output, one can find the _____.

16. _____

17. When all factors can be varied in decisions, then a firm is making _____ decisions.

17. _____

True or False: *Circle your choice.*

T F 1. The shape of the short-run cost curves is determined by the production function, with input prices held constant.

T F 2. The shape of the short-run cost curves results from the fact that as output is increased, input prices fall.

T F 3. The production function shows the maximum amount of a particular good or service that can be produced with given combinations of resources.

T F 4. The production function is synonymous with the production-possibilities curve.

T F 5. The efficiency of resources implied by the production function can be increased by working the labor input harder.

T F 6. In the short run, technology is fixed.

T F 7. If resources are inefficiently combined, society is producing at a point inside the production-possibilities curve.

T F 8. If any factor of production is fixed in a firm's decision-making process, then the firm is making a short-run decision.

T F 9. Marginal physical product is the addition to total output associated with a one-unit increase in all required inputs.

T F 10. Total output may continue to rise even though marginal physical product is declining.

T F 11. Marginal cost is the increase in total cost required to hire one more unit of input.

T F 12. Total cost refers to the market value of all resources used in producing a good or service.

T F 13. Fixed costs are those costs that do not change with the rate of production.

T F 14. Normal profit is an economic cost of production.

T F 15. If output is reduced to zero, total cost falls to zero in the short run.

T F 16. The law of diminishing returns causes both marginal cost and average variable cost to rise.

T F 17. With greater output, falling average fixed costs eventually outweigh falling average variable costs, and then average total cost starts to rise.

T F 18. When marginal cost is rising, average variable cost must be rising.

T F 19. When marginal cost is below average variable cost, average variable cost will be falling.

T F 20. When a factor of production is paid an explicit wage, both the accountant and the economist will include it in their cost calculations.

T F 21. The long-run average cost curve shows the average minimum cost for producing any level of output.

T F 22. Both long-run marginal cost and short-run marginal cost are equal at the minimum of the long-run average cost curve.

T F 23. Economies of scale cause the short-run average cost curve to decline.

T F 24. Economies of scale result from the law of diminishing returns.

T F 25. Improved technology shifts the total product curve upward and the cost curves downward.

Multiple Choice: *Select the correct answer.*

_____ 1. Which of the following is *not* held constant when drawing the short-run cost curves?
(a) Technology.
(b) Input prices.
(c) Fixed factors.
(d) Output.

_____ 2. A production function shows:
(a) The minimum amount of output that can be obtained from alternative combinations of inputs.
(b) The maximum quantities of inputs required to produce a given quantity of output.
(c) The maximum quantity of output that can be obtained from alternative combinations of inputs.
(d) None of the above.

_____ 3. Productivity is a measure of:
(a) Output per unit of input.
(b) Input per unit of output.
(c) Output per dollar of input.
(d) Input per dollar of output.

_____ 4. To be inefficient is to:
(a) Get less output than possible from a given combination of inputs.
(b) Waste resources.
(c) Cause society to operate at a point inside the production-possibilities curve.
(d) Do all of the above.

_____ 5. Marginal physical product is:
(a) The change in total input required to produce one additional unit of output.
(b) The change in total output associated with one additional unit of the variable input.
(c) The number of units of output obtained from all units of input employed.
(d) Another name for total output.

_____ 6. The law of diminishing returns occurs with each additional unit of variable input when:
(a) Total output begins to decline.
(b) Marginal physical product becomes negative.
(c) Total output begins to rise.
(d) Marginal physical product begins to decline.

_____ 7. Declining marginal productivity is the result of:
(a) Inefficiency in the production process.
(b) The use of inferior factors of production.
(c) Laziness.
(d) A rising ratio of variable input to fixed input.

_____ 8. The law of diminishing returns:
(a) Operates in few societies.
(b) Operates in every production process.
(c) Does not apply to command economies.
(d) Can be rendered inoperative with good management techniques.

_____ 9. Marginal cost:
(a) Is the change in total cost from producing one additional unit of output.
(b) Is the change in total variable cost from producing one additional unit of output.
(c) Rises because of declining marginal productivity.
(d) All of the above.

_____ 10. Which of the following statements is correct?
  (a) When marginal physical product is falling, marginal cost is rising.
  (b) When marginal physical product is rising, marginal cost is falling.
  (c) When the law of diminishing returns sets in, marginal costs start to rise.
  (d) All of the above statements are correct.

_____ 11. In the short run, average costs may rise as a firm increases the rate of production because:
  (a) Inflation raises the prices of resources.
  (b) The supply curve for the product is shifting.
  (c) Capital, such as plant and equipment, cannot be varied.
  (d) All of the above are the case.

_____ 12. Which of the following would most likely be a fixed cost?
  (a) The cost of property insurance.
  (b) The cost of water used in the production process.
  (c) The cost of labor used in the production process.
  (d) The cost of electricity used in the production process.

_____ 13. Rising marginal costs result from:
  (a) Rising prices of fixed and variable inputs.
  (b) Rising prices of variable inputs only.
  (c) Falling marginal product.
  (d) None of the above.

_____ 14. For which of the following costs must the associated average curve fall continuously?
  (a) Total costs.
  (b) Variable costs.
  (c) Fixed costs.
  (d) Marginal costs.

_____ 15. Which of the following costs must remain constant at all levels of output?
  (a) Total costs.
  (b) Variable costs.
  (c) Fixed costs.
  (d) Marginal costs.

_____ 16. Which of the following must be variable costs?
  (a) Total costs.
  (b) Economic costs.
  (c) Accounting costs.
  (d) Marginal costs.

_____ 17. Which of the following can you compute if you know total cost at all levels of output?
  (a) Fixed cost.
  (b) Variable cost.
  (c) Marginal cost.
  (d) All of the above.

_____ 18. Which one of the following curves must be falling when marginal cost is below it?
  (a) Average variable cost curve.
  (b) Average total cost curve.
  (c) Average fixed cost curve.
  (d) All of the above.

_____ 19. Which one of the following curves must be rising when marginal cost is above it?
  (a) Average total cost curve.
  (b) Average fixed cost curve.
  (c) Marginal physical product curve.
  (d) All of the above.

20. As the production rate is increased, average fixed costs:
    (a) Are constant.
    (b) First fall, then rise (in a U-shaped curve).
    (c) Decline.
    (d) Determine the shutdown point for a firm.

Problems and Applications

Exercise 1

This exercise shows how to compute and graph the marginal physical product of a factor of production. It also demonstrates the law of diminishing returns.

In the textbook, an example of jeans production was used to show how many sewing machines and workers were needed per day to produce various quantities of jeans per day. The table (20.1 in the text) is reproduced here as Table 20.1.

Table 20.1
The production of jeans
(pairs per day)

Capital input (sewing machines per day)	Labor input (workers per day)							
	0	1	2	3	4	5	6	7
0	0	0	0	0	0	0	0	0
1	0	15	34	44	48	50	51	46
2	0	20	46	64	72	78	81	80
3	0	21	50	73	82	92	99	102

1. Suppose a firm had only two sewing machines and could vary only the amount of labor input. On the basis of Table 20.1, fill in the column 2 of Table 20.2 to show how much can be produced at different levels of labor input when there are only two sewing machines.

Table 20.2
The production of jeans with
two sewing machines

(1) Labor input (workers per day)	(2) Production of jeans (pairs per day)	(3) Marginal physical product (pairs per worker)
0	_____	_____
1	_____	_____
2	_____	_____
3	_____	_____
4	_____	_____
5	_____	_____
6	_____	_____
7	_____	_____

2. Graph the total output curve in Figure 20.1.

Figure 20.1

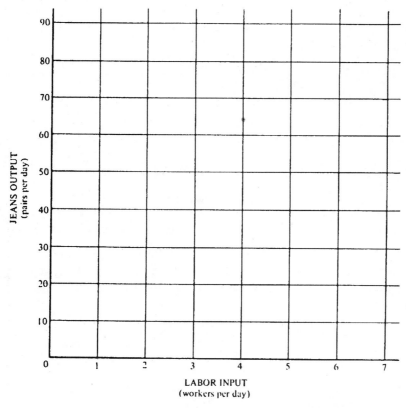

3. Compute the marginal physical product of each extra worker per day. (*Hint:* See Figure 20.2 in the text.) Place the answers in column 3 of Table 20.2.

4. Graph the marginal physical product curve in Figure 20.2.

Figure 20.2

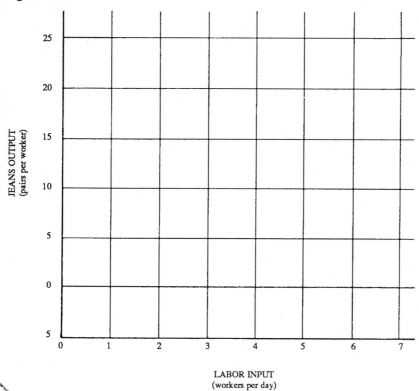

5. The law of diminishing returns states that the marginal physical product of a factor:
    (a) Will become negative as output increases.
    (b) Will decline as output increases.
    (c) Will increase and then decline as output increases.
    (d) Will decline as the amount of a factor used increases.

6. At what amount of labor input does the law of diminishing returns first become apparent in Figure 20.2?
    (a) 0–1   (b) 1–2   (c) 2–3   (d) 3–4

7. In Figure 20.1 at three units of labor, total output:
    (a) Is rising with increased labor usage.
    (b) Is falling with increased labor usage.
    (c) Remains constant with increased labor.

8. T   F   When marginal physical product declines, total output declines.

Exercise 2

This exercise shows the relationship between average and marginal cost curves. Although this example is confined only to average and marginal costs, it can also be applied to average and marginal revenues, average and marginal product, and average and marginal utility.

1. Complete Table 20.3.

Table 20.3
Falling average total cost

Quantity (items per year)	Total cost (TC) (dollars per year)	Average total cost (ATC) (dollars per item)	Marginal cost (MC) (dollars per item)
0	$ 0	$_____	$_____
2	8	_____	_____
4	12	_____	_____
6	15	_____	_____

(*Remember: MC* is the cost of producing *one* more unit, so you must divide the change in total cost by 2 in the problem.)

2. Graph average total cost and marginal cost in Figure 20.3. Label them ATC_1 and MC_1. (Ignore negative values.)

Figure 20.3

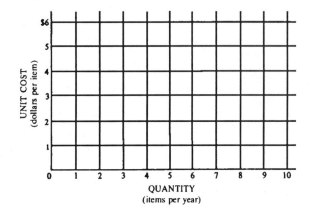

288

3. Complete Table 20.4.

Table 20.4
Constant average total cost

Quantity (items per year)	Total cost (TC) (dollars per year)	Average total cost (ATC) (dollars per item)	Marginal cost (MC) (dollars per item)
0	$ 0	$_____	$_____
1	5	_____	_____
2	10	_____	_____
3	15	_____	_____
4	20	_____	_____
5	25	_____	_____

4. Graph average total cost and marginal cost in Figure 20.3. Label them ATC_2 and MC_2.

5. Complete Table 20.5.

Table 20.5
Rising average total cost

Quantity (items per year)	Total cost (dollars per year)	Average total cost (dollars per item)	Marginal cost (dollars per item)
0	$ 0.0	$_____	$_____
1	0.5	_____	_____
2	2.0	_____	_____
3	4.5	_____	_____
4	8.0	_____	_____
5	12.5	_____	_____

6. Graph average total cost and marginal cost in Figure 20.3. Label them ATC_3 and MC_3.

7. When the average total cost curve is rising, the marginal cost curve is (above, below, the same as) the average total cost curve.

8. When the average total cost curve is falling, the marginal cost curve is (above, below, the same as) the average total cost curve.

9. When the average total cost curve is flat, the marginal cost curve is (above, below, the same as) the average total cost curve.

Correctly answered, Problems 6–9 summarize the relationship of the average total cost curve to the marginal cost curve. These rules are a fast way of checking whether the curves you draw on an examination are correct.

Exercise 3

Using information about output and total costs, this exercise shows how to compute fixed, variable, average fixed, marginal, and average variable costs. It will be helpful in the first exercise at the end of Chapter 20 in the text.

1. Fixed costs are defined as:
   (a) Costs that do not change with inflation.
   (b) Costs that are set firmly (without escalator clauses) in a contract.
   (c) Costs of production that do not change when the rate of production is altered.
   (d) Average costs that do not change when the rate of production is altered.

2. Variable costs include:
   (a) Costs of production that change when the rate of production is altered.
   (b) All costs in the long run.
   (c) The difference between total and fixed costs.
   (d) All of the above.

3. Suppose you decide to go into the parachute business. Table 20.6 shows the expenses you would find in your income statement at various rates of production.

Table 20.6
Expense statements for parachute business
(dollars per week)

	Parachutes produced per week							
Weekly expense	0	100	200	300	400	500	600	700
Leased production facilities	$1,400	$1,400	$1,400	$1,400	$1,400	$1,400	$1,400	$1,400
Sewing machines	600	600	600	600	600	600	600	600
Nylon	0	400	1,150	1,700	2,450	3,200	4,650	6,300
Utilities (electricity, etc.)	0	100	150	200	250	300	350	400
Labor	0	500	500	500	500	1,000	1,000	1,000
Testing and certification	1,000	1,000	1,000	1,000	1,000	1,000	1,000	1,000

Which items are fixed costs? _____

4. Complete Table 20.7 using the information in Table 20.6.

Table 20.7
Summary, expenses for parachute business

	Parachutes produced per week							
Costs	0	100	200	300	400	500	600	700
Fixed costs (dollars per week)	$_____	$_____	$_____	$_____	$_____	$_____	$_____	$_____
Variable costs (dollars per week)	_____	_____	_____	_____	_____	_____	_____	_____
Average variable costs (dollars per parachute)	_____	_____	_____	_____	_____	_____	_____	_____
Total costs (dollars per week)	_____	_____	_____	_____	_____	_____	_____	_____
Average total costs (dollars per parachute)	_____	_____	_____	_____	_____	_____	_____	_____
Marginal costs (dollars per parachute)	_____	_____	_____	_____	_____	_____	_____	_____

5. In Figure 20.4 draw the average variable cost, average total cost, and marginal cost curves. Label them *AVC, ATC,* and *MC,* respectively. You should find the *MC* and *AVC* curves intersecting at point *A*, while the *MC* and *ATC* curves intersect at point *B*.

Figure 20.4

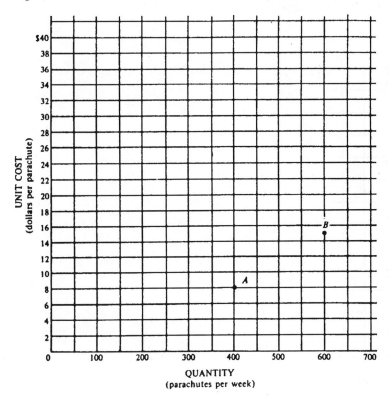

QUANTITY
(parachutes per week)

6. T   F   Since there are no variable costs, the cost curves in Figure 20.4 represent your firm's long-run costs.

7. What is the output at which the lowest unit cost is first attained? (This is referred to as the minimum efficient scale at which the plant can operate.) _____

Exercise 4

Table 20.8 presents the cost data for two alternative technologies that can be used to produce cement. Assume that no other ways of producing cement exist.

Table 20.8
Costs associated with two technologies

Output (tons per day)	Technology 1		Technology 2	
	Total cost (dollars per day)	Average total cost (dollars per ton)	Total cost (dollars per day)	Average total cost (dollars per ton)
0	$ 4	$_____	$ 6	$_____
1	8	_____	10	_____
2	10	_____	16	_____
3	15	_____	18	_____
4	24	_____	20	_____
5	35	_____	20	_____
6	48	_____	24	_____
7	63	_____	28	_____
8	88	_____	32	_____
9	108	_____	36	_____
10	140	_____	60	_____

1. Fill in the blanks in Table 20.8. Then diagram the average total cost curve for both technologies in Figure 20.5. Label them ATC_1 and ATC_2, respectively.

Figure 20.5

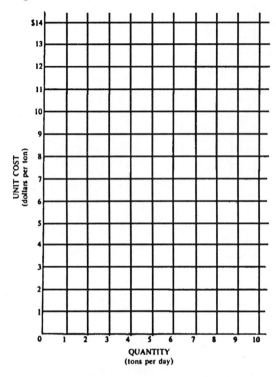

2. If there are only two technologies for making cement, then for an output of between five and nine tons of cement, the long-run average cost curve shows that there are:
   (a) Constant returns to scale.
   (b) Economies of scale.
   (c) Diseconomies of scale.

3. For between nine and ten tons of cement production, there are:
   (a) Constant returns to scale.
   (b) Economies of scale.
   (c) Diseconomies of scale.

4. For between four and five tons of cement production, there are:
   (a) Constant returns to scale.
   (b) Economies of scale.
   (c) Diseconomies of scale.

5. What is the least-cost technology between one and three tons of cement output?
   (a) Technology 1.
   (b) Technology 2.

6. What is the least-cost technology between four and ten tons of cement output?
   (a) Technology 1.
   (b) Technology 2.

Exercise 5

This exercise should test your knowledge of the economic definitions of profit, interest, and rent.

Table 20.9 contains the annual revenues and costs faced by a firm.

Table 20.9
Costs and revenues
(millions of dollars per year)

Costs		Revenues	
Wages and salaries	$100	Sales	$420
Materials	90		
New equipment	30		
Rented property and buildings	50		
Payments on money borrowed to buy inventories of materials	10		

In order to begin operations, the firm had to raise capital by issuing stock. The firm used the money to finance inspections, licenses, and patents. However, the stockholders might have used their money elsewhere; the opportunity cost of these funds is $109 million per year. Furthermore, there is an owner-manager of the firm who could receive income for his services elsewhere; the opportunity cost of his services is $1 million per year.

1. Accountants would compute the annual profit, or net revenue, of the firm to be:
   (a) $140 million.
   (b) $30 million.
   (c) $110 million.
   (d) $40 million.

2. The annual normal profit of the firm would be:
   (a) $140 million.
   (b) $30 million.
   (c) $110 million.
   (d) $40 million.

3. Annual economic profit would be:
   (a) $140 million.
   (b) $30 million.
   (c) $110 million.
   (d) $40 million.

4. Annual explicit costs would be:
   (a) $280 million.
   (b) $390 million.
   (c) $270 million.
   (d) $380 million.

5. Annual implicit costs would be:
   (a) $1 million.
   (b) $10 million.
   (c) $109 million.
   (d) $110 million.

6. Annual labor costs would be:
   (a) $1 million.
   (b) $100 million.
   (c) $101 million.
   (d) $130 million.

Exercise 6

The media often provide information on events that affect productivity. By using one of the articles in the text, this exercise will show the kind of information to look for. If your professor makes a newspaper assignment for this chapter, this exercise will provide an example of how to do it.

Reread the article in Chapter 18 entitled "R & D Spending Seen Growing at Slower Rate" from the *Washington Post*. Then answer the following questions:

1. What phrase indicates the event that would alter productivity or costs?

2. Which of the following statements *best* indicates the effect the event should have on average costs?
   (a) The average cost curve drops below where it would have been if the event had not occurred.
   (b) The average cost curve rises above where it would have been if the event had not occurred.

3. Which of the following statements *best* indicates the effect the event should have on the marginal product curve for labor?
   (a) The marginal product curve drops below where it would have been if the event had not occurred.
   (b) The marginal product curve rises above where it would have been if the event had not occurred.

4. What statement indicates the effect of the event on production rates, prices, unit costs, or productivity?

Common Errors

The first statement in each "common error" below is incorrect. Each incorrect statement is followed by a corrected version and an explanation.

1. Total output starts falling when diminishing returns set in. WRONG!

   Diminishing returns set in when marginal physical product begins to decline. RIGHT!

   The law of diminishing returns describes what happens to *marginal physical product,* not total output. Marginal physical product will typically begin to decline long before total output begins to decline. For total output to decline, the marginal physical product must be negative.

2. A firm's productivity increases when labor is willing to accept lower wages. WRONG!

   A firm's productivity increases when more output can be produced per unit of labor used. RIGHT!

   Productivity is not defined on the basis of the prices of factors of production. Productivity depends simply on the amount of output that is produced by the factors of production.

3. The term "economies of scale" refers to the shape of the short-run average cost curve. WRONG!

   The term "economies of scale" refers to the shape of the long-run average cost curve. RIGHT!

   The short-run average cost curve and the long-run average cost curve may have similar shapes. But the shape of the short-run curve results from the law of diminishing returns. In the long run, all factors, and therefore all costs, are variable. Thus the shape of the long-run average cost curve is the result of other forces such as the specialization and division of labor, the use of different sources of power, and so on. Remember, even though the long-run average cost curve is a summary of many short-run average cost curves, and even though the shapes of the two curves may be similar, the reasons for the shapes of the curves are quite different. The term "economies of scale" applies only to the long-run average cost curve.

4. The marginal cost curve rises because factor prices rise when more of a good is produced. WRONG!

   The marginal cost curve rises because the marginal productivity of the variable factor declines. RIGHT!

   The marginal cost curve moves in the opposite direction to the marginal product curve. Changes in factor prices would shift the whole marginal cost curve but would not explain its shape and would not affect the marginal product curve.

5. Marginal physical product begins to decline because inferior factors must be hired to increase output. WRONG!

   Declining marginal physical product occurs even if all of the factors are of equal quality. RIGHT!

Many people incorrectly attribute diminishing returns to the use of inferior factors of production. Diminishing returns result from an increasing ratio of the variable input to the fixed input. There is always a point where the variable input begins to have too little of the fixed input to work with. Result? Diminishing marginal product! The quality of the factors has nothing to do with it.

■ ANSWERS ■

Key-Term Review

1. marginal cost (*MC*)
2. average variable cost (*AVC*)
3. fixed costs
   variable costs
   total cost
4. constant returns to scale
5. economies of scale

6. marginal physical product (*MPP*)
7. law of diminishing returns
8. productivity
9. production function
10. short run
11. economic cost

12. efficiency (technical)
13. opportunity cost
14. factors of production
15. average fixed cost (*AFC*)
16. average total cost (*ATC*)
17. long-run

True or False

1. T	6. T	10. T	14. T	18. F	22. T
2. F	7. T	11. F	15. F	19. T	23. F
3. T	8. T	12. T	16. T	20. T	24. F
4. F	9. F	13. T	17. F	21. T	25. T
5. F					

Multiple Choice

1. d	5. b	9. d	12. a	15. c	18. d
2. c	6. d	10. d	13. c	16. d	19. a
3. a	7. d	11. c	14. c	17. d	20. c
4. d	8. b				

Problems and Applications

Exercise 1

1. See Table 20.2 answer, column 2.

2. **Figure 20.1 answer**

Table 20.2 answer

(1)	(2)	(3)
0	0	—
1	20	20
2	46	26
3	64	18
4	72	8
5	78	6
6	81	3
7	80	– 1

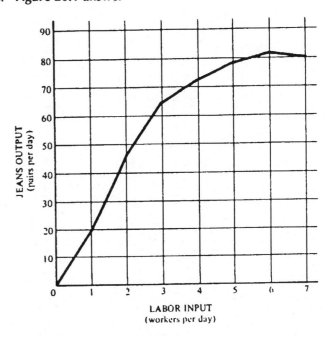

LABOR INPUT
(workers per day)

3. See Table 20.2 answer, column 3.

4. **Figure 20.2 answer**

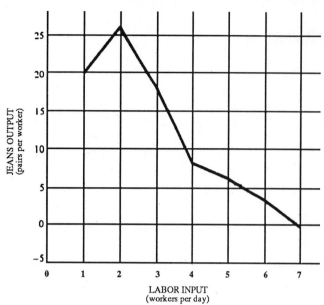

5. d
6. c
7. a
8. F

Exercise 2

1. **Table 20.3 answer**

TC (dollars per year)	ATC (dollars per item)	MC (dollars per item)
$ 0	$—	$—
8	4	4
12	3	2
15	2.5	1.5

2. See lines ATC_1 and MC_1 in Figure 20.3 answer.

Figure 20.3 answer

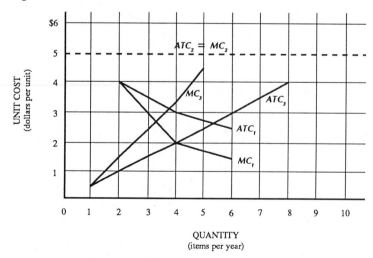

3. **Table 20.4 answer**

TC (dollars per year)	ATC (dollars per item)	MC (dollars per item)
$ 0	$—	$—
5	5	5
10	5	5
15	5	5
20	5	5
25	5	5

4. See lines ATC_2 and MC_2 in Figure 20.3 answer.

5. **Table 20.5 answer**

Total cost (dollars per year)	Average total cost (dollars per item)	Marginal cost (dollars per item)
$ 0.0	$ —	$ —
0.5	0.5	0.5
2.0	1.0	1.5
4.5	1.5	2.5
8.0	2.0	3.5
12.5	2.5	4.5

6. See lines ATC_3 and MC_3 in Figure 20.3 answer.
7. above
8. below
9. the same as

Exercise 3

1. c
2. d
3. leased production facilities, sewing machines, and testing and certification

4. **Table 20.7 answer**

Costs	Parachutes produced per week							
	0	100	200	300	400	500	600	700
Fixed costs	$3,000	$3,000	$3,000	$3,000	$3,000	$3,000	$3,000	$3,000
Variable costs	0	1,000	1,800	2,400	3,200	4,500	6,000	7,700
Average variable costs	—	10	9	8	8	9	10	11
Total costs	3,000	4,000	4,800	5,400	6,200	7,500	9,000	10,700
Average total costs	—	40	24	18	15.5	15	15	15.3
Marginal costs	—	10	8	6	8	13	15	17

5. Figure 20.4 answer

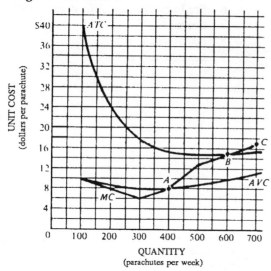

QUANTITY
(parachutes per week)

6. F

7. 400 parachutes, where *ATC* reaches $15

Exercise 4

1. **Table 20.8 answer**

	Technology 1		Technology 2	
Output (tons per day)	TC (dollars per day)	ATC (dollars per ton)	TC (dollars per day)	ATC (dollars per ton)
0	$ 4	$ —	$ 6	$ —
1	8	8	10	10
2	10	5	16	8
3	15	5	18	6
4	24	6	20	5
5	35	7	20	4
6	48	8	24	4
7	63	9	28	4
8	88	11	32	4
9	108	12	36	4
10	140	14	60	6

Figure 20.5 answer

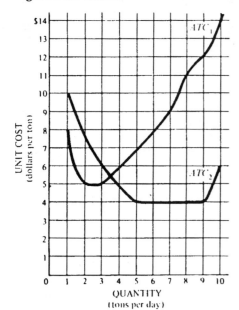

QUANTITY
(tons per day)

2. a
3. c
4. b
5. a
6. b

298

Exercise 5   (answers in millions of dollars per year)

1. a   Total revenues – total costs = $420 – $280 = $140.
2. c   Opportunity costs of stockholders + opportunity costs of owner-manager = $109 + $1 = $110.
3. b   Net revenues – normal profits = $140 – $110 = $30.
4. a   Wages and salaries + materials + equipment + property and buildings + payments on borrowed money = $100 + $90 + $30 + $50 + $10 = $280.
5. d   Opportunity costs of stockholders + opportunity costs of owner-manager = $109 + $1 = $110.
6. c   Wages and salaries + opportunity costs of owner-manager = $100 + $1 = $101.

Exercise 6

1. The phrase "federal budget constraints, economic uncertainty and short-term corporate outlooks" indicates the original problems that will curb R & D and thereby curb productivity and slow the fall of average costs.
2. b   Growth in productivity is reduced, and the rate at which average costs are falling due to productivity is slowed.
3. a
4. "Growth of research and development spending in the United States is likely to slip" indicates a slowing in research and development. This, in turn, should hinder productivity improvements and slow decreases in average costs. Notice that productivity and cost changes are never even mentioned in the article but can be discovered by reading between the lines.

Chapter 21
Profits and the Supply Decision

Quick Review

The pursuit of profits is a motivating, driving force in the management of firms in the U.S. economy. In this chapter we examine the profit motive and pay particular attention to the following questions:

- What are profits?
- How can a firm maximize profits?
- How do profit opportunities affect supply decisions?

To start with, business firms are the suppliers of goods and services. Large and small firms alike want to earn profits. Profits are the difference between total revenue and total cost, and a profit-maximizing firm must consider how revenues and costs change when the rate of production changes. The profit-maximizing producer compares marginal cost with marginal revenue. As long as marginal revenue exceeds marginal cost, profits grow as production increases. This additional profit gives the producer an incentive to speed up production. As the rate of production increases, however, marginal costs rise while prices remain constant or decline.

Why does increased production push up marginal costs? Marginal costs rise when crowding, waste, and exhaustion occur as a result of the increased rate of production. Why does increased production lower prices and marginal revenue? The law of demand is at work: to induce consumers to buy more of its product, a firm usually must lower its prices.

At some rate of production, marginal costs will exceed marginal revenue. Further increases in production will then lower profits. Consequently, a firm reaches maximum profits at the production rate at which marginal cost equals marginal revenue ($MC = MR$).

The elasticity of demand tells a firm the percentage decline in prices that must occur if it is to sell a given percentage increase in the firm's output. The elasticity is simply the ratio of the percentage change in quantity demanded that will occur in response to a percentage change in price:

$$\text{Price elasticity of demand} = \left| \frac{\text{percentage change in quantity demanded}}{\text{percentage change in price}} \right|$$

However, the price elasticity of demand is shown as a positive rather than a negative number.

With information on the price elasticity of demand, the manager can tell how total revenue will change in response to a change in price as shown in Table 21.1.

Table 21.1
Elasticity and price changes

If elasticity of demand is:	Then for a	
	Rise in price:	Decline in price:
Greater than 1 (elastic demand)	Total revenue falls	Total revenue rises
Equal to 1 (unit elasticity)	Total revenue remains the same	Total revenue remains the same
Less than 1 (inelastic)	Total revenue rises	Total revenue falls

Because some firms are such a small part of the market, their prices may not have to be lowered when they increase production. These are called competitive firms. In this case, demand is perfectly elastic, the demand curve is flat, and the marginal revenue curve is equal to the demand curve. Noncompetitive firms, on the other hand, recognize that they can sell additional output only if they lower prices. Their demand curves are downward sloping, and their marginal revenue curves fall below the demand curve.

A firm is faced with various types of costs. Fixed costs, which firms cannot change in the short run, can be altered by the long-run investment decision. Production decisions, however, involve changes in variable costs, which can be manipulated in the short run along with changes in the rate of production. In the short run, a firm continues to operate as long as it can cover its variable costs with something left over to apply to its fixed costs. The firm will thus minimize its losses (which is another way of saying it maximizes profits) when that is the best it can do.

For competitive firms, that part of the marginal cost curve that lies above the average variable cost curve is equivalent to the firm's short-run supply curve. Like the demand curve, the supply curve shifts due to certain determinants. However, the determinants are different from those for demand; the supply determinants include the prices of resources, technology, expectations (about prices, technology, etc.), and the number of suppliers. As in the case of demand it is important to distinguish between the terms *quantity supplied* and *supply*. A change in price causes a movement along the supply curve to a new quantity supplied but no change in the supply curve itself. Finally, as in the case of demand, it is necessary to distinguish the supply for an individual firm from the market supply curve.

The supply curve in the short run may be quite different from the one in the long run. In the short run a firm shuts down if variable costs of production cannot be covered. However, in the long run a firm must cover all costs both explicit and implicit or exit from the market.

Throughout, it will be important to keep in mind that economic and accounting notions of profit and cost are different. Although accountants treat all costs that a firm must explicitly pay to produce a good, economists identify other factors necessary in the production of a good but not explicitly paid for. Because economists include more costs in assessing the costs of production, economic profits will be smaller than accounting profits. Thus, when economists talk about zero profits, they envision that a firm will be able to maintain its operations in the long run. In fact, there may be quite substantial accounting "profits" even when economic profits are zero!

Tax laws are sometimes used to encourage (or discourage) firms in making their investment decisions. Changes in the corporate tax rates, depreciation rules, investment tax credits, and the like affect the business firms' outlook and expected costs and therefore their potential to supply goods and services.

Learning Objectives

After reading Chapter 21 and doing the following exercises, you should:	True or false	Multiple choice	Problems and applications	Common errors	Pages in the text
1. Know how economic profits are defined, how they differ from accounting profits, and how profits are maximized.	10	3,10,17		1,3	515–518, 522–527
2. Be able to compute profits and relate them to prices, costs, and the price elasticity of demand.	2–4,13	11–13	2		518–520

After reading Chapter 21 and doing the following exercises, you should:	True or false	Multiple choice	Problems and applications	Common errors	Pages in the text
3. Know the relationships among total, average, and marginal costs (or revenue).	8,9,12	2,6,7	1		520–522
4. Recognize the difference between long-run and short-run decisions.	7,11	9,14	3		521–522, 532
5. Know the role that marginal revenue and marginal cost play in profit maximization.	1,6,17				521–527
6. Be able to explain the production decision in simple numerical examples.	19				525-527
7. Be able to indicate diagrammatically how a firm determines profit, price, and production in the short run (the production decision).	21–23	22		5	524–525
8. Understand how investment decisions are made.	26,28,29	16			529–532, 534–537
9. Know how changes in the price of a good, technology, the price of resources, expectations, taxes or subsidies, and the number of sellers affect the supply curve.	5,14–16, 18,20	1,4,5, 8,18–20	4	2,4	533–534
10. Know how taxes affect the supply curve.	25,27	15			534–537
11. Understand how tax provisions can be used to encourage investment.	24,26, 28,29	21,23,24			534–537

Key-Term Review

Review the following terms; if you are not sure of the meaning of any term, write out the definition and check it against the Glossary in the text.

competitive firm
depreciation (tax)
economic cost
economic profits
imperfectly competitive firm
investment decision
law of demand
law of diminishing returns
law of supply
long run
marginal cost
marginal revenue

normal profit
production decision
profit
profit-maximization rule
quantity supplied
short run
shutdown point
supply
supply curve
total revenue
variable costs

Fill in the blank following each of the statements below with the appropriate term from the list above.

1. According to the _____, when the price of a good falls, *ceteris paribus*, the quantity demanded rises.

    1. _____

2. The opportunity cost of capital, or average rate of return on an investment, is referred to as _____.

   2. _____

3. _____ is the product of price and quantity.

   3. _____

4. When total costs exceed total revenue, _____ is negative.

   4. _____

5. When price falls below average total costs, then the _____ by a firm may still be greater than zero, as long as price is above the minimum of average _____.

   5. _____

     _____

6. As long as the firm does not have to shut down, it will maximize profits at the production rate where _____ equals marginal cost.

   6. _____

7. When the firm chooses its production rate to meet this condition in the short run, it is making a _____.

   7. _____

8. As long as the demand curve is flat and the firm is at or above minimum average variable costs, the _____ curve will be the same as the _____ curve.

   8. _____

     _____

9. When a firm makes an _____, it has no fixed costs since all factors of production can be varied in the long run.

   9. _____

10. Because _____ is larger than accounting cost, _____ are smaller than accounting profits.

   10. _____

      _____

11. In the _____ the marginal cost curve is upward sloping because by the _____, the marginal product of factors will be falling as more of the variable factors are used.

   11. _____

      _____

12. However, in the _____ the shape of the marginal cost curve is dependent on technological factors, since there are no fixed costs.

   12. _____

13. A firm does not reach the _____ unless price equals minimum short-run average variable costs.

   13. _____

14. By the _____ a firm produces at that rate of output where marginal revenue equals marginal cost.

   14. _____

15. _____ is a tax deduction allowed for the cost of using capital and equipment in production.

   15. _____

16. A firm that has no market power is called a _____; one that has market power an _____.

   16. _____

      _____

17. The quantity of goods that firms are willing and able
to sell at different prices is represented by a

    _____.   17. _____

18. According to the _____, as the price of a good
rises, *ceteris paribus*, the quantity supplied increases.   18. _____

True or False: *Circle your choice.*

T F   1. A firm should produce until the next unit produced would raise added costs above additional revenues.

T F   2. A horizontal demand curve is a unit-elastic demand curve.

T F   3. If demand is elastic, a quantity decrease will more than offset a price increase, causing total revenue to drop.

T F   4. If the price of a good remains the same but the firm's output is changing, *ceteris paribus*, the demand curve facing the firm is infinitely elastic.

T F   5. For a competitive firm, the supply curve is that part of the marginal cost curve that is above the short-run average variable cost curve.

T F   6. Only at the output where marginal revenue equals marginal cost will profits be maximized.

T F   7. Since a firm's goal is to maximize profits, it should expand production as long as it is making profits.

T F   8. The marginal cost curve intersects the average total cost (*ATC*) curve at the lowest point of the *ATC* curve.

T F   9. The marginal cost curve intersects the average variable cost (*AVC*) curve at the lowest point of the *AVC* curve.

T F 10. Economic costs are greater than accounting costs.

T F 11. Fixed costs remain constant at all rates of production.

T F 12. Average fixed costs remain constant at all rates of production.

T F 13. If the price elasticity of demand is larger than 1, a price reduction will always increase profit.

T F 14. A change in the quantity supplied during a given time period indicates that the supply curve has shifted.

T F 15. A shift in the supply curve is likely to change the quantity of a product supplied during a given time period, *ceteris paribus*.

T F 16. When the supply curve of a good shifts downward, the supply of the good falls.

T F 17. Maximizing profits and minimizing losses amount to the same thing; the only difference is that in one case profits are greater than zero and in the other they are less than zero.

T F 18. If the prices of factors used to produce a good change, both the demand curve and the supply curve of the good will shift.

T F 19. All factors are not variable when the firm makes the production decision.

T F 20. Technological change shifts the supply curve and the marginal cost curve.

T F 21. Competitive firms face flat demand curves because they have no market power.

T F 22. The market demand curve slopes downward to the right only in noncompetitive markets .

T F 23. The perfectly elastic demand curve faced by a competitive firm is compatible with a downward-sloping market demand curve for the firm's product.

T F 24. When Congress lengthens the period over which assets are depreciated, investment is encouraged.

T F 25. A change in the tax rate on corporate profits will not change the firm's production decision in the short run.

T F 26. A change in the tax rate on corporate profits will affect the firm's investment decision.

T F 27. A change in the tax rate on corporate profits does not affect marginal costs.

T F 28. Accelerated cost recovery schedules in the tax law resulted in lower tax liabilities for firms.

T F 29. Tax credits for new investment are deducted directly from a firm's tax bill.

Multiple Choice: *Select the correct answer.*

_____ 1. A market supply curve of a product shows, *ceteris paribus:*
  (a) The amount of the product that firms are willing to supply for an industry at various prices.
  (b) The amount of output that will be supplied by firms at various factor costs.
  (c) The quantities that firms are willing and able to supply at various prices in a given time period, *ceteris paribus.*
  (d) The marginal cost curve of a representative firm.

_____ 2. When a firm raises prices, total revenue definitely:
  (a) Increases, thus increasing profits.
  (b) Falls, thus lowering profits.
  (c) Increases, but profits may fall.
  (d) Increases total revenue if demand is inelastic.

_____ 3. When a firm maximizes profits, it is:
  (a) Minimizing losses.
  (b) Maximizing the difference between total revenue and total cost.
  (c) Finding the production level at which its marginal revenue equals its marginal cost above average variable costs.
  (d) Doing all of the above.

_____ 4. When the wage rate paid to the production workers of a firm is increased:
  (a) The firm's marginal cost curve shifts upward.
  (b) Supply increases, and the supply curve rises.
  (c) The supply curve shifts to the right.
  (d) Marginal costs are unaffected.

_____ 5. Which of the following is *not* a determinant of either supply or demand?
  (a) Shortages.
  (b) Technological change.
  (c) Expectations.
  (d) Prices of other goods.

_____ 6. When the average cost curve is flat:
  (a) Marginal costs are rising with output.
  (b) Marginal costs are falling with output.
  (c) Marginal costs equal average costs.
  (d) The curve has been drawn incorrectly.

_____ 7. When a firm's average revenue curve is flat:
  (a) No matter how much the firm produces in a period of time, price remains constant.
  (b) Its marginal revenue curve is equal to its average revenue curve.
  (c) Its demand curve is flat.
  (d) All of the above are the case.

_____ 8. Which of the following is a determinant of both supply *and* demand?
  (a) Technological change.
  (b) The price of resources used in production.
  (c) Expectations.
  (d) The prices of other goods (substitutes and complements).

_____ 9. When a firm minimizes its losses in the short run:
   (a) It is doing the same thing as maximizing profits, except that negative profits are inevitable.
   (b) It will always shut down its production.
   (c) It will exit from the industry.
   (d) All of the above are incorrect.

_____ 10. While consumers try to maximize utility, firms generally try to maximize:
   (a) Profits.
   (b) Revenues.
   (c) Sales.
   (d) Production in a given period of time, *ceteris paribus*.

_____ 11. The price elasticity of demand measures the percentage change in quantity demanded caused by a 1 percent change in the:
   (a) Price of substitutes, *ceteris paribus*.
   (b) Price of resources, *ceteris paribus*.
   (c) Price of the good itself, *ceteris paribus*.
   (d) Prices of all of the above.

_____ 12. The price elasticity of supply measures the percentage change in quantity supplied in a given time period caused by a 1 percent change in the:
   (a) Price of a complementary good, *ceteris paribus*.
   (b) Price of resources, *ceteris paribus*.
   (c) Price of the good itself, *ceteris paribus*.
   (d) Price of a substitute good.

_____ 13. If the price of a good for which demand is highly elastic increases, total revenue:
   (a) Will decline.
   (b) Will remain constant.
   (c) Will increase.
   (d) Cannot be determined.

_____ 14. A firm should shut down (stop producing) whenever:
   (a) Minimum average variable cost exceeds price.
   (b) Minimum average total cost exceeds price.
   (c) It is making a loss.
   (d) Marginal cost exceeds marginal revenue.

_____ 15. A rise in depreciation for tax purposes means:
   (a) A firm has experienced greater losses of capital due to greater production.
   (b) A firm is able to reduce its taxes.
   (c) A firm must buy more capital to replace old capital.
   (d) All of the above.

_____ 16. A firm that makes an investment decision views all factors of production as:
   (a) Variable over the long run.
   (b) Variable over the short run.
   (c) Fixed over the long run.
   (d) Fixed over the short run.

_____ 17. Economic costs and economic profits are:
   (a) Greater and smaller, respectively, than their accounting counterparts.
   (b) Smaller and greater, respectively, than their accounting counterparts.
   (c) Both smaller than their accounting counterparts.
   (d) Both larger than their accounting counterparts.

_____ 18. Which of the following groups of determinants are all supply determinants?
   (a) Technology, price of resources, expectations, and number of buyers.
   (b) Price of other goods, expectations, income, and technology.
   (c) Price of other goods, expectations, technology, and number of sellers.
   (d) Price of resources, technology, expectations, and price of the good itself.

_____ 19. The marginal cost curve and the supply curve are not the same when:
   (a) Price and marginal revenue are not the same.
   (b) A firm has power over the price that is charged for its product (downward-sloping demand curve for the firm).
   (c) The marginal cost curve falls below the average variable cost curve.
   (d) Any of the above are the case.

_____ 20. The supply curve and demand curve are best contrasted by which of the following statements?
   (a) The demand curve reflects what the buyer is willing and able to buy; the supply curve reflects what the seller is willing and able to sell.
   (b) Both the demand curve and the supply curve reflect what a seller is willing and able to make available to the buyer, *ceteris paribus*.
   (c) Both the demand curve and the supply curve reflect what a buyer is willing and able to purchase from the seller, *ceteris paribus*.
   (d) The demand curve reflects what the seller will be able to sell and the supply curve reflects what the buyer will be able to buy, *ceteris paribus*.

_____ 21. Which of the following would encourage firms to invest?
   (a) A lower corporate-profits tax rate.
   (b) A faster depreciation schedule.
   (c) Larger investment tax credits.
   (d) All of the above.

_____ 22. A competitive firm faces:
   (a) A downward-sloping marginal revenue curve and a downward-sloping market demand curve.
   (b) A downward-sloping marginal revenue curve but a flat market demand curve.
   (c) A flat demand curve from the point of view of the firm but a downward-sloping market demand curve.
   (d) A downward-sloping demand curve from the point of view of the firm but a flat market demand curve.

_____ 23. Tax credits alter a firm's investment decision by allowing firms to:
   (a) Deduct depreciation allowances from their tax liability.
   (b) Deduct the tax credits from their tax bill.
   (c) Deduct their tax credits from the income on which the tax is levied.
   (d) Deduct depreciation allowances from their tax liability.

_____ 24. The 1986 Tax Reform Act included provisions that:
   (a) Lengthened the time over which firms may depreciate assets.
   (b) Eliminated the investment tax credit.
   (c) Resulted in greater taxes being paid by corporations.
   (d) Did all of the above.

Problems and Applications

Exercise 1

This exercise gives practice in relating the concepts of supply and marginal cost. It also gives practice in graphing, shifting, and moving along the different curves.

Assume you own a machine tool manufacturing company that produces one standardized type of tool. Your total costs change as shown in Table 21.2. On the basis of Table 21.2, answer the questions below:

Table 21.2
Costs of machine tool manufacturer

(1) Quantity (thousands of machine tools per day)	(2) Total cost (TC) (thousands of dollars per day)	(3) Average cost (AC) (dollars per machine tool)	(4) Marginal cost (MC) (dollars per machine tool)
0	$ 0	$_____	$_____
1	$ 5	_____	_____
2	20	_____	_____
3	60	_____	_____

1. Fill in columns 3 and 4 of Table 21.2.

2. Graph the average and marginal cost curves for the firm in Figure 21.1.

Figure 21.1

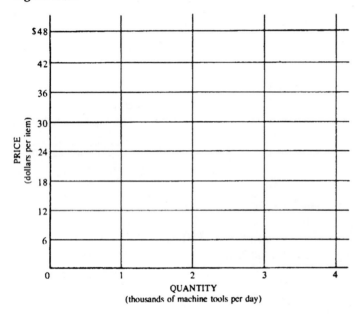

3. Your machine tool firm is characterized by:
   (a) Economies of scale.
   (b) Constant returns to scale.
   (c) Diseconomies of scale.
   (d) None of the above because the cost information is applicable only in the short run.

4. Suppose that total cost increases as shown in Table 21.3. Fill in columns 3 and 4 of Table 21.3, then graph the new average and marginal cost curves using dotted lines in Figure 21.1.

Table 21.3
Costs after a cost increase

(1) Quantity (thousands of machine tools per day)	(2) Total cost (TC) (thousands of dollars per day)	(3) Average cost (AC) (dollars per machine tool)	(4) Marginal cost (MC) (dollars per machine tool)
0	$ 0	$_____	$_____
1	6	_____	_____
2	24	_____	_____
3	72	_____	_____

5. Because of the cost increases:
   (a) The marginal cost curve has shifted upward, but it is uncertain how the supply curve shifts.
   (b) The marginal cost curve has shifted downward, but it is uncertain how the supply curve shifts.
   (c) Since the supply curve and marginal cost curve consist of the same points, both have shifted upward.
   (d) Since the supply and marginal cost curve consist of the same points, both have shifted downward.

6. T F Because the supply curve has shifted upward, there is a greater supply.

7. If you expect prices to fall in the near future because you expect a recession, you might decide to cut back your operations and invest your money in securities. The machine tool supply curve of your firm would:
   (a) Shift to the left.
   (b) Shift to the right.
   (c) Remain unchanged, but you would move to a lower quantity supplied along your supply curve.
   (d) Remain unchanged, but you would move to a higher quantity supplied along your supply curve.

8. If prices do fall in the market for machine tools, you would lower your prices to remain competitive. The machine tool supply curve of your firm would:
   (a) Shift to the left.
   (b) Shift to the right.
   (c) Remain unchanged, but you would move to a lower quantity supplied along your supply curve.
   (d) Remain unchanged, but you would move to a higher quantity supplied along your supply curve.

9. Suppose there were a new technology that made production of machine tools more efficient. If you adopted this new technology, your machine tool supply curve would:
   (a) Shift to the left.
   (b) Shift to the right.
   (c) Remain unchanged, but you would move to a lower quantity supplied along your supply curve.
   (d) Remain unchanged, but you would move to a higher quantity supplied along your supply curve.

Exercise 2

This exercise gives you a chance to sort out all of the different formulas for costs and revenues, to graph them, and then to find the rule that will lead to profit maximization.

1. Several formulas that use symbols with which you should familiarize yourself appear below. Match each formula with the number of one of the columns in Table 21.4. To find what the symbols in the formula mean, look at Table 21.4. (*Note: FC* is a fixed cost, and $\triangle$ means "the change in.")

		Column			Column	
a.	$TC - FC$	_____	f.	$(TC - FC)/q$	_____
b.	$\Delta TC / \Delta q$	_____	g.	$\Delta TR / \Delta q$	_____
c.	$TR - TC$	_____	h.	TR/Q	_____
d.	$p \times q$	_____	i.	$(TR - TC)/q$	_____
e.	TC/q	_____			

Table 21.4
Cost and revenue data

		(1)		(2)	(3)	(4)	(5)	(6)	(7)	(8)	(9)
Quantity (q) (items per week)	Price (p) (dollars per item)	Total revenue (TR) (dollars per week)	Total cost (TC) (dollars per week)	Profit (dollars per week)	Average profit (dollars per item)	Average revenue (AR) (dollars per item)	Average total cost (ATC) (dollars per item)	Total variable cost (TVC) (dollars per week)	Average variable cost (AVC) (dollars per item)	Marginal cost (MC) (dollars per item)	Marginal revenue (MR) (dollars per item)
0	$4	$____	$ 400	$____	$____	$____	$____	$____	$____	$____	$____
100	4	____	1,000	____	____	____	____	____	____	____	____
200	4	____	1,300	____	____	____	____	____	____	____	____
300	4	____	1,500	____	____	____	____	____	____	____	____
400	4	____	1,600	____	____	____	____	____	____	____	____
500	4	____	1,700	____	____	____	____	____	____	____	____
600	4	____	1,850	____	____	____	____	____	____	____	____
700	4	____	2,100	____	____	____	____	____	____	____	____
800	4	____	2,450	____	____	____	____	____	____	____	____
900	4	____	3,600	____	____	____	____	____	____	____	____

2. After checking your answers, complete Table 21.4.

3. In Figure 21.2, diagram the average revenue, average total cost, marginal revenue, average variable cost, and marginal cost curves.

Figure 21.2

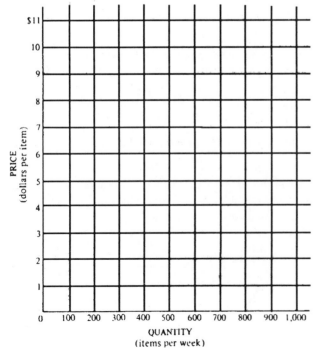

QUANTITY
(items per week)

310

Now you can test to see which rules give you the production rate that earns the greatest profit for the firm. Fill in Table 21.5 with the production rate (one of the ten rates in the rows of Table 21.4) at which the particular rule is satisfied.

Table 21.5

	When this occurs. . .	The production rate is:
4.	Maximum profits	_____
5.	Maximum average profits	_____
6.	Minimum total costs	_____
7.	Maximum revenues	_____
8.	Minimum average total costs	_____
9.	Maximum average revenues	_____
10.	Minimum average variable costs	_____
11.	Minimum marginal cost	_____
12.	Marginal cost = price	_____
13.	Marginal cost = marginal revenue	_____
14.	Marginal cost = average total cost	_____
15.	Marginal cost = average variable cost	_____

Very few rules give the unique profit-maximizing production rate of 800. As a matter of fact, only the $MC = MR$ rule, which applies to all firms, and the $MC = p$ rule, which applies only when the demand curve is flat, yield the production rate at which profits are maximized.

Exercise 3

This exercise will show how to identify the price at which a firm would shut down. It will be helpful in solving the problem at the end of Chapter 21 in the text.

1. The shutdown price for a firm is any price below the minimum of the:
   (a) *ATC* curve.
   (b) *MR* curve.
   (c) *AVC* curve.
   (d) *MC* curve.

2. Suppose the price of parachutes is $6 and there is no way to change that price. Compute total revenue and profits and put answers in Table 21.6.

Table 21.6
Total revenue and profit of parachute business at price of $6 per parachute (dollars per week)

	Parachutes produced per week							
	0	100	200	300	400	500	600	700
Total revenue (*TR*)	$____	$____	$____	$____	$____	$____	$____	$____
Total costs (*TC*)	3,000	4,000	4,800	5,400	6,200	7,500	9,000	10,700
Profit (*TR – TC*)	____	____	____	____	____	____	____	____

3. Draw the new demand curve with a dotted line in Figure 21.3. Label it *D*.

Figure 21.3

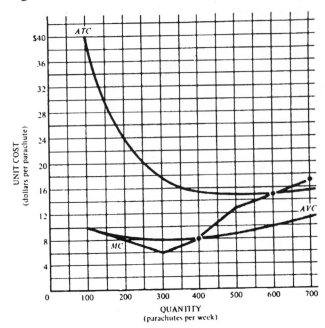

QUANTITY
(parachutes per week)

4. What is the profit-maximizing production rate? (Check Table 21.6.)
   (a   0 parachutes per week.
   (b) 200 parachutes per week.
   (c) 400 parachutes per week.
   (d) 600 parachutes per week.

5. At what production rate does the marginal revenue curve intersect the marginal cost curve?
   (a) 100 parachutes per week.
   (b) 300 parachutes per week.
   (c) 500 parachutes per week.
   (d) 700 parachutes per week.

6. Does the *MR* = *MC* rule indicate correctly the output at which profits are maximized or losses are minimized? _____

7. A supply curve shows, *ceteris paribus*:
   (a) The quantities of a good that a seller is willing and able to sell at various market prices per unit of time.
   (b) The price that sellers demand for producing a specific quantity of a good.
   (c) The quantities of a good that a buyer is willing and able to buy at various market prices.
   (d) None of the above.

8. Refer to the definition of the supply curve again (Question 7). When the price for parachutes is $6 per parachute, does the marginal cost curve accurately show what you are willing and able to supply? _____

9. What is the shutdown price level for parachute production? $ _____
   (*Remember:* Always find the minimum of the average variable cost curve. At any price below that minimum, the marginal cost curve ceases to function like a supply curve.)

Exercise 4

The media often provide information that suggests shifts in a market supply curve or a movement along such a curve. By using one of the articles in the text, this exercise will show the kind of information to look for. If your professor makes a newspaper assignment for this chapter, this exercise will provide an example of how to do it.

Reread the article in Chapter 2 entitled "Surplus Punches Hole in Oil Price," from *USA Today*. Then answer the following questions, using Figure 21.4 to answer Question 1:

1. Which of the four diagrams in Figure 21.4 best represents the movement or shift in supply that the article describes? a b c d (circle one)

Figure 21.4

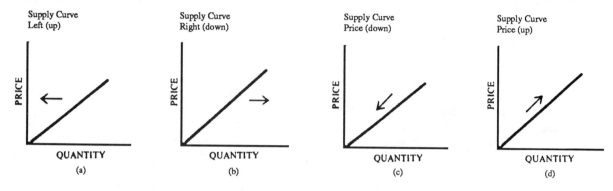

2. What phrase indicates the market in which the supply shift or movement occurred?

3. What sentence indicates the change in the determinant of supply or price that caused the shift or movement you chose in Figure 21.4?

4. What phrase indicates who the seller is?

5. Where does the article mention a change in price or quantity that resulted from the shift in supply or change in quantity supplied?

Crossword Puzzle

Select the economic term in the following list that corresponds with each of the definitions and descriptions below. Then fit the term or one of the words within it into the crossword puzzle at the numbers indicated.

average
  revenue
average total
  cost
depreciation
economic cost
fixed costs
investment
  decision
law of demand
law of
  diminishing
  returns
long run
marginal cost
marginal
  revenue
MR = MC

price
price elasticity
  of demand
production
  decision
profit
profit
  maximization
quantity
  supplied
short run
shutdown
  point
supply
total cost
total revenue
variable cost

Across

2. Total cost divided by quantity.
5. Where price equals minimum short-run average variable cost.
7. Helps firms to decide whether prices should be raised or not.
10. This is always the same thing as average revenue.
11. When the price rises, firms usually increase the _____.
14. The type of horizon a business person has when making an investment decision.
17. The difference between total revenue and total cost.
18. Quantity times unit cost.
19. The amount of additional expense incurred by increasing production by one unit.
20. The total value of all factors used in production, not just explicit costs.
21. The cause of the upward-sloping marginal cost curve in the short run.

Down

1. The chief goal of a firm.
3. When a firm stops producing in the short run, this type of cost is zero.
4. The curve that represents this quantity is equal to or below the demand curve.
5. All factors of production can be changed when a business person makes this kind of choice.
6. A firm has none of these when it makes a long-run decision.
8. What sellers are willing and able to sell.
9. A tax deduction.
11. The type of horizon a business person has when he makes a production decision.
12. When a business person cannot change some factors, his or her choices must be of this type.
13. The basic reason for the downward slope of demand curves.
15. Price times quantity.
16. The algebraic condition that a firm satisfies if it is maximizing profits.

Common Errors

The first statement in each "common error" below is incorrect. Each incorrect statement is followed by a corrected version and an explanation.

1. Higher prices yield greater profits. WRONG!

   The effect of price increases on total revenue depends on the elasticity of demand. RIGHT!

   The law of demand tells us that when prices rise, quantity falls; total revenues may actually decrease (remember the $4 ice cream cones). Costs also change; if they don't fall as quickly as total revenues, then *profits* fall.

2. Surpluses and shortages are determinants of demand and supply that shift demand-and-supply curves. WRONG!

   Surpluses and shortages often result from shifts of demand or supply curves, but do not cause such shifts themselves. RIGHT!

   Surpluses or shortages may appear in a market if the market price does not adjust to the equilibrium price. If there is a shift in demand or supply, shortages or surpluses may temporarily result until the market price reaches its equilibrium.

3. If a firm is taking a loss, it is not maximizing profits. WRONG!

   A firm may be maximizing profits even if it is making zero profits or even taking a loss. RIGHT!

   Minimizing losses is essentially the same as maximizing profits. A firm is maximizing profits as long as there is nothing it can do to make larger profits. Remember, even if the firm is taking a loss, it will not shut down if it can cover variable costs.

4. A change in price changes the supply of goods produced by a firm. WRONG!

   A change in price changes the quantity of a good supplied by a firm in a given time period. RIGHT!

   Be careful! Economists differentiate between the terms "quantity supplied" and "supply." A change in the quantity supplied usually refers to a movement along a supply curve due to a change in price or production rate. A change in supply refers to a shift of the supply curve due to a change in technology, the price of a resource, or the number of sellers.

5. A firm should always increase the rate of production as long as it is making a profit. WRONG!

A profitable firm should increase production rates only as long as additional revenues from the increase in production exceed the additional associated costs. RIGHT!

If the increase in production rates generates more costs than revenue, the firm will be less profitable. In this case, continued expansion will ultimately result in zero profits.

■ ANSWERS ■

Key-Term Review

1. law of demand
2. normal profit
3. total revenue
4. profit
5. quantity supplied
   variable costs
6. marginal revenue
7. production decision

8. marginal cost
   supply
9. investment decision
10. economic cost
    economic profits
11. short run
    law of diminishing returns
12. long run

13. shutdown point
14. profit-maximization rule
15. depreciation
16. competitive firm
    imperfectly competitive firm
17. supply curve
18. law of supply

True or False

1. T	6. T	11. T	16. F	21. T	26. T
2. F	7. F	12. F	17. T	22. F	27. T
3. T	8. T	13. F	18. F	23. T	28. T
4. T	9. T	14. F	19. T	24. F	29. T
5. T	10. T	15. T	20. T	25. T	

Multiple Choice

1. c	5. a	9. a	13. a	17. a	21. d
2. d	6. c	10. a	14. a	18. d	22. c
3. d	7. d	11. c	15. b	19. d	23. b
4. a	8. c	12. c	16. a	20. a	24. d

Problems and Applications

Exercise 1

1. Table 21.1 answer

Quantity	AC	MC
0	$—	$—
1	5	5
2	10	15
3	20	40

2. Figure 21.1 answer

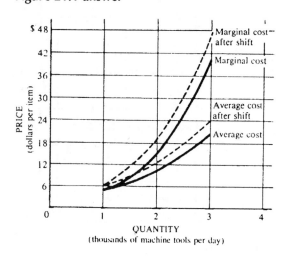

3. c
4.

Table 21.3 answer

Quantity	AC	MC
0	$—	$—
1	6	6
2	12	18
3	24	48

See also the dotted lines in Figure 21.1 answer.

Exercise 2

1. a. 6   d. 1   g. 9
   b. 8   e. 5   h. 4
   c. 2   f. 7   i. 3

2.

Table 21.4 answer

		(1)		(2)	(3) Average	(4)	(5)	(6)	(7)	(8)	(9)
Quantity (items per week)	Price (dollars per item)	TR (dollars per week)	TC (dollars per week)	Profit (dollars per week)	profit (dollars per item)	AR (dollars per item)	ATC (dollars per item)	TVC (dollars per week)	AVC (dollars per item)	MC (dollars per item)	MR (dollars per item)
0	$4	$ 0	$ 400	$—400	$ —	$—	$ —	$ —	$ —	$ —	$—
100	4	400	1,000	—600	—6.00	4	10.00	600	6.00	6.00	4
200	4	800	1,300	—500	—2.50	4	6.50	900	4.50	3.00	4
300	4	1,200	1,500	—300	—1.00	4	5.00	1,100	3.67	2.00	4
400	4	1,600	1,600	0	0.00	4	4.00	1,200	3.00	1.00	4
500	4	2,000	1,700	300	0.60	4	3.40	1,300	2.60	1.00	4
600	4	2,400	1,850	550	0.92	4	3.08	1,450	2.42	1.50	4
700	4	2,800	2,100	700	1.00	4	3.00	1,700	2.43	2.50	4
800	4	3,200	2,450	750	0.94	4	3.06	2,050	2.56	3.50	4
900	4	3,600	3,600	0	0.00	4	4.00	3,200	3.56	11.50	4

3. **Figure 21.2 answer**

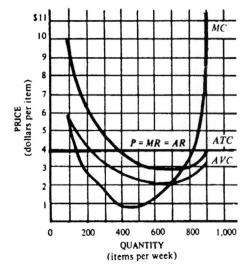

PRICE (dollars per item)

P = MR = AR   ATC   AVC   MC

QUANTITY (items per week)

Problems 4–15 (Table 21.5) are expressed in number of it
per week.

4. 800
5. 700
6. 0
7. 900
8. 700
9. all output levels
10. 600

5. c
6. F
7. a
8. c
9. b

11. 400–500
12. 100–200 when the marginal cost curve falls below price (this is where profits are minimized)
    800–900 when the marginal cost curve rises above price (this is where profits are maximized)
13. 100–200 when the marginal cost curve falls below marginal revenue (this is where profits are minimized)
    800–900 when the marginal cost curve rises above marginal revenue
14. 700–800
15. 100, 600–700

Exercise 3

1. c
2.

Table 21.6 answer

	Parachutes produced per week							
	0	100	200	300	400	500	600	700
Total revenue (TR)	$ 0	$ 600	$ 1,200	$ 1,800	$ 2,400	$ 3,000	$ 3,600	$ 4,200
Total costs (TC)	3,000	4,000	4,800	5,400	6,200	7,500	9,000	10,700
Profit (TR–TC)	–3,000	–3,400	–3,600	–3,600	–3,800	–4,500	–5,400	–6,500

3. **Figure 21.3 answer**

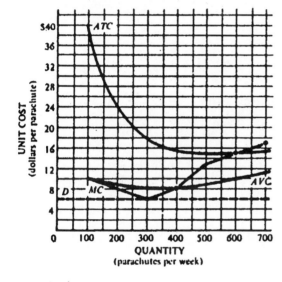

4. a
5. b
6. No. In this case the firm should shut down because $P < AVC$.
7. a
8. No
9. $8 per parachute

Exercise 4

1. Diagram *a* applies to two separate shifts; (a) the effect of the three-week Norwegian oil strike and (b) the drop in the number of oil rigs needed to produce oil in the United States. We'll focus here on the latter shift. Other information indicates that a price change might also be interpreted as diagram *d* when prices were rising and diagram *c* when prices again fell. One of the principal skills in reading media articles is to disentangle each of the separate changes that are described.
2. "West Texas intermediate, the USA's highest quality grade of crude" is one of the indications of the market.
3. "Last week it [count of operating oil rigs] was 754. . . . It was more than 1800 this time last year."

317

4. "Most people in exploration and production" refers to the sellers.
5. "Fueling the earlier price rally" does not explicitly refer to the changes in the number of oil rigs, but it is consistent with the change in prices that would be caused by fewer oil rigs. By implication, fewer oil rigs suggest a reduced supply of oil.

Crossword Puzzle Answer

Across

2. *average* total cost
5. shut*down* point
7. price *elasticity* of demand
10. *price*
11. quantity *supplied*
14. *long* run
17. *profit*
18. total *cost*
19. *marginal* cost
20. *economic* cost
21. law of diminishing *returns*

Down

1. profit *maximization*
3. *variable* cost
4. marginal *revenue*
5. investment *decision*
6. *fixed* costs
8. *supply*
9. *depreciation*
11. *short* run
12. *production* decision
13. law of *demand*
15. *total* revenue
16. MR = MC

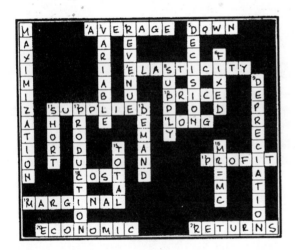

Chapter 22
Competitive Markets

Quick Review

The purely competitive model is a standard by which all other market structures are judged. Other models are labeled efficient or inefficient, depending on how their long-run equilibrium price and output compare with what would be achieved in a competitive market.

The essence of a competitive market is that the actors are powerless to influence product prices and resource flows. They are powerless because such a market is characterized by (1) a product that is homogeneous, (2) a large number of very small buyers and sellers, (3) prices that are free of artificial restrictions, and (4) an absence of barriers to entry into or exit from the industry.

In this chapter our principal interest is to determine:

- How prices and output are determined in competitive markets.
- How competition affects the profits of a firm or industry.
- How prices and profits affect the investment and production decisions of competitive firms.

Of course, firms sometimes incur losses. In that case, the market has sent a signal that some firms should leave the industry. Supply is thereby reduced, price rises, *ceteris paribus,* and long-run equilibrium is established at a higher price. Resources that left the industry will move to higher-valued uses elsewhere. Society's efficient allocation of scarce resources owes as much to losses as it does to profits.

Firms in a competitive market are called "price takers." The price that they "take" is the equilibrium price, at which supply equals demand in the market. Because each firm is so small relative to the market, each entrepreneur recognizes that he or she alone cannot influence the price of the product by altering his or her share of the total supply. The price dictated by the market becomes, therefore, the marginal revenue. Following the rules described earlier, entrepreneurs produce at that rate of production at which $MR = MC$. This is the best they can do.

Let's suppose that at the current market price profits are above the normal rates of return earned by similar resources in alternative uses. Owners of those resources will enter the market, start new firms, and produce output. But by doing so they will increase the supply of the product and, *ceteris paribus,* drive down the market price (each firm's marginal revenue). The entry of firms will continue until the above-normal returns are eliminated. Thus, each firm is forced by the competition (or threat of competition) from other firms to operate efficiently. In other words, the producer is forced to the minimum average total cost *(ATC)* of producing goods.

When the long-run equilibrium is reached in a competitive market, several important conditions result. First, consumers are willing to pay an amount (*p*) for the last unit produced that is just equal to the amount required (*MC*) to get firms to produce it. Furthermore, $MC =$ minimum ATC, because if ATC were any higher, returns would be above average and new firms would enter the industry and drive the price down. Consumers get what they want at the lowest possible price. The economy's resources are used most efficiently in purely competitive markets.

Examples of competitive markets are easy to find. Personal computers, agricultural products, VCRs, and so on, provide excellent examples. This chapter uses the story of the personal computer to illustrate how competitive markets work and how the consumer benefits as a result.

Learning Objectives

After reading Chapter 22 and doing the following exercises, you should:	True or false	Multiple choice	Problems and applications	Common errors	Pages in the text
1. Know how the absence of market power relates to the shape of demand-and-supply curves from the point of view of buyers and sellers.	1	11		1	540–544
2. Be able to list the characteristics of the competitive market structure and describe the role of competition in the U.S. economy.	6,7,17	7,8,10	5		544–553
3. Be able to tell why the demand curve facing a competitive firm is flat.	2,3	1,2			542
4. Know the difference between the firm's demand curve and the market demand curve.	4,5	1	1		541–543
5. Know why above-normal profits disappear in competitive industries.	7–9	5	4	2	543–544, 544–553
6. Know how barriers to entry influence the competitive process.		3			550
7. Understand how a competitive market structure affects prices, cost, output, and profits in the short and long run.	11,12	4,9,13,15			544–557
8. Be able to identify the signals for the entry and exit of firms.	10,18,20			3	552–558
9. Be able to show the effects of shifts of market demand or supply on individual demand or supply.	15,16	6,12,14	2,3		550–553
10. Describe how marginal cost pricing leads to efficiency.	13,14,19				560–561

Key-Term Review

Review the following terms; if you are not sure of the meaning of any term, write out the definition and check it against the Glossary in the text.

average total cost (*ATC*)
barriers to entry
competitive firm
competitive market
economic profit
efficiency (technical)
equilibrium price
long-run competitive equilibrium
marginal cost (*MC*)
marginal cost pricing

marginal revenue
market mechanism
market power
market supply
opportunity cost
production decision
profit per unit
shift of supply
short-run competitive equilibrium
shutdown point

Fill in the blank following each of the statements below with the appropriate term from the list above.

1. The additional cost that would be incurred if the firm were to produce an additional unit of output is called _____.

1. _____

2. In the short run when a competitive firm is at a production rate where $p = MC$, it is in _____.

2. _____

3. When a competitive firm is at the minimum of its long-run average total cost curve, it is in _____.

3. _____

4. When quantity supplied equals quantity demanded, this equivalence establishes the _____.

4. _____

5. A market characterized by large numbers of buyers and sellers, each without any market power, is called a _____.

5. _____

6. When society allows demand and supply to allocate resources, we say society is using the _____.

6. _____

7. The development of a new and efficient technology for producing a product could cause a _____.

7. _____

8. The difference between economic cost and total revenue is called _____.

8. _____

9. The difference between average total cost and average revenue is called _____.

9. _____

10. The total amount supplied to a market by all firms at all possible prices per unit of time, *ceteris paribus*, is called _____.

10. _____

11. When you divide total cost by the quantity produced you get _____.

11. _____

12. A firm that gets the greatest output possible per unit of input used is producing at high _____.

12. _____

13. The best alternative opportunity forgone when you undertake any course of action is your _____.

13. _____

14. When a firm decides what production rate will maximize profits, it is making a _____.

14. _____

15. A firm that is too small to affect prices has no _____.

15. _____

16. An example of this kind of firm is the _____.

16. _____

17. Since there is nothing to prevent firms from entering the industry, there are no _____.

17. _____

18. When price is equal to minimum average variable cost, a competitive firm has reached the _____.

18. _____

19. Setting price equal to the additional cost of producing the last unit of output is called _____.

19. _____

20. The additional revenue gained from selling an additional unit is called _____.

20. _____

True or False: *Circle your choice.*

T F 1. The demand curve faced by an individual competitive firm is determined by the market price and is thus perfectly inelastic.

T F 2. The demand curve faced by the perfectly competitive market slopes downward and to the right.

T F 3. For the perfectly competitive firm, marginal revenue and price have the same value.

T F 4. For the perfectly competitive market, marginal revenue and price have the same value.

T F 5. For the perfectly competitive firm, price and average revenue have the same value.

T F 6. The perfectly competitive model is not useful since it has never existed.

T F 7. In the long-run equilibrium, a competitive market's profits may be above normal.

T F 8. Since perfectly competitive firms earn zero economic profits (no above-normal profits) in the long run, all firms will leave the industry.

T F 9. When resources are earning zero economic profits, they are doing as well as they could in their next best alternative use.

T F 10. If a perfectly competitive firm were to raise its price above the market price, it would lose all of its customers.

T F 11. A necessary condition for the operation of a perfectly competitive market is free entry into, and exit from, the market.

T F 12. When entrepreneurs decide to build a plant, they are making the production decision.

T F 13. In the long-run equilibrium of a purely competitive market, the price of the product will equal the minimum long-run average cost.

T F 14. The marginal cost curve of a purely competitive producer must be perfectly flat.

T F 15. That part of the firm's marginal cost curve that lies above the minimum of the average variable cost curve contains the same points as the firm's short-run supply curve.

T F 16. The short-run market supply curve is a horizontal summation of the *MC* curves above minimum *AVC* of the individual firms.

T F 17. Most markets in the United States are perfectly competitive.

T F 18. Competitive markets are responsive to the desires of consumers.

T F 19. Perfectly competitive firms are forced to be efficient by government regulations.

T F 20. In competitive markets, losses are the signal for firms to exit from the industry.

Multiple Choice: *Select the correct answer.*

_____ 1. Farmer Kitt, as an individual producer, faces a firm demand curve that:
   (a) Slopes downward to the right.
   (b) Slopes upward to the right.
   (c) Appears flat (horizontal).
   (d) Is the same as the market demand curve.

_____ 2. The Ford Motor Company faces a demand curve that is:
   (a) Flat.
   (b) The same as the market demand curve for American-made automobiles.
   (c) Vertical.
   (d) Downward sloping to the right.

_____ 3. Farmer Kitt:
   (a) Is able to keep potential egg producers out of the market.
   (b) Would like to keep potential egg producers out of the market but cannot.
   (c) Will not care if more egg producers enter the market.
   (d) Is powerless to alter his own rate of production.

_____ 4. In the text, the reason cited for the decline in the price of personal computers was basically that:
   (a) Fewer but larger firms were producing them.
   (b) U.S. firms produced them abroad and shipped them into the United States.
   (c) New technology lowered fixed costs.
   (d) More firms produced them and more efficient technologies were developed.

_____ 5. If marginal cost exceeds marginal revenue, a competitive firm can usually increase its profits (or decrease its losses) by:
   (a) Increasing output.
   (b) Raising price.
   (c) Stopping production.
   (d) Decreasing output.

_____ 6. Suppose that the discovery of a new productive technique reduces the costs of production. In a purely competitive market, the short-run effects will be:
   (a) Higher price, greater output, and larger profits.
   (b) Higher price, smaller output, and smaller profits.
   (c) Lower price, smaller output, and smaller profits.
   (d) Lower price, greater output, and larger profits.

_____ 7. Which of the following conditions is *not* characteristic of a perfectly competitive market?
   (a) Competition between sellers is impersonal.
   (b) Products of all sellers in the industry are identical or nearly so.
   (c) The individual sellers do not advertise.
   (d) The market price is determined by an organization of sellers.

_____ 8. The perfectly competitive model is useful because:
   (a) Most industries in the United States are perfectly competitive.
   (b) They provide a good starting point for analysis of the price system.
   (c) A number of market situations approximate perfect competition.
   (d) Both b and c are the case.

_____ 9. In short-run competitive equilibrium, which of the following is *not* true for a firm?
   (a) Marginal cost equals marginal revenue.
   (b) Price equals marginal cost.
   (c) Market price exceeds average cost by the largest possible amount.
   (d) Profit is a maximum (or loss is a minimum) for the market.

_____ 10. Which of the following conditions is characteristic of a perfectly competitive market?
   (a) The seller does not lose all customers when the selling price is raised above the market price.
   (b) The seller can produce and sell as much as desired at the established market price without affecting that price.
   (c) The seller spends large sums of money on advertising.
   (d) The seller is affected by the actions of any competitors.

_____ 11. The demand curve for a competitive market is:
   (a) Flat.
   (b) Downward-sloping because the firms in the industry have market power.
   (c) Downward-sloping because of the law of demand.
   (d) Both b and c.

_____ 12. The marginal cost curve is the same as the firm's supply curve when it is:
  (a) Above minimum average variable costs and the firm's demand curve is downward sloping.
  (b) Below minimum average variable costs and the demand curve is flat.
  (c) Above minimum average variable costs and the firm's demand curve is flat.
  (d) Below minimum average variable costs and the demand curve is downward sloping.

_____ 13. Which of the following conditions always characterizes a firm that is in short-run competitive equilibrium where profits are maximized?
  (a) Price equals minimum average total cost.
  (b) Price equals marginal cost.
  (c) There are no economic profits.
  (d) All of the above are characteristic.

_____ 14. The market supply curve will shift due to all of the following *except:*
  (a) Changes in technology.
  (b) Changes in the number of supplying firms.
  (c) Changes in expectation about making profits in an industry.
  (d) Changes in the current income of buyers.

_____ 15. In a competitive market where firms are incurring losses, which of the following should be expected as the industry moves to long-run equilibrium, *ceteris paribus?*
  (a) A higher price and fewer firms.
  (b) A lower price and fewer firms.
  (c) A higher price and more firms.
  (d) A lower price and more firms.

Problems and Applications

Exercise 1

This exercise provides the link between individual and market demand curves. It shows how the equilibrium in the market determines the demand curve from the seller's point of view. It also shows how the market equilibrium determines the supply curve from the buyer's point of view.

  1. Hard-time Charlie needs psychiatric help. He would like to engage a psychiatrist for four hours per week at the current price of $6 per hour. However, at a price of $12 per hour, Charlie would only want two hours per week. In Figure 22.1 draw Charlie's individual demand curve. (Assume the demand curve is a straight line.)

Figure 22.1
Demand curve of the buyer

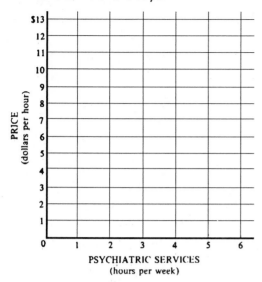

PSYCHIATRIC SERVICES
(hours per week)

2. Suppose that Charlie is not the only one with a problem. There are 9,999 other hard-time Charlies in the same city who have identical demand curves. In Figure 22.2 graph the market demand curve for all of the hard-time Charlies combined and label it *D*.

Figure 22.2
Market demand and supply curves

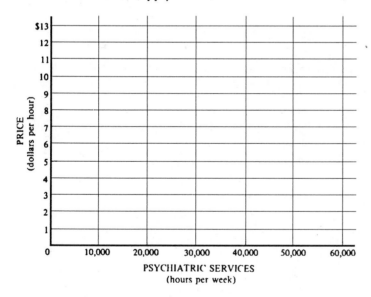

PSYCHIATRIC SERVICES
(hours per week)

3. Lucy is a psychiatrist who is fond of visits from Charlie, particularly at the $12 per hour rate. At that rate she would be willing and able to schedule 50 hours of couch time per week. But at the lower $6 per hour rate she would be willing to schedule only 10 hours per week. In Figure 22.3 draw Lucy's supply curve. (Assume it is a straight line.)

325

Figure 22.3
Supply curve of the supplier

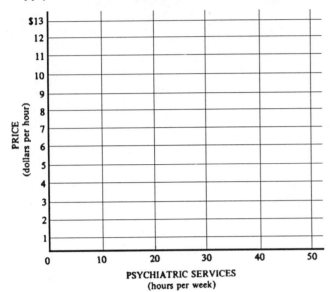

PSYCHIATRIC SERVICES
(hours per week)

4. There are 999 other psychiatrists in the city with supply curves like Lucy's. Draw the market supply curve for psychiatrists in Figure 22.2 and label it *S*. (Assume it is a straight line.)

5. The equilibrium price for psychiatric services for hard-time Charlies in this market is:
   (a) $12 per hour.
   (b) $9 per hour.
   (c) $6 per hour.
   (d) $3 per hour.
   (e) $0 per hour.

6. One of the 10,000 hard-time Charlies is suddenly married and needs no more psychiatric services. Is the new market demand curve for psychiatric services significantly different from that in Figure 22.2? _____

7. Table 22.1 shows how the market equilibrium price changes in response to the quantity demanded by one good-time Charlie before and after his marriage. Fill in the table.

Table 22.1

Psychiatric services (hours per week)	Market equilibrium price (dollars per hour)
0 (after marriage)	$_____
3 (before marriage)	_____

8. Table 22.1 represents psychiatric services sellers are willing and able to sell to Charlie. In Figure 22.4 diagram the supply curve that Charlie is facing.

Figure 22.4
Supply curve from buyer's viewpoint

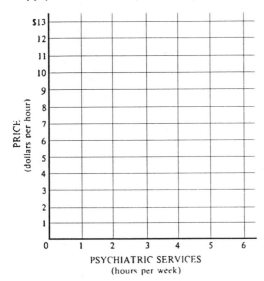

9. When there are many buyers in a market, the quantity bought by any one buyer is likely to have little effect on the market equilibrium price in a given period of time. Each buyer therefore views the supply curve facing him or her as:
   (a) Upward sloping.
   (b) Downward sloping.
   (c) Flat.

10. Our once hard-time Charlie is divorced again, and so there are again an even 10,000 hard-time Charlies. Now Lucy takes a week-long world-wide tour. Is the resulting new market supply curve for psychiatrists much different from the one you labeled S in Figure 22.2, during the week of Lucy's vacation? _____

11. Fill in Table 22.2, which shows how the market equilibrium price changes in response to the quantity supplied by Lucy.

Table 22.2

Psychiatric services (hours per week)	Market equilibrium price (dollars per hour)
0 (during vacation)	$_____
30 (before vacation)	_____

12. Table 22.2 shows what buyers are willing and able to buy of Lucy's services. In Figure 22.5, diagram the demand curve Lucy is facing.

Figure 22.5
Demand curve from seller's viewpoint

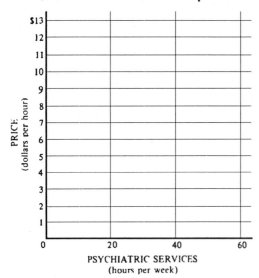

13. When there are many suppliers in a market, the quantity supplied by any one seller is likely to have little effect on market equilibrium price in a given time period. Each supplier therefore views the demand curve facing him or her as:
    (a) Upward sloping.
    (b) Downward sloping.
    (c) Flat.

14. Is the demand curve of the buyer (Figure 22.1) the same as the demand curve facing the individual seller (Figure 22.5)? _____

15. Is the supply curve of the seller (Figure 22.3) the same as the supply curve facing the individual buyer (Figure 22.4)? _____

This exercise should alert you to the importance of distinguishing *individual* (or firm) from market demand-and-supply curves. You should also be aware that a downward-sloping demand curve for an individual buyer is not necessarily the demand curve seen by a supplier. Also the upward-sloping supply curve of an individual seller is not necessarily the supply curve perceived by the buyer.

Exercise 2

Many of the newspaper and magazine articles you have read in the text describe supply-and-demand shifts. This exercise gives you the investigative skills to recognize information about shifts and to correctly identify the kind of shift that is involved.

Find the letter of the diagram in Figure 22.6 that best represents the shift described in each of the following articles. At the beginning of each listed article the appropriate market for examining the shift is indicated. Identify at least one determinant that caused the shift. (Choose from tastes, income, prices of substitutes, prices of complements, expectations, and number of buyers for the demand curve. Choose from technological change, expectations, price of alternative goods, number of sellers, taxes or subsidies, and prices of resources for the supply curve.) Then indicate whether equilibrium price and equilibrium output should go up (↑) or down (↓) because of the shift in demand or supply. Before looking up the article in the text, see if you can answer these questions just by reading the headline of the article.

Figure 22.6

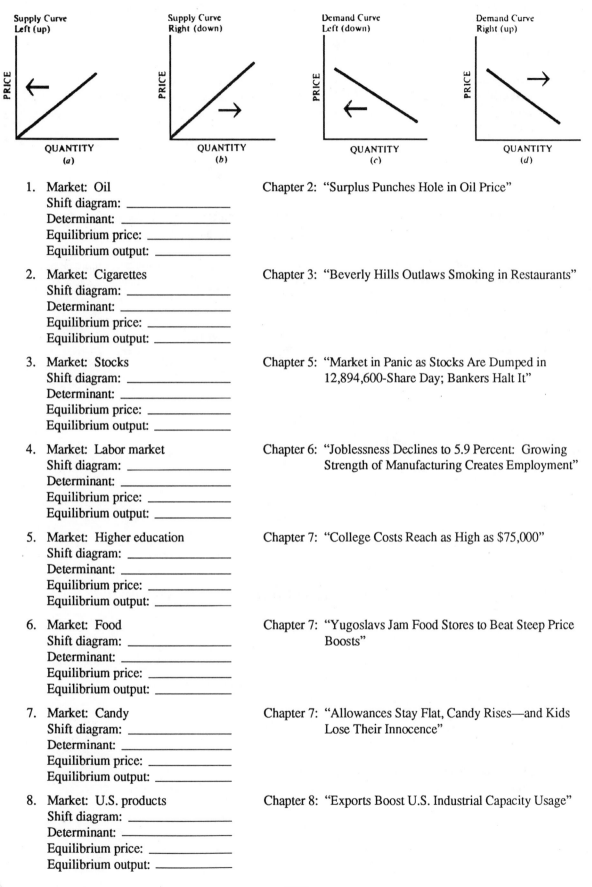

Supply Curve Left (up)	Supply Curve Right (down)	Demand Curve Left (down)	Demand Curve Right (up)

1. Market: Oil
   Shift diagram: _____
   Determinant: _____
   Equilibrium price: _____
   Equilibrium output: _____

   Chapter 2: "Surplus Punches Hole in Oil Price"

2. Market: Cigarettes
   Shift diagram: _____
   Determinant: _____
   Equilibrium price: _____
   Equilibrium output: _____

   Chapter 3: "Beverly Hills Outlaws Smoking in Restaurants"

3. Market: Stocks
   Shift diagram: _____
   Determinant: _____
   Equilibrium price: _____
   Equilibrium output: _____

   Chapter 5: "Market in Panic as Stocks Are Dumped in 12,894,600-Share Day; Bankers Halt It"

4. Market: Labor market
   Shift diagram: _____
   Determinant: _____
   Equilibrium price: _____
   Equilibrium output: _____

   Chapter 6: "Joblessness Declines to 5.9 Percent: Growing Strength of Manufacturing Creates Employment"

5. Market: Higher education
   Shift diagram: _____
   Determinant: _____
   Equilibrium price: _____
   Equilibrium output: _____

   Chapter 7: "College Costs Reach as High as $75,000"

6. Market: Food
   Shift diagram: _____
   Determinant: _____
   Equilibrium price: _____
   Equilibrium output: _____

   Chapter 7: "Yugoslavs Jam Food Stores to Beat Steep Price Boosts"

7. Market: Candy
   Shift diagram: _____
   Determinant: _____
   Equilibrium price: _____
   Equilibrium output: _____

   Chapter 7: "Allowances Stay Flat, Candy Rises—and Kids Lose Their Innocence"

8. Market: U.S. products
   Shift diagram: _____
   Determinant: _____
   Equilibrium price: _____
   Equilibrium output: _____

   Chapter 8: "Exports Boost U.S. Industrial Capacity Usage"

9. Market: Manufacturing goods

   Shift diagram: _____
   Determinant: _____
   Equilibrium price: _____
   Equilibrium output: _____

Chapter 9: "Plants Plan December Shutdowns as the
   Recession Spreads Rapidly"

10. Market: Money

   Shift diagram: _____
   Determinant: _____
   Equilibrium price: _____
   Equilibrium output: _____

Chapter 12: "Fed, Banks Increase Key Interest Rates:
   Moves Expected to Boost Cost of Borrowing"

Exercise 3

When the hand-held calculator was invented in the 1970s, the market responded in competitive fashion. There were numerous producers, prices were forced down as firms entered the market, and so on. This exercise is based on that experience.

Figure 22.7 presents the cost curves that are relevant to a firm's production decision, and Figure 22.8 shows the market demand and supply curves for the calculator market. Use Figures 22.7 and 22.8 and the knowledge of cost curves that you have gained from the text to answer Problems 1–9.

Figure 22.7
Firm

Figure 22.8
Market (all firms)

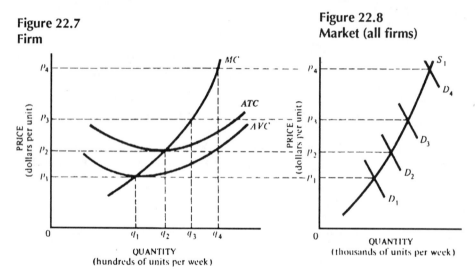

1. If the market demand-and-supply curves are S_1 and D_1, the market price will be:
   (a) P_1.
   (b) P_2.
   (c) P_3.
   (d) P_4.

2. Suppose the demand for calculators shifts to D_4. This shift might be caused by:
   (a) An increase in the number of consumers.
   (b) An increase in consumers' incomes.
   (c) A rise in the price of a substitute good.
   (d) All of the above.

3. If the demand curve is at D_4, the quantity supplied by the *firm* will be:
   (a) q_1.
   (b) q_2.
   (c) q_3.
   (d) q_4.

4. Suppose a recession results in a shift in the demand curve for calculators to D_1. Then the *firm* will produce:

(a) q_1.

    (b) q_2.

    (c) q_3.

    (d) q_4.

5. The firm will continue to produce some output until demand declines enough to drive price to:

    (a) p_1.

    (b) p_2.

    (c) p_3.

    (d) p_4.

6. At prices below p_1, the firm will shut down (produce no output) because:

    (a) Its loss will be less than if it produces at any level of output.

    (b) Its loss will be limited to its fixed costs.

    (c) Total revenue is less than total variable cost.

    (d) All of the above are the case.

7. The fact that the quantity supplied by the firm changes whenever the market price changes indicates that:

    (a) The firm is a price setter.

    (b) The firm is a price taker.

    (c) The firm has monopoly power.

    (d) The firm has no control over the quantity it produces.

8. Since the firm will not produce any output if the market price falls below p_1:

    (a) The firm's supply curve is that part of the MC curve above the minimum point on the ATC curve.

    (b) The average variable cost curve is the firm's supply curve.

    (c) The average total cost curve is the firm's supply curve.

    (d) The firm's supply curve is that part of its marginal cost curve that lies above its average variable cost curve.

9. If the price is p_3, and the demand curve is D_3:

    (a) Returns to the firm are below average, and firms will leave the industry.

    (b) Returns are above average, and new firms will have an incentive to enter the industry.

    (c) Returns are about average, and there is no incentive for firms to move into or out of the industry.

    (d) We really can't say without more information.

Exercise 4

The following exercise shows how long-run equilibrium is related to the shape of the average cost curves associated with different technologies. By doing the exercise you will learn how to do the problem at the end of Chapter 22 in the text.

1. In Figure 22.9, the short-run average cost curves for the only two technologies for producing cement are shown. Draw in the long-run average cost curve for cement production and label it *LRAC*.

Figure 22.9

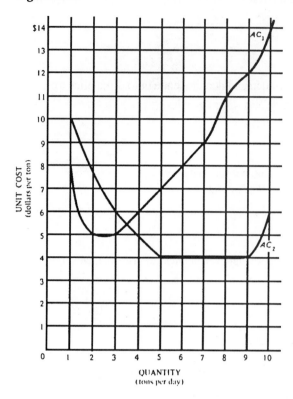

QUANTITY
(tons per day)

2. What would be the *long*-run equilibrium price if this is a competitive market? (Assume all firms have the same cost curves.)
   (a) $3.20 per ton.
   (b) $4.00 per ton.
   (c) $5.00 per ton.
   (d) $3.00 per ton.

3. What would be the minimum profit-maximizing output for the typical firm if the cement market were in long-run equilibrium?
   (a) 0 tons per day.
   (b) 2 tons per day.
   (c) 4 tons per day.
   (d) 5 tons per day.

4. If the long-run price in the market were to fall to $4 and half of the firms were using Technology 1 and half were using Technology 2, firms using Technology 1 would:
   (a) Shut down.
   (b) Exit.
   (c) Enter.
   (d) Increase production.

5. Which technology would firms use in the long run?
   (a) Technology 1.
   (b) Technology 2.
   (c) Neither, because there would not be enough profit.
   (d) A mix of both.

6. If the price in the long run were artificially supported by the government at $12:
   (a) The firms in the market would expand production regardless of the technology they were using.
   (b) There would be increased entry of firms into the cement market.
   (c) Both a and b would be the case.

7. What would be the maximum number of firms that a competitive market could support if at the long-run equilibrium price the quantity demanded were 1,000 tons per day? _____

Exercise 5

Many newspapers provide information from competitive markets, such as the want ads, market prices, and advertising. By using one of the articles in the text, this exercise will show the kind of information to look for to determine if a market is competitive or not. If your professor makes a newspaper assignment for this chapter, this exercise will provide an example of how to do it.

Reread the article in Chapter 31 entitled "Teachers in Greater Demand" from the *New York Times*. Then find an example of each of the following types of information, which can help verify that a market is truly competitive:

1. *Structural characteristics*. What indicates that a large number of teachers are in the teaching market?

2. *Conduct*. What passage indicates entry to or exit from the teaching market? Find another passage that suggests lack of market power (in other words, price taking not price making).

3. *Performance*. What sentence indicates the efficient working of the market mechanism characteristic of competitive markets?

4. *Market boundaries*. Which of the following best characterizes the market boundaries of the teaching market?
   (a) It appears to be strictly a local market.
   (b) It appears to be a regional market.
   (c) It appears to be a national market.
   (d) It appears to be an international market.

5. What phrase provides a clue about the extent of market boundaries?

Common Errors

The first statement in each "common error" below is incorrect. Each incorrect statement is followed by a corrected version and an explanation.

1. The demand curve for a competitive market is flat. WRONG!

   The demand curve for a competitive firm is flat. RIGHT!

   The error above results from failure to distinguish between the market and the firm. Review Exercise 1 if this distinction is not clear.

2. Competitive firms do not make profits. WRONG!

   Competitive firms can make economic profits in the short run. RIGHT!

   In the long run, firms enter an industry and compete away economic profits. In the short run, a change in demand or supply may cause price to change and may bestow temporary economic profits on a firm. In the personal computer example in the text, technological changes shifted the supply curve and provided temporary profits.

   Be careful! Always distinguish short-run profit-maximizing production rates and price levels from long-run equilibrium production rates and price levels. While industries have a tendency to move toward long-run equilibrium, they may never reach it because of shocks that buffet a market.

3. Since competitive firms make zero profits in the long run, they cannot pay their stockholders and so they should shut down. WRONG!

   Since competitive firms make zero economic profits in the long run, they are able to pay all factors of production, including the skill of entrepreneurs, to keep the firms in existence. RIGHT!

333

Be careful! Keep the accounting and economic definitions of such words as "profit" separate and distinct. Keep movements along the supply curve (firms increase production rates) separate from shifts of the supply curve (firms enter or exit). Avoid confusing short-run responses (increasing production rates in existing plants) with long-run responses (entry or exit).

■ ANSWERS ■

Key-Term Review

1. marginal cost (*MC*)
2. short-run competitive equilibrium
3. long-run competitive equilibrium
4. equilibrium price
5. competitive market
6. market mechanism
7. shift of supply

8. economic profit
9. profit per unit
10. market supply
11. average total cost (*ATC*)
12. efficiency (technical)
13. opportunity cost
14. production decision

15. market power
16. competitive firm
17. barriers to entry
18. shutdown point
19. marginal cost pricing
20. marginal revenue

True or False

1. F	5. T	9. T	12. F	15. T	18. T
2. T	6. F	10. T	13. T	16. T	19. F
3. T	7. F	11. T	14. F	17. F	20. T
4. F	8. F				

Multiple Choice

1. c	4. d	7. d	10. b	12. c	14. d
2. d	5. d	8. d	11. c	13. b	15. a
3. b	6. d	9. c			

Problems and Applications

Exercise 1

1. **Figure 22.1 answer**

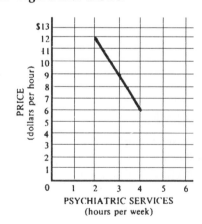

2. **Figure 22.2 answer**

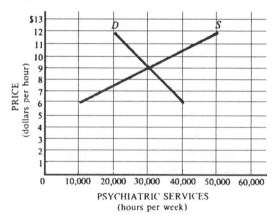

3. **Figure 22.3 answer**

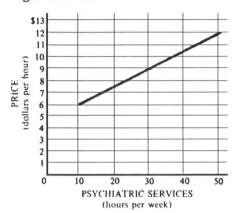

PRICE (dollars per hour)

PSYCHIATRIC SERVICES
(hours per week)

4. See line S in Figure 22.2 answer.
5. b
6. No

7. **Table 22.1 answer**

Hours per week	Price
0	$9
30	9

8. **Figure 22.4 answer**

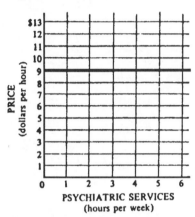

PRICE (dollars per hour)

PSYCHIATRIC SERVICES
(hours per week)

9. c
10. No

11. **Table 22.2 answer**

Hours per week	Price
0	$9
30	9

12. **Figure 22.5 answer**

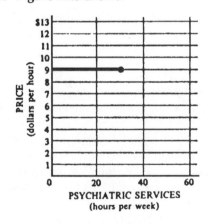

PRICE (dollars per hour)

PSYCHIATRIC SERVICES
(hours per week)

13. c
14. No
15. No

Exercise 2

1. c, Number of buyers, weather, summer travel demand, ↓, ↓
2. c, Number of buyers, ↓, ↓
3. b, Expectations and number of sellers, ↓, ↑
4. d, Number of buyers and income, ↑, ↑
5. a, Not enough information, ↑, ↓
6. d, Expectations (about future prices), ↑, ↑
7. a, Not enough information, ↑, ↓
8. d, Income (exchange rate change increases foreign income measured in dollars), ↑, ↑

9. a, Expectations (about effects of recession), ↑, ↓
10. a, Expectations (about inflation and dollar), ↑, ↓

Exercise 3

1. a	4. a	7. b
2. d	5. a	8. d
3. d	6. d	9. b

Exercise 4

1. **Figure 22.9 answer**

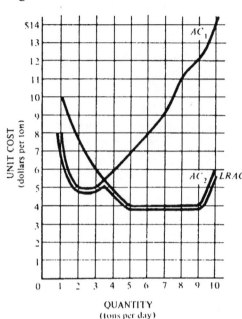

2. b
3. d
4. b
5. b
6. c

7. The minimum size of each firm would be 5 tons per day. With 1,000 tons per day being demanded, 200 firms (=1,000/5) can exist in the market.

Exercise 5

1. "For some years there has been an oversupply of teachers." The plural form, "teachers," indicates more than one. Furthermore, the lack of names of specific teachers or groups of teachers suggests the article is talking about many teachers.
2. The passage "despite the fact that many teachers have retired or grown discouraged by low pay and abandoned the profession" indicates exit from the market. The passage "Many college students were warned away or denied the chance to take education courses needed to qualify for teaching" implicitly refers to the entry process for new teachers. The fact that teachers are retiring because of the low pay (noted in the quotation above) also suggests that teachers have no control over their pay.
3. "All this has engendered a feeling of optimism about teaching as a career, not only concerning job openings but also the prospect of higher salaries." The salaries are seen as rising in the future because of the shortage of teachers beginning in the year the article was written. In other words market supply and demand are determining salaries, thus eliminating inefficiencies resulting from shortages or surpluses. This kind of efficient market mechanism is expected in competitive markets.
4. c
5. No specific phrase indicates the extent of market boundaries. However, there is no mention of foreign countries, which suggests that the market could be national, regional, or local. There is also no mention of a specific region or locality, which suggests the article is talking about education nationally. However, the absence of information on specific regions or localities is not enough to say definitely the market is national.

Chapter 23
Monopoly

Quick Review

In this chapter we are concerned with monopoly—a market structure at the other end of the spectrum from a competitive market. In the former there is a single producer. In the latter, as we learned in the previous chapter, there are a larger number of producers.

Let's focus on the following questions:

- What price will a monopolist charge for his output?
- How much output will he produce?
- Are consumers better off or worse off when only one firm controls the entire market?

The key to each of these questions rests with market power. Market power is the ability to influence significantly the market price of goods and services. The extreme case of market power is monopoly. The demand curve facing the monopolist and the market demand curve are identical. Accordingly, the firm must pay heed to the effect of increased production on the price at which its output may be sold. To sell larger quantities of output in a given time period, it must lower the price of its product. Such price reductions cause marginal revenue and price to diverge. A firm without market power has no such problem: it may sell as much output as it desires at the prevailing market price.

Like all profit-maximizing firms, a monopolist will produce at that rate of output at which marginal revenue equals marginal cost. The monopolist will attain a higher level of profit than a competitive firm because of its ability to equate industry (its own) marginal revenues and marginal costs. By contrast, a competitive firm ends up equating marginal cost and price, since it has no control over the market supply, market demand, or equilibrium price.

The higher profits attained by a monopolist will attract envious entrepreneurs. A market-power position and its related profits can be maintained only if barriers to entry keep other firms out of the market.

Monopolists charge a price higher than marginal cost. They also fail to fully utilize available resources. Finally, monopolists do not necessarily pick the least-cost technologies for production. Competitive firms do achieve these economic objectives.

The principal arguments in favor of market power focus on the alleged ability of large firms to pursue long-term research and development, on the incentives implicit in the opportunity to attain market power, and on the greater efficiency that larger firms may attain. The first two arguments are weakened by the fact that competitive firms are under much greater pressure to innovate and *can stay ahead in the profit game only if they do so*. Nevertheless, larger firms may be able to achieve economies of scale—lower minimum average costs brought about by a larger scale of plant—and thus may be considered desirable on the grounds of efficiency. A firm with economies of scale over the entire range of market output is called a natural monopoly. Larger firms are not necessarily more efficient, however, since either constant returns to scale or even diseconomies of scale may arise as firm size increases. Few firms are natural monopolies.

Recently economists have investigated the restraining power of *potential* competition in markets where the barriers to entry are not too high. This idea is included in the concept of "contestable markets."

Learning Objectives

After reading Chapter 23 and doing the following exercises, you should:	True or false	Multiple choice	Problems and applications	Common errors	Pages in the text
1. Know the meaning of market power.		18	5		564–565
2. Know why a monopolist has market power and a downward-sloping demand curve and why price and marginal revenue diverge.	13	7	5	3	565–567
3. Be able to show the relationship between the market demand and individual demand curve for a monopolist.	14	10, 26–28	2		565–566
4. Know the difference between marginal cost pricing for a competitive firm and profit maximization for a monopoly.	6	8,11,12		2	575–576
5. Be able to determine a monopolist's most profitable rate of production.	18	1,19–21	3	1	567–568
6. Be able to show why monopoly typically results in higher profits, less output, and higher prices than would occur in a competitive market.	2,8,13	4,13			568–574
7. Be able to contrast a competitive industry's long-run behavior with that of a monopoly.	1,15, 18,19	2,5	1		574–575
8. Be able to describe the advantages and disadvantages of monopoly and competition.	4,5,7, 17	3	5		576–578
9. Be able to distinguish price discrimination from other types of pricing.	3,10	9,22–25	4		578–579
10. Be able to distinguish economies of scale from constant returns to scale and diseconomies of scale.	9,11,16	16,17		4	581
11. Be able to explain the differences between the normal monopoly model and that of a natural monopoly.		14,15			581–582
12. Know how and why antitrust policy is used to control monopoly.	12	6			584–588
13. Understand the idea of "contestable" markets.	20–22	29–31	5		582–583

Key-Term Review

Review the following terms; if you are not sure of the meaning of any term, write out the definition and check it against the Glossary in the text.

average total cost (*ATC*)
barriers to entry
contestable market
economies of scale
investment decision
marginal cost pricing
marginal revenue (*MR*)

market power
monopoly
natural monopoly
price discrimination
price elasticity of demand
production decision
profit-maximization rule

Fill in the blank following each of the statements below with the appropriate term from the list above.

1. A firm with no competitors is a _____, and, since such firms can control price, they have _____.

1. _____

   _____

2. A one-unit increase in production will change total revenue by an amount called _____.

2. _____

3. A competitive firm will increase its production rate until price equals marginal cost. Such behavior is called _____.

3. _____

4. To keep out potential competitors, a monopoly firm must erect _____.

4. _____

5. When a firm has _____, then with increased production there will be a decline in _____.

5. _____

   _____

6. If average total costs decline at all levels of production, the market is a _____.

6. _____

7. It suddenly becomes profitable for a firm to export goods to a foreign country. Even though it would be cheaper to produce abroad, the firm does not have time to build a foreign plant, so it chooses to make the goods for export with existing domestic plant and equipment. This choice is its _____.

7. _____

8. At the same time, the firm chooses to start constructing foreign plant and equipment to begin production abroad as soon as possible. This choice is its _____.

8. _____

9. Because there are no laws against the practice in the foreign country, consumers there are charged different prices for the same product. This practice is called _____.

9. _____

10. Such conduct is possible because each consumer has a different _____.

10. _____

11. While only competitive firms use marginal cost pricing, both competitive firms and monopolists use the _____.

11. _____

12. A _____ is a market in which the behavior of even imperfectly competitive firms is constrained by potential competition.

12. _____

True or False: *Circle your choice.*

T F 1. Since competitive firms can sell unlimited quantities of output at the prevailing price, they can affect the market price of a good or service.

T F 2. A monopolist can pick any point on the market supply curve and designate it as a new equilibrium.

T F 3. The more elastic a demand curve is, the more consumers are willing and able to reduce purchases in response to a price increase.

T F 4. Monopolists have a clear advantage over competitive markets in pursuing research and development and receiving the full benefit of research efforts.

T F 5. Absolute expenditures on research and development give an adequate perspective on the incentives that industries have to engage in research and development.

T F 6. Monopolists maximize profits at the output level at which price equals marginal cost.

T F 7. In competitive markets, firms can make profits from innovation because of the amount of time it takes for other competitive firms to catch up.

T F 8. Barriers to entry prevent the use of an invention in a monopolistic market from accruing to firms other than the monopolist.

T F 9. A firm may achieve economies of scale by increasing production in a given plant.

T F 10. Price discrimination can occur because of the differences in demand curves among buyers.

T F 11. The term "constant returns to scale" means that no matter how large a plant is built, the minimum average cost of production will still be the same.

T F 12. By prosecuting illegal anticompetitive market behavior, the antitrust agencies make monopolists competitive.

T F 13. The monopolist has a flat demand curve because of high barriers to entry.

T F 14. The demand curve for the monopolist is exactly the same as the market demand curve.

T F 15. Since both monopolists and competitive firms maximize profits at the output level at which marginal revenue equals marginal cost, monopolists and competitive markets with the same marginal cost curves and demand curves will produce the same output.

T F 16. Diseconomies of scale occur as a firm increases output, and its fixed costs are spread over greater production, causing average fixed costs to decrease in the short run.

T F 17. Monopolists redistribute income when they raise prices and profits above competitive levels.

T F 18. Monopolists shut down in the short run when they are taking losses even though they are covering short-run average variable costs.

T F 19. Firms have an incentive to enter an industry when economic profits are being earned in that industry. Increased entry of new firms, however, reduces prices and profits.

T F 20. The theory of contestable markets focuses on market behavior rather than market structure.

T F 21. Barriers to entry are significant in determining how "contestable" a market is.

T F 22. When markets are contestable, firms *must* behave like pure competitors, even though the market structure is imperfectly competitive.

Multiple Choice: *Select the correct answer.*

_____ 1. In monopoly and competition, a firm should expand production when:
  (a) Price is below marginal cost.
  (b) Price is above marginal cost.
  (c) Marginal revenue is below marginal cost.
  (d) Marginal revenue is above marginal cost.

_____ 2. A monopolist with many plants produces less than would be produced if all of the plants were competing with one another in a competitive market:
   (a) Because the demand curve slopes downward for the monopolistic firm but not for the competitive firms.
   (b) Because the demand curve slopes downward for the monopolistic market and for the competitive market.
   (c) Because the marginal revenue curve is below the demand curve for the monopolistic market but not for the competitive firms.
   (d) For all of the above reasons.

_____ 3. Monopoly may be considered more desirable than competition:
   (a) Because the monopolist has more incentive to keep costs down.
   (b) Because in polluting industries, monopoly is the best way of restricting output below the level of production that would be reached under competition.
   (c) Because monopoly—as, for example, that which comes from the control of patents—is the best way of rewarding inventive efforts.
   (d) Because diseconomies of scale can only be realized by a single firm given the size of the market.

_____ 4. When a monopoly continues to make above-normal profits in the long run, you can be sure that:
   (a) It produces more efficiently than a competitive market can.
   (b) Barriers to entry prevent other firms from competing away the above-normal profits.
   (c) There is a conspiracy between the government and the monopolist to maintain high prices.
   (d) It has an inelastic demand curve, which gives it greater revenues.

_____ 5. Monopoly is said to be inefficient when:
   (a) Price in the long run is not equal to the lowest point of the long-run average cost curve.
   (b) The monopolist does not pick the optimum size of plant because it can maximize profit with a plant of a different size.
   (c) The monopolist does not produce at an output level at which long-run marginal cost equals the minimum of long-run average cost.
   (d) All of the above are the case.

_____ 6. Which of the following is most likely *not* a monopolist?
   (a) The only doctor in a small community.
   (b) A large soft-drink firm such as Coca-Cola.
   (c) The electric power company in your area.
   (d) The water company in your area.

_____ 7. A monopolist has market power:
   (a) Because it faces a downward-sloping demand curve.
   (b) Because when it produces an extra unit of output, it must lower its price on all of its production.
   (c) Because its marginal revenue curve is below its demand curve.
   (d) For all of the above reasons.

_____ 8. Which of the following is the same for monopoly and competition under the same costs?
   (a) The goal of maximizing profits.
   (b) Production levels.
   (c) Long-run economic profits.
   (d) Efficiency of production.

_____ 9. If a monopolist has inelastic demand for its product it can:
   (a) Raise total revenue by lowering price.
   (b) Raise total revenue by raising price.
   (c) Lower total costs by lowering prices.
   (d) Lower total costs by raising production rates.

10. The demand curve and marginal revenue curve are different for a monopoly:
    (a) Because the supply curve is upward sloping for monopoly.
    (b) Because the marginal cost curve is upward sloping for monopoly.
    (c) Because lower revenues due to lower prices must be subtracted from revenue gains due to the greater output.
    (d) For all of the above reasons.

11. Which of the following rules will always be satisfied when a firm maximizes profit?
    (a) p = lowest level of long-run average costs.
    (b) $p = MC$.
    (c) $MR = MC$.
    (d) $p = AC$.

12. The supply curve for a monopolist:
    (a) Slopes upward.
    (b) Is the same as the marginal cost curve.
    (c) Is the same as the marginal revenue curve.
    (d) Doesn't exist.

13. Which of the following is *not* a barrier to entry into a monopoly?
    (a) Profits of the monopolist.
    (b) Advertising.
    (c) Patents.
    (d) Difficulty of obtaining resources.

14. Which of the following types of monopoly always achieves economies of scale?
    (a) A pure monopoly.
    (b) A discriminating monopoly.
    (c) A natural monopoly.
    (d) None of the above.

15. Which of the following types of monopoly has market power?
    (a) Pure monopoly.
    (b) Discriminating monopoly.
    (c) Natural monopoly.
    (d) All of the above.

Choose among the four diagrams presented in Figure 23.1 to answer Questions 16–21.

Figure 23.1

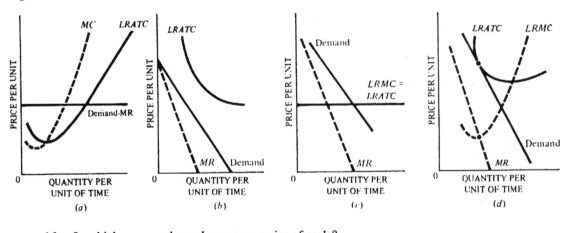

16. In which case are there always economies of scale?

17. In which case are there constant returns to scale?

18. In which case does the firm have no market power?

342

_____19. In which case can a monopolist make only negative profits?

_____20. In which case is the firm making zero profits when it maximizes profits?

_____21. Average profits are computed by:
    (a) $(TR - TC)/q$
    (b) $AR - MC$.
    (c) Demand curve - marginal cost curve.
    (d) $MR - AC$.

In Questions 22–25, decide what type of pricing is being used.

_____22. Farmers plant a particular crop long before they know what price they will receive for it.
    (a) Monopoly pricing (price making).
    (b) Competitive pricing (price taking).
    (c) Price discrimination.
    (d) None of the above.

_____23. Cities often provide their own sewer and water services. Rates are often determined by a board.
    (a) Monopoly pricing (price making).
    (b) Competitive pricing (price taking).
    (c) Price discrimination.
    (d) None of the above.

_____24. A family doctor charges patients for a particular service on the basis of what the patient can afford to pay.
    (a) Monopoly pricing (price making).
    (b) Competitive pricing (price taking).
    (c) Price discrimination.
    (d) None of the above.

_____25. Airlines offer various discount fares, with restrictions on time of departure, advance reservations, and the like.
    (a) Monopoly pricing (price making).
    (b) Competitive pricing (price taking).
    (c) Price discrimination.
    (d) None of the above.

Use the three diagrams in Figure 23.2 to answer Questions 26–28.

Figure 23.2

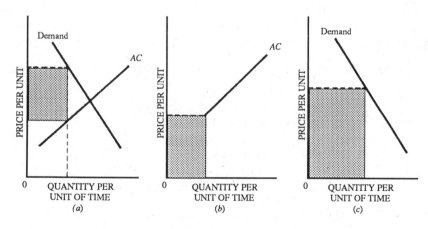

_____26. The shaded area in diagram *a* represents:
  (a) Total revenue.
  (b) Total cost.
  (c) Total profit.
  (d) None of the above.

_____27. The shaded area in diagram *b* represents:
  (a) Total revenue.
  (b) Total cost.
  (c) Total profit.
  (d) None of the above.

_____28. The shaded in area in diagram *c* represents:
  (a) Total revenue.
  (b) Total cost.
  (c) Total profit.
  (d) None of the above.

_____29. The U.S. automobile market is thought to be:
  (a) A monopoly.
  (b) Perfectly competitive.
  (c) Contestable.
  (d) None of the above.

_____30. The theory of contestable markets relies on:
  (a) Market behavior.
  (b) Potential entry.
  (c) Market structure.
  (d) All of the above.

_____31. In the U.S. automobile market, the major restraint on market power is:
  (a) Antitrust legislation.
  (b) Antitrust enforcement.
  (c) Foreign competition.
  (d) None of the above.

Problems and Applications

Exercise 1

The following table should help you to summarize what you have learned (in Chapters 20–23) about the difference between the long run and short run. Insert the letter designating each of the following responses into its proper space in Table 23.1.

a. production
b. shuts down
c. variable costs only
d. investment
e. decreasing short-run average costs
f. lowest point of short-run average variable cost curve
g. economies of scale
h. goes out of business (exits)
i. lowest point of long-run average cost curve
j. all factors are variable
k. existing firms increase production rates
l. some factors are fixed
m. fixed and variable costs
n. new firms enter (if no barriers to entry)

Table 23.1
Short- and long-run decision making

	The short run	The long run
Type of decision	_____	_____
Variability of factors	_____	_____
Types of costs	_____	_____
If prices fall below	_____	_____
Then the firm	_____	_____
If prices rise above minimum average total cost, then	_____	_____
A declining average cost curve means there are	_____	_____

Exercise 2

This exercise shows graphically how to represent total revenues, total cost, and total profit on the basis of average revenue and average cost curves.

1. In Table 23.2, the total revenue and average cost are presented for the Black Jack Playing Card Company, which has a monopoly on the production of playing cards. Fill in the information on average revenue and average costs for the production levels shown in Table 23.2. In Figure 23.3, draw and label the average cost curve and demand (average revenue) curves based on Table 23.2. (Use straight lines for both curves.)

Table 23.2
Revenue and cost from producing and selling cards

Quantity of cards (in millions of decks per month)	Revenue		Cost	
	Total (millions of dollars per month)	Average (dollars per deck)	Total (millions of dollars per month)	Average (dollars per deck)
0	$ 0.0	$_____	$ 0.0	$_____
4	6.4	_____	2.8	_____
10	10.0	_____	10.0	_____
20	0.0	_____	30.0	_____

Figure 23.3
Total profit from average revenue and average cost

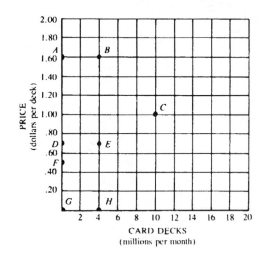

2. In Figure 23.3, shade with vertical lines the total revenue that the Black Jack Playing Card Company would earn by producing and selling 4 million decks of cards per month.

3. Which of the following line segments represents average revenue from selling 4 million decks of cards?
   (a) *BE*.
   (b) *EH*.
   (c) *BH*.
   (d) *AF*.
   (e) None of the above.

4. In Figure 23.3, shade with light horizontal lines the total cost that the Black Jack Playing Card Company would incur to produce 4 million decks of cards per month.

5. Which of the following line segments represents the average cost of producing 4 million decks of cards?
   (a) *BE*.
   (b) *EH*.
   (c) *BH*.
   (d) *AF*.
   (e) None of the above.

6. Which of the following rectangles in Figure 23.3 represents total profit?
   (a) *ABHG* (total shaded area).
   (b) *ABED* (non-cross-hatched shaded area).
   (c) *DEHG* (cross-hatched area).
   (d) None of the above.

7. Which of the following line segments represents the average profit from producing and selling 4 million decks of cards?
   (a) *BE*.
   (b) *EH*.
   (c) *BH*.
   (d) *AF*.
   (e) None of the above.

8. Compute each of the following:
   (a) The area of *ABHG* (total shaded area) in Figure 23.3 under the demand curve.
   (b) The total revenue from selling 4 million decks of cards.
   (c) The length of line segment *BH* multiplied by the length of line segment *GH* in Figure 23.3.
   (d) The average revenue multiplied by the quantity sold (4 million decks of cards).

   Does each of these methods result in the same total revenue calculation? _____

9. Compute each of the following:
   (a) The area of *DEHG* (cross-hatched area) under the average cost curve in Figure 23.3.
   (b) The total cost from selling 4 million decks of cards.
   (c) The length of line segment *EH* multiplied by the length of line segment *GH* in Figure 23.3.
   (d) The average cost multiplied by the quantity sold (4 million decks of cards).

   Does each of these methods result in the same total cost calculation? _____

10. Compute each of the following:
    (a) The area of *ABED* (non-cross-hatched area) between the demand and average cost curves in Figure 23.3.
    (b) The total profit from selling 4 million decks of cards.
    (c) The area *ABHG* (total shaded area) minus area *DEHG* (cross-hatched area) in Figure 23.3.
    (d) The total revenue minus total cost from producing and selling 4 million decks of cards.
    (e) The length of line segment *BE* multiplied by the length of line segment *GH* in Figure 23.3.
    (f) The average profit multiplied by the quantity sold (4 million decks of cards).

    Does each of these methods result in the same total profit calculation? _____

Exercise 3

This exercise is a review of the cost and revenue formulas and gives further experience with profit maximization.

1. Match the algebraic formulas at the right with the equivalent economic terms at the left.

   _____ fixed cost (*FC*)   a. VC/q
   _____ average fixed cost (*AFC*) b. $TR - TC$
   _____ variable cost (*VC*)   c. $FC + VC$
   _____ average variable cost (*AVC*) d. same as total cost at zero production rate
   _____ total revenue (*TR*)   e. $\Delta TC/\Delta q$
   _____ total cost (*TC*)   f. FC/q
   _____ average total cost (*ATC*) g. TC/q
   _____ profit   h. type of cost that is zero at a zero production rate
   _____ price (*p*)   i. $(TR - TC)/q$
   _____ marginal cost (*MC*)   j. $\Delta TR/\Delta q$
   _____ marginal revenue (*MR*)   k. $p \cdot q$ or TC + profit
   _____ average profit   l. TR/q

2. Table 23.3 shows the cost breakdown from projected income statements of the American Ferris Aluminum Company. It shows what costs would be at four levels of production. Using these data, fill in Table 23.4. (*Note:* If you do not remember how to sort fixed and variable costs, look at their definitions in the text. If you still have trouble, see Exercise 3, Chapter 20, in this study guide.)

Table 23.3
Cost of aluminum production, by category, at four production levels

	Aluminum production (tons per week)			
	0	1,000	2,000	3,000
Price (dollars per unit)	$ 120	$ 100	$ 80	$ 60
Cost (dollars per week):				
Production workers	0	15,000	30,000	90,000
Managers, maintenance, interest, and taxes	26,000	26,000	26,000	26,000
Leased equipment payments	34,000	34,000	34,000	34,000
Electricity and bauxite	0	25,000	60,000	120,000

Table 23.4
Costs and revenues, American Ferris Aluminum Company, at four production levels

	Aluminum production (tons per week)			
Cost/Revenue	0	1,000	2,000	3,000
Fixed costs (dollars per week)	$_____	$_____	$_____	$_____
Variable costs (dollars per week)	_____	_____	_____	_____
Average variable cost (dollars per ton)	_____	_____	_____	_____
Total cost (dollars per week)	_____	_____	_____	_____
Marginal cost (dollars per ton)	_____	_____	_____	_____
Average total cost (dollars per ton)	_____	_____	_____	_____
Total revenue (dollars per week)	_____	_____	_____	_____
Marginal revenue (dollars per ton)	_____	_____	_____	_____
Profit (dollars per week)	_____	_____	_____	_____

3. In order to draw a demand curve, you need to have a demand schedule that relates:
   (a) Total revenue to total cost.
   (b) The production rate to each price level.
   (c) The profit to each level of production.
   (d) The marginal cost at each level of production.

4. Using your computations in Table 23.4, graph the demand, marginal revenue, average total cost, average variable cost, and marginal cost in Figure 23.4. In this problem you are dealing with discrete data, *so things don't work out exactly*. Still, you should be able to answer questions based on this graph. In Figure 23.4 your demand curve should pass through point A, your average total cost curve through point B, your marginal revenue curve through point C, your marginal cost curve through point D, and your average variable cost curve through point E.

Figure 23.4

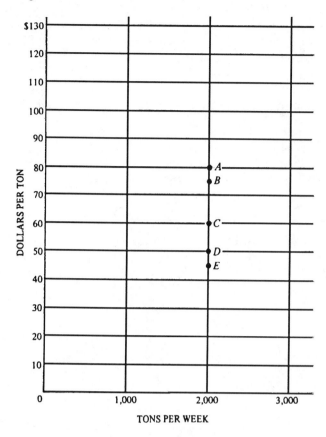

TONS PER WEEK

Profit maximization and representation

5. Which of the four production rates in Table 23.4 comes nearest to the point at which marginal revenue and marginal cost are equal? _____ This is the profit-maximizing production rate.

6. The profit-maximizing price for a monopolist:
   (a) Can be read on the y-axis horizontally from the demand curve, *below* the point where $MR = RC$.
   (b) Is equal to marginal revenue at the point at which $MR = MC$.
   (c) Can be read from the y-axis horizontally to the left of the point where $MR = MC$.
   (d) Can be read on the y-axis horizontally from the demand curve, *above* the point where $MR = MC$.

7. The profit-maximizing price for the monopolist pictured in Figure 23.4 is:
   (a) $100 per ton.
   (b) $80 per ton.
   (c) $70 per ton.
   (d) $60 per ton.

8. In Figure 23.4, shade in total profit at the profit-maximizing production rate. If you have done so correctly, the *area* that you have shaded equals which of the following?
   (a) Profits at a production rate of 2,000 tons per week in Table 23.4.
   (b) Total revenue minus total cost at all rates of production.
   (c) Average revenue minus average cost at all rates of production.
   (d) All of the above.

9. A firm shuts down when:
   (a) Variable costs are greater than total revenue.
   (b) Price equals marginal cost but is less than average variable cost.
   (c) Average revenue is below average variable cost regardless of the production level.
   (d) All of the above are the case.

10. What is the shutdown price for the American Ferris Aluminum Company? _____

Exercise 4

The media occasionally supply information on monopolies because a single firm's decision may be crucial to all firms buying from or selling to the monopolist. By using one of the articles in the text, this exercise will show the kind of information to look for to determine if a market is monopolized or not. If your professor makes a newspaper assignment for this chapter, this exercise will provide an example of how to do it.

Reread the article in Chapter 23 entitled "A New Era of Hot Competition." Then find an example of each of the following:

1. *Structural characteristics.* Which sentence indicates that there is only one firm in the market or that one or more of the following characterize the market: high barriers to entry, significant economies of scale, a product that is unique when compared to anything produced by anyone else, or the unavailability of substitutes?

2. *Conduct.* Which sentence indicates that AT&T was a price maker instead of price taker?

3. *Performance.* Which sentence indicates high, excessively high or rising prices?

4. The evidence in the article suggests that the telecommunications market is:
    (a) Strictly a local market.
    (b) A regional market.
    (c) A national market.
    (d) An international market.

5. What evidence in the article points to the extent of the market boundaries?

Common Errors

The first statement in each "common error" below is incorrect. Each incorrect statement is followed by a corrected version and an explanation.

1. The shaded area in Figure 23.5a shows total profits.

Figure 23.5a

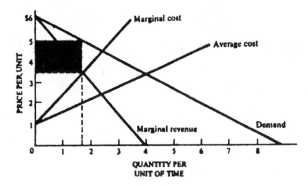

The shaded area in Figure 23.5*b* shows total profits.

Figure 23.5*b*

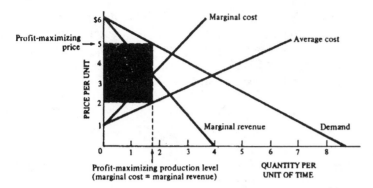

Notice that profit-maximizing production is found at the point where the *MR* curve intersects the *MC* curve. But *after* finding the profit-maximizing output level, forget about *MR* = *MC*. When you're finding profits themselves, don't use marginal curves; use the *average* curves. Simply find the difference between the demand curve (which is also the average revenue curve) and the average cost curve. This procedure gives you average profit. Then shade in everything to the left of the average profit until the *y*-axis is reached.

Here's a little rule to keep things straight:

- Use marginal curves to find profit-maximizing production.
- Use average curves to find profits.

2. Monopolists have supply curves. WRONG!

Monopolists have marginal cost curves, but not supply curves. RIGHT!

The marginal cost indicates the quantity that a competitive firm will supply at a given price. (*Remember:* Price equals marginal cost for the competitive firm.) But we cannot tell what a monopolist will supply at a given price by looking at the marginal cost curve. We need to know marginal revenue and therefore the demand curve before we can tell what quantity the firm will supply. (*Remember:* Marginal cost equals marginal revenue when profits are maximized.)

Be careful! Do not label the marginal cost curve of a monopolist (or any noncompetitive firm) as a "supply" curve in your diagrams.

3. A monopolist wishes to be on the inelastic part of the demand curve. WRONG!

A monopolist will operate on the elastic part of the demand curve. RIGHT!

If demand is inelastic, then the monopoly can usually decrease costs and increase revenues by cutting back production. This procedure means more profits. Remember the total-revenue test for the elasticity of demand. If demand is inelastic, then a firm can raise prices and get more revenues. Of course, with lower production rates, the firm also experiences lower costs. There is no doubt about it, if any firm is on the inelastic portion of its demand curve, it can make greater profits by raising prices.

4. When there are economies of scale, a firm can simply increase production rates in the short run and unit costs will decline. WRONG!

When there are economies of scale, a firm can choose a plant size designed for increased production rates at lower unit costs. RIGHT!

Economies of scale are not realized through production decisions in the short run. They are realized through investment decisions, by the choice of an optimal-sized plant for higher production rates. Scale refers to plant size or capacity, not to production rates within a plant of a given size. Think of economies of scale in terms of investment decisions concerning choices of optimal capacity for the long run, *not* production decisions concerning the lowest cost production in the short run.

■ ANSWERS ■

Key-Term Review

1. monopoly
   market power
2. marginal revenue
3. marginal cost pricing
4. barriers to entry
5. economies of scale
   average total cost (*ATC*)
6. natural monopoly
7. production decision
8. investment decision
9. price discrimination
10. price elasticity of demand
11. profit-maximization rule
12. contestable markets

True or False

1. F	5. F	9. F	13. F	17. T	20. T
2. F	6. F	10. T	14. T	18. F	21. T
3. T	7. T	11. T	15. F	19. T	22. F
4. T	8. T	12. F	16. F		

Multiple Choice

1. d	7. d	12. d	17. c	22. b	27. b
2. d	8. a	13. a	18. a	23. a	28. a
3. c	9. b	14. c	19. b	24. c	29. c
4. b	10. c	15. d	20. d	25. c	30. d
5. d	11. c	16. b	21. a	26. c	31. c
6. b					

Problems and Applications

Exercise 1

Table 23.1 answer

The short run	The long run
a	d
l	j
m	c
f	i
b	h
k	n
e	g

Exercise 2

1. Table 23.2 answer

Quantity	Average revenue	Average cost
—	$ —	$ —
4	1.60	0.70
10	1	1
20	0	1.50

Figure 23.3 answer

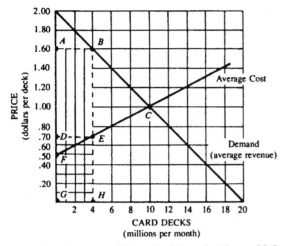

CARD DECKS
(millions per month)

2. See area with vertical lines in Figure 23.3 answer.
3. c
4. See cross-hatched shaded area in Figure 23.3 answer.
5. b
6. b
7. a
8. Each results in same estimate: $6.4 million per month.
   (= 4 million decks per month x $1.60 per deck)
9. Each results in same estimate: $2.8 million per month.
   (= 4 million decks per month x $0.70 per deck)
10. Each results in same estimate: $3.6 million per month.
    (= 4 million decks per month x $0.90 per deck)

Exercise 3

1. *FC*   d   *ATC*   g
    AFC   f   profit   b
    VC   h   *p*   l
    AVC   a   *MC*   e
    TR   k   *MR*   j
    TC   c   average profit   i

2. **Table 23.4 answer**

	Aluminum production (tons per week)			
	0	*1,000*	*2,000*	*3,000*
Fixed costs	$ 60,000	$ 60,000	$ 60,000	$ 60,000
Variable costs	0	40,000	90,000	210,000
Average variable cost	—	40	45	70
Total cost	60,000	100,000	150,000	270,000
Marginal cost	—	40	50	120
Average total cost	—	100	75	90
Total revenue	0	100,000	160,000	180,000
Marginal revenue	—	100	60	20
Profit	– 60,000	0	10,000	– 90,000

3. b
4. **Figure 23.4 answer**

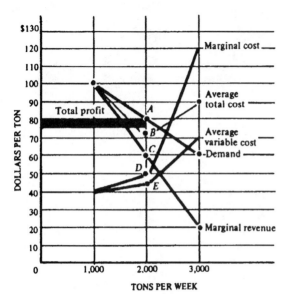

5. 2,000 tons per week
6. d
7. b
8. See Figure 23.3 answer; a
9. d
10. $40 per ton

Exercise 4

1. "For the past 50 years, nearly all the spaces on the board have been occupied by American Telephone and Telegraph Co."
2. "Consumers could benefit from sharply lower long-distance charges, which could fall by 40 percent or more by 1990." The sentence suggests that prices were artificially high under monopoly and would fall under competition.
3. The passage in Question 2 above applies here as well.
4. c   The market boundaries are national although part of the telecommunications business is local or regional.
5. The article is somewhat misleading when it discusses the telecommunications market being among the fastest growing in the "world." This is not equivalent to international market boundaries. Two paragraphs later the article is concerned with AT&T's being split up by the courts. An American court has jurisdiction within the United States but not outside the country. At this point in the article, the focus is implicitly restricted to the United States. The reference to the "split of AT&T's local and long-distance businesses" is the clue that several different markets exist in the telecommunications industry. Some of these markets are local, some regional, and some national.

Chapter 24
Imperfect Competition

Quick Review

Perfectly competitive markets and monopoly represent the two extremes of the spectrum that defines market structure. Between these two extremes most of the firms that we all recognize in the U.S. economy operate. In this chapter, we focus on the following questions:

- What determines how much market power a firm has?
- How do firms with some, but not total (monopoly) power set prices and output?
- How do imperfectly competitive firms compete for sales?
- What impact does imperfect competition have on prices, costs, and the mix of output?

Let's begin by describing imperfect competition. Imperfect competition is found in markets where individual suppliers (firms) have some independent influence on the price at which their output is sold. Two prominent forms of imperfect competition are called oligopoly and monopolistic competition.

An oligopoly is a market structure in which a few firms produce all or most of a particular good or service. Oligopolistic firms are interdependent. A basic conflict exists between the desire of each individual oligopolist to expand its market share and the *mutual* interest of all of the oligopolists in restricting total output so as to maximize industry profits. This conflict may erupt in mutually destructive behavior such as price cutting or cooperative behavior such as price leadership. Sometimes the cooperation is illegal, as in collusion that restrains trade or in price fixing.

A kinked demand curve illustrates a particular kind of oligopoly behavior. In this case, rival oligopolists match price reductions but not price increases. The oddly shaped marginal revenue curve that accompanies the kinked demand curve helps to explain the stickiness of prices in oligopolistic industries. Such barriers to entry as patents, high advertising costs, product differentiation, resource control, control of distribution outlets, and predatory price cutting prevent firms from entering an oligopolistic market and therefore permit the oligopolists to make above-normal profits in the long run.

In monopolistic competition many producers supply the market, so they are not interdependent, as are oligopolists. Each firm retains some independent control of its own price. The demand curve facing each firm slopes downward but is not kinked. Firms in monopolistic competition engage in product differentiation, seeking to maintain and expand "captive" markets (consumers who identify with their particular brand). In the long run, profits are eliminated in monopolistic competition by the entry of additional firms, but unlike perfect competitors, they do not attain minimum average costs.

Learning Objectives

After reading Chapter 24 and doing the following exercises, you should:	True or false	Multiple choice	Problems and applications	Common errors	Pages in the text
1. Know the four different types of market structures that correspond to different degrees of market power and know why they are different.	1,10	5–7, 16–19	1		592–593
2. Be able to describe the determinants of market power, particularly product differentiation.	4,20	9,15,19	4		594–608
3. Be able to give examples of the different types of market structures.	17	15			593–594
4. Know how oligopolies behave.	9			3	594–604,
5. Know the behavioral and market implications of the kinked demand curve.	2,3,5,7	10–13	3		599–602
6. Be able to demonstrate why imperfectly competitive firms may be inefficient, produce less than society desires, sell at higher prices than competitive firms, and make economic profits in the long run.		3,4,23, 27–29, 31		1	604–608
7. Know the distinguishing characteristics of oligopoly and monopolistic competition.	19	1,2,13	4	2	593
8. Be able to explain how oligopolies and monopolistically competitive firms maximize profits as compared to competitive firms.	6,11,14, 18,19	8,14,18, 21,22,26			594–604, 608–610
9. Show how monopolistically competitive firms behave.	8	20	2,4		608–610
10. Be able to describe the effects of nonprice competition.	15,16	20	4		611–612
11. Review Chapters 22 and 23 on market structure, cost curves, and economies of scale.	12,13	20,24,25, 30,32			

Key-Term Review

Review the following terms; if you are not sure of the meaning of any term, write out the definition and check it against the Glossary in the text.

collusion
contestable market
economic profit
law of demand
marginal cost pricing
marginal revenue (MR)
market share
monopolistic competition

monopoly
oligopoly
perfect competition
price leadership
product differentiation
profit-maximization rule
quantity demanded

Fill in the blank following each of the statements below with the appropriate term from the list above.

1. A market composed of few firms is an _____.   1. _____

2. If firms in such a market make explicit agreements to limit production, such behavior is called _____.   2. _____

3. An undeclared pattern in which one firm sets the price for the entire industry is called _____.   3. _____

4. The market power of a firm in such a market is determined by its _____.   4. _____

5. Because firms in this type of market have market power, unlike competitive firms, they do not practice _____.   5. _____

6. Nevertheless, all imperfectly competitive firms still set production at the level at which marginal cost equals _____.   6. _____

7. This is called the _____.   7. _____

8. Many firms are suppliers in imperfectly competitive markets of the type known as _____.   8. _____

9. Each imperfectly competitive firm must lower prices if it wants to increase the _____.   9. _____

10. The reason such firms have some market power is often that they have developed customer loyalty through _____.   10. _____

11. For both competitive and imperfectly competitive markets, price and quantity are inversely related. This relationship is expressed in the _____.   11. _____

12. In long-run equilibrium, monopolistically competitive firms will experience a zero _____.   12. _____

13. When increases in prices or profits may result in competition from new entrants, the market that exists is called a _____.   13. _____

14. When a single firm supplies the entire market, the market structure is known as a _____.   14. _____

15. When a market is structured in such a way that powerless firms are price takers, the market situation is known as _____.   15. _____

True or False: *Circle your choice.*

T F 1. Monopolists do not need to advertise because they have no competitors.

T F 2. All oligopolists face kinked demand curves.

T F 3. Because of their price rigidity, oligopolists always take losses when their marginal costs rise.

T F 4. Monopolies do not have much market power if substitutes are readily available.

T F 5. The kinked demand curve demonstrates that if an oligopolist raises its prices, it is likely to lose market share.

T F   6. When marginal costs rise, monopolistically competitive firms do not change output or price.

T F   7. The reason that costs may have no effect on oligopoly behavior is that the marginal revenue curve contains a vertical segment at the oligopolist's profit-maximizing production rate.

T F   8. In monopolistically competitive markets, product differentiation causes entry to be blockaded.

T F   9. An oligopolistic market may be difficult to enter because of product differentiation or economies of scale.

T F 10. Competitive firms face flat demand curves; imperfectly competitive firms face downward-sloping demand curves.

T F 11. In the long run, monopolistically competitive firms will be forced to the lowest point of their long-run average cost curves.

T F 12. If there are significant economies of scale up to the production rate where all market demand can be satisfied, the market is likely to be composed of many firms.

T F 13. If a firm makes above-normal profits in the long run, price cannot be at the lowest point on the long-run average cost curve.

T F 14. If a firm has a downward-sloping demand curve that is tangent to a U-shaped long-run average cost curve, higher rates of production would result in economic profit.

T F 15. Nonprice competition includes advertising, better service, and greater convenience.

T F 16. Price competition is presumed to be more desirable than nonprice competition.

T F 17. Farmers are in a monopolistically competitive market because they practice product differentiation, as evidenced by differences in the goods they produce.

T F 18. To maximize profits in a market, oligopolists might establish the monopoly price.

T F 19. OPEC's behavior can best be described in terms of the monopolistic competition form of market structure.

T F 20. Research involving generic and brand-name products indicates that market share and brand loyalty are strongly related.

Multiple Choice: *Select the correct answer.*

_____ 1. One of the main differences between oligopoly and monopolistic competition is:
(a) The amount of advertising that firms do.
(b) The amount of nonprice competition that occurs.
(c) The degree of interdependence among firms.
(d) None of the above.

_____ 2. One of the main similarities of oligopoly and monopolistic competition is:
(a) The existence of above-normal profits in the long run.
(b) The number of firms in the industry.
(c) The kinked shape of their marginal revenue curves.
(d) None of the above.

_____ 3. One of the main similarities of competition and monopolistic competition is:
(a) That in the long run, price equals average cost and marginal revenue equals marginal cost.
(b) The amount of product differentiation.
(c) The point on the long-run average cost curve at which firms maximize profits.
(d) None of the above.

_____ 4. One of the main differences between competition and monopolistic competition lies in:
  (a) The degree of product differentiation of goods.
  (b) The number of firms in the market.
  (c) The amount of profits firms make in the long run.
  (d) All of the above.

_____ 5. One of the main similarities of oligopoly and monopoly is usually:
  (a) Collusion and conspiracy in restraining trade in the industry.
  (b) Inefficient production in the long run.
  (c) Low barriers to entry.
  (d) All of the above.

_____ 6. Monopoly is similar to monopolistic competition in:
  (a) That it has a downward-sloping demand curve.
  (b) That it engages in product differentiation.
  (c) That it equates demand and long-run average cost.
  (d) None of the above.

_____ 7. A major difference between monopoly and monopolistic competition is:
  (a) One maximizes profits by setting MR equal to MC, and the other does not.
  (b) In only one of them is the firm's demand curve the same as the market's demand curve.
  (c) One type of firm has market power; the other does not.
  (d) None of the above.

_____ 8. Firms may be willing to enter a market when:
  (a) The market is making above-normal profits.
  (b) Economies of scale do not constitute an important barrier to entry.
  (c) Key resources are not owned by a few existing companies.
  (d) All of the above are the case.

_____ 9. Product differentiation occurs when:
  (a) A completely new process is used to produce a familiar product.
  (b) One firm produces many varieties of a product.
  (c) Buyers, though not necessarily sellers, perceive differences in the products of several companies.
  (d) Sellers, though not necessarily buyers, perceive differences in the products of several companies.

_____ 10. A kinked demand curve indicates that rival oligopolists match:
  (a) All price changes.
  (b) No price changes.
  (c) Price reductions but not price increases.
  (d) Price increases but not price reductions.

_____ 11. The gap in the marginal revenue curve of an oligopolist is caused by:
  (a) The existence of two alternative demand curves that apply to the oligopolist, depending on whether it raises prices or lowers them.
  (b) The failure of the marginal cost curve to intersect the demand curve at the profit-maximizing level.
  (c) The ability of oligopolists to make above-normal profits if they cooperate with each other.
  (d) None of the above.

_____ 12. Because of the gap in the marginal revenue curve, when the marginal cost curve rises, the oligopolist may have an incentive to:
  (a) Speed up production and lower prices—behavior that leads to greater profits.
  (b) Maintain both production rates and prices—behavior that leads to lower profits but not necessarily to losses.
  (c) Lower production rates and maintain prices—actions that raise profits by counteracting cost increases.
  (d) Speed up production rates and maintain prices—actions that result in losses.

_____13. The kinked oligopoly demand curve does not describe the demand curve for monopolistic competition because:
  (a) Monopolistically competitive firms are not as interdependent as oligopolistic firms.
  (b) Monopolistically competitive firms have no market power.
  (c) Entry into a monopolistically competitive market is easy, which means that the demand curve for such a firm is flat.
  (d) Monopolistically competitive firms make profits in the long run.

_____14. In the short run a monopolistically competitive firm:
  (a) May make profits, but it fails to make profits in the long run because of the entry of new firms.
  (b) May make profits just as it does in the long run, because firms can enter.
  (c) Produces at a rate at which long-run average cost equals price, but not at which long-run marginal cost equals marginal revenue.
  (d) Makes profits just as it does in the long run because entry is blocked.

_____15. Which of the following are reasons that OPEC was not able to maintain control over the world price of oil?
  (a) Decline in the world demand for oil.
  (b) Increased production by non-OPEC countries.
  (c) Price discounting and quota violations by OPEC members.
  (d) None of the above.

Match the four diagrams of long-run equilibrium in Figure 24.1 with the appropriate type of market named in Questions 16–19. Use each diagram *only once*.

Figure 24.1

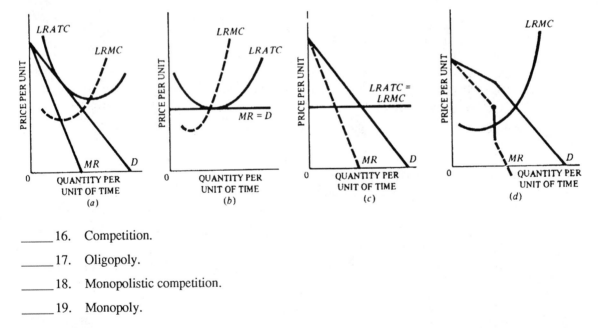

_____16. Competition.

_____17. Oligopoly.

_____18. Monopolistic competition.

_____19. Monopoly.

Select the letter of the diagram(s) in Figure 24.2 that *best* represent the economic concepts named in Questions 20–32. Q^* indicates the profit-maximizing rate of production.

Figure 24.2

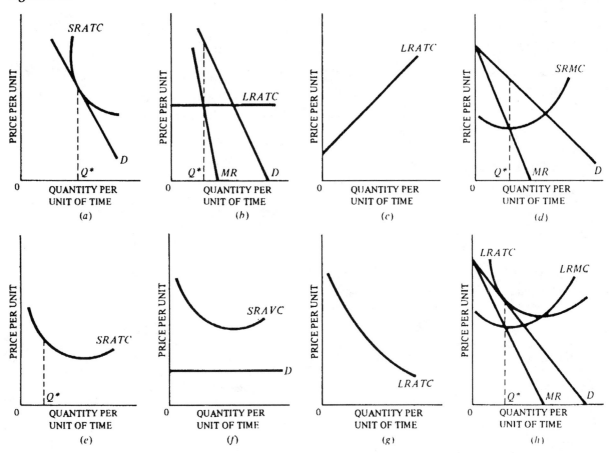

20. Economies of scale.

21. Normal profits (zero economic profits) in the long run.

22. Normal profits (zero economic profits) in the short run.

23. Excess capacity (three answers).

24. Firm shuts down.

25. Constant returns to scale.

26. Situation in which other firms will always enter industry if they can.

27. Inefficient technology is used.

28. Misallocation of resources in the long run (factors not paid their true value to society) (two answers).

29. Misallocation of resources in the short run.

30. Diseconomies of scale at all production rates.

31. Above-normal profits in the long run.

32. Firm has no market power.

Problems and Applications

Exercise 1

This exercise contrasts monopoly, oligopoly, monopolistic competition, and competition, and summarizes their differences.

In Table 24.1 select the appropriate answer given in parentheses at left and fill in the blanks on the right.

Table 24.1
Characteristics of four types of industries

	Monopoly	Oligopoly	Monopolistic competition	Competition
Characteristic				
1. How many firms are there? (many, few, one)	_____	_____	_____	_____
2. Product is _____. (standardized, differentiated, unique)	_____	_____	_____	_____
3. Entry is _____. (blockaded, impeded, easy)	_____	_____	_____	_____
4. Is there market power? (yes, no)	_____	_____	_____	_____
Conduct				
5. Do firms use marginal cost pricing? (yes, no)	_____	_____	_____	_____
6. Is there the possibility of collusion, price leadership, or price wars? (yes, no)	_____	_____	_____	_____
Performance (long run)				
7. Are prices too high? (yes, no)	_____	_____	_____	_____
8. Is market production too low? (yes, no)	_____	_____	_____	_____
9. Is the market efficient? (yes, no)	_____	_____	_____	_____
10. Are profits greater than normal expected in the long run? (yes, no)	_____	_____	_____	_____

Exercise 2

This case study and exercise provides practice in the use of graphs to portray market behavior.

1. The calculator market contains a variety of types of calculators. The electronic calculator has eliminated the firms that produced the mechanical calculators. New firms, such as Casio, challenged older firms, such as IBM, for the growing market. Firms competed using innovations such as reduced size, solar power, programming capabilities, games, and complicated models for special disciplines such as engineering. Rapid price reductions followed the introduction of each new variety as imitators flocked into the market. Nevertheless, some firms were able to hold on to some customers that had become loyal users of their brand. Advertising and quality became an important means to survive in the calculator market. In the calculator market there is evidence of:
   (a) Nonprice competition.
   (b) Easy entry.
   (c) Product differentiation.
   (d) All of the above.

2. On the basis of the information in Problem 1, the calculator market might best be classified as:
   (a) A monopoly.
   (b) An oligopoly.
   (c) A monopolistically competitive market.
   (d) A competitive market.

3. Suppose a calculator producer had the demand and cost curves pictured in Figure 24.3. The firm would be making:
   (a) Economic profits.
   (b) Only normal profits (zero economic profit).
   (c) Losses.

4. Shade in the profits or losses in Figure 24.3 at the firm's profit-maximizing production rate. (Hint: See Figure 24.7 in the text.)

5. Suppose other firms observed that economic profits were being made by the calculator firm in Figure 24.3. These firms would be likely to:
   (a) Exit from the market.
   (b) Enter the market.

6. As new firms enter into the calculator market:
   (a) An existing firm's demand and marginal revenue curves would shift to the left.
   (b) An existing firm's demand and marginal revenue curves would shift to the right.
   (c) An existing firm's average and marginal cost curves would shift upward.
   (d) An existing firm's average and marginal cost curves would shift downward.

7. In Figure 24.3 draw a demand curve that is parallel to the one that is shown and that also represents the demand curve faced by the calculator firms in long-run equilibrium. Assume that entry is unlimited. Label the new demand curve D_2.

8. T F   In the long run, in such a market, economic profits will continue to exist.

Figure 24.3

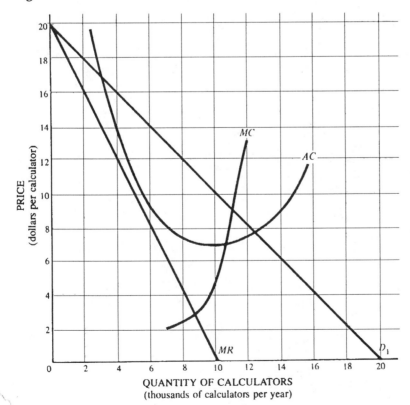

QUANTITY OF CALCULATORS
(thousands of calculators per year)

363

Exercise 3

This exercise gives practice in graphic representations as well as the formulas for examining market structure. It also provides practice with profit maximization in the short and the long run.

1. Corporation NUCAR, Inc., produces small automobiles that currently cost $6,000 each. It finds that its cost and revenues vary as shown in Table 24.2 at various levels of production. Fill in Table 24.2 and refer to it in answering Problem 2. (*Hint:* If you're having difficulties with formulas, review Exercise 3 in Chapter 23 of this study guide.)

Table 24.2
Costs and revenues of NUCAR, Inc. (per year)

	Quantity of cars (thousands)							
	0	50	100	150	200	250	300	350
Price (thousands of dollars)	$ 8.0	$ 7.5	$ 7.0	$ 6.5	$ 6.0	$ 4.0	$ 2.0	$ 0.0
Costs (thousands of dollars)								
Land and buildings, machinery, taxes	240	240	240	240	240	240	240	240
Labor, plastics, rubber, metals	0	100	200	300	400	500	600	700
Transport, business services, utilities	160	160	160	160	160	160	160	160
Variable cost (thousands of dollars)	____	____	____	____	____	____	____	____
Total cost (thousands of dollars)	____	____	____	____	____	____	____	____
Marginal cost (dollars per unit)	____	____	____	____	____	____	____	____
Total revenue (thousands of dollars)	____	____	____	____	____	____	____	____
Marginal revenue (dollars per unit)	____	____	____	____	____	____	____	____
Profit (thousands of dollars)	____	____	____	____	____	____	____	____

2. Draw the demand curve, marginal revenue curve, and marginal cost curve in Figure 24.4, and refer to it in answering Problems 3–6.

Figure 24.4

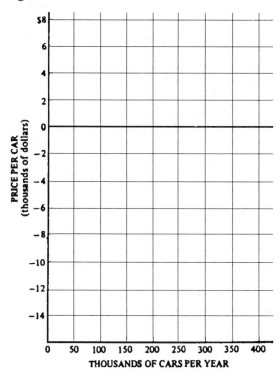

THOUSANDS OF CARS PER YEAR

3. In what kind of market is a firm that has a demand curve like that in Figure 24.4?
   (a) Competitive.
   (b) Monopolistic.
   (c) Oligopolistic.
   (d) Monopolistically competitive.

4. Which of the following does *not* help explain the shape or slope of the demand curve for NUCAR, Inc.?
   (a) Rivals follow price decreases.
   (b) Rivals do not follow price increases.
   (c) The firm has market power.
   (d) The firm can capture the car market by lowering its prices.

Profit maximization

5. The maximum profit for the firm (in thousands of dollars per year) at production rates shown in Table 24.2 is:
   (a) $125.
   (b) $100.
   (c) $400.
   (d) $1,800.

6. The rate of production (in thousands of cars per year) at which maximum profit occurs is:
   (a) 0–50.
   (b) 50–100.
   (c) 100–150.
   (d) 150–200.
   (e) 250–300.
   (f) 300–350.

365

7. Suppose that labor, metals, plastics, and rubber double in price, so that *variable costs* are double those shown in Table 24.2. Complete Table 24.3, taking account of the new *variable* cost at each level of production. (*Hint:* Simply multiply the variable costs in Table 24.2 by 2.) The total-revenue figures are the same as those shown in Table 24.2. Fixed costs are still $400,000 per year.

Table 24.3
Costs and revenues of NUCAR, Inc., after increases in variable costs (per year)

	Quantity of cars (thousands)							
	0	*50*	*100*	*150*	*200*	*250*	*300*	*350*
Variable cost (thousands of dollars)	___	___	___	___	___	___	___	___
Total cost (thousands of dollars)	___	___	___	___	___	___	___	___
Marginal cost (dollars per unit)	___	___	___	___	___	___	___	___
Total revenue (thousands of dollars)	0	375	700	975	1,200	1,000	600	0
Marginal revenue (dollars per unit)	—	7.5	6.5	5.5	4.5	−4.0	−8.0	−12.0
Profit (thousands of dollars)	___	___	___	___	___	___	___	___

8. If we assume the same demand curve as in Figure 24.4, the maximum annual profit that NUCAR can make is:
   (a) $400,000.
   (b) −$100,000.
   (c) $0.
   (d) −$150,000.
   (e) None of the above.

9. Has the profit-maximizing rate of production changed as a result of the doubling of the variable costs?
   (a) Yes.
   (b) No.
   (c) Not possible to tell.

10. T F In this case the firm does not change production when costs change.

11. T F When an oligopolist experiences higher costs, it must go out of business because it can no longer be profitable.

Exercise 4

Monopolistically competitive firms provide us with colorful media advertising meant to differentiate their products from those of others. By using one of the articles in the text, this exercise will show what kind of information to look for to identify if a market is characterized by monopolistic competition or not. If your professor makes a newspaper assignment for this chapter, this exercise will provide an example of how to do it.

Reread the article in Chapter 22 entitled "New Pressures Forcing Down Software Prices" from the *Wall Street Journal*. Then answer the following questions:

1. In the article is there any information on the number of firms in the market?

2. What evidence can be found in the article about product differentiation?

3. Is there evidence of interdependence among the firms in the article?

4. What passage describes entry into or exit from the market?

5. What passage indicates expectations about market prices or profits in this market?

Common Errors

The first statement in each "common error" below is incorrect. Each incorrect statement is followed by a corrected version and an explanation.

1. Because price equals average cost in the long run in a monopolistically competitive firm, such firms must be efficient. WRONG!

   Because price equals average cost in the long run in a monopolistically competitive firm, profits are zero in the long run, but the firm is inefficient. RIGHT!

   Long-run profits are normal (zero economic profits) because competition forces prices to equal long-run average cost. The firm does not reach the *lowest* long-run average cost level, however, and so it is inefficient. The firm's demand curve touches the long-run average cost curve, but not at its lowest point.

2. There are only a few firms in a monopolistically competitive market. WRONG!

   There are many firms in a monopolistically competitive market. RIGHT!

   Don't let the word *monopolistic* fool you. Firms can easily enter or exit from a monopolistically competitive market. Each firm is likely to have excess capacity—which suggests there may be too many firms in a monopolistically competitive market. The restaurant business is a good example of a monopolistically competitive market.

3. Oligopolists have unlimited power to raise prices and curtail production if they cooperate with each other. WRONG!

   Oligopolists' ability to raise prices is limited by demand. RIGHT!

   The demand for oligopolists' products is limited by foreign competition, availability of substitutes, and potential entry by other firms. Such markets as the railroad-car market, the rifle market, and the auto market contain only a few large firms but are limited by potential competition from other countries or at home.

■ ANSWERS ■

Key-Term Review

1. oligopoly	6. marginal revenue (MR)	11. law of demand
2. collusion	7. profit-maximization rule	12. economic profit
3. price leadership	8. monopolistic competition	13. contestable market
4. market share	9. quantity demanded	14. monopoly
5. marginal cost pricing	10. product differentiation	15. perfect competition

True or False

1. F	5. T	9. T	12. F	15. T	18. T
2. F	6. F	10. T	13. T	16. T	19. F
3. F	7. T	11. F	14. F	17. F	20. F
4. T	8. F				

Multiple Choice

1. c	7. b	13. a	18. a	23. a, e, h	28. b, h
2. d	8. d	14. a	19. c	24. f	29. d
3. a	9. c	15. d	20. g	25. b	30. c
4. a	10. c	16. b	21. h	26. b	31. b
5. b	11. a	17. d	22. a	27. h	32. f
6. a	12. b				

Problems and Applications

Exercise 1

Table 24.1 answer

	Monopoly	Oligopoly	Monopolistic competition	Competition
1.	one	few	many	many
2.	unique	standardized or differentiated	differentiated	standardized
3.	blocked	impeded	impeded or easy	easy
4.	yes	yes	yes	no
5.	no	no	no	yes
6.	no	yes	yes	no
7.	yes	yes	yes	no
8.	yes	yes	yes	no
9.	no	no	no	yes
10.	yes	yes	no	no

Exercise 2

1. d
2. c
3. a

4. **Figure 24.3 answer**

5. b
6. a
7. See line D_2 in Figure 24.3 answer.
8. F

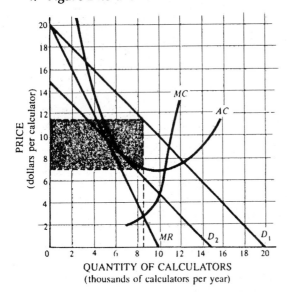

Exercise 3

1. **Table 24.2 answer**

	Quantity of Cars (thousands)							
	0	50	100	150	200	250	300	350
Variable cost	$ 0	$ 100	$ 200	$ 300	$ 400	$ 500	$ 600	$ 700
Total cost	400	500	600	700	800	900	1,000	1,100
Marginal cost	—	2	2	2	2	2	2	2
Total revenue	0	375	700	975	1,200	1,000	600	0
Marginal revenue	—	7.5	6.5	5.5	4.5	−4.0	−8.0	−12.0
Profit	−400	−125	100	275	400	100	−400	−1,100

368

2. **Figure 24.4 answer**

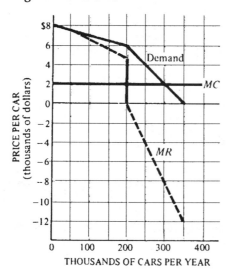

3. c
4. d
5. c
6. d

7. **Table 24.3 answer**

	Quantity of Cars (thousands)							
	0	50	100	150	200	250	300	350
Variable cost (thousands of dollars)	$ 0	$ 200	$ 400	$ 600	$ 800	$ 1,000	$ 1,200	$ 1,400
Total cost (thousands of dollars)	400	600	800	1,000	1,200	1,400	1,600	1,800
Marginal cost (thousands of dollars)	—	4	4	4	4	4	4	4
Total revenue (thousands of dollars)	0	375	700	975	1,200	1,000	600	0
Profit (thousands of dollars)	–400	–225	–100	–25	0	–400	–1,000	–1,800

8. c
9. b
10. T
11. F

Exercise 4

1. The absence of information on market share, the number of firms, or the names of important firms *is itself information.* If no firm has power in a market, it may not be worth mentioning. Articles about competitive firms often do not contain such information. For this reason we might hazard a guess that the article is about competitive firms. This guess is supported by the plural form of words such as "software companies."
2. The reference to "brand names" in paragraph 4 is evidence of product differentiation. This is consistent with either monopolistic competition or differentiated oligopoly.
3. There is no evidence of the interdependence of specific firms; rather, each firm is a price taker that must follow market trends. The "meeting of price discounts" can occur in any market except monopoly.
4. The evidence of entry into the market is contained in the passage "while others are seeking attention with new products" and the reference to "new products." These references are consistent with monopolistic competition and possibly oligopoly.
5. The article suggests that prices are being slashed, which in turn means that long-run profits are not likely to exist. This fact is consistent with competition or monopolistic competition.

Chapter 25

Market Power in the U.S. Economy

Quick Review

Perfect competition, monopoly, oligopoly, and monopolistic competition have been discussed in the last three chapters. Market power is evident in every market except those that are perfectly competitive. In this chapter we look at how market power manifests itself and can be recognized in the U.S. economy. Specifically, we look at the following questions:

- How is market power measured?
- How many firms have market power?
- How do powerful firms use their market power in the marketplace?

We should note to begin with, however, that the market power exercised by imperfectly competitive firms is not socially desirable. The effects of market power include high prices, low output, and a massive transfer of income from the consuming public to a few powerful corporations and the people who own them. Among the policy alternatives used to combat oligopolistic structure or behavior are antitrust action, government regulation, consumer action, and international trade.

A convenient way to measure the extent of market power in a particular product market is to calculate the concentration ratio, the share of total output accounted for by a few of the largest (usually four) firms. When these ratios are calculated, it appears that market power, particularly that of oligopolies, is likely to be found in many of the product markets in the United States. As much as two-thirds of all manufacturing output may be found in markets in which firms possess significant market power. In some cases one firm is so large and powerful as to possess a virtual monopoly over product supply. In addition to those firms with large market shares in one product market, many others have large market shares in several markets. More numerous still are conglomerates, which may have a little power in many markets. Finally, regional and local markets create still more opportunities for market power to develop and to be exploited.

Learning Objectives

After reading Chapter 25 and doing the following exercises, you should:	True or false	Multiple choice	Problems and applications	Common errors	Pages in the text
1. Know the different measures and determinants of market power.	1–3,17	1,2,8			616–621
2. Know why market share and concentration ratios are measures of market power.		12			617, 626
3. Know how to use and interpret concentration and market-share information.	8,18,19		1,2	1,2	617
4. Be able to distinguish the concepts of firm size and market share and know why firm size is important.	15,16			3	617–620
5. Be familiar with the ways in which firms maintain their market power.	9,11,12	3,6,7,9		4	622–635
6. Know how the behavior of firms is related to the structure of their industry.	4–7,10	4,5,10		5	622–635
7. Be able to evaluate the various types of policies that government may use to curb market power.	13,14	11			635–638
8. Be able to analyze market structures from information available in the news media.			3		624–637

Key-Term Review

Review the following terms; if you are not sure of the meaning of any term, write out the definition and check it against the Glossary in the text.

barriers to entry
concentration ratio
conglomerate
contestable market
market power
market share

oligopoly
predatory price cutting
price fixing
price leadership
product differentiation

Fill in the blank following each of the statements below with the appropriate term from the list above.

1. If a market has a high _____, then the market is likely to be an _____.

   1. _____

   _____

2. Such industries experience a range of behavior, including:
   a. Making agreements to hold up prices, which is called _____.

   2a. _____

b. Permitting a single firm to announce a price increase that then becomes the standard for the industry, which is called _____.   2b. _____

c. Spending large amounts of money on advertising to increase market power through _____.   2c. _____

d. Reducing prices in order to drive out competitors, which is called _____.   2d. _____

3. An oligopoly can attain long-run profits if competition is lessened or prevented by significant _____.   3. _____

4. A firm that produces goods in many markets is called a _____.   4. _____

5. Such firms may not have any market power even though they are large because in all markets they have a low _____.   5. _____

6. If a market is a _____, which means it is subject to increased competition if prices or profits increase, then existing firms will suffer a reduction in their _____, their ability to alter market outcomes.   6. _____

_____

True or False: *Circle your choice.*

T F   1. In the U.S. economy, there are more proprietorships than corporations, but corporations have greater dollar assets.

T F   2. If partnerships and proprietorships are lumped together, they have greater sales than corporations in the U.S. economy.

T F   3. Market share and the concentration ratio are used as measures of market power.

T F   4. When oligopolists retaliate against each other in a price war, each forces the others to cut prices to less profitable levels.

T F   5. When oligopolists retaliate against each other in a price war, the oligopoly moves down along the industry demand curve.

T F   6. When firms in a market gather together in a successful conspiracy to fix prices, they are no longer competitive.

T F   7. A market may be characterized by local monopolies and still have a low national concentration ratio.

T F   8. Adding the market share of the top four domestic firms in a market is the same as finding the four-firm concentration ratio in that market.

T F   9. Price-fixing agreements are an important part of price leadership.

T F 10. Predatory pricing occurs in competitive industries.

T F 11. Advertising is a form of nonprice competition.

T F 12. Lobbying for special legislation to protect an industry may prevent competition in that industry.

T F 13. Government restrictions on foreign imports promote competition in this country.

T F 14. If the government prevents entry into a market, it is protecting the competitors in that market, and therefore the government is aiding competition.

T F 15. Market share and concentration measure the sales of a corporation.

T F 16. In business, bigness is badness.

T F 17. If firms can coordinate their actions, they may be able to obtain market power.

T F 18. Local markets may be more concentrated than the national figures on concentration would suggest.

T F 19. The standard measure of concentration gauges the size of any four firms in relation to the size of the total market.

Multiple Choice: *Select the correct answer.*

_____ 1. Which of the following statements is correct?
  (a) There are more proprietorships than corporations in the U.S. economy.
  (b) Corporate assets exceed the combined assets of partnerships and proprietorships in the U.S. economy.
  (c) The combined sales of partnerships and proprietorships are less than those of corporations in the U.S. economy.
  (d) All of the above statements are correct.

_____ 2. The determinants of market power include:
  (a) The number of producers and sellers.
  (b) The relative size of the firms in the industry.
  (c) The extent of barriers to entry.
  (d) All of the above.

_____ 3. Which of the following is *not* a barrier to entry?
  (a) High profits made by existing firms in the industry.
  (b) High capital and advertising costs.
  (c) Economies of scale.
  (d) Ownership of large distribution networks by the existing firms in the industry.

_____ 4. Rival oligopolists face a situation similar to the cold war between major world powers in that:
  (a) Mutual interdependence characterizes oligopolists and world powers.
  (b) If one oligopolist starts a price war, all of the oligopolists will lose, just as the whole world would lose if one nation started a nuclear war.
  (c) If oligopolists cooperate, they can mutually gain.
  (d) All of the above are the case.

_____ 5. A competitive firm does not have to worry about price wars and retaliation because:
  (a) It cannot affect the demand curves of other firms in the industry.
  (b) It recognizes its interdependence with other firms and charges high prices to prevent the market from suffering losses.
  (c) Its profits will change along with those of the firm that starts a price war.
  (d) All of the above are the case.

_____ 6. Collusion is undesirable and illegal because:
  (a) The firms have the market power to raise prices and thus to hurt the consumer.
  (b) Production rates will always be below rates that would persist in a competitive market.
  (c) Above-normal profits may persist in the industry.
  (d) All of the above are the case.

_____ 7. Which of the following is *not* a technique used by oligopolists to maintain prices above long-run competitive levels?
  (a) Price leadership.
  (b) Collusion in the form of price fixing.
  (c) Marginal cost pricing.
  (d) Product differentiation.

8. Which of the following conditions always makes the national concentration ratio an overstatement of true market power in an industry?
   (a) Markets may be local, not national.
   (b) Substitute goods and imports are not reflected in the ratio.
   (c) Barriers to entry are not accounted for in the ratio.
   (d) There may be equal distribution of firm sizes in a market.

9. Which of the following techniques allows monopolists and oligopolists to shift market demand curves outward and increase their profits?
   (a) Restricting what is sold in the marketplace?
   (b) Lowering product quality.
   (c) Advertising.
   (d) Applying their market power to get their suppliers to lower prices.

10. Which of the following types of behavior might be expected in competitive markets?
    (a) Price wars.
    (b) Advertising.
    (c) Frequent entry and exit.
    (d) Collusion in restraint of trade.

11. Alternatives to counteract the market power of oligopolies include:
    (a) International trade.
    (b) Government regulation.
    (c) Consumerism.
    (d) All of the above.

12. Market share and concentration measure market power because:
    (a) They show how large corporations are.
    (b) Control over a large percentage of production allows a firm to influence prices.
    (c) They measure barriers to entry.
    (d) All of the above are the case.

Problems and Applications

Exercise 1

This exercise shows how to compute concentration ratios and market shares for an industry.

1. Market share is:
   (a) The percentage of total market output produced by the largest firms (usually the four largest).
   (b) The percentage of total market output produced by the largest firm.
   (c) The percentage of total market output produced by a given firm.
   (d) A type of stock issued by the firms in a market.

2. Concentration usually refers to:
   (a) The percentage of total market output produced by the four largest domestic firms.
   (b) The percentage of total market output produced by any given four large domestic firms.
   (c) The percentage of total market output produced by a given domestic firm.

3. Table 25.1 presents the sales of the top four firms (A, B, C, D) in a market. Insert the total sales for the top four firms and total sales for the market. Using this information, compute the market share for each firm separately and then add the market shares together to arrive at totals in the last column.

Table 25.1
Sales and market shares of top four firms, by company

Firm	Sales (millions of dollars per year)	Market share
A	$60	_____ %
B	40	_____
C	30	_____
D	20	_____
All top four	$_____	_____ %
All other firms	50	_____ %
All firms	$_____	100 %

4. T F The sum of the market shares of the top four firms is the same as the four-firm concentration ratio.

Exercise 2

This exercise illustrates the importance of knowing whether an industry has a national or regional market.

1. Suppose there are two separate U.S. markets for a product, one on the East Coast and the other on the West Coast. Equal-sized firms A, B, C, and D produce in the eastern market and firms E, F, G, and H produce in the western market. Their sales are shown in Table 25.2. Complete Table 25.2.

Table 25.2
**Annual sales and market shares of top four firms
in East Coast and West Coast markets**

East Coast			West Coast		
Firm	Sales (millions of dollars per year)	Market share	Firm	Sales (millions of dollars per year)	Market share
A	$20	_____ %	E	$20	_____ %
B	20	_____	F	20	_____
C	20	_____	G	20	_____
D	20	_____	H	20	_____
All top four	$_____	_____ %	All top four	$_____	_____ %
All other firms	20	_____	All other firms	20	_____
All firms	$_____	_____ %	All firms	$_____	_____ %

2. What is the concentration ratio in each of the two separate markets? _____ %

3. The Department of Commerce, however, reports concentration ratios for the national market only. *Total sales* for *both* markets together are $_____.

4. What are the sales of the top four firms in the national market (both markets together)? $_____

5. What is the national concentration ratio? (Use information in Problems 3 and 4.) _____ %

6. We may conclude that the national statistics may (overstate, understate, properly represent) the true concentration ratio in regional or local markets.

Exercise 3

Oligopolies provide the battles and rivalry that attract headlines. By using one of the articles in the textbook, this exercise will show the kind of information to look for to determine if a market is an oligopoly or not. If your professor makes a newspaper assignment for this chapter, this exercise will provide an example of how to do it.

Reread the article in Chapter 25 entitled "Wm. Wrigley Boosts Gum Prices in the U.S. Except Orbit Brand" from the *Wall Street Journal*. Then answer the following questions:

1. Is there any information in Table 25.2 on the concentration ratio for the market being described in the article? Is there any information in the article about the number of firms in the market?

2. What evidence does the article contain concerning product differentiation?

3. Is there evidence of interdependence among the firms in the article?

4. Does the article describe entry into or exit from the market? Is there any evidence of barriers to entry?

5. What evidence is there of technological change? Is there information on waste or inefficiency that might be due to lack of competition?

6. What statement, if any, suggests the firm has the ability to influence prices in the whole market?

7. Are long-run profits expected in the market?

Crossword Puzzle

Select the economic term in the following list that corresponds with each of the definitions and descriptions below. Then fit the term or one of the words within it into the crossword puzzle at the numbers indicated.

barrier to entry
collusion
concentration
  ratio (twice)
conglomerate
entry
law of demand
marginal
  revenue
market share
monopoly
oligopoly
opportunity cost
  (twice)

perfect
  competition
  (twice)
predatory price
  cutting (twice)
price fixing
price leadership
product
  differentiation
profit
  maximization
quantity
  demanded

Across

1. The policy of a firm that wants customers to recognize its output and view it as desirable relative to other products.
4. If the firms in an oligopolistic market fail to cooperate, the major firm may discipline the others by engaging in _____.
6. Secret (because illegal) cooperation among firms.
8. Warlike behavior occasionally found when oligopolists vie for market share.
11. As price rises, quantity demanded falls, *ceteris paribus*, according to the _____.
12. A type of firm that contains plants that produce in many different markets.
16. This illegal practice allows firms to charge higher than normal prices and earn higher than normal profits.
18. When many firms are making profits in a market, other firms will try to gain _____.
19. A market structure in which many firms enter the market and vie with each other to sell their goods.
20. A market structure in which only a few firms operate, characterized by interdependent production and pricing decisions.
21. The percentage of total sales made by one firm.

Down

2. A measure of market power by a group of firms in a market.
3. The value of the next best alternative use of a resource.
5. The sum of the market shares of the largest four firms in a market.
7. A measure of the trade-off in production between two goods.
9. The structure of a market in which only one firm operates.
10. The new increase in total revenues that results when production is increased by one unit.
11. Conduct characteristic of an oligopolistic market whereby one firm signals a price change and other firms then follow.
13. A guide for the attainment of the firm's goal.
14. An obstruction that prevents firms from competing in a market or even from getting into the market.
15. A market structure in which many firms operate but none has market power.
17. This changes when there is a movement along a curve.

Common Errors

The first statement in each "common error" below is incorrect. Each incorrect statement is followed by a corrected version and an explanation.

1. The concentration ratio accurately measures market power. WRONG!

   The concentration ratio is a rough, simple measure of market power. RIGHT!

   Information on availability of substitutes, the appropriate market, the relative size of firms in the market, and barriers to entry must be known before we can determine whether or not market power exists. Concentration ratios are usually computed for the nation as a whole, but many industries are characterized by local or regional markets. Also, any given industry may produce a variety of different products, each with a unique concentration ratio. The concentration ratio gives no idea of barriers to entry that may exist, nor does it give any idea whether a market contains one dominant firm or several equally large firms.

2. American industry consists mostly of monopolies. WRONG!

   There are only a few monopolies in the U.S. economy. RIGHT!

   The text has shown that many U.S. markets are imperfectly competitive, but concentration ratios of 100 percent are rare. Monopolies are most likely to occur in the utility industries, which are heavily regulated by government.

3. All large firms have market power. WRONG!

   The largest firms in concentrated markets are likely to have market power. RIGHT!

   Control of a market is more important than bigness in determining market power. Relative size as measured by concentration is more important than absolute size as measured by sales. For example, while conglomerates may be very large, they may play only small roles in many different markets and have no ability to influence prices in any of them.

4. Oligopolists always make huge profits. WRONG!

Oligopolists may use their market power to force each other to experience losses. RIGHT!

Oligopolists may use their market power cooperatively through collusion, price leadership, or indirect means of supporting prices above competitive levels. Such cooperative activity *may* lead to profits in the long run as well as in the short run. Changes in demand and costs, however, can force oligopolists to take losses or even to fail. Most important, oligopolists may not cooperate with each other. They may conduct price wars and engage in nonprice competition in order to erode each other's market share. Such conduct often leads to instability and substantial losses.

5. Oligopolistic firms compete with each other. MISLEADING!

Oligopolies are often characterized by competitive rivalry. RIGHT!

When firms have market power, they become aware of their interdependence. The often warlike or conspiratorial conduct—rivalry—that occurs is quite different from the conduct of competitive firms. Since no competitive firm can affect market prices, no one firm sees any other as a threat, nor is there any possibility of colluding to fix prices. True competition is often marked on the one hand by independent behavior of the competing firms and on the other by cooperation to hold down costs. For example, while farmers rarely succeed in increasing the prices of farm products by cooperative efforts, they may share the use of farm equipment with neighboring farmers to lower costs. There is certainly no reason for one farmer to engage in a price war with another farmer, since both are such small parts of the market.

■ ANSWERS ■

Key-Term Review

1. concentration ratio
   oligopoly
2. a. price fixing
   b. price leadership

2. c. product differentiation
   d. predatory price cutting
3. barriers to entry
4. conglomerate

5. market share
6. contestable market
   market power

True or False

1. T	5. T	8. T	11. T	14. F	17. T
2. F	6. T	9. F	12. T	15. F	18. T
3. T	7. T	10. F	13. F	16. F	19. F
4. T					

Multiple Choice

1. d	3. a	5. a	7. c	9. c	11. d
2. d	4. d	6. d	8. b	10. c	12. b

Problems and Applications

Exercise 1

1. c
2. a

3. **Table 25.1 answer**

Firm	Sales	Market share
A	$60	30%
B	40	20
C	30	15
D	20	10
All top four	$150	75%
All other firms	50	25
All firms	$200	100%

4. T

Exercise 2

1. **Table 25.2 answer (per year)**

East Coast			West Coast		
Firm	Sales (millions of dollars per year)	Market share	Firm	Sales (millions of dollars per year)	Market share
A	$ 20	20%	E	$ 20	20%
B	20	20	F	20	20
C	20	20	G	20	20
D	20	20	H	20	20
All top four	$ 80	80%	All top four	$ 80	80%
All other firms	20	20	All other firms	20	20
All firms	$100	100%	All firms	$100	100%

2. 80 percent
3. $200 million per year
4. $80 million per year
5. 40 percent
6. understate

Exercise 3

1. The concentration ratio is 97 percent, suggesting oligopoly. The names of two firms are mentioned in the article, which suggests duopoly.
2. The discussion of "brands" suggests product differentiation, which is consistent with differentiated oligopoly or monopolistic competition.
3. Graham Morgan of Wrigley shows that he is very much aware of actions by American Chicle Co. His knowledge suggests interdependence and competitive rivalry between the two companies. Such interdependence is consistent with oligopoly.
4. There is evidence of entry with the new "Orbit" brand. "Brands" are mentioned several times. This may indicate a barrier in the form of brand loyalty, advertising, or the like.
5. The article presents no evidence of technological change, inefficiency, or waste.
6. The article shows that Wrigley seems to have the power to decide what gum prices will be. The very fact that its action is important enough to report is also evidence of the firm's market power. This information is consistent with monopoly or oligopoly; the significant number and size of price changes is not likely to indicate monopolistic competition.
7. Profits are not mentioned, but there seems no reason to doubt that they exist and are likely to increase unless costs are increasing more rapidly than revenues.

Crossword Puzzle Answer

Across

1. *product* differentiation
4. *predatory* price cutting
6. *collusion*
8. predatory price *cutting*
11. *law* of demand
12. *conglomerate*
16. price *fixing*
18. *entry*
19. perfect *competition*
20. *oligopoly*
21. market *share*

Down

2. *concentration* ratio
3. opportunity *cost*
5. concentration *ratio*
7. *opportunity* cost
9. *monopoly*
10. *marginal* revenue
11. price *leadership*
13. profit *maximization*
14. *barrier* to entry
15. *perfect* competition
17. *quantity* demanded

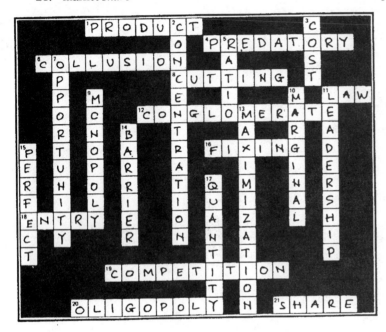

Chapter 26
The Deregulation of Business

Quick Review

The process of deregulating America's "regulated" industries began with the Nixon administration and has continued ever since. The idea is that many regulations, regulatory agencies, and other interferences with market forces have outlived their usefulness or have been found lacking in some respect. The consensus seems to be that markets should be allowed to work more freely in answering the WHAT, HOW, and FOR WHOM questions. Regulation has gone too far.

This chapter considers government's role in the marketplace by discussing the following questions:

- What is the justification for government regulation of a market?
- What form should that regulation take?
- When is it appropriate to deregulate a market?

Historically, economists and politicians have recognized many reasons why an industry should be regulated. "Market failure" means that the market provides an inadequate output mix. Sources of market failure are:

- Externalities
- Public goods
- Market power
- Natural monopoly
- Inequities

The existence of any one of these prevents the market from providing satisfactory answers to the economic problem.

To improve market outcomes where market failure occurs, governments intervene in several ways. Most frequently the intervention takes the form of:

- Taxation
- Public-sector production
- Antitrust activity
- Economic and social regulation

The clearest case for intervention is in "natural monopolies," where a market is best served by a single firm because it alone can capture continuous economies of scale. In regulating natural monopolies, regulators may pursue three basic, but potentially conflicting, goals:

- Price efficiency
- Production efficiency
- Equity

Finding the right combination of policy levers—such as regulating price, output, or profit—is a very difficult job and the risks of regulating badly are unfortunately quite high.

In addition, it has become increasingly clear that regulation itself may impose significant opportunity costs on the economy. Resources are used in devising and administering regulations. The firms in a regulated market use resources to comply with (or get around!) regulations. In addition to these administrative and compliance costs, efficiency costs that result from bad decisions, incomplete information, and so on may worsen the mix of output; moreover, their effects may be compounded over time!

Because many industries are viewed as operating in suboptimal fashion, the process of deregulation has begun. Railroads, trucking, telephone service, airlines, and financial markets are industries in which deregulation is under way. However, there are still many industries that are regulated and even some where regulation has increased, as in the health industry. The question to be answered is always, "Do the benefits of the regulation exceed the cost of regulation?"

Learning Objectives

After reading Chapter 26 and doing the following exercises, you should:	True or false	Multiple choice	Problems and applications	Common errors	Pages in the text
1. Be able to distinguish between administrative, compliance, and efficiency costs of regulation.	8–10,12	1,5,7,8, 15,16	3	1	648–649
2. Know several sources of market failure and several techniques of intervention.	3–5,11	3,4, 8–11,13	1,3		642–644
3. Be able to demonstrate natural monopoly graphically and verbally.	1,2	2,12	2		644–646
4. Understand the potential conflict among the goals of price efficiency, production efficiency, and equity.		6			646–647
5. Know the difficulties associated with regulating the price, output, or profits of natural monopolies.	7,12–18	2,11, 12,14	2		646–648
6. Understand the difficulties associated with devising optimal regulations.	7,9,10,14, 15,19–21	11,12,14, 15,16	3		643,646–649
7. Know the history of regulation and deregulation in the U.S. economy.	6	1			651–658

Key-Term Review

Review the following terms; if you are not sure of the meaning of any term, write out the definition and check it against the Glossary in the text.

antitrust
barriers to entry
contestable market
cross-subsidization
economic profit
government failure
laissez faire

marginal cost pricing
market failure
natural monopoly
opportunity cost
product differentiation
regulation

Fill in the blank following each of the following statements with the appropriate term from the list above.

1. Because of _____, new firms are prevented from competing and eliminating _____.

   1. _____

   _____

2. _____ is a French term meaning "let things alone."

   2. _____

3. When markets do not provide the socially desirable mix of output the reason is _____.

   3. _____

4. When a firm can expand to take over an entire market while simultaneously reducing average cost, then it has a _____.

   4. _____

5. The case for _____ and potential goal conflicts can be demonstrated easily using natural monopoly.

   5. _____

6. Using high prices and profits for one product or service to subsidize low prices on another service is an example of _____.

   6. _____

7. _____ is defined as the best alternative opportunity forgone when one chooses a course of action.

   7. _____

8. Homogeneous products characterize competitive markets; imperfect markets are very often characterized by _____.

   8. _____

9. Firms with monopoly power do not maximize profits by using _____.

   9. _____

10. _____ activity has been used to prevent or dismember concentrations of market power.

    10. _____

11. When regulators produce rules that fail to improve, or even worsen, market performance, their actions point to _____.

    11. _____

12. An imperfectly competitive market subject to potential entry if prices or profits increase is known as a _____.

    12. _____

True or False: *Circle your choice.*

T F 1. All firms that capture economies of scale are natural monopolies.

T F 2. All firms classified as natural monopolies must be able to capture economies of scale.

T F 3. Goods classified as "public goods" will only be produced if government does so.

T F 4. Taxation can be used as a mechanism for correcting market imperfections.

T F 5. Economic regulation focuses on economic outcomes, whereas social regulation is concerned with, for example, the conditions under which production takes place.

T F 6. The argument for regulation is that markets generate imperfect outcomes, and the argument for deregulation is that government worsens market outcomes.

T F 7. Marginal cost pricing implies a loss on every unit of output produced by a natural monopoly.

T F 8. Efficiency costs may result when obsolete regulations are left on the books.

T F 9. Economic regulations may push the physical production-possibilities curve inside the institutional production-possibilities curve.

T F 10. Economic regulation shifts the institutional production-possibilities curve inward.

T F 11. The term "market failure" means that the market mechanism has not generated the best possible mix of output.

T F 12. Since social regulation is concerned with workplace safety, discrimination, and the like, it does not affect prices or output.

T F 13. If an unregulated natural monopolist had society's interest in mind instead of its own self-interest, it would produce where price equals marginal cost even though this would mean lower positive profits.

T F 14. The only safe way to regulate a natural monopoly is to restrict profit to a specific rate of return.

T F 15. Those who seek to regulate a natural monopoly can set both price and output.

T F 16. An *unregulated* natural monopolist will produce and sell an output at which price equals marginal cost.

T F 17. Unregulated natural monopolists produce suboptimal rates of output.

T F 18. For a natural monopolist to earn an economic profit, the demand curve must lie above the average cost curve at some rate of output.

T F 19. To achieve production efficiency, a regulated natural monopolist must be subsidized.

T F 20. Pursuit of society's equity goal requires the elimination of economic profit for regulated natural monopolists.

T F 21. Regulated monopolies that are allowed a specific profit rate have an incentive to hold down costs.

Multiple Choice: *Select the correct answer.*

_____ 1. Which of the presidents before Reagan took steps to deregulate major industries?
   (a) President Nixon.
   (b) President Ford.
   (c) President Carter.
   (d) All of the above.

_____ 2. Which of the following is *not* a form of government intervention?
   (a) Natural monopoly.
   (b) Antitrust activity.
   (c) Regulation.
   (d) Public-sector production.

_____ 3. Which of the following are examples of market failure?
   (a) Inequities in the output mix and the distribution of income.
   (b) Natural monopoly.
   (c) Market power.
   (d) All of the above.

_____ 4. Which of the following leads to a market failure?
   (a) Antitrust activity.
   (b) Public-sector production.
   (c) Natural monopoly.
   (d) All of the above.

_____ 5. The economic cost of a manufacturer complying with an "air bag" law would be:
   (a) The additional money required to buy an automobile with an air bag.
   (b) The resources that were used to produce the air bag.
   (c) The best alternative goods and services forgone when the air bag is produced.
   (d) None of the above.

_____ 6. Consider society's goals of equity, production efficiency, and price efficiency. Which of the following statements is *incorrect* when applied to price regulation of a natural monopolist?
(a) Achieving the equity goal requires that $P = AC$.
(b) Achieving price efficiency requires that $P = MC$.
(c) Achieving production efficiency requires that both $P = MC$ and $P = $ maximum AC.
(d) Achieving the three goals simultaneously using price regulation only is impossible.

_____ 7. Which of the following represents the cost of compliance associated with regulated industries?
(a) The EPA hires a new chemist to assist in devising regulations related to water quality.
(b) Because of a budget cut, the EPA is unable to test new technologies for water treatment.
(c) Ozarka, a company producing and marketing spring water, hires an accountant to set up the data base required to file EPA water-quality reports.
(d) All of the above represent costs of compliance.

_____ 8. Economic regulation focuses on:
(a) Prices in a market.
(b) Production by the market.
(c) Conditions under which firms enter and exit from an industry.
(d) All of the above.

_____ 9. Which of the following is a market imperfection that may justify government intervention?
(a) Taxation.
(b) Antitrust.
(c) Externalities.
(d) All of the above.

_____ 10. Which of the following is a form of government intervention that is designed to correct market imperfections?
(a) Dynamic inefficiency.
(b) Regulation.
(c) Economies of scale.
(d) All of the above.

_____ 11. Which of the following is an undesirable side effect of some types of government intervention?
(a) Dynamic inefficiency.
(b) Lower quality of production.
(c) Shortages.
(d) All of the above.

_____ 12. Which of the following problems results from output regulation of a natural monopoly?
(a) Losses and bankruptcy for the natural monopoly.
(b) Loss of quality.
(c) Excess output.
(d) All of the above.

_____ 13. Which of the following problems results from restrictions on entry to an industry?
(a) Losses and bankruptcy for the natural monopoly.
(b) Lower quality of production.
(c) Higher prices to the consumer and profit to the producer.
(d) All of the above.

_____ 14. Which of the following problems results from a restriction on the profits of a natural monopoly?
(a) Production does not occur at a socially optional rate.
(b) The firm has no incentive to strive for efficiency.
(c) Dynamic inefficiency results.
(d) All of the above are problems.

_____ 15. In the article "The Milking of New York City" on page 651 in the text, it appears that:
   (a) Oligopolists do not have society's interest in mind when they set prices.
   (b) Firms protected from entry by other firms will charge higher prices than if the market was contestable.
   (c) Concern for "quality of service" can be used to serve narrow self-interest.
   (d) All of the above are the case.

_____ 16. Consider the Big Bang described in the article on page 652 of the text. When financial markets were deregulated:
   (a) Established firms welcomed the opportunity to compete with foreign competitors.
   (b) Surprisingly, commission rates went up.
   (c) The daily volume of transactions stayed constant.
   (d) None of the above occurred.

Problems and Applications

Exercise 1

This exercise provides practice in identifying market imperfections, finding an appropriate form of government intervention, and recognizing the possible side effects of government intervention.

Table 26.1 lists market imperfections, means for the government to intervene, and some of the side effects of government policy.

Table 26.1
Market imperfections and government intervention and side effects

Market imperfection	Means of government intervention	Side effects of government policy
I. Externalities	A. Taxes, subsidies, or transfers	1. Inefficiency (unnecessarily high costs)
II. Inequities	B. Regulation of prices, output, or entry	2. Shortages or surpluses
III. Natural monopoly		3. Lack of quality
IV. Nonexclusive goods	C. Antitrust activity	4. Inefficient government bureaucracy
V. Market power	D. Provision of information	5. Dynamic inefficiencies
VI. Lack of information about tastes, costs, or prices	E. Production of goods by the government	
VII. Lack of information about profitability or technology.		

For each of the situations described in Table 26.2, choose the roman numeral(s) for each market imperfection that applies, the letter(s) that represent(s) appropriate action by the government, and number(s) that indicate(s) possible side effects of government involvement.

Table 26.2

Market imperfection	Government intervention	Possible side effects of government policy	Situation
_____	_____	_____	1. Because of severe balance-of-trade deficits, the United States needs to export more goods abroad. If not, foreign exchange markets will be increasingly disrupted. However, many small American companies do not know enough about foreign markets to become exporters of goods and services.

(Continued)

386

Table 26.2 (continued)

Market imperfection	Government intervention	Possible side effects of government policy	Situation
————	————	————	2. It is not economical to have firms compete to provide sewage facilities for residential areas. Each house needs only one set of pipes and it is most efficient to attach all pipes from houses to one major sewer conduit.
————	————	————	3. Many workers at a firm find they are becoming nauseated in the workplace. Furthermore, the cancer rate among the employees appears to be very high. They cannot get management to study the problem because the firm can simply kick them out and hire new employees.
————	————	————	4. Farmers are willing to use the latest techniques for growing crops. However, they have difficulty determining what the newest techniques are by themselves and the market does not adequately provide them with the information.
————	————	————	5. If the farmers do not change continually to the latest disease-resistant seed varieties, it is likely that there will be a disastrous spread of disease that will threaten the economy. However, new varieties of grain are expensive to develop, and the private market would not undertake the continuous research process necessary to develop them.
————	————	————	6. At the beginning of World War II, the United States found that it was cut off from important suppliers of rubber, sugar, and hemp by the Japanese. The private market had not kept enough inventories of these goods on hand in case of war.
————	————	————	7. The St. Joe Mineral Company dumped taconite tailings filled with asbestos into the Great Lakes. While St. Joe suffered no bad side effects from this activity, many people who used the lakes began to suffer such effects.
————	————	————	8. Many older people are poor and as they age and become weaker are beset by various problems and cannot take care of themselves adequately. Private charities do not do enough to maintain a standard of care that society as a whole considers desirable.
————	————	————	9. It is very costly to run electrical lines into a house; thus, it is not economical to put more than one set of electric lines into a home. Electrical services are most economically provided by only one firm.
————	————	————	10. General Electric and Westinghouse decided to coordinate their activities and conspired to set the price of electronic equipment on which they were bidding.

Exercise 2

This exercise explores the implications of downward-sloping average cost curves and monopoly. It will be helpful in solving the problem at the end of Chapter 26 in the text.

Many utilities provide networks that are expensive to put in place and that would be too expensive for a competitor to duplicate. Such networks include local sewage disposal, water, and electricity.

Suppose the annual total cost of installing and maintaining a network was a utility's only cost and that cost was $100 million.

    1. Compute average total cost at the units of output specified in Table 26.3.

Table 26.3

Quantity (units per year)	Total average cost (millions of dollars per unit)
100	$_____
200	_____
300	_____
400	_____
500	_____
600	_____

2. What would marginal cost be at each of those output levels? $_____

Suppose Table 26.4 shows the demand schedule for the utility's services. Costs are $100 million.

Table 26.4

(1) Quantity demanded (units per year)	(2) Price (millions of dollars per unit)	(3) Total revenue (millions of dollars per year)	(4) Marginal revenue (millions of dollars per unit)	(5) Profit (millions of dollars per year)
100	$1.0	$_____	$_____	$_____
200	0.8	_____	_____	_____
300	0.6	_____	_____	_____
400	0.4	_____	_____	_____
500	0.2	_____	_____	_____
600	0.0	_____	_____	_____

3. Fill in columns 3–5 to show the utility's total revenue, marginal revenue, and profit.

4. What is the profit-maximizing production level for the utility? _____

5. What is the revenue-maximizing production level for the utility? _____

6. At what production level does marginal revenue equal marginal cost? _____

7. At what production level are economic profits first eliminated? _____

Exercise 3

The media often provide information about changes in government intervention in the economy. By using one of the articles in the text, this exercise will show the kind of information to look for. If your professor makes a newspaper assignment for this chapter, this exercise will provide an example of how to do it.

Reread the article in Chapter 25 entitled "Greyhound to Purchase Rival Trailways" from the *Washington Post*. Then answer the following questions:

1. Does the article indicate the potential for increased or decreased government intervention?

2. What passage clearly indicates the possibility of increased or decreased government intervention?

3. Which of the following five forms of market failure might justify the intervention?
    (a) Externalities.
    (b) Public goods.
    (c) Market power.
    (d) Natural monopoly.
    (e) Inequities.

4. Which of the following forms of government intervention does the passage you chose in Question 2 indicate?
   (a) Taxation or subsidies.
   (b) Public-sector production.
   (c) Antitrust.
   (d) Economic regulation.
   (e) Social regulation.

5. Which passage indicates a form of government failure inherent in government intervention in the market?

Common Error

The first statement in the "common error" below is incorrect. The incorrect statement is followed by a corrected version and an explanation.

1. Once regulations are in place and enforced, the cost to society is zero. WRONG!

   Regulations impose costs of their own. RIGHT!

   The often-heard phrase "there ought to be a law" implies what is meant here. It seems that the law solves the problem but causes no problems itself. This is an inadequate assessment. It costs society a great deal in the way of opportunity costs to devise, administer, and comply with regulations. In addition, once a regulation is in place, it's very, very difficult to remove because bureaucratic machinery works very slowly. As an example, in the early days of the energy crisis, trucks were allowed to carry freight from point A to point B, but not allowed to haul anything back from point B to point A. Regulations have costs all their own!

■ ANSWERS ■

Key-Term Review

1. barriers to entry
   economic profit
2. laissez faire
3. market failure
4. natural monopoly
5. regulation
6. cross-subsidization
7. opportunity cost
8. product differentiation
9. marginal cost pricing
10. antitrust
11. government failure
12. contestable market

True or False

1. F	5. T	9. F	13. F	16. F	19. T
2. T	6. T	10. T	14. F	17. T	20. T
3. F	7. T	11. T	15. F	18. T	21. F
4. T	8. T	12. F			

Multiple Choice

1. d	4. c	7. c	10. b	13. c	15. d
2. a	5. c	8. d	11. d	14. d	16. d
3. d	6. c	9. c	12. b		

Problems and Applications

Exercise 1

Table 26.2 answer

Market imperfection	Means of government intervention	Side effects of government policy
1. VI, VII	D	1, 4
2. III, V	B or E	1, 2, 3, 4, 5
3. I, IV	B	1, 2, 4, 5
4. VI, VII	D	4
5. I, III, IV, VI, VII	E	1, 3, 4, 5
6. I, IV	E	2, 4, 5
7. I	A or B	2, 4, 5
8. II, IV	A	1, 4, 5
9. III, V	B	1, 2, 3, 4, 5
10. V	C	1, 2, 4, 5

Exercise 2

1. **Table 26.3 answer**

Quantity (units per year)	Total average cost (millions of dollars per unit)
100	$1.0
200	0.5
300	0.33
400	0.25
500	0.2
600	0.17

2. $0

3. **Table 26.4 answer**

(3) Total revenue (millions of dollars per year)	(4) Marginal revenue (millions of dollars per unit)	(5) Profit (millions of dollars per year)
$100	$ 1.0	$ 0
160	0.6	60
180	0.2	80
160	−0.2	60
100	−0.6	0
0	−1.0	−100

4. 300 units
5. 300 units
6. approximately at 300 units
7. 500 units

Exercise 3

1. Prevention of the merger would constitute increased government interference.
2. "If the merger is approved by the ICC ... we wouldn't anticipate any [antitrust] objections by the Department of Justice." This statement indicates potentially increased government interference if the merger is not permitted.
3. c   Market power is indicated by the phrase in the first sentence "leaving a single major company in the business."
4. c
5. "Without the sale, . . . Trailways was headed toward certain bankruptcy." This passage suggests that increased government interference (blocking the merger) would result in a less efficient use of resources.

Chapter 27
The Farm Problem

Quick Review

This chapter discusses the "farm problem." Even the title indicates the need for a solution. The questions that arise in looking for a solution are:

- Why are farm prices and profits so unstable?
- Why has the farm sector shrunk so much?
- How do government farm programs affect farm output, prices, and income?

In answer to the first question, farming has always been an uncertain occupation at best. The recent farm depression, however, seems worse than those that have gone before. The problems this time seem more deep-seated and intractable, and the impact of changes taking place will be felt for a long, long time. Some go so far as to say that farming, as most have known it, is dead.

On the supply side there have always been the forces of nature to deal with. Sudden droughts, freezes, or blights have always raised havoc with supply. On the demand side, both price and income elasticities are perverse. A low income elasticity (low sensitivity of the demand for agricultural goods to changes in income) causes domestic demand to grow slowly. Political considerations have prevented the expansion of export markets, and the period in which the dollar was strong only made exporting more difficult.

In the face of this, tremendous productivity advances, which would be welcome in most other markets, have only resulted in lower prices and farm incomes because the price elasticity of demand is low (low sensitivity of the quantity demanded of agricultural goods to changes in price). In addition, the producers in this competitive, capital- and land-intensive market are beset by the same problems that wrecked firms in many other sectors and brought even giant firms to their knees—high fuel prices, high fertilizer prices, and high interest rates. The results have been falling land prices, continued decline of the farm population, farms lost, and the destruction of a way of life.

Well-intentioned government policy has produced perverse results. The price-support programs encourage production of products already in surplus, raise prices to consumers, and distort the allocation of resources. Direct income-support programs seem to provide more income to those who need it least, set-aside programs pay people for not producing, and Payment-in-Kind (PIK) programs pay farmers for not producing by allowing them to keep previous production. Nothing seems to work well.

Farmers call for price supports to reestablish the relative purchasing power that farm commodities could command some sixty years ago. The Reagan administration, with the Farm Security Act of 1985, moved in the opposite direction, arguing that farmers must be made more responsive to market forces. For example, supporting dairy prices at artificially high prices and then giving away the surplus strikes many as government amok once again.

Learning Objectives

After reading Chapter 27 and doing the following exercises, you should:	True or false	Multiple choice	Problems and applications	Common errors	Pages in the text
1. Know the dimensions and nature of the farm problem.	5	1,13		1,2	661–664, 664–666, 671–676
2. Understand the role of income and price elasticities in the farm problem.	1,2,8,20	13–15		2	662–664
3. Be able to relate the farm problem to forces on both the supply side and demand side of the market.	3,4,12, 16,18	6,7,11, 13,14,17	2	1,2	661–664
4. Know how high petroleum prices, high interest rates, inflation, and other supply-and-demand influences affect the farm economy.	6	16			671–673
5. Be able to describe several types of farm policies and their effects on the farming economy.	6,13–15, 17,19,24	2–5, 9–11	1,2		667–671 673–678
6. Understand how the farmers' problems affect other industries in farm-state economies.	22	7,8			671–675
7. Be able to demonstrate the derived-demand nature of land prices.	9–11				673
8. Know the social and economic characteristics of the farm economy.	7	8,16			666, 674–675
9. Understand the world-wide pervasiveness of agricultural subsidies and other support programs.	21,23	12	1,2		670

Key-Term Review

Review the following terms; if you are not sure of the meaning of any term, write out the definition and check it against the Glossary in the text.

acreage set-aside
barriers to entry
deficiency payment
economic profit
income elasticity of demand

market power
market surplus
parity
price elasticity of demand
profit

Fill in the blank following each of the statements below with the appropriate term from the list above.

1. In agriculture neither buyers nor sellers possess _____.

   1. _____

2. This means in the long run there will be low or zero _____.

   2. _____

3. Even when the economy booms and people have more money to spend, farmers do not make appreciably greater income because of a low _____.

   3. _____

4. In years when there are excellent "bumper" crops, farmers receive very low prices for their crops because of a low _____.

4. _____

5. Farmers argue that what they need are _____ prices that would give them the same ratio of farm to nonfarm prices that existed in the period 1909–14.

5. _____

6. Price-support programs usually result in a _____.

6. _____

7. Recently, farmers have been caught in a cost–price squeeze and net farm income, or _____, has fallen to very low levels.

7. _____

8. _____ programs are designed to restrict the amount of farmland under production.

8. _____

9. _____ are limited to $50,000 per farm.

9. _____

10. Agriculture is characterized by low _____, which is one reason why it is a very competitive industry.

10. _____

True or False: *Circle your choice.*

T F 1. During a recession the demand for food declines very little.

T F 2. The increase in the size of the average-sized farm has been accompanied by a decline in productivity.

T F 3. Quantity supplied in agriculture responds to increased prices with a one-period lag.

T F 4. One way for an individual farmer to protect income is to plant less when prices are low.

T F 5. The farm problem is a post–World War II phenomenon.

T F 6. Under some price-support legislation, farmers have been paid to grow products consumers do not want and paid again to store those crops.

T F 7. The farm population declined from 1940 to 1960 but has remained fairly constant since then.

T F 8. When prices for farm commodities fall, total revenue will go down because the market demand for farm commodities is price inelastic.

T F 9. The average number of acres in a farm has increased during the most recent farm recession.

T F 10. Declining prices for agricultural commodities have been followed by declining prices for farmland.

T F 11. The demand for farmland is derived from the demand for agricultural commodities.

T F 12. Agricultural production in the U.S. economy has been characterized by great increases in output per worker.

T F 13. The milk price support has raised the price of dairy products, reduced consumption, and encouraged production.

T F 14. Deficiency payments are designed to establish the same ratio of farm to nonfarm income as would parity prices.

T F 15. Direct income payments to farmers are more efficient than price-support programs at raising farm incomes.

T F 16. Farming is quite labor intensive.

T F 17. Fortunately for American farmers, a strong U.S. dollar does not hurt exports.

T F 18. When a large crop is produced by American farmers, farmers receive higher incomes.

T F 19. Large stockpiles of government commodities lead to depressed prices as consumers anticipate lowering of stockpiles.

T F 20. If income increases by 20 percent and the quantity demanded at constant prices increases by 10 percent, the income elasticity is 2.0.

T F 21. As a result of U.S. farm subsidies, which lower agricultural prices abroad, Japan's food prices are much lower than those in the United States.

T F 22. Subsidies for agricultural production result in distortions of the production decision in industries that use agricultural products as inputs.

T F 23. Because it subsidizes member nations' wheat producers, the European Community is a major world importer of wheat.

T F 24. To be eligible for any government price supports, farmers must agree to acreage set-asides.

Multiple Choice: *Select the correct answer.*

_____ 1. During which year were relative farm prices at historical highs?
  (a) 1919.
  (b) 1910.
  (c) 1932.
  (d) 1914.

_____ 2. The U.S. government restricts imports of:
  (a) Sugar.
  (b) Beef.
  (c) Cotton.
  (d) All of the above.

_____ 3. Which of the following would result from a price-support program when the support price is set above the equilibrium price?
  (a) The price paid by consumers would be higher.
  (b) The consumption of the product would be reduced.
  (c) Output would increase, *ceteris paribus*.
  (d) All of the above would result.

_____ 4. When government subsidizes the purchase of irrigation water by farmers, the result is:
  (a) Higher marginal costs of production.
  (b) Lower fixed costs to farmers.
  (c) Increased output because marginal costs are lower.
  (d) None of the above.

_____ 5. Which of the following programs will raise farm incomes without generating market distortions?
  (a) Set-aside programs.
  (b) Direct income-support programs.
  (c) Import restrictions.
  (d) None of the above.

_____ 6. Farming is intensive in the use of which of the following factor combinations?
  (a) Labor and land.
  (b) Land and capital.
  (c) Labor and capital.
  (d) Only labor.

_____ 7. Increased oil and fertilizer prices for farmers:
   (a) Raised the farmers' fixed costs of production.
   (b) Lowered the farmers' variable costs of production.
   (c) Raised the farmers' marginal costs of production.
   (d) Raised profit margins of production.

_____ 8. The effect of low crop prices in recent years has been to:
   (a) Reduce farm income.
   (b) Reduce farm wealth.
   (c) Cause an exodus of farmers.
   (d) Do all of the above.

_____ 9. The surplus induced by farm price-support programs can be eliminated by all of the following _except_:
   (a) Export sales.
   (b) Reduced demand.
   (c) Government purchases and stockpiling.
   (d) Supply restrictions.

_____ 10. The Reagan administration's Payment-in-Kind program may be classified as:
   (a) A direct income-support program.
   (b) A price-support program.
   (c) A set-aside program.
   (d) None of the above.

_____ 11. The policy reform programs proposed by the second Reagan administration:
   (a) Were aimed at reducing support prices.
   (b) Proposed to reduce deficiency payments received by farmers.
   (c) Were supposed to make farmers more responsive to market forces.
   (d) Were aimed at all of the above.

_____ 12. Which of the following is _incorrect_?
   (a) In 1983 U.S. farmers kept idle more acreage than all of Western Europe planted.
   (b) In Europe the subsidy for each cow is greater than the personal income of half of the people in the world.
   (c) Japan's rice industry is so efficient it needs no protection.
   (d) U.S. sugar policy has inflicted heavy losses on developing countries.

_____ 13. Which of the following is _not_ generally a characteristic of agriculture?
   (a) Ease of entry and exit.
   (b) Market power.
   (c) Homogeneous products.
   (d) Artificial restraints on prices.

_____ 14. The individual farmer views the demand curve he faces for agricultural commodities as very price elastic, and:
   (a) He is correct even though the market demand curve tends to be quite inelastic.
   (b) He is correct, and the market demand curve is quite elastic as well.
   (c) He is incorrect because the market demand curve tends to be price inelastic.
   (d) He is incorrect because price and quantity demanded are inversely related in the product market.

_____ 15. Which of the following characterizes the price and income elasticities for farm products?
   (a) When prices fall, buyers respond by buying a great deal more; when income increases, buyers respond by buying less.
   (b) When prices and income fall, buyers respond by buying less.
   (c) When prices fall, farmers get less revenue; and when income rises, buyers do not change purchases much.
   (d) All of the above are characteristic.

_____ 16. Which of the following groups have contributed substantially to the technological advances in agriculture?
  (a) Government-sponsored research.
  (b) Research sponsored by those selling equipment to farmers.
  (c) Improvements made by individual farmers.
  (d) All of the above.

_____ 17. During the current farm crisis, the farm population has declined and as a result:
  (a) The marginal productivity of labor should rise.
  (b) The wages of vocational agriculture instructors will not be likely to increase.
  (c) The tax base of farm states has been seriously eroded.
  (d) All of the above are the case.

Problems and Applications

Exercise 1

This exercise shows how to analyze and compare agricultural subsidy programs. It will aid in solving Problem 3 at the end of Chapter 27 in the text.

Reread the article in Chapter 27 of the text entitled "Milk Taxpayers Instead of Cows?" from *U.S. News and World Report*. Assume the supply schedule shown in Table 27.1 for milk prior to the government's actions.

Table 27.1
Supply schedule for milk before government action

Quantity supplied (billions of pounds per year)	Price (dollars per pound)
42	$.05
53	.066
63	.08
76	.10
103	.14

1. Draw the supply curve for milk in Figure 27.1 and label it S_1. Assume that the demand for milk is perfectly inelastic and consumers will buy 53 billion pounds of it. Draw the demand curve and label it D. What is the equilibrium price? $_____

396

Figure 27.1

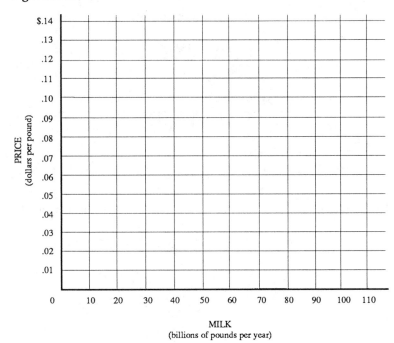

MILK
(billions of pounds per year)

2. Suppose that the farmers' response to the government's offer to pay them for not producing milk results in the supply schedule shown in Table 27.2.

Table 27.2
Supply schedule for milk after government action

Quantity supplied (billions of pounds per year)	Price (dollars per pound)
19	$.05
30	.066
40	.08
53	.10
80	.14

Draw this new supply curve in Figure 27.1 and label it S_2. What is the equilibrium price following the government's intervention? $_____

3. What would be the total amount of the subsidy if the government were to pay farmers the difference between the equilibrium support price (Question 2) and the price that would occur without government interference (Question 1)? $_____

4. Shade in the area in Figure 27.1 that represents the total cost of the government subsidy in Problem 3.

5. According to the article, the government will pay 10 cents for every pound cut from producers' normal production. How much must the government pay to remove 30 percent of the milk (23 billion pounds) from the market, as shown in Figure 27.1 from S_1 to S_2? $_____

6. Use a cross-hatched pattern in Figure 27.1 to show the cost to the government (taxpayers) of cutting normal milk production by 23 billion pounds, from S_1 to S_2, at the 10-cent price.

7. Because it seems stupid to pay farmers not to produce, assume the government allows the farmers to produce the milk and then simply buys 30 percent of the production at 10 cents per pound. The cost of storing that production is 1.74 cents per pound. What would be the total cost of both purchasing *and* storing the milk? $_____

8. Does the estimate of the cost in Question 7 correspond to the estimate of the cost in the article? _____

9. Assume that demand and supply remain the same over four years. How much could be saved by paying farmers to cut production by 30 percent rather than buying and storing 30 percent of their production? (*Hint:* Compare the answers to Questions 5 and 7, and don't forget that the savings over four years must be calculated. _____

10. Does the estimate in Question 9 correspond to the Congressional Budget Office estimate of the savings? _____

11. Which of the three programs described below would be the cheapest means of assuring a price of 10 cents per pound for milk producers?
    (a) Paying the difference between the 10-cent price and the market price paid by consumers. (See the answer to Question 3.)
    (b) Paying farmers not to produce 30 percent of their output. (See the answer to Question 5.)
    (c) Buying 30 percent of farmers' output and storing it. (See answer to Question 7.)

Exercise 2

Articles about agriculture often provide information about shortages or surpluses. By using one of the articles in the textbook, this exercise will show the kind of information to look for to determine whether shortages or surpluses exist. If your professor makes a newspaper assignment for this chapter, this exercise will provide an example of how to do it.

Reread the article in Chapter 27 entitled "Milk Taxpayers Instead of Cows?" from *U.S. News and World Report.* Then answer the following questions:

1. The article indicates there are:
   (a) Shortages.
   (b) Surpluses.

2. What passage in the article indicates the existence of the shortage or surplus?

3. Which of the graphs in Figure 27.2 best represents the shortage or surplus mentioned in the article?
   a   b   (circle one)

Figure 27.2   Shortages or surpluses

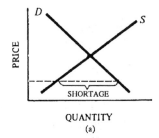
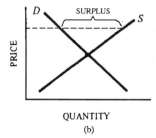

4. Which sentence mentions what is being done or can be done to eliminate the shortage or surplus?

5. Figure 27.3 shows the ways in which demand or supply curves for agriculture can be shifted by a policy to eliminate a shortage or surplus. Which of the diagrams best represents the shift resulting from the passage you indicated in Question 4?   a   b   c   d   (circle one)

Figure 27.3   Shifts of curves

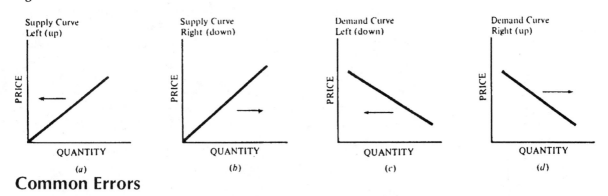

(a) Supply Curve Left (up) *(b)* Supply Curve Right (down) *(c)* Demand Curve Left (down) *(d)* Demand Curve Right (up)

Common Errors

The first statement in each "common error" below is incorrect. Each incorrect statement is followed by a corrected version and an explanation.

1. Advances in farm productivity should be accompanied by improved profitability. WRONG!

   Competition translates improved productivity into lower prices, which can cause lower profitability. RIGHT!

   The spectacular increases in farm productivity that have occurred in the past decades have resulted in lower prices and lower incomes. Increases in supply coupled with price inelastic and slow growing demand have lowered rather than raised net farm income. Yet competition forces the adoption of the newest techniques of scientific farming.

2. When farmers have a bumper crop because of good weather, they will receive high incomes. WRONG!

   When farmers have a bumper crop, their income is likely to fall to low levels. RIGHT!

   Because demand is inelastic for farm goods, a larger percentage rise in output will cause an even larger percentage drop in price.

■ ANSWERS ■

Key-Term Review

1. market power
2. economic profit
3. income elasticity of demand
4. price elasticity of demand
5. parity
6. market surplus
7. profit
8. acreage set-aside
9. deficiency payments
10. barriers to entry

True or False

1. T
2. F
3. T
4. F

5. F
6. T
7. F
8. T

9. T
10. T
11. T
12. T

13. T
14. F
15. T
16. F

17. F
18. F
19. T
20. F

21. F
22. T
23. F
24. T

Multiple Choice

1. a
2. d
3. d

4. c
5. b
6. b

7. c
8. d
9. b

10. c
11. d
12. c

13. b
14. a
15. c

16. d
17. d

Problems and Applications

Exercise 1

1. See Figure 27.1 answer. The equilibrium price is 6.6 cents.

Figure 27.1 answer

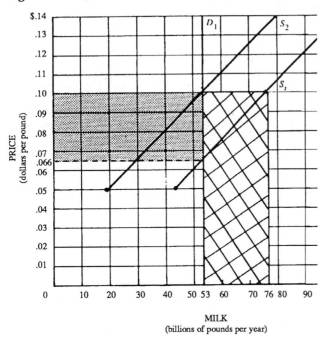

MILK
(billions of pounds per year)

2. See Figure 27.1 answer, line S_2. The equilibrium price is 10 cents.
3. 53 billion pounds x (10.0 cents − 6.6 cents) = $1.8 billion. (This is the same amount that Stockman estimated consumers would lose in the article.)
4. See the shaded area ($1.8 billion) in Figure 27.1 answer.
5. 23 billion pounds x 10 cents per pound = $2.3 billion.
6. See the cross-hatched area in Figure 27.1 answer.
7. Purchase cost is $2.3 billion (See Problem 5). Storage cost is $0.4 billion (1.74 x 23 billion pounds). Total cost is $2.7 billion.
8. yes
9. $2.7 billion − $2.3 billion = $0.4 billion. Multiplying $0.4 billion by the four years shows a saving of $1.6 billion.
10. The estimate in Problem 9 is $100,000 less than the $1.7 billion saving estimated by the Congressional Budget Office as stated in the article.
11. a

Exercise 2

1. b
2. The article says, "and surpluses remained as big as ever."
3. b   Surpluses
4. "Reagan signed legislation to pay dairy producers not to produce milk."
5. a

Chapter 28
Pollution

Quick Review

The word "pollution" is a part of nearly everyone's vocabulary these days. It wasn't always that way. Before the 1960s it wasn't a widely used or widely understood term. The purpose of this chapter is to consider from a systematic economic perspective the following questions:

- What are the major types and sources of pollution?
- What role, if any, do markets play in the creation or abatement of pollution?
- How much of our scarce resources should we devote to cleaning up the environment?

Today we speak easily of many kinds of pollution—air pollution, water pollution, and noise pollution, to name a few. Each imposes opportunity costs on society. Equipment and labor to collect litter, medical services made necessary by unclean air, and engineering services and equipment to clean up rivers and lakes are examples of resources absorbed in the fight against pollution. These resources have valuable alternative uses.

One wonders why producers pollute (although we all contribute to the problem in one way or another). The answer lies in market incentives. In making production decisions, producers will choose the profit-maximizing rate of output and, of course, produce it at the lowest possible cost—even if by doing so they push some real costs onto society as a whole. When they are successful in pushing these costs onto third parties, we say that an "externality" has been created. It represents a divergence between social cost (the full resource cost of an economic activity) and private costs (those borne directly by the producer or consumer of a good).

The solutions to the pollution problem lie in two basic areas: (1) using market incentives and (2) bypassing the market and using direct controls. We shouldn't lose sight of the fact that a pollution-free economy would be very difficult and expensive to achieve. Resources would have to be reallocated to fight pollution and would have to be taken away from the production of other goods and services that we also desire. Prices and patterns of employment would change. That partly explains *why we do not desire to eliminate all pollution*. Indeed, the optimal rate of pollution would be one at which the marginal costs of cleaning up the environment would equal the value of the marginal benefits from cleaning it up.

Learning Objectives

After reading Chapter 28 and doing the following exercises, you should:	True or false	Multiple choice	Problems and applications	Common errors	Pages in the text
1. Know the principal types and sources of pollution.	8	7	4		681–686
2. Understand how to apply the notion of opportunity cost to the pollution problem.	8–11, 13–16		4		686–687
3. Understand how market forces influence the efficiency decisions in producer and consumer behavior.	1	9			687–689
4. Understand the term "externality."	3,4	1			689–693
5. Be able to distinguish between private costs and social costs.	2,7, 11,18	6,8, 11,12	3,4		691
6. Be able to show how taxes, emission charges, and effluent charges can be used to control pollution.	5,6,9,10, 14,15	2–4, 14,15			693–694
7. Be able to show how regulation can be used to control pollution.		5,13	4		694–697
8. Understand how the optimal rate of pollution is determined and know why it is *not* zero.	13	10	1,2,4	1,2	697–700
9. Understand the international dimensions of the pollution problem.	12,17		4		683, 692

Key-Term Review

Review the following terms; if you are not sure of the meaning of any term, write out the definition and check it against the Glossary in the text.

efficiency decision
emission charge
externalities
opportunity cost
optimal rate of pollution

price elasticity of demand
private costs
production decision
social costs

Fill in the blank following each of the statements below with the appropriate term from the list above.

1. When firms equate marginal cost and marginal revenue to determine the profit-maximizing level of output, they are making the _____.

1. _____

2. When firms decide which production process to use to produce a given rate of output, they are said to be making the _____.

2. _____

3. The value of the best alternative use of resources that has been forgone for any course of action is said to be the _____ of that course of action.

3. _____

4. One way to force firms to internalize the costs of pollution would be to levy an _____.

4. _____

5. If the marginal cost of cleaning up the environment equals the marginal benefits *from* cleaning up the environment, society has achieved the _____.

5. _____

6. When the activity of a producer imposes costs (or benefits) on a third party, we refer to the costs or benefits as _____.

6. _____

7. The resource costs actually incurred by a producer are referred to as _____.

7. _____

8. Private costs incurred by a producer plus any external costs imposed on others are called _____.

8. _____

9. The extent to which the cost of cleaning up the environment can be passed along to consumers is determined by the _____.

9. _____

True or False: *Circle your choice.*

T F   1. Pollution results from the rational response of producers to market incentives.

T F   2. Firms that are able to push part of their costs onto society by polluting will produce a greater output of their product than society desires.

T F   3. When externalities exist, firms will not allocate their resources so as to maximize social welfare.

T F   4. Externalities are a measure of the divergence between social costs and private costs.

T F   5. The key to pollution abatement lies in forcing polluters to externalize their internal costs.

T F   6. Market forces brought about the demise of the nonreturnable bottle.

T F   7. When a firm pollutes, its marginal cost curve no longer intersects the average variable cost curve at its lowest point.

T F   8. The existence of a serious pollution problem influences the answer to the WHAT question in the United States.

T F   9. Pollution-abatement programs lead to increases in the prices charged for the products of the polluting industry.

T F 10. Pollution-abatement programs cost jobs in the polluting industries.

T F 11. Social costs of an economic activity include the activity's private costs.

T F 12. The greenhouse problem shows the difficulty of dealing with an externality that is world-wide in size.

T F 13. The optimal rate of pollution will be attained when the total benefits received by lowering the pollution level are equal to the total costs that must be incurred to achieve it.

T F 14. Returnable bottles are not a source of pollution; nonreturnable bottles are a source of pollution.

T F 15. If the cost of cleaning up the air should be borne by those who pollute it, then automobile prices should be increased to cover the costs of including smog devices.

T F 16. Pollution abatement imposes opportunity costs on society.

T F 17. The greenhouse problem is evidence of market failure in both the United States and other countries.

T F 18. Social costs are the sum of private costs and external costs.

Multiple Choice: *Select the correct answer.*

_____ 1. When external costs result from the production of some good, the output level of that good tends to be:
   (a) Larger than is desirable.
   (b) Smaller than is desirable.
   (c) Neither too small nor too large.
   (d) Too large if the external costs exceed the private costs.

_____ 2. It has been suggested that owners of private automobiles should be taxed in proportion to the amount of their exhaust emissions. If this policy were implemented:
   (a) Consumers would insist on truly effective smog-control devices, no matter what the cost.
   (b) The demand for public transportation would probably rise.
   (c) The efficiency of automobiles as measured by gallons per mile would increase.
   (d) None of the above would be the case.

_____ 3. Which of the following means will contribute to a reduction in the amount of solid waste generated within the economy?
   (a) An across-the-board reduction in production and consumption.
   (b) A tax on the disposal of solid-waste materials.
   (c) The outright prohibition of production of certain products.
   (d) All of the above.

_____ 4. If emission charges were affixed to all production and consumption activities:
   (a) The relative price of highly polluting activities would increase.
   (b) People would stop producing and consuming.
   (c) Pollution would be eliminated.
   (d) There would be no redistribution of income.

_____ 5. Pollution levels can be reduced by:
   (a) Transforming waste materials for which the environment has little assimilative capacity into forms for which the environment has a greater assimilative capacity.
   (b) Reducing the levels of production and consumption.
   (c) Stricter enforcement of clean-air laws.
   (d) All of the above.

_____ 6. A firm that can dump its unfiltered waste products into our waterways will be:
   (a) Paying the full cost of production.
   (b) Paying more than the full cost of production.
   (c) Enabled to sell its product at a lower price than if it filtered its wastes.
   (d) Doing none of the above.

_____ 7. The "materials-balance problem" refers to:
   (a) Choosing the most cost-efficient technology to produce a given level of output.
   (b) Choosing a balance of materials so that pollution from any given level of output is minimized.
   (c) The fact that in the production process the physical form of resources changes, but little is actually lost.
   (d) None of the above.

_____ 8. When firms are allowed to pollute the environment without bearing the costs of polluting, then:
   (a) Their marginal cost curve is too low.
   (b) Their average variable cost curve is too low.
   (c) Their average total cost curve is too low.
   (d) All of the above are the case.

_____ 9. When firms acquire the capability of polluting, this capability affects:
   (a) Their production and efficiency decisions.
   (b) Their production decision but not the efficiency decision.
   (c) Their efficiency decision but not the production decision.
   (d) None of the above.

_____10. In making the production decision, polluting firms equate:
   (a) Marginal social cost with marginal social benefits.
   (b) Marginal revenue and internal marginal costs.
   (c) Marginal social cost and marginal revenue.
   (d) Marginal private costs and marginal social costs.

_____11. Which of the following statements concerning social cost is true?
   (a) It excludes private costs.
   (b) It includes private costs.
   (c) It is unrelated to private costs.
   (d) None of the above statements is true.

_____12. When social costs and private costs of consumption and production diverge, then inevitably:
   (a) Producers have an incentive to pollute.
   (b) Consumers have an incentive to pollute.
   (c) Both producers and consumers have an incentive to pollute.
   (d) None of the above statements is true.

_____13. The solution to the pollution-abatement problem lies in:
   (a) Eliminating the divergence between internalized private costs and social costs.
   (b) Compelling firms to internalize all costs resulting from their production.
   (c) Forcing polluters to pay both private and social costs.
   (d) Doing all of the above.

_____14. A required deposit on beverage containers purchased by consumers will:
   (a) Increase beverage consumption.
   (b) Increase beverage production.
   (c) Raise the opportunity cost of polluting.
   (d) Eliminate container waste pollution.

_____15. The use of emission charges to control pollution can have an impact on:
   (a) A firm's production decision because marginal costs are involved.
   (b) A firm's efficiency decision because technology may be affected.
   (c) A firm's investment decision because future profitability may be affected.
   (d) All of the above.

Problems and Applications

Exercise 1

This exercise shows how to compute the optimal rate of pollution.

Table 28.1 indicates various levels of pollution that might be experienced in a lake near your home. It also contains information concerning the value of damages imposed on society by the pollution and the cost to society of cleaning the lake to particular levels. For example, the lake could be made pollution-free with an expenditure of $280,000. The question is: "Is it worth it?" Complete Problems 1–7 to find out.

Table 28.1
**Annual value of damages associated with polluted water
and costs of reducing pollution**

(1) Quantity of pollution (units of waste material per 100 cubic feet of water)	(2) Monetary value of damages (thousands of dollars)	(3) Marginal benefits of pollution abatement (thousands of dollars)	(4) Costs of treating polluted water (thousands of dollars)	(5) Marginal cost of pollution abatement (thousands of dollars)
6	$140	$ —	$ 0	$ —
5	100	40	5	5
4	70	_____	15	_____
3	45	_____	30	_____
2	25	_____	50	_____
1	10	_____	100	_____
0	0	_____	280	_____

1. Assume that without any controls, polluters will annually impose $140,000 of damages on the lake's users by generating 6 units of waste for every 100 cubic feet of water. To clean out the sixth unit of pollutants (that is, lower the quantity of pollution from 6 units to 5) costs $5,000. The value of the benefits gained is $40,000. Complete the rest of column 3.

2. Complete column 5 in Table 28.1 in the same way. The first calculation has been done for you.

3. Should the annual level of pollution be reduced from 6 units to 5? _____

4. Which of the following reasons explains why annual pollution should (or should not) be reduced from 6 to 5 units of pollution?
   (a) The optimal rate of pollution has been reached.
   (b) The marginal social benefits exceed the marginal social cost from reducing the pollution.
   (c) The marginal social costs exceed the marginal social benefits from reducing the pollution.

5. Should pollution be reduced annually from 5 units to 4? _____

6. What is the optimal rate of pollution? _____

7. Which of the following reasons explains why the lake should not be made free of pollution?
   (a) The optimal rate of pollution has been reached when the lake is free of pollution.
   (b) The marginal social benefits incurred in eliminating the pollution would exceed the marginal social benefits achieved.
   (c) The marginal social costs incurred in eliminating all of the pollution would exceed the marginal social benefits achieved.

Exercise 2

This exercise shows how externalities affect third parties.

A chemical plant and a plastics factory are located adjacent to the same stream. The chemical plant is located upstream. The downstream plastics factory requires pure water for its production process. Its basic supply is the stream that runs past both firms.

Figure 28.1

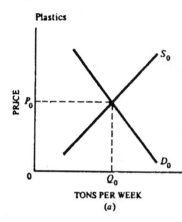

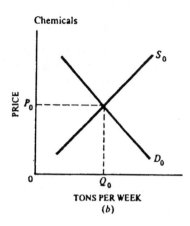

In Figure 28.1a and b, S_0 and D_0 represent the supply and demand for plastics and chemicals, respectively. Assume that the economy is initially competitive and resources are allocated efficiently. Equilibrium price and quantity are P_0 and Q_0 in each case. But then the chemical producer decides to dump waste products into the stream rather than dispose of them with the costly process that had been used.

1. In Figure 28.1b draw in a new private supply curve for chemicals after the dumping in the stream begins. Label it S_1. (*Hint:* It is not possible to draw it in the exact location.)

2. The pollution from the chemical plant forces the plastics manufacturer to use a costly water-purifying system. Draw a new private long-run supply curve for plastics in Figure 28.1a. Label it S_1.

3. The effect of pollution on the quantity of chemicals sold is as if:
   (a) A new, improved technology were discovered.
   (b) Wages to its labor force were reduced.
   (c) The social security tax had been abolished.
   (d) All of the above were the case.

4. As a result of the chemical plant's polluting activities:
   (a) The price of chemicals has risen.
   (b) The price of chemicals has fallen.
   (c) The price of plastics has not changed.
   (d) None of the above is the case.

5. As a result of the chemical plant's activities:
   (a) More chemicals are produced and sold than society desires.
   (b) More labor is used to produce chemicals than society desires.
   (c) More capital inputs are used to produce chemicals than society desires.
   (d) All of the above are the case.

6. The effect of the chemical firm's pollution is to:
   (a) Raise the price of plastics and reduce the quantity sold.
   (b) Lower the price of plastics and increase the quantity sold.
   (c) Raise the price of plastics and increase the quantity sold.
   (d) Do none of the above.

7. The impact of the pollution on the plastics industry in this example is to:
   (a) Reduce the output of plastics below the level that society desires.
   (b) Reduce the employment possibilities in the plastics industry.
   (c) Raise the price of products made with plastics.
   (d) Do all of the above.

Exercise 3

This exercise shows the difference between private marginal costs and social marginal costs.

1. An iron-producing firm mines iron ore. Assume the iron ore industry is competitive. Table 28.2 depicts the private (internalized) costs and social costs of the firm's iron production at each daily production rate. Complete Table 28.2.

Table 28.2
Costs of producing iron

Production rate (tons per day)	Total private cost (dollars per day)	Private marginal cost (dollars per ton)	Total social cost (dollars per day)	Social marginal cost (dollars per ton)
0	$ 0	$ —	$ 0	$ —
1	40	_____	80	_____
2	90	_____	170	_____
3	150	_____	270	_____
4	220	_____	380	_____
5	300	_____	500	_____
6	390	_____	630	_____
7	490	_____	770	_____
8	600	_____	920	_____
9	720	_____	1,080	_____
10	850	_____	1,250	_____
11	990	_____	1,430	_____
12	1,140	_____	1,620	_____

2. In Figure 28.2 graph the demand and marginal cost curves facing the firm for its iron if the price of the iron in the market is $140 per ton. Label the private marginal cost curve *PMC*. Label the social marginal cost curve *SMC*. Label the demand curve "Demand."

Figure 28.2

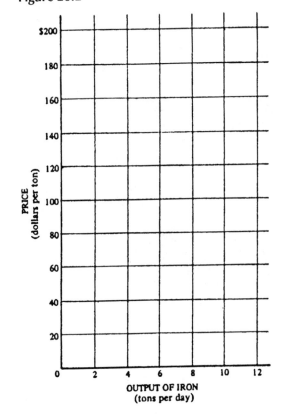

408

3. What is the profit-maximizing production rate for the firm if it considers only its private costs?
   (a) 5 tons per day.
   (b) 7 tons per day.
   (c) 9 tons per day.
   (d) 11 tons per day.

4. What is the profit-maximizing production rate if the firm is required to pay all social costs?
   (a) 5 tons per day.
   (b) 7 tons per day.
   (c) 9 tons per day.
   (d) 11 tons per day.

5. What tax should be charged per ton of iron produced in order to induce the iron-producing firm to pay the true social costs of its production?
   (a) $4 per ton.
   (b) $40 per ton.
   (c) $100 per ton.
   (d) $50 per ton.

Exercise 4

The effects of pollution have become an increasingly important topic in the media. By using one of the articles in the textbook, this exercise will show the kind of information to look for to identify the effects of pollution. If your professor makes a newspaper assignment for this chapter, this exercise will provide an example of how to do it.

Reread the article in Chapter 28 entitled "Effects of SO_2 and NO_x Emissions" from *Science*. Then answer the following questions using Figure 28.3 (which shows possible shifts in the social marginal cost curve from S_0 to S_1 because of a change in pollution levels).

Figure 28.3

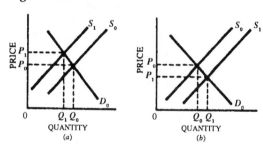

1. What passages indicate a change in pollution levels? (Ignore actions taken by government.)

2. Which graph (a,b) shows the impact of government action on polluting industries?

3. What should happen to the market price as a result of the change in pollution levels?
   (a) The price should rise.
   (b) The price should fall.

4. What should happen to the quantity of product produced at the new equilibrium?
   (a) The quantity should rise.
   (b) The quantity should fall.

5. What passage indicates an action that government can take to correct the problem?

Common Errors

The first statement in each "common error" below is incorrect. Each incorrect statement is followed by a corrected version and an explanation.

1. We should eliminate all pollution. WRONG!

   There is an optimal rate at which pollution can take place given the limited resources of our economy. RIGHT!

   Eliminating pollution involves some significant costs. Would it be practical to make sure that every cigarette butt on campus was picked up—even those that might have been flipped into the bushes? No, because the additional costs necessary to achieve a 100 percent pollution-free environment would exceed the additional benefits of doing so. We stop short of that 100 percent pollution-free level—at the point where the marginal social benefits equal the marginal social costs. It would be inefficient to do otherwise.

2. If business firms have a social conscience, they won't pollute. WRONG!

   Even if business firms have a social conscience, there will still be pollution. RIGHT!

   Firms produce goods and services to make profits. In so doing, they serve the rest of society by providing the goods and services society wants and jobs for millions in the process. To avoid polluting the firms would have to raise their own costs, and there would always be the danger that their competition would not follow suit. Then they would be driven out of business and the pollution problem would still be there.

■ ANSWERS ■

Key-Term Review

1. production decision
2. efficiency decision
3. opportunity cost
4. emission charge
5. optimal rate of pollution
6. externalities
7. private costs
8. social costs
9. price elasticity of demand

True or False

1. T	4. T	7. F	10. T	13. F	16. T
2. T	5. F	8. T	11. T	14. F	17. T
3. T	6. F	9. T	12. T	15. T	18. T

Multiple Choice

1. a	4. a	7. c	10. b	12. c	14. c
2. b	5. d	8. d	11. b	13. d	15. d
3. d	6. c	9. a			

Problems and Applications

Exercise 1

1. Table 28.1 answer

Marginal benefits of pollution abatement	Marginal cost of pollution abatement
$ —	$ —
40	5
30	10
25	15
20	20
15	50
10	180

410

2. See Table 28.1 answer.
3. Yes, because the marginal benefits are worth $40,000 annually, while the marginal costs are only $5,000 annually.
4. b
5. yes
6. When pollution has been reduced to 2 parts per 100 cubic feet of water annually.
7. c

Exercise 2

1. **Figure 28.1 answer**

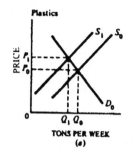 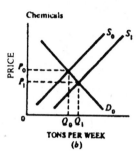

Plastics

Chemicals

2. See Figure 28.1 (*a*), line S_1.
3. d   4. b   5. d   6. a   7. d

Exercise 3

1. **Table 28.2 answer**

Production rate	Private marginal cost	Social marginal cost
0	$ —	$ —
1	40	80
2	50	90
3	60	100
4	70	110
5	80	120
6	90	130
7	100	140
8	110	150
9	120	160
10	130	170
11	140	180
12	150	190

2. **Figure 28.2 answer**

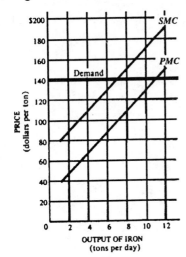

3. d
4. b
5. b

Exercise 4

1. The first two paragraphs contain several examples of increasing pollution levels. One of the most telling examples is the statement "In just a few years observed occurrences of pathology in the forests there have increased from a few percent to more than 50 percent."

2. a
3. a
4. b
5. The article states the government can "enact legislation designed to curtail it."

Chapter 29
Productivity of the Firm

Quick Review

Until now we have assumed that firms are profit maximizers and hence that they minimize their costs for any given level of production. In this chapter these assumptions are held up for scrutiny.

Our discussion will be guided by the following questions:

- What is an "efficient" firm?
- What forces enhance or impede efficiency?
- How can managers improve a firm's performance?

Our discussion necessarily begins with the production function, which indicates maximum output rates for any level of inputs. The cost function, on the other hand, indicates minimum costs for any given level of production. In this chapter we define inefficiency as a condition of the firm producing less than its maximum (technical inefficiency) or with costs greater than its necessary minimum (cost inefficiency). Harvard Professor Harvey Leibenstein coined the term "x-inefficiency" to refer to both.

Efficiency is often measured as the difference between potential and actual productivity. Productivity and (in)efficiency changes are not the same thing. Productivity refers to output per unit of labor, output per unit of capital, or output per unit of labor and capital. Productivity *changes* are the result of changes in technology or in the amount of inputs used. By contrast, efficiency refers to the use of an input *relative* to its potential usefulness. Hence, *changes* in efficiency come about when *given* amounts of inputs working with *given* technology produce either more or less output.

Increased efficiency is essential to survival. Many case studies from publications such as the *Wall Street Journal, Fortune, Forbes,* and *Business Week* have shown that firms have drastically increased their output or produced at lower costs. Often such improvements may come about either through the threat of job and income loss or when a (new) management team applies a system of motivation that produces more work effort from its employees.

What causes a firm to be x-efficient? The sociology of the firm, unions, market power, government regulation and buying procedures, and management performance all play a role. The sociology of the firm is important for two reasons. First, individuals have some discretion or control over how much effort they use on the job. Second, the managers are very often not the owners and hence will seek to achieve goals other than maximum profits for the firm.

Market power also has an effect on productivity. Unions will affect productivity through work rules such as seniority and their receptivity to technological changes. If a firm has market power, then it is sheltered from competitive pressure and hence from the strict requirement of being x-efficient. In a similar manner, government regulation may give the firm monopoly status while its buying procedures often exclude a concern for cost efficiency.

Management is seen as ultimately responsible for the firm's level of efficiency. There are many different types of managers and ways they prod firms to be more efficient. There are different theories about how to manage, including X, Y, and Z (the Japanese model of the firm). While Theory X assumes that workers are lazy and irresponsible, Theory Y assumes the opposite along with the further assumption that workers are motivated by more than money. Theory Z takes this one step further by viewing the firm as a family, by emphasizing consensus and cooperation, and by training employees to be part of the firm, not part of their own profession.

However, the keys to efficiency are elusive. Firms that seem to be x-efficient this year are found x-inefficient the next. We close by noting, however, that greater effort at work not only increases available output but may often increase job satisfaction as well.

Learning Objectives

After reading Chapter 29 and doing the following exercises, you should:	True or false	Multiple choice	Problems and applications	Common errors	Pages in the text
1. Understand the relationship between technical efficiency and cost efficiency.	1–6	6,7,9	1	1	702–705
2. Know some of the barriers that prevent firms from achieving maximum productivity from a set of inputs.	7–13	1,8,11	3	1,2	705–715
3. Be able to measure productivity in a simple problem.	15	5	1,3		703–704
4. Be familiar with theories of management behavior.	8,14,18	1–4, 10,11	2		711–717
5. Be aware of differences between Japanese and American philosophies and styles of management.	16,17	12,13			711–716

Key-Term Review

Review the following terms; if you are not sure of the meaning of any term, write out the definition and check it against the Glossary in the text.

cost inefficiency
discretionary effort
diseconomy of scale
labor supply

management
production function
productivity
technical inefficiency

Fill in the blank following each of the statements below with the appropriate term from the list above.

1. The _____ matches the maximum output that can be achieved to a given set of inputs.

1. _____

2. _____ is the ratio of output produced to the unit of a specified input or set of inputs used to produce the output.

2. _____

3. When a firm is operating with _____, it must also suffer from _____, because one implies the other.

3. _____

   _____

4. _____ is the difference between maximum effort on the part of the employee and the level of effort that allows him or her to keep his or her job.

4. _____

5. When the size of the firm increases, individual work effort may be reduced, and a _____ is the result.

5. _____

6. The _____ curve is thought to slope upward and to the right.

6. _____

7. _____ controls the inputs into the production process.

7. _____

True or False: *Circle your choice.*

T F   1. If a firm is operating in a technically inefficient manner, more output can be produced only if more inputs are used.

T F   2. Inefficiency is measured by the amount by which actual productivity exceeds potential productivity.

T F   3. When a firm is using "best practices," its *ATC* curve cannot be forced any lower.

T F   4. Cost inefficiency results from technical inefficiency.

T F   5. The past existence of x-inefficiency can be inferred when firms are "turned around" by new management.

T F   6. Increasing productivity in the upswing of the business cycle implies inefficiency in the contraction phase of the cycle.

T F   7. Economic theory traditionally has assumed managers' primary motivation is profit, but recently this assumption has been questioned.

T F   8. Owner-managed firms tend to be more cost efficient than those of nonowner managers.

T F   9. The smaller the commitment gap, the more inefficient the firm will be.

T F 10. Union work rules are a significant source of inefficiency.

T F 11. Cost-plus contracting rewards inefficiency because the higher costs bring greater absolute profit.

T F 12. Firms with market power are likely to be more efficient than competitive firms that have less control over the market.

T F 13. New technology that lowers average costs also increases the productivity of all factors.

T F 14. Theory Y managers rely on fear.

T F 15. Increasing one factor, such as capital, relative to another, such as labor, should shift the production function upward.

T F 16. When Japanese firms have been established in America, they have been much more successful than their American counterparts.

T F 17. According to Martin Starr and Nancy Bloom, Japanese-owned firms in the United States have lower absenteeism but higher turnover than American firms.

T F 18. Because stock ownership is so widely dispersed in the United States, corporate management is becoming more insulated from stockholder control.

Multiple Choice: *Select the correct answer.*

_____ 1. Which of the following is *not* a management function?
(a) Forecasting.
(b) Planning.
(c) Organizing.
(d) Controlling.

_____ 2. Which of the following types of managers would be most likely to say the following: "If you come to work late one more time, it'll be the last time you come to work"?

(a) A theory X manager.
(b) A theory Y manager.
(c) A theory Z manager.
(d) A cost-plus contract manager.

_____ 3. Which of the following managers would be most likely to say the following: "We're not producing what we should on the third shift. Check with the guys on the line and see if you can solve the problem together"?

(a) A theory X manager.
(b) A theory Y manager.
(c) A theory Z manager.
(d) A cost-plus contract manager.

_____ 4. Which of the following managers would be likely to say the following: "The home office may be forced to close the plant if we don't become profitable. Let's all get together to see if, as a group, we can work it out"?

(a) A theory X manager.
(b) A theory Y manager.
(c) A theory Z manager.
(d) A cost-plus contract manager.

_____ 5. Productivity is measured by:

(a) The decline in labor cost per unit of output.
(b) The output divided by the amount of factor that is used to produce it.
(c) The change in output that results from a change in inputs.
(d) All of the above.

_____ 6. Inefficiency means:

(a) That more output could be produced with the resources that are being used.
(b) That a smaller amount of resources could be used to produce the same output.
(c) That the same output could be produced at a lower cost.
(d) All of the above.

_____ 7. Which of the following concepts can be illustrated by the shape of the long-run average cost curve?

(a) Technical inefficiency.
(b) x-inefficiency.
(c) Cost inefficiency.
(d) Diseconomies of scale.

_____ 8. To measure discretionary effort, it is necessary to know:

(a) The maximum effort an individual can bring to a job.
(b) The minimum effort needed to keep a job.
(c) The commitment gap.
(d) All of the above.

_____ 9. Diseconomies of scale occur when a long-run average cost curve is:

(a) Flat.
(b) Downward sloping.
(c) Upward sloping.
(d) None of the above.

_____ 10. Unfriendly takeovers can be beneficial to stockholders when:

(a) Current management is inefficiently managing the firm to be taken over.
(b) The firm that is attempting the takeover is managed inefficiently.
(c) There are tax advantages from taking over a company.
(d) All of the above are the case.

_____11. Which of the following is always a barrier to productivity improvement?
   (a) Unionization.
   (b) Competition.
   (c) Government interference.
   (d) Larger commitment gaps.

_____12. Which of the following does *not* justify foreign investment by the Japanese in the United States?
   (a) Japanese trade barriers to American goods.
   (b) Avoiding the costs of shipping goods from Japan to the United States.
   (c) Producing in the United States allows the Japanese firms to avoid U.S. trade restrictions.
   (d) All of the above justify such investment.

_____13. According to Martin Starr and Nancy Bloom, which of the following statements is true concerning differences between Japanese and American management styles?
   (a) Japanese put work before family; Americans do not.
   (b) Japanese are group oriented; Americans are more individualistic.
   (c) Japanese are open and cooperative; Americans are less open and cooperative.
   (d) All of the above are the case.

Problems and Applications

Exercise 1

The relationship of efficiency, production curves, and cost curves is examined in this exercise. After doing this exercise, you will find the problem at the end of Chapter 29 in the text easier to complete.

1. Table 29.1 and Table 29.2 represent a firm's experience in two different time periods even though the level of its inputs is the same in both periods. Complete the tables assuming that wages for labor are $30 per day and material costs are $5 per unit of output produced. The two periods differ in fixed costs; the first period has a fixed cost of $200 while the second period has a fixed cost of $100.

Table 29.1
Period 1

(1) Labor (workers per day)	(2) Total product (units per day)	(3) Marginal product (units per worker)	(4) Fixed cost (dollars per day)	(5) Labor cost (dollars per day)	(6) Material cost (dollars per day)	(7) Total cost (dollars per day)	(8) Average cost (dollars per unit)	(9) Marginal cost (dollars per unit)
0	0	_____	$_____	$_____	$_____	$_____	$_____	$_____
2	20	_____	_____	_____	_____	_____	_____	_____
4	30	_____	_____	_____	_____	_____	_____	_____
6	36	_____	_____	_____	_____	_____	_____	_____
8	40	_____	_____	_____	_____	_____	_____	_____

Table 29.2
Period 2

(1) Labor (workers per day)	(2) Total product (units per day)	(3) Marginal product (units per worker)	(4) Fixed cost (dollars per day)	(5) Labor cost (dollars per day)	(6) Material cost (dollars per day)	(7) Total cost (dollars per day)	(8) Average cost (dollars per unit)	(9) Marginal cost (dollars per unit)
0	0	_____	$_____	$_____	$_____	$_____	$_____	$_____
2	16	_____	_____	_____	_____	_____	_____	_____
4	24	_____	_____	_____	_____	_____	_____	_____
6	30	_____	_____	_____	_____	_____	_____	_____
8	32	_____	_____	_____	_____	_____	_____	_____

2. For period 1 draw the total product curve in Figure 29.1 and label it OU_1. In the same figure draw the total product curve for period 2, and label it OU_2.

Figure 29.1
Total product curves

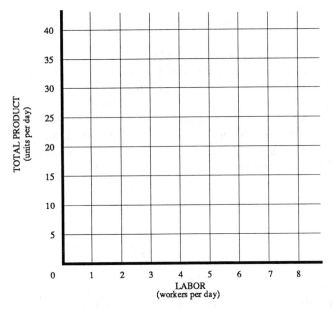

3. Which period shows the most technically efficient use of the labor input?
   (a) Period 1.
   (b) Period 2.

4. In Figure 29.2, for period 1 draw the average cost curve (label it AC_1) and marginal cost curve (label it MC_1). In the same figure, for period 2 draw the average cost curve (label it AC_2) and marginal cost curve (label it MC_2).

Figure 29.2
Average and marginal cost curves

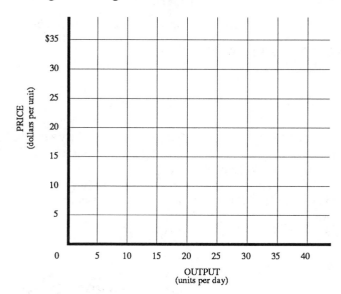

5. Which period was most cost efficient for the firm?
   (a) Period 1.
   (b) Period 2.

6. Suppose the firm experienced x-inefficiency in both periods. In which period is the x-inefficiency most attributable to lazy management of the labor resource?
   (a) Period 1.
   (b) Period 2.

7. In which period is the x-inefficiency most attributable to lazy management of the fixed capital resource?
   (a) Period 1.
   (b) Period 2.

Exercise 2

This exercise should help you remember the individuals whose ideas were discussed in the text.

Match the names of the individuals with the descriptive statements which describe their theories, ideas, evidence, or experience. Place your answers in the blanks provided.

a. W. Edwards Deming   e. John Shelton
b. Martin Starr and Nancy Bloom   f. Walter Primeaux
c. Kenichi Yamamoto   g. Frederick Taylor
d. Harvey Leibenstein   h. Abraham Maslow

_____ 1. The changing pattern of world economic conditions will dictate new management styles for Japanese firms in the future.

_____ 2. Utility companies that compete directly will have lower costs than those sheltered as natural monopolies.

_____ 3. "Piece rates" did not yield the response hoped for.

_____ 4. Workers don't want to be identified with defective parts. The system is to blame for quality problems.

_____ 5. Japanese management techniques can be used to advantage in other countries.

_____ 6. Technical inefficiency and cost inefficiency are two sides of the same coin.

_____ 7. When companies buy back franchised restaurants and provide an employee-manager, costs go up.

_____ 8. Managers must respond to workers' needs. Basic needs must be satisfied first. Higher-level needs must be satisfied in other ways.

Exercise 3

The media often provide information on changes within a firm that are expected to affect its productivity. By using one of the articles in the text, this exercise will show the kind of information to look for. If your professor makes a newspaper assignment for this chapter, this exercise will provide an example of how to do it.

Reread the article from Chapter 25 entitled "Business Journal to Buy, Then Close, Business Review" from the *Washington Post*. Then answer the following questions:

Figure 29.3
Shifts of curves

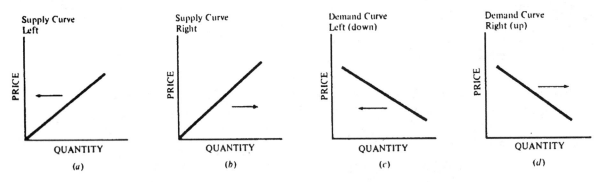

1. What sentence indicates a change in technology or productivity?

2. What is the product for which the change in technology or productivity will have an effect?

3. Which diagram in Figure 29.3 shows the direction of the shift of the supply or demand curve as a result of the change in productivity?   a   b   c   d   (circle one)

Common Errors

The first statement in each "common error" below is incorrect. Each incorrect statement is followed by a corrected version and an explanation.

1. Technological change means increased productivity. WRONG!

   Technological change may increase the productivity of some factors, but it may increase the productivity of none of them. RIGHT!

   Sometimes "change" in an industry, such as mining, involves increasing inefficiency through time. Even with better techniques it may not be possible to produce as much output per unit of the inputs. Furthermore, even if productivity increases with respect to some inputs, there are others in which it is likely to decrease. When technological change involves the use of more of a factor, diminishing returns are likely to lower the marginal productivity of that one factor and possibly productivity as well.

2. Workers can be made more productive if their wages are lowered. WRONG!

When workers are given the incentive to produce more or when technology changes so that they can produce more, their productivity changes. RIGHT!

Productivity is measured as the amount of output divided by the amount of input. Wages do not appear in the measure of productivity. Lower wages may actually hurt productivity by giving less incentive to workers to work.

■ ANSWERS ■

Key-Term Review

1. production function
2. productivity
3. technical inefficiency

cost inefficiency
4. discretionary effort
5. diseconomy of scale

6. labor supply
7. management

True or False

1. F	4. T	7. T	10. T	13. F	16. F
2. F	5. T	8. T	11. T	14. F	17. T
3. T	6. T	9. F	12. F	15. T	18. F

Multiple Choice

1. a	4. c	6. d	8. d	10. a	12. a
2. a	5. b	7. d	9. c	11. d	13. d
3. b					

Problems and Applications

Exercise 1

1. Table 29.1 answer

(3) Marginal product (units per worker)	(4) Fixed cost (dollars per day)	(5) Labor cost (dollars per day)	(6) Material cost (dollars per day)	(7) Total cost (dollars per day)	(8) Average cost (dollars per unit)	(9) Marginal cost (dollars per unit)
—	$200	$ 0	$ 0	$200	$ —	$ —
10	200	60	100	360	18.00	8
5	200	120	150	470	15.67	11
3	200	180	180	560	15.55	15
2	200	240	200	640	16.00	20

Table 29.2 answer

(3) Marginal product (units per worker)	(4) Fixed cost (dollars per day)	(5) Labor cost (dollars per day)	(6) Material cost (dollars per day)	(7) Total cost (dollars per day)	(8) Average cost (dollars per unit)	(9) Marginal cost (dollars per unit)
—	$100	$ 0	$ 0	$100	$ —	$ —
8	100	60	80	240	15.00	8.75
4	100	120	120	340	14.20	12.50
3	100	180	150	430	14.30	15.00
1	100	240	160	500	15.63	35.00

2. **Figure 29.1 answer**

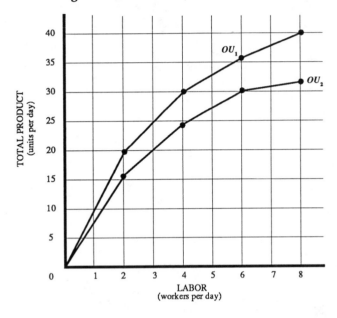

3. a The production curve for period 1 is above that for period 2.
4. **Figure 29.2 answer**

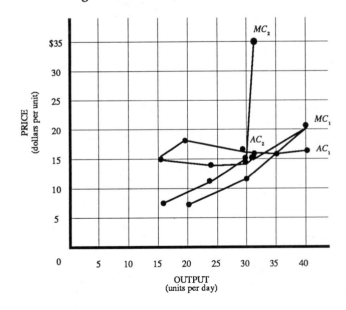

422

5. b   The average cost is lowest for period 2.
6. b   See Problem 3.
7. a   There were higher fixed costs for managing the fixed amount of capital in both periods.

Exercise 2

1. c   5. b
2. f   6. d
3. g   7. e
4. a   8. h

Exercise 3

1. The key sentence is, "they will buy and close down their competitor." Since one firm will take over the customers of the other firm, it will be able to spread its costs over a wider circulation. This will probably lower the average cost of delivering each paper. Furthermore, the firm will very likely have the ability to choose the best employees from its competitor, which may lead to greater employee productivity. However, the capacity to produce newspapers will be reduced with the closing down of one firm, which could also alter productivity.
2. The product is a business journal.
3. Demand from the firm's viewpoint increases because a substitute has been eliminated. However, if the reorganization allows better personnel to be employed then the shift would be rightward from the viewpoint of the firm (answer b). From the viewpoint of the market, there is a shift of the supply curve to the left (answer a) because there are fewer firms.

Chapter 30
The Supply of Labor

Quick Review

Most of us do not think of ourselves in the abstract as "inputs," or factors of production, but in the language of the circular flow of economic activity, that's what we are. In the circular flow model there are markets for products and markets for factors. People are demanders in the product market but suppliers in the factor market. This chapter discusses the supply side of that market; the next chapter looks at the demand side.

The "supply" questions that need to be answered are:

- What are the motivations for working?
- How do people decide how much time to allocate to work?
- How do wage rates and other firms of compensation affect the quantity of labor supplied to the market?

Let's begin with the first question. People choose between leisure and the satisfaction of material needs. Given the institutional structure of our economy, material needs are satisfied mainly by working for income. When we work, however, we sacrifice leisure. Hence, the opportunity cost of goods and services obtained by working is the number of hours of leisure that must be sacrificed to earn the required income. Conversely, the opportunity cost of leisure is the amount of goods and services that cannot be bought because of the time not spent working. Psychological and social needs may also motivate people to work. These needs affect the utility of both leisure and the income gained from work.

The marginal utility of labor reflects the satisfaction to be gained from added income as well as any direct pleasure a job may provide. A worker compares the marginal utility of labor with that of leisure and chooses either more labor or more leisure, depending on which offers greater marginal utility. An individual's work effort is optimal when the marginal utility of labor equals the marginal utility of leisure.

The supply curve of labor reflects the trade-off between material needs and leisure. People feel two conflicting emotions when they receive an increase in the wage they are paid for working.

1. The substitution effect makes a person want to work more. (An hour of work is worth more in terms of goods and services that can be obtained; the opportunity cost of leisure has risen.)
2. The income effect diminishes the need to work. (The same quantity of goods and services can be obtained with less labor after the wage increase.)

Usually these two effects result in an upward-sloping supply curve for labor; a wage increase encourages a person to work more hours. But if a person dislikes work or feels enough of his or her needs are already met, a higher wage may result in fewer hours worked, so that his or her supply curve bends backward. In this case the income effect overpowers the substitution effect.

Learning Objectives

After reading Chapter 30 and doing the following exercises, you should:	True or false	Multiple choice	Problems and applications	Common errors	Pages in the text
1. Know what the labor-supply curve is and the determinants that cause it to shift.	1,4,9,10, 16,18	1,4,5,8, 14–18	1,3	1,2,4	720–724
2. Be able to explain the trade-off between leisure and labor.		2,12			724–728
3. Be able to explain the importance of the marginal utility of leisure and labor to the labor-supply curve.	11,15	7,13	1	3	726–728, 730–731
4. Be able to apply the law of diminishing marginal utility to the labor market.	2,3,13,14		2		727–728
5. Know the condition that must be satisfied if the optimum choice is to be made between leisure and work.	13	7,11	2	3	728
6. Be able to explain the shape of the labor-supply curve, including its backward-bending segment.	6,17, 20,21		1		729–731
7. Be able to describe the substitution effect and income effect.	5,7,8, 20,21	3,10	1		730–731
8. Be able to describe the institutional constraints on the supply of labor.		9			734
9. Be able to show how the government can alter the labor-market outcomes, particularly with respect to supplying labor to the military.	19	6	3		735–737
10. Be able to describe the market supply of labor and calculate the elasticity of supply.	8,9	20,21	3		731–732

Key-Term Review

Review the following terms; if you are not sure of the meaning of any term, write out the definition and check it against the Glossary in the text.

elasticity of labor supply
income effect of wages
labor supply
labor-supply curve
law of diminishing marginal utility
marginal utility of labor

market mechanism
market supply of labor
optimal work effort
substitution effect of wages
utility
wage rate

Fill in the blank following each of the statements below with the appropriate term from the list above.

1. The increment of satisfaction gained by giving up leisure in order to work an extra hour is the
_____ .

1. _____

2. The more hours you work, the more you appreciate an extra hour of leisure. This is consistent with the _____.

2. _____

3. If your marginal utility of labor is the same as your marginal utility of leisure, then you have reached the _____.

3. _____

4. Marginal utility gained from the goods and services will rise when you have fewer goods and services, but total _____ may decline.

4. _____

5. As long as the government does not interfere with the factor payment to labor—in other words, the _____—then people will tend to achieve the optimal work effort through the workings of the _____.

5. _____

_____

6. In the labor market, changes in the number of workers, expectations, and working conditions will alter _____.

6. _____

7. However, if there is not a strong _____, then there may be a backward-bending _____ because of the overpowering _____.

7. _____

_____

_____

8. By summing the individual supply curves for labor, we can obtain the _____.

8. _____

9. The _____ is a measure of the responsiveness of the quantity of labor supplied to changes in the wage rate.

9. _____

True or False: *Circle your choice.*

T F 1. The fact that you are willing to have leisure time and are able to pay for it by working means that you have a supply curve for labor.

T F 2. An increase in wages raises the marginal utility of work.

T F 3. According to the law of diminishing marginal utility, the higher the wage rate, the lower the utility of leisure.

T F 4. The chief reason people work is that work itself has utility.

T F 5. The supply curve for labor bends backward when the substitution effect of wages exceeds the income effect of wages.

T F 6. On the portion of the supply curve for labor that bends backward, a decline in wages means that there is an increase in the quantity of labor that would be supplied in a given time period.

T F 7. If wages rise and the quantity of labor supplied remains unchanged, the income effect of the wage change must exactly cancel the substitution effect of the wage change.

T F 8. If the income effect is ignored, the substitution effect of a wage decrease always encourages a worker to work less.

T F 9. Increasing the status of a job does not shift the labor-supply curve.

T F 10. Employees demand work during a recession.

T F 11. The demand curve and the marginal utility curve are the same.

T F 12. The market supply of labor curve is the horizontal summation of the individual labor-supply curves of laborers in the labor market.

T F 13. If a person is making an optimal work effort, an increase in the prices of goods and services that he or she purchases should initially decrease the marginal utility of work below that of leisure.

T F 14. According to the law of diminishing marginal utility, the marginal utility of leisure falls as a person has more of it.

T F 15. Laborers move down their marginal utility of labor curves as wages fall.

T F 16. A change in wage rates causes a shift in labor supply.

T F 17. The backward-bending supply curve is caused by a shift in workers' attitudes toward work.

T F 18. A change in job status shifts both the marginal utility of labor curve and the labor-supply curve.

T F 19. A military draft is an example of how the market mechanism allocates scarce resources.

T F 20. Although the market supply of labor curve may bend backward, the individual supply curves cannot.

T F 21. If the market supply of labor were to bend backward, employers would have to reduce wages to obtain larger quantities of labor.

Multiple Choice: *Select the correct answer.*

_____ 1. The main reason that people work is:
   (a) The work ethic.
   (b) Materialistic wants.
   (c) That too much leisure is not good.
   (d) None of the above.

_____ 2. The constraint that is *most* important in determining the trade-off between leisure and work is:
   (a) Income.
   (b) Time.
   (c) Available goods and services.
   (d) Satisfaction from working.

_____ 3. If wages rise and the quantity of labor supplied falls, then:
   (a) The income effect overpowers the substitution effect.
   (b) The substitution effect overpowers the income effect.
   (c) The two effects cancel each other out.
   (d) The effect that prevails cannot be determined.

_____ 4. Upgrading the status of a job does not shift the labor-supply curve:
   (a) Because tastes are not a determinant of supply curves.
   (b) Because such an action affects only the demand for labor.
   (c) Because such an action does not alter wages.
   (d) For none of the above reasons, because upgrading a job *does* shift the labor supply curve.

_____ 5. Because of the work ethic, the *supply curve* for labor is:
  (a) Higher than it would be if people had only materialistic needs.
  (b) Lower than it would be if people had only materialistic needs.
  (c) Higher than it would be if the United States were a slaveholding society, as ancient Greece was.
  (d) None of the above.

_____ 6. Which of the following examples *best* suggests that the marginal utility of work is higher than the marginal utility of leisure?
  (a) At the end of the 1960s, many college students did not bother to get jobs.
  (b) During the Vietnam War, many young men were drafted into the army in order to provide the necessary military personnel.
  (c) During 1972–73, union representatives pushed for optional overtime in contracts with several major companies that previously had required involuntary overtime.
  (d) During the recession of 1974–75, some unions had to accept lower pay in order to maintain jobs.

_____ 7. Which of the following is *incorrect*? According to the Bureau of Labor Statistics survey presented on page 734 of the text:
  (a) The older the worker, the more satisfied he or she is with his or her work-leisure mix.
  (b) Over all age groups, nearly two-thirds of the workers are satisfied with their work–leisure mix.
  (c) Most of those who are dissatisfied with their current work-leisure mix prefer more leisure.
  (d) All of the above are correct.

_____ 8. Shifts of the labor-supply curve are caused by:
  (a) Changes in tastes for jobs.
  (b) Wage increases.
  (c) Changes in the number of job vacancies.
  (d) All of the above.

_____ 9. The reason that few people can achieve the optimal work effort is:
  (a) Their inability to control the number of hours to be worked.
  (b) Their inability to control the marginal utility of leisure.
  (c) The low wages available to them.
  (d) None of the above.

_____ 10. The decline in the average workweek that has accompanied the increase in real income since the beginning of the twentieth century is most consistent with:
  (a) The income effect of wages.
  (b) The substitution effect of wages.
  (c) The law of diminishing marginal utility.
  (d) The law of demand.

_____ 11. By definition, the optimal work effort occurs:
  (a) When the marginal utility of labor equals the marginal utility of leisure.
  (b) When the opportunity cost of labor equals the marginal cost of leisure.
  (c) When the labor-supply curve intersects the labor demand curve.
  (d) Under none of the above circumstances.

_____ 12. In the trade-off between leisure and work, economists must assume that:
  (a) Leisure cannot occur simultaneously with work.
  (b) Work is not desired for its own sake.
  (c) The availability of leisure is unlimited.
  (d) People can pay for leisure.

_____ 13. Which of the following changes the marginal utility of leisure for an employee who has achieved the optimal work effort?
  (a) A change in the wage rate.
  (b) Increased status of the job performed.
  (c) Higher prices of goods and services.
  (d) All of the above.

Figure 30.1 shows possible movements along or shifts of the market labor-supply curve.

Figure 30.1

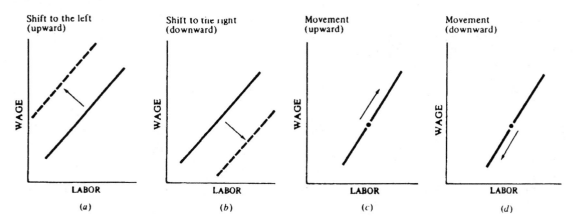

Choose the letter of the diagram that best represents what would happen to the private labor market in Questions 14–18, *ceteris paribus.*

_____14. The wage rate rises.

_____15. Job status increases.

_____16. There is a reduction in the size of the labor force.

_____17. Wage controls push wages below market levels.

_____18. Women are legally permitted to serve in combat functions in the armed forces for the first time.

Problems and Applications

Exercise 1

This exercise shows the relationship between marginal utility and the supply of labor. It provides practice in graphing labor supply and examines backward-bending supply curves, the substitution effect, and the income effect.

Suppose you came to school without any means of support. The employment office suggests that you take a job at the school. Your only task is to correct true–false examinations (the professors give you all of the answers to the exams), add up the scores, and figure out everyone's grade (except your own). You can work as many hours as you wish because opportunities are plentiful.

Drawing labor-supply curves

If the work were offered to you on a volunteer basis, you would not work at all. But at $2 an hour you might work one hour per day—just to see how well your classmates are doing. Only at $4 an hour would it be worthwhile to work many hours—perhaps four hours per day. At $8 an hour you would work six hours per day and at $16 an hour you would make it a full-time job of eight hours per day. But at $32 an hour you would decide to spend more time at leisure and work only six hours per day.

1. Fill in column 1 of Table 30.1, your labor-supply schedule using the information in the paragraph above.

Table 30.1
Supply of labor

(1) Hourly wage (dollars per hour)	(2) Work effort (hours worked per day)	(3) Elasticity of supply
$ 0	_____	—
2	_____	_____
4	_____	_____
8	_____	_____
16	_____	_____
32	_____	_____

2. Graph the labor-supply curve in Figure 30.2. Be sure to label the axes and the curves. (The curve should pass through point A.)

Figure 30.2

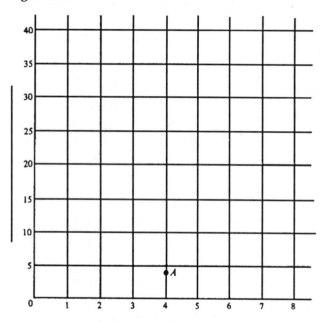

Backward-bending supply curves

3. On the backward-bending segment of a supply curve, price and quantity are:
   (a) Directly (positively) related.
   (b) Inversely related.
   (c) Related by a horizontal line.
   (d) Related by a vertical line.

4. Which of the following circumstances might explain a backward-bending supply curve such as the one you have drawn in Figure 30.2?
   (a) You want to make a certain amount of income, and like Freddie in the text, you want to spend the rest of your time sleeping, listening to the stereo, and playing video games.
   (b) Because of the increased income you receive from a raise in wages, you can increase your leisure without losing any income.
   (c) The marginal utility of income falls as income rises.
   (d) All of the above might explain such a curve.

5. An increase in wage rates:
   (a) Definitely increases hours worked through both the substitution and income effects.
   (b) Tends to increase hours worked through the substitution effect but may tend to decrease hours worked through the income effect.
   (c) Tends to increase hours worked through the substitution effect but definitely decreases hours worked through the income effect.
   (d) Tends to decrease hours worked through the substitution effect and may increase hours worked through the income effect.

6. On the backward-bending portion of the supply curve:
   (a) The income effect overpowers the substitution effect.
   (b) The substitution effect overpowers the income effect.
   (c) Both effects tend to decrease the quantity of labor supplied as a result of a wage increase.

7. In column 3 of Table 30.1, show the elasticity of supply between each successful rate.

The relation of marginal utility to supply

Table 30.2 presents the labor–leisure trade-off and the marginal utilities of labor and leisure at two wage rates.

Table 30.2
Hours spent at work and at leisure and marginal utilities of labor and leisure at two wage rates

Total hours		Marginal utility		
			Labor	
Leisure	Labor	Leisure	Wage = $4	Wage = $8
24	0	20	—	—
23	1	30	200	400
22	2	45	150	310
21	3	70	120	240
20	4	90	90	180
19	5	105	60	150
18	6	130	40	130
17	7	180	32	90
16	8	260	24	70
15	9	300	18	50
14	10	350	12	35
13	11	410	7	20
12	12	490	3	10
11	13	600	0	0
.	.	.	.	.
.	.	.	.	.
.	.	.	.	.
0	24		0	0

8. At a wage of $4, how many hours would be worked? _____ (Find the optimal work effort in much the same way as was done with Table 30.2 in the text.) Plot the point in Figure 30.2 and label it *A*. (*Note:* The point you have drawn in should be the same as that which is shown on the graph.)

9. What is the optimal work effort at the $8 wage rate? _____ Plot the point in Figure 30.2. Label it *B*. Connect this point with a straight line to point *A* (Problem 8).

10. T F The choices made by the use of marginal utility analysis are reflected in the labor-supply curve of Figure 30.2.

11. T F The marginal utility for labor (Table 30.2) does not follow the law of diminishing marginal utility.

12. T F The opportunity cost of labor is one hour of leisure per hour of labor.

Exercise 2

This exercise shows the relationship between marginal utility and the optimal work effort.

Optimal work effort

People work for many things besides money. Students, for example, work (sacrifice leisure) in order to get higher grades. Let's return to Freddie, the economics student mentioned in the text. Suppose Freddie believes that for each extra hour of study per day he can raise his grade average for the semester by a full letter grade. If he spends one hour, he can have a D average. Two hours earns a C average, and so on. He doesn't have to hold a job because his parents still give him his allowance, so he has twenty-four hours of leisure time. But every hour of study means one less hour of leisure time.

1. The optimal work effort is attained at that amount of work at which:
   (a) The marginal utility of income from another hour of work equals the marginal utility of another hour of work.
   (b) The marginal utility of another hour of work equals the marginal utility of another hour of leisure.
   (c) The marginal utility of income divided by income equals the marginal utility of products that can be bought with that income divided by the price of those products.

2. Table 30.3 shows the change that takes place in the marginal utility of leisure with each additional hour that Freddie studies. What is Freddie's optimal study effort? _____

Table 30.3
Marginal utilities of leisure and study and grade average, by hours of study

Leisure	Study	Leisure	Study	Grade average
24	0	2	—	F
23	1	11	150	D
22	2	39	70	C
21	3	68	68	B
20	4	104	20	A
19	5	196	0	A

3. Suppose that Freddie's classes become more difficult so that each extra hour of study time raises his grade average by only half a grade, as shown in Table 30.4. What will his optimal study time be under these conditions? _____

Table 30.4
Effect of study time on grade average

Leisure	Study	Leisure	Study	Grade average
24	0	2	—	F
23	1	11	111	D–
22	2	39	39	D
21	3	68	35	C–

Table 30.4 (continued)

Leisure	Study	Leisure	Study	Grade average
20	4	104	35	C
19	5	196	34	B–
18	6	213	34	B
17	7	232	15	A–
16	8	247	5	A

4. **T F**   Under a stricter grading standard, Freddie's optimal study effort is less. (*Hint*: Compare your answer to Problem 3 with your answer to Problem 2.)

5. Which of the following are nonmonetary incentives to studying?
   (a) Pleasant surroundings.
   (b) Meaningful course content.
   (c) Course material that will help you get promotions in a future job.
   (d) All of the above.

6. After observing Freddie's study behavior under a stricter grading system, a manager of a firm would not recommend:
   (a) Making promotions difficult for workers to get.
   (b) Providing nonmonetary incentives such as contests and awards for work.
   (c) Making a comfortable work environment for employees.
   (d) Providing game and exercise rooms in the workplace.

Law of diminishing marginal utility

7. The law of diminishing marginal utility does *not* mean that:
   (a) Each successive unit of a good yields diminishing utility.
   (b) The marginal utility of a good declines as more of it is consumed in a given time period.
   (c) Total utility of a good declines as a person consumes more of it.

8. Which of the following activities provides evidence that Freddie obeys the law of diminishing marginal utility?
   (a) Studying.
   (b) Leisure.
   (c) Both a and b.
   (d) Neither a nor b.

Exercise 3

Changes in labor supply can be very disruptive to organizations and major changes are covered in the media. This exercise will show the kind of information to look for to identify and analyze changes involving labor supply. If your professor makes a newspaper assignment for this chapter, this exercise will provide an example of how to do it.

Reread the article in Chapter 14 entitled "Mexico Freezes Peso, Prices to Slow Rampant Inflation" from the *Washington Post*. Then answer the following questions, using Figure 30.3 for Question 1.

Figure 30.3

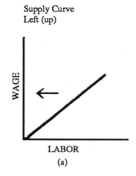

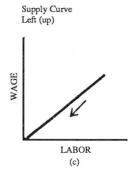
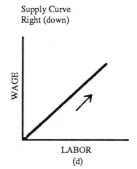

1. Which of the four diagrams in Figure 30.3 best represents the government's order to raise wages by 3 percent? a b c d (circle one)

2. What phrase indicates the specific labor market to which the change applies?

3. What phrase describes the change in the determinant of supply or wages that has caused the shift or movement you chose in Figure 30.3?

4. What sentence identifies the buyer of labor?

5. What sentence indicates the change in wages or quantity of labor that results from the shift in supply or that causes the movement along the supply curve?

Common Errors

The first statement in each "common error" below is incorrect. Each incorrect statement is followed by a corrected version and an explanation.

1. People work because they have to. WRONG!

   Generally people work in order to buy the goods and services they want. RIGHT!

   People have flexibility in choosing the conditions under which they will work. What they *choose* to do reflects their utility of leisure compared to their utility of the goods and services they can buy with their income from work. If their needs for goods were satisfied, they might not work at all.

2. People who work more enjoy their work more. WRONG!

   The reasons that people work as long as they do differ from person to person. RIGHT!

   The "busy hands are happy hands" adage easily leads us astray here. Some people do work because they like it. Others work solely because they like the goods they can buy with money. The time spent working tells little if anything about the reasons people work. Even less can be said about comparisons of the utility of work for different people. We cannot tell if people who work more enjoy it more than people who work less.

3. Marginal utility curves and demand curves are the same. WRONG!

   Marginal utility curves reflect the law of diminishing marginal utility while demand curves reflect the law of demand. RIGHT!

   Remember, utility refers only to our wants. Demand refers to our wants and our ability to pay for their satisfaction. Table 30.5 presents a summary of the two curves' differences and similarities.

Table 30.5
Characteristics of marginal utility and demand curves

Characteristic	Marginal utility curve	Demand curve
x-axis	Quantity of good or service in a given time period	Quantity of good or service in given time period
y-axis	Marginal utility (change in satisfaction for each extra unit of product consumed)	Price (price per unit that a buyer is willing and able to pay for a given amount of product)
Slope	Downward slope, according to the law of diminishing marginal utility	Downward slope, according to the law of demand
Meaning	Declining satisfaction with each extra unit of product consumed	Declining satisfaction and declining ability to pay for larger amounts of product

4. The labor-supply curve is the same as the supply curve of the products that labor produces. WRONG!

    The labor-supply curve is a supply curve of a factor market, while a product-supply curve applies to a product market. RIGHT!

    Supply curves in different markets are not the same curves, although they may look the same. The chief difference is found on the axes, as shown in Table 30.6.

Table 30.6
Axes of labor-supply and product-supply curves

Axis	Labor-supply curve	Product-supply curve
x-axis	Labor services in a given time period	Output in a given time period
y-axis	Wage for labor	Price of product

5. Workers demand jobs. WRONG!

    Employers demand labor services and workers (employees) supply them. RIGHT!

    Demand refers to what a buyer is willing and able to buy. Certainly workers are not seeking to pay their employers. Rather the workers are trying to find someone who is willing and able to pay them for their labor.

■ ANSWERS ■

Key-Term Review

1. marginal utility of labor
2. law of diminishing marginal utility
3. optimal work effort
4. utility
5. wage rate
    market mechanism
6. labor supply
7. substitution effect of wages
    labor-supply curve
    income effect of wages
8. market supply of labor
9. elasticity of labor supply

True or False

1. T	5. F	9. F	13. T	16. F	19. F
2. T	6. T	10. F	14. T	17. F	20. F
3. F	7. T	11. F	15. F	18. T	21. T
4. F	8. T	12. T			

Multiple Choice

1. b	4. d	7. c	10. a	13. d	16. a
2. b	5. b	8. a	11. a	14. c	17. d
3. a	6. d	9. a	12. a	15. b	18. b

Problems and Applications

Exercise 1

1. **Table 30.1 answer**

(1)	(2)	(3)
	Work effort	
Hourly wage (dollars per hour)	(hours worked per day)	Elasticity of supply
$ 0	0	—
2	1	1.0
4	4	1.8
8	6	0.6
16	8	0.429
32	6	−0.429

2. **Figure 30.2 answer**

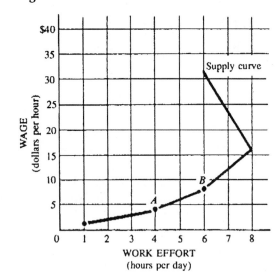

3. b
4. d
5. b
6. a

7. See Table 30.1 answer, column 3. The formula for the elasticity of labor supply is:

$$\frac{\text{Percentage change in quantity of labor supplied}}{\text{Percentage change in wage rate}}$$

The elasticity of labor supply can be estimated (just as the elasticity of demand was estimated) by using the following midpoint formula:

$$\frac{(L_2 - L_1)/[1/2 \times (L_2 + L_1)]}{(W_2 - W_1)/[1/2 \times (W_2 + W_1)]} = \frac{(6 - 8)/[1/2 \times (6 + 8)]}{(32 - 16)/[1/2 \times (32 + 16)]} = -\frac{3}{7}$$

In the formula, L_1 is the amount labor offered at the wage W_1 in period 1 and L_2 is the amount labor offered at the wage W_2 in period 2.

8. 4 hours; see Figure 30.2 answer, point A.
9. 6 hours; see Figure 30.2 answer, line segment AB.
10. T
11. F
12. T

436

Exercise 2

1. b
2. 3 hours
3. 2 hours
4. T
5. d
6. a
7. c
8. c

Exercise 3

1. d
2. The phrase "across-the-board hike for all wage earners" points to the labor market.
3. The answer is the same as in Question 2 above. The change in the determinant is a rise in wages.
4. "Veteran labor boss Fidel Velazquez warned today, however, that if business does not keep its promise to hold down prices 'it will have to pay the consequences' with higher wages."
5. The sentence in Question 4 indicates there will be less labor at lower real wage rates—wages that do not rise as fast as prices. Implicitly the 3 percent increase in wages makes more labor available.

Chapter 31

The Demand for Labor

Quick Review

The great disparities in incomes earned in the United States lead us to ask the following questions:

- What determines the wage rate an employer is willing to pay?
- How many workers will be hired at any given wage rate?
- Why are some workers paid so much and others so little?

To answer the first question, the demand for labor depends on the demand for the goods that labor produces. The demand for labor is thus a derived demand; the demand for a factor of production is derived from the demand for the product itself.

The marginal revenue product curve is a derived demand curve. It shows the additional revenue generated by an additional unit of labor. An employer will not want to pay a worker more than the extra revenue that the worker creates. Hence, the marginal revenue product curve sets an upper limit to wages. Shortages and surpluses can occur if wages are not at equilibrium.

The more labor a business employs, the less revenue each additional unit of labor brings to the firm. This reflects the law of diminishing returns: employing more workers in a given firm implies that each worker has less plant and equipment with which to work. As a result, each worker's marginal product declines as more workers are hired.

The demand for other factors is similarly derived. Their demand curves also slope downward and to the right as a result of the workings of the law of diminishing returns. Firms choose among factors on the basis of the increase in product that each extra factor generates for the input price. A profit-maximizing producer will always choose the most cost-efficient input, that is, the one with the highest ratio of marginal product to factor price (not necessarily the factor with the lowest price).

The marginal revenue product is not the only means by which wage rates are determined, however. Wage rates also reflect market power, custom, discrimination, and the opportunity wage.

Learning Objectives

After reading Chapter 31 and doing the following exercises, you should:	True or false	Multiple choice	Problems and applications	Common errors	Pages in the text
1. Understand how demand for a product determines the derived demand for the factors that are used to make the product.	1,2, 17,18	2,9, 17,20	1,3		740–741
2. Understand the concept of marginal physical product.					742–743
3. Be able to derive the marginal revenue product curve from information on product price and factor productivity.	3,4, 12,20	3,5,16, 18,19	2,3	2	743
4. Understand the law of diminishing returns.	15	4,15		3	744–745
5. Understand why the demand curve for a factor slopes downward.	5,16		3		745–746
6. Be able to describe how supply and demand interact to determine wages.	9,11	1	1,4		746–749
7. Be able to apply the concepts of shortages and surpluses in reference to government policies such as the minimum wage.		21,22			749–750
8. Be able to trace the effects of shifts of the labor-demand and labor-supply curves on wages.	13,14	6–8	4	5	749
9. Understand the concept of cost efficiency.	6,8,19	10		1	751–752
10. Know what the efficiency decision is and how it is made.	7,10	11–13		4	752–755
11. Recognize in the concept of "opportunity wage" that wages reflect the opportunities of workers to work elsewhere.		14			756–757
12. Understand the implications of the "comparable worth" doctrine.	21,22	23,24			755–759

Key-Term Review

Review the following terms; if you are not sure of the meaning of any term, write out the definition and check it against the Glossary in the text.

cost efficiency
demand for labor
derived demand
efficiency decision
equilibrium wage
investment decision
law of demand

law of diminishing returns
marginal physical product (MPP)
marginal revenue product (MRP)
opportunity wage
production decision
production process
shift in demand

Fill in the blank following each of the statements below with the appropriate term from the list above.

1. Since the marginal revenue product is computed on the basis of the demand for the product produced, it is referred to as a _____.

    1. _____

2. The choice between production processes is the _____.

    2. _____

3. In order to make this choice, a firm must know, in addition to the input cost, the amount of output each additional factor provides, which is the _____.

    3. _____

4. As more of a factor is used, its marginal productivity will probably fall, in accordance with the _____.

    4. _____

5. As the marginal productivity of labor declines, a downward slope will appear in the curve that represents the _____.

    5. _____

6. Automation increases labor productivity, which in the labor market causes a _____.

    6. _____

7. The decision to put new technology to use is called the _____.

    7. _____

8. If we know input prices and marginal productivity of inputs then we can compare each input or input process for its _____.

    8. _____

9. The amount of labor used is directly affected by the choice of output levels in a given time period. The choice of the output rate to be reached is called the _____.

    9. _____

10. The downward slope of the marginal revenue product curve reflects the law of diminishing returns and also, in the product market, the _____.

    10. _____

11. If you know the marginal physical product and the price of the product, then for any factor you can compute the _____.

    11. _____

12. The highest pay that an individual can earn in alternative jobs is his or her _____.

    12. _____

13. A specific combination of resources used to produce a good or service is known as the _____.

    13. _____

14. Because the minimum wage exceeds the _____, unemployment is the obvious result.

    14. _____

True or False: *Circle your choice.*

T F   1.   The demand curve for factors of production is derived from the demand curve for the products that the factors produce.

T F   2.   When a firm is taxed by the government, employees do not feel the effects of the tax; only a firm's profits are affected.

T F   3.   A firm's upper limit of willingness to pay labor is determined by the marginal revenue product curve.

T F   4.   The marginal revenue product curve and the derived demand curve for a factor are the same thing.

T F   5.   The relation between the marginal physical product curve and the marginal revenue product curve is determined by the demand curve for the product produced by the firm.

T F   6.   When production processes are compared, the principle of cost efficiency can no longer be applied, since a marginal revenue product can be computed only for one factor of production.

T F   7.   Automation is desired when labor-intensive processes have higher costs per unit produced than capital-intensive processes, *ceteris paribus*.

T F   8.   The relative cost efficiency of various factors is measured by the ratio of marginal physical product to the price of each factor of production.

T F   9.   The average value of the product that people produce is a major determinant of the wages that they receive.

T F 10.   In order to maximize profits in the long run, a firm must make efficiency decisions, a production decision, and an investment decision.

T F 11.   In a competitive market economy, the equilibrium wage may be at or above the marginal revenue product.

T F 12.   The demand curve for labor is labor's marginal revenue product curve.

T F 13.   A derived demand curve shifts in the same direction as the demand curve from which it is derived, *ceteris paribus*.

T F 14.   When the demand for a firm's product changes, the firm's demand for factors of production changes as well.

T F 15.   The law of diminishing returns suggests that the fewer the workers employed, the more total output they can produce in a given time period, *ceteris paribus*.

T F 16.   If a firm's marginal physical product curve slopes downward, its marginal revenue product curve must also slope downward.

T F 17.   Because of the law of diminishing returns, the demand curve for a product slopes downward.

T F 18.   Unlike most demand curves, derived demand curves may not be governed by the law of demand.

T F 19.   The ratio of marginal physical product to factor cost may not be the same for all factors because of institutional constraints in the economy.

T F 20.   The seller in the product market is the buyer in the factor market.

T F 21.   Advocates of comparable worth use supply and demand to establish pay scales.

T F 22.   The U.S. Commission on Civil Rights has rejected the comparable-worth doctrine.

Multiple Choice: *Select the correct answer.*

_____ 1.   Which of the following is essential in explaining the wage level in a market economy?
   (a) The opportunity wage.
   (b) The marginal revenue product.
   (c) The degrees of market power of the buyer and supplier of a factor.
   (d) All of the above.

_____ 2. The differences between demand in the product market and demand in the factor market include:
    (a) The fact that the demand curve for the product is governed by the law of demand and the derived demand curve is not.
    (b) The fact that the demand curve for a product is the same as the marginal revenue product curve, but the derived demand is not the same as the marginal revenue product.
    (c) The fact that the axes of the two demand curves are labeled differently.
    (d) All of the above.

_____ 3. In order to calculate marginal revenue product, we need to know:
    (a) The marginal physical product and the marginal revenue of the product.
    (b) The marginal physical product and the unit price of the factor.
    (c) The marginal revenue and the amount of the product produced.
    (d) The marginal revenue and the cost of the factor.

_____ 4. The diminishing returns to a factor may be due to:
    (a) The declining utility of a good as we consume more of it.
    (b) Crowding or overuse of other factors as production is increased.
    (c) The decline in the demand curve for a product.
    (d) The decline in the marginal revenue curve for a product.

_____ 5. The marginal revenue product curve and marginal physical product curve have similar shapes:
    (a) Because marginal revenue product depends on marginal physical product.
    (b) Because the product demand curve slopes downward in accordance with the law of diminishing returns.
    (c) Because the law of demand and the law of diminishing returns are due to the same economic behavior.
    (d) For all of the above reasons.

_____ 6. Employment will definitely rise when:
    (a) Productivity and wages rise.
    (b) Productivity rises and wages fall.
    (c) Productivity falls and wages rise.
    (d) Productivity and wages fall.

_____ 7. A change in wages causes a shift in:
    (a) The marginal revenue product curve for labor.
    (b) The marginal physical product curve for labor.
    (c) The derived demand curve for labor.
    (d) None of the above.

_____ 8. A change in productivity causes a change in:
    (a) The marginal revenue product of labor.
    (b) The marginal physical product of labor.
    (c) The derived demand for labor.
    (d) All of the above.

_____ 9. A change in the demand for a product usually causes a shift in:
    (a) The marginal revenue product curve for labor.
    (b) The marginal physical product curve for labor.
    (c) The demand curve for labor.
    (d) Both a and c.

_____ 10. When two factors are used efficiently, then:
    (a) The ratio of marginal physical product to unit factor cost will be the same for both factors.
    (b) The same amount of each factor will be used.
    (c) The marginal revenue products of both factors will be the same.
    (d) The ratio of marginal physical product to product price will be the same for both factors.

_____ 11. An example of an "efficiency decision" is:
   (a) Automation.
   (b) Product decisions.
   (c) Investment decisions.
   (d) Short-run revenue maximization.

_____ 12. The groups that lose out from automation include:
   (a) Workers replaced in automated plants.
   (b) Consumers of products from newly automated plants.
   (c) Owners of newly automated plants.
   (d) The whole society.

_____ 13. Methods used to alleviate the problems of automation include:
   (a) Unemployment benefits.
   (b) Retraining programs.
   (c) Relocation assistance.
   (d) All of the above.

_____ 14. Which of the following help to explain why the wages received by two workers with different jobs are not the same?
   (a) Differences in marginal revenue products at their respective jobs.
   (b) Wages that they would receive in alternative jobs.
   (c) The prices of the products they produce.
   (d) All of the above.

Figure 31.1

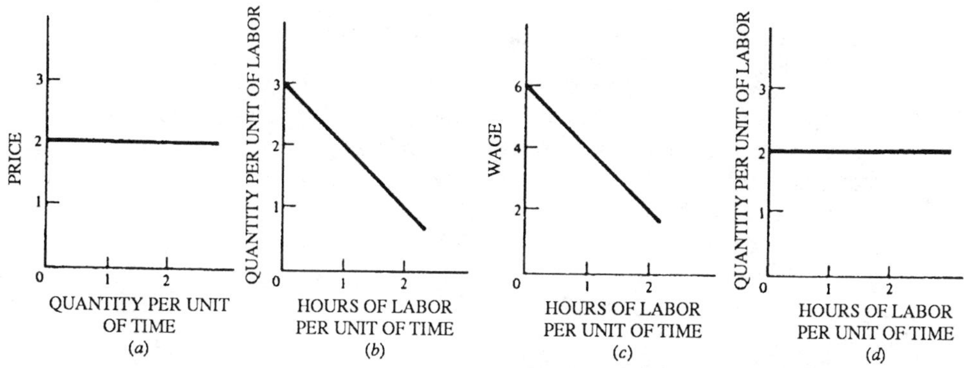

Figure 31.1 presents four diagrams. Pick the diagram that best illustrates:

_____ 15. The law of diminishing returns.

_____ 16. The demand curve in a factor market.

_____ 17. The derived demand curve.

_____ 18. The marginal revenue product curve.

_____ 19. The curve that one can always find by multiplying the marginal physical product by marginal revenue.

_____ 20. The demand curve for a product.

_____ 21. Which of the following policies is consistent with shortages of labor in the labor market?
   (a) Wage controls (ceilings).
   (b) Price controls (ceilings).
   (c) Minimum wage legislation.
   (d) None of the above.

_____22. Which of the following policies is consistent with surpluses of labor in the labor market?
  (a) Price supports in the product market.
  (b) Minimum wage legislation.
  (c) Wage controls (ceilings).
  (d) All of the above.

_____23. The economic theory of wage determination and the comparable-worth doctrine:
  (a) Can be reconciled since both depend on supply and demand.
  (b) Cannot be reconciled because the former depends on demand and supply and the latter depends on subjective evaluations.
  (c) Cannot be reconciled because one depends on free markets and the other depends on market intervention.
  (d) Have been reconciled by the city of Los Angeles.

_____24. If the comparable-worth doctrine was widely adopted, economic theory would predict:
  (a) Surpluses in those occupations where the wage was raised.
  (b) Shortages in those occupations where the wage was not raised.
  (c) That a new mechanism would be required to eliminate the shortages and surpluses.
  (d) All of the above.

Problems and Applications

Exercise 1

This exercise gives practice in the formulas for and graphing of derived demand.

1. Match the formulas on the right with the appropriate economic term on the left. (*Note:* q refers to the quantity of a product, and L refers to the amount of labor services during a given time period. Assume labor is the only cost. Remember that the symbol Δ refers to a small change in a variable.)

_____ total cost (*TC*)	a. $p \times q$
_____ marginal cost (*MC*)	b. $\Delta TR / \Delta L$
_____ total revenue (*TR*)	c. Wage $\times L$
_____ marginal revenue (*MR*)	d. $\Delta TC / \Delta q$
_____ marginal revenue product (*MRP*)	e. $\Delta TR / \Delta q$

Refer to the diagrams in Figure 31.2 in answering Problems 2–6.

Figure 31.2

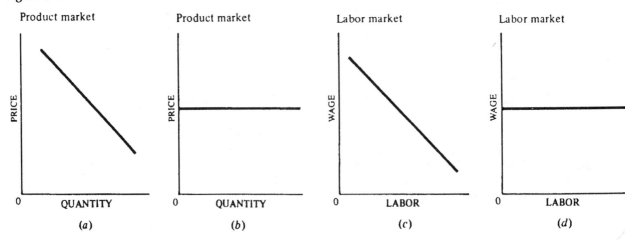

(*a*)   (*b*)   (*c*)   (*d*)

2. Which curve might represent a firm's marginal revenue in a competitive market? _____

3. Which curve represents marginal revenue product when marginal physical productivity is declining? _____

4. Which curve represents the supply curve of labor (wage rate) when a firm does not have the market power to alter the wage rate?

5. Which curve might represent the demand curve for labor in a perfectly competitive labor market? _____

6. Which curve might represent the demand curve for a product of a competitive firm? _____

Exercise 2

This exercise provides experience in computing and graphing derived demand as well as determining the profit-maximizing wage. It shows that a solution in the product market is the same as the solution in the labor market.

Profit maximization in the product market: review

1. You are a producer of Rotgut Ripple, which sells for $1 per gallon. In its desire to lend some local color to your country, the government permits you to produce it in the hills, where the ingredients cost nothing. It is hard to get people to work for you. You have to pay $3 an hour for labor, which is your only cost. Table 31.1 shows your costs and revenues according to the amount of labor you hire. Complete Table 31.1.

Table 31.1
Cost and revenue of Rotgut Ripple production, by labor hours

Wage (dollars per hour)	Labor (workers per hour)	Quantity produced (gallons per hour)	Total cost (dollars per hour)	Marginal cost (dollars per gallon)	Price (dollars per gallon)	Total revenue (dollars per hour)	Marginal revenue product (dollars per worker)
$3	0	0	$_____	$ —	$1	$_____	$ —
3	1	15	_____	_____	1	_____	_____
3	2	27	_____	_____	1	_____	_____
3	3	36	_____	_____	1	_____	_____
3	4	42	_____	_____	1	_____	_____
3	5	45	_____	_____	1	_____	_____
3	6	46	_____	_____	1	_____	_____

2. Draw your demand and marginal cost curves in Figure 31.3, using the information in Table 31.1. Your marginal cost curve should slope upward if you compute it correctly. (Remember to divide by the *change* in q— not L!) Label your demand curve D and your marginal cost curve MC.

Figure 31.3

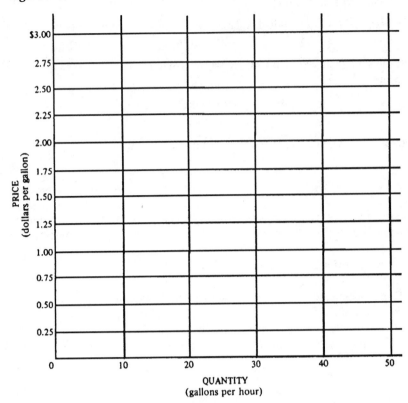

3. You would maximize profits at the production level at which:
   (a) Demand equals average cost.
   (b) Demand equals marginal revenue.
   (c) *MR* equals *MC*.
   (d) *AC* equals *MC*.

4. How many gallons of Ripple would you produce each hour to maximize profits?
   (a) 0.
   (b) 15.
   (c) 27.
   (d) 36.
   (e) 42.
   (f) 45.
   (g) 46.

5. That means you will hire how many workers per hour?
   (a) 0.
   (b) 1.
   (c) 2.
   (d) 3.
   (e) 4.
   (f) 5.
   (g) 6.

Profit maximization in the labor market

6. T F The demand curve for Ripple workers is found by plotting the marginal revenue product curve.

7. T F The supply curve for Ripple workers is the marginal cost curve.

8. In Figure 31.4, draw the demand curve for labor. Lable it *DL*.

Figure 31.4

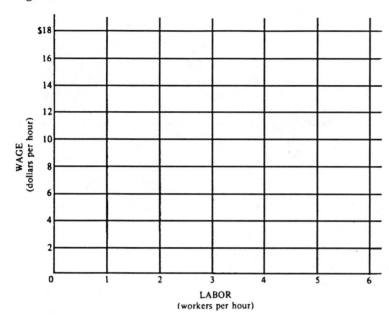

LABOR
(workers per hour)

9. Draw the supply curve for Ripple workers at the wage of $3 in Figure 31.4 and label it *LS*.

10. How many workers will be hired if you are to maximize profits?
    (a) 0.   (e) 4.
    (b) 1.   (f) 5.
    (c) 2.   (g) 6.
    (d) 3.

11. How much Ripple will be produced per hour? _____

12. T F By using either the labor or product market, it is possible to find how much product will be produced and how much labor will be used by a profit-maximizing firm.

Exercise 3

This exercise illustrates the relationship between marginal productivity, marginal revenue, and marginal revenue product by letting you compute each from the same data.

1. T F The marginal physical product (*MPP*) measures the change in total output that occurs when one additional worker is hired.

2. Which of the following formulas would provide a correct calculation of the marginal physical product? (Remember that the symbol $\triangle$ refers to a small change in a variable.)
   (a) q/L (c) $\triangle q/\triangle L$
   (b) $\triangle q/L$ (d) $\triangle TR/\triangle L$

3. In column 3 of Table 31.2 compute marginal physical product associated with each unit of labor that is used.

447

Table 31.2
Marginal physical product and marginal revenue product

(1) Labor (workers per hour)	(2) Quantity produced (gallons per hour)	(3) Marginal physical product (gallons per worker)	(4) Price (dollars per gallon)	(5) Total Revenue (dollars per hour) (2) x (4)	(6) Marginal revenue (dollars per gallon)	(7) Marginal revenue product (dollars per worker) (3) x (6)
0	0	———	$1	—	—	—
1	15	———	1	———	———	———
2	27	———	1	———	———	———
3	36	———	1	———	———	———
4	42	———	1	———	———	———
5	45	———	1	———	———	———
6	46	———	1	———	———	———

4. The law of diminishing returns states that:
   (a) The marginal revenue declines as additional labor is employed in a given production process.
   (b) The marginal revenue product declines as additional labor is employed in a given production process.
   (c) The marginal physical product of labor declines as additional labor is employed in a given production process.

5. T F There are diminishing returns to labor with increased production in this example.

6. Marginal revenue product can be computed by multiplying marginal physical product by the marginal revenue. Complete Table 31.2.

7. The reason the demand curve for labor in Figure 31.4 slopes downward is:
   (a) Diminishing returns to labor.
   (b) The market power of labor in labor markets.
   (c) The market power of the Ripple firm in labor markets.
   (d) Declining demand for Ripple.

8. T F The derived demand for labor is downward sloping because of diminishing returns to labor.

Exercise 4

The media often report shifts in the supply and demand for labor that affect workers' jobs, their livelihood, and even their mental health. By using one of the articles in the text, this exercise will show the kind of information to look for to identify such shifts. If your professor makes a newspaper assignment for this chapter, this exercise will provide an example of how to do it.

Reread the article in Chapter 31 entitled "Mighty Microchip Derails the Caboose" from the *Washington Post.* Then answer the following questions, using Figure 31.5 to answer Question 1:

Figure 31.5

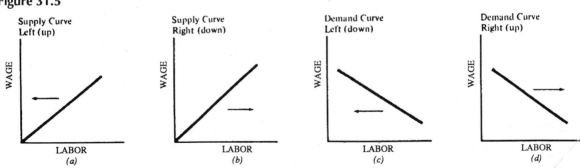

1. Which of the four diagrams in Figure 31.5 best represents the change in demand or supply for labor?
   a b c d (circle one)

2. Which sentence mentions the specific categories of labor that are affected?

3. What sentence describes the change in the determinant of demand or supply that has caused the shift you chose in Figure 31.5?

4. Through whom does the change in the determinant of demand or supply initially affect the market?
   (a) The buyer.
   (b) The seller.

5. What sentence indicates a change in the wage rate or quantity of labor that results from the shift in demand or supply?

Common Errors

The first statement in each "common error" below is incorrect. Each incorrect statement is followed by a corrected version and an explanation.

1. Employers employ those factors that are least expensive. WRONG!

   Employers want to employ those factors that are most cost-effective. RIGHT!

   If a factor is cheap there may be a reason. It may not last long, may not work correctly, or may require heavier use of other factors of production—for example, maintenance workers. The marginal productivity of the cheap factor may therefore be low. An apparently more expensive factor might perform its proper function well and even save on the costs of other factors. The marginal productivity of the more expensive input would more than make up for its higher cost. Businesses would choose the more expensive factor of production.

2. Marginal revenue product is the same as marginal revenue. WRONG!

   The marginal revenue product curve applies to the factor market while the marginal revenue curve applies to the product market. RIGHT!
   The formula for marginal revenue product is:

   $$\frac{\text{Change in total revenue}}{\text{Change in quantity of input}}$$

   while that for marginal revenue is:

   $$\frac{\text{Change in total revenue}}{\text{Change in quantity of output}}$$

   Marginal revenue shows changes in total revenue due to increased output and therefore is appropriate in analyzing what happens in the product market.
   Marginal revenue product shows changes in total revenue due to the increased use of a factor and therefore is appropriate in analyzing what happens in the factor market. Both curves are derived from the demand curve in the product market. However, in order to find marginal revenue product, it is necessary also to know the relationship between the quantity of input and quantity of output. That is why the marginal physical product becomes important.

3. The law of diminishing returns means that average total costs will rise as a firm expands. WRONG!

   The law of diminishing returns applies only to changes in the use of one factor while all others remain constant. RIGHT!

   If a firm could expand all factors of production proportionately, there might be no decline in productivity at all, and thus no increase in average total cost. If the firm could do so without affecting factor prices, there would then be no change in unit costs either. The law of diminishing returns applies to changes of only one factor or group of factors, *ceteris paribus* (all other factors being held constant).

4. Because automation increases efficiency, it is good for society as a whole. WRONG!

   Automation results in the use of less labor per unit of output; some workers will therefore be hurt by automation. RIGHT!

   Automation increases the efficiency of the economy. However, when some people are hurt by a change, society must make a hard choice. Many criteria, such as equity and minimum welfare, may enter into this choice.

5. No one is hurt when companies are taxed except the companies themselves. WRONG!

   Part of the burden of taxes on a company may fall on the factors of production that a company employs. RIGHT!

   Remember that the demand for factors is derived from the product market. If the sales tax, for example, alters the demand curve for a product, it will alter the demand curve for the factors used to produce the product.

■ ANSWERS ■

Key-Term Review

1. derived demand	6. shift in demand	11. marginal revenue product (*MRP*)
2. efficiency decision	7. investment decision	12. opportunity wage
3. marginal physical product (*MPP*)	8. cost efficiency	13. production process
4. law of diminishing returns	9. production decision	14. equilibrium wage
5. demand for labor	10. law of demand	

True or False

1. T	5. T	9. F	13. T	17. F	20. T
2. F	6. F	10. T	14. T	18. F	21. F
3. T	7. T	11. F	15. F	19. T	22. T
4. T	8. T	12. T	16. T		

Multiple Choice

1. d	5. a	9. d	13. d	17. c	21. a
2. c	6. b	10. a	14. d	18. c	22. b
3. a	7. d	11. a	15. b	19. c	23. b
4. b	8. d	12. a	16. c	20. a	24. d

Problems and Applications

Exercise 1

1. *TC*   c
   MC   d
   TR   a
   MR   e
   MRP b
2. b
3. c
4. d
5. d
6. b

Exercise 2

1. **Table 31.1 answer**

Labor	Total cost	Marginal cost	Total revenue	Marginal revenue product
0	$ 0	$ —	$ 0	$—
1	3	1/5	15	15
2	6	1/4	27	12
3	9	1/3	36	9
4	12	1/2	42	6
5	15	1	45	3
6	18	3	46	1

2. **Figure 31.3 answer**

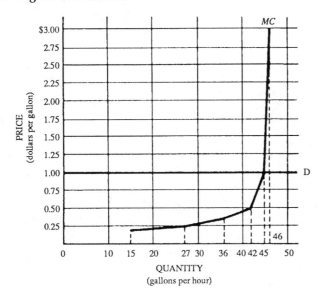

QUANTITY
(gallons per hour)

3. c
4. f
5. f
6. T
7. F

8. **Figure 31.4 answer**

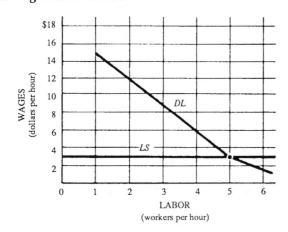

LABOR
(workers per hour)

9. See line *LS* in Figure 31.4 answer.
10. f
11. 45 gallons per hour
12. T

451

Exercise 3

1. T
2. c
3. **Table 31.2 answer**

(1)	(3)	(5)	(6)	(7)
	Marginal physical product	Total Revenue	Marginal revenue	Marginal revenue product
Labor		(2) x (4)		(3) x (6)
0	—	—	—	—
1	15	$15	$1	$15
2	12	27	1	12
3	9	36	1	9
4	6	42	1	6
5	3	45	1	3
6	1	46	1	1

4. c
5. T
6. See columns 6 and 7 in Table 31.2 answer.
7. a
8. T

Exercise 4

1. c
2. "A crew member, either the conductor or the rear brakeman, was assigned to sit there and keep an eye out for derailments, dragging equipment and overheated axles, called 'hot boxes.' "
3. "The venerable piece of Americana . . . . is headed for extinction, replaced by a shoebox-size microelectronic monitor . . . designed to do the work traditionally entrusted to a crew member perched in the caboose's cupola." The determinant is the availability of a substitute good or service.
4. a   The buyer is the one who buys the microchip and no longer needs the labor.
5. See the sentence in Question 3 or either of the following sentences: "With computerized record-handling, train personnel no longer needed a rolling office. Changing work rules meant crews no longer spent the night on the caboose."

Chapter 32
Power in Labor Markets

Quick Review

The outcomes in the labor market, including the wage rate and level of employment, can be distorted by market power on either the supply or demand side. This chapter investigates power in labor markets and addresses the following questions:

- How do large and powerful employers affect market wages?
- How do labor unions alter wages and employment?
- What outcomes are possible from collective bargaining between management and unions?

Power in labor markets means the ability to influence wage rates. Where the labor market is segmented by geographical, occupational, or industrial boundaries, a very few firms or unions may have market power. In extreme cases, a single labor union may contract all of one type of labor and thus be a monopoly, or a single firm may be the only buyer in a particular market, thereby becoming a monopsonist. Table 32.1 summarizes the names applied to buyers, depending on the number of unions or firms in a market.

Table 32.1
**Types of firms having power in labor market,
by number of firms and market role**

Number of firms or unions	Market role	
	Buyers	Suppliers
One	Monopsony	Monopoly (union)
Few	Oligopsony	Oligopoly
Many	Competitive buyers	Competition

Unions typically negotiate for a large number of objectives. The most important is usually the wage rate. But a union's power is based on its membership. If wages rise, the number of workers hired may decline (law of demand). Unions therefore tend to reduce the number of people they permit to be employed and to bargain for higher wages than they would seek if the labor market were competitive.

In a competitive labor market the supply of labor is equated with the demand for labor to determine the equilibrium wage. However, unions may behave like monopolists; they restrict employment so that supply and the marginal wage rate are equated. The marginal wage rate is the change in total wages that results from employment of an extra unit of labor. The union tries to negotiate a wage as far above this marginal wage rate as possible. If a firm has market power, it will try to keep wages down to the marginal wage rate.

The dilemma faced by firms that have market power is the opposite of the one confronting labor unions: the more labor an employer seeks, the higher the wages will have to be. And when wages are raised for any worker, they must be raised for everyone. The marginal factor cost is therefore higher than the market wage rate. The marginal factor cost is the change in total wage costs that results from the hiring of an extra unit of labor. It is the marginal factor cost, not the market wage rate (found on the labor-supply curve), that a firm equates with marginal revenue product (found on the labor-demand curve). Like unions, monopsonists fail to employ the amount of labor that would be employed in a competitive labor market. Unlike unions, employers will try to pay *less* than the competitive wage. They will force the wage somewhere between the marginal revenue product of labor and the market wage rate.

In bilateral monopolies, where power exists on both sides of the labor market, unions and employers engage in collective bargaining to negotiate a final settlement.

Learning Objectives

After reading Chapter 32 and doing the following exercises, you should:	True or false	Multiple choice	Problems and applications	Common errors	Pages in the text
1. Understand the characteristics that are used to define the boundaries of labor markets.	16				761–763
2. Be able to demonstrate the meaning of the equilibrium wage rate.	1	6	1		767,773, 775
3. Be able to describe the various types of labor buyers and suppliers.		7–10,19	3		763–764
4. Be familiar with the history of labor unions and their role in the economy.	2,9, 11–14,24	1,11–14			763–764, 768–771, 776–780
5. Be able to define, compute, and graph the marginal wage curve and the demand curve for labor.		3,5,16	2		765
6. Be able to determine the optimal level of employment from a union point of view.	4,6,7	2,4		3	764–767
7. Know how to measure union power using the unionization ratio.	15,17				768–771
8. Be able to define, compute, and graph the marginal cost of labor and the supply of labor.	8		2	1	771–773
9. Be able to describe the monopsonist's desired equilibrium.	3,5,10	15	3		773–774
10. Be able to describe how wages are determined in a market characterized by bilateral monopoly.	18–20, 21, 23,25	17,18,20, 21,22	4	2	774–776
11. Understand some of the differences between the role and objectives of unions in the U.S. and those abroad.	24	23			777

Key-Term Review

Review the following terms; if you are not sure of the meaning of any term, write out the definition and check it against the Glossary in the text.

bilateral monopoly
collective bargaining
demand for labor
equilibrium wage
labor supply
marginal factor cost (*MFC*)
marginal revenue product (*MRP*)

marginal wage
market power
monopsony
productivity
unionization ratio
union shop

Fill in the blank following each of the statements below with the appropriate term from the list above.

1. The control that a union exercises over wage rates reflects its _____.

    1. _____

2. The market power of a union can be measured in a rough way by the _____.

    2. _____

3. When a union negotiates with an employer to determine wages, it is participating in _____.

    3. _____

4. When there is only one employer and one union in such negotiations, the market structure is that of

    _____.

    4. _____

5. If there were many nonunion sources of labor in a market, then a single buyer of labor in that market would be a _____.

    5. _____

6. A monopsonist will hire labor up to a level where its marginal revenue product equals the _____.

    6. _____

7. A union may negotiate to make it mandatory for workers to join a union within a certain number of days after the workers are employed. Such an employment setting is called a _____.

    7. _____

8. No matter how powerful a union is, it is limited by the _____.

    8. _____

9. The demand for labor can be found if it is known how total revenues change with an increment of labor, which is the _____.

    9. _____

10. A union with market power may restrict _____ to the level at which the supply curve of labor is intersected by a curve representing the _____.

    10. _____

    _____

11. If neither employer nor employee has market power, then at the level where the quantity of labor supplied and demanded are equal, we can find the _____.

    11. _____

12. Union-negotiated work rules may have a substantial negative impact on worker _____.

    12. _____

True or False: *Circle your choice.*

T F 1. The equilibrium wage rate is the rate at which the quantity of labor demanded equals the quantity supplied.

T F 2. An industrial union is a labor organization that represents people with a particular skill.

T F 3. Monopsonists attempt to equate the marginal wage with the supply curve.

T F 4. Monopolists in the labor market equate the marginal wage with the marginal revenue product.

T F 5. When monopsony power is present in a labor market, the wage can be read off the supply curve.

T F 6. In a monopoly labor market, the wage can be read off the marginal revenue product curve.

T F 7. Labor unions will not allow the labor force to grow so large that the marginal wage becomes negative.

T F 8. A buyer in a competitive labor market sees only a flat supply curve.

T F 9. Unions do not need to control the labor supply in order to have market power.

T F 10. If buyers in the labor market have market power, then the more labor they hire, the higher the wage that must be paid.

T F 11. The Taft-Hartley Act prohibits union shops.

T F 12. Reform unions were designed to unify workers as a political force to accomplish broad social objectives.

T F 13. The AFL began as a reform union and evolved into a trade union.

T F 14. Wars have aided union development, whereas depressions tend to hurt the union movement.

T F 15. The U.S. unionization ratio is about one-fourth of the labor force.

T F 16. There are thousands of labor markets, owing principally to differences in age, sex, and race in the labor force.

T F 17. Both the unionization and concentration ratios are measures of market power.

T F 18. In bilateral monopoly, price and output are determined by the intersection of demand-and-supply curves.

T F 19. The collective bargaining process results in prices above the marginal revenue product curve.

T F 20. The collective bargaining process will not result in a wage below the supply curve of labor.

T F 21. The UAW–GM contract signed in September 1987 generally contained increases in wages and benefits.

T F 22. Franchise owners exercised monopsony power during the 1987 NFL strike.

T F 23. Two-tier contracts are compatible with the doctrine of comparable worth.

T F 24. American unions tend to have a broader political orientation than their European counterparts.

T F 25. Work rules that are designed to protect jobs and maximize employment at any level of output are thought to improve worker productivity.

Multiple Choice: *Select the correct answer.*

_____ 1. Typical goals of a labor union in the United States include:
(a) Recognition.
(b) Wages.
(c) Fringe benefits.
(d) All of the above.

_____ 2. The reason that a union may worry about having too many members is that:
  (a) The union faces a downward-sloping marginal revenue product curve.
  (b) It may be unable to control all of its members.
  (c) It may not be able to reach optimal employment, at which the marginal labor cost curve intersects the demand curve.
  (d) None of the above.

_____ 3. The formula for the marginal wage is:

  (a) $\dfrac{\text{Change in total wages paid}}{\text{Change in total quantity of product}}$

  (b) $\dfrac{\text{Change in total wages paid}}{\text{Change in quantity of labor employed}}$

  (c) $\dfrac{\text{Change in total cost}}{\text{Change in total quantity of product}}$

  (d) The same as that for the marginal cost of labor.

_____ 4. Unions must distinguish between marginal wage and the market wage, but nonunion workers generally do not:
  (a) Because the demand curve for labor from the union point of view slopes downward.
  (b) Because for a nonunion worker who has no market power, the demand curve appears flat.
  (c) Because for a nonunion worker who has no market power, the demand curve is the same as the marginal wage curve.
  (d) For all of the above reasons.

_____ 5. The marginal revenue curve in the product market is similar to the marginal wage curve in the labor market:
  (a) Because they equal the demand curves in their respective markets when those demand curves are flat.
  (b) Because they are below the demand curves in their respective markets when those demand curves slope downward.
  (c) Because they both take account of the gains in total revenue (total wage bill) due to a greater quantity as well as the losses due to a lower price (wage).
  (d) For all of the above reasons.

_____ 6. If a union contract fixes a particular wage and then the demand curve for the product that the workers produce suddenly shifts to the left:
  (a) There will be a surplus of workers.
  (b) There will be a shortage of workers.
  (c) The derived demand curve will shift rightward.
  (d) The derived demand curve will shift upward.

Select the answers for questions 7–10 from the following five responses:
  (a) Union shop.
  (b) Apprenticeship program.
  (c) Apprenticeship program linked to a certification program.
  (d) Open shop.
  (e) Closed shop.

_____ 7. Which of the five structures is the most effective and legal method of controlling the labor supply?

_____ 8. Which structure is illegal in all states but would be very effective if it were allowed?

_____ 9. In which structure is the union weakest in controlling the labor supply?

_____ 10. Which structure requires workers to join a union thirty days after being employed, but not necessarily one particular union?

_____ 11. Which of the following would unions regard most favorably?
   (a) Yellow-dog contracts.
   (b) Right-to-work laws.
   (c) Certification programs.
   (d) Scabs.

In Questions 12–14 match each of the following acts with its key provisions:
   (a) Taft-Hartley Act.
   (b) National Industrial Recovery Act.
   (c) Right-to-work laws.
   (d) Wagner Act.

_____ 12. Closed shops are illegal.

_____ 13. Membership in a union is completely voluntary.

_____ 14. Employees may bargain collectively (two possible answers).

_____ 15. The difference between a competitive labor market and a monopsonistic labor market is:
   (a) That the monopsony will attempt to charge a higher wage than will be charged in a competitive market, *ceteris paribus*.
   (b) That the monopsony will hire less labor than will be hired in a competitive market, *ceteris paribus*.
   (c) That the shape of the marginal revenue product curve of a monopsony will differ from that of a competitive industry.
   (d) None of the above.

_____ 16. The difference between a competitive labor market and a monopolistic one is:
   (a) That the monopoly will attempt to obtain a higher wage than will be obtained in a competitive market, *ceteris paribus*.
   (b) That less labor will be hired in a monopoly than will be hired in a competitive market, *ceteris paribus*.
   (c) That in the monopoly an insufficient and inefficient amount of labor will be used.
   (d) All of the above.

_____ 17. In bilateral monopoly it is certain that:
   (a) The optimum employment level in the labor market occurs where the marginal wage curve intersects the marginal labor cost curve.
   (b) The wage occurs somewhere between the marginal revenue product curve and the labor-supply curve.
   (c) The employment level will be lower than in the case of either a monopoly or a monopsony individually.
   (d) All of the above are the case.

_____ 18. Monopoly, monopsony, and monopolistic competition are all characterized by:
   (a) The existence of only one firm on either the buyer's or the supplier's side of the market.
   (b) Market power on the buyer's or the supplier's side of the market.
   (c) Application only to the product market.
   (d) All of the above.

_____ 19. Which of the following unions probably has the greatest market power in its labor market?
   (a) Shoe Workers' Union.
   (b) United Farm Workers.
   (c) Textile Workers.
   (d) Teamsters.

_____ 20. Which of the following statements is true concerning two-tier contracts:
   (a) They are the natural result of market forces.
   (b) They are compatible with the comparable-worth doctrine.
   (c) They cannot be maintained in a free market.
   (d) None of the above is true.

_____21. Two-tier contracts:
(a) Discriminate against the most recently hired workers.
(b) Increase the number of workers hired.
(c) Create tensions between those paid at the upper wage and those paid at the lower wage.
(d) Do all of the above.

_____22. The three-year 1987 UAW– GM contract provided for:
(a) A 3 percent increase in the base wage in the first year.
(b) A total of forty-one paid holidays annually.
(c) A cost-of-living adjustment tied to increases in the CPI.
(d) All of the above.

_____23. Which of the following is *incorrect*?
(a) Swedish unions lobby for liberal social policies.
(b) The Solidarity union in Poland was successful in achieving legal status at one time.
(c) French unions formulate their demands after the national economic plan has been formulated.
(d) U.S. unions tend to focus on bread-and-butter issues, such as wages and benefits.

Problems and Applications

Exercise 1

This exercise should help you to relate all of the different models of buyer and seller market power. It should also help you to remember the graphic representation of long-run equilibrium.

Figure 32.1 represents long-run equilibrium for different types of firms or labor suppliers.

Choose the letter of the diagram in Figure 32.1 (p. 460) that best represents the long-run equilibrium for firms in the following types of industry:

1. _____ monopsony
2. _____ monopolistic competition
3. _____ oligopoly
4. _____ competitive buyers
5. _____ competitive suppliers
6. _____ monopoly

Figure 32.1

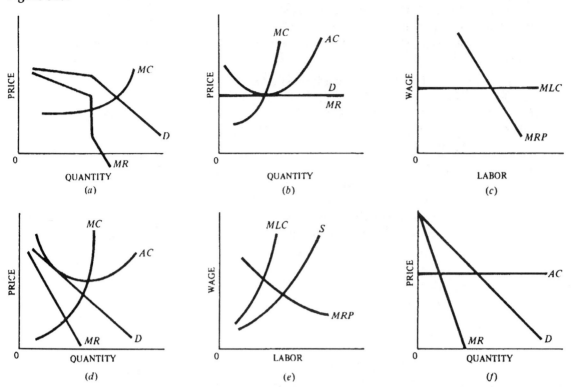

7. The marginal cost of labor is:
   (a) The change in total cost resulting from a unit increase in the product produced.
   (b) The change in total cost resulting from a unit increase in use of labor services.
   (c) The total cost divided by the amount of product produced.
   (d) The total cost divided by the amount of labor services used.

8. The marginal revenue product is:
   (a) The change in total revenue resulting from a unit increase in the quantity of product produced and sold.
   (b) The change in total revenue resulting from a unit increase in the labor services used.
   (c) The total revenue divided by the amount of product produced.
   (d) The total revenue divided by the amount of labor services used.

Exercise 2

This review of different formulas contains every formula that is needed for the different models in the product and labor markets ($\triangle$ = a small change in). Answers may be used more than once, or not at all.

Match the formula at the right with the appropriate concept at left:

1. _____ marginal cost   a. TC/q
2. _____ marginal cost of labor (MCL)   b. TC/L
3. _____ marginal revenue   c. TR/q
4. _____ marginal revenue product   d. TR/L
5. _____ derived demand   e. $\triangle TC/ \triangle q$
6. _____ marginal wage   f. $\triangle TR/ \triangle L$
7. _____ average revenue   g. $\triangle TR/ \triangle q$
8. _____ average cost   h. $\triangle TC/ \triangle L$
9. _____ demand for the product   i. $\triangle$ Total wage/ $\triangle L$

Exercise 3

This exercise provides practice with formulas and graphs in monopsony situations.

1. Let's return to the Rotgut Ripple firm you owned in Chapter 31. Suppose the data in Table 32.2 represents the wages, number of workers, and prices that you face when producing different amounts of Ripple. Complete Table 32.2.

Table 32.2
Labor market with variable wage

(1) Labor (workers per hour)	(2) Wage (dollars per hour)	(3) Ripple (quarts per hour)	(4) Price (dollars per quart)	(5) TC (dollars per hour) (1) x (2)	(6) MCL (dollars per worker) ($\Delta TC/\Delta L$)	(7) TR (dollars per hour) (3) x (4)	(8) MRP (dollars per worker) ($\Delta TR/\Delta L$)
0	$1	0	$1	$ ____	$ —	$ ____	$ —
1	2	15	1	____	____	____	____
2	6	27	1	____	____	____	____
3	9	36	1	____	____	____	____

2. Your firm has market power:
   (a) In both the product and labor market.
   (b) In the market for Ripple only.
   (c) In the labor market only.
   (d) In neither market alone.

   (*Hint:* What changes with production?)

3. In Figure 32.2, diagram the demand and supply of labor that is facing your firm. Label the supply curve *S* and the demand curve *D*. Also diagram the marginal cost of labor curve, and label it *MCL*.

Figure 32.2

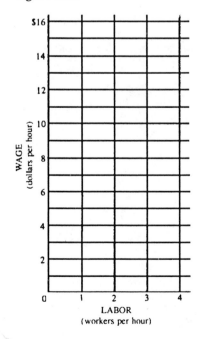

461

4. The amount of Ripple you will produce to maximize your profits is _____; the wage you will pay your workers is _____; the marginal cost of labor will be _____; the number of employees you will hire will be _____.

5. T   F   For each new worker you hire, you must raise wages for all of the workers together, which means that the marginal cost of labor is different from the supply curve of labor.

6. T   F   The wage at which the marginal cost of labor curve intersects the marginal revenue product curve is the equilibrium wage rate.

7. You firm can best be classified as:
   (a) A monopolist in the Ripple market and monopsonist in the labor market.
   (b) A monopolist in the labor market and monopsonist in the Ripple market.
   (c) A monopolist in the Ripple market and competitive buyer in the labor market.
   (d) A competitive supplier in the Ripple market and monopsonist in the labor market.
   (e) Competitive in both the Ripple and labor markets.

8. Which *best* describes your firm based on Table 32.2?
   (a) The Ripple market is a national market with many competitive varieties of Ripple, but the labor market contains only a few people who depend on you for their income.
   (b) Only people in your village buy Ripple and they have great loyalty to your product, but you are competing with other wine producers for people to work at your winery.
   (c) The Ripple is highly profitable over the long run, but it is very difficult to find workers to produce all that you want to produce.

Exercise 4

In stories about specific markets, the media often provide enough information to classify the market that is involved as to structure. By using one of the articles in the text, this exercise will show the kind of information to look for to identify and classify markets. If your professor makes a newspaper assignment for this chapter, this exercise will provide an example of how to do it.

Reread the article in Chapter 24 entitled "Marketing: Cold Cures Spread Like Flu as Companies Fight for Sales" from the *Wall Street Journal*. Then answer the following questions:

1. Are cold cures a differentiated or standardized product?

2. Use Table 25.2 on pages 618–619 of the text to find the concentration ratio in the aspirin market.

   Concentration ratio: _____

   What other evidence of a concentrated market does the article provide?

3. Are there long-run profits in the market? _____

   What passage in the article provides evidence of this fact?

4. Is there evidence of interdependent behavior in the article? _____

   What is the evidence?

5. Did firms enter and exit from the market? _____

   What passage provides evidence of this?

6. What indicates that technological change prevails in this market?

7. This market is an example of:
   (a) Monopoly.
   (b) Oligopoly.
   (c) Monopolistic competition.
   (d) Competition.
   (e) Monopsony.
   (f) Bilateral monopoly. (two possible answers)

8. Which of the diagrams in Figure 32.1 (p. 460) best represents long-run equilibrium in this market?
   a   b   c   d   e   f   (two possible answers)

Common Errors

The first statement in each "common error" below is incorrect. Each incorrect statement is followed by a corrected version and an explanation.

1. The marginal cost of labor curve is the same as the marginal cost curve, and therefore it is also the supply curve for a firm. WRONG!

   The marginal cost of labor curve is derived from the supply of labor and is applicable only to the labor market, not to the product market. RIGHT!

   The marginal cost of labor is given by the formula

$$\frac{\text{Change in total wage costs}}{\text{Change in quantity of labor}}$$

   while the marginal cost curve is given by

$$\frac{\text{Change in total wage costs}}{\text{Change in quantity of product}} .$$

   While the marginal cost of labor applies to labor costs in the labor market, the marginal cost curve applies to all costs in the product market.

2. In bilateral monopoly the optimal level of employment occurs where the marginal cost of labor curve intersects the marginal wage curve. WRONG!

   In bilateral monopoly, it is possible to determine the limits between which the labor and wage levels will fall but not the precise optimal levels. RIGHT!

   The buyer wishes to buy labor at the point where the marginal cost of labor curve intersects the labor-demand curve. The labor supplier wishes to offer services at the point where the marginal wage curve intersects the labor-supply curve. Only through negotiation can a compromise be worked out. The final outcome reflects the relative market power of supplier and buyer.

3. Powerful unions can get whatever wage they want. WRONG!

   Powerful unions are limited by the demand for labor. RIGHT!

   If unions make and receive exorbitant wage demands, they may find the union membership dwindling as more employees are laid off. Frequently unions moderate wage demands in order to prevent employers from going out of business, foreign competition from undercutting prices, and nonunionized workers from becoming attractive to employers. All of these considerations reflect the law of demand.

Crossword Puzzle

Select the economic term in the following list that corresponds with each of the definitions and descriptions below. Then fit the term or one of the words within it into the crossword puzzle at the numbers indicated.

bilateral
monopoly
closed shop
collective
bargaining
craft union
equilibrium
wage rate
fixed costs
fringe benefits
industrial union
labor demand
labor supply
marginal cost of
labor
marginal
physical
product

marginal
productivity
marginal
revenue
product
marginal wage
market power
market wage
monopoly
monopsony
nominal wage
rent
right-to-work
laws
unionization
ratio
union shop

Across

1. The change in total wages paid associated with a one-unit increase in the quantity of labor employed.
4. The fraction of the labor force that belongs to a union.
5. The degree to which a firm can increase total output by adding one unit of input.
8. Current wage rate paid by the employer and received by individual workers.
11. The change in total wage costs that results when the quantity of labor employed is expanded by one unit.
12. The change in total revenue associated with one additional unit of input.
13. A market structure in which one buyer faces one supplier.
16. The process by which an agreement is worked out between members of a bilateral monopoly.
18. A company that agrees to employ only union members from one union.
20. Derived from the demand for products that are produced by labor.
21. A market structure in which there is only one seller.
22. Legislation that makes union membership voluntary.

Down

2. A factor payment to land.
3. The money value of wages uncorrected for inflation.
5. The ability to influence price or wage.
6. An organization of workers with a particular skill that has the purpose of altering wage and employment conditions.
7. An organization of workers in a particular industry that has the purpose of altering wage and employment conditions.
9. The wage rate at which the quantity of labor supplied in a given time period equals the quantity of labor demanded.
10. Nonwage compensation, such as pensions and paid holidays.
12. The change in total output associated with one additional unit of input.
14. A firm that is the only buyer of a product in a particular market.
15. Costs that do not vary with production rates.
17. An employment setting in which all workers must join a particular labor organization within thirty days after being employed.
19. The quantity of labor that would be supplied at alternative wage rates, *ceteris paribus*.

■ ANSWERS ■

Key-Term Review

1. market power
2. unionization ratio
3. collective bargaining
4. bilateral monopoly
5. monopsony
6. marginal factor cost (*MFC*)
7. union shop
8. demand for labor
9. marginal revenue product (*MRP*)
10. labor supply
    marginal wage
11. equilibrium wage
12. productivity

True or False

1. T	6. T	10. T	14. T	18. F	22. T
2. F	7. T	11. F	15. F	19. F	23. F
3. F	8. T	12. T	16. F	20. T	24. F
4. F	9. F	13. F	17. T	21. T	25. F
5. T					

Multiple Choice

1. d	5. d	9. d	13. c	17. b	21. d
2. a	6. a	10. a	14. b, d	18. b	22. d
3. b	7. c	11. c	15. b	19. d	23. c
4. d	8. e	12. a	16. d	20. c	

Problems and Applications

Exercise 1

1. e
2. d
3. a
4. c

5. b
6. f
7. b
8. b

Exercise 2

1. e
2. h
3. g

4. f
5. f
6. i

7. c
8. a
9. c

Exercise 3

1. **Table 32.2 answer**

(1) Labor	(2) Wage	(5) TC	(6) MCL	(7) TR	(8) MRP
0	$1	$ 0	$—	$ 0	$—
1	2	2	2	15	15
2	6	12	10	27	12
3	9	27	15	36	9

2. c

3. **Figure 32.2 answer**

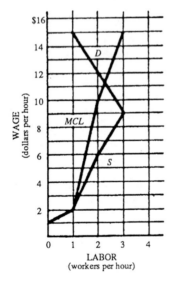

4. 27 quarts per hour; $6 per hour; $10 per hour; 2 employees per hour
5. T
6. F
7. d
8. a

Exercise 4

1. Differentiated. The last paragraph shows that there are many varieties of cold medicine that can be geared to get a consumer response, even though the product is not much different from that produced and marketed by others. This suggests differentiation. In the third paragraph different "brands" are mentioned. Monopolistic competition or differentiated oligopoly may be the appropriate market structures.
2. The concentration ratio is 78 percent, which is consistent with oligopoly. The last paragraph shows that one company has a major share of the market.
3. Yes. "The prize is a piece of the $1.2 billion cold-remedy market" implies a profitable market worth competing for.

4. Yes. Interdependence is suggested in quotations such as "brands succeed at the expense of others" and the title that refers to the "fight" in which the companies are engaged. The "prize" goes to the winner of the fight. This is an article about oligopolistic interdependence.
5. No. Significant barriers to entry are suggested by the amount of effort that companies must put into coming up with new products. The Federal Drug Administration (FDA) is part of that entry barrier. While there are new brands of cold products, it is not clear that the brands are from newly entering firms. Oligopoly or monopolistic competition would be a good bet.
6. The article suggests that there is technological change, but it is a very minor change.
7. b or c
8. a in the case of oligopoly or d for monopolistic competition.

Crossword Puzzle answer

Across

1. *marginal* wage
4. unionization *ratio*
5. marginal *productivity*
8. market *wage*
11. marginal cost of *labor*
12. marginal revenue *product*
13. *bilateral* monopoly
16. collective *bargaining*
18. *closed* shop
20. labor *demand*
21. *monopoly*
22. *right*-to-work laws

Down

2. *rent*
3. *nominal* wage
5. market *power*
6. *craft* union
7. *industrial* union
9. *equilibrium* wage rate
10. *fringe* benefits
12. marginal *physical* product
14. monopsony
15. *fixed* costs
17. *union* shop
19. *labor* supply

Chapter 33
Rent, Interest, and Profit

Quick Review

The income of the economy is distributed to the factors used in production of goods and services. These factors are land, labor, capital, and entrepreneurship. Each factor has a corresponding factor payment: rent for land, wages for labor, interest for capital, and profit for entrepreneurship. Each factor payment rises or falls according to the demand for and supply of the factor.

Chapters 30–32 focused on labor. This chapter is devoted to the other factors, but the same principles are used to explain the payments they receive. Our discussion focuses on the following questions:

- What is economic "rent," and how is its level determined?
- What function do interest rates serve, and how is their level determined?
- What justifies an economic profit?

The economic meanings of the words used for the various types of factor payment differ from their meanings in ordinary usage:

- "Rent" refers to the payments to a factor above the amount that will induce it to be supplied, *not* a payment to a landlord. For such factors as land (not land alone!), which are in fixed supply, all factor payments are rent. Such rent is important in allocating the factor to its most valuable users.
- In both common and economic usage, "interest" is the return for the use of money. The return for the use of money is the opportunity cost of investing in capital. In equilibrium the market interest rate should equal the return to capital. Economists therefore use the term "interest" in a broader sense than that in which it is normally used.
- "Economic profit" refers to the revenue left over after implicit as well as explicit costs have been subtracted from total revenue. Instead of thinking of economic profit as an unfair distribution of income, economists view it as a payment for risk taking.

Economists often use discounting to determine the present value of an income stream. This allows an accurate comparison of the present cost of purchasing an asset with the present value of the income the investor will receive from it.

It is apparent that the high incomes of superstars in many fields are economically justified. It is equally obvious that interference with the market, as in the case of rent control, reduces incentives to increase supply.

Learning Objectives

After reading Chapter 33 and doing the following exercises, you should:	True or false	Multiple choice	Problems and applications	Common errors	Pages in the text
1. Be able to distinguish between the economic meaning of the term "rent" and the everyday use of the term rent.	3,7,20	2			785–788
2. Be able to explain the high incomes observed in selected industries, like professional sports and entertainment, using economic theory.					787–788
3. Understand the allocating function of economic rent.	1,5,6,9, 10,21	3–6,14, 15,17,20	1	4	787–788
4. Be aware of the payment to capital and understand how it is derived.	4,13, 14,25	7–10, 16–19,22			790–792
5. Comprehend the economic impact of regulations such as rent controls.	22–24	21			788–789
6. Be able to calculate the present value of an income stream.		23,24	2,4	2	792–793
7. Know the role of entrepreneurs and the reward they receive in the economy.	12,13, 16,17			3	793–794
8. Understand how implicit and explicit costs are treated by economists in computing profit.	15,18, 19	11–13, 25	3		793–795
9. Be able to distinguish and explain each factor of production, its factor payment, and its factor share in national income.	2,8,11	1		1	783–784
10. Understand the vertical relationships between markets.			5		788–790

Key-Term Review

Review the following terms; if you are not sure of the meaning of any term, write out the definition and check it against the Glossary in the text.

economic costs
economic profit
factor share
fixed costs
functional distribution of income
interest rate

marginal cost
marginal revenue product (*MRP*)
market mechanism
opportunity cost
price elasticity of supply
rent

Fill in the blank following each of the statements below with the appropriate term from the list above.

1. The factor payment to money (and, in equilibrium, to capital) is the _____.

   1. _____

2. The factor payment to land or other factors fixed in supply is _____.

   2. _____

3. When revenues exceed the total of implicit and explicit costs, the residual is _____.

   3. _____

4. Economic profit is a residual that remains if one subtracts from total revenues all _____.

4. _____

5. For a person investing in capital, interest rates are a measure of the incurred _____.

5. _____

6. All factor payments are likely to be rent when there is nearly a zero _____.

6. _____

7. In the short run the production rate will not change even though a firm experiences an increase in _____.

7. _____

8. By computing the change in cost resulting from a change in quantity produced, you have found the _____.

8. _____

9. The fraction of income that goes to a particular resource is known as the _____.

9. _____

10. When an input is increased by one unit, the increase in revenue obtained is called the _____.

10. _____

11. The _____ indicates how much income goes to each factor of production.

11. _____

12. In the United States a large part of our scarce resources are allocated by the _____.

12. _____

True or False: *Circle your choice.*

T F 1. The government can tax rents without decreasing the quantity of a factor supplied in the short run.

T F 2. Wages and salaries account for about one-fourth of national income.

T F 3. "Rent" refers to the returns to capital.

T F 4. Interest is what labor receives in return for its services.

T F 5. David Ricardo showed that the rising price of land reflected the rising price of corn.

T F 6. The price of land is not determined by supply and demand because the supply curve for land is vertical.

T F 7. Rent is the surplus above the price needed to bring forth a factor of production to the market.

T F 8. The marginal revenue product alone determines the actual price for a factor if the buyer has no market power.

T F 9. All factors of production are inelastically supplied.

T F 10. In the long run the high fixed costs of land will affect the amount of land that is used for agricultural purposes.

T F 11. Money is a form of capital and can be considered a factor of production.

T F 12. Interest is a return on the use of money.

T F 13. Interest is the opportunity cost of investing in capital when the market is in equilibrium.

T F 14. The rate of return to capital is the same as the interest rate when markets are in equilibrium.

T F 15. Economic profit and net revenue are the same by definition.

T F 16. The reward for risk taking is economic profit.

T F 17. Economic profit results only from market power.

T F 18. Economic profits should not be taxed because such taxation alters the quantity supplied of those factors with inelastic supply curves.

T F 19. Economic profit does not contain implicit or explicit costs.

T F 20. All economic rent is a "surplus" payment.

T F 21. Falling commodity prices in the 1980s were followed by falling prices for agricultural land.

T F 22. Rent controls ultimately reduce the quality of rental units and encourage attempts to convert apartment houses to condominiums.

T F 23. More apartment buildings will be built if rents are held below the equilibrium price with controls.

T F 24. Rent controls distort the allocation of resources.

T F 25. When the interest rate rises, the supply of loanable funds increases.

Multiple Choice: *Select the correct answer.*

_____ 1. Which of the following are viewed as contributing to capital's share of income?
(a) Rent.
(b) Interest.
(c) Profit.
(d) All of the above.

_____ 2. Which of the following represents rent in an economic sense?
(a) Returns from improvements to land.
(b) Payments to landlords.
(c) Payments for corn in the market.
(d) None of the above.

_____ 3. The value of land is determined by:
(a) The value of the uses to which it can be put.
(b) The whim of landlords.
(c) Those who assess the value of land for property taxes.
(d) None of the above.

_____ 4. Which of the following *best* represents David Ricardo's explanation of the rising costs of farmland?
(a) The marginal cost curve of land shifted upward.
(b) The marginal revenue product curve of land shifted upward as a result of rising corn prices.
(c) The marginal cost curve of land shifted downward.
(d) Landlords were able to exercise their market power because of the limited available amount of land and raised prices to extract economic profits.

_____ 5. An economic justification for allowing rent to exist is that:
(a) Without it, there would be inadequate amounts of fixed factors.
(b) Such rents allocate scarce resources among competing uses.
(c) It represents payments to the risk of holding land.
(d) It tends to create an optimal distribution of income.

_____ 6. Factors to which rent may be paid have:
(a) Elastic supply curves.
(b) Elastic demand curves.
(c) Highly inelastic supply curves.
(d) Highly inelastic demand curves.

_____ 7.   Interest is:
(a) Money paid for the use of money.
(b) A measure of the opportunity cost of investing in capital.
(c) Equivalent to the rate of return on capital when the market is in equilibrium.
(d) All of the above.

_____ 8.   When interest rates rise, _ceteris paribus:_
(a) Borrowers must agree to pay back more money in the future in order to take out a loan.
(b) Savers will tend to decrease the amount of money they save.
(c) Investors will tend to increase the amount of money they borrow.
(d) All of the above are the case.

_____ 9.   In the loanable funds market:
(a) The suppliers are savers and the buyers are investors.
(b) The buyers are savers and the suppliers are investors.
(c) There is a shortage of loanable funds when there is excess saving.
(d) The equilibrium market price is the price of capital goods.

_____ 10.   When the market rate of interest is above the rate of return on capital goods:
(a) There will be excess saving.
(b) There will be excess consumption.
(c) There will be excess investment.
(d) None of the above will be the case.

_____ 11.   Economic profit is:
(a) Total revenue minus explicit costs.
(b) Total revenue minus explicit and implicit costs.
(c) Total revenue minus explicit, implicit, and factor costs.
(d) Total revenue.

_____ 12.   Economic profit may result from:
(a) Market power of the supplier.
(b) Risk taking.
(c) Entrepreneurship.
(d) All of the above.

_____ 13.   The effect of taxing away excess profits would be (in the short run):
(a) To change the amount of output produced and the amount of factors used.
(b) To interfere with the allocation of resources to their most profitable uses.
(c) To leave the distribution of income unchanged.
(d) None of the above.

Choose the diagram in Figure 33.1 that illustrates the economic concept in each of the following items.

_____ 14.   An inelastic supply curve of labor.

_____ 15.   The supply curve of a factor that can yield substantial rent.

_____ 16.   The marginal revenue product curve facing a powerful union.

_____ 17.   The supply curve of a fixed factor.

_____ 18.   The labor-demand curve facing a worker who has no market power.

_____ 19.   The labor-supply curve facing a buyer who has no market power.

Figure 33.1

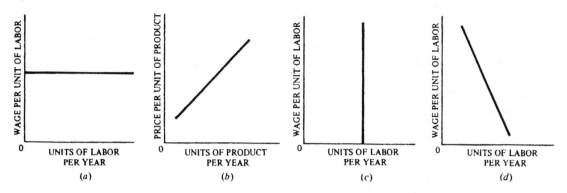

(a)	(b)	(c)	(d)

_____20. Falling prices for U.S. farmland in the 1980s are a consequence of:
   (a) A reduced demand for farmland coupled with an increased supply of farmland.
   (b) Increased rents demanded by landlords.
   (c) Weak demand for farm products coupled with huge harvests.
   (d) None of the above.

_____21. Rent controls result in windfall gains for:
   (a) Landlords.
   (b) Those who seek new apartments.
   (c) Those who own "occupancy rights" to rent-controlled apartments.
   (d) All of the above.

_____22. When the interest rate rises:
   (a) The demand for loanable funds falls and the supply of loanable funds falls.
   (b) The demand for loanable funds rises and the supply of loanable funds rises.
   (c) The demand for loanable funds falls and the supply of loanable funds rises.
   (d) The quantity of loanable funds demanded falls and the quantity of loanable funds supplied rises.

_____23. The present value of $100,000 to be received every year for three years when the discount rate is 10 percent is:
   (a) $300,000.
   (b) $248,742.
   (c) $133,100.
   (d) None of the above.

_____24. The present value of any income stream will be:
   (a) Greater than the sum of the amounts in the income stream.
   (b) Equal to the sum of the amounts in the income stream.
   (c) Less than the sum of the amounts in the income stream.
   (d) None of the above.

_____25. Which of the following statements about windfall profits is true?
   (a) They can be taxed away without causing output to fall.
   (b) They are a form of economic rent.
   (c) They resulted when President Reagan eliminated controls on crude oil prices in 1981.
   (d) All of the above statements are true.

Problems and Applications

Exercise 1

This exercise should serve as a review of cost and revenue formulas and the idea of derived demand.

Match the formula at the right with the appropriate economic concept at the left. TR = total revenue; TC = total cost; p = price; q = quantity; L = land; Δ = a small change in a variable.

1. _____ profit   a. $\Delta\,TR/\,\Delta L$
2. _____ marginal revenue product   b. $\Delta\,TC/\,\Delta q$
3. _____ marginal revenue   c. $TR - TC$
4. _____ marginal cost of land   d. $p \times q$
5. _____ marginal cost   e. $\Delta\,TR/\,\Delta q$
6. _____ total revenue   f. $\Delta\,TC/\,\Delta L$

7. Suppose the government owns 5,000 acres of virgin forest in Colorado and only one lumber company has the ability to use the forest for commercial purposes. The demand schedule for the lumber company's products is shown in Table 33.1. Complete Table 33.1. (*Remember:* Marginal revenue is not the same as marginal revenue product.)

Table 33.1
Demand schedule for lumber company (per year)

Quantity of wood (thousands of tons)	Price (dollars per ton)	Total revenue (thousands of dollars)	Land (thousands of acres)	Marginal revenue product of land (dollars per acre)
0	$60	$_____	0	$_____
4	60	_____	1	_____
7	60	_____	2	_____
9	60	_____	3	_____
10	60	_____	4	_____
10	60	_____	5	_____

8. T F The lumber firm experiences diminishing returns to its use of land in producing wood products.

9. The derived demand schedule for land is:
   (a) The marginal revenue schedule.
   (b) The marginal revenue product schedule.
   (c) Neither a nor b.

10. Diagram the derived demand curve for land in Figure 33.2 and label it D.

Figure 33.2

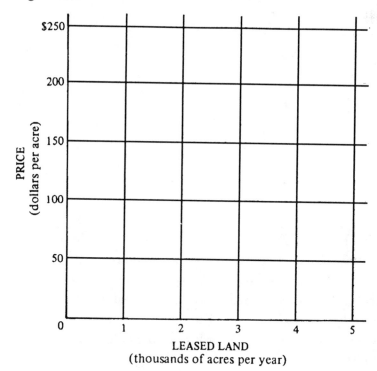

PRICE (dollars per acre)

LEASED LAND
(thousands of acres per year)

11. Assume the government leases the land at $120 per acre per year. Draw the supply curve for the land in Figure 33.2 and label it S.

12. How many thousands of acres would the lumber company lease at the $120 price?
    (a) 1.
    (b) 2.
    (c) 3.
    (d) 4.
    (e) 5.

Exercise 2

This exercise shows how market interest rates determine what investments will be made.

1. You have just inherited $1 million. Suddenly you discover you have ten new friends—each of whom suggests how you might invest $100,000. Each one promises you returns next year as shown in Table 33.2. Compute the rate of return on each project in column 3 of Table 33.2. The formula is

$$\left[\left(\frac{\text{Amount promised in one year}}{\text{Amount invested this year}}\right) - 1\right] \times 100\%$$

Table 33.2
Promised return on investment of $100,000 after one year

(1) Project	*(2)* Amount promised in one year	*(3)* Rate of return on $100,000
a. Construction firm	$120,000	_____ %
b. Fast-food chain	170,000	_____
c. Auto-repair shop	110,000	_____
d. Record studio	190,000	_____
e. Clothing-design center	140,000	_____
f. Whiskey still	200,000	_____
g. Photographic studio	160,000	_____
h. Warehouse	150,000	_____
i. Clinic	180,000	_____
j. Travel agency	130,000	_____

2. Arrange the letters designating each of the projects in Table 33.2 from the most desirable investment to the least desirable. _____

3. T   F   The more of your $1 million that you put into your friends' projects, the lower the rate of return on the next most desirable project.

4. You remember that your bank will also pay you money if you put your money into savings deposits. This rate of return on the use of your money is called the _____.

5. In column 2 of Table 33.3, compute the amount of income you would be able to withdraw if you had deposited $100,000 a year earlier at the bank interest rate shown in column 1.

Table 33.3
Return obtainable on $100,000 deposited in a bank

(1) Interest rate (percent per year)	*(2)* Total amount withdrawable after one year	*(3)* Projects you would invest in at each interest rate	*(4)* Total amount you would invest in chosen projects
100%	$_____	_____	$_____
90	_____	_____	_____
80	_____	_____	_____
70	_____	_____	_____
60	_____	_____	_____
50	_____	_____	_____
40	_____	_____	_____
30	_____	_____	_____
20	_____	_____	_____
10	_____	_____	_____
0	_____	_____	_____

6. In column 3 of Table 33.3 enter the letters of the projects you would invest in before putting your money into a savings account at each interest rate. (*Hint:* You should invest in those projects that give at least as high a return as you could receive on your savings.)

7. In column 4 of Table 33.3 compute how much of your $1,000,000 would go to your friends' projects at each interest rate that the bank might offer. (*Hint:* Count the number of projects that you have entered in each row of column 3 and multiply by the amount you would invest in each.)

8. In Figure 33.3 graph the relationship between the interest rate (column 1, Table 33.3) and the total amount that you would invest in your friends' projects (column 4, Table 33.3).

Figure 33.3

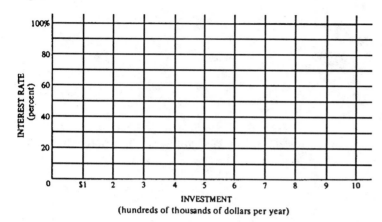

INVESTMENT
(hundreds of thousands of dollars per year)

9. As the interest rate rises:
   (a) Your investment in your friends' capital projects falls.
   (b) Your savings at the bank rise.
   (c) The capital projects in which you invest will have a higher rate of return.
   (d) All of the above.

10. T   F   Higher interest rates mean lower rates of return for capital projects.

11. The supply and demand of loanable funds is shown in Figure 33.4. If the supply of loanable funds is S_1, then the equilibrium interest rate is:
    (a)   30 percent.
    (b)   40 percent.
    (c)   60 percent.
    (d) 100 percent.

Figure 33.4

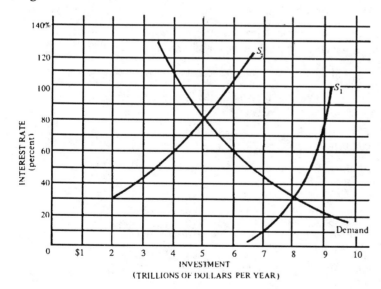

INVESTMENT
(TRILLIONS OF DOLLARS PER YEAR)

12. At the equilibrium interest rate, how many of your friends' capital projects would you invest in? (*Hint:* Find your answer using Figures 33.4 and 33.3.)
    (a)   6.
    (b)   7.
    (c)   8.
    (d) 10.

477

13. If the supply of loanable funds is cut back to S_2, in how many of your friends' capital projects would you invest?
    (a) 3.
    (b) 5.
    (c) 8.
    (d) 10.

Exercise 3

Use Exercise 6 in Chapter 20 (p. 293) to review how to calculate economic profit, explicit costs, implicit costs, and opportunity costs.

Exercise 4

This exercise shows how to compute the present value of different investments. It also shows how important the interest rate is in the choice of present values.

1. Suppose you buy 1,000 acres of forest land for $100,000 in the current year. Next year you could have the trees cut down for lumber for $1,320,000 (after taxes and all other expenses). The interest rate is 10 percent. Find the present value of your 1,000 acres of forest land. (*Hint:* Remember that in the first year you are spending money for the land; this appears as a negative number. Since the costs appear only in the first year, there is no need to discount them.)

2. However, you do not like the idea of cutting down the trees, and so you decide to open the land up for multiple uses including recreation. By charging user fees you can receive rent of $130,000 a year forever. Compute the present value of holding the land for recreational uses. (*Hint:* Remember that it is still necessary to subtract the cost of the land in the first year.)

3. Which of the following is the *most* profitable use of the land to you?
    (a) Not buying the land in the first place because its present value is negative.
    (b) Cutting the forest down for lumber.
    (c) Using the forest for recreational purposes.

4. Suppose interest rates rose to 20 percent. What would the present value of turning the forest to lumber be at 20 percent interest rate if the cost and profit were the same as at 10 percent?

5. At the 20 percent interest rate what would the present value of the land be for recreational uses?

6. Which is the *most* profitable use of the land at the 20 percent interest rate?
    (a) Not buying the land because its present value is negative.
    (b) Cutting down the forest for lumber.
    (c) Using the forest for recreational purposes.

7. T F When the interest rate rises, the present value of investments rises. (*Hint:* Compare answers to Problems 1 and 4.)

8. T F When the interest rate rises, the value of land falls.

9. T F The present value of long-run projects is more sensitive to interest rates than short-run projects.

Exercise 5

The media often provide evidence of vertical relationships between markets—that is, the relationship between outputs and the inputs used to make those products. By using one of the articles in the text, this exercise will show the kind of information to look for to identify such relationships. If your professor makes a newspaper assignment for this chapter, this exercise will provide an example of how to do it.

Reread the article in Chapter 9 entitled "Plants Plan December Shutdowns as the Recession Spreads Rapidly" from the *Wall Street Journal*. Look particularly at the following two quotations:

> The hard-hit auto, truck, farm equipment and construction machinery industries . . . will take a lot of extra time off this year, as will a number of their suppliers.

> There will be a lot of shutdowns and short workweeks this month as companies adjust to the rapidly spreading recession.

Try to construct the vertical relationships between the market participants—(a) labor, (b) consumers, (c) "auto, truck, farm equipment and construction machinery" companies, and (d) suppliers to those companies—and the markets—(A) "auto, truck . . ." market, (B) labor market, and (C) machinery-supplier market—that they buy from or sell to.

Table 33.4
Vertical relationships between market participants and markets

(1) Market participant	(2) Buyer or seller	(3) Market
_____	Seller	
_____	Buyer	_____
_____	Seller	
_____	Buyer	_____
_____	Seller	
_____	Buyer	_____

In Table 33.4 write in the buyers and sellers in column 1 and the market in column 2. In column 1 you should have a list of four participants, and in column 2 you should show the three vertically related markets. Each of the participants must take title to the good or service and each market must have a buyer and seller.

Common Errors

The first statement in each "common error" below is incorrect. Each incorrect statement is followed by a corrected version and an explanation.

1. Money is capital. WRONG!

    Money is a medium of exchange; it has no physical return. Capital is a factor of production; it has a physical return in the flow of goods produced by it. RIGHT!

    Common usage of the word "capital" often leads people to treat money itself as a factor of production and interest as a return to the factor. While it is easy to confuse capital as an asset and money as a store of value, the two have quite different physical properties and make quite different contributions to production. However, in equilibrium the return to capital and the interest rate will be the same.

2. Interest is a return on capital. WRONG!

    Interest is a return on money. RIGHT! See explanation above.

3. Profits are evil. WRONG!

    Profits are payments for services but are undesirable when they lead to inefficient or inequitable distributions of income. RIGHT!

In the common usage of the word "profits," implicit costs, which are payments for resources such as entrepreneurship, are often ignored. When profits result from market power, they may lead to undesirable inefficiency. The market mechanism that generates profits may not equitably distribute those profits; in that case, transfers must be made to redistribute the profits. The possibility of economic profits may be quite important in providing incentives for risk taking.

4. Rent is a payment to a landlord. WRONG!

Rent is a payment above what is needed to coax a factor into the market. RIGHT!

Payments made for the use of land include payments to factors that are on or accessible to the land—for example, an apartment in a house built on the land. Only the unimproved land itself is in fixed supply, however. Other factors of production that are in fixed supply may also accrue rent.

■ ANSWERS ■

Key-Term Review

1. interest rate	5. opportunity cost	9. factor share
2. rent	6. price elasticity of supply	10. marginal revenue product (*MRP*)
3. economic profit	7. fixed costs	11. functional distribution of income
4. economic costs	8. marginal cost	12. market mechanism

True or False

1. T	6. F	10. F	14. T	18. F	22. T
2. F	7. T	11. F	15. F	19. T	23. F
3. F	8. F	12. T	16. T	20. T	24. T
4. F	9. F	13. T	17. F	21. T	25. F
5. T					

Multiple Choice

1. d	6. c	10. a	14. c	18. a	22. d
2. d	7. d	11. b	15. c	19. a	23. b
3. a	8. a	12. d	16. d	20. c	24. c
4. b	9. a	13. d	17. c	21. c	25. d
5. b					

Problems and Applications

Exercise 1

1. c
2. a
3. e
4. f
5. b
6. d

7. **Table 33.1 answer**

Quantity	Total revenue	Marginal revenue product
0	$ 0	$ —
4	240	240
7	420	180
9	540	120
10	600	60
10	600	0

8. T
9. b
10. **Figure 33.2 answer**

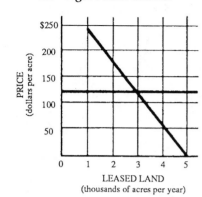

PRICE (dollars per acre)

LEASED LAND
(thousands of acres per year)

11. See Figure 33.2 answer, line *S*.
12. c

Exercise 2

1. **Table 33.2 answer**

(1) Project	(2) Rate of return (percent)
a	20%
b	70
c	10
d	90
e	40
f	100
g	60
h	50
i	80
j	30

2. f, d, i, b, g, h, e, j, a, c
3. T
4. interest rate

5. **Table 33.3 answer**

(1) Interest rate (percent per year)	(2) Total amount withdrawable after one year	(3) Projects you would invest in at each interest rate	(4) Total amount you would invest in chosen projects
100%	$200,000	f	$ 100,000
90	190,000	f, d	200,000
80	180,000	f, d, i	300,000
70	170,000	f, d, i, b	400,000
60	160,000	f, d, i, b, g	500,000
50	150,000	f, d, i, b, g, h	600,000
40	140,000	f, d, i, b, g, h, e	700,000
30	130,000	f, d, i, b, g, h, e, j	800,000
20	120,000	f, d, i, b, g, h, e, j, a	900,000
10	110,000	f, d, i, b, g, h, e, j, a, c	1,000,000
0	100,000	f, d, i, b, g, h, e, j, a, c	1,000,000

6. See Table 33.3 answer, column 3.
7. See Table 33.3 answer, column 4.

8. **Figure 33.3 answer**

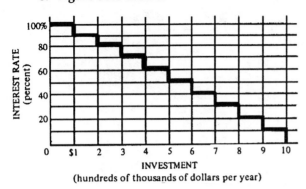

INTEREST RATE (percent)

INVESTMENT
(hundreds of thousands of dollars per year)

9. d
10. F The rates of return on projects are not changed by interest rates. However, investors' willingness to invest in them when there are alternatives with higher-paying interest rates does change.
11. a
12. c Count the number of your friends' projects that are equal to or above the 30 percent equilibrium interest rate.
13. a

Exercise 3

See answers to Exercise 6 in Chapter 20 (p. 299).

Exercise 4

1. $-\$100,000 + \dfrac{\$1,320,000}{1.10} = \$1,100,000$

2. $-\$100,000 + \dfrac{\$130,000}{.10} = \$1,200,000$

3. c

4. $-\$100,000 + \dfrac{\$1,320,000}{1.20} = \$1,000,000$

5. $-\$100,000 + \dfrac{\$130,000}{.20} = \$550,000$

6. b
7. F
8. T
9. T

Exercise 5

Table 33.4 answer

(1) Market participant	(2) Buyer or seller	(3) Market
(a) labor	Seller	(B) Labor market
(d) suppliers	Buyer / Seller	(C) Machinery-supplier market
(c) "auto, truck . . ."	Buyer / Seller	(A) "Auto, truck . . ." market
(b) consumers	Buyer	

Chapter 34

Taxes: Equity vs. Efficiency

Quick Review

Taxes are a fact of life. They are a way of transferring command of resources from the private sector to the public sector and of redistributing income from rich to poor. The impact of taxes on the economy is not always easy to determine, and there appears to be a trade-off between society's goals of equity and efficiency. Let's examine the equity–efficiency trade-off by focusing on the following questions:

- How are incomes distributed in the United States?
- How do taxes alter that distribution?
- How do taxes affect the rate and mix of output?

The distribution of income is a major concern of public policy; it concerns the FOR WHOM question. It should be remembered, however, that income is sometimes not required to get goods and services; welfare payments, for example, are sometimes made in kind. It is also necessary to distinguish between income and wealth, even though the two are obviously related, and both have implications for one's command over goods and services. Income is a flow and is measured over time; wealth is a stock and is measured at a point in time.

The size distribution of income concentrates on the way income is distributed among income-receiving units, such as households. For example, one may be interested in the fraction of total income received by those who comprise the lowest 20 percent of income recipients (households).

The Lorenz curve is a graph that compares the actual distribution of income with a distribution of income in which everyone receives the same income. The Lorenz curve is particularly useful in comparing income distribution before and after taxes. It is generally observed that in the United States, income is distributed somewhat more equally after taxes than before.

One must be extremely careful in talking about taxes and the tax system. Provisions in the tax law called "loopholes" allow individuals to reduce the amount of income subject to tax. The loopholes also result in a violation of two important principles of taxation—horizontal equity and vertical equity. Because of this, economists use several tax rates—average tax rate, nominal tax rate, effective tax rate, and so on—to analyze the tax system. In addition, taxes may be shifted from one group to another. Even the employer's portion of the social security tax is thought to be borne by the employee. We should also not lose sight of the fact that other levels of government (state and local) tax income and property too.

While the overall degree of inequality is difficult to determine, one cannot argue with the fact that income is distributed unequally in the United States. Whether the distribution is fair or not is an entirely different matter. Some feel more *should* be transferred from those with higher incomes to those with lower incomes. Others argue that such a redistribution of income would so damage the incentives of productive, high-income people that total production and income would decline.

Because of the many concerns about such issues as equity, efficiency, and the erosion of the tax base, Congress passed the Tax Reform Act of 1986. This act closed loopholes, reduced marginal tax rates, reduced the number of tax brackets, increased the tax burden of corporations relative to individuals, and provided tax relief for the poor.

Learning Objectives

After reading Chapter 34 and doing the following exercises, you should:	True or false	Multiple choice	Problems and applications	Common errors	Pages in the text
1. Be able to distinguish between wealth and income.	1–3	2	1	1	800–802
2. Understand the size distribution of income and be able to interpret a Lorenz curve.	8,11, 12,17	3,5, 6–8,10	1		802–805
3. Be aware of the impact of taxes and transfers on the distribution of income.	13,14, 18,23	9			805–807
4. Understand the principles of horizontal and vertical equity.	6,9	16–18	2,3		806
5. Be able to distinguish the marginal and average tax rates, and nominal and effective tax rates.	4,5,7,9,10, 19–22	13–15			806–807
6. Understand the impact of tax "loopholes."	14,16	1			807–809
7. Be able to distinguish arguments for equality from arguments for equity.		11			812–814
8. Recognize that the most serious potential cost of greater equality would be damaged incentives.	15			2	813
9. Recognize the trade-off between greater equality and efficiency.	7			2	813–814
10. Be aware of major reforms embodied in the Tax Reform Act of 1986.	19,20	19,20			807–809
11. Be able to distinguish among progressive, regressive, and proportional taxes.	4,21–25	4			805,809, 810,812

Key-Term Review

Review the following terms; if you are not sure of the meaning of any term, write out the definition and check it against the Glossary in the text.

effective tax rate
horizontal equity
income share
income transfers
Lorenz curve
marginal revenue product (*MRP*)
marginal tax rate
nominal tax rate

personal income (*PI*)
progressive tax
regressive tax
size distribution of income
tax base
tax incidence
vertical equity

Fill in the blank following each of the statements below with the appropriate term from the list above.

1. Plotting percent of income received against the percent of families receiving the income yields a _____.   1. _____

2. That part of income or property which is subject to tax is known as the _____.

    2. _____

3. The grouping of households according to income class, so that the share of total income received by each class may be observed, yields the _____.

    3. _____

4. A tax that takes a greater fraction of income as income rises is called a _____.

    4. _____

5. The flow of income received before the payment of personal income taxes is called _____.

    5. _____

6. The increase in revenue generated by an additional unit of an input is called the _____ of the input.

    6. _____

7. The proportion of income received by a particular group is called an _____.

    7. _____

8. Social security contributions are an example of a _____.

    8. _____

9. The federal income tax imposes a progressively higher _____.

    9. _____

10. The total taxes divided by total income is a measure called the _____.

    10. _____

11. After all deductions and exemptions have been taken from income, it is possible to find the _____.

    11. _____

12. The idea that individuals with high incomes should pay greater taxes than those with low incomes is referred to as _____; that individuals with the same income should pay the same tax is called _____.

    12. _____

    _____

13. Because the burden of a given tax may not reside where a tax is levied, care must be taken in determining the _____.

    13. _____

14. Social security payments, welfare payments, and unemployment compensation are examples of _____.

    14. _____

True or False: *Circle your choice.*

T F 1. Wealth and income are the same thing.

T F 2. A person can have a great deal of wealth but have very little income.

T F 3. Income is a flow and wealth is a stock.

T F 4. Marginal tax rates must increase for a tax to be progressive, *ceteris paribus.*

T F 5. When total income exceeds taxable income, the effective tax rate will be less than the nominal tax rate.

T F 6. A flat tax would take the same dollar amount from each taxpayer.

T F 7. The efficiency issue in taxation refers to the impact of higher marginal rates on the incentive to produce.

T F 8. The size distribution of income focuses on the size of the share going to labor, capital, and land.

T F 9. Because of numerous exemptions and deductions, the effective tax rate often exceeds the nominal tax rate.

T F 10. The nominal tax rate cannot exceed the effective tax rate.

T F 11. The top 20 percent of income recipients in the United States get about one-fifth of total income.

T F 12. If everyone had equal income, the Lorenz curve would coincide with the line of equality.

T F 13. The combined effect of federal, state, and local taxes is to increase the degree of income inequality in the United States.

T F 14. Loopholes, exemptions, and deductions cause an erosion of the tax base.

T F 15. The potential cost of greater equality is thought to be the damage done to incentives of productive individuals.

T F 16. Tax loopholes are illegal techniques typically used by the rich to avoid taxes.

T F 17. Since income is simply a dollar measure of output produced, the distribution of money income is synonymous with the distribution of goods and services.

T F 18. Money income statistics give a misleading picture of the income distribution of real income.

T F 19. The Tax Reform Act of 1986 broadened the tax base by closing many loopholes.

T F 20. One effect of the Tax Reform Act of 1986 was to increase the tax burden on those with lowest incomes.

T F 21. Since a sales tax takes a flat percentage of income, it is a proportional tax.

T F 22. The incidence of a tax depends on the elasticity of the supply and demand of the base on which the tax is levied.

T F 23. Because higher property taxes are reflected in higher rents, the property tax is progressive.

T F 24. The employee portion of the social security tax is progressive because the higher one's income, the more dollars one pays.

T F 25. The employer portion of the social security tax is proportional because the employer pays the same number of dollars on each individual employed.

Multiple Choice: *Select the correct answer.*

_____ 1. Which of the following can be perceived as an income distribution issue?
  (a) Tax reform.
  (b) Affirmative action.
  (c) Social security.
  (d) All of the above.

_____ 2. The distribution of income is basically the answer to:
  (a) The WHAT question for society.
  (b) The HOW question for society.
  (c) The FOR WHOM question for society.
  (d) None of the above.

_____ 3. In which of the following countries is the percent of income received by the top ten percent of income recipients the smallest?
  (a) The United States.
  (b) Sweden.
  (c) Brazil.
  (d) Australia.

_____ 4. Which of the following is typically a progressive tax?
(a) A sales tax.
(b) A property tax.
(c) The social security tax.
(d) None of the above.

_____ 5. The size distribution of income concerns the:
(a) Share of income going to labor.
(b) Median income.
(c) Average income.
(d) Share of income going to various income classes.

_____ 6. If your family's income was $51,000 in 1986, you were in the:
(a) Highest quintile.
(b) Top 5 percent.
(c) Second highest quintile.
(d) Middle of the distribution.

_____ 7. In 1986 the share of total income of the lowest quintile was:
(a) 10.8 percent.
(b) 16.8 percent.
(c) 4.6 percent.
(d) 24.0 percent.

_____ 8. Which of the following statements is _incorrect_?
(a) If income were distributed equally, the Lorenz curve would be a straight line.
(b) When income is distributed unequally, the line of equality sags below the Lorenz curve.
(c) When income is distributed unequally, the Lorenz curve sags below the line of equality.
(d) The Gini coefficient is zero when income is distributed equally.

_____ 9. The U.S. tax system results in a slight reduction in inequality of after-tax income because:
(a) Of the progressive nature of state and local taxes.
(b) Of the progressive nature of the federal income tax.
(c) The rich have fewer available loopholes than the poor.
(d) The poor receive such generous welfare benefits.

_____ 10. The argument _against_ greater equality in the distribution of income in the United States hinges basically on:
(a) Productivity concerns.
(b) The Equal Rights Amendment.
(c) The underground economy.
(d) None of the above.

_____ 11. The argument in favor of greater equality of income distribution in the United States hinges on:
(a) The idea that the present degree of inequality is more than necessary to maintain incentives.
(b) The idea that low-income earners would be more willing and able participants in the economy if income were distributed more equally.
(c) The idea that those with high incomes wield greater political power and weaken the democratic process.
(d) All of the above.

_____ 12. In making comparisons of income among countries, care must be exercised because:
(a) In poor countries much of what is produced does not pass through markets and thus does not get counted in the nation's income.
(b) In countries such as Sweden and Great Britain, the government provides more goods and services directly than in the United States.
(c) In-kind benefits should be included in real income in all countries.
(d) All of the above are true.

Use the following information to answer Questions 13–15. The tax schedule is hypothetical to keep the calculations simple.

Suppose an individual has a total income of $100,000, has a taxable income of $50,000, and pays taxes of $5,000.

_____ 13. For this individual the difference between his total income and his taxable income is:
   (a) $45,000.
   (b) $50,000.
   (c) $95,000.
   (d) None of the above.

_____ 14. This individual's (choose one) tax rate is 5 percent.
   (a) Nominal tax rate.
   (b) Effective tax rate.
   (c) Marginal tax rate.
   (d) None of the above.

_____ 15. This individual's (choose one) tax rate is 10 percent.
   (a) Nominal tax rate.
   (b) Effective tax rate.
   (c) Average tax rate.
   (d) None of the above.

_____ 16. The principle of taxation that says people with equal incomes should pay equal taxes is called:
   (a) Vertical equity.
   (b) Horizontal equity.
   (c) Progressivity.
   (d) Regressivity.

_____ 17. The principle of taxation that says that people with higher incomes should pay more in taxes than those with lower incomes is called:
   (a) Vertical equity.
   (b) Horizontal equity.
   (c) Progressivity.
   (d) Regressivity.

_____ 18. The federal income tax is a:
   (a) Flat tax.
   (b) Proportional tax.
   (c) Progressive tax.
   (d) Regressive tax.

_____ 19. Which of the following was accomplished by the Tax Reform Act of 1986?
   (a) Closing loopholes.
   (b) Reducing the number of tax rates.
   (c) Reducing marginal tax rates.
   (d) All were accomplished.

_____ 20. Which of the following statements is true? The 1986 Tax Reform Act:
   (a) Reduced the tax base while increasing marginal tax rates.
   (b) Increased the tax base while reducing the number of brackets.
   (c) Increased the burden on individuals by increasing marginal tax rates.
   (d) Increased the number of individuals who will have to pay taxes.

Problems and Applications

Exercise 1

This exercise will help you understand the Lorenz curve and the problem at the end of Chapter 34 in the text.

1. The information given in Table 34.1 is reprinted from Table 34.1 in the text (p. 803). Fill in column 3 of Table 34.1, then use it to draw a Lorenz curve in Figure 34.1.

Table 34.1
Size distribution of personal income, by household income group, 1986

(1) Quintile of income recipients (households)	(2) Percent of total household income received	(3) Percent of income received (cumulative)
Lowest fifth	4.6%	_____%
Second fifth	10.8	_____
Third fifth	16.8	_____
Fourth fifth	24.0	_____
Highest fifth	43.7	_____

Figure 34.1

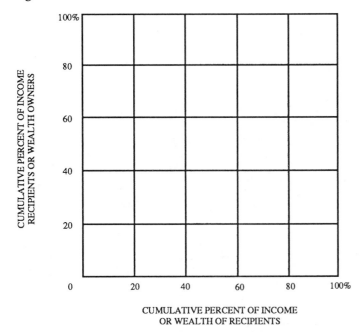

CUMULATIVE PERCENT OF INCOME
OR WEALTH OF RECIPIENTS

2. The information given in Table 34.1 is for 1986 income. Income in 1986 was distributed (equally, unequally).

3. Draw the line of absolute equality in Figure 34.1 and label it. Shade in the area between the Lorenz curve and the line of equality. The shaded area is a measure of the degree of _____.

4. In Figure 34.1 draw a second Lorenz curve that indicates the distribution of wealth in the United States for the same year. Use the hypothetical data from Table 34.2. Calculate column 3 first.

489

Table 34.2
Hypothetical size distribution of wealth, by wealth-holding group

(1) Quintile of wealth owners	(2) Wealth owned	(3) Wealth owned (cumulative)
Lowest fifth	0.5%	_____ %
Second fifth	5.0	_____
Third fifth	12.0	_____
Fourth fifth	20.0	_____
Highest fifth	62.5	_____

5. Although the data in Table 34.2 are hypothetical, they do actually indicate the direction of inequality of wealth ownership relative to the distribution of income. Wealth is (more, less) equally distributed than income.

Exercise 2

By using an example from the tax reform for the 1987 tax year this problem will show how to determine the impact of a tax change on vertical and horizontal equity.

For the 1986 tax year the federal tax liability for single individuals was computed on the basis of the schedule shown in Table 34.3.

Table 34.3

If your taxable income Is above:	But below:	Then your tax is:
$11,650	$13,920	$1,297.70 + 18% of anything over $11,650
13,920	16,190	1,706.30 + 20% of anything over $13,920
16,190	19,640	2,160.30 + 23% of anything over $16,190

For the 1987 tax year the corresponding federal tax liability for single individuals was computed with the schedule found in Table 34.4.

Table 34.4

If your taxable income Is above:	But below:	Then your tax is:
$ 1,800	$16,800	$ 198.00 + 15% of anything over $1,800
16,800	27,000	2,448.00 + 28% of anything over $16,800

1. What would the marginal tax rates be for a single taxpayer with a taxable income of $17,000 in 1986? _____ % In 1987? _____ % On the basis of this information does it appear that the tax reform of the Reagan administration increased work incentives for single taxpayers with a taxable income of $17,000?   yes   no   (circle one)

2. For the three taxpayers listed in Table 34.5, compute the taxable income, taxes in the years 1986 and 1987, and difference in taxes for the two years.

Table 34.5
Taxable income and tax computations

Taxpayer	Gross income	Exemptions and deductions	Taxable income	1986 Tax	1987 Tax	Difference
1	$30,000	$18,000	$_____	$_____	$_____	$_____
2	30,000	13,000	_____	_____	_____	_____
3	50,000	38,000	_____	_____	_____	_____

3. On the basis of Table 34.5 did the tax reform package lower taxes for single taxpayers in the taxable income range of $12,000 to $17,000?   yes   no   (circle one)

4. In Table 34.6 rank each taxpayer on the basis of the nominal tax rate, effective tax rate, and marginal tax rate for 1987.

Table 34.6
Rankings for 1987

Rank	Taxpayer	Nominal tax rate	Effective tax rate	Marginal tax rate
1	____ (highest)	_____%	_____%	_____%
2	____ (middle)	_____	_____	_____
3	____ (lowest)	_____	_____	_____

5. How should horizontal equity be determined?
   (a) The two taxpayers with the same nominal incomes should be compared for their marginal tax rates.
   (b) The two taxpayers with the same nominal incomes should be compared for their effective tax rates.
   (c) The effective tax rate of the taxpayer with the highest nominal income should be compared to the effective tax rates of taxpayers with lower nominal income.
   (d) The marginal tax rate of the taxpayer with the highest nominal income should be compared to the marginal tax rates of taxpayers with lower nominal incomes.

6. How should vertical equity be determined?
   (a) The two taxpayers with the same nominal incomes should be compared for their marginal tax rates.
   (b) The two taxpayers with the same nominal incomes should be compared for their effective tax rates.
   (c) The effective tax rate of the taxpayer with the highest nominal income should be compared to the effective tax rates of taxpayers with lower nominal incomes.
   (d) The marginal tax rate of the taxpayer with the highest nominal income should be compared to the marginal tax rates of taxpayers with lower nominal incomes.

7. T   F   For single taxpayers with taxable incomes between $12,000 and $17,000, the tax-reform package reduced vertical equity.

Exercise 3

Around April 15 of every year many articles appear about changes in the tax laws from the previous year. By using one of the articles in the text, this exercise will show the kind of information to look for to identify and classify changes in the tax system. If your professor makes a newspaper assignment for this chapter, this exercise will provide an example of how to do it.

Reread the article in Chapter 3 entitled "Some Taxing Facts about Lotteries" from *NBER Digest*. Then answer the following questions:

1. What passage indicates a change in the tax law has occurred or has been proposed?

2. What sentence indicates a change in horizontal or vertical equity resulting from the tax change?

3. The change in equity indicated in the article concerns:
   (a) Vertical equity.
   (b) Horizontal equity.

Common Errors

The first statement in each "common error" below is incorrect. Each incorrect statement is followed by a corrected version and an explanation.

1. Income and wealth are the same thing. WRONG!

   Income and wealth mean distinctly different things. RIGHT!

   The distinction between income and wealth is critical to sound economic analysis. Income is a flow and has a time dimension. For example, one states one's income in dollars *per year*. Wealth is a stock and is measured at a point in time; for example, you may say you have $5,000 in your savings account *today*. Some people with apparently great wealth may have very little income, as in the case of someone who owns land known to contain oil. On the other hand, someone who has much income may have little wealth; some famous entertainers earn large incomes, save little (accumulate no wealth), and wind up in bankruptcy. Of course, wealth and income may go hand in hand: the incomes of some oil magnates flow *from* their wealth. But clearly the two terms imply different things about one's economic well-being and command over goods and services.

2. Equity and equality of income distribution mean the same thing. WRONG!

   Equity and equality of income distribution mean different things. RIGHT!

   Many arguments over the division of the income pie, whether at the national level, the corporate level, or the university level, are laced with the terms *equity* and *equality* used interchangeably. They are not interchangeable. Equality of income distribution means that each person has an equal share. Equity of income distribution implies something about fairness. In a free society some will surely be more productive than others at doing what society wants done. The brain surgeon's services have greater value than the hairdresser's. The surgeon's income will exceed that of the hairdresser—that is, they'll be unequal. But is that inequitable? This is a matter of judgment. It's safe to say, however, that if one were not allowed to keep some of the rewards for being more productive than average, our economy would suffer. An equitable distribution of income in our society will require some inequality. How much? There is no sure answer to that question, only a series of compromises.

■ ANSWERS ■

Key-Term Review

1. Lorenz curve	6. marginal revenue product (*MRP*)	11. nominal tax rate
2. tax base	7. income share	12. vertical equity
3. size distribution of income	8. regressive tax	horizontal equity
4. progressive tax	9. marginal tax rate	13. tax incidence
5. personal income (*PI*)	10. effective tax rate	14. income transfers

True or False

1. F	6. F	10. F	14. T	18. T	22. T
2. T	7. T	11. F	15. T	19. T	23. F
3. T	8. F	12. T	16. F	20. F	24. F
4. T	9. F	13. F	17. F	21. F	25. F
5. T					

Multiple Choice

1. d	5. d	9. b	12. d	15. a	18. c
2. c	6. a	10. a	13. b	16. b	19. d
3. a	7. c	11. d	14. b	17. a	20. b
4. d	8. b				

Problems and Applications

Exercise 1

1. **Table 34.1 answer**

(1) *Quintile of* *income recipients* *(households)*	*(3)* *Income* *received* *(cumulative)*
Lowest fifth	4.6%
Second fifth	15.4
Third fifth	32.2
Fourth fifth	56.2
Highest fifth	99.9

Figure 34.1 answer

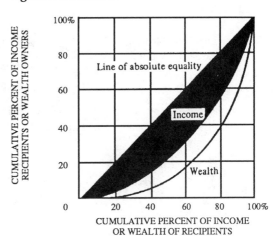

2. unequally
3. See shaded area in Figure 34.1 answer; inequality.
4. See Table 34.2 answer and Figure 34.1 answer.

Table 34.2 answer

(1) *Quintile of* *wealth owners*	*(3)* *Wealth owned* *(cumulative)*
Lowest fifth	0.5%
Second fifth	5.5
Third fifth	17.5
Fourth fifth	37.5
Highest fifth	100.0

5. less

Exercise 2

1. 23 percent for 1986 (the percentage used in the formula is the marginal tax rate); 28 percent for 1987; no

2. **Table 34.5 answer**

Taxpayer	Taxable income	1986 Tax	1987 Tax	Difference
1	$12,000	$1,360.70	$1,728	$367.30
2	17,000	2,346.60	2,504	157.40
3	12,000	1,360.70	1,728	367.30

3. no

4. **Table 34.6 answer**

Rank	Taxpayer	Nominal tax rate	Effective tax rate	Marginal tax rate
1	2	(2,504/17,000 = 14.7%)	(2,504/30,000 = 8.35%)	28%
2	1	(1,728/12,000 = 14.4%)	(1,728/30,000 = 5.76%}	15
3	3	(1,728/12,000 = 14.4%)	(1,728/50,000 = 3.46%}	15

5. b
6. c
7. T The difference in total taxes paid was greater at a $12,000 taxable income than it was at a $17,000 taxable income as shown in the last column of Table 34.5 answer.

Exercise 3

1. "Per capita lottery ticket sales averaged $88 in 1985, up from $23 in 1975."
2. "The transfer of these revenues to state treasuries is an important tax on lottery bettors and that tax is 'decidedly regressive.' "
3. a

Chapter 35
Work vs. Welfare

Quick Review

Poverty is an age-old problem. Even in the most affluent societies some people, although they work, have income and living standards that society feels are too low. Very often some form of assistance such as welfare is provided. In this chapter we discuss the relationship between work, income, and welfare by examining the following questions:

- How many Americans are poor?
- How much assistance do they get from the welfare system?
- How does the welfare system discourage work and so perpetuate the welfare problem?

As recently as 1986 over 32 million Americans were classified as poor. They were a heterogeneous group when classified by age, sex, race, employment history, and the like. Surprisingly, many were employed full-time the year round. Whether someone is poor or not (in the official sense) depends on cash income, family size, and place of residence (urban or rural).

Poverty has three principal causes: (1) human-capital deficiencies, (2) insufficient demand for labor, and (3) discrimination. Public policy can help eliminate poverty by providing people with the skills and opportunities they need to earn an income that will push them above the poverty line. But some people—the very old, the very young, the infirm—cannot be helped in this way.

The policy alternatives available to us are varied, but the predominant programs involve income transfers (e.g., AFDC benefits) and in-kind transfers (such as food stamps and Medicaid). Welfare programs are administered at the federal, state, and local levels. Each of the welfare programs must attempt to achieve three goals: (1) to provide incentives to those who are still able to work, (2) to minimize the cost of the program, and (3) to provide adequate income support to the individuals involved. Because these goals tend to conflict and because jurisdictions overlap, our nation's welfare program is under almost constant review and revision.

The administration changed the welfare eligibility and benefit rules in 1981. Major changes involved limiting gross income, limiting allowable work expenses, raising the marginal tax rate, and placing restrictions on the assets one may own and still be eligible for AFDC benefits. An additional change suggested, but not adopted, was compulsory work at the minimum wage.

Congress did allow states the opportunity to experiment with the last option, which came to be called "workfare." Between 1981 and 1988, thirty states instituted programs of this type, with results that were encouraging. Recently, a policy option called "EDfare" has received some attention. Its focus is the development of the recipient's human capital as a condition for continued benefits.

Learning Objectives

After reading Chapter 35 and doing the following exercises, you should:	True or false	Multiple choice	Problems and applications	Common errors	Pages in the text
1. Know how the poverty count is made and how many are "officially poor."	2,9–11	1,9,10, 14,15		2	817–820
2. Be able to distinguish between cash transfers and "in-kind" transfers.	1,16	11,13			818–820
3. Understand the role of human capital and derived demand in the poverty dilemma.	3,4	3,4,12, 18			820–821
4. Know what the basic government welfare programs are, which level of government administers them, and who is eligible for the various programs.	12,16	1,2, 16–18		1	818–819, 823
5. Be able to describe and give examples of three conflicting goals that an antipoverty program may have.	5,6,8, 13,15, 17	6–8, 20–22			826–829
6. Understand how welfare eligibility changes as income increases.		5,19	1		823–826
7. Be able to describe how a welfare recipient's real income may decline as money income increases.	7		1		823–826
8. Know some of the recent initiatives to reform the welfare system.	14,17	23	2		829–831

Key-Term Review

Review the following terms; if you are not sure of the meaning of any term, write out the definition and check it against the Glossary in the text.

cyclical unemployment
human capital
income transfers
in-kind transfers
labor-force participant

marginal productivity
marginal tax rate
marginal utility of labor
workfare

Fill in the blank following each of the statements below with the appropriate term from the list above.

1. When someone enhances his or her productivity by obtaining an education or training, we say that person is investing in _____.

1. _____

2. Social security payments and AFDC payments are both _____.

2. _____

3. When a poor person's income subsidy is reduced by $0.50 for each $1.00 he or she earns, we can say that 0.50 is the _____.

3. _____

4. The addition to total satisfaction derived from working an additional hour is called the _____.

    4. _____

5. Such benefits as medical care and food stamps are called _____.

    5. _____

6. Someone who is employed or is actively seeking employment is said to be a _____.

    6. _____

7. If labor markets are competitive, participants are paid according to their _____.

    7. _____

8. If, because of economic fluctuations, aggregate demand is not sufficient to provide a job for everyone who wants one, there is said to be _____.

    8. _____

9. Compulsory community service at the minimum wage was part of the Reagan administration's welfare initiative called _____.

    9. _____

True or False: *Circle your choice.*

T F 1. The social security payments received by retired persons are an in-kind transfer payment.

T F 2. Whether a given family is below the official poverty line depends only on its money income and the number of family members.

T F 3. Monetary and fiscal policies that encourage a high growth rate for the economy are a means of alleviating the sluggish demand for labor.

T F 4. There is a direct and positive relationship between educational level attained and the incidence of poverty.

T F 5. Programs that guarantee a certain minimum level of income may induce individuals to give up low-paying jobs.

T F 6. The higher the marginal tax rate of any given welfare program, the greater the damage to the work incentives of recipients, *ceteris paribus*.

T F 7. It is possible under current programs for the money income of a welfare recipient to rise while his or her real income declines.

T F 8. Large in-kind benefits tend to diminish the incentive to seek employment.

T F 9. The official poverty index is based on a comparison of cash and in-kind benefits to family size.

T F 10. Nonfarm families may have higher cash incomes than farm families of the same size and still be counted as poor.

T F 11. The number of poor people is exaggerated because in-kind transfers are included in calculating their income.

T F 12. Medicaid provides cash to the poor so that they may purchase medicine and doctors' services.

T F 13. The higher the marginal tax rate on earned income, the greater the incentive to work.

T F 14. Increasing "disregards" will raise the break-even level of income.

T F 15. Increasing welfare benefits may worsen the problem of poverty by damaging work incentives.

T F 16. Aid to Families with Dependent Children (AFDC) is the largest in-kind welfare program in the United States.

T F 17. Congress attempted to improve work incentives for welfare recipients by increasing income "disregards."

Multiple Choice: *Select the correct answer.*

_____ 1. Most of the poor:
   (a) Are poor for life.
   (b) Come from minority families.
   (c) Do not work.
   (d) Are characterized by none of the above.

_____ 2. Which of the following statements most accurately characterizes the American "poor"?
   (a) Most work at least part-time.
   (b) Most are white.
   (c) They move in and out of the "poor" category with great frequency.
   (d) All of the above statements are characteristic.

_____ 3. "Human capital" refers to:
   (a) The size of a person's investments.
   (b) The bundle of skills that a person carries with him or her to the labor market.
   (c) The ability of the worker to handle capital equipment.
   (d) The ability of the entrepreneur to substitute capital for labor in the production process.

_____ 4. A person who has a job may earn a low income because:
   (a) His or her marginal physical productivity is low.
   (b) The price of the product he or she produces is low.
   (c) His or her marginal revenue product is low.
   (d) Both a and b, which together imply c.

_____ 5. Male-headed poor families usually receive no welfare benefits because:
   (a) The male head is too lazy to earn an income.
   (b) The male head is not seeking work.
   (c) The male head is supported by other family members.
   (d) Society feels that able-bodied males can support their households.

_____ 6. A high marginal tax rate is thought to damage:
   (a) The adequate-income goal.
   (b) The cost-minimization goal.
   (c) The work-incentive goal.
   (d) All of the above.

_____ 7. Suppose a poverty program has an income floor of $4,000, a zero disregard, and a marginal tax rate of 0.50. The break-even level is:
   (a) $2,000.
   (b) $4,000.
   (c) $20,000.
   (d) None of the above.

_____ 8. A low break-even level can be achieved by means of a low income floor or:
   (a) A low marginal tax rate.
   (b) A high marginal tax rate.
   (c) Strict enforcement procedures.
   (d) None of the above.

_____ 9. The official poverty index is based on:
   (a) Family size.
   (b) Cash income.
   (c) Type of residence (urban or rural).
   (d) All of the above.

_____10. If a person is a labor-force participant:
    (a) That person may be working.
    (b) That person may be looking for work.
    (c) That person may be poor even though he or she is employed.
    (d) All of the above may be the case.

_____11. A good reason for excluding in-kind transfers from income calculations is:
    (a) That the more poor there are, the more jobs there will be for bureaucrats.
    (b) That people would be forced above the poverty line by consuming things like medical services.
    (c) That it is impossible to place a value on most of the services provided.
    (d) None of the above.

_____12. Cyclical unemployment is typically the result of:
    (a) A lack of human capital.
    (b) Labor-market discrimination.
    (c) Deficient aggregate demand.
    (d) Low productivity.

_____13. Which of the following statements applies to income transfers?
    (a) Income transfers increase upward job mobility.
    (b) Income transfers are typically used to remedy human-capital deficiencies.
    (c) Income transfers conflict with work incentives.
    (d) All of the above apply.

_____14. Which of the following are included in the poverty population?
    (a) Aged persons.
    (b) Single-parent families.
    (c) Two-parent families.
    (d) All of the above.

_____15. In terms of numbers, the poverty population is dominated by:
    (a) Families with aged parents.
    (b) Families with several infirm members.
    (c) Families with younger children.
    (d) None of the above.

_____16. Which of the following programs does _not_ provide in-kind benefits?
    (a) The food stamp program.
    (b) The housing assistance program.
    (c) Aid to Families with Dependent Children (AFDC).
    (d) Medicaid.

_____17. Which of the following programs provides aid to the aged, blind, and permanently disabled?
    (a) SSI.
    (b) AFDC.
    (c) General Assistance.
    (d) The food-stamp program.

_____18. Which of the following is _not_ a welfare myth?
    (a) The poor are mostly white.
    (b) People are poor because they are lazy and don't want to work.
    (c) The poor don't know how to spend their money.
    (d) Most of the poor are poor for life.

_____19. When authorities choose to "disregard" income earned by welfare recipients, they are:
    (a) Intentionally helping the welfare recipient cheat.
    (b) Attempting to improve work incentives.
    (c) Looking out for their own jobs because the more income they disregard, the more poor there will be.
    (d) Being arbitrary in their administration of the program.

_____20. Reducing the marginal tax rate has the effect of:
   (a) Increasing the cost of the program.
   (b) Improving work incentives.
   (c) Raising the amount of income the program participant may keep.
   (d) Doing all of the above.

_____21. The break-even level of income is:
   (a) The amount of income a person must have to reach the poverty line.
   (b) The level of income a person may earn before losing all welfare benefits.
   (c) The level of income at which an individual household begins to have some discretionary income.
   (d) The level of income at which in-kind benefits are no longer necessary.

_____22. Based on the results of several experiments, which of the following statements is correct?
   (a) High marginal tax rates increase the quantity of labor supplied.
   (b) The labor supply of husbands is affected more than that of wives by high marginal tax rates.
   (c) The labor supply of wives is affected more than that of husbands by high marginal tax rates.
   (d) The results of the experiments are suspect since there were only two of them.

_____23. President Reagan felt:
   (a) The welfare system was too stingy.
   (b) The income limits in the existing programs were too low.
   (c) The existing programs focused too narrowly on the truly poor.
   (d) None of the above.

Problems and Applications

Exercise 1

This exercise helps in analyzing welfare plans. It will be helpful with the problem at the end of Chapter 35 in the text.

For each of the plans mentioned in Problems 1–3, compute the implicit marginal tax rate, the break-even level of income, the basic benefit (income floor), and the amount of earnings disregards.

1. Marginal tax rate: _____
   Break-even level
      of income: _____
   Basic benefit
      (income floor): _____
   Amount of earnings
      disregard: _____

   People receive a level of income of $4,000, which the government decrees as the minimum acceptable poverty-level income. People can make as much as they want above the $4,000 level and therefore do not need to report the income to the government.

2. Marginal tax rate: _____
   Break-even level
      of income: _____
   Basic benefit
      (income floor): _____
   Amount of earnings
      disregard: _____

   The whole welfare system is eliminated in favor of using the tax system. People with income up to a maximum of $8,000 a year automatically receive one exemption of $2,000 in computing their taxable income. They then receive money from the government (a negative tax) in the amount of 50 percent of the difference between $6,000 and their taxable income.

3. Marginal tax rate: _____   People receive $4,000 in benefits automatically, but every dollar they
    Break-even level   earn above $4,000 must be subtracted from the $4,000 benefit and must
       of income: _____   be returned.
    Basic benefit
       (income floor): _____
    Amount of earnings
       disregard: _____

4. Which of the plans is likely to put the fewest people on welfare?   1   2   3   (circle one)

5. Which plan is likely to put the most people on welfare?   1   2   3   (circle one)

6. Which plan is likely to be cheapest to the government?   1   2   3   (circle one)

7. Which plan is likely to be the most expensive?   1   2   3   (circle one)

Exercise 2

In election years the welfare system often becomes a hot topic in the press. By using one of the articles in the text, this exercise will show what kind of information to look for to recognize the impacts of different proposals on welfare recipients. If your professor makes a newspaper assignment for this chapter, this exercise will provide an example of how to do it.

Reread the article in Chapter 35 entitled "Breaking Through the Welfare Myths" from the *Washington Post*. Then answer the following questions:

1. What passage indicates a criticism of the current welfare system?

2. Which of the following four aspects of welfare would the critic most likely want changed or actually mentions should be changed?
    (a) Marginal tax rate.
    (b) Earnings disregard.
    (c) Income floor.
    (d) Break-even level of income.

3. The critic wants the item in Question 2 to be:
    (a) Raised.
    (b) Lowered.

4. Which passage provides evidence for your answers to Questions 2 and 3?

Common Errors

The first statement in each "common error" below is incorrect. Each incorrect statement is followed by a corrected version and an explanation.

1. The federal government runs the welfare system. WRONG!

    The welfare system consists of programs administered by federal, state, and local governments. RIGHT!

    It's true that the federal government is heavily involved in the welfare system, but state and local governments are involved as well. As a matter of fact, the benefits that a poor person may receive vary from state to state. The differentials in benefits have been the proximate cause of the migration of some poor people from low-benefit states to high-benefit states.

2. Welfare recipients are typically minority families headed by able-bodied males. WRONG!

There is no average welfare recipient. RIGHT!

The stereotype of the welfare recipient seems firmly entrenched in the minds of American taxpayers. The poor are a very heterogeneous group, however, with many more whites than minority-group members. Most work when they can find employment. Some work all year long and are still poor.

■ ANSWERS ■

Key-Term Review

1. human capital
2. income transfers
3. marginal tax rate
4. marginal utility of labor
5. in-kind transfers
6. labor-force participant
7. marginal productivity
8. cyclical unemployment
9. workfare

True or False

1. F	4. F	7. T	10. T	13. F	16. F
2. F	5. T	8. T	11. F	14. T	17. T
3. T	6. T	9. F	12. F	15. T	

Multiple Choice

1. d	5. d	9. d	13. c	17. a	21. b
2. d	6. c	10. d	14. d	18. a	22. c
3. b	7. d	11. b	15. c	19. b	23. d
4. d	8. b	12. c	16. c	20. d	

Problems and Applications

Exercise 1

1. 0; none; $4,000; all income
2. 50 percent; $8,000; $3,000 [50% x ($6,000 – 0 taxable income)]; $2,000 (exemption)
3. 100 percent; $8,000; $4,000; $4,000
4. 2 or 3   Both plans apply to the same number of people because they have the same break-even level.
5. 1   Everyone is on welfare.
6. 2 or 3   Plan 2 might be cheapest because of its low disregard. On the other hand, plan 3 might be cheapest because of the high marginal tax rate. The answer depends on the income distribution of the population.
7. 1   It is most expensive because everyone is on welfare.

Exercise 2

1. "The combined benefits of Aid for Families with Dependent Children and food stamps total less than three-fourths of the official poverty-income level."
2. c
3. a
4. "And that poverty level was *only* $5,500 for a family of four in 1975" (emphasis added). "Only" indicates the direction Califano thinks the income floor should go.

SECTION IV INTERNATIONAL ECONOMICS AND COMPARATIVE SYSTEMS

Chapter 36

International Trade

Quick Review

Even the most casual observer of economic activity understands that trade between the United States and other nations is very important. Hardly a day goes by without hearing or reading some reference to exports, imports, the "trade deficit," the value of the dollar in foreign-exchange markets, and the like. In this chapter we ask some basic questions on trade, such as:

- What benefit, if any, do we get from international trade?
- How much harm do imports cause, and to whom?
- Should we protect ourselves from "unfair" trade by limiting some or all imports?

In recent decades the United States has become much more dependent on foreign trade than ever before. We export a wide variety of goods, especially agricultural products and capital goods, to many countries, and import from such advanced industrial nations as Japan and such poor countries as Uruguay. Oil has become our most important import.

Countries are motivated to trade because by doing so they can produce together more total output than they could in the absence of trade. Specialization and trade allow both members of a trading partnership to consume beyond their respective production-possibility curves. That is, consumption possibilities exceed production possibilities when countries specialize and trade. The economic reason for this situation is rooted in what is called the "law of comparative advantage." This dictum says that as long as the opportunity costs of producing goods in two countries differ, it will always be possible for those countries to specialize and trade to their mutual advantage. Neither the absolute size of the countries nor their absolute costs are important. What does count is the relative (comparative) cost of producing alternative goods.

Although undoubtedly specialization and trade benefit trading nations, special-interest groups often exert strong pressure against foreign trade. Those who would lose their markets and jobs to imported goods and foreign workers may oppose free trade.

Industries that need raw materials that are being exported may also exert pressure on government to place restrictions on the export of them. The government may place a tariff or quota on imported goods or provide aid to the affected domestic industry. The government may subsidize industries that are hurt by foreign trade. We have occasionally asked our trading partners to voluntarily limit their exports to us so as to ease the pressure on threatened firms and industries. The government has sometimes made assistance (cash, training, or relocation) available to those whose jobs were lost to foreign competition.

Under Ronald Reagan the administration took a rather dim view of adjustment-assistance programs, arguing that they slow down the adjustment process rather than assisting it. It also argued that a worker displaced by imports should be treated like any other unemployed worker.

Learning Objectives

After reading Chapter 36 and doing the following exercises, you should:	True or false	Multiple choice	Problems and applications	Common errors	Pages in the text
1. Know some basic facts about U.S. trade patterns.	1–3,19	17–19, 23		4	835–838
2. Understand the macroeconomic impact of international trade.	4–9	11,20	2		837–838
3. Understand why specialization and trade increase both production possibilities and consumption possibilities.	10		1	3,4	840–844
4. Be able to explain comparative advantage using opportunity costs.	11,12	1–3,5,7, 12–14	1	1	844–846
5. Know how to determine the limits to the terms of trade.	13	4,15	2		846–849
6. Be able to calculate the gains from specialization and trade at a given exchange rate.		16	2		841–844
7. Be able to show how trade allows a country to consume beyond its production-possibilities curve.	10		1,2		846–849
8. Recognize the sources of pressure that result in restricted trade.	14,16		3	2	849–853
9. Know some of the arguments used by those wishing to restrict trade.	17	6,8,9	3	2	851–853
10. Be able to discuss nontariff barriers to trade.	15,18,20	20			854–859, 860
11. Know the basis for programs that provide assistance to workers displaced by imports.		10			861–862

Key-Term Review

Review the following terms; if you are not sure of the meaning of any term, write out the definition and check it against the Glossary in the text.

absolute advantage	opportunity cost
adjustment assistance	production possibilities
comparative advantage	quota
consumption possibilities	tariff
embargo	terms of trade
equilibrium price	trade deficit
exports	trade surplus
imports	voluntary restraint agreement (VRA)

Fill in the blank following each of the statements below with the appropriate term from the list above.

1. The slope of the production-possibilities curve indicates the quantity of one good that must be given up in order to produce one more unit of another good, or in other words, the _____. 1. _____

2. The leakages from the income stream consist of savings, taxes, and _____.

2. _____

3. When the opportunity cost of producing a good is lower in one country than in another, the first country is said to have a _____.

3. _____

4. A country that can produce more of a good than another country with the same amount of resources is said to have an _____.

4. _____

5. U.S. firms manufacture computers and produce agricultural goods and ship them to France. Computers and agricultural goods are U.S. _____.

5. _____

6. The various combinations of two goods that a country can produce and consume without trade constitute its _____.

6. _____

7. The various combinations of two goods that a country can consume when it engages in trade is called its _____.

7. _____

8. An absolute limit imposed by a government on the quantity of a specific item that may be imported is called a _____.

8. _____

9. A tax on imported goods is known as a _____.

9. _____

10. In 1973 the Arab members of OPEC agreed not to sell oil to the United States. This action was called an _____.

10. _____

11. Two countries producing two goods must decide how much of one good will trade for a unit of the other good. This ratio indicates the _____.

11. _____

12. A country that imports more than it exports over a given period of time is said to have a _____.

12. _____

13. When a country's exports exceed its imports, it is said to have a _____.

13. _____

14. Under a freely flexible exchange-rate system, the market price will approach the _____.

14. _____

15. A quota placed by a country on its own exports is called a _____.

15. _____

16. Workers who are aided because their jobs were lost when imported goods replaced domestically produced goods are said to receive _____.

16. _____

True or False: *Circle your choice.*

T F 1. U.S. merchandise exports are less than 10 percent of the total GNP.

T F 2. The main reason that countries specialize and trade with each other is that by doing so they can get things they cannot produce themselves.

T F 3. The trade balance is calculated by subtracting exports from imports.

T F 4. Any change in exports has a multiplier effect on the aggregate level of income, *ceteris paribus*.

T F 5. Any change in imports has a multiplier effect on the aggregate level of income, *ceteris paribus*.

T F 6. Net increases in exports tend to lower national income; net increases in imports tend to raise the level of national income.

T F 7. If exports increase while imports remain constant, a trade surplus will increase.

T F 8. A trade deficit means that imports exceed exports over some relevant time period.

T F 9. Since one country's exports are another country's imports, overall world trade must balance.

T F 10. Specialization and trade allow countries to consume beyond their own respective production-possibility curves.

T F 11. If the opportunity costs of producing goods in two countries are the same, there is no incentive to trade.

T F 12. Straight-line production-possibility curves imply that the law of diminishing returns does not operate.

T F 13. The terms at which countries will trade one good for another will occur between their respective domestic opportunity costs.

T F 14. Since free trade is beneficial to society as a whole, it benefits each individual group in society as well.

T F 15. From the consumer's point of view, quotas are more onerous than tariffs.

T F 16. The pressure for restrictions on trade tends to increase when the economy is operating near capacity.

T F 17. In countries where they are imposed, tariffs and quotas raise the price of imported goods to consumers.

T F 18. Voluntary restraint agreements are, in reality, "voluntary quotas."

T F 19. Bilateral trade balances refer to trade between two countries.

T F 20. Voluntary export restraints by Japanese auto manufacturers result in higher prices for automobiles purchased by U.S. consumers.

Multiple Choice: *Select the correct answer.*

_____ 1. Suppose the production of one ton of steel in the United States requires the same amount of resources as the production of 100 gallons of oil. In Canada, two tons of steel might require the same amount of resources as 200 gallons of oil. This means that:
(a) The United States has the comparative advantage in steel.
(b) Canada has the comparative advantage in steel.
(c) The United States has an absolute advantage in steel.
(d) None of the statements above is correct.

_____ 2. In Germany, six cameras or four bicycles can be produced with one unit of labor. In Japan, nine cameras or five bicycles can be produced with one unit of labor. Therefore:
(a) Germany has an absolute advantage in the production of both goods.
(b) Japan has a comparative advantage in the production of both goods.
(c) Germany has a comparative advantage in the production of bicycles.
(d) Japan has a comparative advantage in the production of bicycles.

_____ 3. Given the conditions listed in Question 2, what is the opportunity cost of producing one bicycle?
(a) In Germany, 1.5 cameras.
(b) In Germany, 2/3 camera.
(c) In Japan, 5/9 camera.
(d) In Japan, 8.1 cameras.

_____ 4. Given the conditions listed in Questions 2 and 3, the terms of trade at which these two goods would be traded between Germany and Japan would be one bicycle to:
   (a) More than 1.8 cameras.
   (b) More than 1.5 cameras but less than 1.8 cameras.
   (c) Less than 1.5 cameras.
   (d) None of the above, because Japan has an absolute advantage in both goods.

_____ 5. Suppose that France and the United States do not trade and that the competitive price of an ordinary bottle of wine is 20 francs in France and $2 in the United States; the price of wheat per bushel is 40 francs in France and $6 in the United States. This information is sufficient to enable us to state that:
   (a) France has a comparative advantage in the production of wine.
   (b) France has a comparative advantage in the production of wheat.
   (c) Neither country has a comparative advantage in the production of either good.
   (d) The United States has an absolute advantage in the production of both goods.

_____ 6. A person who accepts the arguments for freer trade:
   (a) Will oppose all tariffs, whatever the arguments in their favor.
   (b) Will favor tariffs because they will raise the real income of the countries levying them.
   (c) Could favor tariffs if he or she thought the objectives of policy served by such tariffs were more important than raising real income.
   (d) Will oppose all tariffs but will favor selective quotas.

_____ 7. To say that a country has a comparative advantage in the production of wine is to say that:
   (a) It can produce wine with fewer resources than any other country can.
   (b) Its opportunity cost of producing wine is greater than any other country's.
   (c) Its opportunity cost of producing wine is lower than any other country's.
   (d) The relative price of wine is higher in that country than in any other.

_____ 8. Which of the following statements about tariffs is likely to be true?
   (a) Tariffs result in lower prices than those that would prevail in their absence.
   (b) Tariffs encourage the growth of our efficient industries.
   (c) Tariffs cause employment and output to be higher in protected industries than would otherwise be the case.
   (d) Tariffs result in a more efficient allocation of resources than would result in their absence.

_____ 9. A principal objective of GATT is to:
   (a) Protect domestic producers from foreign competition.
   (b) Settle domestic tax disputes internationally.
   (c) Equalize income tax structures in various countries.
   (d) Reduce barriers to trade.

_____10. Adjustment assistance is designed to:
   (a) Ease the adjustment problems confronting consumers when a tariff or quota is levied.
   (b) Assist producers and those workers who are adversely affected by a reduction in tariffs or quotas.
   (c) Assist producers and those workers who are adversely affected by an increase in tariffs or quotas.
   (d) Increase the revenues received by the government.

_____11. A beggar-my-neighbor policy is:
   (a) An attempt by a poor country to get more foreign aid and assistance.
   (b) The imposition of trade barriers for the purpose of expanding exports.
   (c) The imposition of import barriers for the purpose of curbing inflation.
   (d) The imposition of trade barriers to increase domestic demand and employment.

Suppose the productivities of Japanese and U.S. producers are as indicated in Table 36.1. Refer to Table 36.1 in answering Questions 12–16.

Table 36.1
**Output per worker-day in the
United States and Japan**

Country	TV sets (per day)	Bicycles (per day)
Japan	2	10
United States	1	8

_____ 12. Which of the following statements is true?
(a) The United States has an absolute advantage in the production of bicycles.
(b) Japan has an absolute advantage in the production of bicycles only.
(c) Japan has an absolute advantage in the production of TV sets only.
(d) Japan has an absolute advantage in the production of both bicycles and TV sets.

_____ 13. Which of the following is a true statement?
(a) The opportunity cost of TV sets is higher in Japan than in the United States.
(b) The opportunity cost of TV sets is lower in Japan than in the United States.
(c) It is impossible to tell anything about opportunity cost from the information given.
(d) The United States has a comparative advantage in the production of TV sets.

_____ 14. Which of the following statements is true?
(a) Japan has an absolute advantage in the production of both products but a comparative advantage in bicycles.
(b) Japan has a comparative advantage in both products and an absolute advantage in the production of TV sets.
(c) The United States has an absolute advantage in neither product but a comparative advantage in the production of bicycles.
(d) The United States has an absolute advantage in neither product but a comparative advantage in TV sets.

_____ 15. Suppose the terms of trade are established in such a way that 1 TV set equals 5 bicycles. Which of the following statements would be true?
(a) These terms of trade provide gains for the United States, but Japan is worse off.
(b) These terms of trade provide gains for Japan, but the United States is worse off.
(c) These terms of trade provide gains for the United States, and Japan is no worse off.
(d) These terms of trade provide gains for Japan, and the United States is no worse off.

_____ 16. Which of the following terms of trade would provide gains for both countries?
(a) One TV set equals five bicycles.
(b) One TV set equals eight bicycles.
(c) One TV set equals six bicycles.
(d) None of the above would provide such gains.

_____ 17. Which of the following statements is correct?
(a) The United States is becoming increasingly dependent on foreign trade.
(b) The United States is becoming less dependent on foreign trade.
(c) U.S. dependence on trade has remained relatively constant for the past decade.
(d) None of the above statements is correct.

_____ 18. When Japan "voluntarily" restrained exports to the United States between 1981 and 1985:
(a) U.S. auto producers became more profitable.
(b) Firms importing Japanese cars became more profitable.
(c) Consumers paid higher prices for both U.S. and Japanese cars.
(d) All of the above were true.

_____19. Which of the following countries has the *lowest* export-to-GNP ratio?
  (a) The United States.
  (b) Japan.
  (c) Great Britain.
  (d) Canada.

_____20. Which of the following statements concerning the use of nontariff barriers is correct?
  (a) They have been used as a substitute for tariff barriers.
  (b) Many countries, including the United States, use them.
  (c) Since GATT negotiated tariff reductions, they have been used more often.
  (d) All of the above statements are correct.

Problems and Applications

Exercise 1

This exercise shows how trade leads to gains by all trading partners through specialization and comparative advantage.

1. Suppose that Japan has 20 laborers in total and that the United States has 40 laborers. Suppose their productivities are as indicated in Table 36.2. (*Be careful:* The table tells you that a worker in Japan can produce two TV sets per day *or* ten bicycles per day, *not* two TV sets and ten bicycles!)

Table 36.2
Output per worker-day in the
United States and Japan

Country	TV sets (per day)	Bicycles (per day)
Japan	2	10
United States	1	8

Draw the production-possibilities curves for each country in Figure 36.1. Assume constant costs of production.

Figure 36.1

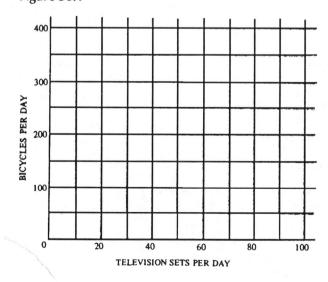

509

2. Suppose that before trade Japan uses 12 laborers to produce bicycles and 8 laborers to produce television sets; suppose also that in the United States 20 workers produce bicycles and 20 produce television sets. Complete Table 36.3.

Table 36.3
Output produced and consumed without trade

Country	TV sets (per day)	Bicycles (per day)
Japan	_____	_____
United States	_____	_____
Total	_____	_____

3. Before trade, the total output of television sets is _____; of bicycles, _____.

4. What is the opportunity cost of one television set in Japan? _____. In the United States? _____.

5. What is the opportunity cost of one bicycle in Japan? _____. In the United States? _____.

6. If Japan and the United States specialize according to their respective comparative advantages, Japan will produce _____ and the United States will produce _____. They will do so because the opportunity cost of bicycles in terms of television sets is (lower, higher) in the United States than in Japan, and the opportunity cost of television sets in terms of bicycles is (lower, higher) in Japan than in the United States.

7. After specialization, the total output of televisions sets is _____ and the total output of bicycles is _____. (*Hint:* Twenty Japanese produce only TV sets, and 40 Americans produce only bicycles.)

8. This output represents an increase of _____ bicycles and _____ television sets over the pre-specialization output. (*Hint:* Compare answers to Problems 3 and 7.)

Exercise 2

This exercise will help you understand how the terms of trade are determined. Refer to Exercise 1 for the data.

If Japan and the United States are to benefit from the increased production, trade must take place. The Japanese will be willing to trade television sets for bicycles as long as they get back more bicycles than they could get in their own country.

1. The terms of trade will be between one television set equals _____ bicycles and one television set equals _____ bicycles.

2. If the terms of trade were four bicycles equals one television set,
   (a) Neither country would buy bicycles but both would buy TV sets.
   (b) Neither country would buy TV sets but both would buy bicycles.
   (c) Both countries would buy bicycles and TV sets.
   (d) Neither country would buy TV sets or bicycles.

3. Suppose that the two countries agree that the terms of trade will be six bicycles equals one television set. Let Japan export 20 television sets per day to the United States. Complete Table 36.4. Assume that Japan produces 40 television sets per day and the U.S. produces 320 bicycles.

Table 36.4
Consumption combination after trade

Country	TV sets	Bicycles
Japan	_____	_____
United States	_____	_____
Total	40	320

4. As a result of specialization and trade, the United States has the same quantity of television sets and _____ more bicycles per day. (Compare Tables 36.3 and 36.4.)

5. As a result of specialization and trade, Japan has the same number of bicycles and _____ more television sets per day.

Now suppose that at the exchange rate of six bicycles to one TV set, Japan would like to export 10 TV sets and import 60 bicycles per day. Suppose also that the United States desires to export 90 bicycles and import 15 television sets per day.

6. At these terms of trade there is a (shortage, surplus) of television sets.

7. At these terms of trade there is a (shortage, surplus) of bicycles.

8. Which of the following terms of trade would be more likely to result from this situation?
   (a) Five bicycles equal one television set.
   (b) Six bicycles equal one television set.
   (c) Seven bicycles equal one television set.

Exercise 3

As protectionist spirit rises in the United States, the media concentrate more on ways to protect American producers. By using a newspaper cartoon found in the text, this exercise will show how to evaluate the effects of such proposals on trade. If your professor makes a newspaper assignment for this chapter, this exercise will provide an example of how to do it.

Study the cartoon in Chapter 36 from the *Washington Post* about auto protectionism. Then answer the following questions:

1. How does the cartoon indicate which product or products are the subject of protectionism?

2. What form of protectionism is changing according to the cartoon?
   (a) Quotas.
   (b) Tariffs.
   (c) Export subsidies.
   (d) Other (specify: _____).

3. How does the cartoon identify the form of protectionism?

4. How does the cartoon indicate whether protectionism is increasing or decreasing?

5. How does the cartoon indicate the effects of the change in protectionism on quantities or prices of the good, exports or imports of the good, trade relations between countries, or diplomatic relations?

Common Errors

The first statement in each "common error" below is incorrect. Each incorrect statement is followed by a corrected version and an explanation.

1. A country must have an *absolute advantage* in order to gain from trade with another country. WRONG!

    A country must have a *comparative advantage* in order to gain from trade with another country. RIGHT!

    Mutually advantageous trade requires only that the opportunity costs of producing goods differ in the two countries. Another way of stating this is that the production-possibility curves of the two countries must have different slopes. These two circumstances are indicated in Figure 36.2.

Figure 36.2

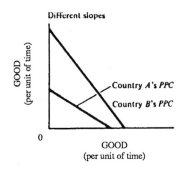

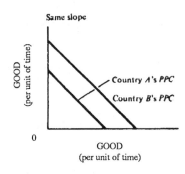

(*a*) Different slopes. Mutually advantageous trade *is* possible.

(*b*) Same slope. Mutually advantageous trade is *not* possible.

2. Foreign trade costs a country jobs. WRONG!

    Although jobs may be lost, new ones will be created by the opportunities opened up by trade. RIGHT!

    When countries specialize and trade according to the law of comparative advantage, some particular workers and firms may be hurt by imports, but the economy as a whole gains by trade. More output per resource input will be attainable. Because the economy is able to reach full employment with trade as well as without trade, there is no reason to assume there will be fewer jobs.

3. A country is well off only as long as it exports more than it imports. WRONG!

    Countries may, at times, be well off when they experience a trade surplus; they may also be well off when they have a trade deficit. RIGHT!

    Both trade deficits and trade surpluses can be problems if either situation persists for a long period of time. Trade surpluses mean that a country is giving more of its limited, precious resources in trade than it is acquiring from other countries. The currencies of deficit countries tend to depreciate, which means they will be unable to buy as many foreign goods with a unit of currency.

4. Countries tend to enter into trade to get the things they cannot produce themselves. WRONG!

    Countries very often trade for things they could produce themselves. RIGHT!

    Be careful! Countries often trade for things they could produce themselves, because the relative costs of domestic production would be prohibitive. Take baskets as an example. We could certainly produce baskets if we really wanted to. The skill is not difficult to learn and the materials are abundant. But baskets do not lend themselves to machine production, and hand labor is expensive. The cost in terms of goods forgone would be tremendous. (So would the price of the baskets.) We're better off specializing in something like computers, where we have a comparative advantage, and trading for baskets, where we clearly do not have a comparative advantage.

■ ANSWERS ■

Key-Term Review

1. opportunity cost
2. imports
3. comparative advantage
4. absolute advantage
5. exports
6. production possibilities

7. consumption possibilities
8. quota
9. tariff
10. embargo
11. terms of trade

12. trade deficit
13. trade surplus
14. equilibrium price
15. voluntary restraint agreement (VRA)
16. adjustment assistance

True or False

1. T
2. F
3. F
4. T

5. T
6. F
7. T
8. T

9. T
10. T
11. T

12. T
13. T
14. F

15. T
16. F
17. T

18. T
19. T
20. T

Multiple Choice

1. d
2. c
3. a
4. b

5. b
6. c
7. c
8. c

9. d
10. b
11. d

12. d
13. b
14. c

15. c
16. c
17. a

18. d
19. a
20. d

Problems and Applications

Exercise 1

1. **Figure 36.1 answer**

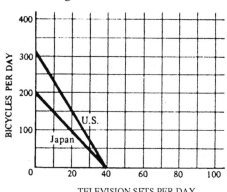

2. **Table 36.3 answer**

Country	TV sets	Bicycles
Japan	16	120
United States	20	160
Total	36	280

3. 36; 280
4. 5 bicycles; 8 bicycles
5. one-fifth television set; one-eighth television set
6. television sets; bicycles; lower; lower
7. 40; 320
8. 40; 4

Exercise 2

1. 5; 8
2. a
3. **Table 36.4 answer**

Country	TV sets	Bicycles
Japan	20	120
United States	20	200
Total	40	320

4. 40
5. 4
6. shortage   The Japanese wish to export fewer (10) TV sets than Americans want (15).
7. surplus   The Americans wish to export more (90) bicycles than the Japanese want (60).
8. c

Exercise 3

1. The drawing is of an automobile dealership, and the product is therefore automobiles.
2. a
3. "Tell me again how the quotas . . ." is the quotation.
4. The "higher prices" shown in the car windows indicate a recent change upward.
5. See the answer to Question 4.

Chapter 37

International Finance

Quick Review

All of the trade between nations discussed in Chapter 36 must somehow be financed. Of course, since each country has its own money, we have to ask several critical questions:

- What determines the value of one country's money in terms of other national currencies?
- What causes the international value of currencies to change?
- Can we limit the fluctuations in the value of the dollar; and should we try to do so?

To facilitate trade and to eliminate the need for barter, markets for foreign exchange have developed. Their function is to determine the exchange rate at which two currencies will trade. The foreign-exchange market is like any other market—it consists of a supply schedule and a demand schedule. Supply and demand mean the same thing here as they do in any other market. The commodity being traded in this case is the money of one country for the money of another. Demand and supply determine the equilibrium price (exchange rate) and quantity of foreign exchange that is traded.

When the international value of a currency increases, the currency is said to appreciate. When a currency's international value decreases, the currency is said to depreciate. The exchange rate responds to changes in underlying forces, as reflected in shifts of the supply-and-demand curves. Changes in relative income levels, changes in relative prices, and technological change are examples of the underlying forces that cause supply-and-demand curves to shift, and alter exchange rates.

To keep track of the foreign exchange flows that accompany the flow of goods and services, each country summarizes its transactions in a statement called the "balance of payments." The balance of payments is based on double-entry bookkeeping and must therefore balance, even though individual accounts may not. The primary balances struck are the balance of trade, the current account, and the capital account.

Governments do not always like the way the exchange rates for their currencies change. Depending on their interests at the moment, they may intervene to support their currencies or those of other countries. In some situations a government may set a fixed price for its currency. Although the world's major currencies are basically free to float, governments still sometimes interfere.

A government enters on the demand side when the price of its currency falls below the level it considers to be appropriate. It enters on the supply side when the exchange rate rises above the level it considers to be appropriate. When governments do interfere, we call the resulting situation a managed-rate system, or a "dirty float." In recent years, the U.S. government and the governments of its major trading partners have intervened several times to prevent undesired fluctuations in the value of the dollar.

Learning Objectives

After reading Chapter 37 and doing the following exercises, you should:	True or false	Multiple choice	Problems and applications	Common errors	Pages in the text
1. Understand that an exchange rate is simply a price.		1,11,16, 17	1	3	866–868
2. Know the forces that operate on the demand side of the foreign-exchange market.	1,2,7	7,12,13	1–3	3	867
3. Know the forces that operate on the supply side of the foreign-exchange market.	3		1–3	3	867–868
4. Understand how supply and demand interact to determine the equilibrium exchange rate.	14	2,4	1–3		869–872
5. Be able to demonstrate graphically the forces that cause a currency to appreciate or depreciate.	5,6, 8–11,13	8	1–3	2	872–874
6. Understand some elements of balance-of-payments accounting.		22–24			868–869
7. Be able to describe several exchange-rate systems and their consequences.	4	6,7,19			876–883
8. Understand the macroeconomic and microeconomic consequences of exchange-rate movements.	12,14–16, 23,24	9,10, 14,15		1	875–876
9. Be able to describe a balance-of-payments problem.		18,20,21	3	1,2	868–869, 876–883
10. Understand rudimentary balance-of-payments accounting.	17–20, 22,25–28	3,5			868–869
11. Be aware of the recent history of the international value of the dollar.	21		2		872–873

Key-Term Review

Review the following terms; if you are not sure of the meaning of any term, write out the definition and check it against the Glossary in the text.

appreciation
balance of payments
balance-of-payments deficit
balance-of-payments surplus
demand for foreign exchange
depreciation
equilibrium price
exchange rate
flexible exchange rates
foreign-exchange markets

foreign-exchange reserves
gold reserves
gold standard
law of demand
managed exchange rates
market shortage
shift in demand
supply of foreign exchange
trade deficit

Fill in the blank following each of the statements below with the appropriate term from the list above.

1. Places where foreign currencies are bought and sold are called _____.

1. _____

2. The quantity of foreign currency that buyers are willing and able to buy over a given period of time at alternative exchange rates (prices), *ceteris paribus*, is the _____.

2. _____

3. The quantity of foreign currency that sellers are willing and able to sell over a given time period at alternative exchange rates (prices), *ceteris paribus*, is the _____.

3. _____

4. The price of one country's currency expressed in terms of another country's currency is the _____.

4. _____

5. The price (exchange rate) at which quantity demanded equals quantity supplied over a given time period is called the _____.

5. _____

6. A change in the quantity demanded at every price (exchange rate) is called a _____.

6. _____

7. A rise in the price of one currency relative to other currencies is referred to as _____.

7. _____

8. A fall in the price of one currency relative to other currencies is referred to as _____.

8. _____

9. When the quantity of imports demanded exceeds the quantity supplied at a given exchange rate, there is a _____.

9. _____

10. The amount by which the value of imports exceeds the value of exports is called the _____.

10. _____

11. An agreement by countries to fix the prices of their currencies in terms of gold is called the _____.

11. _____

12. Excess demand by foreigners for domestic currency at current exchange rates causes a _____.

12. _____

13. Excess demand by domestic residents for foreign currency at current exchange rates causes a _____.

13. _____

14. Holdings of the currencies of other countries by an official government agency, usually the controller, central bank, or treasury, are called _____.

14. _____

15. Stocks of gold held by government to purchase foreign exchange are called _____.

15. _____

16. When exchange rates are permitted to vary with market supply and demand, they are called _____.

16. _____

17. Government intervention in foreign-exchange markets to limit but not eliminate exchange-rate fluctuations produces _____.

17. _____

18. The demand for foreign exchange has a negative slope, which would be expected because of the _____.

18. _____

19. The _____ provides a summary of a country's economic transactions over a given period of time.

19. _____

True or False: *Circle your choice.*

T F 1. When a U.S. corporation builds a plant in Germany, it demands foreign currency (marks) to pay for the inputs.

T F 2. When Russian gymnasts tour the United States, they create a demand for dollars by supplying rubles.

T F 3. The U.S. demand for French francs represents a supply of dollars to the French.

T F 4. The present system of exchange-rate determination is free of government intervention.

T F 5. When the supply of foreign exchange increases, *ceteris paribus*, the demand for foreign exchange also increases.

T F 6. When the supply of foreign exchange increases, *ceteris paribus*, the quantity of foreign exchange demanded increases.

T F 7. Increased foreign travel by Americans tends to cause the dollar to appreciate, *ceteris paribus*.

T F 8. When the dollar price of German marks increases, BMW autos become cheaper to U.S. residents.

T F 9. When the dollar price of German marks increases, BMW autos become more expensive to Germans relative to U.S. cars.

T F 10. If the dollar appreciates against the French franc, this change will be favorable to U.S. importers of French wine.

T F 11. If the dollar appreciates against the franc, this change will be favorable to California vintners.

T F 12. An appreciation of the French franc against the U.S. dollar will be favorable to French vintners.

T F 13. If income in Japan rises faster than income in the United States, *ceteris paribus*, the yen should appreciate against the dollar.

T F 14. If the U.S. price level rises more rapidly than the Japanese price level, *ceteris paribus*, U.S. exports to Japan will rise.

T F 15. Generally, exporters will favor a depreciation of their own currency.

T F 16. A country that experiences a depreciation in the value of its currency over a long period of time will, *ceteris paribus*, be faced with the problem of underemployment in exporting industries.

T F 17. When the value of exports exceeds the value of imports, a country is said to have a balance-of-payments surplus.

T F 18. When the value of exports exceeds the value of imports, a country is said to have a balance-of-payments deficit.

T F 19. When the value of exports exceeds the value of imports, a country is said to have a deficit in its balance of trade.

T F 20. When the value of imports exceeds the value of exports, a country is said to have a trade deficit.

T F 21. In 1987 the United States alone spent over $100 billion of reserves to prop up the value of the dollar.

T F 22. The overall "balance of payments" must be zero.

T F 23. U.S. exporters become better off when the dollar appreciates.

T F 24. Imports are an injection into the income stream.

T F 25. The current account includes both trade and merchandise and services.

T F 26. Since every transaction must have two sides, the current account can never be in deficit.

T F 27. In the current account a deficit in the trade balance is necessarily offset by a surplus in the service balance.

T F 28. If there is a deficit in the capital account, it must be offset by a surplus in the current account.

Multiple Choice: *Select the correct answer.*

_____ 1. An increase in the dollar price of other currencies will tend to cause:
  (a) American goods to be cheaper to foreigners.
  (b) American goods to be more expensive to foreigners.
  (c) Foreign goods to be cheaper to residents of the United States.
  (d) Foreign goods to be more expensive to residents of foreign countries.

_____ 2. Suppose that there exists a flexible exchange rate between the U.S. dollar and the Japanese yen. An increase in the supply of yen (a rightward shift in the supply curve of yen) will tend to:
  (a) Increase U.S. imports of Japanese goods.
  (b) Push the U.S. balance of trade in the direction of a surplus.
  (c) Lower the yen price of the dollar.
  (d) Raise the dollar price of the yen.

_____ 3. A U.S. balance-of-payments deficit suggests that:
  (a) U.S. imports exceed U.S. exports.
  (b) U.S. exports exceed U.S. imports.
  (c) Total payments made by residents of the United States to foreigners exceed total payments made by foreigners to residents of the United States.
  (d) Total payments made by residents of the United States to foreigners are less than total payments made by foreigners to residents of the United States.

_____ 4. Suppose newsprint sells in the United States for $100 per ton. The cost of shipping newsprint to and from France is $10 per ton. The exchange rate between the French franc and the U.S. dollar is $1 : Fr20. Thus the United States will:
  (a) Export newsprint to France if the price of newsprint exceeds Fr2,000 per ton in France.
  (b) Export newsprint to France if the price of newsprint exceeds Fr2,200 per ton in France.
  (c) Import newsprint from France if the price of newsprint exceeds Fr2,000 per ton in France.
  (d) Import newsprint from France if the price of newsprint exceeds Fr2,200 per ton in France.

_____ 5. A country will experience a reduction in its balance-of-payments deficit, *ceteris paribus*, if:
  (a) Its level of GNP rises relative to foreign levels of GNP.
  (b) Its prices fall relative to foreign price levels, *ceteris paribus*.
  (c) The domestic price of the foreign currency falls.
  (d) It lowers its tariffs.

_____ 6. Under a system of fixed exchange rates, if the rate of price increase in the United States exceeds the rate of price increase of its trading partners:
  (a) U.S. exports will tend to rise and imports to fall.
  (b) U.S. exports will tend to fall and imports to rise.
  (c) U.S. foreign-exchange reserves will tend to rise.
  (d) The dollar price of foreign currencies will tend to fall.

_____ 7. Under a system of flexible exchange rates, if the rate of price increase in the United States is less than the rate of price increase of its trading partners:
   (a) The dollar will strengthen against foreign currencies.
   (b) The dollar will weaken against foreign currencies.
   (c) The dollar will maintain its value against foreign currencies.
   (d) The United States will run a balance-of-payments deficit.

_____ 8. Which of the following changes will tend to cause a shift in the domestic demand curve for foreign currencies?
   (a) Changes in domestic incomes, _ceteris paribus_.
   (b) Changes in domestic prices, _ceteris paribus_.
   (c) Changes in consumer taste for foreign goods, _ceteris paribus_.
   (d) All of the above.

_____ 9. Depreciation of the dollar refers to:
   (a) A loss of foreign-exchange reserves.
   (b) An increase in the dollar price of foreign currency.
   (c) Intervention in international money markets.
   (d) A fall in the dollar price of foreign currency.

_____ 10. Import-competing industries in the United States are likely to resist:
   (a) Appreciation of the dollar.
   (b) Depreciation of the dollar.
   (c) Devaluation of the dollar.
   (d) Evaluation of the dollar.

_____ 11. American citizens planning a vacation abroad would welcome:
   (a) Appreciation of the dollar.
   (b) Depreciation of the dollar.
   (c) Devaluation of the dollar.
   (d) None of the above.

_____ 12. Suppose researchers discover that Scotch whiskey causes cancer when given in large doses to Canadian mice. This finding would be likely to:
   (a) Increase the demand for British pounds.
   (b) Decrease the demand for British pounds.
   (c) Increase the supply of British pounds.
   (d) Decrease the supply of British pounds.

_____ 13. Suppose that real incomes rise faster in the United States than in England. In the United States, this situation would likely cause:
   (a) An increase in the demand for pounds.
   (b) A decrease in the demand for pounds.
   (c) A decrease in the supply of pounds.
   (d) An increase in the supply of pounds.

_____ 14. Orderly marketing arrangements are often described as:
   (a) Involuntary quotas.
   (b) Burial insurance.
   (c) Embargos.
   (d) Voluntary quotas.

_____ 15. Adjustment assistance is _sometimes_ used to:
   (a) Assist in retraining workers displaced by exports.
   (b) Assist in retraining workers displaced by imports.
   (c) Assist foreign firms injured by our quotas.
   (d) Do none of the above.

_____ 16. Suppose the franc–dollar exchange rate is 5 : 1. Suppose a Renault automobile costs 20,000 francs in France. If the other costs that might be involved are ignored, what would be the dollar price of the automobile?
  (a) $4,000.
  (b) $10,000.
  (c) $20,000.
  (d) $100,000.

_____ 17. If French speculators believed the yen was going to appreciate against the dollar, they would:
  (a) Purchase francs.
  (b) Purchase dollars.
  (c) Purchase yen.
  (d) Sell yen.

_____ 18. Suppose that at the prevailing yen–dollar exchange rate there is an excess demand for yen. To prevent the dollar from depreciating, the United States might:
  (a) Raise taxes.
  (b) Reduce government spending.
  (c) Raise interest rates.
  (d) Do all of the above.

_____ 19. Under a fixed exchange rate, a country can avoid an appreciation of its currency by:
  (a) Decreasing the supply of foreign exchange.
  (b) Using deflationary policies.
  (c) Using inflationary policies.
  (d) Raising tariff barriers.

_____ 20. Which of the following would be appropriate monetary and fiscal policies for a surplus country to follow?
  (a) Reduce taxes.
  (b) Purchase securities in the open market.
  (c) Increase government spending.
  (d) Do all of the above.

_____ 21. Which of the following would *not* be appropriate monetary and/or fiscal policies for a deficit country to follow?
  (a) Raise taxes.
  (b) Sell securities in the open market.
  (c) Increase government spending.
  (d) Lower the reserve requirement.

_____ 22. The overall "balance" of the balance of payments must be:
  (a) Equal to zero.
  (b) Positive if exports of goods and services exceed imports of goods and services.
  (c) Positive if the capital account is in surplus.
  (d) Negative if the current account is in deficit.

_____ 23. The current account includes:
  (a) Trade in goods.
  (b) Trade in services.
  (c) Unilateral transfer.
  (d) All of the above.

_____ 24. If the balance of trade is positive:
  (a) The capital account may be in surplus.
  (b) The capital account may be in deficit.
  (c) The current account may be in surplus or deficit.
  (d) All of the above may be the case.

Problems and Applications

Exercise 1

Equilibrium exchange rates

This exercise provides practice in determining exchange rates.

1. Table 37.1 depicts the hypothetical demand for and supply of British pounds in terms of U.S. dollars. Use the information in Table 37.1 to plot in Figure 37.1 the demand and supply of British pounds at the exchange rates indicated. Then answer Problems 2–4.

Table 37.1
Monthly demand for and supply of British pounds in the United States

Dollars per British pound	Quantity demanded	Quantity supplied
4.50	100	700
4.00	200	600
3.50	300	500
3.00	400	400
2.50	500	300
2.00	600	200
1.50	700	100

Figure 37.1

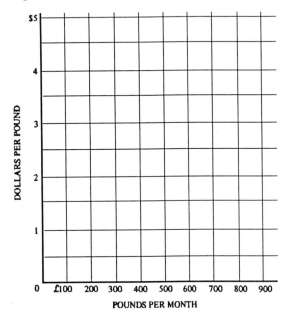

2. What is the equilibrium rate of exchange? $_____

3. At a price of $2 per pound there would be excess:
   (a) Demand, and the exchange rate for pounds would rise.
   (b) Demand, and the exchange rate for pounds would fall.
   (c) Supply, and the exchange rate would rise.
   (d) Supply, and the exchange rate would fall.

4. Suppose that Americans suddenly increased their demand for English woolens. What prediction would you make concerning the exchange rate between the dollar and the pound?
   (a) The dollar price of pounds would fall.
   (b) The dollar price of pounds would rise.
   (c) The pound price of dollars would rise.
   (d) This event should not affect the dollar–pound exchange rate.

Exercise 2

This exercise shows how to analyze the foreign-exchange market using supply-and-demand curves. The effects of several historical events in United States–Japanese relations are analyzed.

For each of the following, choose the letter of the appropriate diagram in Figure 37.2 that best describes the kind of shift that would occur in the foreign-exchange market. The market should be looked at from the U.S. point of view, that is, the shifts represent changes in the demand and supply of dollars. Think of the price of a dollar as being measured in yen per dollar. Remember that exchange rates were fixed until 1971, which prevented them from reflecting supply-and-demand changes.

Figure 37.2
Shifts in the demand and supply of a currency

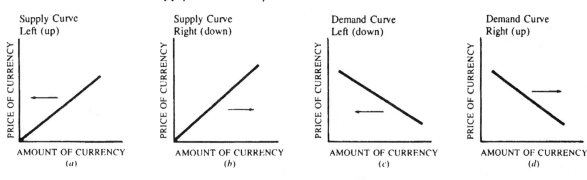

The demand for dollars originates with the Japanese who wish to buy goods and services produced by U.S. firms or who wish to purchase assets through U.S. markets (e.g., stocks, real estate, bank deposits). The supply of dollars to the foreign-exchange market originates with U.S. residents who wish to purchase Japanese goods and services or who wish to purchase Japanese assets.

Indicate whether the shift described in each of the questions below would cause the equilibrium price of the dollar to appreciate (increase in value) or to depreciate (decrease in value). Also, indicate with an arrow whether the equilibrium quantity of dollars would increase (↑) or decrease (↓). Finally, indicate in the blanks provided which of the following determinants of demand and supply had changed:

(a) Relative income changes and demand for goods and services.
(b) Relative price changes.
(c) Changes in product availability.
(d) Change in relative interest rates.
(e) Change in speculative activity.

(*Hint:* Do not confuse the demand and supply for imports and exports with the demand and supply for dollars.)

1. Shift: _____

   Change in value: _____
     Appreciate/Depreciate
   Change in equilibrium
     quantity: _____
   Determinant: _____

   After World War II the Japanese had little wealth. The U.S. economy had been left intact and experienced strong growth in both income and wealth.

2. Shift: _____

   Change in value: _____
     Appreciate/Depreciate
   Change in equilibrium
     quantity: _____
   Determinant: _____

   The Japanese replaced capital destroyed in World War II with the most modern production techniques available and began to produce goods for export.

3. Shift: _____

   Change in value: _____
     Appreciate/Depreciate
   Change in equilibrium
     quantity: _____
   Determinant: _____

   The Japanese protected their emerging industries from foreign (U.S.) competition.

4. Shift: _____

   Change in value: _____
     Appreciate/Depreciate
   Change in equilibrium
     quantity: _____
   Determinant: _____

   The U.S. engaged in the Korean War in the early 1950s and the Vietnam War in the early 1970s and had to import goods to make up for what it could not produce.

5. Shift: _____

   Change in value: _____
     Appreciate/Depreciate
   Change in equilibrium
     quantity: _____
   Determinant: _____

   The United States began to experience high inflation rates, while Japan continued to have low rates in the 1970s.

6. Shift: _____

   Change in value: _____
     Appreciate/Depreciate
   Change in equilibrium
     quantity: _____
   Determinant: _____

   Many people anticipated that the United States would go off the gold standard and expected the dollar to float and become much cheaper relative to the yen. In order to make a profit from these anticipated events, they entered the foreign-exchange market.

7. Shift: _____

   Change in value: _____
     Appreciate/Depreciate
   Change in equilibrium
     quantity: _____
   Determinant: _____

   When the United States went off the gold standard in 1971, commodity prices began to rise rapidly and the United States curtailed exports of scrap steel, soybeans, and logs to Japan. The United States further reneged on commitments to sell grains and oil.

8. Shift: _____

    Change in value: _____
       Appreciate/Depreciate
    Change in equilibrium
       quantity: _____
    Determinant: _____

In the mid-1970s Japan and other countries cut their demand for the basic commodities on which the United States had placed restrictions. (This shift showed up after the United States tried once again to sell commodities to Japan.)

9. Shift: _____

    Change in value: _____
       Appreciate/Depreciate
    Change in equilibrium
       quantity: _____
    Determinant: _____

In the late 1970s and early 1980s, the United States became concerned about its trade deficit and the competition from Japanese goods in domestic markets. Protectionist sentiment mounted and the United States placed additional restrictions on imports from Japan.

10. Shift: _____

    Change in value: _____
       Appreciate/Depreciate
    Change in equilibrium
       quantity: _____
    Determinant: _____

In 1988 the United States was successful in getting the Japanese to lift some of the barriers that prevented American goods from entering the Japanese market.

Exercise 3

The media often feature articles about negotiations concerning international financial issues. By using one of the articles in the text, this exercise will show how to use supply-and-demand curves to test the accuracy of reporting on international financial events. If your professor makes a newspaper assignment for this chapter, this exercise will provide an example of how to do it.

Reread the article in Chapter 37 entitled "Japan's Big Economic Debate" from the *New York Times*. Then answer the following questions:

1. What sentence or sentences describe the effect on the dollar of Japan's stimulation of its own economy?

2. Figure 37.2 (p. 523) shows the possible shifts of demand and supply for a nation's currency. Which shift best represents the expected shift in the supply or demand for the dollar due to the event described in Question 1?   a   b   c   d   (circle one)

3. The dollar should (rise, fall) in value relative to the yen if exports to Japan increased.

4. Which shift in Figure 37.2 best represents the impact on the supply or demand for yen caused by the event you chose in Question 1?   a   b   c   d   (circle one)

5. The yen should (rise, fall) in value relative to the dollar if exports to Japan increase.

6. What sentence indicates the direction of the shift in the demand for the dollar?

7. T   F   The article's prediction that dollar demand would fall contradicts the expected direction for dollar demand in response to Japan's stimulation of its own economy.

Reread the statement that begins, "Although most economists attribute Japan's large and growing trade surpluses to the strong dollar and other macroeconomic factors. . ." Decide the truth of the following statements in Questions 8–10.

8. T F If the Japanese stimulate their own economy, the demand for the dollar should become stronger.

9. T F If a stronger dollar causes growing trade surpluses as the article suggests, then stimulation of the Japanese economy should increase the surplus.

10. T F As suggested in the article, a more expansionary posture in Japan would help to reverse trade and currency imbalances. (*Hint:* Compare this statement with your previous conclusion.)

Common Errors

The first statement in each "common error" below is incorrect. Each incorrect statement is followed by a corrected version and an explanation.

1. A country is well off if its currency appreciates steadily over a long period of time. WRONG!

Both appreciating currencies and depreciating currencies create problems. RIGHT!

Be careful! There are problems associated with steadily appreciating currencies *and* with steadily depreciating currencies. The problems that accompany depreciating currencies are more obvious to most people because they are typically, and mistakenly, associated with trade deficits. The export industries in countries with appreciating currencies will ultimately have employment problems; countries with depreciating currencies will suffer from inflation.

2. When countries have trade deficits, money really flows out. When they have surpluses, money really flows in. WRONG!

Money does not *really* flow in most transactions, but the claim to ownership does. RIGHT!

This is a conceptually difficult problem. Most foreign trade is transacted by check and is just a "flow" of bookkeeping entries. Even when gold is sold, it seldom *physically* flows anywhere. In the case of the United States, it stays in Fort Knox, though someone else owns it. Thus, it is the claim to ownership that flows, not the money. When countries run trade deficits, their trading partners add to their claims against them. For countries with a trade surplus, the reverse is true.

3. Economic sanctions are an effective political weapon. WRONG!

Economic sanctions can only sometimes bring pressure on another country, but even then their effects are difficult to control. RIGHT!

It was very popular in the early days of the energy crisis to talk about withholding wheat or some other commodity from Arab countries in an attempt to coerce them into lowering the price of oil.

Of course, in the case of wheat and other agricultural products alternative suppliers exist, the market is competitive, and the price is determined in world markets. In the case of oil we were on the demand side and had few acceptable alternatives but to pay the price at which oil was offered. However, even this powerful political weapon has lost its potency. The oil market is in disarray. The supply has increased; demand has retreated. We've come full circle in ten years. Instead of running surpluses, many oil-producing countries are running deficits in the balance of payments and have become desperate to sell oil.

The United States used oil as a political weapon against Japanese expansion. Unfortunately, our embargo contributed to Pearl Harbor and the U.S. entrance into World War II. Similarly, in 1973 and again in 1978, many Americans wished to retaliate with war against the OPEC nations.

■ ANSWERS ■

Key-Term Review

1. foreign-exchange markets
2. demand for foreign exchange
3. supply of foreign exchange
4. exchange rate
5. equilibrium price
6. shift in demand
7. appreciation

8. depreciation
9. market shortage
10. trade deficit
11. gold standard
12. balance-of-payments surplus
13. balance-of-payments deficit

14. foreign-exchange reserves
15. gold reserves
16. flexible exchange rates
17. managed exchange rates
18. law of demand
19. balance of payments

True or False

1. T	6. T	11. F	16. F	21. F	25. T
2. T	7. F	12. F	17. F	22. T	26. F
3. T	8. F	13. F	18. F	23. F	27. F
4. F	9. T	14. F	19. F	24. F	28. T
5. F	10. T	15. T	20. T		

Multiple Choice

1. a	5. b	9. b	13. a	17. c	21. c
2. a	6. b	10. a	14. d	18. d	22. a
3. c	7. a	11. a	15. b	19. c	23. d
4. b	8. d	12. b	16. a	20. d	24. d

Problems and Applications

Exercise 1

1. **Figure 37.1 answer**

2. $3
3. a
4. b

POUNDS PER MONTH

Exercise 2

1. b, Depreciate, ↑, a
   With higher incomes, Americans could buy more Japanese goods and assets. They therefore supplied more dollars to the foreign-exchange market.
2. b, Depreciate, ↑, c
   With more Japanese goods to purchase, Americans were willing to supply more dollars to the foreign-exchange market.

3. c, Depreciate, $\downarrow$, c

   With fewer sales to Japan, there was less need for U.S. dollars from the foreign-exchange market.
4. b, Depreciate, $\uparrow$, a

   To buy more Japanese goods, the United States had to supply more dollars to the foreign-exchange market.
5. c or b, Depreciate, uncertain, b and e

   Not wishing to hold dollars that would purchase less due to inflation, speculators would supply these dollars to the foreign-exchange market, to buy more stable currencies such as the yen.
6. b or c, Depreciate, uncertain, b and e

   Not willing to hold dollars that would purchase less due to the expectations of the depreciating dollar, speculators would supply these dollars to the foreign-exchange market, to buy more stable currencies.
7. c, Depreciate, $\downarrow$, c and b

   As the Japanese curtailed purchases of American goods, they did not need to buy as many American dollars in the foreign-exchange market.
8. c, Depreciate, $\downarrow$, a or c

   As the Japanese curtailed purchases of American goods, they did not need to buy as many American dollars in the foreign-exchange market.
9. a, Appreciate, $\downarrow$, a or c

   The United States submitted fewer dollars to the foreign-exchange market, since there was less product to purchase from Japan.
10. d, Appreciate, $\uparrow$, a or c

    The Japanese could buy more American goods and therefore needed more dollars from the foreign-exchange market with which to buy the goods.

Exercise 3

1. "United States officials . . . have suggested that a more expansionary posture domestically would help to reverse trade and currency imbalances." More specifically, "If Japan took steps to stimulate its domestic economy . . . [Japanese] consumers would have more money to spend on imports."
2. d   The Japanese need to buy more dollars to buy more American imports.
3. rise
4. b   The Japanese buy dollars in the foreign-exchange market by supplying more yen.
5. fall
6. "Less demand for the dollar might also spur its fall against the yen, making American products less expensive in Japan, and Japanese products more expensive in the United States." This sentence comes right after the statement "If Japan took steps to stimulate its domestic economy, . . . consumers would have more money to spend on imports." This statement suggests the two concepts are related to each other when, in fact, they are contradictory.
7. T   See the answer to Question 6.
8. T   This is consistent with our analysis that demand for the dollar will shift to the right as the Japanese import more from the United States.
9. T   The logic of this statement is impeccable, but the article's statement about the existence of a strong dollar is misleading and the source of the problem. The dollar may become even stronger as a result of Japanese stimulation of its economy. Perhaps the dollar is not strong enough. The key is that Americans will wish to export more to Japan, despite a strong dollar, if the Japanese stimulate their economy.
10. T   The imbalances will be redressed but not by a weaker dollar. The trade balances will be redressed because of greater Japanese income. The article has confused a shift in demand for dollars because of growing Japanese incomes with a movement along the demand curve because of a change in the value of the dollar.

Chapter 38
International Development

Quick Review

This chapter is about poverty and despair on a world-wide scale. The questions that drive the description and analysis are:

- How poor are Third World countries?
- Why have they not developed faster?
- What policies might accelerate their economic growth?

To begin with, we find commonality among the less developed or Third World countries because they have extremely low per capita incomes and slow GNP growth rates. These two characteristics are more often than not combined with low life expectancy, illiteracy, and the like—all symptoms of extreme poverty. What's more, their prospects for improvement are poor because there are many barriers to development.

Some of the barriers have to do with domestic resources—land, labor, and capital. Sometimes, but not always, the country does not have fertile land or mineral resources. Less developed countries (LDCs) frequently have populations that are young, large, and growing more rapidly than the labor force. Thus, it is very difficult for them to produce a surplus that can be saved and invested to form capital.

The need for additional resources and the reallocation of existing ones permeates development policy. Both require saving by some group so that resources somewhere are released from current uses to more productive long-term uses. Financing is thus a key ingredient.

External financing, both public and private, has been made available to such countries for a long time. The amounts provided have usually been very small relative to the global problem. The debts owed to multilateral public agencies or to private lenders must be paid back. Very often this requires hard currency earnings, which can only be acquired by exporting or incurring more debt.

Many LDCs have tried to develop through export-led growth, but even here there are barriers. The markets they enter may grow very slowly, have inelastic demand, or be characterized by such barriers as quotas and tariffs.

Advances in technology are also very difficult to achieve. Sometimes ingrained attitudes prevent the adoption of new techniques; sometimes the required infrastructure is not in place. Nevertheless, the desire for development is strong, and many countries have adopted strategies and made difficult choices in an attempt to move forward.

Learning Objectives

After reading Chapter 38 and doing the following exercises, you should:	True or false	Multiple choice	Problems and applications	Common error	Pages in the text
1. Know some of the economic characteristics of poor countries.	1	1–3			886–890
2. Understand some of the barriers to economic growth in poor countries.	2–5, 7,8	10	2		890–896
3. Be able to discuss and describe some of the difficulties encountered with various types of private external financing.	6	4–6, 11–14			893–897
4. Know some of the sources for public external financing.	9–14		1		897–898
5. Understand the constraints that inhibit the introduction of new technology in poor countries.	15,16	7			898–899
6. Be able to describe some of the strategic questions that must be answered before choosing a growth strategy.	17	8			899–904
7. Know some of the issues relating to reliance on foreign and domestic markets.	18	9,13		1	904–906
8. Be able to discuss the debt crisis.		11	1		896–897

Key-Term Review

Review the following terms; if you are not sure of the meaning of any term, write out the definition and check it against the Glossary in the text.

barter
comparative advantage
debt servicing
disguised unemployment
GNP per capita
market mechanism

market shortage
price elasticity of demand
production possibilities
productivity
quota

Fill in the blank following each of the statements below with the appropriate term from the list above.

1. Individuals who are working but producing little or nothing are an example of _____.

1. _____

2. When output per unit of input declines, it is correct to say there is falling _____.

2. _____

3. The savings–investment process is made difficult in economies that rely on _____.

3. _____

4. LDCs, as well as other countries, must allocate resources by tradition, command, or the _____.

4. _____

5. In economies using the market mechanism as an allocating device, the signal for greater production is a _____.

5. _____

530

6. Governments have sometimes responded to increased competition from imports by imposing a _____.

6. _____

7. Quotas and other impediments to trade have sometimes prevented LDCs from developing production in products in which they have a _____.

7. _____

8. One impediment to export-led development is that LDC products may face a low _____.

8. _____

9. Long-term growth of an LDC requires an expansion of the country's _____.

9. _____

10. Countries are classified from rich to extremely poor on the basis of their _____.

10. _____

11. One of the difficulties faced by Third World countries is that their _____ requirements are in hard currencies.

11. _____

True or False: *Circle your choice.*

T F 1. Developing countries are those with high growth rates.

T F 2. Disguised unemployment in poor countries is synonymous with discouraged workers in developed countries.

T F 3. The introduction of child labor laws would not affect output in poor countries.

T F 4. The WHAT question is determined largely by the requirements for subsistence in poor countries.

T F 5. In poor countries the inefficiency of a money economy is overcome by barter.

T F 6. Although barter is less efficient than money exchange, it does speed up the savings–investment process.

T F 7. The Soviet Union and the People's Republic of China have very high voluntary savings ratios, as evidenced by their high savings rates.

T F 8. Inflation is a way to "force" saving on the economy.

T F 9. The term "hard currency" refers to money that is based on precious metals.

T F 10. The World Bank provides poor countries with general balance-of-payments assistance.

T F 11. A soft loan can be made with hard currency.

T F 12. Because loans must often be repaid in hard currency, export-producing projects will often be favored over domestic projects.

T F 13. In 1988 poor countries as a group had export earnings roughly four times that required to service their debt.

T F 14. Based on the percent of total GNP given as foreign aid, the United States rates as one of the most generous of the developed countries.

T F 15. Lack of infrastructure is often an impediment to foreign investment.

T F 16. Emphasis on the agricultural sector can be justified because the balance of trade may improve if imports of food decline.

T F 17. Balanced growth is a viable approach to development in poor countries.

T F 18. The "infant industry" argument has led to inefficient industrial development in many LDCs.

Multiple Choice: *Select the correct answer.*

_____ 1. Which of the following problems do less developed countries face?
   (a) Low per capita incomes and high GNP growth rates.
   (b) Low population growth and low per capita income.
   (c) Low per capita incomes and slow GNP growth rates.
   (d) Low per capita incomes and high saving rates.

_____ 2. Poor countries are characterized by:
   (a) A low caloric intake.
   (b) A low ratio of doctors to population.
   (c) A low energy consumption per capita.
   (d) All of the above.

_____ 3. Which of the following would be classified as a "low-income country"?
   (a) Singapore.
   (b) Brazil.
   (c) India.
   (d) All of the above.

_____ 4. Which of the following would be likely to make a hard-currency loan for a specific project?
   (a) IBRD.
   (b) IDA.
   (c) IFC.
   (d) Exim Bank.

_____ 5. Which of the following agencies would be most likely to participate in equity financing for a specific project?
   (a) IBRD.
   (b) IDA.
   (c) IFC.
   (d) The Asian Development Bank.

_____ 6. Which of the following would most likely be classified as a hard-currency loan?
   (a) A loan repayable in the borrower's own currency over a twenty-year period.
   (b) A loan repayable in dollars over a twenty-year term.
   (c) Cofinancing of an equity investment project through the IFC.
   (d) None of the above.

_____ 7. In which of Walter W. Rostow's stages is the savings–investment process alleged to increase?
   (a) Preconditions to takeoff.
   (b) Takeoff into sustained growth.
   (c) Drive to maturity.
   (d) High mass consumption.

_____ 8. LDCs that attempt to enter export markets often face which of the following challenges?
   (a) Competition from other LDCs.
   (b) Competition from developed countries.
   (c) Restricted access to developed-country markets.
   (d) All of the above.

_____ 9. The demand for food tends to be:
   (a) Price elastic.
   (b) Price inelastic.
   (c) Income elastic.
   (d) None of the above.

_____10. Capital formation is difficult in LDCs because:
  (a) The savings rate is low.
  (b) If a barter system exists, saving often takes illiquid forms.
  (c) Borrowing abroad at reasonable terms is very difficult.
  (d) All of the above are the case.

_____11. The term "debt service" means:
  (a) Debtors' prison awaits those who cannot repay their loans.
  (b) Those who cannot repay their debts have the option of entering public service to pay off lenders.
  (c) The ability to repay both interest and principal.
  (d) All of the above.

_____12. A hard currency is one that is:
  (a) Backed by a precious metal.
  (b) Made up of coin, as opposed to cash.
  (c) Traded internationally.
  (d) Hard to come by, that is, a collector's item.

_____13. Multilateral loans are:
  (a) Preferred to bilateral loans by poor countries.
  (b) Made only by the IBRD.
  (c) No-strings-attached loans.
  (d) All of the above.

_____14. Which of the following projects would be a suitable candidate for a loan to a poor country to be repaid in U.S. dollars?
  (a) A loan to build a new school.
  (b) A loan to install a new sewer system.
  (c) A loan to purchase equipment to produce textiles for sale abroad.
  (d) A loan to purchase emergency medical supplies.

Problems and Applications

Exercise 1

This exercise will show how the debt of underdeveloped countries can get out of hand because of high interest payments. Many Latin American countries have problems meeting even the interest payments on their foreign debt, not to mention paying anything on the amount borrowed (the principal). They must be able to make payments on their foreign debt using foreign currencies that they earn by exporting goods and services.

1. Table 38.1 shows estimated data on key economic statistics compiled by international organizations for four Latin American countries for 1983. Compute (to the nearest tenth of a billion dollars) the interest that must be paid on this debt at an interest rate of 10 percent per year and place your answers in row 2 of the table.

Table 38.1
Burden of the debt

	Mexico	Venezuela	Brazil	Argentina
Total debt (billions of dollars)	$ 89	$ 34	$ 93	$ 48
Interest (billions of dollars per year)	$_____	$_____	$_____	$_____
Export earnings (billions of dollars per year)	$ 21.0	$ 13.7	$ 21.4	$ 8.3
Growth rates in gross domestic product (per year)	−4 %	−2 %	−5 %	+2 %
Inflation rate (per year)	91.9 %	6.4 %	21.1 %	401.6 %

2. Of course, a country cannot spend all of its export earnings on debt repayment. It must also import goods and services. This means that the country can only use the surplus of exports over imports to service the debt. If it cannot run such surpluses, it must borrow again just to make interest payments. Let's see what happens to the debt of Argentina if it simply borrows to make yearly interest payments.

   In Table 38.2, column 1 shows the year, column 2 shows the debt existing at the beginning of that year, column 3 shows the interest payment on that debt, and column 4 shows what the new debt will be if Argentina borrows in order to pay off the interest. In the years following 1983, assume that the interest rate on the total debt is 10 percent. The first row has been done for you. Complete the other rows. (Round off to the nearest tenth of a billion dollars.)

Table 38.2

(1) Year	(2) Debt (see col. 4 of previous year) (billions of dollars)	(3) Interest on debt (10% of col. 2) (billions of dollars per year)	(4) Total debt after borrowing to pay interest [(2) + (3)] (billions of dollars)
1983	$48.0	$4.8 (.10 x 48)	$52.8
1984	52.8	_____	_____
1985	_____	_____	_____
1986	_____	_____	_____
1987	_____	_____	_____
1988	_____	_____	_____
1989	_____	_____	_____

3. By what percentage will the debt at the end of 1989 (see column 4 for 1989 in Table 38.2) exceed the debt at the beginning of 1983 (see column 2 for 1983 in Table 38.2)? _____%

4. If Argentina is able to sustain a real growth rate in gross domestic product (GDP) of 2 percent per year, by what percentage will the GDP of 1989 exceed the GDP of 1983? _____%

5. Between 1983 and 1989, the ratio of the external debt will grow relative to GDP by:
   (a) 0–10 percent.
   (b) 10–30 percent.
   (c) 30–50 percent.
   (d) 50–80 percent.

6. The situation in Argentina deteriorated in 1985 as the following *Business Week* article (July 1, 1985, p. 34) recounts:

   On June 14, Argentine President Raul Alfonsin . . . decreed . . . a series of draconian economic measures to throttle the country's 1,010% rate of inflation. . . . While dramatic, the introduction of australes (a new currency) and a wage and price freeze may turn out to be the least important reforms. They do little to get at the root of the problem: government printing of money to finance an $8.4 billion budget deficit. . . . Economy Minister Sorrouille insists that from now on state agencies will be funded only from their own tariffs and foreign borrowing. "The printing machine will cease to function," vows Sorrouille.

   From this article it can be concluded that Alfonsin's new austerity program will:
   (a) Increase the debt/GDP ratio.
   (b) Decrease the debt/GDP ratio.
   (c) Leave the debt/GDP ratio unchanged.

7. Suppose the interest rate is 15 percent per year, not 10 percent. Fill in Table 38.3 in the same way you completed Table 38.2, using an interest rate of 15 percent.

Table 38.3

(1) Year	(2) Debt (see col. 4 of previous year) (billions of dollars)	(3) Interest on debt (15% of col. 2) (billions of dollars per year)	(4) Total debt after borrowing to pay interest [(2) + (3)] (billions of dollars)
1983	$48.0	$_____	$_____
1984	_____	_____	_____
1985	_____	_____	_____
1986	_____	_____	_____
1987	_____	_____	_____
1988	_____	_____	_____
1989	_____	_____	_____

8. If the interest rate rises from 10 percent per year to 15 percent per year, by 1989 the debt will also rise. By what percentage would the debt at the higher interest rate (Table 38.3) exceed the debt at the lower interest rate (Table 38.2) by the end of 1989? _____%

9. Table 38.1 shows the inflation rates and the rate of growth in GDP for four Latin American countries. Which of the following statements is *false*?
   (a) Because of the negative growth rates, these countries have a difficult time preventing the debt/GDP ratio from expanding and placing even greater burdens on the economy.
   (b) Because these countries are unable to use the debt-repayment funds for internal growth, the growth rate in GDP suffers.
   (c) Because internal needs cannot be met with foreign funds, the government issues more money, which stimulates inflation.
   (d) The high inflation rate means that the value of the debt in real terms is becoming smaller.

Exercise 2

Except for a few key newspapers like the *New York Times*, the media do very shallow reporting on less developed countries. However, careful reading of those articles that are found can provide a wealth of information on the barriers to a country's economic growth. By using one of the articles in the text, this exercise will show the kind of information that can be found by careful reading of an article about a less developed country. If your professor makes a newspaper assignment for this chapter, this exercise will provide an example of how to do it.

Reread the article in Chapter 38 entitled "China to Levy Tax as Birth Check" from the *Oregonian*. Then answer the following questions:

1. What is the first sentence that indicates a barrier to the country's growth?

2. What sentence indicates actions designed to overcome the barrier to growth?

Common Error

The first statement in the "common error" below is incorrect. The incorrect statement is followed by a corrected version and an explanation.

1. Foreign aid has been a huge give-away program for poor countries. WRONG!

   Foreign aid has not been large relative to the development problem, and much of this aid is in the form of loans, not "gifts." RIGHT!

Foreign aid has sometimes been large in absolute dollars, but it has never reached the magnitude envisioned by its early proponents. It has really been quite small relative to the global problem it is designed to alleviate. Moreover, much of it is not "given" but takes the form of loans, sometimes on onerous terms and with many strings attached. The "strings" may take the form of requirements that purchases must be made in the donor country, shipped in donor country ships, and the like. Often these requirements result in inefficiency and high prices. For these and many other reasons, one can say foreign aid is not large and much is not a gift.

■ ANSWERS ■

Key-Term Review

1. disguised unemployment
2. productivity
3. barter
4. market mechanism
5. market shortage
6. quota
7. comparative advantage
8. price elasticity of demand
9. production possibilities
10. GNP per capita
11. debt servicing

True or False

1. F	4. T	7. F	10. F	13. T	16. T
2. F	5. F	8. T	11. T	14. F	17. F
3. F	6. F	9. F	12. T	15. T	18. T

Multiple Choice

1. c	4. a	7. b	9. b	11. c	13. a
2. d	5. c	8. d	10. d	12. c	14. c
3. b	6. b				

Problems and Applications

Exercise 1

1. Table 38.1 answer

	Mexico	Venezuela	Brazil	Argentina
Interest (billions of dollars per year)	$8.9	$3.4	$9.3	$4.8

2. Table 38.2 answer

Year	Debt (billions of dollars)	Interest on debt (billions of dollars per year)	Total debt (billions of dollars)
1983	$48.0	$4.8	$52.8
1984	52.8	5.3	58.1
1985	58.1	5.8	63.9
1986	63.9	6.4	70.3
1987	70.3	7.0	77.3
1988	77.3	7.7	85.0
1989	85.0	8.5	93.5

3. $\dfrac{93.5 \text{ billion } 1989}{\$48.0 \text{ billion } 1983} = 1.948$

In other words, the debt has increased by 94.8 percentage points.

4. (1.02) x (1.02) x (1.02) x (1.02) x (1.02) x (1.02) x (1.02)
   1983   1984   1985   1986   1987   1988   1989
   = 1.149

In other words, GDP has increased by 14.9 percentage points.

5. There will be a 69 percent (1.948/1.149) increase in the debt/GDP ratio, because the debt will grow by 94.8 percent while GDP only grows 14.9 percent.

6. a   The internal policies will lower GDP (because of reduced government spending) without changing the debt.

7. **Table 38.3 answer**

Year	Debt (billions of dollars)	Interest on debt (billions of dollars per year)	Total debt (billions of dollars)
1983	$48.0	$7.2	$55.2
1984	55.2	8.3	63.5
1985	63.5	9.5	73.0
1986	73.0	11.0	84.0
1987	84.0	12.6	96.6
1988	96.6	14.5	111.1
1989	111.1	16.7	127.8

8. $\dfrac{\$127.8 \text{ billion debt at } 15\% \text{ interest rate}}{\$93.5 \text{ billion debt at } 10\% \text{ interest rate}} = 1.367$

There will be a 36.7 percent increase in debt by 1989 because of the 5 percentage point rise in interest rate.

9. d   Debt is denominated in foreign currencies such as the dollar, which is not affected by inflation in Latin American currencies.

Exercise 2

1. "Birth control was an 'urgent problem' in China."
2. "China . . . will begin taxing families who have too many children."

Chapter 39

Socialist Planning

Quick Review

Some of the world's largest economies rely on "planning," rather than the market mechanism, to allocate their scarce resources in answering the WHAT, HOW, and FOR WHOM questions. Their reasons for doing so are rooted in their socialist or communist political ideology. In this chapter we study how centrally planned economies deal with the following questions:

- What basic economic decisions must be made by the government in a centrally planned economy?
- How can these decisions be implemented?
- How does central planning work, in comparison to decentralized markets?

Every economy has to answer the WHAT, HOW, and FOR WHOM questions. In the United States these questions are answered when consumers attempt to maximize satisfaction with limited incomes, business people attempt to maximize profits, and voters express their preferences about the way they are governed. In planned economies, the big decisions, such as the division of output between capital goods and consumer goods, are made by a central authority.

The central authority (that is, the planners) attempts to allocate resources to achieve specific objectives. Very often these objectives include a particular income distribution and a strong military establishment. Planners use such techniques as input–output analysis to allocate their scarce resources; in contrast, in a market economy prices automatically signal where resources are to move. Prices are used in planned economies to perform a rationing function, but not the allocation function that they perform in a market economy.

Since prices are not allowed to provide incentives in a planned economy, the planners have to invent other ways to bring about desired outcomes. Sometimes force is used, but more recently bonuses and ideological appeals have been used in the two largest planned economies, the Soviet Union and the People's Republic of China.

It is difficult to say that one system is clearly superior to the other. Comparisons show that each system has strengths and weaknesses.

Learning Objectives

After reading Chapter 39 and doing the following exercises, you should:	True or false	Multiple choice	Problems and applications	Common errors	Pages in the text
1. Recognize that every economy is restricted by its production-possibilities curve and the choices that result.	1,2	13	2		910-913

538

2.	Recognize the very serious difficulties encountered in "planning" for large economies.		2	2	918–925
3.	Recognize that every economy, no matter how it's organized, must answer the WHAT, HOW, and FOR WHOM questions.	3,4,7	3–6	1	911–913, 918
4.	Understand the roles that prices play in market and planned economies.	5,6,8,9	1	1,3	1	916–918
5.	Know what input–output analysis is and how it is used by planners.			2	914–916
6.	Know the objectives of socialist planning.	10			909–918
7.	Know the relative strengths and weaknesses of market and planned economies.	11	7–9,11,14	2,3	918–932
8.	Know the relative living standards of the United States, China, and the Soviet Union.	14–18	10,12		2	925–931
9.	Recognize the trend toward a greater role for markets in the Soviet Union and the People's Republic of China.	12,13, 19,20	15		931–932

Key-Term Review

Review the following terms; if you are not sure of the meaning of any term, write out the definition and check it against the Glossary in the text.

capitalism
communism
counterplanning
economic growth
investment
market economy

market mechanism
production possibilities
production process
socialism
underemployment
unemployment

Fill in the blank following each of the statements below with the appropriate term from the list above.

1. An outward shift of the production-possibilities curve indicates that an economy is experiencing _____.

1. _____

2. Workers who are producing substantially below their capability are said to experience _____.

2. _____

3. Market economies sometimes have large numbers of jobless workers. The Soviet Union and China do not experience a problem with _____.

3. _____

4. The stage of the Marxist revolution in which resources are allocated by the state is called _____.

4. _____

5. The system of organization that relies on the market mechanism to allocate resources is called _____.

5. _____

6. Those economies that desire to grow more rapidly must devote substantial amounts of resources to _____.

6. _____

7. A particular combination of resources used to produce a particular output is called a _____.

7. _____

8. The final stage of the Marxist revolution is called _____.

8. _____

9. The negotiation of plan targets between central planners and local production managers is called _____

9. _____

10. The alternative combinations of final goods and services that could be produced in a given time period within the limits imposed by available resources and technology are called _____.

10. _____

11. In a _____ resources are largely allocated by the _____.

11. _____

_____

True or False: *Circle your choice.*

T F 1. Both planned and market economies are subject to limited production possibilities.

T F 2. In a fully employed economy, the cost of greater output of investment goods is measured in terms of output of consumer goods forgone.

T F 3. In the immediate postrevolutionary period, the Chinese devoted more resources to investment goods than did the Soviet Union.

T F 4. Input–output coefficients indicate the dollars of output per dollar of input used in the production process.

T F 5. The basic function of prices in a nonmarket economy is to signal to producers that some products are relatively scarce and others are relatively plentiful.

T F 6. The efficiency of a market economy might be considered undesirable because of distributional effects of letting the market determine prices.

T F 7. In a socialist society the profit motive can still be effective as long as steeply progressive income taxes are used to eliminate economic profits.

T F 8. In a planned economy prices can signal where resources should move, but they do not serve to ration consumer goods.

T F 9. In a capitalist economy prices perform the function of increasing efficiency; in a planned economy they fail to perform this function.

T F 10. Soviet leader Mikhail Gorbachev has advocated a greater role for market forces in the Soviet economy.

T F 11. In the Soviet Union, the productivity of "worker-owned" land is significantly greater than the productivity of state-owned land.

T F 12. Soviet five-year plans chart the direction the economy should take but leave it entirely up to the workers to decide how it should be done.

T F 13. Chinese planning is more centralized than Soviet planning.

T F 14. After adjustments for differences in economic organization, government subsidies, and the like, it appears the average city dweller in China has an income roughly equivalent to that of his or her American counterpart.

T F 15. The Soviet living standard is thought to lie somewhere between that of the United States and China.

T F 16. Income distribution is more egalitarian in the United States than in the planned economies.

T F 17. In planned economies unemployment is not so severe a problem as in capitalist economies.

T F 18. Underemployment is a greater problem than unemployment in a planned economy.

T F 19. *Perestroika* is the Russian word for centralized planning.

T F 20. The market for college graduates in the Soviet Union must be very efficient, because every graduate gets a job.

Multiple Choice: *Select the correct answer.*

_____ 1. Which of the following statements *best* describes the role(s) played by prices in a planned economy?
   (a) Prices play the same role as in a market economy.
   (b) Prices are used to allocate resources but not to ration final goods and services.
   (c) Prices are used to ration final goods and services but not to allocate resources.
   (d) None of the above statements is descriptive.

_____ 2. In market economies the coordination of producers' and consumers' decisions is accomplished by markets; in a planned economy such decisions are typically coordinated by:
   (a) The workers.
   (b) The plant managers.
   (c) A central planning authority.
   (d) None of the above.

_____ 3. Which of the following economies is the most centralized?
   (a) The United States.
   (b) The Soviet Union.
   (c) The People's Republic of China.
   (d) Yugoslavia.

_____ 4. The Soviet Union has for decades emphasized the production of military and capital goods. This priority has *greatest* implications for which of the following?
   (a) The answer to the WHAT question.
   (b) The answer to the HOW question.
   (c) The answer to the FOR WHOM question.
   (d) The answer to the WHERE question.

_____ 5. Which of the following is *most* responsible for revolutions that lead to planned economies?
   (a) The answer to the WHAT question.
   (b) The answer to the HOW question.
   (c) The answer to the FOR WHOM question.
   (d) All of the above.

_____ 6. Which of the following statements justifies the rejection of the market mechanism by planned economies?
(a) If prices were used to allocate resources, planning goals would be jeopardized.
(b) If prices were used to allocate resources, capital-goods production would fall.
(c) If prices were used to allocate resources, income-distribution goals would be impaired.
(d) All of the above justify such a rejection.

_____ 7. Which of the following has been used as incentives to increase worker productivity in the Soviet Union?
(a) Terror.
(b) Income bonuses.
(c) "Ownership" of small plots of land.
(d) All of the above.

_____ 8. Which of the following statements is correct?
(a) Land owned by workers is more productive than land owned by the state in the Soviet Union.
(b) Land owned by the state is more productive than that owned by workers in the Soviet Union.
(c) It's impossible to measure the productivity of land in the Soviet Union because prices are not attached to outputs.
(d) None of the above statements is correct.

_____ 9. Which of the following accounts for the decentralization observed in the Chinese planning process?
(a) The successful experience during the period of guerrilla warfare.
(b) The sheer size of the Chinese economy.
(c) The effectiveness of decentralization in helping workers to identify with communal goals.
(d) All of the above.

_____ 10. The average Chinese city dweller has an income equivalent to a small fraction of that of his or her U.S. counterpart. This statement is misleading because:
(a) There is a problem in determining the exchange rate between the two currencies.
(b) Many goods and services carry artificially low prices in China.
(c) Many goods and services are provided without charge in China.
(d) All of the above are the case.

_____ 11. Planned economies typically suffer from:
(a) Both unemployment and underemployment.
(b) Neither unemployment nor underemployment.
(c) Unemployment but not underemployment.
(d) Underemployment but not unemployment.

_____ 12. It is likely that output per worker in the United States exceeds that in China because:
(a) Chinese workers are lazy and American workers are not.
(b) Chinese workers have more capital than American workers.
(c) American workers have more capital than Chinese workers.
(d) Chinese workers are not unionized.

_____ 13. In both planned and market economies, the only way to increase capital formation is to:
(a) Lower interest rates.
(b) Increase saving.
(c) Increase consumption.
(d) Reduce business taxes.

_____ 14. Recent pronouncements by China's Central Committee indicate that tight state controls are to blame for:
(a) Stifling initiative.
(b) Encouraging waste.
(c) Ignoring market demand.
(d) All of the above.

_____15. Which of the following would violate the intent of *perestroika*?
   (a) Wage rates based on performance.
   (b) Factories retaining "profit" to be used for bonuses.
   (c) A requirement that factories sell their output to the state.
   (d) None of the above.

Problems and Applications

Exercise 1

The production-possibilities curve for a planned economy is shown in Figure 39.1. Assume that the economy is operating at point A. Suppose the planners decide that the society must increase its production of defense goods from the amount indicated by D_1 to the amount indicated by D_2.

Figure 39.1

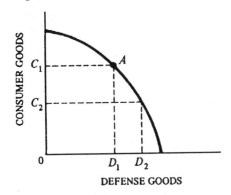

Production possibilities and opportunities

1. The opportunity cost of increasing the output of defense goods from D_1 to D_2 is:
   (a) Zero, since there are unemployed resources in the economy.
   (b) $0C_2$ of consumer goods.
   (c) $0C_1$ of consumer goods.
   (d) C_1C_2 of consumer goods.

2. To get the workers to switch from the production of consumer goods to the production of defense goods, the planners will be most surely successful if they:
   (a) Raise the wages of workers who produce defense goods.
   (b) Lower the wages of workers who produce consumer goods.
   (c) Raise the wages of workers who produce defense goods relative to those of workers who produce consumer goods.
   (d) Raise the wages of workers who produce consumer goods relative to those of workers who produce defense goods.

3. If more defense goods are to be produced, resources will have to be taken away from consumer goods, and consumers will have fewer consumer goods to purchase. Suppose the demand and supply of consumer goods are as indicated in Figure 39.2.

Figure 39.2

QUANTITY OF CONSUMER GOODS PER YEAR

The equilibrium price–quantity combination is:
(a) P_2, C_1.
(b) P_1, C_1.
(c) P_2, C_2.
(d) P_3, C_2.

Taxes and price limitations (ceilings)

4. To prevent producers from having an incentive to produce too many consumer goods, the planners might hold prices down to P_3. Which of the following results would you expect?
   (a) Excess inventories.
   (b) Excess profits.
   (c) Long queues of people waiting to buy.
   (d) All of the above.

5. When the planners cut production from C_1 to C_2 the result is a:
   (a) Surplus at prices below P_1.
   (b) Shortage at prices below P_2.
   (c) New equilibrium at P_3, C_2.
   (d) None of the above.

6. To get consumers to restrain their consumption to output C_2, the planners could levy a tax equal to the distance:
   (a) $0P_3$.
   (b) $0P_1$.
   (c) $P_2 P_3$.
   (d) $P_1 P_2$.

Subsidies, price supports, and floors

7. Suppose the government wishes to control diseases by making more medical services available. Figure 39.3 shows the demand and supply curves for medical services. The equilibrium price–quantity is:
   (a) P_1, M_1.
   (b) P_2, M_2.
   (c) P_3, M_3.
   (d) P_1, M_3.

Figure 39.3

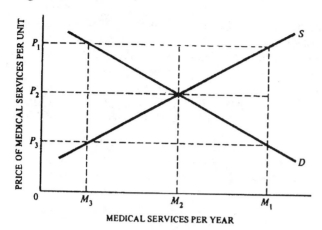

MEDICAL SERVICES PER YEAR

8. Suppose the government wants M_1 of medical services produced. If the government sets a price like P_1 so that the desired medical services would be produced, you would expect:
   (a) Underemployment of medical personnel.
   (b) Shortages of medical services.
   (c) Improvements in health to the degree that the government targets.
   (d) All of the above.

9. In order to encourage fuller use of the services available at M_1, the government could introduce a subsidy per unit of medical service of:
   (a) $P_1 P_3$.
   (b) $M_3 M_1$.
   (c) $P_2 P_3$.
   (d) $P_1 P_2$.

10. If the government wanted M_1 of medical services to be offered, wanted to subsidize no one, and wanted to keep the price at P_3, it would have to build medical facilities to provide:
    (a) $M_3 M_1$ of medical services.
    (b) $0M_1$ of medical services.
    (c) $0M_2$ of medical services.
    (d) $0M_3$ of medical services.

11. At the price of P_3, private medical practices would provide:
    (a) $M_3 M_1$ of medical services.
    (b) $0M_1$ of medical services.
    (c) $0M_2$ of medical services.
    (d) $0M_3$ of medical services.

    (*Hint:* The supply curve reflects what would be provided in the private market.)

Exercise 2

This exercise should give you an idea of how to use input–output analysis. It should also give you an idea of how difficult it is to allocate resources without the use of prices.

Input–output application

1. You are a planner faced with the Soviet input–output relationships shown in Table 39.1 in the text (pp. 914–915). You are responsible for ensuring that the bread, flour, and confections industry (sector 46 in column 3) has all of the required goods needed to produce 100,000 rubles of bread, flour, and confections. You succeed in obtaining all of the necessary requirements except those produced by three industries. Table 39.1 shows the amounts of the various requirements in these three industries that you are able to obtain. In column 3 write down the input–output coefficients for each of these sectors (use the bread, flour, and confections column of Table 39.1 in the text.)

2. You should be able to calculate the amounts of the three requirements in Table 39.1 that you would need to produce 100,000 rubles of bread, flour, and confectionery goods. Place these amounts in column 4 of Table 39.1. (*Hint:* The coefficients in column 3 tell the fraction of the total cost of bread, flour, and confectionery goods that goes into each input.)

Table 39.1
Shortfall for requirements in three industries
to produce bread, flour, and confections

(1) Industry	(2) Amount obtained (rubles)	(3) Input– output coefficient	(4) Amount (rubles) needed to produce 100,000 rubles of output 100,000 × (3)	(5) Fraction of target that can be met (2) ÷ (4)	(6) Maximum production possible given input available 100,000 × (5)
Specialized M & E (sector 17)	45.0	_____	_____	_____	_____
Fish products (sector 43)	30.0	_____	_____	_____	_____
Sugar (sector 45)	533.4	_____	_____	_____	_____

3. You are now ready to find the percentage of bread, flour, and confectionery goods you can make with the available inputs that you have. In column 5 of Table 39.1 you can compute the ratio of what you have available of each input to the amount needed to reach your target of 100,000 rubles of bread, flour, and confection output. This same ratio tells the fraction of your 100,000-ruble production target that you will be able to produce. Compute this maximum production in column 6, Table 39.1.

4. Which input causes the production of bread, flour, and confectionery goods to be the lowest?
   (a) Specialized M & E.
   (b) Fish products.
   (c) Sugar.

5. Assuming that production can be increased only if you have enough of each and every input and that production can be expanded only in proportion to the available inputs, the maximum output of bread, flour, and confectionery goods that can be produced with available inputs is:
   (a) 1,000 rubles.   (d) 90,000 rubles.
   (b) 10,000 rubles.   (e) 83,333 rubles.
   (c) 100,000 rubles.   (f) 75,000 rubles.

6. Since you are able to meet only one-tenth of your target for bread, flour, and confectionery products, you will have (surpluses, shortages) of all of the inputs to these products except sugar.

7. For each of the commodities in Table 39.2, compute the amount of surplus you have of each of the listed inputs as a result of your inability to use them. Since you had enough of each of these inputs to produce 100,000 rubles of bread, flour, and confectionery goods, you can assume that column 3 in Table 39.2 represents the amount of each input you were allocated. (*Hint:* Find the input coefficient and then compute the amount of factor needed as you did in Table 39.1.) Since you can use only 10 percent of the factors you were allocated, because of the sugar shortages, your surplus will be 90 percent (column 4) of what you were allocated (column 3).

Table 39.2
Excess inputs due to sugar shortage

(1) Input	(2) Input coefficient	(3) Amount (rubles) needed to produce 100,000 rubles of output	(4) Amount unused 0.9 x (3)
Coal (sector 5)	_____	_____	_____

Electric and
  thermal power
  (sector 9)
	_____	_____	_____

8. You are also the planner for automobile production. You have to produce 1 million rubles of output of automobiles. If you fail you will go to Siberia. You receive the allocation that you need from all sectors except for the two shown in Table 39.3. Complete Table 39.3 as you did Table 39.1 of this study guide, this time using the automobile column (column 1) in Table 39.1 of the text to find the input–output coefficients.

Table 39.3
Shortfall of requirements to produce one million rubles of automobiles

(1) Input	(2) Amount obtained (rubles)	(3) Input– output coefficient	(4) Amount (rubles) needed to produce one million rubles of output 1,000,000 x (3)	(5) Fraction of target that can be met (2) ÷ (4)	(6) Maximum production possible given available inputs 1,000,000 x (5)
Coal (sector 5)	1,945.8	_____	_____	_____	_____

Electric and
  thermal power
  (sector 9)
	11,592.9	_____	_____	_____	_____

9. How would you be able to reach your automobile target?
   (a) Transfer bread, flour, and confectionery products to the automobile industry.
   (b) Transfer cars to the bread, flour, and confectionery industry.
   (c) Transfer sugar, fish products, and specialized M & E to the automobile industry.
   (d) Transfer coal and electric and thermal power from the automobile industry to the bread, flour, and confectionery industry.
   (e) Transfer coal and electric and thermal power from the bread, flour, and confectionery industry to the automobile industry.

10. How much more coal (in rubles) does the automobile industry need from the bread, flour, and confectionery industry in order to reach its target without any waste?
   (a) 1,171 rubles.   (c) 117.1 rubles.
   (b) 214.2 rubles.   (d) 2,160 rubles.

11. Are there still surpluses of inputs for any industry after the automobile target is reached?
    Yes   no   (circle one)

Exercise 3

The media often compare foreign economies to the United States economy. By using one of the articles in the text, this exercise will show the kind of information to look for to identify the type of economic system used in another country. If your professor makes a newspaper assignment for this chapter, this exercise will provide an example of how to do it.

Reread the article in chapter 39 entitled "Soviets Find Job for Every College Grad" from the *Los Angeles Times*.

1. How would you classify the way in which the economy of the Soviet Union is organized? (two possible answers)
    (a) Communist.
    (b) Socialist.
    (c) Mixed.
    (d) Free market.

2. What sentence from the article is consistent with the way you classified the economy?

Common Errors

The first statement in each "common error" below is incorrect. Each incorrect statement is followed by a corrected version and an explanation.

1. Prices serve no function in a planned economy. WRONG!

    Prices are used to allocate resources and goods in accordance with central plans. RIGHT!

    In planned economies prices are not allowed to perform the same functions as in a market economy. Prices do not generally provide the signal for resources to move (their allocation function), but they do perform the rationing function. Luxury goods have high prices, and necessities carry lower price tags.

2. The average city dweller in China subsists on an income of approximately $340 per year. WRONG!

    The average Chinese city dweller is at about the U.S. poverty line. RIGHT!

    This "common error" points up the difficulty of making comparisons of living standards across international boundaries. Simple dollar comparisons gloss over the radical differences in economic organization. Some of the things that carry high price tags in the United States, such as medical services, carry low price tags in China. Housing is another example. Many services that are provided without charge by the state in China must be paid for by the consumer in the United States. Such differences create significant distortions, so simple comparisons are very misleading. After adjustments, it appears that the average Chinese city dweller has an income roughly equivalent to that at the U.S. poverty line.

■ ANSWERS ■

Key-Term Review

1. economic growth
2. underemployment
3. unemployment
4. socialism

5. capitalism
6. investment
7. production process
8. communism

9. counterplanning
10. production possibilities
11. market economy
    market mechanism

True or False

1. T	5. F	9. T	12. F	15. T	18. T
2. T	6. T	10. T	13. F	16. F	19. F
3. F	7. F	11. T	14. F	17. T	20. F
4. F	8. F				

Multiple Choice

1. c	4. a	7. d	10. d	13. b
2. c	5. c	8. a	11. d	14. d
3. b	6. d	9. d	12. c	15. d

Problems and Applications

Exercise 1

1. d	4. c	7. b	10. a
2. c	5. b	8. a	11. d
3. b	6. c	9. a	

Exercise 2

1–3. **Table 39.1 answer**

(1)	(2)	(3)	(4)	(5)	(6)
Specialized M & E	45.0	0.00054	54	5/6	83,333
Fish products	30.0	0.00040	40	3/4	75,000
Sugar	533.4	0.05334	5,334	1/10	10,000

4. c
5. b
6. surpluses
7. **Table 39.2 answer**

(1)	(2)	(3)	(4)
Coal	0.00238	238	214.2
Electric and thermal power	0.00284	284	255.6

8. **Table 39.3 answer**

(1)	(2)	(3)	(4)	(5)	(6)
Coal	1,945.8	0.00216	2,160	0.9008	900,800
Electric and thermal power	11,592.9	0.01171	11,710	0.9900	990,000

9. e
10. b
11. yes

Exercise 3

1. a or b
2. "And many wind up with jobs only remotely related to their studies." This sentence indicates underemployment. The fact that the state finds jobs for the students is evidence of state ownership or direction of enterprises.